THE
MAGNIFICENT
ACTIVIST

THE MAGNIFICENT ACTIVIST

The Writings of
Thomas Wentworth Higginson
(1823–1911)

EDITED BY

Howard N. Meyer

DA CAPO PRESS

Higginson, Thomas Wentworth, 1823–1911
   The magnificent activist : the writings of Thomas Wentworth Higginson (1823–1911)/
edited by Howard N. Myer. — 1st DaCapo Press ed.
     p. cm.
   Includes bibliographical references and index.
   ISBN 0-306-80954-0 (paperback)
    1. Higginson, Thomas Wentworth, 1823–1911—Political and social views.
2. Afro-Americans—Civil rights—History—19th century.   3. Antislavery movements—United States—History—19th century.   4. United States—History—Civil War, 1861–1865—Participation, Afro-American.   5. Women's rights—United States—History—19th century.   6. United States—Social conditions—1865–1918.   7. American literature—19th century—History and criticism.
I. Meyer, Howard N.   II. Title.

E185.18.H54   2000
818'.409—dc21

                                        00-024267

Text design by Jeff Williams
Set in 11-point Minion by the Perseus Books Group

Published by Da Capo Press
A Member of the Perseus Books Group
http://www.dacapopress.com

1 2 3 4 5 6 7 8 9 10—04 03 02 01 00

For Gertrude Lang
with Love

Thomas Wentworth Higginson, 1846

CONTENTS

Anti-Imperialist

PART V
NATURALIST *411*

PART VI
CRITIC AS ESSAYIST *483*

ACKNOWLEDGMENTS

When assembling a representative selection of the out-of-print work of a writer who worked at his craft for sixty years, an anthologist cannot go it alone. First, a word must be said for the shops that stock and sell previously owned books. These shops are the repositories of a unique segment of our history and culture.

Thomas Wentworth Higginson's writings appear in many bound volumes, but of his uncollected papers—speeches, magazine and newspaper articles, and more—most are accessible only on microfilm. Thanks are due to the Central Research librarians and the microfilm section of the New York Public Library. For manuscripts and rare and valuable clippings, I am indebted to Harvard's Houghton Library, especially for the effort of Reading Room Associate Jennie Rathbun, a librarian who located the manuscript of "The Clergy and Reform," and for the Houghton's consent to publish this document, only brief selections of which have previously appeared. I also found some items in the rare-book rooms of Columbia University's Butler Library and the New York Public Library.

Anna Mary Wells, formerly a professor of American literature at Rutgers University, was a generous source of clues and shared her notes with me. Her Higginson biography, *Dear Preceptor*, is important to those interested in facts rather than speculations regarding Higginson's relationship with Emily Dickinson. Professor James M. McPherson of Princeton University and Professor Joel Myerson at the University of South Carolina furnished leads that reflect their important work in American history and American studies.

Of the many who helped to sustain my morale, I'd like to mention especially the playwright Lorraine Hansberry; the editor of the *Negro Digest*, Hoyt Fuller; and John Morsell, the assistant executive director of the National Association for the Advancement of Colored People. All were crucial during the early years of my interest in Higginson as he was a nineteenth-century writer who should be remembered better for judgments that would have been useful during the twentieth, and whose relevance to the twenty-first century should be appreciated.

I owe affectionate thanks to Gert Lang for editorial assistance supplemented by a constant boost to morale, as well as to Michael Dorr, former editor at Da Capo Press, for his part in reviving the idea for this collection. The help given by Senior Editor Andrea Schulz was substantial and important.

CHRONOLOGY

NOTE: Only a representative sampling of Higginson's publications is given here; the complete bibliography of his works (published in 1906) is forty-six pages long. There were more to come in 1906–1911.

1823   Thomas Wentworth Higginson (TWH) born on December 23 in Cambridge, Massachusetts.

1834   Father, Stephen Higginson, dies; TWH grows up in all-female household.

1835   TWH, aged twelve, attends lecture given by Ralph Waldo Emerson.

1837   Registers as undergraduate at Harvard College.

1841   Graduates from Harvard; visits Virginia relatives and sees actuality of slavery.

1843   Enters Harvard Graduate School.

1842   Visits Transcendentalist-oriented Brook Farm with Barbara Channing, his future sister-in-law.

1843   First publications: four poems and a review of Lydia Maria Child's *Letters from New York*.

1844   Enters Harvard Divinity School.

1845   Drops out of Divinity School but reenters in 1846.

1846   Sonnet in honor of William Lloyd Garrison published in the magazine *Liberty Bell*.

1847   Graduates from Harvard Divinity School. Delivers Visitation Day student sermon, "The Clergy and Reform," whose message is that Christlike love requires capacity for moral indignation at social wrongs.

Called to serve as pastor at the Unitarian church in Newbury-port, after two trial Sunday visits.

Marries Mary Channing.

1848   Sermon after Thanksgiving: "Man Lives Not by Bread Alone."

1849   Obliged to resign pulpit because of radical views; remains in Newburyport vicinity. Begins lecture career; some newspaper writing.

1850   Signs call to convene Worcester Woman's Rights Convention.

Runs for U.S. Congress on new Free Soil party ticket. Gets 21 percent of the vote.

New Fugitive Slave Law includes federal enforcement of earlier law. TWH helps form Boston-based Vigilance Committee to resist.

1851   With Vigilance Committee attempts to free runaway slave Thomas Sims.

Delivers "Merchants," a Sunday evening lecture.

1852   Called to serve at Worcester's Free Church.

1853   Addresses the Massachusetts Constitutional Convention on the subject "Woman and Her Wishes."

When World Temperance Convention refuses to seat Lucy Stone on the platform, TWH leads delegates to walk out and form Whole World's Temperance Convention.

1854   Leads Vigilance Committee attempt to free ex-slave Anthony Burns from detention in the federal courthouse in Boston. TWH is indicted but the case is not prosecuted.

Delivers sermon "Massachusetts in Mourning" in response to enforcement of Fugitive Slave Act in Burns case.

1855   Travels with wife to the Portuguese island of Fayal, for her health.

1856   Recruits and arms settlers in Kansas who will vote against Kansas's becoming a slave state (Kansas-Nebraska Act of '54 repealed the Missouri Compromise); TWH appointed agent of Massachusetts Kansas Aid Committee.

TWH writes "A Ride Through Kanzas."

1857   Helps initiate and addresses Massachusetts Disunion Convention.

Address to Antislavery Society: "The New Revolution."

1858   Writes "Saints and Their Bodies," the first of many essays for the *Atlantic Monthly*. "Water Lilies" is the first of many nature essays.

Collaborates with Lucy Stone on *Woman's Rights Almanac*.

Meets with John Brown and agrees to support his cause financially.

1859   After John Brown's attack on Harpers Ferry fails, TWH tries to plan rescue of Brown and aids his family.

"Ought Women to Learn the Alphabet?" published in the *Atlantic Monthly;* reprinted as pamphlet.

1860   Writes essays: "Visit to John Brown's Household"; "The Maroons of Jamaica" and "The Maroons of Surinam" are examples of Brown's aim: slaves revolt and run away to form autonomous community in mountains.

1861   Essays on slave revolt leaders Nat Turner, "Gabriel," and Denmark Vesey are companion pieces to "Maroon" essays.

"A New Counterblast" presents facts on dangers of tobacco including French surgeon's report that it is a carcinogen. Writes "My Outdoor Study" and other essays.

Civil War begins in April; in November, TWH asks for and receives authority to form (white) Massachusetts regiment.

1862   "Letter to a Young Contributor," "Life of the Birds," and other essays.

Accepts post as colonel of First South Carolina Volunteers, regiment of freed slaves.

Receives letter from Emily Dickinson; beginning of their friendship, conducted mainly by letters.

1863   Publication of first book, *Outdoor Papers*, a collection of essays, including nature studies.

Trains black regiment on the Sea Islands and begins engagements with enemy.

1864   Medical discharge from service after wound on upriver raid. Fights for his men to receive pay equal to white soldiers'.

Joins wife in Newport residence.

Articles on commanding black troops start to appear in *Atlantic Monthly*.

1865 As member of Newport School Board, helps integrate local schools.

Translates the works of the Stoic philosopher Epictetus.

1866 Editor of *Harvard Memorial Biographies,* on alumni lost in Civil War (author of thirteen of the tributes).

Helen Hunt moves into Newport boarding house where the Higginsons live.

1867 Writes "Driftwood Fire" and other Newport essays later published in the collection *Oldport Days*.

Is a founder of and active in Boston-based Radical Club and Free Religious Association.

1868 Writes essays on Margaret Fuller and the abolitionist and writer Lydia Maria Child for *Eminent Women*.

1869 Publication of *Malbone,* a novel set in Newport.

1870 First meeting with Emily Dickinson, in Amherst.

Publication of *Army Life in a Black Regiment;* also, "A Shadow" and other essays.

1871 Publication of *Atlantic Essays*.

"Sympathy of Religions," an early ecumenical statement, published as a pamphlet. (Special edition appears later for the 1893 Parliament of Religions.)

The essay "Sappho" published.

1873 Publication of *Oldport Days,* collection of Newport essays.

1875 Publication of TWH's best-seller, *Young Folks' History of the United States*.

"English Statesmen."

Publishes essay "The Word Philanthropy," the best statement of his outlook.

1877 Publicly approves President Hayes's withdrawal of federal troops from three southern states.

Mary Channing Higginson dies after a long illness.

Begins fourteen years as contributing editor of the *Woman's Journal,* the organ of the American Woman Suffrage Association.

Begins twenty-six years as poetry editor of *The Nation*.

1878   "Some War Scenes Revisited," a report on life in the Sea Islands.

1879   Publication of *Short Studies of American Authors.*

      "The Other Side of the Woman Question" published in the *North American Review.*

      Marries Mary Thacher; moves back to Cambridge.

1880   Begins two-year term in upper house of Massachusetts legislature.

1881   Publishes *Common Sense About Women,* mainly pieces written for the *Woman's Journal.*

      His daughter, Margaret, is born.

      Second edition of *Young Folks' History of the United States.*

1882–83 Publication of some pieces that will become chapters of *Larger History of the United States,* a book for adults.

1884   Publication of *Margaret Fuller Ossoli,* full-length biography in Houghton Mifflin's American Men of Letters series.

      Defends presidential candidate Grover Cleveland, attacked for immorality.

1885   Begins to write a column, "Women and Men," for the periodical *Harper's Bazar* (*sic*).

      Death of Helen Hunt Jackson.

      TWH's warm obituaries of Helen Hunt Jackson appear in several publications.

1886   Death of Emily Dickinson. Her family requests TWH's presence at the funeral.

1887   Publication of *Women and Men,* a collection of feminist pieces published in *Harper's Bazar* (*sic*).

      "Hints on Writing and Speech Making."

1888   TWH runs for U.S. Congress; loses.

1889   Publication of essay collection *Travelers and Outlaws.*

      Becomes involved with Edward Bellamy's socialist "Nationalist" movement after reading his utopian novel, *Looking Backward: 2000–1887.*

1890   Finds publisher for and coedits first volume of Emily Dickinson's poems.

      Publication of second volume of Dickinson's poems.

Invited to speak at Boston's municipally sponsored memorial for John Boyle O'Reilly, Irish-born rebel, poet, naturalized American, and editor of the Boston *Pilot*.

1891   Essay "Emily Dickinson" published in the *Atlantic Monthly*.

1892   *Concerning All of Us*.

1895–96 Writes two-volume *Massachusetts in the Army and Navy During the Civil War*, commission by publishers Wright & Potter.

1897   Publication of essay collection *Book and Heart*.

1898   Publication of *Cheerful Yesterdays*, an autobiographical memoir.

Receives honorary degree from Harvard.

1899   Cofounds the Anti-Imperialist League to protest U.S. military activity to suppress Philippine independence movement.

Publication of *Contemporaries*, profiles of fellow Transcendentalists, abolitionists, and others.

1900   Publication of seven-volume selected works, *Definitive Edition*. Vol. 1: *Cheerful Yesterdays*; vol. 2: *Contemporaries*; vol. 3: *Army Life in a Black Regiment*; vol. 4: *Women and the Alphabet*; vol. 5: *Studies in Romance*; vol. 6: *Outdoor Studies*; vol. 7: *Studies in History and Letters*.

1902   Publication of biographies of Longfellow and Whittier.

1903   Publication of *Reader's History of American Literature* (co-author: Henry Walcott Boynton).

1905   Publication of *Part of a Man's Life*, containing recent essays such as "Intensely Human" and "Butterflies and Poetry."

1907   Publication of biography of his father, Stephen Higginson.

1908   Publication of essay collection *Things Worth While*.

1909   Publication of collection of recent essays, *Carlyle's Laugh and Other Surprises*.

1910   "In After Days," a contribution TWH was invited to make to a collection of essays on beliefs about immortality.

1911   TWH dies, aged 87, having been active until the end. At his funeral is an honor guard of blacks serving in the U.S. Army—all born years after the Civil War.

INTRODUCTION

~~~~~~~~~~~~~~~~~~~~~~~

It has been said of the American writer Thomas Wentworth Higginson (1823–1911) that his whole life was a "sermon on freedom." He aimed always to help achieve a more just, a more humane, a more egalitarian society in America. But that is not all his life was about. He was a reformer—indeed, a militant one—in America's Age of Reform (1830–60). And though the word "activist" was not used then with the meaning we give it today, in his time he was an activist in our modern sense. His activism took many forms and ranged across an extraordinary number of causes. He lectured against fundamentalism ("Scripture Idolatry," Part IV, Chapter 3) in 1850 and against the subjugation of Philippine freedom fighters by U.S. troops in 1899.

He protested against the exclusion of women from a meeting's platform by leading a faction that seceded and withdrew from the meeting. Another time he broke down a courthouse door in an effort to rescue a fugitive slave. And he commanded the first black regiment to fight for the U.S. Army.

Yet all this was less important to him in his lifetime than that he was a writer, and it is as a writer that he deserves to be remembered. He was an inimitable chronicler of large swaths of our history, chapters that are now imperfectly recalled. He should be read for the sheer joy of the reading itself, and his works should be respected enough to serve as models for teaching writing to both writers and students generally.

Higginson's writing was a tool of his activism, but did not dominate it and was not corrupted by it or prostituted to it. And it is not a relic of the past or a museum piece: he has much to say to our time, often suggesting the need to modify self-congratulation on gains we are pleased to think we have achieved.

On some subjects he might be considered avant-garde today—certain of his essays might possibly be banned in not a few school districts. Consider what he wrote in 1904 in his essay "The Black Troops: 'Intensely Human' " (Part II, Chapter 1) in the teeth of a society that had come to the nadir of its shame in interracial justice: "As the memories of the slave period fade away the mere fetich [*sic*] of colorphobia will cease to control society; and marriage may come to be founded, not on the color of the skin, but on the common courtesies of life, and upon genuine sympathies of heart and mind."

An even more startling contemporary relevance is found in an address he made at a suffrage meeting a century before the phrase "affirmative action" became current:

> We men have been standing for years with our hands crushing down the shoulders of woman, so that she should not attain her true altitude; it is not so easy, after we have dwarfed and crippled her, to get rid of our responsibility by standing back and saying: "There, we will let you go; stand up for yourself." . . . We have got to do more than mere negative duty. By as much as we have helped to wrong them, we have got to help right them (*History of Woman Suffrage,* vol. 1, Fowler & Wells, NY, 1882, p. 657).

The selections from Higginson's work in this volume will show a diversity of interest and subject matter that is well nigh staggering.

Higginson wrote on abolition, women's suffrage, and public health (he was one of the first to link smoking and cancer), but his writing was not confined to social or political issues. He was a literary critic, a historian, and a biographer whose work has been a resource for many. As a writer on nature Higginson is widely considered to have been outdone only by John Burroughs and John Muir.

When a writer's work lies before us, the testimony of an expert witness is not ordinarily called for. An exception may be made when the writer has been neglected for years and the witness in his favor is Edmund Wilson. The generally accepted grand master of literary criticism discovered Higginson in the course of reading for his book on writers of the Civil War era, *Patriotic Gore* (1962). He salutes Higginson's "graceful and elegant style . . . The phrases are shapely and trim. . . . One hardly notices, in fact, that one is reading."

Memory of Higginson did not altogether "perish" (as he said the French nineteenth-century journalist Pierre-Joseph Proudhon would have put it), but in light of all the credentials sketched above and the further evidence provided in this book, it seems odd that he is not better known, both as a contributor to the fabric of American liberty and as a writer. (He lived long enough to observe repeatedly the phenomenon of a writer's posthumous fall from grace or rise to fame, and remarked on it with more than one apt metaphor.)

When Higginson died, in 1911, his memory earned hosannas, most of them echoing tributes paid already on the occasions of his seventy-fifth and eightieth birthdays. Not long afterward, however, he seemed to sink from view, as his books went out of print one by one—even the record of his Civil War service, *Army Life in a Black Regiment,* which by itself should have placed its author in the American literary pantheon.

Theories have been advanced for his departure from the radar screen of history. One was that he was identified indiscriminately with an out-of-fashion "genteel" tradition, a supposition hardly plausible in the light of his radical record and persistent nonconformity. Another is that his social and political goals, all very commendable, had been attained. That does not seem even superficially plausible for two reasons: Whatever progress may be noted, there is much to be done before we can be said to have justice as well as genuine equality in race relations or gender equity. Furthermore, it is not in the American tradition to dismiss innovators when their contributions have been accepted.

But what if their contributions are later spurned? The role of black soldiers in winning the Civil War was recognized by the Fourteenth Amendment; its "equal protection" pledge implemented a promise Higginson's deputy made expressly to Higginson's troops on their discharge: "The nation guarantees to you full protection and justice" (*Army Life in a Black Regiment,* Norton, 1962, p. 279). One who breaks a promise will tend to forget why it was made.

This discussion is best closed on an optimistic note, one of Higginson's felicitous passages: "Happy is the author who comes to be benefited by an actual return of reputation,—as athletes get beyond the point of breathlessness and come to their 'second wind.'"

Has the time come for a new recognition of Thomas Wentworth Higginson's life and works?

John T. Bethell, editor of *Harvard Magazine,* has observed that Higginson has "something meaningful to say to our times." I thank him for coining the phrase "the magnificent activist."

FROM CAMBRIDGE TO NEWBURYPORT

Thomas Wentworth Higginson was born in Cambridge, Massachusetts, in 1823, when Thomas Jefferson was still alive. He died in 1911, when Woodrow Wilson was campaigning for the 1912 presidential nomination, and conflicts in the Balkans foreshadowed World War I. His life spanned the period in which America emerged from a primitive, postrevolutionary condition, survived the Civil War, and became a great industrial and agricultural nation, a world power.

His paternal ancestor Francis Higginson, a Puritan clergyman, arrived in Massachusetts not long after the landing of New England's first settlers. Among his mother's ancestors were eminent colonials, including English king's governors, and a British prisoner-of-war who subsequently married a daughter of the clan. His paternal grandfather served in the Revolution as a privateer, attacking British shipping, then became a member of the Continental Congress, and later was a wealthy shipping merchant.

Jefferson's Embargo, before the War of 1812, led to the destruction of the Higginson family's fortune. They left Boston to seek refuge in nearby Bolton, west of Boston, where friends had offered them a sheep farm where they could live. The move to Cambridge was made possible when other friends obtained for Higginson's father the post of bursar at Harvard.

Harvard dominated Cambridge then more than it does now. Life as a child in a college town, in what was in effect a college family, left its mark on young Higginson. Later he was to call himself a "child of the college," as indeed he was; his playmates were the children of faculty members, and he had access to their homes and libraries and occasionally their parents.

In his own household, life changed when his father died. Thomas, the youngest child, was eleven. His nine older siblings were already married, at graduate school, or away on business at sea or on State Street. The family at home now consisted of his mother, an aunt, and two younger sisters. The impression he recalled of all of them was as independent, self-respecting, intelligent women.

As a somewhat sickly baby and the youngest, he had received special attention and concern, especially from his mother. When he was nine she expressed satisfaction with what she had accomplished in his upbringing with the appraisal: "He has genuine refinement and delicacy, with manliness and a power of controlling himself. A sense of right governs his thought and action which commands my respect as much as if he had been a grown man."

She had begun his education well before he attended any school. She once observed that books had been her own recreation and, next to her children, her "greatest source of pleasure." In consonance with her own sense of the value of books, she read aloud to her children every evening. She thus covered, as Higginson later recalled, all of Sir Walter Scott's Waverly novels.

That preschool education was not the only asset Higginson's mother provided him. More than sixty years later, in an essay titled "The Woman Who Most Influenced Me," he said he traced to his mother's direct influence "three leading motives of her youngest son's life—the love of personal liberty, of religious freedom, and of the equality of the sexes."

She may not, however, have directly influenced his development of a lifelong love for the outdoors. Though organized sports were not a part of the curriculum of the preparatory schools he attended, he found his way to playing football and cricket and to enjoy boxing, swimming, and ice-skating.

Even more important to him in later life was the early appearance of a love for nature and nature studies. This came with a talent for attentive appreciation. A generalist in regard to nature, he specialized in no particular branch, but was grateful for any opportunities for study and observation in wood, field, and stream.

Higginson was the youngest in his Harvard class. But apparently this didn't cause him to suffer academically: at graduation, in 1841, he ranked second in his class. He had a gift for languages and became conversant in several. In both mathematics and natural history (the latter not at all unexpectedly) he did unusually well, so much so that he won extracurricular appointments as aide to professors in each subject. He was active as well in the college's Natural History Society.

He thought it an important asset of his college days to have studied with Edward T. Channing, professor of English language and literature. Channing has the distinction of having instructed more great American writers than anyone else before or since in any U.S. university. Gaining the distinction could be attributed somewhat to the good fortune of having students like Thoreau, Emerson, James Russell Lowell, Oliver Wendell Holmes (senior), Edward Everett Hale, John Lothrop Motley, and Charles Sumner.

As graduation approached in 1841, Higginson faced a decision as to a career or calling. This was not easy. His education had advanced his literary skill, had provided equipment for life's tasks. But the development of his personality or character was shaped mainly by his response to the world about him.

In the twenty years 1821–41, the state of the nation had changed. The so-called "Era of Good Feelings," of contentment with things as they were, had ended. As the Harvard senior saw it, "a period of general seething" had come over the nation. More specifically, as he was to write later, "there was passing through the community a wave of desire for a freer and more ideal life."

Ralph Waldo Emerson, whom Higginson had first heard lecture when he was twelve years old and for whom he repeatedly expressed admiration, described this period in a letter to an English friend: "We are all a little wild here with numberless projects of social reform; not a reading man but has a draft of a new community in his waistcoat pocket." He could have added that he himself was one of the instigators.

American historians have called the period from 1830 to 1860 the Era of Reform. In its day many called it the "period of the newness." At its peak, in the 1840s, the period immediately after Higginson graduated from college, it constituted an environment that a young man could not disregard. As one who in his teens had read every word published by Emerson, he had a more than rudimentary understanding of what was going on. But he did not grasp at once what effect it should have on his life, what part he should play in the society that he was about to enter.

Not yet eighteen when he graduated from college, Higginson was reluctant to commit himself to a choice of life's work. He chose to postpone his decision. Instead he took temporary employment as a teaching aide at a boys' school. When that did not work out he transferred to a position as tutor to children of a cousin who lived in Brookline, then a suburb of Boston.

The Brookline job provided ample leisure time to look around, in and outside Boston, and learn some things that he had been too young to pay attention to at college. There was much to see and hear in Boston in the spring and summer of 1842 that could not be known behind the sheltering walls of Harvard Yard.

The United States was beginning to recover from its second major business depression. There were shocking scenes of women and children begging on the streets of Boston. Housing for the poor was abominable. Little help came from the state government, and at that time the federal government took absolutely no interest in the matter.

The young tutor's diaries and correspondence during this period reflected the course of his entry into the spirit of the Era of Reform. He resolved, on paper at least, to starve if it were necessary in order for him to "do his duty to the world in whatever manner he can use his talents" (he often referred to himself in the third person). He declared in another entry that he had to rise above "following Ambition," because "neither Wealth nor Fame will, I trust, make me happy or satisfy me."

As he developed from romantic abnegation to advocacy and activism for change in social arrangements, he was not oblivious to the consequences. He resolved "never to be intimidated against opening my eyes or my mouth." He did not take long to recognize the consequences: "The moment any person among us begins to broach any 'new views' and intimates that all things are not exactly right, the conservatives lose no time in holding up their fingers and branding him an unsafe person— fanatic, visionary and all the rest of it."

This last was written in a letter to a young woman, Mary Channing, a second cousin, who was a frequent visitor to the household where Higginson had been serving as tutor. Their friendship ripened into an attachment that culminated in engagement to marry, although his economic situation deferred that happy outcome for years.

Mary, slightly older than he, provided a source of stability, as well as being a companion and comrade who joined in his free-time pursuits.

Their activities together included frequent attendance at churches where the radical preachers of that era sermonized. Together they attended "a series of exciting meetings for Reform," as he described them, "where the battle raged high between Associationists and Communists. Defenders of the established order also took part." At one meeting, he recalled half a century later, he heard a speech "so thrilling and effective" that it helped make him "at least a halfway socialist for life." (Marx was not to publish the *Communist Manifesto* for another five years.)

"Reform" as advocated by Emerson was the focus and preoccupation of Boston-based groups of people who were dissatisfied with the institutions and civic arrangements that had been passed on to them. It is important to understand the difference between reform as Higginson and his generation understood it and what we think of as reform today.

What we see in movements for reform in our times is attractive, non-controversial (almost), and ameliorative in a gentle way. Reform's object is not to eliminate an institution, practice, or policy, or to change society radically. Reformers today usually agree with or are devoted to—or at least respect—the object of their endeavor, for example, the educational system. They want to improve it, to help it function more efficiently to accomplish its stated aims.

Twentieth-century reformers are usually "liberals." Liberals are often reformers, but radicals and radicalism do not enter the picture.

In the United States before the Civil War, the terms were different. Efforts toward "reform" most often involved a fundamental, even revolutionary purpose. Its aim was to overthrow institutions or substantially alter policies and practices. What Emerson meant and what his generation took him to mean by "reform"—to remake what others had made—required nothing less.

The efforts of the reformers in Higginson's day had such targets as the abolition of slavery, which would require (as they knew) not merely emancipation of individual slaves, but eradication of the slave system, the political and social incubus that dominated the national government and the "better classes" in both the North and South, which were economically dependent on slavery.

An almost equivalent upheaval would have been brought about by achievement of the aims of the movement for equal treatment of women. Well before the beginning of the formal establishment of a "women's" movement led organizationally by women, there were both men and women activists who denounced and sought the removal of the props and barriers that had, in the nineteenth century, continued women's status as a disadvantaged class.

These were not the only targets of activists. There was a whole "sisterhood of reforms," as Higginson called them later. Many were directed at the social evils so characteristic of eighteenth-century English society, brought here by the colonists and untouched by the independence movement that styled itself a revolution (1776). They included prison reform, abolition of the death penalty, electoral reform, extending the franchise, temperance reform (thereby abolishing an entire industry), abolishing imprisonment for debt, elimination of child labor, ending the common law treatment of labor unions as "conspiracies," and, not least, the establishment of public education for all.

Higginson's response to all this he acknowledged later and with no regrets. "During all this time I was growing more, not less radical." Studying society was a useful occupation; learning from the reformers and sympathizing with their aims was well enough, but where was he to make his contribution? "I crave action, unbounded action," he mused. "I love men passionately. I feel intensely their suffering and shortcomings and yearn to make all men brothers."

First came a decision not to follow a proposed career. It was thought by some in the family and hoped by all that in his various positions he was making and saving money to go to law school. But what he had come to know of the laws of Massachusetts by 1842 was enough to turn him away from this idea. He perceived that the law was an organized system of rules for the protection of property interests, and this was not for him. "I could not surrender my life to what Blackstone [a law textbook] represented."

Clues as to what path he would follow came from the church services he was attending with Mary, not only in what was being preached but in the impressive personae of the radical pastors of the period.

Notable among the liberal activist pastors were his cousin, William Henry Channing, and the even more radical James Freeman Clarke, to whose sermons Mary Channing introduced him. She was a communicant at the church of Reverend Clarke and something of a radical. More instructive—and radical—than either Channing or Clarke was Theodore Parker, whose unusual scholarship enhanced his sermons.

Parker's radical ministry, his talent, and his eloquence were drawing overflow crowds to the services over which he presided at Boston's old Melodeon Building. He was world-famous, and noted visitors from abroad, such as the English novelist William Makepeace Thackeray, came to Boston determined to hear Parker preach.

Higginson's experience with these pastors convinced him that by becoming a pastor himself he would be best able to aid the antislavery cause and other social causes to which he had been drawn. He entered Harvard Divinity School to find out. A year later, however, he dropped out, expressing impatience with the instructors, his fellow students, and the courses of study. After a year as an independent scholar, he reconsidered and returned to the Divinity School.

During this period his ambition to become an activist increased. One of his diary entries reads:

> I cannot remain in the background.
> Something more will be sought of me—
> the life of a Reformer, a People's
> guide, "fighting for the right,"
> Glorious, but how hard.

By the time he was ordained, he had become convinced that abolition of slavery was the most urgent cause of all.

As graduation from the Divinity School approached, members of his class went out to deliver demonstration sermons. Higginson had a favorable reception for his in Newburyport, a small and attractive port north of Boston, at the mouth of the Merrimack River, and was engaged as pastor to the Newburyport Unitarian Church. The elders of the congregation, the more affluent members of the community, were primarily active and retired sea captains and mates and men in business occupations whose work had maritime connections.

Their tendency to conservatism was enhanced by the role American shipping had played in the slave trade, and in carrying to the port the products of slavery, raw materials from the South and products manufactured in the North.

He had not concealed his radicalism when it came to slavery and other issues that were part of the sisterhood of reforms. The elders decided to take the risk of engaging the young man, whose appearance and eloquence charmed the women of the congregation and were not displeasing to the men.

Higginson has been described as unusually handsome. His good looks were enhanced by his tall and stately figure. He avoided provoking the conservatives among the congregation, but not to the point of abandoning his beliefs.

Eventually, though, his opposition to and criticism of slavery began to build discontent. So too did his championing of temperance, especially with regard to hard liquor. Working people, urban and rural, had used whiskey and rum to excess and the problem increased as the Industrial Revolution progressed, bringing harder working conditions and long working hours. Temperance was a liberal idea. But the successful local factory that made Caldwell's Old Newburyport rum was a valued community asset.

Higginson won no favor among the elders of the church by his open advocacy of the reduction of the factory day to ten hours. The radical pastor concerned himself also with the condition of the poor, whose numbers increased with Irish immigration. He introduced adult education, and taught adult education classes himself.

Resentment of radicalism increased. The local upper class, a minority of the congregation but a majority of the elders, decided they could stand no more. To the dismay of many, they demanded and secured Higginson's resignation.

He left with an aphorism: "An empty pulpit can speak more loudly than a live minister."

FROM NEWBURYPORT TO WORCESTER AND WAR

One will not find in any of Higginson's published reminiscences an expression of concern about his first experience with unemployment. He was not likely, having been forced out of the pulpit, to find a church willing to overlook his unconcealed radicalism.

When first called to the ministry in Newburyport, he had married his fiancée of some years, Mary Channing. She was his second cousin and a niece of the famed minister Dr. William Ellery Channing. In the biography of Higginson written by his second wife, Mary Thacher Higginson, his first wife was described as "intelligent and brilliant in conversation."

Mary Channing's sister Barbara knew members of the Brook Farm socialist community experiment, located in West Roxbury, Massachusetts, and had escorted Higginson to visits there. Brook Farm, sometimes known as The Community, was an experiment in cooperative living. It was an offshoot of what came to be known as Transcendentalism, a name flippantly given to the group whose thinking was stimulated—but not controlled—by Emerson and Thoreau. Although Higginson was a latecomer to the movement, his own philosophy was influenced by what they wrote and said. The Transcendentalists were a potent force among the reformers of the 1830–60 period.

The Higginsons liked the Newburyport area and a relative's offer of a rent-free home enabled them to stay. He found several ways to earn a living. He had started to write, mainly poetry at first, even before the Divinity School, and his sermons and Sunday night lectures were published as pamphlets and sold well. He wrote for newspapers and even got to write a regular newspaper column. He also taught in private schools.

Then a new opportunity presented itself: in that era, inadequate newspapers and the absence of other communications media resulted in a hunger for information about the changing world. To meet this need a lecture circuit presenting traveling lecturers had developed. While Higginson was still a pastor, he and his wife often had welcomed into their home traveling luminaries such as Charles Sumner, Louis Agassiz, the feminist Lucy Stone, and Ralph Waldo Emerson himself.

Having acquired some celebrity of his own, Higginson was eligible for and was accepted into the lecture circuit, which was usually referred to as the "Lyceum."

He and his wife stayed on in the Newburyport area for two years after he had been forced to give up his pulpit. He had not thought of a career in politics as a way to advance his views as a reformer, but that lack of ambition did not prevent his being nominated as the newly formed Free Soil party's candidate for the United States House of Representatives. Indeed he was not quite eligible, being under twenty-five years of age, but was named at the insistence of John Greenleaf Whittier, an abolitionist as well as poet. He came in third.

In 1850 he ran again, on his own initiative this time, but it was not yet possible to challenge the two major parties of the day, Democratic and Whig. (The Whig party was to disappear in a few years, split by the slavery issue. The branch of the party that called itself "conscience Whigs" joined with the Free Soil supporters in 1854 to form the new Republican party.)

Higginson and other antislavery advocates were helping fugitive slaves to find refuge as they made their way to Canada—the so-called Underground Railroad. Although those aided were a comparative trickle, the slave states feared that recognition of fugitives' freedom eroded slavery's legitimacy. As part of the Compromise of 1850, the slave states won passage of a new Fugitive Slave Act, whereby the federal government assumed responsibility to return fugitives. Federal courts and federal troops were to enforce the law commanding return of the self-freed. In his 1850 run for Congress, Higginson focused his campaign on attacking this law.

Though the abolition movement was divided by a number of issues concerning both the strategy and tactics to be used in the struggle, its members joined forces to oppose what they viewed as an abuse of federal power, clearly unauthorized by the Constitution. They argued that if court action failed to overturn the law, a "higher law" would justify resistance to its enforcement. After discussing the law in one of his newspaper columns, Higginson closed with the simple phrase: "Disobey it."

Perceiving that there was a need for organized action, he helped to form the Boston-based Vigilance Committee, whose members' mission was simple and direct: whenever a fugitive was seized to be returned to slavery, it was a call to action and all members who heard it pledged to respond by doing everything possible to prevent the fugitive from being returned to bondage.

Higginson had feared that he would have to give up preaching for good after he was forced out of the Newburyport pulpit, but he had a pleasant surprise. Without having searched for or solicited another position, he received an invitation to serve as pastor of a newly formed Free Church in Worcester. That central Massachusetts city had radicals enough to support a new house of worship where they would be comfortable with their pastor, and he with them. Higginson accepted with pleasure.

In his installation sermon, Higginson made a principal point of warning that the Bible narratives were not to be taken as literally true. (This part of the sermon was later developed as "Scripture Idolatry" [see Part IV, Chapter 3], a lecture also published in pamphlet form.) He covered the entire field of reforms currently being agitated for, telling the congregation that there was more to do than oppose slavery. The rights of women, land reform, the ten-hour day, prison conditions, and child labor were all on the list.

As published and distributed, the sermon had a fine reception in and out of Worcester, advancing Higginson further along the road to national recognition.

Worcester was to be his home for the next ten years. It was there, between the ages of twenty-eight and thirty-eight, that he proved to be an activist-militant, not merely an advocate of using force against slavery, but a practitioner himself, risking harm and arrest and encountering both.

In that decade he matured as a writer and became a first-class popular essayist. In finely crafted nature studies he matched Thoreau and was admired by him. In advocating attention to and action for people's health, he created a new cause, and many of the ideas in his articles remain relevant today.

When he joined the struggle for women's rights, he became the most notable male in our history to champion the right of women to equality of treatment in every respect: home, school, workplace, ballot box. His efforts were expended in both writing and overt actions; he was America's male feminist without peer.

In addition to his public commitment and advocacy, he served privately as instigator, inspiration, and impresario for individual women of talent who otherwise, in the face of the obstacles inherent in an age of male supremacy, might never have been able to work or be appreciated for what they did.

Higginson continued to speak on the Lyceum lecture circuit. He taught in his church's Sunday School. He served on the public school board, the first of many he served on over the years. He was active in the defense of the right of a Roman Catholic child to choose to read only the version of the Bible approved by the priest, in defiance of local school authorities. For this action challenging the anti-Catholic and anti-immigrant "Know Nothing" movement, he was ousted from his school-board post, but was later reinstated.

Now the pastor had a congregation that could be expected solidly to back his radicalism. He had a freedom not previously experienced: he lived as he had advocated that others should live. He was not deterred or diverted by the distractions of his developing career as a writer.

Having helped launch the women's movement at its first national convention, held in Worcester in 1850, he stayed involved with the movement, addressing legislative committees as well as public meetings. He lectured regularly against slavery. He organized a boat club and participated in outings on Lake Quinsigamond, and these furnished material for his nature essays. He was president of an athletic association and prime mover in the formation of the Worcester Natural History Society—and found time to help organize and manage Worcester's first free public library.

This was a period during which the Underground Railroad was in full operation and fugitive slaves often sought aid from him and his fellow abolitionists. From time to time, appeals appeared in Boston and Worcester newspapers, over his signature, asking for financial aid. He personally helped find work or hiding places for escapees.

Ignoring the Fugitive Slave Act was one thing. Openly defying it and forcibly resisting officials who, under the flag of the United States, sought to seize and send back to bondage those who had freed themselves was another. This was the business of his Boston-based Vigilance Committee.

The case of Anthony Burns well illustrates what the committee faced. Burns was a Bostonian by adoption who had freed himself from a Virginia plantation and made his way north. Not expecting or wishing to live on handouts, he gained employment in a Boston tailor shop. He disclosed his whereabouts in a letter to a brother, which was illegally intercepted by the U.S. Post Office.

A Boston policeman located and seized Anthony Burns. Massachusetts would not permit slave hunters to use its state jails to hold those who had been seized, and so Burns was taken to the federal courthouse and held in its detention pen until a semblence of a hearing could take place at which an order of deportation to Virginia would be signed.

The Vigilance Committee scheduled a public meeting to protest this action. Reverend Higginson was notified and took the first train to Boston. The committee's scheme was for a squad of protesters to storm the lightly guarded courthouse and spirit Burns off to safety before the order could be signed. All was set, Higginson bought a dozen axes to be used if needed, and the voluntary rescue group was selected.

The success of the protest brought failure of the rescue.

Higginson had never seen Faneuil Hall as crowded as it was by the protest meeting called in behalf of freedom for Anthony Burns. The plan of action could not be explained to enough of the core committee members present because it was impossible to move through the crowd. Some entrances were hopelessly blocked. Higginson, with the agreed-upon advance group at the courthouse, decided to act without waiting for the aid they had expected from Faneuil Hall.

Reverend Higginson led the group in breaking down the door and he and another protester rushed in; the entrance was too narrow to let more people follow unless the first two moved forward, but their path was blocked by a pack of club-wielding marshals. Higginson suffered a blow on the chin and a cut that left a lifelong scar. A pistol shot rang out, no one then knew from where, and one of the federal defenders fell. The shot had killed a U.S. deputy marshal; its effect was to cause the support crowd to melt away. The rescue had failed.

The hearing proceeded, with the foreordained result. Two companies of U.S. marines were sent to Boston to support local army units mobilized to ensure one man's return to bondage. They lined the streets to hold back the crowds, said to be 50,000-strong, of those who had come to witness the tragedy. Buildings were festooned with black crepe as for a funeral procession as Burns was forced to board a ship that would take him back to slavery in Virginia.

Higginson was arrested and indicted—although for riot, not for murder, as he feared—for his role in the incident in which the marshal had been shot. He refused advice and assistance from those who felt he should flee. Lucy Stone, a feminist leader, said to him, "It would be good for the cause if they were to hang you"—he would become one of its martyrs. But the case never came to trial, as the indictment was dismissed on a legal point. Lawyers for Higginson included John A. Andrew, who was to be governor of Massachusetts during the Civil War; it was Andrew who authorized the creation of the 54th Massachusetts Regiment, the black regiment whose story is told in the movie *Glory*.

The Congress that passed the Fugitive Slave Act of 1850 can be blamed for the violence of the Burns confrontation. The Kansas-Nebraska Act of 1854 produced much more widespread and deadly violence as anti- and pro-slavery forces battled for control of the Kansas territory—"Bleeding Kansas," as it came to be called. Here too Higginson was in the forefront of the fight for freedom.

The Kansas-Nebraska Act of 1854 repealed the so-called Missouri Compromise, the 1820 law that had brought an uneasy truce between slave and free states by drawing a line between the two regions (Kansas and Nebraska both lay north of it) and providing that as the nation expanded west, one slave state should be admitted to the union for every free state added.

The 1854 act, however, meant that the decision of whether a state should be slave or free was to be made by a vote of the inhabitants of the state. The flaw in this seemingly democratic idea (if anything condoning slavery can ever be called democratic) was that Kansas's then most populous border was with the slave state Missouri. Emigrants from the free eastern states who had traveled long and far to settle in good faith in a free state were outvoted (and terrorized) by "Border Ruffians," as pro-slavery Missourians who traveled to Kansas to vote in the 1855 election came to be known.

Many in the northeastern part of the United States, especially in Massachusetts—including some who had not been in sympathy with the abolitionists—were outraged by what they saw as slavery advocates' move to open aggression against the free states. Community organizations were formed to collect funds and equipment to aid the legitimate settlers.

Higginson was sent by a group calling itself the Kansas Aid Committee to take supplies, including rifles and ammunition, to the bona fide settlers. Armed and in danger more than once, he wrote home: "Imagine me patrolling as one of the guard for an hour every night, in high boots amid the dewy grass, rifle in hand and revolver in belt."

The story of his expedition is told in "A Ride Through Kansas" (he originally spelled it "Kanzas"), which is a collection of the dispatches he sent to the *New York Tribune* from the field (see Part I, Chapter 4).

The next step toward war soon followed. In Kansas, John Brown and his sons, who were free-state settlers, had engaged with and battled the Border Ruffians. Higginson and Brown had naturally become aware of each other's activities.

Later, in 1858, Brown asked Higginson for help "for the perfection of by far the most important undertaking of my life," which turned out to be the raid on Harpers Ferry, Virginia. This help was given by Higginson and five like-minded comrades—a group that some later called the Secret Six.

But Brown's attempted raid at Harpers Ferry failed. After this failure Higginson was the only one of the Secret Six who neither flinched nor fled. Others went into hiding, went abroad, or took refuge in madness. He was later saluted for his stand in Stephen Vincent Benet's epic poem, "John Brown's Body," as "swart-minded Higginson."

Higginson raised funds for the defense of Brown and those taken with him, and he planned an armed expedition to invade Virginia to rescue the prisoner. When Brown learned this he stopped it. Brown's act and his execution energized the antislavery movement and won sympathy for it among previously nonaligned citizens.

Higginson was as loyal to the cause of freedom for women as he steadfastly was to the cause of freedom for African Americans. The fame he gained in consequence of the Burns case was paralleled by unflagging public service to the infant women's movement, which he had helped to launch.

In addition to lecturing and counseling, Higginson participated in two cases of open activism for the feminist cause, nonviolent but effective in their day. When Lucy Stone and Henry Blackwell were to be married they asked Reverend Higginson to officiate; they planned to make the nuptials a protest demonstration of the injustice inherent in the marriage relationship under current law. Having participated as clergyman, he endorsed their formally written protest. He released his statement supporting Stone's position—among other things she insisted on using her own last name—to the press, along with her statement, and it won some attention at the time. Higginson's role in this episode does not usually earn mention in accounts of the history of the fight for women's equality.

More sensational reverberations ensued when women delegates were excluded from a committee meeting at the World Temperance Convention in New York, in 1853. Higginson, a member of the organizing committee, proposed that Susan B. Anthony be placed on the Arrangements Committee. This was refused, and the convention was in an uproar when the chairman upheld the refusal. Higginson then called out supporters of women's rights, and under his initiative about fifty delegates left the hall. They proceeded to another hall, hired it for their meeting, elected Higginson as chairman, and named their meeting the Whole World's Temperance Convention.

The jeers in the street and in the press outnumbered the expressions of approval and understanding, but at that time nothing different could have been expected. Even so, many who had been passive or critical concerning women's equality came to think about the issue and to accept, even if not advocate, the point made by Thomas Wentworth Higginson.

Higginson was soon to become an ex-minister, so that he could devote more time to writing. His writing career had been advanced by an invitation to be among the first regular writers for the newly founded periodical *Atlantic Monthly.*

Soon he won fame with his writings in the national publication. By the beginning of 1860 eight major essays had been published in the new magazine. Several of them created something of a sensation.

These included "Saints and Their Bodies," an effort to draw attention to and popularize proper health care and health maintenance. Another essay on a health-related subject was "A New Counterblast," in which Higginson criticized tobacco as being addictive and as a reported cause of cancer. But the most successful at that period was "Ought Women to Learn the Alphabet?" a clever and seriously humorous essay that was of considerable value to the feminist cause and was often reprinted. Sophia Smith said it moved her to found the college in Northampton, Massachusetts, that bears her name.

He did not allow the memory of John Brown to die. Established as a successful writer, he began research on the subject of slave rebellions.

What he found enabled him to write an essay about two successful slave revolts in the Caribbean. He then turned to slave revolts in the United States. His research was diligent.

In five essays written over a three-year period he testified to the existence of a will and the courage of Africans and their descendants in this hemisphere. Implicitly these essays defended John Brown. In the last essay, "Nat Turner's Insurrection," he addressed himself to the case of Nat Turner's revolt in Virginia. Over a century later, Dr. John A. Morsell of the NAACP, in congressional testimony, saluted Higginson's work as an early effort to bring about the integration of history teaching in the United States. (Higginson's slave revolt essays have been collected and published as *Black Rebellion* [Da Capo Press, 1998].)

THE PIONEER BLACK REGIMENT AND ITS COLONEL

As the years passed in Worcester, the activist-pastor began to recognize that striving on so many fronts, possible at age twenty-eight, was becoming more difficult. By 1858, his income from writing and Lyceum circuit lecturing had relieved him of the need to serve full time for the Free Church. But he would not curtail his abolition and women's rights activities.

Higginson began early in 1861 to prepare for the war that seemed inevitable. As he wrote later, "From the time of my Kansas visit, I never doubted that a further conflict of some sort was pending." While signs of the "coming storm" multiplied, he began "to read military books, take notes on fortifications, strategy, and the principles of attack and defense."

When the war started, later in 1861, he was thirty-seven years old and ambivalent about volunteering. Contributing to Higginson's doubt about serving was a sad change in his home life. His wife suffered an illness that became permanently disabling (probably a form of arthritis). This did not prevent—indeed, she encouraged—his forays into Boston, New York, and Kansas. Though her illness didn't interfere with his life as a writer, it discouraged him from volunteering—a step that would put his life at risk and be marked by long absences.

President Abraham Lincoln's first response to the threat of secession by Southern states was an attempt to appease the slave states. A proposed Thirteenth Amendment offered an unrepealable guaranty against emancipation. Passed by Congress, it failed to be ratified by the states. Eleven states proceeded to secede from the Union in early 1861, and war broke out on April 12, 1861, when Southern forces opened fire on Fort Sumter, South Carolina. As the war went on it became clear that defeats and hardship would increase, unless the Union's war effort was directed toward striking directly at slavery, the economic basis of the South and hence of its ability to make war. His policy of leaving slavery alone shattered, Lincoln now declared free all slaves whose labor was being used to support the rebellion (transporting supplies, building fortifications, etc.).

Higginson's hesitation ended and he decided to volunteer. He now focused on the study of drill, manuals of arms, and marching, instead of his physical culture classes. He requested and received authority to raise a Massachusetts regiment, the 51st Massachusetts, and was commissioned captain of one of its companies. His regiment was soon ready for its marching orders.

Then, in the autumn of 1862, as he dined one evening with his fellow officers, he received a letter containing an invitation that "took his breath away." It changed his military career, his life, and the course and, it may reasonably be contended, the very outcome of the war.

The nation's conduct of the war had been suffering a self-imposed handicap. Thousands of Americans of African descent who lived in the free states were qualified to serve as soldiers, yet their representatives' offers to enlist them and their individual attempts to volunteer had been rebuffed repeatedly. Prevailing prejudices raised doubts as to whether they were fit to serve as soldiers. Moreover, Lincoln worried that the support from the nonseceding slave states would be endangered by putting blacks in Union uniforms.

Then, events made possible an important advance in Lincoln's policy. After a string of reverses, the United States military at last won an encouraging victory. Off the coast of South Carolina lie the Sea Islands; here there were a number of plantations and, at Beaufort, a fine harbor for seagoing vessels. Here the United States Navy secured a beachhead, from which the army fanned out to conquer and hold the rest of the islands. They were to remain Union territory for the rest of the war. The islands were strategically located among the Confederacy's great ports, and so securing them enhanced the U.S. Navy's ability to enforce the Union blockade that prevented the import of arms and supplies and the export of goods that helped the rebel states to survive.

The plantation owners fled to the mainland, some with their household slaves. But they left behind thousands of field slaves, and these men represented a great opportunity. Washington was tempted to make an exception to its policy barring soldiers of African descent; the former slaves on the Sea Islands were to be empowered to make permanent their own freedom—and to help transform the sectional conflict into a struggle for the freedom of hundreds of thousands of their brothers, sisters, and children.

The letter that Captain Higginson received that autumn afternoon was from General Rufus Saxton, the military governor of the Sea Islands. He was the first Union commander with full legal authority to place rifles in the hands of ex-slaves and muster them into the U.S. Army.

Saxton was a Massachusetts man, a good antislavery man. His concern was not only the military mission of the new soldiers. He was aware that their performance could affect the decision to recruit more black soldiers, and it would help persuade a reluctant and prejudiced population to treat slaves as men, as equal humans.

Special qualifications were needed for a commander of the regiment. This commander would have to supervise closely and direct the training of men who as ex-slaves could genuinely be called disadvantaged. He would have to relate to the men in a manner that won not only their respect but their affection. He would also have to inspire them.

When a chaplain who was a former abolitionist minister suggested that Saxton seek out Thomas Wentworth Higginson for the assignment, there was no need for further inquiry. Saxton knew Higginson personally, as well as by reputation, and felt sure he was the best man for the assignment. That was how a Massachusetts captain, with flimsy military experience, with no military training, came to become the instant colonel of a regiment. Higginson quickly accepted General Saxton's offer of the command of the First South Carolina Volunteers. Whatever self-doubt he might have had as to his ability to accomplish the mission was overcome by his feeling that he "had been an abolitionist too long and had known and loved John Brown too well, not to feel a thrill of joy at last on finding myself in the position where he only wished to be."

Within three weeks he had been relieved of his Massachusetts post and was on his way to the island headquarters at Beaufort, to put on his colonel's eagles and to take command of his regiment.

Professor Dudley T. Cornish, a professor of history and sometime instructor at the Army General Staff College at Ft. Leavenworth, Kansas, wrote about this venture in his book *The Sable Arm* (Longmans, Green, New York, 1956), which is still cited as the most complete and authoritative work on the role of the African Americans in the U.S. Civil War. (The phrase "sable arm" was coined by Frederick Douglass in his call—one of many—to employ blacks in the Union Army.) Cornish's assessment of Saxton's choice of Higginson:

General Saxton had made a superb choice in the man to lead the 1st South Carolina: he was Thomas Wentworth Higginson of Massachusetts, abolitionist and old friend of John Brown, a man with an excellent reputation throughout the North because of his intellectual and literary attainments.

Higginson was exactly what the situation demanded. He lent the enterprise a respectability it had previously lacked and he quickly brought the regiment into a state of training and morale equal to that of any white regiment of similar experience. His intelligence, imagination, devotion to duty, and military experience provided the right mixture.

He had soon won the confidence and affection of his men, and he gradually restored the regiment and the whole enterprise of arming Negroes in the opinion of the white officers and men of the department by seeing that his men did their fair share and more of the fatigue duty and unloading supply ships.

For Higginson, the entire experience was novel and challenging and he gave it his best. He was aware more than anyone else of the signal importance of making the regiment a good one, aware that the organization "was watched with microscopic scrutiny by friends and foes."

Higginson the soldier never forgot that he was a writer and recorded his experience in his journals and letters home, and eloquently told his story in articles in the *Atlantic Monthly.* These were published in 1869 as the book *Army Life in a Black Regiment* (W. H. Norton/Norton Library, 1984). (And Higginson the writer never forgot that he had been a soldier: not only in the immediate postwar years, but for the rest of his life, he was addressed or referred to in print or speech as "Colonel Higginson" and he must have preferred it that way.)

The book is an extraordinary record of a unique experience: the encounter of a New England intellectual with almost a thousand African Americans, and his experiences in training and leading them. But it was, as Higginson intended, effective proof that African Americans can fight, die, or kill for their country as heroically as whites. And it was considerably more than that.

Higginson's production of this work gave us an important asset for combating prejudice, and as such it is no less valuable than the regiment itself, which opened the way for the two hundred thousand black troops that arguably made the difference between victory and stalemate in the Civil War.

His articles in the *Atlantic Monthly*, and later his book, constitute a "document in desegregation," as the critic Howard Mumford Jones has said of *Army Life in a Black Regiment.* The portrayal of the interrelation and the developing mutual affection of the white colonel and the black troops can still help eradicate all the misconceptions that have barred full recognition of racial equality.

One of the salient characteristics of Higginson's account was his continual self-analysis, as the experience of command and cohabitation caused him to rethink and discard some stereotypes he had continued to harbor, even while, with all the goodwill in the world, he had been fighting to eliminate them and cure their consequences.

One or two academics, diligent in rummaging about among diaries, letters, drafts of manuscripts, and the like, have questioned *Army Life* on one point—portions of the book as published are not compatible with some phraseology in Colonel Higginson's unpublished journals. They suggest that his omission of expressions of impatience with his white junior officers and doubts about his black privates impair the book as history.

Such "discoveries" do not in the least detract from the value of *Army Life in a Black Regiment* as a "document in desegregation." Whatever may have been noted as an expression of impatience, under tension or in moments of stress, is not necessarily any more accurate as a factual statement than a later, calm reappraisal.

As the century-old civil rights struggle intensified in the 1960s, an essay by the novelist Jackson Stanley appeared in *The New Republic;* it began: "Thomas Wentworth Higginson's *Army Life in a Black Regiment*, first published in 1869, is probably the finest personal history to come out of the Civil War, but who knows anyone who ever heard of it?"

But Stanley's question elicited no response. It was ignored during the 1990 release and reception of the film *Glory*, which was publicized with indifference to the truth—characteristic of Hollywood—as the story of the true "first" black regiment.

The very organization of the 54th Massachusetts Regiment, the "*Glory*" regiment, was not initiated and authorized until Higginson's regiment had proved its mettle. Higginson tells in his book of how Colonel Robert Gould Shaw, the young commander of the newly mustered 54th, sought him out for advice on how a white officer should relate to his troops of African descent.

A more authoritative evaluation of Higginson and his regiment has recently been provided by Professor Barbara Jeanne Fields. Invited to address a "rededication" in Boston of the eloquent Saint-Gaudens monument erected in front of the State House in memory of Shaw and the 54th Massachusetts Regiment, she frankly criticized the sad consequence of the misrepresentations propagated by the film *Glory:* "It is to bury even further from sight the remarkable history of the First South Carolina Volunteers, organized in mid-October 1862 and commanded by the Unitarian minister and man of letters, Thomas Wentworth Higginson."

NEWPORT: "THE WOMEN'S HOUR" AND SOME OTHERS

Higginson, wounded slightly in an upriver raid into the mainland South Carolina, was discharged in 1864, before the war was over.

He did not, as he would have preferred, return to Massachusetts. Even before his return, his semi-invalid wife had decided that Newport, Rhode Island, was to be their new home. She had many relatives there, and she hoped that she would get some relief for her condition from living near the sea. But her health did not improve.

Higginson was to live in Newport for fourteen years, until Mary's death. She had chosen to live in a boarding house, a decision that deprived him of the amenities of home life and, especially important to a writer, provided room for only a few books and limited space for handling papers. As if unwilling to relive those days, he omitted the whole period from his own informally written biography, *Cheerful Yesterdays.*

But Newport life was not wholly without cheer. Working under cramped conditions, he continued to write and to be published at the pace maintained at Worcester. He did not lack opportunity for activism, in town and out of it. He developed friendships with women writers and assisted them by helping them develop and being supportive of their morale. He had a not inconsiderable social life as well.

He did not have to wait long to resume the good fight, his reputation having preceded him to Newport. Soon after Higginson joined his wife at the boarding house, a member of the school committee, a local judge who planned to resign, nominated Higginson to fill the vacancy.

Soon there developed a clash that was a local preview of the struggle that was supposed to, but didn't, end with *Brown vs. Board of Education* a century later. First there was a small but revealing misunderstanding. The school committee was elected by the city council, but if vacancies occurred during the term, the committee filled them itself. The judge who was resigning lobbied his fellow committee members to vote for Higginson as the replacement for himself, and in a conversation with one member he said, "He would be a very useful member on the board."

"Don't know about that," said his colleague, "but I am not going to sit on the same committee with a black man."

This assumption that Higginson was a black man was corrected, and Higginson joined the school committee. (This was not the only time, during his life and long after he was dead, that that mistake was made.)

Things did not remain quiet for long. George T. Downing was a successful businessman who as an abolitionist in Boston in 1854 had been with Higginson in the group that broke down the courthouse door in the failed attempt to secure Anthony Burns's freedom. Now living in Newport, Downing sought to enter his children in the nearest school. He was twice defeated; he was black.

When Downing heard that Higginson was in Newport and was on the school committee, he lost no time in making a new application. The school superintendent chose not to act on it and referred the case to the school committee. Higginson was prepared. He had already lined up two allies who fought vigorously at the decisive meeting. A week of successful lobbying by a celebrated commander of black soldiers who had fought for freedom and equal treatment carried the day by a vote of seven to three.

There was a temporary backlash at City Hall, and in the next election of the full school committee by the city council, Higginson was dropped—despite the fact that dozens more black children had been admitted to local schools and peacefully integrated. But vindication ultimately came when a fully democratic process was instituted, in which citizens themselves voted for the school committee members. Not only was Higginson returned to the committee, the panel itself was integrated by the election of a black clergyman.

Higginson was eager to rejoin the effort to win for women not only the vote, but more: fully equal treatment. Wishing to keep his options open, he declined an offer of a full-time position as agent for the New England Freedman's Aid Society. He avowed continued attachment to the black freedom cause, but said he could not give his life to it exclusively; that did not mean he would abandon it.

This became evident when some of the woman activists began to protest what they saw as unfair provisions in the new amendment, the Fourteenth Amendment, proposed by abolitionists and their allies in the Republican party to safeguard Emancipation. To understand Higginson's stance on the issue of suffrage as it applied to women and the just-emancipated male slaves, some background is necessary.

The need for this amendment arose after Lincoln's death and the accession of Andrew Johnson to the presidency. From his residence in

Newport Higginson observed the Johnson administration with increasing concern.

Johnson had been accepted by Lincoln as a patriotic Southern "moderate"—born in Raleigh, North Carolina, as a U.S. senator representing Tennessee he was the only Southern senator to support the Union during the Civil War. When he took office after Lincoln's death he seemed to be just this, declaring, "Treason is treason and must be punished." In the spirit of Lincoln he believed in a "mild" Reconstruction, yet the Radical Republicans and many in the North felt he went too far in his leniency. For example, ex-Confederate officers were allowed to resume participation in the governments of states whose secession from the Union they had supported. The period that followed, until an aroused Congress stepped in, could well be termed "racist reconstruction."

The reinstated Confederates knew they could not restore slavery, but they sought ways to effectively stall, through so-called Black Codes, most of the positive consequences for ex-slaves of their emancipation. The codes were a series of laws designed to bring about a state of affairs described by Higginson in a letter to *The Nation* (see Part I, Chapter 11): "to keep the [N]egroes in a condition just as near slavery as possible; to limit their right of contract; their right of locomotion; and their range of labor; to have, in short, a separate [N]egro code."

In a letter to a friend he wrote that Johnson's program amounted to "the pardon of every rebel for the crime of rebelling, and the utter refusal to pardon a single black loyalist for the 'crime' of being black."

When Congress reconvened later that year (1865), it created a Joint Committee on Reconstruction to examine the situation; its searching inquiry found the situation pretty much as Higginson had described it.

Congress mounted a program to check the kinds of abuses Higginson had referred to. As part of this program it began a process that culminated in the Fourteenth Amendment, which declared "all persons" born in the United States of America to be citizens and assured equal protection of the laws. For the first time in our history the sense of the phrase used in the Declaration of Independence in 1776, "created equal," had been put into law.

The first and principal clause of the proposed Fourteenth Amendment, which guarantees due process and equal protection of the laws to all persons, was acceptable to the women's rights advocates. (Indeed, it is the basis on which most of women's gains of the last thirty years have been won.)

The second clause of the Fourteenth Amendment was the one that troubled women activists. It was intended to discourage interference with the new citizens' vote. Any denial of the right to vote would be punished by reduction of a state's representation in Congress in proportion to the extent of the offense. But the clause stipulated that the punishable offense was denial of the vote "to any of the male inhabitants" of the state. Of course it was unfair to women, but in 1866 women did not have the vote in any state.

Two feminist leaders, Susan B. Anthony and Elizabeth Cady Stanton, saw the preparations for passage of the Fourteenth Amendment as an opportunity to advance woman suffrage. They wanted to eliminate the word "male," for they viewed that word's presence as a wrong against women. Theoretically it was, and one could hold that women's rights, not being inferior to Negro rights, required changing the wording of the amendment.

Higginson, a participant in the women's freedom fight and a valued counselor to women struggling for equal rights, agreed that they were right to attempt to eliminate the word "male." But when this attempt failed, he felt it was wrong to continue to oppose the ultimate adoption of the amendment. He saw that nothing would be gained for women if the Fourteenth Amendment were defeated. Equal rights for women had not been the objective or issue of the Civil War. Higginson felt that the struggle's main object—removal of slavery and all of its consequences— was now in jeopardy because of actions taken by the former rebels and secessionists. Former slaves needed protection most urgently. The effort to get that protection would have been endangered had the opponents of the word "male" succeeded.

In the shorthand of the day the whole controversy was summarized by the aphorism "This is the Negro's hour and not the women's hour."

A parallel fight erupted when the word "male" was put in the Fifteenth Amendment, which forbade abridgment of any male suffrage on account of a man's having been a slave.

So sharp was the controversy, so bitter the feeling it generated, that it caused a split in the women's movement. Anthony and Stanton, who now opposed passage of the Fourteenth Amendment, formed their own group, the National Woman Suffrage Association. Lucy Stone and many others supported passage of the amendment and sent out a call for others to join their cause, which resulted in the birth of the American Woman Suffrage Association. Higginson, who had supported the Fourteenth Amendment and was also recognized as a staunch supporter of the feminist cause, was elected president of this group's founding convention.

Higginson became a member of the editorial staff of the American Woman Suffrage Association's organ, the *Woman's Journal,* and a regular columnist. The *Woman's Journal* was an important influence in the women's rights field for the next fifty years. Higginson's column was widely read and often quoted. He never attacked or even mildly criticized the Stanton-Anthony group.

Unlike some of his early associates in the A.W.S.A., he remained on good terms with Stanton and Anthony. In Stanton's autobiography she pointedly tells us that in 1872, when Anthony was jailed for "illegally" trying to vote under the umbrella of the Fourteenth Amendment, "financial aid was given, unsolicitedly, by Thomas Wentworth Higginson." His persistent efforts to bring about unification contributed to the ultimate merger of the two groups twenty years later.

Higginson always respected women as individuals, and his friendships with them developed on the basis of mutual recognition that such relations were possible without sexual overtones. In the Newburyport years, Higginson was an early and sometimes important supporter of woman writers. His interest in supporting them continued in the Newport period; it was from Newport that he traveled for the first of his two meetings with Emily Dickinson, in 1870.

As one surveys the whole panorama of Higginson's work and achievements as a reformer, fighter, and man of letters, his connection with Dickinson would not ordinarily occupy a dominant position. But this relationship earns our attention because for a long time the Dickinson connection has been the principal feature of his life and work for which he has been remembered. It is also the aspect that has been more unfairly judged than any other.

Two *Atlantic Monthly* essays begin and end the story. "Letter to a Young Contributor" was published in April 1862; the other, "Emily Dickinson," published in 1891, sums up Higginson's involvement with the young poet of Amherst and her works. (See Part VI, Chapters 5 and 6.)

One April morning in 1862, Higginson took his usual stroll to the Worcester Post Office. One of the letters he received had no return address, and was postmarked Amherst, Massachusetts. It contained four poems in a barely legible hand, and a brief letter that began "Mr. Higginson, are you too deeply occupied to say if my verse is alive?"

Dickinson's letter was sent in the month in which Higginson's "Letter to a Young Contributor" was published, and the former has usually been thought to have provoked the latter. The timing and the content of the "Letter" make that suggestion plausible, but its content suggests otherwise. It is addressed to unknown, aspiring, hitherto unpublished writers in general, not to a specific person—a courteous expression of advice to would-be writers. The opening paragraph of the "Letter" shows it to be an answer to a number of letters asking advice and help, the sort that begin to flood the boxes of established writers as they get to be known. It decidedly was not an invitation for more such letters.

It has been said that Higginson "discovered" Emily Dickinson, but perhaps the opposite is more accurate: she discovered him. The essay "Emily Dickinson" (Part VI, Chapter 6) contains ample evidence—Higginson's report of their talks and of the tenor of her letters—that Dickinson admired Higginson's writing, agreed with much of his political thought, and read every word of his that was published. Dickinson evaluated what the man *was* on the basis of what he had *written*. As far as she was concerned, they were not strangers: she knew enough about him, what he had done and what he believed, to entrust to him, wholesale, as it were, the treasured product of her seclusion. Two or three other people had seen a couple of her poems; Samuel Bowles or Josiah Holland allowed or caused one of the poems, "I Taste a Liquor Never Brewed," to be published without her permission.

Dickinson's tentative inquiry to Higginson began a correspondence that continued for more than twenty years. An adequate sampling of her letters is contained in the essay "Emily Dickinson"; few of Higginson's letters to her have survived. Careful and thoughtful examination of the letters will give a better idea of their tenor and significance than any commentary or summary can provide. They offer evidence to refute as unwarranted the scorn that has marked many discussions of what Higginson meant to her.

It is demeaning to and disrespectful of Dickinson to assume that her repeated expressions of confidence, respect, and affection were insincere or without justification. Her simple statement "You were not aware that you saved my life," an impulsive expression of gratitude for helping her to recoil at self-destruction, does not stand alone as an expression of Higginson's importance to her.

The letters reproduced and the conversations reported in "Emily Dickinson" are rich in signs of a friendship marked by trust, confidence, mutual respect, and affection. (As we have already noted, this was not the only friendship Higginson had with women that was free of any romantic overtone.) Dickinson expressed her regard for Higginson in numerous ways: "I have had few pleasures as deep as your opinion"; "Will you be my preceptor, Mr. Higginson?"; "If at any time you regret you received me, or I give you a different fabric to that you supposed, you must banish me."

This was a relationship that made possible, after her death in 1886, the rescue of the body of her work. Higginson was to play a significant, perhaps indispensable, part in that rescue. When Dickinson died, her sister and sister-in-law found the hundreds of poems, written over a period of many years, in the room in which she had lived and died, out of communication with the world and yet incredibly aware of the emotions and ways of people and their relation to their environment. They thought the little bundles of paper might have some value; but living in a village with no significant communication with the world in which publication might be possible, what were they to do?

They had never met Higginson, nor had they seen him during the two visits he paid to Emily, but they knew of his standing as writer, critic, and public figure. His correspondence with Emily was known well enough for him to have been invited to her funeral and to participate in the obsequies. They brought the poetry to him. He in turn took it to his own publisher, Houghton Mifflin. He was rejected there—reportedly one member of the firm said to another after his visit, "Higginson must have been out of his mind to think we would publish that stuff."

Ultimately he secured a publisher, Roberts Brothers, and acted as coeditor of the first volumes, and the genius that was Emily Dickinson became a significant part of America's and the world's literature. During her lifetime she was ahead of her time, ahead of the standards and customs of the day and of the prevalent expectations of poetry. After her death, literary taste adjusted to her work.

From her letters and Higginson's recounting of their relationship in "Emily Dickinson," a number of conclusions can be fairly drawn: Dickinson greatly admired Higginson as a writer and chose him to be the one friend and adviser she felt she needed. His letters and conversation gave her exactly what she sought, undiminished by any criticism that missed the point of what she was doing. Her strength and self-respect as an artist were such that her morale was unaffected by such criticism. Because of Higginson's advocacy, her work survived and became available to us very much as she would have wished; if not for what he did for her in life and death, this would have been unlikely.

Nevertheless Higginson has generally been viewed as something of a villain in relation to Dickinson. Dr. Howard W. Hintz noted, in a 1939 dissertation, a tendency to treat Higginson's relation with Dickinson with utter condescension and scorn. The poet Genevieve Taggard said in her 1930 biography of Dickinson, *The Life and Mind of Emily Dickinson* (A. A. Knopf, NY, 1934), that "Higginson botched things badly." The literary historian George Whicher wrote in his book about Dickinson, *This Was a Poet,* that "more than most poets, she had been exposed to the attacks of formal critics. . . . At the head of this list must be placed her chosen guide, Thomas Wentworth Higginson." As a result of this type of comment, a view of Higginson as a critic so narrow and conventional that he lacked literary acumen became widely accepted.

"*Dear Preceptor*" (Houghton Mifflin, 1968), by Anna Mary Wells, is a Higginson biography that, as the title indicates (it was the salutation Dickinson used in her letters to him), is shaped to give special emphasis to their friendship. It is a bright, scholarly, and readable work. Wells finds on the evidence that the critics all erred who said that the poet was wrong to revere Higginson, that her poetry was marred by his criticism, and that the decision not to publish during her lifetime was his, not hers. Wells satisfied the critics, but the miasma hanging over Higginson has not been dissipated.

This was painfully demonstrated by the writing and reception of the play *The Belle of Amherst*, by William Luce, which had a successful run on Broadway in 1976 and has since been seen on broadcast TV and published as a book (also by Luce). Luce accepted and used as a basis all the elements of the old misconceptions regarding Higginson and compounded the harm by writing lines that give a distorted picture of the character of the man he calls Professor Higginson.

There have been attempts to redress the balance, however. Critiques of the play and its underlying premises were published in the 1986 volume *19th Century Women Writers of the English Speaking World* (Rhoda Nathan, ed.; Greenwood). It contains three papers presented at a conference at Hofstra University offering detailed and documented refutations of the play: "A Second Look at the Belle," by Howard N. Meyer; "T. W. Higginson and Emily Dickinson in Feminist Perspective," by Tilden G. Edelstein; and "The Soul's Society: Emily Dickinson and Colonel Higginson," by Anna Mary Wells.

Helen Hunt Jackson was an important but less remembered woman writer of the nineteenth century who was greatly indebted to Higginson. She happened to be a childhood friend of Dickinson's (and could testify to her disinclination to publish her poems). Bereaved of both husband and child, she landed at the Newport boarding house where Mary and her husband stayed. In spite of her loss she carried herself with such courage that he noted in his diary, "She seems very bright and social and may prove an accession."

He was right. Her relationship with him was to remake her life and lead her to realize her potential as a writer.

It did not take Higginson long to perceive Hunt's capacity for self-expression and to learn of a talent to write that had already produced a few poems. With his guidance and encouragement, she developed quickly, constantly consulting him as an editor. She repeatedly expressed her gratitude, in the most affectionate terms. They spent much of their time together and among other things went to Boston to hear Charles Dickens lecture when he came to the United States in 1868. Higginson was openly fond of her and frank in his appreciation of her company. At the time their association was not the subject of gossip; yet viewing it through a twentieth-century lens might lead to speculation as to the character of their friendship—which might be sufficiently justified to warrant a fictional treatment, perhaps a movie.

Helen Hunt left Newport in 1872, and after some travels (about which she wrote) she settled in Colorado Springs. There she met and ultimately married William Sharpless Jackson, a banker and rail magnate. In the American West, Helen Hunt Jackson observed with such repugnance the treatment of Native Americans that she became what she had once told Higginson she would not: a "woman with a cause." Her indignation found expression in the novel *Ramona* and in the monograph to which she gave the eloquent title *A Century of Dishonor.*

AND WRITING ALL THE WHILE

Neither politics nor personalities could have distracted the ex-colonel from his desire or need to write, a need that was financial as well as emotional.

There was no doubt in the Newport years—if ever there had been— that whatever Higginson's distractions might be, he was primarily a writer. Some work was commissioned and of course he continued to conceive of projects and to undertake them on his own initiative.

In 1867 he accepted a publisher's commission to edit the two-volume *Harvard Memorial Biographies,* which profiled and paid tribute to the Harvard men who had lost their lives in the Civil War (he wrote thirteen of the contributions himself). During one period, from approximately 1868 to 1869, his usual work of writing nonfiction was derailed by his hopeful attempt to write fiction. One result was a novel, *Malbone,* published in 1869, that disappointed the writer and his readers. A few of his short stories had some merit, but the reception did not encourage his writing more of them.

There was a gym in Newport where Higginson worked out regularly, which helped him recover from the effects of his war wound and gave him an escape from the difficult life at the boarding house. Other welcome distractions were the backcountry and woods, where he hiked and botanized, and the seaport and its waterfront, with its ancient wharves, where he roamed about. He was often seen out in the bay in a dory.

It was in Newport that he organized part of his journals and some of the essays he had sent back from the Sea Islands, to put together the book that was published as *Army Life in a Black Regiment.* He wrote sketches and sometimes obituaries of his contemporaries that for their keen observations have been seen as an incomparable collection (in quality and in quantity) of profiles of American men and women of the nineteenth century. This body of his work not only makes for good reading about people not necessarily covered elsewhere, but also is a resource for scholars.

In addition to the articles in the *Atlantic Monthly, Scribner's,* and smaller and specialized journals, he published a translation of the works of Epictetus; *Army Life;* his failed novel, *Malbone;* a collection of essays, *Atlantic Essays* (in 1871); *English Statesmen* (1875); and *American Explorers* (1877).

Another project, to which he devoted two years of research, was to prove to be his best-seller. An inspired suggestion by a Boston educator who was repelled by the history texts being used in the schools led to a commission from Lee and Shepard to write a *Young Folks' History of the United States.* In his unfailingly elegant style, he made history a narrative illuminated with images producing interest, not boredom.

Possibly more than two hundred thousand copies of the work were sold. It was adopted by many school districts, and was translated into French, German, and Italian. The work is eminently readable, informal, and anecdotal and places more emphasis on periods of peace than on war. Many have said that the book led to the discarding of old forms and replaced them with a better style of history writing.

The Newport years ended in 1877 with the death of Mary Channing Higginson; death ended her suffering and lifted a burden from Higginson, who had been her diligent and unfailing caretaker for so many years.

JOURNEY'S END: BACK TO CAMBRIDGE

Two further events of signal importance in the life of Colonel Higginson took place in 1877. One was a change in his personal life that made it brighter; the other was a change in our nation's political course that marred our history.

As he had long wished, he moved back to Cambridge. There a young woman, Mary Thacher, who had sent him some of her manuscripts, won his heart, and they married. Not long afterward, in 1881, she presented him with his first and only child, Margaret.

On the national scene, the new president, Rutherford B. Hayes, ordered the withdrawal of troops that had been stationed in Louisiana and South Carolina to enforce the so-called "Reconstruction amendments," the Fourteenth and Fifteenth Amendments.

The "radical" amendments, the Fourteenth and Fifteenth, were the prize that Higginson had been fighting and risking his life for during most of the thirty years of his adult life. Yet in April 1877 he wrote a statement, published as a letter in the *Tribune,* declaring that he approved "heartily, cordially, and unreservedly" of President Hayes's order for a troop withdrawal. This was seen by some to be a reversal of position regarding the need for and justice of the Reconstruction amendments. The record needs to be carefully examined before Higginson is written off as one of those indifferent to the "betrayal of the Negro."

During his Newport years, Higginson had no illusions about what was happening in the former slave states. He did what he could to protest. He denounced Andrew Johnson's cave-in to Reconstruction, Confederate style, whereby rebel leaders were back in power; former masters were to be allowed to exploit their former slaves; and the latter were denied basic rights. He supported ratification of the Fourteenth and Fifteenth Amendments, the latter enfranchising male former slaves.

He called for the enforcement of equal rights and saw and deplored the consequences of nonenforcement: the treatment of blacks as a lower caste. The 1868 attempt to remove Andrew Johnson failed; his remaining in office as president meant that enforcement continued to be ineffective, owing to a lack of forceful leadership at the top.

A tide of resistance to equal treatment of blacks and whites had risen that was later to thwart President Grant's good-faith efforts to bring about compliance with the laws and constitutional provisions that Congress had established to provide for an equitable Reconstruction of the Southern states.

Grant's leadership as president could not match his effectiveness as a general. Higginson saw the step-by-step reconquest of most of the South by the self-styled "redeemers" who displaced the legitimate Reconstruction governments. They were winning by force or fraud; by terrorism at the polls and corruption of the electoral process.

In 1869, President Grant had deployed United States Army troops to enforce Reconstruction's constitutional guaranties, but this effort was failing. In the former slave states, local forces succeeded in placing unreconstructed whites in power, and each time this occurred, the federal troops were withdrawn. As of 1876, they remained in only three states, Louisiana, South Carolina, and Florida.

Many people—including even some former abolitionists—started to ask: What was the point of keeping troops in three minor states if federal guardianship was lacking in the rest? That question was produced by a virus infecting the nation whose symptoms were a feeling of being "tired of Reconstruction," and a readiness to argue that it would be "good for business" if differences about civil rights could be smoothed over. The process of surrendering the nation's commitment to racial equality for the sake of national white unity is detailed in Paul Buck's *The Road to Reunion* (Little, Brown, 1937).

Higginson was aware of, but not in agreement with, this trend. But even though he remained unaffected by the virus as such, he ultimately came to believe that further force was futile. The present course had failed; but he felt there might be a chance of success if an appeal were made to the sense of fairness of the more enlightened of the former rebel citizens, some of whom he had met. He knew the incoming President Hayes had served in the war as a major in a volunteer regiment, had risen to the rank of brigadier general, and when elected to Congress after the war had supported the Reconstruction amendments and attendant legislation.

When Hayes announced the troop withdrawal—as part of a deal that made him president, of which Higginson was ignorant—Higginson wrote, in a letter to the editor of the *New York Tribune* (Part I, Chapter 9): "[U]nder the present circumstances the President had no alternative. Let the immediate consequences be good or bad—I firmly believe they will be good—there was nothing else to be done. . . . [I]t is necessary to maintain the right of each state to manage its affairs in its own way, well or badly, as long as the peace is kept *and the Constitution obeyed*" (emphasis added).

But Higginson, to his discredit, failed for many years to react openly when it became clear that the Constitution was not being obeyed. But in the 1890s, reports of southern barbarity against blacks became so frequent that some of his old fire returned (see Part I, Chapters 9, 10, 11, and 12).

In the 1870s a new cause won his interest and support: reform of the civil service, and eliminating corruption from public life. In his *Young Folks' History of the United States* he told of how the "spoils system" had begun during Andrew Jackson's presidency: the practice of disregarding merit and tenure in favor of finding jobs for the adherents of the winner of an electoral contest. "The practice has never before existed on any large scale but it has unfortunately continued ever since," he commented.

Later, in *Larger History of the United States,* a book for adults that he was invited to write on his return to Cambridge and that built on the success of the *Young Folks' History,* he wrote, "[I]t was simply a disease which the nation must undergo—must ultimately get rid of indeed, unless destroyed by it."

He took very seriously the threat of the nation's destruction by corruption of the public service, and civil service reform was an objective that he addressed himself to, and that sometimes overshadowed his commitment to earlier reforms.

Public employment across the nation had expanded with the economic expansion that marked the period after the war. With the advent of the so-called Gilded Age, the public became aware of the problem of corrupt public officials and the need for reform of the civil service. President Grant had responded by calling for the formation of a Civil Service Commission, but Congress, the locus of much of the corruption, killed the commission by cutting off appropriations for it.

Carl Schurz was a soldier, statesman, and journalist who had emigrated from Germany in the wake of the failed German revolution of 1848 and had become an American citizen and then a hero in the Civil War. After his election to the Senate from Missouri in 1870, he was a member of a group of so-called Liberal Republicans who opposed reelection of Grant in 1872. They blamed him, perhaps unjustly, for much of the corruption in Washington.

Convinced of Grant's integrity, and the sincerity of his effort to enforce reconstruction rights, Higginson had backed Grant when the Liberal Republicans broke with their party in 1872 to vote for Horace Greeley.

As Grant's second term was ending in 1876, Schurz and his comrades of 1872 came back to the party to support Rutherford B. Hayes, who had expressed strong support for civil service reform. Invited to address one of their meetings, Higginson said the civil service reform issue was "more important than the results of the reconstruction—for what is reconstruction worth if the government that you have reconstructed is not an honest one."

Soon afterward Higginson was to return to electoral politics. He was invited by the Massachusetts Republican organization—without any solicitation on his part—to run for the upper house of the state legislature as a representative from the district that included Cambridge, and he won the seat. Once more he had the opportunity to agitate for votes for women. He also stood up for reform of the civil service and, in a move reminiscent of his school board activities, blocked a bill to curtail freedom of management in Catholic parochial schools.

The woman suffrage bill failed, but there was a modest silver lining: when the vote on the suffrage bill was called, three Irish Catholic legislators who opposed it left the hall without voting. They later told him that in view of his record on freedom of religion, they did not want to oppose a measure that he had done so much to support.

Senator Higginson did not seek reelection at the end of his two-year term. His work as a writer continued; his outside interests and activities did not diminish the volume of his output. Although he was afflicted after sixty by a variety of illnesses, there was no perceptible reduction in his activities.

In the early years of the second Cambridge period he published the *Larger History of the United States* and a biography of the writer and feminist Margaret Fuller (1884); this biography was enriched so much by firsthand knowledge, as well as insight and empathy, that it remains one of the best introductions to Fuller's life. He was regularly publishing new essays as well as collections of earlier work. Especially notable were *Travelers and Outlaws* (the source of the selections in the 1998 book *Black Rebellion*), and *Common Sense About Women,* a selection of columns from the *Woman's Journal.*

He published speeches and lectures he had delivered at woman suffrage conventions and elsewhere as well as standard talks he continued to give when he addressed the still popular Lyceum sessions.

With all this, in 1878 he accepted an appointment as the poetry editor for *The Nation* magazine, and continued in this role until 1903, eight years before his death in 1911.

As he aged he was transformed into a more conventional person, a process that was accompanied in Cambridge with a more conventional family life than he had ever had. This is not to imply any insensitivity to injustice, or silence in the face of it. He often spoke out to comment on issues related to immigration, or to protest instances of anti-Catholic bias. But though he intermittently deplored, even denounced, racial injustice, he abstained from active engagement in organized opposition.

His daughter's birth in 1881 was greeted by a letter from Emily Dickinson—were any others ever? She wrote, "I am very glad of the Little Life. I know but little of little ones, but love them very softly." That he was old enough to be his daughter's grandfather did not at all interfere with his role as her playmate, and their comradeship lasted beyond her marriage and the birth of grandchildren.

When in his eighties, Higginson continued to write essays and reviews, and published biographies of Henry Wadsworth Longfellow, John Greenleaf Whittier, and two ancestor Higginsons. He would credit this output to the fact that a young lady with a typewriter had replaced his own longhand late in the nineties.

In his later years, our man of action and letters encountered and joined two new causes, socialism and anti-imperialism.

His interest in socialism was prompted by a book. In 1888, the author Edward Bellamy published a utopian novel called *Looking Backward: 2000–1987*. It described the coming of a cooperative commonwealth, socialism in action. In the novel, a young New Englander awakens, after a long Rip Van Winkle type of slumber, to discover a happy land in which there is no want, no unemployment, no waste of natural resources, a happy life for all. He called this social system nationalism (unaware, of course, of the tendency, then barely beginning, to use that word with the ultrapatriotic connotation now familiar).

The idea took hold, spread across the country, and was carried forward by a flock of "Nationalist" clubs that met to discuss and plan ways and means of achieving the desired end. Higginson was interested and lectured favorably about the idea, but didn't quite join the movement, expressing his sentiment in a poem of which two lines were: "The children of each outcast heir / The harvest fruits of time shall reap." (See Part IV, Chapter 8, Higginson's critical but sympathetic analysis of the movement, "Edward Bellamy's *Nationalism*.")

In 1906—at age eighty-three—he joined with the authors Jack London and Upton Sinclair, self-proclaimed and active socialists, to found the Intercollegiate Socialist Society. In a letter to an editor he said his purpose was not so much to advance socialism as to defend the teaching of it.

At the turn of the century, Higginson became critical of U.S. policy in the Philippines in the wake of the Spanish-American War. In a move reminiscent of his activities as a pre–Civil War militant, he became a founder and activist supporter of an organization, the Anti-Imperialist League, that organized dissent against the U.S. Philippines policy and opposed the presence of U.S. troops there. This protest and opposition to U.S. military action, as eloquent as those protesting the Vietnam intervention, was a response to the aftermath of the war of 1898 against Spain. Supposedly to aid Cuban Independistas, the U.S. military attacked all vulnerable Spanish overseas possessions; some, like Puerto Rico, were seized. The case was particularly bad in the Philippines, where the American ouster of the Spanish was aided by the native independence freedom fighters. Once the Spanish were out, the Americans wanted in, and in order to achieve the aim of occupying the islands indefinitely, the freedom fighters who had helped the Americans eliminate the Spanish were slaughtered.

Higginson's writing activities continued unabated during his last decade, which was the first decade of the twentieth century. He also continued to respond to invitations to deliver lectures, which he prepared for later publication. His contemporaries from the "flowering of New England" were dying, and he wrote appreciations of their lives and works that were rich in anecdote and reminiscences, veins of ore that many historians have mined.

In his eighty-seventh year he delivered a talk, "Dickens in America," inspired by the appearance in Boston of the English author whose lecture he'd come up from Newport with Helen Hunt to attend thirty years before. It was to be published posthumously.

Thomas Wentworth Higginson died on May 9, 1911, "his last days painless and serene," as his widow wrote in a biography published three years later. At the farewell service the casket was borne up the aisle of the church to the sound of muffled drums, carried by a squad of young black soldiers.

The many obituary notices, some very long, celebrated his life and work with appropriate respect and appreciation. To see them and then recall the oblivion that subsequently closed over him is a source of amazement.

To the extent that Higginson has been treated by literary historians, he has been classified as a "minor writer." Some others whose works are not read much lately are considered "major," but there is no need to quibble about that: Higginson was a major American, one of whom his country can be proud but whom it nevertheless forgot. Emerson once said: "Better that the book should not be quite so good and the bookmaker abler and better and not himself a ludicrous contrast to all he had written." These words were heeded by Higginson and guided his life, as he once said. He anticipated his place—and thus served properly those who are said to have written better but to have failed to address or act upon society's ills.

He was not the initiator of a great movement, like William Lloyd Garrison, or a leader of his people, like Frederick Douglass, or the founder of an organization, like Stanton and Anthony—whose cause he nevertheless aided more than any other man and many women. His efforts to combat neglect of the health of individuals' bodies were pioneering but without enduring direct effect—although more than one president has returned to the subject without acknowledging Higginson's path-breaking role. Many of his observations on such subjects as the stereotyping of women's roles in society and the use of force by the United States not so much for defense as to impose its will are acutely relevant today.

Anticipating curiosity as to his own hopes for the future, he wrote in 1890: "Personally I should like to live to see international arbitration secured, civil service reform completed, free trade established; to find the legal and the educational rights of the two sexes equalized . . . to see natural monopolies owned by the public, not in private hands . . . to live under absolute as well as nominal religious freedom."

TAKING STOCK

As we enter a new century, we can measure the state of the reforms Higginson proposed for America as the twentieth century began.

International arbitration, the idea of peaceful conflict resolution among nations that America succeeded, early in the century, in embodying in the World Court, by century's end had been displaced by a unilateralism that embraces the use of force to impose solutions.

Free trade advances, but the globalization that comes with it is a mixed blessing.

Reform of the civil service is on the statute books, but is not everywhere accepted or applied.

Equality of the sexes has come a long way—but has quite a way to go.

Public ownership of natural monopolies is undermined by the recently fostered notion of privatization.

Racial justice (unmentioned on Higginson's list) to solve the problems bequeathed by slavery and segregation has advanced to the extent that the Fourteenth and Fifteenth Amendments are formally recognized as the law of the land; the problem Higginson did not anticipate, of finding remedies for the legacy of the many decades during which they were not, is with us still.

America would be a better place if we were to remember what Thomas Wentworth Higginson did to help remove the wrongs he saw a century and a half ago, and the need he felt for individual commitment to continue a process that can never be complete.

PART ONE

Abolitionist and Champion of Human Rights

> It had been my privilege to live in the best society all my
> life—namely that of Abolitionists and fugitive slaves.
>
> THOMAS WENTWORTH HIGGINSON,
"A VISIT TO JOHN BROWN'S
HOUSEHOLD IN 1859," Contemporaries (1899)

> It may be said you cannot expect at once to convert the
> white Southerner to loyal ideas. . . . We do not expect to
> let all the burglars to remain at large till they have
> experienced religion.
>
> THOMAS WENTWORTH HIGGINSON,
LETTER TO "SOUTHERN DOUGHFACES,"
COMMONWEALTH, AUGUST 19, 1865

The essays selected from Higginson's writings for this segment come from both his prewar and postwar writings.

Under "Activism and Advocacy" I discuss essays from the years before the war, which are fairly consistent in outlook.

Under "Witness to a Counterrevolution" I discuss items taken from Higginson's postwar writings and statements addressed to the problem of civil rights of the emancipated slaves, and southern white resistance. Here Higginson's heart is in the right place, but his mind's choices reflect the complexity of our nation's difficulty in dealing with the massive resistance of the unreconstructed South—and the victory, complete by the time of his death in 1911, of the white-supremacy South.

1. ACTIVISM AND ADVOCACY

Even before Higginson entered college in 1841, the basic premises and doctrinal underpinning of the branches of the divided movement to abolish slavery had been developed and propounded. As a second-wave recruit to the movement, he did not have to suffer through the "Martyr Age" of the thirties, when mere antislavery evolved to radical abolitionism, "immediatism" as its leaders described it in their shorthand.

But he became an activist supporter whose deeds, the events he initiated and led, were more important for the cause than what he wrote. Indeed, as he put it, there was no need for theoretical foundation. By its very nature it was less complicated than women's rights: "Once recognize the fact that man could have no right of property in man, and the whole affair was settled; there was nothing left but *to agitate, and if need be, to fight.*"

And fight he did.

From the fighting words of the sermon "Man Cannot Live by Bread Alone" to the charge against the courthouse door in the vain effort to free the self-liberated and recaptured Burns, Higginson was an exemplar of militant activism.

Relevant, if somewhat overstated, is the remark of the once-noted poet Genevieve Taggard, who simplistically as well as hyperbolically said, "Higginson, unwittingly, may have done more than any man in New England to precipitate the Civil war."

Though this exaggerates the case as much as it ignores the social-economic causes of the war, it nevertheless is a sort of tribute to what he accomplished by deed and word in the struggle.

He was not only a writer of fighting words and persuasive polemics; his role as historian and memoirist is impressive.

And though he did not originate the doctrine of "disunion" as an antislavery theme—the notion that the North should secede from the South to free itself of slavery—he was a foremost advocate of the idea. He headed a Massachusetts Disunion Convention in 1856, and one of his statements explaining his position is offered in "The New Revolution: What Commitment Requires" (Chapter 6). There the reader will find a more than adequate exposition of the difference between the proposed Free State secession (without aggression) movement of 1855–60 and the Slave State secession (with aggression) of 1860–61.

Whereas American history in its treatment of interracial relations and injustice has been thoroughly revised—at least at the university level—in the thirty years of the Second Reconstruction that began in the 1960s, there is one case of cultural lag. This is in regard to John Brown and his initiative at Harpers Ferry.

A substantial portion, possibly still the majority, of published historical work presents one form or another of the "madman or murderer (or both)" thesis that came to be the prevailing view of John Brown. (No African American historian that I've seen has condemned John Brown.) Higginson was not an impartial observer, to put it mildly. But his testimony to the character and motivation of John Brown in Kansas and at Harpers Ferry has the ring of truth.

"A Ride Through Kansas" and "Assorted Lots of Young Negroes (Chapters 4 and 5) speak for themselves in explaining and justifying extremism in abolitionism and the world in which John Brown at Harpers Ferry won not merely applause but reverence from the best minds of the nonslavery states, a reverence that was dissipated after the overthrow of Black Reconstruction.

WITNESS TO A COUNTERREVOLUTION

"Revolutions can go backwards," observed Colonel Higginson. This he learned by observation, not merely by deduction. The Civil War was followed by a period often called merely Reconstruction. This is an over-simplification. There was the initial Reconstruction—Confederate style, for which President Andrew Johnson was responsible; then Radical Reconstruction, carrying out the revolution begun with the war, which culminated in passage of the Fourteenth and Fifteenth Amendments, later to become our proud heritage from that period; then came the Counter-Reconstruction, the period during which by force or fraud the democratic state governments created in former rebel states were replaced by regimes intent on re-creating a two-caste society.

Higginson had been militant, steadfast, and no-holds-barred in the fight against the existence of slavery in the United States. He was the same in opposition to Andrew Johnson's policy that allowed restoration of rebel regimes as the seceded returned to the Union they had sought to destroy. He supported unconditionally the civil rights protective program that we know now as Radical Reconstruction, including the Fourteenth and Fifteenth Amendments, designed to make equal justice permanent. The period and his response are described in James M. McPherson's *The Struggle for Equality* (Princeton University Press, 1964) and Tilden Edelstein's biography of Higginson, *Strange Enthusiasm* (Yale University Press, 1968). Edelstein cites a Higginson article of October 1865 that shows him attributing to the Johnson administration (which had come into power in April, after Lincoln's assassination) "the re-establishment of slavery under the name of 'apprenticeship.'" Higginson concluded: "What has made the nation despise its President is not a political but a moral difference; not merely that he misuses his office but that he degrades it."

Therefore, a decade later it came as a shock to many of his former abolitionist comrades when Higginson expressed his approval (Chapter 9) of the action of the newly elected president, Rutherford B. Hayes, in withdrawing federal troops from South Carolina, Mississippi, and Louisiana, where President Ulysses S. Grant had posted them to enforce compliance with the civil rights guaranties of the new amendments. This letter has been cited as evidencing a change in heart on the part of Higginson, an acquiescence in the success of the counter reconstruction.

The historical context sheds light on—although to many it may not justify—Higginson's position. The very fact that the elements of Radical Reconstruction remained in only three states illuminates that context.

President Grant had succeeded Johnson in 1869. His own intentions were honorable; indeed he helped complete the states' ratification of the Fifteenth Amendment, designed to protect against interference with the voting rights of the new citizenry created by the Fourteenth Amendment, the ex-slaves. But Grant the president lacked the skill needed to combat civilian resistance to the fulfillment of the pledges of the Constitution. The ability to organize, to lead, to inspire that Grant the general had possessed for military action was not the same as that needed for civilian government. Moreover, as president Grant lacked the absolute authority he enjoyed as a general to exercise command and to enforce discipline. Civilian rule lacks the efficiency of the military.

In consequence, by 1876 it was evident that Grant had failed to bring life into the Fourteenth and Fifteenth Amendments. The most significant evidence of that failure was that by the end of his administration in 1876, troops had already been withdrawn from all but three of the former rebel states. Their presence had not prevented the overthrow of state governments that accepted in good faith the Civil War amendments, and their replacement by regimes hostile to equal justice.

While this was happening, Higginson was neither quiet nor indifferent. Chapter 10 is a letter protesting a racist editorial in The Nation (which had formerly been sympathetic to abolition); the editor responded to it with repeated use of the slurs employed to justify replacement of the reconstruction governments.

In this letter—written not long before Higginson's acceptance of Hayes's abandonment of the few remaining republican governments—he recognized that "the real source of the trouble" was the refusal of the white leaders of the South . . . to accept in good faith the result of emancipation."

That said, the pro-Hayes letter nevertheless recognizes the reality of the situation: that "the President had no alternative." On that assumption, Higginson acquiesced in Hayes's troop withdrawal, provided that "the Constitution [be] obeyed."

The genesis of that forlorn hope was in the developing view that there were some enlightened former Confederate leaders whose influence would bring about compliance with the two amendments. His belief in that was confirmed by what he saw in his return to South Carolina, where he had led his black soldiers, in 1878. This is described in "Fourteen Years Later" (Chapter 15).

He wrote that he had seen signs of social progress; he felt that he was observing "a finer example of self-respecting peasant life" than elsewhere in the world. There was no sign of strained relations between the races. Some former slaves were prosperous, moving into the middle classes. He saw no evidence of "a covert plan for crushing or re-enslaving the colored race." He stressed the contrast between the kind of discriminatory exclusions from police forces, trains, and schools in the North as against comparable cases of enlightened treatment at the South. Much of what he said, in hindsight, was wishful thinking.

This is precisely the kind of evidence used by C. Vann Woodward in *The Strange Career of Jim Crow* to argue that the segregation and massive injustice that developed late in the eighties and climaxed by the turn of the century did not spring up immediately on emancipation. It was only after the Supreme Court, in 1882, misinterpreted the Fourteenth Amendment and struck down the first wave of civil rights laws, or disemboweled them, that the overt and obvious mischief followed.

Higginson for a time did not want to see what was happening in the former slave states for the first decade after his trip to South Carolina. He had other interests, not only the women's movement, but civil service reform and his career as a writer, on which he was dependent for a living.

His support for Hayes was not clearly an error, absent any real alternate course to follow at the time; furthermore, he was ignorant of the deal that had been made to turn a contested election to Hayes's favor, the price that Hayes would pay. As to that, Hayes himself repented, and

sooner than Higginson, of his acceptance of the condition of withdrawing the troops. He was then incapable of overcoming the now consolidated public sentiment in favor of a Union restored at the expense of the
African American segment of the population.

Higginson's restraint ended before the turn of the century. In a letter
to *The Nation* (Chapter 11) headed "The Case of the Carpet-baggers," he
speaks out. Of the conventions called by President Andrew Johnson to
repeal the secession ordinances, he asserts that their object was "to keep
the [N]egroes in a condition just as near slavery as possible." He attributes the "misdeeds of the so-called carpet-baggers" to their treatment by
the people of the South, adding: "There never was a Western State which
received into itself a better class of immigrants than those who entered
the South after the Civil War."

In the following year he presided at a protest demonstration that was
reported in the Boston *Transcript* under the headline "Southern Barbarity: Lynching Outrages Vigorously Denounced." He was identified as one
"who came to the rescue of Anthony Burns . . . and answered the call of
his country in '61. The Colonel said: 'The trouble is that the freedom of
these people in the South is the nominal, not the real freedom.' "

Profiles of two abolitionists, William Lloyd Garrison and Lydia Child
(Chapters 13 and 14), are but a fraction of the numerous contributions
to history and understanding of the times to be found in Higginson's
writings. Bowing to Higginson as a "man of letters and an accomplished
one, as well as a fighting reformer," Edmund Wilson added, in his *Patriotic Gore,* that "his memoirs of his New England contemporaries have
survived as something more than documents. His limpid and elegant
style has a flavor of artistic personality."

1

Not by Bread Alone

There are two kinds of what may be called Thanksgiving.

There is a gratitude which, showing itself in thought and works, as love for the giver of all good things, temporal and things spiritual— shows itself whenever occasion is found, in love for man and unfailing service in the unrestrained imparting to others of whatever good is given, in wide philanthropy, in remembering those in bonds as "bound with them," the poor as having them always with us,—and this Thanksgiving, whether it show itself in its practical attitude, or its devotional, is especially bestowed and accepted.

There is another kind which is less worthy. Its gratitude is superficial, or at least self-deceptive. Recognizing temporal goods as the beginning and the end of all blessing, the one thing needful in life, it dwells on its happiness in securing them, if it does secure them with such intense vividness *that it seems like thankfulness;* it calls itself grateful because it is glad, and exults that it is not as other men are. It forgets that Christ said "a man's life consisteth not in the abundance of things which it possesseth," and values itself above others by comparative worldly possessions. It forgets that we are "not to live by bread alone," and by bread alone,

---

A Thanksgiving Sermon preached at Newburyport Nov. 30, 1848. — Ed.

47

that is by the body, its comforts and luxuries, by material acquisitions and triumphs does it live. This kind of Thanksgiving is in fact vainglory, material enslavement of the mind.

Yet it is the ordinary vice of our society . . . this avarice, this materialism, this money-getting, this "living by bread alone," is our peculiar sin and must be recognized as such and especially today, because, as I said, it comes so close to our Thanksgiving, as often to counterfeit it, intercept it, and take its place. And this temptation to to fall in with the popular estimate, and sacrifice conscience to comfort, the soul to "bread" is very terribly strong.

It takes many shapes.

It comes to the mechanic in the form of poor work and mind puffing; it comes to the merchant in the form of buying too cheap and selling too dear; it comes to the lawyer and the preacher in the form of supporting bad causes and opposing good ones; it comes finally, to the majority of the community in their political relations, just now in a peculiar form, which, because it is very important and very apparent, I shall take as the illustration of my text. Another presidential election has just passed. The plans I spoke of long since (a year ago, last August, you may remember) as being made to place another slaveholding president at the head of this nominally free republic, have been developed, consummated, carried through, with the consent and approval, nay the enthusiasm, of a majority of you.

If the fact seemed important enough to allude to it *then* when I was here as an occasional preacher, and had no ties with you, you can hardly think it is strange if I hold it enough so to speak of it now, when the majority of you have defined your position on it, and that position, so widely different (as you know) from mine. . . .do you not see that by *your expressions of delight at at the result of the election,* you have voluntarily foregone all the defense you had when you endlessly lamented for the "necessary evil,. . . " you have accepted the triumph as your triumph, and rejoiced over it and for that you are now to be held accountable. . . . you knew that the ultra slave men of the South electioneered for and chose him on this ground—bargaining, however, for as many northern votes as they wanted. You knew that he was a man professedly of not the smallest political knowledge, a mere warrior, a mere slaveholder and never could have been nominated or chosen but by this ultra slave influence.

You knew all this or ought to have known it, and yet when the time came, and this humiliating stroke of the slave power triumphed you accepted it as your triumph and illuminated your houses! And why did you triumph? Why did the North or any part of it feel this way?

Other reasons may have mingled, but I do from my soul believe blush as I may say it, that this one great reason stood and forever will stand in history—underlying all, overtopping all,—this—that slavery or no slavery, consistency or inconsistency, honor, or dishonor, that spirit in the Northern people which "lives by bread alone" has secured the PROTECTIVE TARIFF. . . . my soul is weary of these degrading facts. Enough that under these circumstances, led by these influences, we are entering upon the thirteenth slave-holding administration out of a total of sixteen.

Meanwhile slavery exists with all its horrors,—already the slave power turns upon us and says "You have chosen our candidate, knowing what we wanted him for, and now prepare to go on and give us our new territory . . ." Already the new-born anti-slavery movement of the northern slave states beginning to pause at the prospect of a new slave market given by your compromise;—the three millions of sufferers are destined to expand, perhaps, to four; and Massachuesetts smiles on, secure in possession of her Tarriff. Slavery is to her still a distant abstraction; protection, "bread alone," a present practical result.

Slavery a distant abstraction!

I listened this week to Frederick Douglass and I sat and looked at that extraordinary man and trembled before the volcanic words in which the accumulated wrongs of an outraged race burnt their way through his soul—and heard the depth of fiery earnestness with which he depicted his own and his brothers' bondage; and the withering sarcasm with which he denounced the hypocritical religion of this slaveholding nation—when I heard this and remembered that this man himself, body, soul, God-given genius and all was himself once the victim of this terrible institution (and that three millions were there still—and more coming) I felt, good heaven, as if I were a recreant to humanity, to let one Sunday pass in the professed practice of Christianity and leave the name of Slavery unmentioned. I felt it was a base, selfish, sluggishness in me even to let that fearful institution so pass from my thoughts as to omit the mention of its *name* at least, in prayer or in preaching: so help me God I never will again.

And when, farther, I thought of the position of this man among us with his genius, his virtue, his burning eloquence, his sacred cause—coming and going without enthusiasm, without applause—almost without a friendly hand to grasp his in sympathy—and when on the other side, I recall the enthusiasm you had called up within but a few days, at the name of a man you never saw—a man with no genius, no eloquence, no sacred cause—not a known virtue even, (save brute courage and that common honesty you would feel insulted if I denied you)—when I looked at this picture and then at this—I felt how low, how base our moral standard—and how thankful I should be that God placed me where even my weak voice might be a gain to the cause of the oppressed against the oppressor.

You call this fanaticism, I do not wish to *be* a fanatic—but I have no fear of being called so.

These are unpleasant things, unpleasant to introduce today, but I do not see how it can be helped. It would be pleasanter to bury all our sins and not give thanks, but it cannot be. . . . I cannot encourage you to pour out your souls in gratitude for temporal blessings without reminding you how great the price you have been paying for mere temporal blessings.

I cannot congratulate you on the reunion of families and the return of happy associates, without thinking of the very many families (of darker hue but light enough souls) to whom it brings no gleam of joy; and who are destined for aught we know, to a longer and worse slavery because of the coalition you have just effected with their oppressor effected first and then triumphed in.

Side by side with the liberty we are grateful for, stands now, if ever before, the slavery we are made responsible for,—by consenting for value received to its bold demands. If there is to be Thanksgiving for this, it must be by fasting and prayers for the others.

God forbid that I should give only a dark picture, or do injustice to any. I feel very sure that this is "the darkest hour which precedes the dawn." We could go no further in subservience to the Slave Power and the reaction has already come.

It is seen in the grand uprising of the Free Soil movement; one based on a noble principle (not perfectly satisfactory, for no movement is, but very noble) and destined under some form for a sure triumph. But how can I speak to you of that, when scarce a dozen of you own to any sympathy with it? Yet how far any individual of you is accountable for all this, I do not judge.

I know the mad atmosphere in which we live, and how hard it is for individuals to change it or resist. But wrong is wrong, none the less., and who is to say so if not the preacher.

[end of Thanksgiving sermon, "Man shall not live by bread alone."]

2

THE SCHOOL OF MOBS

Higginson was a teenager during the 1830s, the period that Harriet Martineau described in the title of her work on the travails of abolitionism during that period as The Martyr Age in the United States *(New York, 1839). He did not have to endure the mob scenes described in the following chapter from his Whittier biography. He recalled, more than once, later in life, the other type of mob scene he viewed at age eleven in Cambridge. In his memoir* Cheerful Yesterdays *he wrote, ". . . all that I had read of persecution did not implant so lasting a love of liberty as that one spectacle."*

Mr Chairman; I took my first lesson in religious liberty when I stood by my mother's side and watched the burning of the Ursuline Convent in Charleston, a Catholic convent burned by a Protestant mob; I took my second lesson when in the know-nothing days I saw procession after procession of Protestants marching through the streets then occupied by Irish Catholics, with torchlight and using every form of insult, banners in their hands, and making every effort to taunt the Catholics out of the houses and bring them into a street fight which, thanks to the self-control of those naturalized foreigners, they failed to do. I hope never to see a renewal of those actions, for if those scenes were to be renewed it would not be necessary to go further than this [house Hearing] room to find those who would lead the mob.

From official report of Massachusetts House Hearing on proposed bill for harassment of Parochial schools by state agents. (March 1889, bound as a pamphlet, "A Protest.")—Ed.

A ll this was, however, but the peaceful early stage of the antislavery movement; the mob period was approaching. It was a time peculiarly trying to those who had been bred in the non-resistance theory, and had to choose for themselves among the three alternatives, resistance, endurance, and flight. Those who in later years read the fine dramatic delineations in the poem "Barclay of Ury" do not quite appreciate the school in which Whittier learned what life meant to Barclay. The first time that actual violence came near Whittier, in his own town of Haverhill, though it missed him, was after there had been established (on April 3, 1834) an antislavery society of which he was secretary. A year or so later, in August, 1835, the Rev. Samuel J. May of Syracuse, N.Y., preached in the Unitarian pulpit at Haverhill and announced that he should give an antislavery address in the evening. The result is thus described by the historian of Haverhill:

> The evening meeting was entirely broken up by a mob outside, who threw sand and gravel and small stones against the windows, breaking the glass, and by their hootings frightened the female portion of the audience, and led to the fear on the part of all, that more serious assaults would follow if the meeting was continued. It was therefore summarily dissolved. It was perhaps fortunate that this course was adopted, as a loaded cannon was then being drawn to the spot, to add its thunderings to the already disgraceful tumults of that otherwise quiet Sabbath evening.[1]

The preacher thus mobbed was, by universal admission, the most moderate, disarming, and courteous of all antislavery lecturers, indeed so eminent for these particular virtues as almost to constitute a class by himself. His reception shows how absolutely unjust was the charge that the abolitionists brought upon themselves, by their mere manner, the persecution they often received. In this case the meeting was broken up in uproar, and Mr. May was roughly handled as he went out, but as he had Elizabeth Whittier on one arm and her friend Harriet Minot on the other, he escaped actual violence. Less fortunate was George Thompson, the distinguished English antislavery orator, who had been the leader of the agitation for the abolition of slavery in the English colonies, and who came to America by invitation of Garrison. He acted on the fine principle laid down for all time by the so-called infidel Thomas Paine, who, when some one quoted to him the Latin motto, "Where liberty is, there

---

[1] Chase's "History of Haverhill," p. 505.

is my country" (*Ubi libertas, ibi patria*) replied that this was a coward's phrase, since the brave man's watchword would be, "Where liberty is *not*, there is my country." Thompson was of course received with peculiar hostility as a foreigner, a feeling not yet extinct, for it is not many years since I saw him disdainfully classed as "a foreign carpet-bagger," and that by one of the most eminent of Boston philanthropists. He had been mobbed, accordingly, in one place after another, including Salem, whence he had escaped with difficulty and had been afterward secreted by Whittier for two weeks in East Haverhill. He and Whittier had personally undertaken a few antislavery meetings, and had set out for that purpose. I take what followed from the excellent description of their friend, Mrs. Cartland:

. . . Thinking themselves secure because personally unknown, the two friends drove to Plymouth, N.H., to visit Nathaniel P. Rogers, a prominent abolitionist. On their way they stopped for the night in Concord at the house of George Kent, who was a brother-in-law of Rogers. After they had gone on their way, Kent attempted to make preparations for an antislavery meeting to be held when they should return. There was furious excitement, and neither church, chapel, nor hall could be hired for the purpose. On their arrival Whittier walked out with a friend in the twilight, leaving Thompson in the house, and soon found himself and friend surrounded by a mob of several hundred persons, who assailed them with stones and bruised them somewhat severely. They took refuge in the house of Colonel Kent, who, though not an abolitionist, protected them and baffled the mob. From thence Whittier made his way with some difficulty to George Kent's, where Thompson was. The mob soon surrounded the house and demanded that Thompson and "the Quaker" should be given up. Through a clever stratagem the mob was decoyed away for a while, but, soon discovering the trick, it returned, reenforced with muskets and a cannon, and threatened to blow up the house if the abolitionists were not surrendered.

"A small company of antislavery men and women had met that evening at George Kent's, among whom were two nieces of Daniel Webster, daughters of his brother Ezekiel. All agreed that the lives of Whittier and Thompson were in danger, and advised that an effort should be made to escape. The mob filled the street, a short distance below the gate leading to Kent's house. A horse was quietly harnessed in the stable, and was led out with the vehicle under the shadow of the house, where Whittier and Thompson stood ready. It was bright moonlight, and they could see the gun-barrels gleaming in the street below them. The gate was suddenly opened, the horse was started at a furious gallop, and the two friends drove off amidst the yells and shots of the infuriated crowd. They left the city by the way of Hookset Bridge, the other avenues being guarded, and hurried in the direction of Haverhill. In the morning they stopped to refresh themselves and their tired horse. While at breakfast they found that 'ill news travels fast,' and gets worse as it goes; for the landlord told them that there had been an abolition meeting at Haverhill the night before, and that George Thompson, the Englishman, and a young Quaker named Whittier, who had brought him, were both so roughly handled that they would never wish to talk abolition again. When the guests were about to leave, Whittier, just as he was stepping into the carriage, said to the landlord, 'My name is Whittier, and this is George Thompson.' The man opened his eyes and mouth with wonder as they drove away.

When they arrived at Haverhill they learned of the doings of the mob there, and the fortunate escape of their friend May.[2]

Another of these Thompson mobs, at which Whittier was not present, is thus described by Mrs. Lydia Maria Child, who was there. I insert her account, because it describes the period better than any other narrative I know, and gives the essential atmosphere of the life amid which Whittier was reared.

My most vivid recollection of George Thompson is of his speaking at Julian Hall on a memorable occasion. Mr. Stetson, then keeper of the Tremont House, was present, with a large number of his slaveholding guests, who had come to Boston to make their annual purchases of the merchants. Their presence seemed to inspire Mr. Thompson. Never, even from his eloquent lips, did I hear such scathing denunciations of slavery. The exasperated Southerners could not contain their wrath. Their lips were tightly compressed, their hands clinched; and now and then a muttered curse was audible. Finally, one of them shouted, 'If we had you down South, we'd cut off your ears.' Mr. Thompson folded his arms in his characteristic manner, looked calmly at the speaker, and replied, 'Well, sir, if you did cut off my ears, I should still cry aloud, 'He that *hath* ears to hear, let him hear.'

Meanwhile my heart was thumping like a sledge-hammer; for, before the speaking began, Samuel J. May had come to me, and said in a very low tone: 'Do you see how the walls are lined by stout truckmen, brandishing their whips? They are part of a large mob around the entrance in Federal

[2]Underwood's "Whittier," pp. 116–18.

Street, employed by the Southerners to seize George Thompson and carry him to a South Carolina vessel in waiting at Long Wharf. A carriage with swift horses is at the door, and these Southerners are now exulting in the anticipation of lynching him. But behind that large green curtain at the back of the platform there is a door leading to the chamber of a warehouse. We have the key to that door, which leads to a rear entrance of the building on Milk Street. There the abolitionists have stationed a carriage with swift horses and a coloured driver, who of course will do his best for George Thompson. Now, as soon as Mr. Thompson ceases speaking, we want antislavery women to gather round him and appear to detain him in eager conversation. He will listen and reply, but keep imperceptibly moving backward toward the green curtain. You will all follow him, and when he vanishes behind the curtain you will continue to stand close together, and appear to be still talking with him.'

At the close of the meeting twenty-five or thirty of us women clustered around Mr. Thompson and obeyed the instructions we had received. When he had disappeared from our midst there was quiet for two or three minutes, interrupted only by our busy talking. But the Southerners soon began to stand on tiptoe and survey the platform anxiously. Soon a loud oath was heard, accompanied by the exclamation, 'He's gone!' Then such a thundering stampede as there was down the front stairs I have never heard. We remained in the hall, and presently Samuel J. May came to us, so agitated that he was pale to the very lips. 'Thank God, he is saved!' he exclaimed; and we wrung his hands with hearts too full for speech.

The Boston newspaper press, as usual, presented a united front in sympathy with the slaveholders. . . . But they were all in the dark concerning the manner of his escape; for as the door behind the curtain was known to very few, it remained a mystery to all except the abolitionists.[3]

Garrison wrote of the Concord mob to his brother-in-law, Sept. 12, 1835, "Our brother Thompson had a narrow escape from the mob at Concord, and Whittier was pelted with mud and stones, but he escaped bodily damage." Thompson wrote to Garrison, Sept. 15:

You would have been delighted to have shared our adventures in *Concord* (?) on the memorable night of the 4th inst. The mirthful and the melancholy were so strangely and equally blended throughout, that I scarcely know which had the advantage, and certainly could not tell the story of our 'hairbreadth 'scapes' without exciting your risibility. However, my es-

---

[3]Underwood's "Whittier," pp. 118–20.

cape from the ignorant and murderous rabble that clamoured and thirsted for my blood was very providential, and I desire to feel grateful to Him who I believe watches over our persons and our cause, and will restrain the malice of our foes, or cause our sufferings to advance His glory.

Poor Whittier was compelled to receive a tithe of the vengeance accumulated for me. I had really little expectation and less desire to be stoned by proxy, but such is the fruit of keeping bad company.[4]

Next followed the Garrison mob, properly so called, during which Whittier happened to be in Boston, in attendance at an extra session of the state legislature, of which he was then a member. His sister being at the women's antislavery convention, he went in search of her, and found that the meeting had been broken up by a mob, or dispersed by the mayor to quiet those outside, and that the rioters had been allowed by the mayor to take down the very sign, "Female Antislavery Society" and break it to pieces, thus lynching George Thompson by proxy, as he expresses it, in a bit of harmless board. Whittier saw Garrison hurried through the street with a rope round him, and taken for safety to jail, where Whittier and May visited him in his cell; then, being warned that the house which was their own stopping-place might also be attacked, they removed Elizabeth Whittier without her knowing the reason, while they themselves mounted guard all night. This was the ordeal by which Whittier's Quaker training was tested, but it rang true. He would not arm himself, but he did not flinch where others were arming.

His courage was to be once more tested, however, in Philadelphia, while he edited the *Pennsylvania Freeman*. A hall had been erected by the antislavery people and other reformers, and was first opened on May 15, 1838. There was an address by the eminent lawyer, David Paul Brown, and a poem of a hundred and fifty lines by Whittier, whose publishing office was in the building. It was not one of his best poems, and he excluded it from his complete edition; but it was enough, with other things, to call out the gradually increasing wrath of a mob which hooted, yelled, and broke windows. On the third day the president of the Pennsylvania Hall Association called for the intervention of the mayor and sheriff. About sunset the mayor replied that, if the building were vacated and given into his possession, he would disperse the rioters. The keys were given up to him, and he addressed the mob as "Fellow-citizens." Deprecating disorder in general terms, he added: "There will be no meeting here this evening. The house has been given up to me. The

[4]"Garrison's Life," I. 520.

managers had the right to hold the meeting, but as good citizens they have, at my request, suspended their meeting for this evening. We never call out the military here. We do not need such measures. Indeed, I would, fellow-citizens, look upon you as my police! I trust you will abide by the laws and keep order. I now bid you farewell for the night."

Since mob law began on this planet there probably was never a more dastardly invitation to outrage. Three cheers were given for the mayor, and the mob went at once to its work. Ransacking the antislavery bookstore and office, they carried all combustibles to the platform and set the building on fire. Two Southern witnesses will best tell the tale.

A Southern account of the fire appeared in a New Orleans paper, as follows:

At 8.30 P.M. the people, feeling themselves able and willing to do their duty, burst open the doors of the house, entered the Abolition book-store, and made complete havoc of all within. They then beat out all the windows, and, gathering a pile of window-blinds and a pile of abolition books together, they placed them under the pulpit, and set fire to them and the building. . . . The multitude, as soon as they saw the building on fire, gave a loud shout of joy. A large number of splendid fire-engines were immediately on the spot, many of which could throw water more than a hundred feet high; but the noble firemen, to a man, of all the companies present, refused to throw one drop of water on the consuming building. All they did was to direct their engines to play upon the private buildings in the immediate vicinity of the blazing hall, some of which were in danger, as they were nearly joining the hall. . . . Such conduct in the Philadelphia fire companies deserves the highest praise and gratitude of all friends of the Union, and of all Southerners in particular; and I hope and trust the fire companies of New Orleans will hold a meeting, and testify in some suitable manner to the Philadelphia fire companies their sincere approbation of their noble conduct on this occasion.

Another Southerner wrote to a Georgian paper how he and a friend helped, and enjoyed the spectacle:

We lent our feeble efforts to effect the demolition of this castle of iniquity. . . . The fire companies repaired tardily to the scene of action, and not a drop of water did they pour upon that accursed Moloch until it was a heap of ruins. Sir! it would have gladdened your heart to have beheld that lofty tower of mischief enveloped in flames. The devouring clement seemed to wear, combined with its terrible majesty, beauty and delight. To witness those beautiful spires of flame gave undoubted assurance to the heart of the Southron that in his brethren of the North he has friends.[5]

This shows what the mob discipline was. It did not drive Whittier from his non-resistant principles, as was the case with most of the men of that stamp who went nearly thirty years later to Kansas; it only made him more absolutely sure and resolute in proclaiming the antislavery gospel.

Nor was this the whole story. The next day a "Shelter for Coloured Orphans" was burned, and a church of the coloured people attacked and damaged. The day before the first attack the Pennsylvania Antislavery Society had announced a meeting at the hall for the election of officers, and at the appointed hour it met by the smoking ruins and went through its business amid the howling of the mob. The tumults lasted a week, and at the end of this time the mayor offered a reward for the arrest of the rioters, from which nothing followed. The summary of the whole affair in the *Pennsylvania Freeman* was written by Whittier and Charles Burleigh. It was practically the record of the poet's baptism into the second degree of reform—the period of mob violence.

Years after, Whittier had a curious memorial of this period:

Once when he was passing through Portland, Me., a man, seeing him go by, stepped out of his shop and asked if his name were Whittier, and if he were not the man who was stoned, years ago, by a mob at Concord. The answer being in the affirmative, he said he believed a devil possessed him that night; for he had no reason to wish evil either to Whittier or Thompson, yet he was filled with a desire to kill them, and he thought he should have done so if they had not escaped. He added that the mob was like a crowd of demons, and he knew one man who had mixed a black dye to dip them [the abolitionists] in, which would be almost impossible to get off. He could not explain to himself or to another the state of mind he was in.[6]

---

[5]Linton's "Whittier," pp. 74–76.
[6]Fields's "Whittier," p. 47.

3

OBEYING THE HIGHER LAW

The Fugitive Slave Law had just passed, and a year or two after Garrison had proudly showed a row of escaped negroes sitting on the platform of an anti-slavery convention, and had defied the whole South to reclaim them, these very men were fleeing to Canada for their lives. When the storm first broke, on February 15, 1851, in the arrest of Shadrach, Boston had a considerable colored population, which handled his rescue with such unexpected skill and daring that it almost seemed as if Garrison were right; yet it took but a few days for their whole force to be scattered to the winds. The exact story of the Shadrach rescue has never been written. The account which appears most probable is that on the day of the arraignment of the alleged fugitive, the fact was noted in a newspaper by a colored man of great energy and character, employed by a firm in Boston and utterly unconnected with the Abolitionists. He asked leave of absence, and strolled into the Court-House. Many colored men were at the door and had been excluded; but he, being known and trusted, was admitted, and the others, making a rush, followed in behind him with a hubbub of joking and laughter. There were but a few constables on duty, and it suddenly struck this leader, as he and his followers passed near the man under arrest, that they might as well keep on and pass out at the opposite door, taking among them the man under arrest, who was not handcuffed. After a moment's beckoning the prisoner saw his opportunity, fell in with the jubilant procession, and amid continued uproar was got outside the Court-House, when the crowd scattered in all directions.

It was an exploit which, as has been well said, would hardly have furnished a press item had it been the case of a pickpocket, yet was treated at Washington as if it had shaken the nation. Daniel Webster called it "a case of treason;" President Fillmore issued a special proclamation; and Henry Clay gave notice of a bill to lend added strength to the Fugitive Slave Law, so as to settle the question "whether the government of white men is to be yielded to a government of blacks." More curious even than this was the development of antislavery ethics that followed. The late Richard H. Dana, the counsel for various persons arrested as accomplices in the rescue of Shadrach, used to tell with delight this tale of a juryman impaneled on that trial. To Dana's great surprise, the jury had disagreed concerning one client who had been charged with aiding in the affair and whose conviction he had fully expected; and this surprise was all the greater because new and especial oaths had been administered to the jurymen, pledging them to have no conscientious scruples against convicting, so that it seemed as if every one with a particle of anti-slavery sympathy must have been ruled out. Years after, Dana encountered by accident the very juryman—a Concord blacksmith—whose obstinacy had saved his client; and learned that this man's unalterable reason for refusing to condemn was that he himself had taken a hand in the affair, inasmuch as he had driven Shadrach, after his rescue, from Concord to Sudbury.[1]

I fear I must admit that while it would have been a great pleasure to me to have lent a hand in the Shadrach affair, the feeling did not come wholly from moral conviction, but from an impulse perhaps hereditary in the blood. Probably I got from my two soldier and sailor grandfathers an intrinsic love of adventure which haunted me in childhood, and which three-score and fourteen years have by no means worn out. So far as I can now analyze it, this early emotion was not created by the wish for praise alone, but was mainly a boyish desire for a stirring experience. No man so much excited my envy during my whole college life as did a reckless Southern law student, named Winfield Scott Belton, who, when the old Vassall House in Cambridge was all in flames, and the firemen could not reach the upper story with their ladders, suddenly appeared from within at an attic window, amid the smoke, and pointed out to them the way to follow. Like most boys, I had a passion for fires; but after this the trophies of Belton would not suffer me to sleep, and I often ran miles towards a light in the horizon. But the great opportunity never oc-

---

[1]See Adams's *Life of Dana*, i. 217. The story there is related from Mr. Adams's recollection, which differs in several respects from my own, as to the way in which Dana used to tell it. Possibly, as with other good *raconteurs*, the details may have varied a little as time went on. I write with two MS. narratives before me, both from well-known Concord men.

curs twice, and the nearest I ever came to it was in being one of several undergraduates to bring the elder Professor Henry Ware out of his burning house. It was not much of a feat,—we afterwards risked ourselves a great deal more to bring some trays of pickle-jars from the cellar,—but in the case of the venerable doctor the object was certainly worth all it cost us; for he was the progenitor of that admirable race upon which, as Dr. Holmes said to Professor Stowe, the fall of Adam had not left the slightest visible impression.

This combination of motives was quite enough to make me wish that if there should be another fugitive slave case I might at least be there to see, and, joining the Vigilance Committee in Boston, I waited for such an occasion. It was not necessary to wait long, for the Shadrach case was soon to be followed by another. One day in April, 1851, a messenger came to my house in Newburyport and said briefly, "Another fugitive slave is arrested in Boston, and they wish you to come." I went back with him that afternoon, and found the Vigilance Committee in session in the "Liberator" office. It is impossible to conceive of a set of men, personally admirable, yet less fitted on the whole than this committee to undertake any positive action in the direction of forcible resistance to authorities. In the first place, half of them were non-resistants, as was their great leader, Garrison, who stood composedly by his desk preparing his next week's editorial, and almost exasperating the more hotheaded among us by the placid way in which he looked beyond the rescue of an individual to the purifying of a nation. On the other hand, the "political Abolitionists," or Free-Soilers, while personally full of indignation, were extremely anxious not to be placed for one moment outside the pale of good citizenship. The only persons to be relied upon for action were a few whose temperament prevailed over the restrictions of non-resistance on the one side, and of politics on the other; but of course their discussion was constantly damped by the attitude of the rest. All this would not, however, apply to the negroes, it might well seem; they had just proved their mettle, and would doubtless do it again. On my saying this in the meeting, Lewis Hayden, the leading negro in Boston, nodded cordially and said, "Of course they will." Soon after, drawing me aside, he startled me by adding, "I said that for bluff, you know. We do not wish any one to know how really weak we are. Practically there are no colored men in Boston; the Shadrach prosecutions have scattered them all. What is to be done must be done without them." Here was a blow indeed!

What was to be done? The next day showed that absolutely nothing could be accomplished in the court-room. There were one or two hundred armed policemen in and around the Court-House. Only authorized persons could get within ten feet of the building. Chains were placed across the doors, and beneath these even the judges, entering, had to stoop. The United States court-room was up two high and narrow flights of stairs. Six men were at the door of the court-room. The prisoner, a slender boy of seventeen, sat with two strong men on each side and five more in the seat behind him, while none but his counsel could approach him in front. (All this I take from notes made at the time.) The curious thing was that although there was a state law of 1843 prohibiting every Massachusetts official from taking any part in the restoration of a fugitive slave, yet nearly all these employees were Boston policemen, acting, so the city marshal told me, under orders from the mayor and aldermen. Under these circumstances there was clearly nothing to be done at the trial itself. And yet all sorts of fantastic and desperate projects crossed the minds of those few among us who really, so to speak, meant business. I remember consulting Ellis Gray Loring, the most eminent lawyer among the Abolitionists, as to the possibility of at least gaining time by making away with the official record from the Southern court, a document which lay invitingly at one time among lawyers' papers on the table. Again, I wrote a letter to my schoolmate Charles Devens, the United States marshal, imploring him to resign rather than be the instrument of sending a man into bondage,—a thing actually done by one of the leading Boston policemen. It is needless to say to those who knew him that he answered courteously and that he reserved his decision. No other chance opening, it seemed necessary to turn all attention to an actual rescue of the prisoner from his place of confinement. Like Shadrach, Thomas Sims was not merely tried in the United States Court-House, but imprisoned there, because the state jail was not opened to him; he not having been arrested under any state law, and the United States having no jail in Boston. In the previous case, an effort had been made to obtain permission to confine the fugitive slave at the Navy Yard, but Commodore Downes had refused. Sims, therefore, like Shadrach, was kept at the Court-House. Was it possible to get him out?

There was on Tuesday evening a crowded meeting at Tremont Temple, at which Horace Mann presided. I hoped strongly that some result might come from this meeting, and made a vehement speech there myself, which, as Dr. Samuel Gridley Howe honored me by saying, was bringing the community to the verge of revolution, when a lawyer named Charles Mayo Ellis protested against its tone, and threw cold water upon all action. It was evident that if anything was done, it must be done by a very few. I looked round, during the meeting, for a band of twenty-five men from Marlborough, who had seemed to me to show more fighting quality than the rest, but they had probably gone home. Under this conviction half a dozen of us formed the following plan. The room where Sims was confined, being safe by reason of its height from the ground, had no gratings at the windows. The colored clergyman of Boston, Mr. Grimes, who alone had the opportunity to visit Sims, agreed to arrange with him that at a specified hour that evening he should go to a certain window, as if for air,—for he had the freedom of the room,— and should spring out on mattresses which we were to bring from a lawyer's office across the way; we also providing a carriage in which to place him. All was arranged,—the message sent, the mattresses ready, the carriage engaged as if for an ordinary purpose; and behold! in the dusk of that evening, two of us, strolling through Court Square, saw men busily at work fitting iron bars across this safe third-story window. Whether we had been betrayed, or whether it was simply a bit of extraordinary precaution, we never knew. Colonel Montgomery, an experienced guerrilla in Kansas, used to say, "It is always best to take for granted that your opponent is at least as smart as you yourself are." This, evidently, we had not done.

I knew that there was now no chance of the rescue of Sims. The only other plan that had been suggested was that we should charter a vessel, place it in charge of Austin Bearse, a Cape Cod sea-captain and one of our best men, and take possession of the brig Acorn, on which Sims was expected to be placed. This project was discussed at a small meeting in Theodore Parker's study, and was laid aside as impracticable, not because it was piracy, but because there was no absolute certainty that the fugitive would be sent South in that precise way. As no other plan suggested itself, and as I had no wish to look on, with my hands tied, at the surrender, I went back to my home in deep chagrin. The following extract from a journal written soon after is worth preserving as an illustration of that curious period:—

"It left me with the strongest impressions of the great want of preparation, on our part, for this revolutionary work. Brought up as we have all been, it takes the whole experience of one such case to educate the mind to the attitude of revolution. It is so strange to find one's self outside of established institutions; to be obliged to lower one's voice and conceal one's purposes; to see law and order, police and military, on the wrong side, and find good citizenship a sin and bad citizenship a duty, that it takes time to prepare one to act coolly and wisely, as well as courageously, in such an emergency. Especially this is true among reformers, who are not accustomed to act according to fixed rules and observances, but to strive to do what seems to themselves best, without reference to others. The Vigilance Committee meetings were a disorderly convention, each man having his own plan or theory, perhaps stopping even for anecdote or disquisition, when the occasion required the utmost promptness of decision and the most unflinching unity in action. . . . Our most reliable men were non-resistants, and some who were otherwise were the intensest visionaries. Wendell Phillips was calm and strong throughout; I never saw a finer gleam in his eyes than when drawing up that stirring handbill at the antislavery office."

During the months which followed, I attended anti-slavery conventions; wrote editorially for the newly established "Commonwealth," the Boston organ of the Free Soil party; and had also a daily "Independent Column" of my own in the "Newburyport Union," a liberal Democratic paper. No other fugitive slave case occurred in New England for three years. The mere cost in money of Sims's surrender had been vast; the political results had been the opposite of what was intended, for the election of Charles Sumner to the United States Senate practically followed from it. The whole anti-slavery feeling at the North was obviously growing stronger, yet there seemed a period of inaction all round, or of reliance on ordinary political methods in the contest. In 1852 I removed to Worcester, into a strong anti-slavery community of which my "Free Church" was an important factor. Fugitives came sometimes to the city, and I have driven them at midnight to the farm of the veteran Abolitionists, Stephen and Abby Kelley Foster, in the suburbs of the city. Perhaps the most curious case with which we had to deal was that of a pretty young woman, apparently white, with two perfectly white children, all being consigned to me by the Rev. Samuel May, then secretary of the Boston Anti-Slavery Society, and placed by him, for promptness of transportation to Worcester, under the escort of a Worcester merchant, thoroughly pro-slavery in sympathy, and not having the slightest conception that he was violating the laws in finding a seat for his charge and holding the baby on his knee. We had them in our care all winter. It was one of those cases of romantic incident which slavery yielded. She was the daughter of her former master, and was the mistress of her present owner, her half-brother; she could scarcely read and write, but was perfectly ladylike, modest, and grateful. She finally married a tradesman near Boston, who knew her story, and she disappeared in the mass of white population, where we were content to leave her untraced.

All this minor anti-slavery work ended when, on Thursday evening, May 25, 1854, I had a letter by private messenger from the same Samuel May just mentioned, saying that a slave had been arrested, and the case was to be heard on Saturday morning; that a meeting was to be held on

Friday evening at Faneuil Hall, and it was important that Worcester should be well represented. Mr. A. B. Alcott also came thither on the same errand. I sent messages to several persons, and especially to a man of remarkable energy, named Martin Stowell, who had taken part in a slave rescue at Syracuse, New York, urging them to follow at once. Going to Boston on the morning train, I found myself presently in a meeting of the Vigilance Committee, not essentially different from those which had proved so disappointing three years before. There was not only no plan of action, but no set purpose of united action. This can be imagined when I say that at one moment when there seemed a slight prospect of practical agreement, some one came in to announce that Suttle and his men, the slave-catchers, were soon to pass by, and proposed that we should go out and gaze at them, "pointing the finger of scorn,"—as if Southern slave-catchers were to be combated by such weapons. This, however, had an effect in so far that the general committee adjourned, letting those alone remain who were willing to act personally in forcible resistance. This reduced our sixty down to thirty, of whom I was chosen chairman. Dr. Howe was then called on to speak, and gave some general advice, very good and spirited. Two things were resolved on,—to secure the names of those willing to act, and to have definite leadership. One leader would have been best, but we had not quite reached that point, so an executive committee of six was chosen at last,—Phillips, Parker, Howe, Kemp (an energetic Irishman), Captain Bearse, and myself; Stowell was added to these at my request. Even then it was inconceivably difficult to get the names of as many as twenty who would organize and obey orders. The meeting adjourned till afternoon, when matters were yet worse,—mere talk and discussion; but it seemed to me, at least, that something must be done; better a failure than to acquiesce tamely as before, and see Massachusetts henceforward made a hunting-ground for fugitive slaves.

All hopes now rested on Stowell, who was to arrive from Worcester at six P. M. I met him at the train, and walked up with him. He heard the condition of affairs, and at once suggested a new plan as the only thing feasible. The man must be taken from the Court-House. It could not be done in cold blood, but the effort must have behind it the momentum of a public meeting, such as was to be held at Faneuil Hall that night. An attack at the end of the meeting would be hopeless, for the United States marshal would undoubtedly be looking for just that attempt, and would be reinforced accordingly; this being, as we afterwards found, precisely what that official was planning. Could there not be an attack at the very height of the meeting, brought about in this way? Let all be in readiness;

let a picked body be distributed near the Court House and Square; then send some loud-voiced speaker, who should appear in the gallery of Faneuil Hall and announce that there was a mob of negroes already attacking the Court-House; let a speaker, previously warned,—Phillips, if possible,—accept the opportunity promptly, and send the whole meeting pell-mell to Court Square, ready to fall in behind the leaders and bring out the slave. The project struck me as an inspiration. I accepted it heartily, and think now, as I thought then, that it was one of the very best plots that ever—failed. "Good plot, good friends, and full of expectation." Why it came within an inch of success and still failed will next be explained.

The first thing to be done—after providing a box of axes for attack on the Court-House doors, a thing which I personally superintended—was to lay the whole matter before the committee already appointed and get its concurrence. This committee was to meet in the ante-room of Faneuil Hall before the general meeting. As a matter of fact it never came together, for everybody was pushing straight into the hall. The moments passed rapidly. We caught first one member of the committee, then another, and expounded the plot. Some approved, others disapproved; our stout seacaptain, Bearse, distrusting anything to be attempted on land, utterly declining all part in it. Howe and Parker gave a hasty approval, and—only half comprehending, as it afterwards proved—were warned to be ready to give indorsement from the platform; Phillips it was impossible to find, but we sent urgent messages, which never reached him; Kemp stood by us: and we had thus a clear majority of the committee, which although it had been collectively opposed to the earlier plan of an attack at the end of the meeting, was yet now committed to a movement half way through, by way of surprise. We at once found our gallery orator in the late John L. Swift, a young man full of zeal, with a stentorian voice, afterwards exercised stoutly for many years in Republican and temperance meetings. He having pledged himself to make the proposed announcement, it was only necessary to provide a nucleus of picked men to head the attack. Stowell, Kemp, and I were each to furnish five of these, and Lewis Hayden, the colored leader, agreed to supply ten negroes. So far all seemed ready, and the men were found as well as the general confusion permitted; but the very success and overwhelming numbers of the Faneuil Hall meeting soon became a formidable obstacle instead of a help.

It was the largest gathering I ever saw in that hall. The platform was covered with men; the galleries, the floor, even the outer stairways, were absolutely filled with a solid audience. Some came to sympathize, more to look on,—we could not estimate the proportion; but when the speaking was once begun, we could no more communicate with the platform than if the Atlantic Ocean rolled between. There was then no private entrance to it, such as now exists, and in this seemingly slight architectural difference lay the failure of the whole enterprise, as will be presently seen.

Those of us who had been told off to be ready in Court Square went there singly, not to attract attention. No sign of motion or life was there, though the lights gleamed from many windows, for it happened—a bit of unlooked-for good fortune—that the Supreme Court was holding an evening session, and ordinary visitors could pass freely. Planting myself near a door which stood ajar, on the east side of the building, I waited for the trap to be sprung, and for the mob of people to appear from Faneuil Hall. The moments seemed endless. Would our friends never arrive? Presently a rush of running figures, like the sweep of a wave, came round the corner of Court Square, and I watched it with such breathless anxiety as I have experienced only twice or thrice in life. The crowd ran on pell-mell, and I scanned it for a familiar face. A single glance brought the conviction of failure and disappointment. We had the froth and scum of the meeting, the fringe of idlers on its edge. The men on the platform, the real nucleus of that great gathering, were far in the rear, perhaps were still clogged in the hall. Still, I stood, with assumed carelessness, by the entrance, when an official ran up from the basement, looked me in the face, ran in, and locked the door. There was no object in preventing him, since there was as yet no visible reinforcement of friends. Mingling with the crowd, I ran against Stowell, who had been looking for the axes, stored at a friend's office in Court Square. He whispered, "Some of our men are bringing a beam up to the west door, the one that gives entrance to the upper stairway." Instantly he and I ran round and grasped the beam; I finding myself at the head, with a stout negro opposite me. The real attack had begun.

What followed was too hurried and confusing to be described with perfect accuracy of detail, although the main facts stand out vividly enough. Taking the joist up the steps, we hammered away at the southwest door of the Court-House. It could not have been many minutes before it began to give way, was then secured again, then swung ajar, and rested heavily, one hinge having parted. There was room for but one to pass in. I glanced instinctively at my black ally. He did not even look at me, but sprang in first, I following. In later years the experience was of inestimable value to me, for it removed once for all every doubt of the intrinsic courage of the blacks. We found ourselves inside, face to face with six or eight policemen, who laid about them with their clubs, driving us to the wall and hammering away at our heads. Often as I had heard of clubbing, I had never before known just how it felt, and to my surprise it was not half so bad as I expected. I was unarmed, but had taken boxing lessons at several different times, and perhaps felt, like Dr. Holmes's young man named John, that I had "a new way of counterin' I wanted to try;" but hands were powerless against clubs, although my burly comrade wielded his lustily. All we could expect was to be a sort of clumsy Arnold Winkelrieds and "make way for liberty." All other thought was merged in this, the expectation of reinforcements. I did not know that I had received a severe cut on the chin, whose scar I yet carry, though still ignorant how it came. Nor did I know till next morning, what had a more important bearing on the seeming backwardness of my supposed comrades, that, just as the door sprang open, a shot had been fired, and one of the marshal's deputies, a man named Batchelder, had fallen dead.

There had been other fugitive slave rescues in different parts of the country, but this was the first drop of blood actually shed. In all the long procession of events which led the nation through the Kansas struggle, past the John Brown foray, and up to the Emancipation Proclamation, the killing of Batchelder was the first act of violence. It was, like the firing on Fort Sumter, a proof that war had really begun. The mob outside was daunted by the event, the marshal's posse inside was frightened, and what should have been the signal of success brought, on the contrary, a cessation of hostilities. The theory at the time was that the man had been stabbed by a knife, thrust through the broken panel. The coroner's inquest found it to be so, and the press, almost as active as now, yet no more accurate, soon got so far as to describe the weapon,—a Malay kris, said to have been actually picked up in the street. For years I supposed all this to be true, and conjectured that either my negro comrade did the deed, or else Lewis Hayden, who was just behind him.[2] Naturally, we never exchanged a word on the subject, as it was a serious matter; and it was not till within a few years (1888) that it was claimed by a well-known journalist, the late Thomas Drew, that it was Martin Stowell who shot, not stabbed, Batchelder; that Drew had originally given Stowell the pistol; and that when the latter was arrested and imprisoned, on the night of the outbreak, he sent for Drew and managed to hand him the

---

[2]Lewis Hayden apparently fired a shot in my defense, after entrance had been made, but this was doubtless after the death of Batchelder; and the bullet or slug was said to have passed between the arm and body of Marshal Freeman. When Theodore Parker heard this statement, he wrung his hands and said, "Why did he not hit him?"

weapon, which Drew gave to some one else, who concealed it till long after the death of Stowell in the Civil War. This vital part of the facts, at the one point which made of the outbreak a capital offense, remained thus absolutely unknown, even to most of the participants, for thirty-four years. As Drew had seen the revolver loaded in Worcester, and had found, after its restoration, that one barrel had been discharged, and as he was also in the attacking party and heard the firing, there can be no reasonable doubt that the revolver was fired. On the other hand, I am assured by George H. Munroe, Esq., of the "Boston Herald," who was a member of the coroner's jury, that the surgical examination was a very thorough one, and that the wound was undoubtedly made by a knife or bayonet, it being some two inches long, largest in the middle and tapering towards each end. A similar statement was made at the time, to one of my informants, by Dr. Charles T. Jackson, the reported discoverer of etherization, who was one of the surgical examiners. It is therefore pretty certain that Stowell's bullet did not hit the mark after all, and that the man who killed Batchelder is still unknown.

All this, however, was without my knowledge; I only knew that we were gradually forced back beyond the threshold, the door standing now wide open, and our supporters having fallen back to leave the steps free. Mr. Charles E. Stevens, in his "Anthony Burns, a History," published in 1856, says that I said on emerging, "You cowards, will you desert us now?" And though his narrative, like most contemporary narratives, is full of inaccuracies, this statement may be true; it was certainly what I felt, not knowing that a man had already been killed, and that Stowell and others had just been taken off by the police. I held my place outside, still hoping against hope that some concerted reinforcement might appear. Meanwhile the deputy marshals retreated to the stairway, over which we could see their pistols pointing, the whole hall between us and them being brightly lighted. The moments passed on. One energetic young lawyer, named Seth Webb, whom I had known in college, ran up the steps, but I dissuaded him from entering alone, and he waited. Then followed one of the most picturesque incidents of the whole affair. In the silent pause that ensued there came quietly forth from the crowd the well-known form of Mr. Amos Bronson Alcott, the Transcendental philosopher. Ascending the lighted steps alone, he said tranquilly, turning to me and pointing forward, "Why are we not within?" "Because," was the rather impatient answer, "these people will not stand by us." He said not a word, but calmly walked up the steps,—he and his familiar cane. He paused again at the top, the centre of all eyes, within and without; a revolver sounded from within, but hit nobody; and finding himself wholly unsupported, he turned and retreated, but without hastening a step. It seemed to me that, under the circumstances, neither Plato nor Pythagoras could have done the thing better; and the whole scene brought vividly back the similar appearance of the Gray Champion in Hawthorne's tale.

This ended the whole affair. Two companies of artillery had been ordered out, and two more of marines, these coming respectively from Fort Warren and the Charlestown Navy Yard. (Here again I follow Stevens.) Years after, the successor of the United States marshal, the Hon. Roland G. Usher, said to me that his predecessor had told him that the surprise was complete, and that thirty resolute men could have carried off Burns. Had the private entrance to the platform in Faneuil Hall existed then, as now, those thirty would certainly have been at hand. The alarm planned to be given from the gallery was heard in the meeting, but was disbelieved; it was thought to be a scheme to interrupt the proceedings. Phillips had not received notice of it. Parker and Howe had not fully comprehended the project; but when the latter could finally get out of the hall he ran at full speed up to the Court-House, with Dr. William Francis Channing at his side, and they—two of our most determined men—found the field lost. Had they and such as they been present, it might have been very different.

The attempt being a failure and troops approaching, I went down the steps. There is always a farce ready to succeed every tragedy, and mine occurred when a man in the crowd sidled quietly up to me and placidly remarked, "Mister, I guess you've left your rumberill." It flashed through my mind that before taking hold of the beam I had set down my umbrella—for it was a showery day—over the railing of the Court-House steps. Recapturing this important bit of evidence, I made my way to Dr. W. F. Channing's house, had my cut attended to, and went to bed; awaking in a somewhat battered condition the next morning, and being sent off to Worcester by my advisers. Then followed my arrest after a few days,—a matter conducted so courteously that the way of the transgressor became easy.

Naturally enough, my neighbors and friends regarded my arrest and possible conviction as a glory or a disgrace according to their opinions on the slavery question. Fortunately it did not disturb my courageous mother, who wrote, "I assure you it does not trouble me, though I dare say that some of my friends are commiserating me for having a son 'riotously and routously engaged,'"—these being the curious legal terms of the indictment. For myself, it was easy to take the view of my old favorite Lamennais, who regarded any life as rather incomplete which did not, as in his own case, include some experience of imprisonment in a good cause. ("Il manque toujours quelque chose à la belle vie, qui ne finit pas sur le champ de bataille, sur l'échafaud ou en prison.") In my immediate household the matter was taken coolly enough to suggest a calm inquiry, one day, by the lady of the house, whether all my letters to her from the prison would probably be read by the jailer; to which a young niece, then staying with us, replied with the levity of her years, "Not if he writes them in his usual handwriting."

It was left to my honor to report myself at the station in due time to meet the officers of the law; and my family, responding to this courtesy, were even more anxious than usual that I should not miss the train. In Boston, my friend Richard Henry Dana went with me to the marshal's office; and I was seated in a chair to be "looked over" for identification by the various officers who were to testify at the trial. They sat or stood around me in various attitudes, with a curious and solemn depth of gaze which seemed somewhat conventional and even melodramatic. It gave the exciting sensation of being a bold Turpin just from Hounslow Heath; but it was on a Saturday, and there was something exquisitely amusing in the extreme anxiety of Marshal Tukey—a dark, handsome, picturesque man, said to pride himself on a certain Napoleonic look—that I should reach home in time for my Sunday's preaching. Later the long trial unrolled itself, in which, happily, my presence was not necessary after pleading to the indictment. Theodore Parker was the only one among the defendants who attended steadily every day, and he prepared that elaborate defense which was printed afterwards. The indictment was ultimately quashed as imperfect, and we all got out of the affair, as it were, by the side-door.

I have passed over the details of the trial as I omitted those relating to the legal defense of Burns, the efforts to purchase him, and his final delivery to his claimant, because I am describing the affair only as a private soldier tells of what he personally saw and knew. I must, however, mention, in closing, a rather amusing afterpiece to the whole matter,—something which occurred on October 30, 1854. A Boston policeman, named Butman, who had been active at the time of Burns's capture, came up to Worcester for the purpose, real or reputed, of looking for evidence against those concerned in the riot. The city being intensely anti-slavery and having a considerable colored population, there was a strong disposition to lynch the man, or at least to frighten him thoroughly, though the movement was checked by a manly speech to the crowd by George Frisbie Hoar, now United States Senator, but then a young lawyer; the ultimate result being that Butman was escorted to the railway station on

Mr. Hoar's arm, with a cordon of Abolitionists about him, as a shelter from the negroes who constantly rushed at him from the rear. I was one of this escort, and directly behind Butman walked Joseph Howland, a non-resistant of striking appearance, who satisfied his sensitive conscience by this guarded appeal, made at intervals in a sonorous voice: "Don't hurt him, mean as he is! Don't kill him, mean though he be!" At Howland's side was Thomas Drew, a vivacious little journalist, already mentioned, who compounded with his conscience very differently. Nudging back reprovingly the negroes and others who pressed upon the group, he would occasionally, when the coast was clear, run up and administer a vigorous kick to the unhappy victim, and then fall back to repress the assailants once more. As for these last, they did not seem to be altogether in earnest, but half in joke; although the scene gave the foundation for a really powerful chapter, called "The Roar of St. Domingo," in the now forgotten novel "Harrington," by W. D. O'Connor.

4

A Ride Through Kanzas

I. — Nebraska City.

Nebraska City, Sept. 12, 1856.

Nebraska City is a handful of one-story cabins, interspersed with an equal number of magnificent distances, all beautifully situated on a bluff overlooking the muddy Missouri. It has one or two groves of "timber" about it, and there are noble woods on the rich bottom-land across the river. The village itself, like other Western villages, has a tavern and three or four land offices, and the principal pursuit of the inhabitants consists in sitting on the doorsteps of these structures, waiting for real estate to rise. It does rise, however, very fast, and the name of the settlement may be more veracious at some future time. At present, in this region, if a place is tolerably large, it is called a town. If otherwise, something must be done for it, and it is christened Something City.

This is a good way into the Far West. From childhood I had learned by Worcester's Geography that Council Bluffs was the extreme verge of the imaginable horizon. When at last the stage rolled me in there, I felt as strangely as a little boy on the Canada Railway, who, as the conductor shouted the name of the little village of London, sprang up, half awake, behind me, exclaiming, "Do we really pass through LONDON, that great city!"

Set it down as a general rule that all statements of Iowa Kanzas Committees in regard to stage routes are incorrect; and in fact those of everybody else, for the only fixed rule of the Western Stage Company is to do

---

The following letters were originally published, with the signature of Worcester, in the New York Tribune. — Ed.

74

nothing to-day, as it was done yesterday. And as each driver goes but ten or fifteen miles, and knows nothing beyond his own route, and as the agent at each end hardly knows *that,* it is impossible to state at any given moment what will be done. When the stage ought to go, it stops, and when it should stop, it goes. No wonder, then, if Kanzas Committees are wrong, when nobody is right. But it may save some disappointment if I say that there is not a single direct stage route across Iowa to Nebraska City, of any sort, and that whether one starts from Iowa City or Mount Pleasant, it is equally necessary to bring up at Council Bluffs, and thence get down the river as one can, the best way being to take a stage which leaves twice a week for Sidney, at the convenient hour of midnight. Sidney is fifteen miles from this city, and one must choose between a private conveyance thence, and a hack which is *said* to run twice a week with the mails.

There is thus no stage line over the greater part of either route, and this is a great inconvenience. A route has been talked of in the newspapers, and even announced in handbills, running directly from Mount Pleasant to this place, through the second tier of Iowa counties, but I am satisfied that there is no prospect of its being opened. In the mean time, the one hope of Kanzas emigration is the Burlington and Missouri Rivers Railroad. Let Eastern capitalists remember this.

At present no person, without actually travelling across Iowa, can appreciate the injury done by the closing of the Missouri River. Emigrants must toil, week after week, beneath a burning sun, over the parched and endless "rolling prairie," sometimes seeing no house for a day or two together, camping often without wood, and sometimes without water, and obliged to carry with them every eatable they use. It is no wonder that they often fall sick on the way; and when I consider how infinitely weary were even my four days and nights of staging, (after as many more of railroad travel,) I can only wonder at the patience and fortitude which the present emigrants have shown.

As soon as one approaches the Missouri River, even in Iowa and Nebraska, he begins to feel as if he were in France or Austria. Men are very cautious in defining their position, and wait to hear what others will say. Then, perhaps, their tongues are slightly loosed, if they think there are no spies about them. But it is no slight risk when a man may have to pay with his life, further down the river, for a free word, spoken at Council Bluffs or Sidney, both Pro-Slavery towns.

The first night I spent in this place, it seemed as if a symbolical pageant had been got up to remind me where I was. I sat writing by an open window in the beautiful moonlight. A party of boys in the street were shouting and screeching, playing "Border Ruffian," and "storming a fort." In a building beyond, two very inexperienced performers played martial tunes with a drum and fife. Within, the small tavern rocked with the music and dancing of a border ball. Thus I sat between tragedy and comedy.

But there is plenty of genuine tragedy. Coming from a land where millionaires think themselves generous in giving fifty dollars to Kanzas, I converse daily with men who have sacrificed all their property in its service, and are ready at any hour to add their lives. Refugees come every few days from Leavenworth City, and tell, with a quiet desperation, of the wrongs and outrages there transacted. "Come, Uncle George," says the latest informant, "have a seat on this log, and I'll tell you all about it." So Uncle George sits down, takes out his long jack-knife, selects a convenient stick, and begins to whittle. The informant takes out his knife, and follows suit, and a few bystanders settle down and begin to whittle likewise. Then comes the story, "all which he saw, and part of which he was"—how the Missourians came over to vote, and voted—how enraged they were that the Free State men would not vote—how they collected in mobs at last, maddened by whiskey—how they went from house to house and shop to shop, while men took their wives and children to the fort, and fled themselves—how they tarred and feathered one of Uncle George's friends, and ran another out of town, and murdered another—how, like devils, they behaved inside his handsome house, destroying what they could not steal, and trying at last to set it on fire. "Your loss can't be less than $6,000, old fellow," concludes his frank informant, who has himself lost that or more, "even if they didn't burn your block of stores, which they *allowed* to do after I left." Uncle George hears it all in silence, whittles faster or slower according to the excitement of the narrative, and quietly says at last, with a slight moisture in the corner of either eye, "Well, my old woman was out of it, anyhow."

Meantime, in regard to Topeka and Lawrence, the accounts are somewhat confused even here, only one hundred and twenty-five miles off. The last arrival left Topeka on Friday, Sept. 5. He reports the condition of affairs such as you have doubtless had narrated before now. The fortifications around Lawrence, and so on;—the people provided with beef and potatoes, but entirely out of flour and of *lead*. As to the road between here and there, he saw fewer Missourians than previous parties have seen; and there is reason to think that Richardson's bands have been drawn off for a time, to re-enter at a time agreed upon—probably when their spies report that our emigrant train in ready to set forth—

though if it amounts to half their number, it is not likely that they will dare to attack it.

The train is passing through here piecemeal, on its way from a temporary encampment at Tabor to another at the Little Nemaha, twenty-five miles south of this place. The largest section of it is a party of some fifty Massachusetts and Maine men. Having personally assisted in organizing this party and starting them from Boston, I can testify to their character. Some of them own their own wagons and bring pecuniary means with them; others have only brave hearts and strong bodies; and they complain of nothing but the long delay, as they left July 24. Beside these, there are smaller parties from Vermont, Ohio, Illinois, and Iowa, who bring much valuable property. When we are all collected on the Little Nemaha, I shall, perhaps, have time to write more definitely as to the numbers of the train, which will probably count up to several hundred.

Every one admits the fine appearance and excellent conduct of the whole party thus far. Even the mean editor of *The Nebraska News,* a little Administration paper published here, can find nothing against the emigrants, except that they look dusty and ragged. Probably he would prefer them if they had tramped across three hundred miles of prairie in ruffles and patent leather. But the article has been of use in the reaction which it has produced. Even Pro-Slavery men here see that it may injure the place, though not the emigrants, and the first citizens are signing a protest against it. The fact is, that an effort is already being made to turn the emigration through Plattsmouth, (where the ferry is better than here,) and the people of this village perceive where their interest lies. The train will spend some $2,500 or more here, first and last, and not the slightest disorder has yet been charged on a single member of the company. If the market were larger, our purchases would be larger also. I have myself bought up for the emigrants all the cowhide boots to be found in town, (except extra sizes,) and nearly all the flannel shirts and blankets.

Missouri, however, expects to rule Iowa and Nebraska, as well as Kanzas. It is openly threatened that the new steam ferry boat, now being built at St. Louis, shall never come up the river to be used in carrying emigrants; and this is fast converting the owner of the ferry, born in Missouri, and hitherto Pro-Slavery, into an Anti-Slavery man. The Missourians also threaten to attack Tabor, Iowa, which is only some twenty miles from the border, and which is an Anti-Slavery town. Indeed, the citizens of Tabor are entitled to everlasting gratitude for their unwearied kindness to our emigrants. The sick have been cared for, clothing has been made, and every house, stable, and melon-patch, has been common property. Let the Eastern States hold this thriving little village in grateful remembrance.

I am here as a sort of General Agent, to put the train through, and shall, of course, go in with it, to Kanzas.

II. — NEBRASKA TO KANZAS.

TOPEKA, Sept. 25, 1856.

I wrote last from Nebraska City, just before the train of emigrants left that place for this. I reached here yesterday, a day or more in advance of them, having pushed through, for the last two days, with a few companions. The distances on the route are about as follows:—To Camp Creek, or Worcester, twelve miles; thence to Little Nemaha River and Village, fifteen miles; to Archer, fifteen miles; to Plymouth, (Kanzas,) twelve miles; to Lexington, ten miles; to Indian Village, thirty-five miles; to Topeka, fifteen miles. This would make the whole distance one hundred and fourteen miles, and it is variously estimated from that up to one hundred and forty. The route is also somewhat circuitous, and will be shortened hereafter. The road is uniformly a good prairie road, except where a creek is to be crossed, and there is a steep pitch on each side, with a slough between. No serious accident, however, occurred to any of our teams. Of the localities above-named, Nemaha and Archer are thriving little Nebraska settlements, each with lodging-house and store. Worcester, in Nebraska, is one log-house. Plymouth consists of an earthen redoubt on a hill, and two log-houses in the distance. Lexington is a log-fort in the centre of a prairie, where seven of our brave Worcester boys were laboriously digging the best well I have seen in this region—thirty-five feet deep and nine wide. Both Plymouth and Lexington, however, are very favorable town sites, and well laid out. The companies who settled them are now returning from the seat of war, and if they can only obtain food and clothing during the winter, (a doubtful prospect,) these will yet be flourishing towns. That well of water, at least, will be a clear gain to Kanzas in all coming time.

Except these, there are no settlements over this long route till Indianola, a few miles from Topeka. There are occasional log-houses, however, and it is, on the whole, more inhabited than the western part of Iowa.

Our train included about one hundred and forty men and some twenty women and children. There were twenty-eight wagons—all but eight being horse-teams. Our nightly tents made quite a little colony, and presented a busy scene. While some watered and fed the stock, others brought wood for the fires; others prepared the tents and wagons for sleeping; others reloaded pistols or rifles, and the leaders arranged the nightly watch or planned the affairs of the morrow. Meanwhile, the cooks fried pork, made coffee, and baked bread, and a gaping crowd, wrapped in blankets, sat around the fire. Women brought their babes, and took the best places they could find, and one worthy saddler brought out his board and leather every night and made belts and holsters for the men. We slept soundly in spite of the cold and of the scarcity of wood, and each kept watch for an hour, striding in thick boots through the grass, heavy with frost. Danger always seemed before us, though we never actually got into it, and we were never far from our rifles and revolvers. Truth compels the admission that my rifle was never pointed at anything more formidable than a superb hawk, which it brought down, and even that shot was disputed by a comrade, who fired at the same time. However, I have the wings.

We came through without attack from the Missourians, as General Lane assured us that we should; we had had their spies among us, but they had seen that we were well armed, and that our men, though quiet, were determined.

The one thing that discouraged our party, however, was to meet other parties, day after day, returning. Men on horseback and on foot, with wagons and without, came along in ominous numbers. All told the same story. "What the Missourians have been trying for two years to do, Governor Geary has done in two weeks at last," said one man; "*the Free State men are driven out.*" It was like entering Hungary just after the treachery of Görgey. Each had his story to tell of arrests and tyrannies; how a Pro-Slavery witness had only to point at a man as identified with any measure of public defense, and he was seized at once. Several whom we met had been arrested in person, herded with a hundred others, like cattle, on the bare prairie, been scantily fed once a day, and escaped by rolling half a mile through the grass while the sentinels' backs were turned. The bravest young men of Lawrence were put under arrest, charged with treason, murder, arson, robbery, and what not; while not a Pro-Slavery man was seized. This was the penalty they had to pay for defending themselves vigorously at last, and clearing their own soil from the invading Missourians. "The worst enemy Kanzas had ever had," they pronounced Governor Geary to be; and they were going into Iowa to wait for better times. "Will you give up Kanzas?" I asked. "Never!" was the reply from bronzed and bearded lips, stern and terrible as the weapons that hung to the saddle-bow. "We are scattered, starved, hunted, half-naked, but we are not conquered *yet.*"

Some of these were young men, whom I had seen go from prosperous homes, well clothed and cared for. I had since heard of them performing acts of heroic courage in this summer's battles. Lane had praised them to me, and declared that there never was such courage in the world as that of the Free State men of Kanzas. "I saw one of them," said he, "ride up alone within thirty yards of a body of a hundred and fifty men, during an engagement, take deliberate aim, and bring one down." I now saw that very man—that boy rather, a Worcester boy—retreating from his adopted country, hungry, ragged, and almost barefooted, walking wearily on, with others hunted like himself, while some, who had been less scrupulous, rode by on horses which they had plundered from the Missourians, who had first plundered them.

It was such processions as this which welcomed us to unhappy Kanzas. And when we reached the muddy banks of the world-famous river, we found not less than nineteen wagons of emigrants, fleeing with heavy hearts from the land of promise they sought so eagerly two years ago; a sad greeting for the families we brought in. "Truly," said our informant, again, "the Free State men are leaving Kanzas at last; Governor Geary has conquered them."

As Hungary, having successfully resisted her natural enemy, Austria, yielded at length to the added strength of Russia; so the Kossuths of Kanzas, just as they had cleared her borders of Missourians, are subdued by the troops of the United States at last.

III. — AN ARREST.

LAWRENCE, KANZAS, Sept. 28, 1856.

It produces a singular effect upon the mind to awake in the morning, before daybreak, and find the house surrounded by a cordon of dragoons, each sitting silent on his horse. This was my experience this morning, followed by the information that they intended at daylight to search the house for the leaders of the party of immigrants of which I had been one of the conductors. Sallying forth and inquiring for the commanding officer, I was astonished at being accosted by name and discerning an old acquaintance. I then ascertained that the man chiefly aimed at was our common friend Redpath. Then appeared a gentlemanly young Virginian, Colonel Preston, who introduced himself to me as the marshal who was to make the arrest, and gave further elucidation.

I must go back and say that, as the emigrant train was arriving on the previous day, one hundred and forty United States dragoons had come riding through the town, followed by baggage wagons enough for a winter's campaign. They passed us with such unconcern that we regarded them with much the same indifference; but Colonel Preston explained all that. It seems that the vigilant Governor had sent him in pursuit of an armed force of terrific numbers, said to be entering the Territory from Nebraska, under the most ferocious leaders. Therefore a special marshal was sent, clothed with almost unlimited powers, which he showed me, to arrest any or all of this party, and by all means to secure the leaders, especially Redpath. So the marshal rode past our peaceful train, looking for the warlike one, and happening to inquire at the last wagon, found that we, and none but we, were the expected army. Either the bird had flown, or it was a dove, and not a hawk. True, the dove carried a Sharp's rifle under his wing, but it was for defensive purposes only. So Colonel Preston and Captain Walker halted their force, unloaded their baggage wagons, camped uncomfortably on the prairie, and waked sadder and wiser men next morning.

True, they still wished to arrest Redpath, but after some courteous debate with Governor Robinson and myself, it was finally agreed, especially as the victim could not be found, that he should be amicably *invited* to drive down to Lecompton with us, and call on the Governor. This seemed very natural and proper to me, as I had been twice arrested myself, in the same amicable manner, in the Bay State region. (Being brought before potentates in that manner suggests the same criticism made on the sedan chair with no bottom to it—"If it were not for the name of it, it is very much like walking.")

So we four rode down behind the Governor's pair of horses (respectable, but not dashing steeds, well worked); and the traitor and the captor rode on the back seat together, and they interchanged cigars, and Redpath, who would be on easy terms with the Great Mogul at the second whiff, joked the young Colonel rather closely, and put in little keen questions about the decay of Virginia, and the good, generous, manly Governor Robinson had always a sensible word to add; and we told our guest that we didn't approve of stealing horses, but approved particularly of "stealing niggers," and I really was pleased with his exemplary courtesy. I must, however, put in the brief Yankee criticism of Captain W., a staunch Free State man, on my praising these attributes in the young Virginian: "Confound him, *does the manners well;* so they all do, and shoot you the next minute, if they dare."

We rode into the little village of Lecompton, caught a glimpse of the prisoners (whom I shall visit to-morrow), and found the Governor in a house pleasantly situated by the river. Poor man, there is nothing else that is pleasant in his situation.

There is much more harmony in the opinions held here about the Governor than appears to have existed a week or two ago. It does not take long to see through him. When you see that a man *makes an effort* to be dignified and commanding, it is all over with him. The new Governor's eyes look at you, as a certain poet once described somebody's to me, "with a very intensified *nothing* in them." He impressed me as a man who intends to do the right thing, and is profoundly convinced that he has the full ability to do it, and is profoundly mistaken in that belief. He appears to have energy of will, without real energy of character; can do single acts of decision, and has done them already; but has neither the mental ability to understand the condition of Kanzas, nor the moral power to carry out any systematic plan for its benefit. His present plan, to coerce both parties and play a little Napoleon at Lecompton, will inevitably fail, and is failing already. Both sides will cease to respect him as soon as they understand him, and it is mere chance which he will fall out with first. But he will be the last person in the Territory to discover his own failure.

He thinks he has plenary power, commits the most despotic acts without apparently understanding what he does, sets aside the Territorial laws at pleasure, and the United States laws, and all other laws, and yet cannot be made to see that he does so. He puts Pro-Slavery militia over Free State men, and is organizing bodies of Free State men to keep down Pro-Slavery men, and all without law or precedent. So far, he has only arrested Free State men; but I shall not be at all surprised if he arrests others. Still, the Free State men cannot consistently make complaints under the Territorial laws, and they do not; and as they keep aloof from him, and are learning to despise him, he is almost wholly under the influence of the other party.

What can be expected from a man who proclaims in presence of a dozen people, as I heard him, in the most grandiloquent manner, "Gentlemen, rely upon it that I watch over you always; my information extends everywhere; my spies are everywhere; I shall spend $10,000, if necessary, in obtaining information; two men cannot talk together in the streets of Kanzas without my knowing the subject of their machinations; in fact, a man can scarcely *think,* without my knowing the subject of his thoughts." Yet these are almost his precise words, not in private conversation, but delivered in an almost public manner, and written down by me directly after.

I give this description of the new Governor of Kanzas, because there is no public man in the United States whose blunders or errors may be more destructive. Of his private life I have nothing to say, and indeed know nothing; but he has undertaken a position so inconsistent and difficult that the wisest man could not fill it; and he is a great way from being the wisest.

As to Redpath's case it was soon dismissed, but not till his keen wit had had ample play upon the lofty Governor, who did not for some time discover whom he had to deal with; and when they finally parted, Redpath assured the Governor that he need not apologise for his treatment of him, and if their positions were ever reversed, he would certainly treat him with the same generosity. It was impossible not to laugh, and his Excellency bowed us out, looking a little puzzled, and I closed the door, feeling that pity one entertains for a man not without good intentions, but who has undertaken a task utterly out of proportion to his calibre.

We came down to Lawrence that night in the Governor's carriage, (the *real* Governor, who by the way made a noble speech to our emigrants, the day before, in his own simple way,) and it was through the most tremendous, sudden storm I was ever out in. It was just after sunset, and in an instant all was absolute darkness around us, and the lightning came in such intensity that we could see no more than we saw without it. The hail came in sheets upon the roof of the vehicle, then the rain saturated even its interior; the horses had to be held in their fright; it was uncomfortable. But I reflected that I had come to Kanzas expecting adventures, and here was one; and then I was being driven by a Governor, in his own carriage, moist though it might be. And we arrived safely at last.

Lawrence is three times the size of Topeka, and delightfully situated; hills, river, and "timber" in plenty; more in this vicinity than I have seen anywhere else. Things look less utterly paralyzed than in Topeka, where I counted forty-four occupied buildings, and nineteen on which work had been begun and abandoned. Here there seems to be some employment, but the ruins of the large hotel, and the bare spot where Governor Robinson's house stood, and the fortifications across some of the principal streets, tell a tale about as sad. There has also been far more suffering here. Flour has just arrived in abundance, and sells at $5.00 per sack of 100 lbs., but, where to get the money!

Never have I been in such a community as this; never seen such courage, such patience, such mutual generosity, such perfect buoyancy of spirit. Not a man nor a woman seems bent or depressed by all that they have suffered; and they speak of the attack upon the town, a fortnight ago to-day, with two thousand eight hundred Missourians outside and two hundred and fifty fighting men inside, as lightly as I can now speak of the prairie tempest last night.

IV. — THE PRISONERS.

TOPEKA, Sept. 30, 1856.

Yesterday I visited the prisoners of State, now under confinement at Lecompton. It was my second visit to that forlorn little Virginia town. I call it thus because the whole sensation is that of the Old Dominion. Instead of the rising school-houses and churches of Lawrence, the little street is lined with bar-rooms, whereof the chief is the "Virginia Saloon." The tavern is true Virginia—bacon, corn-bread, and dirty negro boys and girls to wait at table. Southern provincialisms strike one's ear at every moment, and the town is garrisoned by Colonel Titus's militia, re-enforced yesterday by twenty-five precious youths from Georgia, in a high state of whiskey.

The Governor disavows all control over the prisoners, but Marshal Donelson was very ready to admit me to see them. In fact, they were very visible, being allowed an area of a square rod or so before their prison door, guarded by a few young Missourians, who paced up and down with loaded muskets. I met one of the poor fellows, allowed for some reason to cross the street, pursued by an evil-looking scoundrel with fixed bayonet. It is singular how much alike all Slavery's officials look. I saw half a dozen times repeated the familiar features of my Boston friend, Mr. Asa O. Butman.

The hundred and five prisoners lounged about, looking as prisoners everywhere do. They are kept in a large unfinished wooden building, without an atom of furniture of any description. They do their own cooking, with very scanty utensils, and such provisions as I shall here-after describe. They have obtained with great difficulty fifteen straw pallets for the whole company. Some have no blankets; but the majority possess the luxury of one apiece. It was an exceedingly cold, windy day, when I was there; the exposed side of the house was unfinished, and about half its superficial extent consisted of great gaps through which the wind whistled. A few of the men lay about on the floor sick with fever and ague.

Most of them are young men, the flower of the youth of Lawrence. They are a light-hearted set of boys, and are resolved to avenge themselves on their captors by perfect indifference to captivity. It comes hard, however, on some fathers of families and owners of farms, which are alike suffering from their absence. Three weeks labor of a hundred men, all lost, in the busiest season of the year, for it is the only time to get in the hay for the Winter's supply.

One man had left six children, all sick, and his wife accidentally absent from home; he said he *supposed* some of the neighbors would look after them! Another carried in his arms a child, who was, I was told, the first child born in Lawrence, and was christened with the name of the town. The poor little thing looked rather forlorn, as its pallid father carried it up and down the bare prison room; an early initiation into the sorrows of Kanzas.

Among the crowd I found two of the best emigrants whom Worcester had sent, and others who belonged to companies which I had organized. Not one of these seemed depressed, but all appeared proud of being there. At first, they said, while in the care of the United States troops, and encamped on the prairie, there were many escapes; now the guard was so close that it was almost impossible. Colonel Titus, who has charge of these men, is the head of one division of Kanzas militia, his force being chiefly from Missouri and other Southern States; he is the man whose life was humanely spared by the Free State men when they broke up his camp of outlaws. He showed his gratitude by informing his Free State prisoners that if one of them attempted to escape, he should blow the building to atoms. I looked and saw the cannon actually pointed, not upon the entrance, but so as to command the main portion of the building. There stood the emblem of despotism, with its conical pile of balls beside it. I never saw but one cannon, before, that looked so detestable. That was employed in the same cause, but in Boston instead of Lecompton.

Even now, the men say that some could escape by killing a few sentinels; but this they will not do, for a true Kanzas reason—they would lose their rifles; whereas, if liberated, Governor Geary assures them that they shall be restored. I doubt this prospect, however, from the fact that out of fourteen horses, possessed by different individuals of the number when captured, only three can now be found; and a horse ranks second to a Sharp's rifle in the affections of a Kanzas man.

All these prisoners are bound over for trial in October, on the charge of murder in the first degree. You are aware of the brilliant series of engagements in which the freemen of Kanzas had driven the invaders from their borders before Governor Geary appeared. In most of these a few Missourians were killed. In return for this, every Free State man who is accused by anybody of having taken part in those engagements is in danger of arrest. The greater part, however, were taken after the battle at Hickory Point, while of the Pro-Slavery men, who still had the black flag flying when these were taken, not one was captured.

If each of these prisoners had, in broad daylight, deliberately murdered a man, they could have been placed in no worse position than they are now, for simply defending the liberties of their country under most fearful provocation.

For instance, in the attack on Osawkee, the Free State men, on entering the Pro-Slavery fort, found a man *chained to the floor,* by a heavy log chain, about eight feet long, which was riveted to his leg. In this position he had been kept for six weeks, on the charge of stealing a horse. In all the exasperation produced by this discovery, no man was killed; but the Missourians were compelled to perform the labor of detaching the chain from the leg. My informant saw it done. For this affair, some of those whom I saw at Lecompton were imprisoned, and others in this place are hiding from arrest, or working on their farms with a horse ready saddled for instantaneous escape from any suspicious visitors.

All these arrests have been made by the United States troops, whom it is the present policy of the people not to resist. But this patience cannot last forever; and I only repeat, what I have every day asserted, when I say that the election of Fremont is the only thing that can avert a bloodier conflict than has ever yet stained this soil. For myself, I do not believe that even that will do it. When not a single Pro-Slavery man is arrested, how can men help seeing that the power of the Union is sustaining Missouri?

The Governor excuses himself by saying that the Free State men make no complaints. But he does not wait for complaints on the other side, and he admitted to me that he sent up to arrest the leaders of our train of emigrants without an affidavit from any one. He has been repeatedly informed of the reason why the Free State men do not make complaints—namely, that they repudiate the bogus laws and despise the Judges. But he never will understand it, if it is stated to him every day during his stay in Kanzas.

I think he *means* to be kind to the prisoners, and he readily consented to order some additional blankets for them, and to suggest some improvement in their fare; he also, on being requested, directed the Marshal to close up the chinks in the building above referred to.

I took down a list of the prisoners. They came from the following States: Maine three, New Hampshire one, Vermont three, Massachusetts twelve, Rhode Island two, Connecticut one, New York thirteen, Ohio twelve, Michigan five, Indiana twelve, Illinois twenty-three, Wisconsin five, Iowa nine, Missouri six; total, one hundred and seven. I took pains to collect their names and origin, from their own lips, that we of the Free States may see that these are our own follow-citizens.

The first prisoners were captured September 10, kept by the United States troops ten days, (having on one occasion but one biscuit each for thirty-six hours,) and then transferred to their present position, of which I add a further illustration from another source.

Statement of Provisions furnished the Prisoners for their first week at Lecompton.

Monday, Sept. 20.—Received no rations from United States Camp. Moved to Lecompton. Received at 5 o'clock, 1 sack of 'shorts,' baked into bread—1 do. not baked; 75 lbs. of bacon; 6 candles. 103 men. No coffee or sugar.

Tuesday Evening.—1 sack of shorts, 103 lbs. of bacon, 4 lbs. of coffee, 6 lbs. of sugar, 8 or 10 lbs. of salt, 1 lb. of saleratus, 1 gallon of molasses. 103 men.

Wednesday Evening.—1 sack of shorts, 5 lbs. of coffee, 5 lbs. of sugar, 1 gallon of molasses, 1 lb. of saleratus. 105 men.

Thursday Evening.—1 sack of flour, 50 lbs. of bacon, 6 lbs. of coffee, no sugar, 1 lb. of saleratus, 1 gallon of vinegar, 3 candles, 1 gallon of molasses. Provisions brought after dark. 105 men.

Friday, 2 o'clock.—Called on Sergeant of the Guard for provisions: was informed that he had spoken to the Marshal and that we were curtailed to two meals per day. Half past 4, Marshal came, brought 50 lbs. of bacon, fore-quarter of beef, about 110 lbs., 125 lbs. of flour, 1 bushel of green beans in the pod, 6 lbs. of coffee, no sugar, no salt; we got about 1 quart of salt from a neighbor. 7 o'clock, fresh arrival of nine prisoners. Marshal brought 3 candles for the whole amount of us, 111 men; furnished 15 mattresses to sleep on.

Saturday.—Received 25 lbs. of beef, 125 lbs. of flour, one small sack of salt, one gallon of molasses, 6 lbs. of coffee. [111 men.] Spoke to Marshal in behalf of nine men brought here yesterday, who had no blankets, and was told that it was impossible to furnish any for them. He afterwards brought three quilts for them.

Sunday.—About 100 lbs. of beef, much damaged, 125 lbs. of flour, 6 lbs. of coffee, 1/2 lb. saleratus, 1 peck of beans, 3 candles, 4 lbs. of sugar.

"We give the above as the amount of provisions received by the prisoners since coming to Lecompton, and are willing to make oath to the same.

E. R. FALLEY,
ARTEMAS H. PARKER,
"Commissaries for the prisoners to distribute their provisions."

N. B.—Mr. Parker is well known to me as a worthy citizen of Clinton, Mass., who emigrated this Spring.

V. — THE PEOPLE.

LAWRENCE, October 4, 1856.

Ever since the rendition of Anthony Burns, in Boston, I have been looking for *men.* I have found them in Kanzas. The virtue of courage (for although these two words originally meant the same thing, they have become separated now) has not died out of the Anglo-American race, as some have hastily supposed. It needs only circumstances to bring it out. A single day in Kanzas makes the American Revolution more intelligible than all Sparks or Hildreth can do. The same event is still in progress here.

I have always wondered whether, in the midst of war, tumult, and death, the same daily current of life went on, and men's hearts accommodated themselves to the occasion. In heroic races, I now see that it is so. In Kanzas, nobody talks of courage, for every one is expected to exhibit it.

Take, for instance, the Sunday attack on Lawrence, a fortnight ago. The army which approached it consisted of 2,800 by the estimate here—3,000 by Governor Geary's estimate, and 3,200 by the statement of *The Missouri Republican,* in a singular article, which described the capture of the town, although it never happened. This force was in sight the greater part of the day, and though Governor Geary's aid was invoked, it was known that it could not arrive till evening; thus allowing time for the destruction of everything.

Against this force, the number at first counted upon was *one hundred;* that being the supposed number of fighting men left, after the arrest of the hundred about whom I wrote to you, as prisoners. To the surprise of all, however, more than two hundred rallied to the fort. The lame came on crutches, and the sick in blankets.

Two hundred men against fourteen times their number! And the fort a mere earthen redoubt, of no pretensions—for the only fort worth the name is on the hill above the town, and was at this time useless. And yet (here comes the point) I was assured by Governor Robinson and a dozen others, that among this devoted handful the highest spirits prevailed; they were laughing and joking as usual, and only intent on selling their lives as dearly as possible.

They had no regular commander, any more than at Bunker Hill; but the famous "Old Captain Brown" moved about among them, saying,

"Fire low, boys; be sure to bring down your eye to the hinder sight of your rifle, and aim at the feet rather than the head."

A few women were in the fort that day—all who could be armed. Others spent the whole Sunday making cartridges. I asked one of these how she felt: "Well, I can't remember that I felt any way different from usual," answered the quiet housekeeper, after due reflection. So they all say. One young girl sat at her door, reading, a mile or so from the scene of action. "Once in a while I looked up," she said, "when there was a louder shot than usual."

The chief fighting was among skirmishers, and there was no actual attack on the fort. The newspapers have had the particulars before, and I only mention the affair to show the spirit of buoyant courage which almost universally prevails. It must be remembered, also, that even now these people are poorly armed, and still worse off for ammunition. On this occasion they had but a few rounds apiece.

Persons at the North who grudge their small subscriptions to Kanzas, should remember that a few dollars may sometimes save a thousand. Osawatamic was sacrificed, after one of the most heroic defences in history, for want of ammunition. Brown and twenty-seven others resisted two hundred, killing thirty-three and wounding forty-nine, (eighty-two in all, by the Pro-Slavery statement,) and then retreated through these, with the loss of but one man, shot as he was swimming the creek. A hundred dollars worth of ammunition would have prevented, on that occasion, the destruction of $60,000 worth of property.

I walked out yesterday to the scene of the last fight at Franklin, and heard the narrative from one of the Pro-Slavery men who had defended the fort. He said "he didn't like those d—d Sharp's rifles; didn't mind the ball so much, but hated the *whizzing* of them"—just, I suppose, as the hum of a mosquito is more annoying than the bite. He said also: "As soon as they shoved up the wagon-load of hay, and set it on fire, we boys cried for quarter, and *then we all ran*." I saw where the hay was taken from, a very exposed place, and where the door had been burned by it. He showed also the narrow space through which the defenders fired, and I observed that nearly all the rifle balls of the assailants went above it, the tendency of Sharp's rifles in inexperienced hands. My Pro-Slavery friend dug out one of these for me, as a memorial.

Franklin was the place where the Free State men were charged with plundering the letters from the Post-Office. I suppose it will not have the smallest effect on the Democratic newspapers when I say that this young man, the postmaster's son, entirely denied this story. He only charged them with stealing sixty dollars worth of stamps. But as the village of

Franklin consists of less than a dozen houses, and as I have found it hard to buy a dollar's worth of stamps at much larger places in this region, I must doubt the precise accuracy of these figures, and I told him so.

Since breaking up this den of thieves, the vicinity has been quiet, except when the noble army of two thousand eight hundred, on returning, burnt a large mill close by, on which the whole neighborhood depended for meal and lumber. It is not far from here to Blanton's Bridge, which the Grand Jury declared a nuisance, because it gave aid and comfort to Free State men. I suppose that this mill was a nuisance for the same reason. The heaps of sawdust of the building were still in flames as I stood before them.

The owner of this mill was a Pennsylvanian, named Straub. We saw his daughter, a noble looking girl of 20, but rather unnecessarily saucy and spirited in her replies, I at first thought. Presently she said, with surprise, "Why, I thought you were Missourians, and I was resolved that you should hear the truth." This was a piece of genuine Kanzas pluck, as it was a lonely place, and we were three to one. Afterward, we found that this girl had walked alone into the midst of the Missourians, while the house and mill were burning, and demanded her horse from one of them with such spirit that the others compelled him to dismount. She mounted it and rode away—he presently followed and attempted to get the halter from her hand. She held on. He took his bowie-knife and threatened to cut her hand off; she told him to do it if he dared; he cut the rope close to her hand, and led the horse away. She slipped off, and presently two of the man's companions rode up and brought her the horse once more. A horse is worth more than a life in this region, and you can estimate the extent of such a triumph.

As for Lawrence, it has one of the most beautiful situations I ever looked upon. It stands on a bank above a bend in the river; across the river are miles of woods, while behind the town rise two beautiful hills, which *are* hills, and not merely the endless swells of rolling prairie of which my Eastern eyes have grown so tired. Indeed, this whole region far surpasses, in respect to hills and forest, both Iowa and Nebraska, and even Northern Kanzas, while the prairies are richer, and coal and stone are interspersed. Give it freedom, and a few years will make Kanzas the garden of America. This year the Missourians have almost ruined the corn; but never have I seen such luxuriance of melons, squashes, and pumpkins. I have seen some fine stock, too, on the more favored farms; but that kind of riches soon takes to itself legs, more dangerous, in the present state of Kanzas, than the proverbial wings.

Lawrence is three times as large as Topeka, and at present much more busy. It has, however, suffered much more from want of food. For instance, I have just talked with a man whom I knew at the East. "I came out here," said he, "with $1,500 in money. I have served through the whole war. My wife and nine children have lived more than two weeks on green corn and squash. I have in my house no meat, no flour, no meal, no potatoes, no money to buy them, no prospect of a dollar; but *I'll live or die in Kanzas!*"

Afterwards this man's wife wrote to me in almost the same words.

Such is the spirit of multitudes, many of whom are as badly off as this man. There is the greatest generosity, and men share with each other while anything is left; but after that, what then?

The State Committee works with energy and system to relieve distress, and may be entirely relied upon, but its funds are also exhausted. The expense of sending emigrants, arms, and ammunition, through Iowa and Nebraska, has been so enormous, that but little has yet reached Kanzas in any other form; and the cost of supporting the army here has been also enormous—some $300 per day. At the very time when farm labor was most needed, all the able-bodied men have been obliged to live for weeks in camp, at the public expense—they themselves being the principal public.

This discourages and drives out the timid and lukewarm, and educates the remainder to endurance. People in Kanzas are like Indians—they eat what they can, and sleep where they can; and when they have no house and no food they wait awhile till something turns up. I can see that this state of things brings out some bad qualities, but far more good ones.

Last Sunday I preached in this place (though I must say that I am commonly known here by a title which is elsewhere considered incompatible with even the Church Militant). It was quite an occasion; and I took for my text the one employed by the Rev. John Martin the Sunday after he fought at Bunker Hill—Neh. iv: 14; "Be not ye afraid of them; remember the Lord, which is great and terrible, and fight for your brethren, your sons and your daughters, your wives and your houses."

To-night I speak again, and leave to-morrow for Leavenworth, there to witness a Border Ruffian election, as there is to be no voting at Lawrence.

VI.—A KANZAS ELECTION.

LEAVENWORTH, K. T., Oct. 6, 1856.

I have come over to see the election. The road from Lawrence runs thirty-three miles through the most beautiful region of Kanzas, the Delaware Reserve. It is mostly well wooded, and all the soil is luxuriant. There are only a few Indian cabins on the way, but some points of the

road have a sad celebrity. In the hospital, at Lawrence, I saw two men recovering from terrible wounds in the head, inflicted, not by P. S. Brooks,
M. C., but by his humbler imitators in Missouri. The case was this. Three
men were riding, unarmed, from Lawrence to Leavenworth. They were
captured by a small posse of the enemy, and shot in cold blood the next
morning. One had his jaw terribly broken, and was left for dead. Another lay wounded and the wretches felt his pulse, as is their practice,
and finding it still beating, knocked him on the head with their guns, till
life seemed extinct. These were the two I saw; the third was killed; and
amid those lovely woods and fields, a pile of earth and a roadside stake
are his only memorial.

We passed also the spot where Mr. Hops was murdered and scalped,
for a bet of a pair of boots. Now the road is comparatively safe, or what
the stage-driver calls safe: "last week there was only *one* man taken off
the stage, who hasn't since been heard from." But I rode across with an
old farmer and his boy, unmolested, though we met a few small parties
of Missourians on horseback, some of them riding double, as they occasionally do.

The Free State hotels in Leavenworth are broken up. (Don't be surprised to hear of a "Free State hotel" in regions where men distinguish
between a Pro-Slavery and an Anti-Slavery *cow.*) The chief tavern at
present is kept by a man named McCarty, who is building a large new
brick one. He is desperately Pro-Slavery, and in conjunction with Majors
and Russell, the great Government contractors, originated the late riots
in the town.

Leavenworth is twice as large as Lawrence, has a fine situation on the
river and fine scenery around. The landing is good, and with New England enterprise it would be destined to greatness, and by the aid of
Government business it may yet attain it. But never did I see such universal drinking. There must be more than fifty liquor shops for some
two thousand inhabitants; the doors of the Leavenworth Hotel are
adorned with a row of whiskey casks and of barrels full of empty bottles;
and the bar-room is crowded all day.

Despite this, it is said to be the quietest election-day ever known.
None of the Anti-Slavery men vote, very properly declining to recognize
the validity of an election under the bogus laws, and there is but one
ticket running, which I send [see "Law and Order Ticket," p. 93].

There are local interests and jealousies for particular candidates, four
only out of ten being eligible, but the Slavery question is not raised. The
favorite candidate, Martin, is captain of the atrocious Kickapoo Rangers,
and the character of the whole may be easily inferred.

LAW AND ORDER TICKET.

For Congress.
Gen. J. W. WHITFIELD.

———

For Convention.

———

Legislature.

———

No Regular Nomination.

———

Four to be elected.

W. G. MATHIAS,	A. PAYNE,
J. W. MARTIN,	D. J. JOHNSTON,
MAT. WALKER	A. R. KELLUM,
L. F. HOLLINGSWORTH,	E. M. KENNEDY,
S. J. KOOKOGY,	MOSES YOUNG.

As for the voting, nothing can be more free and easy. Strangers are pressed to take a share in it, as if it were something to drink. Nothing seems necessary except to hand in a ticket at a small office window, and announce one's name; no questions appeared to be asked. I was urged to do this by bystanders, in spite of my assurances that I was merely a traveller, not a resident; they assured me it made no difference. I saw the same persuasions succeed with persons who obviously did not come in for the purpose. But many openly proclaimed that as the only object of their visit, and coolly debated the most available points to throw Pro-Slavery votes, just as a knot of country merchants might debate whether to go to New York or Boston for their purchases.

Indeed, there is a delightful absence of hypocrisy in all this region. They leave all that to Eastern politicians, editors, and clergymen. There is very little dispute about the main facts of the case. Every Pro-Slavery man admits the important ones, and defends them. "The end (i.e. Slavery) justifies the means." I wish some of our beclouded and befogged Democratic brethren could sit for an hour or two on McCarty's door steps, of an evening. For instance, last night there was general applause when a leading man said, "By———, I wish the Abolitionists would just kill one or two of our men, moderate men, you know, not good for much, but just enough to let us claim them as ours—*anything to give us a handle.*" And yet the political allies of this worthy personage are every day declaring that the whole excitement is only kept up to make capital for the Fremont party.

Once the conversation began to grow rather personal. Said one man, just from Lecompton, "Tell you what, we've found out one thing, there's a preacher going about here preaching politics." "Fact?" and "is that so?" was echoed with virtuous indignation on all sides. "That's so," continued he, "and he fixes it this way; first, he has his text and preaches religion; then he drops that and pitches into politics; and then he drops that, too, and begins about the sufferin' niggers" (with ineffable contempt); "and what's more, he's here in Leavenworth now." "What's his name?" exclaimed several, eagerly. "Just what I don't know," was the sorrowful reply, "and I shouldn't know him if I saw him, but he's here, boys, and in a day or two there'll be some gentlemen here that know him." (N. B. At my last speech in Lawrence, I was warned that three Missouri spies were present.) "It's well we've got him here, to take care of him," said one. "Won't our boys enjoy running him out of town?" added another, affectionately; while I listened with pleased attention, thinking that I might, perhaps, afford useful information. But the "gentlemen" have not yet appeared, or else are in search of higher game.

The causes of the quiet which reigns to-day are apparently the presence of a few United States troops, and the absence of provocation from the non-voting party. That the latter cause would not be alone sufficient is manifest from the fact that the last riots were produced merely by a similar refusal to vote.

I observe here a large class of young men who are evidently not Missourians, but from other Southern States—a slender, puny race, with good manners and bloated faces. One of them, a Virginian, bearing the appropriate name of Stringfellow, has apparently felt called upon, in a drunken fit, to vindicate the character of the peculiar institution, and has, therefore, just summoned before him his slave, a neat-looking boy of sixteen. "B-B-Bill," says the representative of chivalry, "do you know me?" "Yes, mas'r," returns Bill, respectfully. "Have you ever been in chains, Bill?" stammers out the specimen of the superior race, with the impressive seriousness of inebriation. "Never, sir." "Ever expect to be in chains, Bill?" "Never, sir." "G-g-good boy, Bill, take something to drink, Bill?" Which offer Bill declines, rather to my surprise, and is dismissed with a slight contempt as being after all a poor creature, chains or no chains.

A party of these gentry leave with me, to-night, in the boat for St. Louis, and I shall make further acquaintance with them.

VII.—DOWN THE RIVER.

STEAMBOAT CATARACT, **Missouri River, Oct. 9, 1856.**

We have left Kanzas behind, and my last association with it is of three pistol-shots which killed, in a drunken row, one of the self same company of Virginia and South Carolina youths who were swaggering in our cabin when I went to bed. I did not, however, know of the catastrophe till the next morning. I am told that the remains of the poor young man were taken into a gambling-room and laid upon a table, after which the gambling went on as before.

We are gliding down the rapid Missouri, now shouldering over a sandbank, now shuddering over a snag; while the endless woods look dewy and beautiful in early morning or moonlight, and very hot at noon. The yellow dust drifts over the bare islands which the shrinking water has left, and buzzards and wild geese shriek and soar away through its midst.

The tumultuous steamboat dinner is despatched with that rushing rapidity which is usual on such occasions, where people, having nothing to do afterward, are in a proportionate hurry to do it. As I look up and down the long table, and at the row of guests who sit with their glasses of Missouri water like tumblers of lemonade before them, it is sad to think that among those sixty men there are not half a dozen who belong to the same nation with myself. For what constitutes a common nationality except common ideas, principles, habits, and purposes? and in all these I find myself more alone than I should be among English, French, or Russians.

The majority are young men from various Southern States—Virginia, Kentucky, the Carolinas, and Georgia—who have been to Kanzas expressly to fight men from Maine, Massachusetts, Vermont, New York, Michigan, Illinois, and so on. And yet people speak of civil war as only a thing that may be, when there is scarcely a State in the Union which has not been already involved in civil war, through its representatives here. The simple fact is, that slaveholders and freemen are always two nations. I could speak my whole thoughts more safely in Berlin or St. Petersburg than here, except indeed that these enemies are more susceptible of fear.

By their own account, indeed, they show a poor record in this respect. Yesterday they were declared by their lieutenant, who alone wears a military coat, to be a pack of cowards; and he further asserted that in the point of danger they had been accustomed to take a vote whether to fight or run, and always ran!

Most of them are quite young and slender, with a dull, profligate look, while a few have open, simple faces, that seem strangely out of place. They have an easy, natural politeness, and swear, chew, and play cards enormously.

They are not in the least hypocrites or doughfaces; too uninstructed for that. One of them said, naively, in my hearing, with a sort of tender regret, "Don't you remember when we went up the river, we were all of us drunk all the time?" "So we were," replied another, himself not far from that condition, "and so we should be now, only we've got no money."

They proclaim openly that they went to Kanzas to fight and vote for Slavery. All finally voted at Leavenworth; and, having done that, are going home. But they complain bitterly of Atchison and others, who induced them to go; they say they were promised support for a year and fifty dollars in money, and yet they have had to support themselves almost entirely; and now very few have more than enough to take them to St. Louis, and some were unable to leave Leavenworth for want of even that. "Let me once get home," said the same youth who made the above confession, "and I'll stay at home, sure. It's cost me the price of one good nigger, just for board and liquor, since I left home."

"Woe unto them, for they have cast lots for my people and sold a girl for wine, that I may drink." Let me confess that this apt bit of Scripture I obtain not from memory but from "Dred," of which I bought an early copy at Lawrence. Several of the passengers have borrowed and examined it, with various comments, but no threatening ones. I could easily fill the margin of the book with sketches of illustrative faces, especially those of Ben Dakin, Jim Stokes, and the unfortunate Cripps. The romance reads well in the midst of the reality, though to be sure we have no actual slaves on board, except one young Topsy in a yellow apron, who stands as patiently as her nature permits, behind the chair of a stout lady, in the consecrated upper end of the long cabin. (I never saw the aesthetic inequality of the sexes so fully recognised as in a Missouri River steamboat.)

OCTOBER 11.—Yesterday we spent on a sand-bank, till at nightfall the steamer F. X. Aubry came along and pulled us off. We proceeded in company till at another difficult place the two boat-loads were disembarked, and we all walked half a mile along the shore. Then came out a startling story; how H. Miles Moore, Esq., Secretary of the Kanzas State Committee, had taken passage on board the other boat—after being released from a malicious arrest at Kanzas City; how the South Carolina and Virginia rowdies on the boat, finding him alone and unarmed, had threatened to hang him, and were proceeding to actual violence, when Governor Cobb, of Alabama, and the captain interfered and put him, for protection, in a state-room in the ladies' cabin; and how all thought he actually owed his life to them. Seeking him out, I found that it was all true; although the "honor" of Governor Cobb and some of the rowdies themselves was now pledged for his safety. It appeared to me, however, that a transfer to our boat and the loan of a revolver would be a better security; and that night he availed himself of it, there being fortunately a vacant berth in my state-room. The men on our boat were quite as far gone with whiskey as those on the other, and made common cause with them; but these were fewer in number, and we had three or four very reliable New England men, who kept a good lookout. And caution was needed, for the excitement rose again as we lay at Jefferson City over night, and inquiry began to be made as to the whereabouts of Moore. But Governor Cobb got up a visit to Governor Price, on the part of the passengers; and then there was a dance in the other boat; and when, about 10 ¹/₂ o'clock, the ringleaders began to whisper mischief again, part of their men were asleep and part in a worse condition, and the noble design fell through and we were undisturbed. I was glad to have him there, for I could not bear that he should owe his safety to the protection of a slaveholder.

We reached St. Louis this afternoon, four days and a half from Leavenworth, a trip which usually takes less than three. Kanzas and its perils lie behind, and there is no excitement but elections. Well, one does feel a little homesick for Kanzas, I can assure you, and at some future day The Tribune may hear again from its correspondent.

I did not, however, go out as a settler, but simply to see the country for myself. Yet if I did not live in Massachusetts, I would live in Kanzas.

VIII. THE FUTURE.

WORCESTER, MASS., October 20, 1856.

I find that my letters from Kanzas seem incomplete without a final appendix, in regard to the immediate future of that region. Perhaps the observation of a visitor to the Territory may have seen some things in a different light from that of its residents, or from that of those who have never been there.

Moreover, I have observed for many years that the more thorough an Abolitionist any man is, the more correct are his prophecies as to American affairs; and in this respect, at least, the present writer is pretty well qualified. I will therefore give the reasons which lead me to think, contrary to the opinions of many at the East, that the present comparative quiet of Kanzas is only the prelude to a severer struggle than any she has yet seen; that this struggle will occur soon after the Presidential election; and that it will be almost equally certain to occur, whether Fremont or Buchanan be elected.

The foundation for these opinions can be made very intelligible.

1. The real question at issue is, not the invasions of Missourians, nor the blockading of the river, but the enforcing of the bogus laws. The laws still exist, the Courts are still controlled by Missouri, and this is the real root of the difficulty, over which neither Governor Geary nor any one else (except Congress) has any legitimate control. The essential trouble, therefore, must either remain unsettled till Congress meets again, or be settled by force.

2. There is not the slightest increase of harmony between the parties, but the contrary. Both sides expect to see the contest renewed. I did not hear of a single man, on either side, except Governor Geary and his satellites, who thought otherwise.

3. Both sides are making actual preparations for a renewal. The settlers are collecting arms, ammunition, and fresh men. The Missourians are doing the same. True, men from both sides are leaving the country; but they are going, either with the design to return soon after the election, or else from personal dissatisfaction—not because they expect permanent peace.

4. Neither party *desires* peace, under the present auspices. The Missourians do not desire it, until they see that it involves the speedy introduction of Slavery. And the settlers do not desire it, when it means submission to the laws which a foreign State imposed upon them, and the daily arrest of their own men while Pro-Slavery men go free.

5. War always educates men to itself, disciplines them, teaches them to bear its fatigue, anxiety, and danger, and actually to enjoy them. I saw abundant instances of this on the Free State side; and I believe it to be so with the Missourians. Everybody testified that the army of two thousand eight hundred, which last besieged Lawrence, was better armed and better drilled than any previous invading force; and all agreed that at the battle of Hickory Point the Missourians showed more courage than ever before.

6. The whole tendency of Governor Geary's policy is to exasperate both sides, and, indeed, actually to strengthen both. Take a single instance: What can be more preposterous than his plan of organizing the two parties, "man for man," (as he expressed it to me,) into military companies? Imagine an Irish mob, and the Governor stopping them to say, "Hold on my hearties! lay down your shillelahs, while I give you Sharp's rifles, teach you the art of war, and pick out your bravest men to lead you properly!" Yet

this is precisely what Geary has done. He has organized two companies of Free State men, and two of Pro-Slavery men; he arms them, pays them, and officers them with the very leaders who have been foremost in the fray. At Lawrence, Captain Walker, who led the attack on Titus's fort, now heads one company under the Governor's system, while Titus heads another. Lieutenant Harvey, of the new Lawrence company, is the Colonel Harvey of Hickory Point notoriety. His men lie in prison, while he is put in office: but there is no change in him, only in the Governor. And in Topeka, with the other Free State company, the same folly is played over. The Governor may fancy this a peace measure, if he will; I call it a war measure, and confidently expect to see the conflict recommence *among his own troops.*

7. The reason why the strife is postponed, by tacit agreement, is easily told. The Missourians are waiting, in stronger and stronger hopes that Geary will do their work. The Free State men submit to his aggressions, *only* because the election is coming. That, and that only, gives them patience; precisely as the hope of flight to Canada keeps slaves from insurrection. They cling to the hope, not of escaping the contest, but of placing it on a more favorable footing. Take away the dream of Fremont, and no power could make these injured men endure a week longer the combined oppression of the Administration and of Missouri. Besides, every letter that comes to them from the East, exhorts them to "endure till November, and all will be well." Is it strange, then, if they seem almost too submissive, with such a prospect?

8. The trial of the Lecompton prisoners will furnish fuel to the flames, and perhaps the final explosion. Most of them will, no doubt, be acquitted. But the Pro-Slavery men will not submit to the liberation of all, nor the Anti-Slavery men to the execution of any.

9. Look out, therefore, for trouble in Kanzas, in November. Elect Fremont, and there will be a last desperate effort of Missouri to obtain possession of Kanzas. In this they will rely on the aid of the United States Courts and troops, and will have it, whatever Gov. Geary says. The policy of the Administration will be unchanged. It is absurd to suppose that Pierce, Cushing, and Douglass will not still bid for Southern favor, after the election of Fremont. *They will have nothing else left to do.* They will look

out for a Pro-Slavery reaction four years afterward, (and it will come then, if not sooner,) and steer for that wave. Still, the Kanzas men will have a great advantage, for the United States troops will not in that case act against them *with a will*, and they have nothing else to fear.

In case of Buchanan's election, the whole power of Missouri, backed by the whole power of the Administration, will be directed upon Kanzas. The two forces will be identified. They will be brought to bear as one; and, thank God, *resisted as one*. The defenders of Freedom will fight, at last, as they never yet have fought. Heretofore, they have submitted to injuries from the weakest United States official, which they would never have borne from whole armies of Missourians. They will not make this nice distinction much longer. Oppression is oppression, wherever it comes from, they will say. "If that is treason, make the most of it."

We must have a new dictionary, and the definition of this much abused word must be: "Treason, the rope by which the real traitors seek to hang those who resist them."

Such treason as this is fast ripening in Kanzas. Call it revolution if you please.

If the United States Government and Border-Ruffianism are to mean the same thing, the sooner the people of Kanzas have revolution the better. So they will say, and who shall gainsay it? They have borne to the utmost. Another ounce of weight, and they will bear it no longer; and a less thing than the dispersion of their Legislature, or the destruction of their hotel, will be the signal.

Before I went to Kanzas I feared that her children would gradually scatter and flee, rather than meet a final, *desperate* struggle. I stand corrected. They will stay and meet it. They will meet it, if need be, unaided.

Will they be unaided? Ask Governor Grimes and the thousands of freemen of Iowa. Ask every man who has a heart left in his bosom.

Kanzas may be crushed, but not without a final struggle more fearful than that of Hungary; a struggle which will convulse a continent before it is ended, and separate forever those two nations of North and South, which neither Union nor Constitution has yet welded into one.

5

ASSORTED LOTS OF
YOUNG NEGROES

While in St. Louis in 1856, Mr. Higginson attended the slave market, and wrote the following description of the scene under the title "Assorted Lots of Young Negroes." This was printed in the "Tribune" at the time and widely copied, both in America and in England.

I have before been in other slave States, but never in Missouri. The first thing that struck me on arriving in this city was the apparent absence of the Negro race. In a crowd of a thousand persons on the levee this morning, assembled to witness the burning of six steamboats, I could not count ten black faces. I was told, in explanation, that the colored people were all "uptown," not in the business part of the city.

So, too, I searched the newspapers for slave advertisements, though I knew this city not to be a great mart for those commodities like Richmond; but in vain. At last, in a corner of the "Republican," I discovered the following:

Negroes Wanted.—I wish to purchase a large lot of Negroes, expressly for the Louisiana and Mississippi market, for which I will pay the highest cash prices. All those who have Negroes for sale would do well to give me a call. I can always be seen at the City Hotel, or at Mr. Thompson's Negro-yard, No. 67, Locust St., St. Louis, Mo.

JOHN MATTINGLY

Negroes wanted and for sale.—Wanted and for sale Negroes of all kinds, at my office, No. 67, Locust St., between 2d and 3d Sts., St. Louis, Mo. Having a good and safe yard to board and keep Negroes, I will buy and sell on commission as low as any other house in this city. Please to give me a call.

CORBIN THOMPSON

I took an early opportunity to call on Mr. Corbin Thompson. I found him in the doorway of a little wooden office, like a livery-stable office in one of our cities; he being a large, lounging, good-natured looking man, not unlike a reputable stable-keeper in appearance and manner. Inside his stable, alas! I saw his dusky "stock," and he readily acceded to my desire to take a nearer look at them.

Behind the little office there was a little dark room, behind that a little kitchen, opening into a dirty little yard. This yard was surrounded by high brick walls, varied by other walls made of old iron plates, reaching twenty feet high. These various places were all swarming with Negroes, dirty and clean, from six years old to forty—perhaps two dozen in all, the majority being children under fourteen.

"Fat and sleek as Harry Clay's," said my conductor, patting one on the head patriarchally.

Most of them had small paper fans, which they used violently. This little article of comfort looked very odd, amid such squalid raggedness as most of them showed. One was cooking, two or three washing, and two playing euchre with a filthy pack of cards. The sun shone down intensely hot (it was noon) in the little brick yard, and they sat, lounged, or lay about, only the children seeming lively.

I talked a little with them, and they answered, some quietly, some with that mixture of obsequiousness and impudence so common among slaves. Mr. Thompson answered all questions very readily. The "Negroes" or "Niggers," he said (seldom employing the Virginia phrases "servants" or "people"), came mostly from Missouri or Virginia, and were with him but a little while. "Buy when I can and sell when I can, that's my way; and never ask no questions, only in the way of trade. At this season, get a good many from travellers."

On inquiry, he explained this mystery by adding that it was not uncommon for families visiting Northern watering-places to bring with them a likely boy or girl, and sell them to pay the expenses of the jaunt! This is a feature of the patriarchal institution which I think has escaped Mrs. Stowe. Hereafter I shall never see a Southern heiress at Newport without fancying I read on her ball-dress the names of the "likely boy or girl" who was sold for it. "As for yonder Sambo and Dinah" (I meditated), "no doubt, young Bulford Dashaway, Esq., is at this moment driving them out to Saratoga Lake, as a pair of blood-horses. O Miss Caroline Pettitoes, of Fifth Avenue, how odd it would be if, as you sit superb by his side, those four-legged cattle suddenly resumed the squalid two-legged condition in which I now behold them, in Thompson's Negro-yard, No. 67, Locust Street."

I strolled back into the front office and sat down to see if anything turned up. The thing that turned up was a rather handsome, suburban-looking two-horse carriage, out of which stepped lazily a small, spare, gentlemanly man, evidently a favored patron of my host. After a moment's private talk Thompson went out, while the gentleman said abruptly to me, "Well, it is all bad enough, housekeeping, marketing, and all, but I'm—if servants ain't the worst of all." We then talked a little, and I found him the pleasantest type of a Southerner—courteous, kind, simple, a little imperious—finally, a man of property, member of the city Government, and living a little out of town.

Thompson came in and shook his head. "Can't let Negroes to anybody, Mr.——. Glad to sell, anyhow."

"Got a good article of a small girl?" said the gentleman suddenly.

"Martha!" shouted the slave-dealer, and presently three good articles, aged eleven, nine, and seven, came trotting in. I had not seen them before. Nice little pink frocks, not very dirty—barefooted, of course, but apparently well taken care of, and evidently sisters. With some manœuvring, they were arranged in a line before my new acquaintance, the purchaser.

He fixed his eyes on Sue, a black marble statue, aged seven. Nothing could have been kinder than Mr.——'s manner in addressing the little thing. "Will you like to come and live with me, and have some little girls to play with?"

(It is a little patriarchal, I said. That kind voice would win any child.)

I looked to see the merry African smile on the child's face. But no smile came. There was a moment's pause.

"Speak up, child," said the merchant roughly. But she did n't speak up, nor look up, either. Down went the black marble face, drooping down, down, till the chin rested on the breast of the little pink frock. Down, down came one big tear, and then another over the black marble cheeks; and then the poor little wretch turned away to the wall, and burst into as hearty an agony of tears as your little idol Susy, or yours (my good New-England mother), might give way to, at such an offer from the very kindest man who ever chewed tobacco in the streets of Missouri!

Human nature is a rather unconquerable thing, after all, is n't it?

My kind purchaser looked annoyed, and turned away. The slave-trader gave an ominous look to the poor child, such as I had not seen on his face before. "Beg pardon, sir" (said he gruffly); "they only came from Virginia yesterday, and have n't learnt how to treat gentlemen yet" (with an emphasis).

Poor little Sue!

The purchaser next turned to Martha, the elder sister, a bright Topsy-looking thing.

"What's that on her cheek," he asked, pointing to a sort of scar or streak of paleness. Martha grinned.

"Somebody's whacked her chops, most likely," said the slave-trader, coolly (in whose face I saw nothing good-natured after that). Nothing more was said about it.

The gentleman drew the child to him, felt the muscles of her arm, and questioned her a little. Her price was 700 dollars, and little Sue's 450 dollars.

"Well, Martha," said he at last, "would n't you like to go with me and have a pleasant home?"

Strange to say, the African smile left Martha's merry face, too. "Please, sir," said she, "I wish I could stay with my mother."

"Confound the girls," said the good-natured purchaser, turning to me in despair; "they must be sold to somebody, you know. Of course, I can't buy the whole of them, and the mother, too." Of course not; and there was the whole story in a nutshell.

"Nonsense, gals," said Thompson; "your mother'll be up here, maybe, some day." (Pleasant prospect, in the lottery of life, for three "articles" under twelve years.)

On inquiry it appeared that the mother was in Virginia, and might or might not be sent to St. Louis for sale. The intention was, however, to sell the children in a day or two, together or separately, or else to send them south with Mr. Mattingly.

To avert this, I hoped earnestly that my good-natured friend would buy one or more of the poor things. "For," said he to me, "I mean to bring her up well. She'll be a pet for the children—black or white it will make no difference—and while I live I shan't sell her—that is while it is possible to help it." (A formidable reservation, considering the condition of most Southern estates.)

The little pink frocks were ordered to stand off, and a bargain was finally struck for Martha, quite to Mr. Thompson's chagrin, who evidently hoped to sell Sue, and would, no doubt, have done so, but for her ignorance "how to treat gentlemen."

"Girl is sound, I suppose?" carelessly inquired the purchaser.

"Wind and limb," responded the trader. "But strip her naked and examine every inch of her, if you wish," he quickly added; "I never have any disguises with my customers."

So ended the bargain, and I presently took my leave. I had one last glance at little Sue. It is not long since I set foot on the floating wreck of an unknown vessel at sea, and then left it drifting away in the darkness alone. But it was sadder to me to think of that little wreck of babyhood drifting off alone into the ocean of Southern crime and despair.

St. Louis must unquestionably be a very religious place, however, for in returning to my hotel I passed a church with inscriptions in four different languages. There was Jehovah in Hebrew, "Deo Uno et Trino," "In honorem S. Ludovici." Finally in English and French, "My house shall be called the house of prayer," with the rest of the sentence, in both cases, omitted. Singular accident, is n't it?

I forgot to mention that I asked Mr. Thompson, out of the dozen children in his "yard," how many had their parents or mothers with them. "Not one," he answered, as if rather surprised at the question; "I take 'em as they come, in lots. Hardly ever have a family."

"I suppose you would rather keep a family together?" I put in, suggestively.

"Yes," he answered carelessly. "Can't think much about that, though. Have to shut up shop pretty quick, if I did. Have to take 'em as they come."

This was evident enough, and I only insert it in the faint hope of enlightening the minds of those verdant innocents who still believe that the separation of families is a rare occurrence, when every New Orleans newspaper contains a dozen advertisements of "Assorted lots of young Negroes."

6

THE NEW REVOLUTION: WHAT COMMITMENT REQUIRES

I supposed, until within a few moments, that I was to follow Mr. Garrison in speaking. It is the next most honorable thing to that, to come at his word of command. There is an old Greek proverb which says, It is an honor to be a patriot; it is an honor even to come when a patriot call. A patriot has called me, and I have come. It is not without meaning or consideration that I select that name for our great leader. It is not merely because, in the words of the resolutions, this Society has but one standard of patriotism—the slave. But I have high authority for the epithet which I choose; for it was the leader of the Republican party in this nation, its great manager, its most skillful wire-puller, who, in the best speech he ever made—it is Henry Wilson of whom I am speaking—at *The Liberator* festival, six years ago, after boasting of having read *The Liberator* for twelve years, and attributing to its teachings the greater part of his own love of freedom, ended by choosing out of our friend's virtues to extol, not his truthfulness, not his courage, not his zeal, but the "patriotism" of the disunionist, Mr. Garrison. I have, therefore, high political authority for what I say.

I stand here upon this platform with pleasure, for two reasons. The first is this: We hear it said every day, that the Abolitionists of the American Anti-Slavery Society are stern, narrow, sectarian, illiberal, intolerant of any man or of any opinion which does not fully coincide with them or theirs. I stand here a living witness of the falsehood of the charge. From the moment when first, in an obscure country parish of New England, I ventured to peep and mutter upon the subject of American Slavery, the support, the unfailing friendship, of the Abolitionists around me has been mine. Never agreeing with them wholly, never asked to agree with them wholly, never accepting that special dogma of the interpretation of the Constitution, which is supposed to be the narrow standard by which they try all virtues, I have always found from them a sympathy more than my deserts, a friendliness which I never earned. I could not in words, perhaps, refute the charge of illiberality against them; but it is refuted by my standing here.

I have another reason for being here. I look in vain throughout the nation for another place, to find men and women who see slavery as it is, and in its full strength. I have co-operated with political abolitionists all my life; I may still co-operate with them, if they will be kind enough to pass by my door. I have co-operated all my life with antislavery clergymen also. But I have looked in vain for a body of men who understand slavery in its depth, except the Abolitionists of this Anti-Slavery Society. With all others, it is a superficial thing. Every man who has been in Republican meetings knows it, if he himself knows slavery as it is. Every man who has been in the habit of talking anti-slavery with those who talk it loudly and habitually in the streets and the caucuses, knows the shallowness of their perception of this giant evil. A young New Yorker whom I met last year, in a foreign country, told me he was an Abolitionist. 'I am from America; I am from New York; of course I am an Abolitionist,' said he; 'but then I am not an ultra Abolitionist, like Seward and Greeley.' (Laughter.) Well, we have come here among a class of men also not ultra Abolitionists, *like* Seward and Greeley; of quite a different stamp; but Seward and Greeley are ultra-Abolitionists in their manner, in their earnestness, in their fidelity—ultra-abolitionists compared with the mass of the Republican Party. The mass of the Republican party have only begun to open their eyes to the grasp that slavery has taken upon the nation. The great number of Republican speakers see slavery, after all, as a trivial evil compared with its reality. Of course they see, for he must be blind who does not see, that it is the first political question before the nation, simply because there is no other. It needs no insight to see that slavery is more important than the bank or the tariff, because the tariff is settled, and so is the bank. They are no questions at all. They paint slavery, therefore, as the first question before the nation; they paint the Slave Power as something strong indeed, but not colossal; powerful indeed, but not frightful. They think it is a demon, but that it is a kind of demon that goes out, after all, very easily by prayer and fasting,—the prayer of three thousand Yankee clergymen, and the fasting from the loaves and fishes, of the Republican party, for four years more. (Laughter.)

They do not see it, they never have seen it, as it is. This very morning, I read in an able Republican journal, the statement that, after all, however it may have seemed in times past, the Slave Power is 'a weak thing' when you come to look it in the face. 'A weak thing,' Mr. Chairman? If the power that has governed this nation since its formation, that has for half a century elected every President, dictated every Cabinet, controlled every Congress, the power that has demoralized the religion of the nation, and emasculated its literature, the power that outwitted Clay and stultified Webster, the power that has ruled as easily its Northern creditors as its Northern debtors, the power that at this moment stands with all the patronage of the greatest nation of the world in its clutches, and with the firmest financial basis in the world—so George Peabody says—beneath its feet—if this power be weak, where on the wide earth will you look for any thing strong? Weakness? Why, slavery is king; king *de facto.* It is as strong now, as it was before the thirteen hundred thousand freemen rallied to the support of John C. Fremont. It is as strong now as it was, when Fremont was only known as the explorer of the Rocky Mountains, and the millionaire of California. It is absolute in its strength before us to-day. It knows the folly of those who think it weak, and it laughs at them. What does it fear? It has forgotten God, and there are only two things in the universe that it does fear, and those are the devil and William Lloyd Garrison. Out in Kansas, my brilliant friend, Gen. Jas. H. Lane, was making one of his characteristic speeches to the people, and he wanted words to describe the position of the two leaders of Kansas; for Kansas, like Rome of old, has two consuls, one for war, and one for peace. He characterized the attitude of the Border Ruffians towards Charles Robinson and himself by saying, 'The Missourians hate Jim Lane as they hate the devil; Charles Robinson they hate'—and he paused to think of something that the Missourians hated worse than the devil, and said,—'Charles Robinson they hate as they hate virtue;' and every body agreed that it was the best description of the men ever given. The Missourians of Washington, the Missourians of the South, have the same twin hostility, and it is equally well deserved. They know whom they have to fear.

Mr. Chairman, I began by saying that I never had accepted the opinion which prevails on this platform of the character of the Constitution. A few words only upon that. I never have held, and I hope I never shall hold, that the Constitution, or any thing else, is to be interpreted in a proslavery manner, if you can possibly find any other sense in it. I never have held, and I trust I never shall hold, that it is to be interpreted by what its framers meant to put in it, but only, like all other legal instruments, by what they succeeded in getting in. Some regard it as strongly proslavery, and others as strongly anti-slavery, and others as Talleyrand regarded the French Constitution, when he said it meant nothing, and never would mean anything, because he had made it himself on purpose. (Laughter.) I think that hits the nail upon the head. But there is one fixed rule in the interpretation of documents, where liberty is concerned, and that is, to put in liberty wherever there is a loophole to cram it in by. The authority best adapted to our purpose, so far as I know, is the very memorable decision rendered in the case where Shylock was the plaintiff, Portia the judge, and William Shakespeare the reporter of the court. If there be in that Constitution any space left, if there be an ounce of flesh or a drop of blood, if there be the drachm of a scruple, or a scruple itself, where you can force an anti-slavery meaning into it, you have a right to put that meaning in, and every honest man will justify you in the effort. The mightiest intellect, or the profoundest moral sense, for such a purpose as that, may narrow itself down to microscopic investigation. It may pass through as delicate a fissure as that which held Ariel in the cloven pine, if by so doing it can transform one slave into a freeman.

It is only a question of will, whether it shall be done or not. No instrument, framed as the Constitution was, is without the opportunities which that gives. I do not care where the loophole is found; there may be one in the word 'law;' there may be another in the word 'due.' I do not care how small it is; give us a Supreme Court that is favorable to liberty, and the Constitution is an anti-slavery document tomorrow. (Applause.)

But the difficulty lies elsewhere, not in the law, but in the fact. It is not a question of the meaning of words, as yet. I do not know of any question that this nation can discuss, so utterly unimportant for all practical purposes as the question of the meaning of the Constitution of the United States. It is a dead letter. It is a piece of parchment riddled through and through. Where is the man who obeys it? Where is the Southerner who obeys it? Where is the Northern Republican who means to obey it, if the fugitive slave takes refuge in his house? Nobody means to obey it. I see no difference of practical importance between Wendell Phillips and Gerritt Smith. One thinks the Constitution is pro-slavery; the other thinks the *existing interpretation* of the Constitution is pro-slavery. Each of them admits that it will cost a revolution to get either the Constitution or its interpretation set aside. Both of them believe in carrying that revolution to the point of the bayonet, if necessary. Where is the difference as a question of fact? Nothing. All the intellect, all the genius, all the learning ever expended upon the point of Constitutional interpretation, are not worth, in the practical solution of the slavery question, a millionth part so much as the poorest shot that ever a fugitive slave fired at his master—not worth the thrust of the dagger that made Margaret Garner's child a free being in Heaven, instead of a slave upon earth. The one is a word; the other is a fact. The one is a theory; the other is one of those stern realities that revolutionize nations, and upon which Constitutions only wait.

The question of slavery is a stern and practical one. Give us the power, and we can make a new Constitution, or we can re-interpret the old one. How is that power to be obtained? By politics? Never. By revolution, and that alone. There is the issue, Mr. Chairman. That is what makes men Disunionists, Constitution or no Constitution. It is a question of fact. I cannot bear to waste time in debating the Constitution, because I see that while the Constitution is being talked about, there is a crack in the nation that is growing wider, and wider, and wider apart. When I look at this fact, I do not care for the theory. We talk about a Constitution and a nation; but we are not a nation; we are two nations, whom this frail paper bond has vainly tried to weld together into one. We are diverging more and more every day. Every thing separates us. Birth, tradition, laws, education, social habits, institutions—every thing separates us, nothing brings us nearer together. The reason why Free-State men and Slave-State men hate each other in Kansas, is because all the institutions of their respective nations have for years been training them to hate each other. When they come face to face, it is only the old hostility breaking out again. It is not only the difference in birth, although still the Puritan stock remains upon the one side, and the Cavalier stock upon the other. It is not merely that in Kansas you see on the one side the traces of the Puritan, softened and improved, and upon the other the traces of the Cavaliers, degraded and deteriorated; it is not that even now in Kansas, as during the English civil wars, you may know one side from the other, because the one side wears long hair, and the other does not; because when you meet a party there with long hair, you may suspect they are Missourians, and when you meet a party with short hair, you may know that they are Round-heads, Puritans, Yankees; it is not that alone, strange though that coincidence is, after the lapse of centuries; but it is because something stronger than parties is separating them.

Slaveholders and Freemen are always two nations. There is no power or force that can unite them. There are no two nations in Europe so absolutely antagonistic as the Free-State and the Slave-State men of this Union. All that any town in Massachusetts or New York asserts by its institutions,—that every settlement in South Carolina, every plantation in Virginia denies. How are you to unite these opposing forces? By a Union and a Constitution? Read Olmstead's admirable book on Texas, and you will find that the young New Yorker, travelling among the American settlements of Texas, felt himself a stranger; but, coming into a German settlement, he felt himself among kindred and friends. Germany, far off, dreamy, visionary, poetical Germany, was nearer in national sympathy to the young New Yorker, than the Texans and the Mississippians, who called themselves his brothers. I knew a young man born in South Carolina and educated in Massachusetts. He travelled abroad, and visited half the nations of Europe. When he came back, he entered, for the first time in eight years, his own birth-place, Charleston, S. C.; and he told me that he had not, at Vienna, or Rome, or Paris, the sense of strangeness that he had there. He was a foreigner in his birthplace, because his birth-place was South Carolina, and Massachusetts trained him. Tell me, if you can, in the history of the world, of a nation with such antagonisms as that within its bosom, which has permanently held together.

It is not a question of this or that measure. It is a question of permanent, absolute, irreconcilable distinctions, growing with the growth of the people, showing themselves more and more every year, since every year slavery is more truly slavery, and freedom is more truly freedom. I ask nothing more than the evidence I see with my own eyes of this antagonism, to show me that politicians dream in vain of permanently keeping the Union together. But why should the Union be kept together? What are the objects, the arguments, the advantages? I see the weakness of this Union the moment any man undertakes to defend it, because I see the poverty of the arguments he uses. He asks, for instance, how are you going to dissolve the Union, not seeing that it is dissolving itself. Every time a blow is struck, in Kansas or in Washington, it splits further apart. We must separate, when we have learned to hate each other.

They ask whether you are not deserting the slave by dissolving the Union. The best anti-slavery lecturer I know of upon that point, is one Thomas H. Benton, of St. Louis. If he does not satisfy the people of the Northern States that it is best for them to dissolve the Union, I do not know who will. He came to Worcester the week after we had the Disunion Convention there: A great many people had shaken their heads at that Convention. The argument had been potent with some uninstructed or hasty persons, that if the Union were dissolved, it would be the desertion of the slave, and a baseness unworthy of us. Sir, Mr. Benton settled all that in about five minutes, before one of the largest audiences ever collected in Worcester; and he settled it by the very argument with which he undertook to produce quite a different result. He stood before the people of that city, and tried to startle them by the consequences that would flow from a separation between these States. Said he (his eyes opening wide, and his face growing longer and longer,) 'If you dissolve this Union, friends and fellow-citizens, twenty slaves will run away where one does now'; and a general chuckle of satisfaction ran through the audience. Thinking himself misunderstood, and wishing to deepen the impression, he said, 'If you dissolve the Union, you will bring Canada practically down to the line of Maryland and Virginia;' and when he looked for sorrow and mourning, the house shook with applause.

> 'She went to the undertaker's to buy him a coffin,
> And when she got back, the poor dog was laughing.'

Every body agreed that if we had driven the nail of Disunion, he had clinched it. How idle is it for us, standing here at the North—and I use now the argument familiar to the conservative press—to suppose that we can be better acquainted with the subject of slavery, than Thomas H. Benton.

All the arguments have the same weakness. The real opposition to disunion is a vague, an indeterminate opposition. People shrink from dissolving the Union, because they do not know what the result will be. They see the danger now; they shrink from incurring that which they do not understand. They are about on a level with the old stage-coach driver in England, who had his private opinion of the superiority of stages to rail cars; 'There are as many accidents, in proportion to the travel, upon the stages as upon the railroads,' it was said to him. 'Yes, said old Weller, 'but that is not the thing; don't you see the difference; if you are upset in a stage coach, and find yourself flying over a hedge somewhere, there you are; but if the train runs off the track, and smashes to atoms, *where are you?*' That is about as clear a view as most persons have, of the effect of dissolving the Union. It is a vague impression, a dim apprehension, and we would rather bear those ills we have, than 'fly to others that we know not of.'

Others, sheltering themselves behind the same uncertainty, and the same *laissez faire* doctrine, suppose that as the Union has stood a great while, it will stand a great while longer. No notice has been given, no trumpet sounded; and the Union which has borne a great many shocks, will bear a great many more. These men do not know that a revolution is always half finished, before the majority of the community have found out that it is begun. They do not know that it is not the conscious action of the people, but their unconscious action, that determines the course of events. It was after the battle of Bunker Hill that Congress met and deliberately voted that they "had not taken up arms with the intent and impious purpose of separating themselves from the mother country;" and then they went on and separated. That is the way we are doing. We pledge ourselves against Disunion, and still, after all, every earnest anti-slavery man, calling himself Republican, Union-saver, or what you please, keeps in the corner of his heart a little willingness, like Mr. Banks down in Maine, "in a certain contingency, to let the Union slide." He keeps a place for a disunion argument, just as our friends of *The Tribune* are willing that 'J. S. P.,' of Washington, should have his little column to preach a little of the leaven of disunion, although the editors have not approved it yet. In our more earnest moments, when a fugitive slave case is before us, or when Charles Sumner is struck down, or when a new tragedy takes place in Kansas, we are all disunionists. When sober reflection comes, many a man who thinks himself so, finds that he is not ready for that, quite yet. He finds that, after all, the danger is not so imminent as he supposed, and he says, like the man in the story—'Go along with your old ark: I guess it won't be much of a shower after all.' (Laughter.) It is like the ferryman out West, of whom I heard the other day. He had taken a great many across in his old canoe, and he wanted mightily to cross once more when he had a profitable job to do. 'You had better not go,' said they. 'Yes,' said he, 'I am going.' 'You had better not go; you will be drowned.' 'Never was drowned in my life,' said the man as he went into the boat; and he lost the chance to say that again. It is so with every revolution in the world. Just as some leader of the people has the words upon his lips, 'There is to be no revolution,' he turns round and finds himself in the midst of it.

We are in the midst of a revolution. The anti-slavery movement is not a reform; it is a revolution. It is a revolution when Garrison defies the United States Government in Boston, outside the Constitution; or when Gerrit Smith, in New York, defies it in his way. So long as the Jerrys are rescued, it is of no consequence whether they are rescued with law or without law; it is equally revolution.

> 'Treason, they say, ne'er prospers; what's the reason?
> Why, when it prospers, none dare call it treason.'

Let the radical anti-slavery men come to the epoch of success, and the Henry Wilsons will cease to talk about hanging Disunionists, and will come back to their old (opinion of the patriotism of the Garrisons).

In the meantime, there are two things especially to be done by Abolitionists, in the States where they live. It often happens, in the progress of institutions, Mr. Chairman, that the very thing which at one period is a bulwark for freedom, becomes at a later period, and upon further experience, a check and a hindrance to it. There are two institutions in our free States now, founded with the noblest purposes, sustained with the bravest energies, but both of them grown antagonistic to freedom, by the progress of things,—both destined, I trust, to be abolished.

The first of these institutions, once noble, now out-grown and objectionable, is the Underground Railroad, to Canada. God grant that we may see an end to that very soon! The Underground Railroad, as I have believed for years, and, believe more and more every day, is demoralizing the conscience of our people, accustoming them to think that all their duty to freedom consists, not in making their own soil free, but in pointing the way to some other. I want, and you want if there is any manhood or womanhood in you, to live upon free earth; but the soil which we tread is not free, if, when a man comes to your door and asks for your protection, in the dusk of the evening, all you can do for him is to say, There is a dollar, and that railroad leads to Canada. That is not freedom. It is not freedom, so long as there is any difference between Canada and Broadway to a single human being who has a right to tread God's earth. (Applause.) To establish freedom anywhere, begin by establishing it where you stand. If you cannot make free the soil upon which your own feet tread, it may be a necessary evil to recognize something better somewhere else; but it is a disgrace to you, so long as the fact remains. It is ignoble; it is dishonorable; it is worse than that, because it is demoralizing. The Underground Railroad makes cowards of us all. It makes us think, and hesitate, and look over our shoulders, and listen, and fear, and not care to tell the truth to the man who stands by our side. It may be a necessary evil, but an evil it was. I do not know how it is elsewhere, but I can say that in the city where I live, there has been from year to year, a deepening conviction, that it is degrading to send a man out of the city, merely because he came into it upon the Southern track. It is degrading, dishonorable, demoralizing.

There came some time ago, a black man of herculean proportions, who had earned his right to freedom by brave labors. That man had gone from city to city in the free States, seeking rest and finding none: because, though he was willing to stay and run the risk himself, the best advice he could get at any of these places was, to push a little further along. He came to Worcester at last. We looked at the man, and took the measure of him. Such sinews I never saw. That man could take a barrel of flour in his arms, lift it easily, and hold it out at arm's length. We looked at him, and we said to him, "Those arms are better arguments for staying, than your legs are for going, (laughter and applause,) so stay where you are." He stayed and in order that there might be no uncertainty as to the fact that he was there, some of us took pains to allude to it in the Boston papers, for the benefit of any United States official who might feel disposed to come and make a call upon him; but there is something in the air of Worcester a little prejudicial to the health of that class of officers, and none of them ever came. I thank God that other slaves have done the same thing since. He was not the first, nor is the latest one, I trust, the last. I hope that the time will come in Massachusetts, if nowhere else, when we can call every fugitive slave within her borders to meet in Convention under his own proper name, and hold deliberation in the light of day; yes, and to advertise the Convention in the proslavery issues of the widest circulation, in the New York papers, in the well-named *Journal of Commerce* and the ill-named *Journal of Civilization,* to advertise in them all; and, Mr. Chairman, in the name of the citizens of Worcester, I demand that that Convention shall be held in our City Hall. (Applause.)

So far, so good. There is something else to be abolished besides the underground Railroad, and that is Personal Liberty Bills, as we frame them now. I do not know a Personal Liberty Bill in any State in this Union, that is not as it stands, a refuge for cowards; because they all imply, every one of them, that if a man slips through the defences they offer him, he is a slave, and must be sent southward as such. Mr. Chairman, I do not want to see the fugitive slaves that come into Massachusetts protected only at the cost of perjury on the jury trial. I do not want to see any jury trial for fugitive slaves. Slavery and juries are two things irreconcilable. They have nothing in common. If a human being is to be declared a slave, I would rather have only one man's conscience darkened by the guilt of it, though it be dark as Loring's, than have twelve men in the community put into the dilemma either of perjuring themselves upon their oath to try the case according to the law and the evidence, or of sending the man into slavery. I do not want to see Personal Liberty Bills based upon any narrower ground than the absolute right of every man to freedom law or no law, slavery or no slavery, Constitution or no Constitution. (Applause.) There is growing up, I rejoice to say, in Massachusetts, in New York, in Wisconsin, a protest against these laws. The only true law is the law which makes the difference between the criminal and the slave, not in favor of the criminal, but in favor of the slave. What we want is a law, which makes escape from slavery not the proof of crime, but the crowning fact of virtue. We want a law in the spirit of the old Quaker who was sheltering a colored man under the Fugitive Slave Law, but not knowing who he was. His neighbors were frightened at last, and came and remonstrated with him. 'Why,' said they, 'that man has broken the law.' 'O,' said the Quaker, 'I think not; he seems a good man.' 'But,' said they, 'if you did but know it, he is actually a thief.' 'O no,' said the Quaker, 'I cannot believe that, he seems such a good man.' 'Why, yes he is,' said they, 'he is a fugitive slave; he has stolen himself from his master.' 'Well,' said the Quaker, 'he is a better man than I thought he was.' I want a law based on that principle. The key-note is struck, I rejoice to say, in the State in which we stand now. I must go back, Mr. Phillips must go back, and tell Massachusetts to look to her laurels. We have not even had proposed in the Massachusetts Legislature any point, so high and so honorable as the resolution proposed in New York:—

'Resolved, That this State will not allow slavery within her borders, in any form, under any pretense, for any time, however short.' (Great applause.)

There is a Personal Liberty Bill, indeed! Give a man such a State as that to live in, and the soil he treads upon, though part of a Republic, is as free as if it were ruled by a Queen. It is as free as Canada itself. God speed the time when the Littlejohns of New York shall be the great men of the State. Speaker Littlejohn, like his namesake in old English times, may be an outlaw temporarily. No matter; his arrow has cleft the wand, and with Gerrit Smith for his Robin Hood, and—shall I say it—Henry Ward Beecher for his Friar Tuck, his ultimate victory is sure. (Laughter and applause.)

7

WHY BACK JOHN BROWN?

It will doubtless seem to some readers a very natural transition to pass from this assertion to the later events which brought some of the above-named men into intimate relations with Captain John Brown. It has never been quite clear to me whether I saw him in Kansas or not; he was then in hiding, and I remember to have been taken somewhat covertly to a house in Lawrence, for an interview with a fugitive slave who was being sheltered by a white man; and though this man's name, which I have forgotten, was certainly not Brown, it may have been one of Brown's aliases. My first conscious acquaintance with that leader was nearly a year and a half later, when I received from him this communication, implying, as will be seen, that we had met before:

ROCHESTER, N. Y.   *2d Feb'y*, 1858.
MY DEAR SIR,—I am here *concealing my whereabouts* for good reasons (as I think) not however from any anxiety about my personal safety. I have been told that you are both a true *man:* and a true *abolitionist;* "and I partly believe," the whole story. Last fall I undertook to raise from $500 to $1000, for *secret service,* and succeeded in getting $500. I now want to get for the *perfecting* of *by far* the most *important* undertaking of my whole life; from $500 to $800 within the next sixty days. I have written Rev. Theodore Parker, George L. Stearns and F. B. Sanborn Esqrs. on the subject; but do not know as either Mr. Stearns or Mr. Sanborn are abolitionists. I suppose they are. Can you be induced to opperate at Worcester and elsewhere during that time to raise from *anti*-slavery *men* and *women* (or any other parties) some part of that amount? I wish to keep it entirely still about where I am; and will be *greatly obliged* if you will consider this

communication *strictly confidential:* unless it may be with such as you are *sure* will *feel and act and keep very still.* Please be so kind as to write N. Hawkins on the subject, Care of Wm. I. Watkins, Esqr. Rochester, N. Y. Should be most happy to meet you again; and talk matters more freely. Hope this is my last effort in the begging line.

VERY RESPECTFULLY YOUR FRIEND,

JOHN BROWN.

This name, "N. Hawkins," was Brown's favorite alias. The phrase "partly believe" was a bit of newspaper slang of that period, but came originally from Paul's First Epistle to the Corinthians (xi. 18) whence Brown may well have taken it. I wrote in return, wishing for farther information, and asking if the "underground railroad" business was what he had in view. In a few days came this reply:

ROCHESTER, N. Y.   *12th Feb'y,* 1858.

MY DEAR SIR,—I have just read your kind letter of the 8th inst., and will now say that Rail Road business on a *somewhat extended* scale is the *identical* object for which I am trying to get means. I have been connected with that business as *commonly conducted* from my boyhood and *never* let an opportunity slip. I have been opperating to some purpose *the past season;* but I now have a measure on *foot* that I feel *sure* would awaken in you something more than a *common interest* if you could understand it. I have just written my friends G. L. Stearns and F. B. Sanborn asking them to meet me for consultation at Gerrit Smith's, Peterboro' [N. Y.]. I am very anxious to have *you come along; certain as I feel,* that you will never regret having been one of the council. I would most gladly pay your expenses had I the means to spare. *Will you come on?* Please write as before.

YOUR FRIEND

JOHN BROWN.

As I could not go to Peterboro', he made an appointment in Boston, and I met him in his room at the American House in March, 1858. I saw before me a man whose mere appearance and bearing refuted in advance some of the strange perversions which have found their way into many books, and which have often wholly missed the type to which he belonged. In his thin, worn, resolute face there were the signs of a fire which might wear him out, and practically did so, but nothing of pettiness or baseness; and his talk was calm, persuasive, and coherent. He was simply a high-minded, unselfish, belated Covenanter; a man whom Sir Walter Scott might have drawn, but whom such writers as Nicolay and

Hay, for instance, have utterly failed to delineate. To describe him in their words as "clean but coarse" is curiously wide of the mark; he had no more of coarseness than was to be found in Habakkuk Mucklewrath or in George Eliot's Adam Bede; he had, on the contrary, that religious elevation which is itself a kind of refinement,—the quality one may see expressed in many a venerable Quaker face at yearly meeting. Coarseness absolutely repelled him; he was so strict as to the demeanor of his men that his band was always kept small, while that of Lane was large; he had little humor, and none of the humorist's temptation towards questionable conversation. Again, to call him "ambitious to irritation," in the words of the same authors, is equally wide of the mark. I saw him afterwards deeply disappointed and thwarted, and this long before his final failure, but never could find in him a trace of mere ambition; he lived, as he finally died, absolutely absorbed in one idea; and it is as a pure enthusiast—fanatic, if you please—that he is to be judged. His belief was that an all-seeing God had created the Alleghany Mountains from all eternity as the predestined refuge for a body of fugitive slaves. He had traversed those mountains in his youth, as a surveyor, and knew points which could be held by a hundred men against a thousand; he showed me rough charts of some of those localities and plans of connected mountain fortresses which he had devised.

Of grand tactics and strategy Brown knew as little as Garibaldi; but he had studied guerrilla warfare for himself in books, as well as in Europe, and had for a preceptor Hugh Forbes, an Englishman who had been a Garibaldian soldier. Brown's plan was simply to penetrate Virginia with a few comrades, to keep utterly clear of all attempt to create slave insurrection, but to get together bands and families of fugitive slaves, and then be guided by events. If he could establish them permanently in those fastnesses, like the Maroons of Jamaica and Surinam, so much the better; if not, he would make a break from time to time, and take parties to Canada, by paths already familiar to him. All this he explained to me and others, plainly and calmly, and there was nothing in it that we considered either objectionable or impracticable; so that his friends in Boston—Theodore Parker, Howe, Stearns, Sanborn, and myself—were ready to coöperate in his plan as thus limited. Of the wider organization and membership afterwards formed by him in Canada we of course knew nothing, nor could we foresee the imprudence which finally perverted the attack into a defeat. We helped him in raising the money, and he seemed drawing toward the consummation of his plans, when letters began to come to his Massachusetts supporters from Hugh Forbes, already mentioned, threatening to make the whole matter public unless we could satisfy certain very unreasonable demands for money. On this point our committee was at once divided, not as to refusing the preposterous demands, but because the majority thought that this threat of disclosure made necessary an indefinite postponement of the whole affair; while Howe and myself, and Brown also, as it proved, thought otherwise.

He came again to Boston (May 31, 1858), when I talked with him alone, and he held, as I had done, that Forbes could do him no real harm; that if people believed Forbes they would underrate his (Brown's) strength, which was just the thing he wished; or if they overrated it, "the increased terror would perhaps counterbalance this." If he had the means, he would not lose a day. But as I could not, unaided, provide the means, I was obliged to yield, as he did. He consented to postpone the enterprise and return to Kansas, carrying with him $500 in gold, and an order for certain arms at Tabor, which had belonged originally to the State Kansas Committee, but had since been transferred, in consideration of a debt, to our friend Stearns, who gave them to Brown on his own responsibility. Nearly a year now passed, during which I rarely heard from Brown, and thought that perhaps his whole project had been abandoned. A new effort to raise money was made at Boston in the spring of 1859, but I took little part in it. It had all begun to seem to me rather chimerical. The amount of $2000 was, nevertheless, raised for him at Boston, in June, 1859, and I find that Sanborn wrote to me (June 4), "Brown has set out on his expedition;" and then on October 6, "The $300 desired has been made up and received. Four or five men will be on the ground next week from these regions and elsewhere." Brown's address was at this time at West Andover, Ohio, and the impression was that the foray would begin in that region, if at all. Nobody mentioned Harper's Ferry.

Ten days later the blow came. I went into a newspaper shop in Worcester one morning, and heard some one remark casually, "Old Osawatomie Brown has got himself into a tight place at last." I grasped eagerly at the morning paper, and read the whole story. Naturally, my first feeling was one of remorse, that the men who had given him money and arms should not actually have been by his side. In my own case, however, the justification was perfectly clear. Repeated postponements had taken the edge off from expectation, and the whole enterprise had grown rather vague and dubious in my mind. I certainly had not that degree of faith in it which would have led me to abandon all else, and wait nearly a year and a half for the opportunity of fulfillment; and indeed it became obvious at last that this longer postponement had somewhat disturbed the delicate balance of the zealot's mind, and had made him, at the very outset, defy the whole power of the United States government, and that within easy reach of Washington. Nothing of this kind was included in his original plans.

At any rate, since we were not with him, the first question was what part we were now to take. It will be remembered that the explosion of the Brown affair caused at once a vast amount of inquiry at Washington, and many were the threats of prosecuting Brown's previous friends and supporters. There was some talk of flight to Canada, and one or two of these persons actually went thither or to Europe. It always seemed to me undesirable to do this; it rather looked as if, having befriended Brown's plans so far as we understood them, it was our duty to stand our ground and give him our moral support, at least on the witness-stand. This view was perhaps easier for me to take, as my name was only incidentally mentioned in the newspapers; and it is only within a few months that I have discovered that it had been early brought, with that of Sanborn, to the express attention of Governor Wise, of Virginia. Among his papers captured at Charlestown, Va., by Major James Savage, of the Second Massachusetts Infantry, was this anonymous letter, received by the Virginia governor, and indorsed by him for transmission to some one else, probably in Congress,—but perhaps never forwarded. It read as follows: "There are two persons in Massachusetts, and I think only two, who, if summoned as witnesses, can explain the whole of Brown's plot. Their names are Francis B. Sanborn, of Concord, and T. W. Higginson, of Worcester, Mass. No time should be lost, as they may abscond, but I do not think they will, as they think you would not think it best to send for them. A Friend of Order." This was indorsed "A Friend to Gov. Wise, Oct., 1859. Call attention to this." And just below, "Sent to me, now sent to you for what it is worth. Richmond, Oct. 29, H. A. W. [Henry A. Wise.] A. Huntin [presumably the name of a secretary]."

This communication was written during the trial of Captain Brown, and a few days before his sentence, which was pronounced on November 2. It is hard to say whether it had any direct bearing on the arrest of Sanborn at Concord in the following April. It is very probable that it had, and if so, his arrest, had it been sustained by the court, might have been followed by mine; but it would have been quite superfluous, for I should at any time have been ready to go if summoned, and should, in fact, have thought it rather due to the memory of Brown. I could at least have made it plain that anything like slave insurrection, in the ordinary sense of the word, was remote from his thoughts, and that his plan was wholly different. He would have limited himself to advising a fugitive slave, if intercepted, to shoot down any one who attempted to arrest him; and this advice would have been given by every Abolitionist, unless a non-resistant.

There was, of course, an immediate impulse to rescue Brown from prison. I do not know how far this extended, and can only vouch for myself. The primary obstacle to it was that one of Brown's first acts, on meeting a Northern friend in his prison, had been positively to prohibit any such attempt; the message being sent North by Judge Thomas Russell, from whom I received it at the railway station on his arrival. This barred the way effectually, for after Brown had taken that position he would have adhered to it. It occurred to me, however, that his wife's presence would move him, if anything could, and that she might also be a valuable medium of communication, should he finally yield to the wishes of his friends. For this purpose I went to North Elba, New York, the mountain home of the Browns, to fetch her, and wrote, after that memorable trip, a full account of it, which was prefixed to Redpath's "Life of Brown." Upon entering for the first time the superb scenery of the Adirondacks, I saw myself in a region which was a fit setting for the heroic family to be visited. I found them poor, abstemious, patient, unflinching. They felt that the men of their household had given their lives for freedom, and there was no weak regret, no wish to hold them back. In the family was Annie Brown, who had been with the conspirators in Virginia, and had kept house and cooked for them. There were also the widows of the two slain sons, young girls of sixteen and twenty, one of them having also lost two brothers at Harper's Ferry. It illustrates the frugal way in which the Browns had lived that the younger of these two widows was not regarded by the household as being absolutely destitute, because her husband had left her five sheep, valued at two dollars apiece.

On my return, Mrs. Brown the elder rode with me for a whole day on a buckboard to Keeseville, and I had much talk with her. I have never in my life been in contact with a nature more dignified and noble; a Roman matron touched with the finer element of Christianity. She told me that this plan had occupied her husband's thoughts and prayers for twenty years; that he always believed himself an instrument in the hands of Providence, and she believed it too. She had always prayed that he might be killed in fight rather than fall into the hands of slaveholders, but she "could not regret it now, in view of the noble words of freedom which it had been his privilege to utter." She also said, "I have had thirteen children, and only four are left; but if I am to see the ruin of my house, I cannot but hope that Providence may bring out of it some benefit for the poor slaves." She little foresaw how, within two years, her dead husband's name would ring through the defiles of the Virginia mountains in the songs of the Union soldiers. When, the next day, I had to put into her hands, in the railway-car, the newspaper containing his death-warrant, she bent her head for a few moments on the back of the seat before us, and then lifted it again unchanged. Her errand was absolutely in vain, Brown refusing even to see her, possibly distrusting his own firmness, or wishing to put it above all possibility of peril; and she returned to her mountain home.

MISS FORTEN ON THE
SOUTHERN QUESTION

Were it only as an example of calm and courteous reasoning, on a subject where fervor of feeling could hardly bring reproach, it would be worth while to read the letter of Miss Charlotte Forten, in the last *Commonwealth* [December 30, 1876]. It is in the form of a criticism on Rev. Mr. Savage's sermon, "The Problem of the Hour." There are few persons whose opinion on the Southern question should have more weight than this lady's. Linked in blood and in experience to the two alienated races; herself trained as a pupil and teacher in Massachusetts schools and long connected both with the organization and the instruction of schools for the freedmen: a woman withal of high refinement and cultivation; the friend of Whittier and a contributor to the *Atlantic Monthly*; she is especially fitted, after years of residence at the South since the war, to testify as to its present condition. She now writes, evidently under a strong feeling of injustice, to dissent from the views recently expressed by Mr. Savage; and she does it in a tone of singular calmness, even of sweetness, while fully expressing her entire feeling.

And her line of argument is especially valuable, because, in going behind the merely political aspect of the matter, she touches with firm hand the real sources of the trouble; shows how the white leaders of the South have thrown away their opportunity, and by refusing to accept, in good faith, the results of emancipation, have thrown their former slaves into the hands of bad advisers, and have brought long evils upon all concerned. She says, with singular clearness:

In judging of the misgovernment of which some of the freedmen have been guilty, it should be remembered that this is, in a large measure, due to the ex-slave-holders themselves. Had they, at the close of the war, shown a friendly feeling toward their former slaves, the latter, who, as a rule, had no bitter feeling against masters who had treated them kindly, would doubt-less have chosen many of them for their political leaders, if convinced that they would deal with perfect justness and fairness towards them. Had they pledged themselves to secure to the colored people every civil and political right, they would be at the head of the government in South Carolina to-day, working in perfect harmony with their former slaves, to whom their superior intelligence and political experience would be a constant source of education. But they did not do this, because they had not, and have not, any desire to grant their rights to the colored people; but, on the contrary, a determination to reduce them to a condition as nearly like that of slavery as possible. Thus the freedmen were thrown into the hands of adventurers, Northern and Southern, who took advantage of their ignorance to use them as tools for their own private advantage.

And she justly points out how wrong it is for us to accept the common definition by which "the people of the South" means the whites only. She points out how our Northern men are influenced, in spite of themselves, by the tie of race, so that it is easy for them to think of the whites who fought them, rather than of the blacks who befriended them. How large a part of what is called "magnanimity" in our late discussions really has this for its root.

To the late General Bartlett, for instance, "the South" meant a body of brave men of his own color whom he had helped to conquer and would now receive with open arms. That was his feeling, and he urged it with generous ardor. But that "the South" included about an equal number of a different complexion, who had fought beside General Bartlett instead of against him, and whom these chivalrous opponents had by no means forgiven for that offence—to this he rarely referred. His magnanimity, however sincere and generous, had, therefore, a flaw at its foundation. However unconsciously to himself, it was too much like the pecuniary generosity of a man on whom his own family has a prior claim. "Be just before you are generous" is as true in dealing with human beings as with gold and silver. As Miss Forten tersely says:

Magnanimity is fine and praiseworthy; servility is not. Nor does the Scripture enjoin upon us to love our enemies more than our friends. In the long dark struggle with rebellion the colored people of the country, though so long the objects of oppression, in which the North shared the blame with the South, faltered not in their loyalty to a government to which they owed but little, and, by their active aid, helped to save the country. This especially embittered the Southerners against them. Do not these loyal blacks, and the loyal Northern whites living in the South, who not only lost all their property, but were imprisoned and subjected to suffering and indignity of all sorts for their devotion to the Union—do not these deserve some of the sympathy which has been lavished so freely upon the rebels who outraged them?

What Miss Forten sees plainly and what the *Nation* and the *Springfield Republican* fail to see, is that it was not the will of Republican managers that changed all the course of the Presidential campaign. It was the Hamburgh massacre which did all that; as was pointed out, by many of us, the day after it happened. That event showed that, however it might be elsewhere, the old barbarous spirit prevailed in South Carolina, and, this being exhibited, the whole course of the campaign had to be altered. No doubt many of the Republican leaders were glad to have it so; but those Republicans who were very sorry to have it so,—like the present writer,—were compelled to admit the fact and act accordingly. If a drunken man pushes you into the fire, and you get out a little singed, you can afford to forgive him; but if he avails himself of the moment of forgiveness to push you toward the fire again, your first business is to extricate yourself. One of the worst evils of the Hamburgh massacre was that it instantly postponed for at least four years all those fine questions of civil service reform, and the rest, on which many Republicans, with Governor Hayes at their head, were sincerely desirous to employ themselves. No man saw more clearly this inevitable change in the tone of argument than Mr. Bristow, who had been the especial candidate of the Republican reformers.

If it be said "South Carolina has been under government by the Republican party: in Georgia, in Alabama, there is peace," Miss Forten has an answer, which is as true and weighty, as it is calm.

One Northern minister said, not long ago, that he hoped Wade Hampton would be elected Governor of South Carolina, because in the States where the Southern whites had control of the government there was more tranquility than in the others, and the negroes had their rights, and were better off. Had he said that the negroes in those States had all the rights to which he and their former masters considered them entitled, he would have been nearer the truth. In Georgia, one of these "tranquil States," no colored person, however respectable, can ride in a first-class railway car, and women of respectability, refinement, and even beauty, apparently not "disagreeable, or barbarous, or ape-like," although colored, have been thrust from a car, and forced to ride with the lowest, roughest men in a smoking-car, dirty and disgusting to an extent of which Northern people have no idea. This is a specimen of "equality" in Georgia and other States in which the ex-rebels have the control. Would the minister to whom I have referred be satisfied with such equality for himself, his family, or his friends? Fortunately, God does not see even as Northern Christian ministers see. I have too deep a reverence for Him to believe that He intends one kind of treatment for the white man and another for the black!

This assertion of peace and order in Southern States controlled by the whites is precisely like the old assertions of Northern travelers that the slaves were happy and well off in slavery. "Who knows? Who has heard the slave's side?" said the abolitionists. Horace Mann said that a single slave, on a Georgia plantation, had about as much chance of making his wrongs known as has a man falling overboard in the middle of the Atlantic of swimming to the shore. The chance is not much greater now. Every white man in South Carolina, cheated out of a dollar by the government, has a tongue to speak and a newspaper to record his wrongs. A thousand black men in Georgia may still be wronged out of earnings and out of life; a thousand women may have their virtue insulted; and the news may never travel so far as to the next post village. Rev. Mr. Savage, having lived at the North, does not know this; Miss Forten, who has lived for years at the South, since the war, knows it too well. When the question is, in which Southern States are the colored people treated with most justice and propriety, she, as a cultivated and refined lady has a right to speak; and she has spoken well.

9

LETTER TO THE EDITOR

To THE EDITOR OF THE TRIBUNE:

SIR: I observe in a Republican newspaper, opposed to the Southern policy
of President Hayes, an appeal to the old Abolitionists and original Republicans to stand up and be counted. As one of those addressed, I gladly respond. I wish to be counted as one who approves, heartily, cordially, and
unreservedly the action of the President in withdrawing the garrisons
from the State Houses of South Carolina and Louisiana. I approve not
only what he has done, but the way in which be has done it;—with a wise
delay, giving time, in President Lincoln's fashion, for public sentiment to
crystallize into a firm support behind him.

It seems to me, however, a mistake in some of President Hayes's special
supporters to speak of this action as if it were "an experiment," and something that "could be receded from." It cannot be receded from, and it is
not an experiment. It is no more an experiment than to risk the assertion
that two and two make four, "and enforce it by appropriate legislation."
Under the precise circumstances, the President had absolutely no alternative. Let the immediate consequences be good or bad—I firmly believe
that they will be good, but no matter for that—there was nothing else to
be done. The proof of this lies in the fact that every one who opposes his
action has to begin by assuming that South Carolina and Louisiana are
still provinces. But suppose they are not provinces, what then! They have
been readmitted as States; and being such, they have absolutely the same
rights with New-York and Ohio. For the President to perform within their
borders one act of arbitrary authority endangers the liberties of every
State in the Union. For him, in time of peace, to keep troops in any State
House, in order to determine a disputed claim to the Governorship, is a

stretch of power so great that no State in the Union ought to tolerate it; so great that it ought to be resisted by every peaceful means.

I say "in time of peace." To my mind all turns upon that. Whatever may have been the case in the past, these States have now been for months at peace. No matter from what motives that peace has been kept, the fact remains. There were outrages last year; there may be outrages this year; but neither retrospective nor possible outrages can constitute insurrection. Once recognize that there can be such a thing as "constructive insurrection" or "latent insurrection," and you give a pretext under which the whole nation may at any time be converted into a consolidated despotism at short notice. In the very State where I am writing, during the Dorr rebellion, Mr. Webster, then Secretary of State, took the just ground that the Federal Government had absolutely no power to interfere in a case of "merely threatened domestic violence," or to "anticipate insurrectionary movements;" there must be "actual insurrection" and "lawless assemblages." It is absurd to say that any such condition of things now exists, or has for a long time existed, in South Carolina or Louisiana. Call it a hollow peace, if you please, it is still peace. Say that it is properly to be called insurrection because there were sets of violence last Autumn, and because there are people ready, on slight provocation, to commit such acts again; and you create a precedent under which some future National Administration may garrison the State House of every State where there has been an election riot within the year. There is one thing more important than even the immediate welfare of the colored people of South Carolina and Louisiana; and that is, to maintain the right of each State in the Union to manage its own local affairs in its own way, well or badly, so long as the peace is kept and the Constitution obeyed. On no other conditions can a republic which covers the breadth of a continent be maintained. And of all people in that republic, the colored men of the South can least afford to benefit by any arbitrary stretch of power which may, in other hands, be used to crush them.

THOS. WENTWORTH HIGGINSON,
NEWPORT, R. I., APRIL 26, 1877.

10

The South Carolina Blacks

To the Editor of the Nation:

Sir: I wish respectfully to offer some criticism, based on personal experience, upon a single passage in the *Nation* of April 18, waiving all comment on the rest of the editorial article in which it occurs. The passage to which I refer is as follows:

"There is undoubtedly a good deal of difference among the South Carolina negroes in intelligence and morality. Among the small number of negroes in the cities who have always been free there is a good deal of industry, intelligence, and good conduct. But the average of intelligence among the rest is very low—so low that they are but slightly above the level of animals. On the sea-coast and on the rivers they talk an outlandish idiom which is so different from English that in the witness-box they are with difficulty understood by judge or jury; and when on the jury itself, they must certainly be very far from understanding either the address of counsel or the charge of the judge."

The assertion is here distinctly made—not in an electioneering speech, not in a newspaper-correspondent's hurried letter, but in a journal claiming some deliberation and something of a judicial character—that the majority of the adult population of a State, all those in South Carolina, namely, who were born slaves, "are but slightly above the level of animals." I think that I should mentally question this statement if made of any race nominally professing the Christian religion, even if I had never seen that race. But when I remember that the class here mentioned is one which I have known very intimately, and have reason to remember all my life with love and gratitude, I certainly ought not to withhold my frank dissent.

It was my lot, during the late civil war, to be for two years the colonel of a colored regiment, enlisted chiefly in the Sea Islands of South Carolina. There were times when, for weeks together, I hardly saw a white face, except those of my own commissioned officers. There were other times when I had white troops also under my command, or was placed side by side with them. I thus saw the colored race under the conditions of solitude and of society, and saw them tried by one of the severest of all tests—that of military discipline. I also knew a great deal about the family affairs and social relations of my men, and of the life on the plantations, where the slaves were just freed. And so unlike was my whole experience to the verdict of the *Nation*, as above quoted, that I should almost suppose that we were speaking of different races of men.

"But slightly above the level of animals." If the religious sentiment is the lowest in our nature, and that which especially links us with brutes, then this phrase is appropriate to the Sea-Island negroes—not otherwise; for the religious sentiment is an essential part of their temperaments, and there is nothing in history more wonderful than the manner in which their unfaltering faith has held them up during long years of oppression. I observe that the same number of the *Nation* which I have quoted contains a courteous notice of a late book upon the "Hampton Singers." If the music of the "Hampton" and the "Jubilee" singers puts its authors near the level of the brute creation, then the negroes of South Carolina are there; for it was among them that these plaintive melodies were first studied, recorded, and published to the world.

It may be said that this was a merely sentimental piety, which found no outlet in action. Even if it were so, it would not, perhaps, be a combination altogether inconsistent with human attributes. But it was not so. There was no more of lying, stealing, or unchastity in the regiment of which I speak than in the average of white regiments. There was decidedly less of drunkenness; and the absence of profanity was remarked by all visitors. I did not create this state of things; I found it on arriving. Nor did I find it in consequence of expecting it, for it was quite unexpected. I was prepared to see much more degradation than ever showed itself, and to use much severer discipline than was ultimately needful. And if this was the condition of the people after years of slavery, it is impossible for me to believe that the few years since the war have deprived them of human attributes, and even of intelligible speech.

As to the matter of language, I can only say that I never found any serious difficulty, from the beginning, in making them understand me or in understanding them; nor can I see how any man of fair education should find such difficulty. I often see Irish men and women who are far more obtuse, and who use a far more perplexing dialect than I ever encountered on the Sea Islands; and, if this is the experience of a Northern man, it is inconceivable that a Southern judge or jury should have any serious difficulty in understanding the South Carolina negroes in court.

It may not be improper to point out, in conclusion, that no testimony to mental or moral character can be more unimpeachable than that of officers as regards their soldiers, for no other class of men are put under such heavy bonds to form correct judgments. Every officer risks his life on his own knowledge of his men. With others, it is merely a matter of more or less curious observation; with him it is life or death. He never lies down to sleep that he does not risk all on the vigilance and courage of his sentinels. There is not a day when mere stupidity, the mere misconstruction of an order, may not involve him in disaster. That he has survived to tell his story is indeed some evidence that his story is true, and that he really found his men to be what he claims that they were. It is one of the merits of war that its tests are sharp and unequivocal.

T. W. H.

NEWPORT, R. I., APRIL 30, 1874.

11

LETTER TO *THE NATION*: "THE CASE OF THE CARPET-BAGGERS"

To the Editor of The Nation:

Sir: The new novel called 'Red Rock,' by Thomas Nelson Page, has again brought up the old question of Southern reconstruction and the Northern carpet-baggers. It shows how hard it is to write history that so able a man, and one who obviously wishes to be candid, should yet leave out of sight some of the essential points on which the whole matter turned. The author has the candor to make two of the worst men of his story, Still and McRaffle, Southerners, while one of the best is a Northern settler, Major Welch. This shows that he wished to be fair; and yet he absolutely overlooks two points which make the key to the whole situation.

The first of these points is the fact that negro suffrage was absolutely the only method by which the negroes, who had proved almost the sole Southern friends of the Union, could be protected in their most ordinary rights from those who had tried to destroy it. Anything less would have been an act of desertion on the part of the nation which would have disgraced it for ever. The fact of this necessity will be clear to any one who will read the reports of the conventions called in 1865 by President Andrew Johnson to repeal the secession ordinances and reorganize the Southern States. A good abstract of these conventions will be found in a book called 'The South Since the War,' by Sidney Andrews, a newspaper correspondent of the highest character (Boston: Ticknor & Fields, 1866). He shows conclusively that the apparent object of all these conventions was to keep the negroes in a condition just as near slavery as possible; to limit their right of contract, their right of locomotion, and their range of labor; to have, in short, a separate negro code. It was even proposed in the South Carolina Convention that, "The Legislature shall have power to make laws applicable to colored persons alone, and shall enact such laws as are needful to prevent negroes and persons of color from engaging in any business or pursuit but such as involves manual labor, mining, road-making, agriculture, and the production of naval stores" (Andrews, p. 60). This was not passed, but the general tone of all the legislation was in the direction of "some system of peonage or apprenticeship" (p. 178). The conclusion of Mr. Andrews, who was anything but an extreme abolitionist, was as follows: "If the nation allows the whites to work out the problem of the future in their own way, the negro's condition in three years will be as bad as it was before the war" (p. 225). This he writes after attending the conventions in three Southern States in the very year (1865) in which the scene of 'Red Rock' is laid. In view of these facts, the enfranchisement of the blacks was a simple necessity. It followed logically from the attitude of these Southern conventions.

Again, it is equally unquestionable that the persons mainly responsible for the misdeeds of the so-called "carpet-baggers" were the people of the South themselves. There never was a Western State which received into itself a better class of immigrants than those who entered the South after the civil war. In both cases there was, of course, a mixture of good and poor elements; but from the beginning, in the Western States, this material was sifted by natural processes and the fittest survived. In the Southern States, on the other hand, the immigration was equally sifted, but in the reverse direction, by the bitter hostility of the former slaveholders, who were equally intolerant to the best and the worst. I myself was at the South on military duty, from 1862 to 1864, and saw the beginning of the whole process. I knew, then and afterwards, repeated instances of men of the highest character who came in good faith to bring their capital and energy to South Carolina or Georgia, but who were simply frozen out by the bitter hostility of those among whom they purposed to live. Instead of being welcomed and encouraged, such men found themselves received with suspicion and aversion; and it was a common thing for well-dressed women to hold away their skirts from touching them as they passed in the street. The very people who came to them to borrow money would ostentatiously exclude them from their own doors. Under these circumstances, no man of self-respect could think of bringing his wife and children to such an atmosphere; and the men of the better class who would have been useful citizens more commonly sold out their purchases at a sacrifice and went North again. The cheats and bullies, on the other hand, were less scrupulous, and stayed to revenge themselves amply on their persecutors. It must, therefore, always be borne in mind—though it seems to be easily forgotten—that the typical carpet-bagger, of evil reputation, was simply the man who was left behind to do mischief after the better class of immigrants had been driven out.

THOMAS WENTWORTH HIGGINSON
CAMBRIDGE, MASS., MARCH 2, 1899

12

SOUTHERN BARBARITY

LYNCHING OUTRAGES
VIGOROUSLY DENOUNCED

The chairman then introduced as the presiding officer Col. Thomas Wentworth Higginson, "one who comes to us as he came to the rescue of Anthony Burns some forty years ago and answers the call of his country as he did in '61."

Col. Higginson, on assuming the chair, said that it was his fortune to lead for two years a regiment of colored troops and his only protection against them was the fact that they were in U.S. uniform. He learned to trust colored men then, and he saw no reason to distrust them now. If they were distrusted now it was the fault of those who distrust them and not theirs.

He went on to describe the experiences he had in a camp of colored soldiers, where he had no security save their courage and fidelity, although they were taken out not from the class you represent, but from the lowest and most ignorant of the cotton plantations of Carolina. I shall always feel free for the future that they are to be trusted by their fellow citizens.

If they had those innate tendencies to a licentious self-indulgence which are constantly announced in some newspapers, it is absolutely impossible that I should not have found it out. That I should have been with them for those two years, and never have had even a charge brought against their integrity, their honor and their chastity, is suffi-

---

A report on a speech given by Higginson at a protest meeting in Boston on March 10, 1899.

cient proof, to my mind, that there is no occasion for these charges. You can demoralize any people in this planet by treating them with distrust. The great Lord Bacon said suspicion was the way to lose that which we fear to lose; on the other hand confidence in any people on the face of the earth is to make that people worthy of confidence. And, wherever that has been done to the colored people, they have taken care of the rest.

Col. Higginson finally considered the course to be pursued. "We have a duty," said he, to be wise and patient—not in the sense of a patience that lasts forever and does nothing, but of a patience which studies as well as it can, what to do. These people have a right to the freedom of civilization, the freedom of political rights, the freedom not merely to escape being held as slaves, but to have a position as free men that is worth having. The trouble is that the freedom of these people in the South is the nominal, not the real freedom. Even patience may have its limits, and we know not how long that patience can be continued. We have no right to forget that the colored people are also men and have the rights of men, and there is a limit to even the patience which a great Christian civilization can demand of them.

Col. Higginson then introduced as the first speaker. . .

13

LYDIA MARIA CHILD

To those of us who were by twenty years or more the juniors of Mrs. Child, she always presented herself rather as an object of love than of cool criticism, even if we had rarely met her face to face. In our earliest recollections she came before us less as author or philanthropist than as some kindly and omnipresent aunt, beloved forever by the heart of childhood,—some one gifted with all lore, and furnished with unfathomable resources,—some one discoursing equal delight to all members of the household. In those days she seemed to supply a sufficient literature for any family through her own unaided pen. Thence came novels for the parlor, cookery books for the kitchen, and the "Juvenile Miscellany" for the nursery. In later years the intellectual provision still continued. We learned, from her anti-slavery writings, where to find our duties; from her "Letters from New York," where to seek our highest pleasures; while her "Progress of Religious Ideas" introduced us to those profounder truths on which pleasures and duties alike rest. It is needless to debate whether she did the greatest or most permanent work in any especial department of literature, since she did pioneer work in so many. She showed memorable independence in repeatedly leaving beaten paths to strike out for herself new literary directions, and combined the authorship of more than thirty books and pamphlets with a singular devotion both to public and private philanthropies, and with almost too exacting a faithfulness to the humblest domestic duties.

Lydia Maria Francis was born at Medford, Mass., February 11, 1802. Her ancestor, Richard Francis, came from England in 1636, and settled in Cambridge, where his tombstone may still be seen in the burialground. Her paternal grandfather, a weaver by trade, was in the Concord fight, and is said to have killed five of the enemy. Her father, Convers

Francis, was a baker, first in West Cambridge, then in Medford, where he first introduced the article of food still known as "Medford crackers." He was a man of strong character and great industry. Though without much cultivation, he had uncommon love of reading; and his anti-slavery convictions were peculiarly zealous, and must have influenced his children's later career. He married Susannah Rand, of whom it is only recorded that "she had a simple, loving heart, and a spirit busy in doing good."

They had six children, of whom Lydia Maria was the youngest, and Convers the next in age. Convers Francis was afterwards eminent among the most advanced thinkers and scholars of the Unitarian body, at a time when it probably surpassed all other American denominations in the intellectual culture of its clergy. He had less ideality than his sister, less enthusiasm, and far less moral courage; yet he surpassed most of his profession in all these traits. He was Theodore Parker's first scholarly friend, and directed his studies in preparation for the theological school. Long after, Mr. Parker used still to head certain pages of his journal, "Questions to ask Dr. Francis." The modest "study" at Watertown was a favorite headquarters of what were called "the transcendentalists" of those days. Emerson, Margaret Fuller, Ripley, and the rest came often thither, in the days when the "Dial" was just emancipating American thought from old-world traditions. Afterwards, when Dr. Francis was appointed to the rather responsible and conservative post of professor in the Harvard Theological School, he still remained faithful to the spirit of earlier days, never repressing free inquiry, but always rejoicing to encourage it. He was a man of rare attainments in a variety of directions; and though his great reading gave a desultory habit to his mind, and his thinking was not quite in proportion to his receptive power, he still was a most valuable instructor, as he was a most delightful friend. In face and figure he resembled the pictures of Martin Luther, and his habits and ways always seemed like those of some genial German professor. With the utmost frugality in other respects, he spent money profusely on books, and his library—part of which he bequeathed to Harvard College—was to me the most attractive I had ever seen; more so than even Theodore Parker's.

His sister had, undoubtedly, the superior mind of the two; but he who influenced others so much must have influenced her still more. "A dear good sister has she been to me; would that I had been half as good a brother to her." This he wrote, in self-depreciation, long after. While he was fitting for college, a process which took but one year, she was his fa-

vorite companion, though more than six years younger. They read together, and she was constantly bringing him Milton and Shakespeare to
explain. He sometimes mystified her,—as brothers will, in dealing with
maidens nine years old,—and once told her that "the raven down of
darkness," which was made to smile, was but the fur of a black cat that
sparkled when stroked; though it still perplexed her small brain why *fur*
should be called *down*.

Their earliest teacher was a maiden lady, named Elizabeth Francis,—
but not a relative,—and known universally as "Ma'am Betty." She is described as "a spinster of supernatural shyness, the never-forgotten
calamity of whose life was that Dr. Brooks once saw her drinking water
from the nose of her tea-kettle." She kept school in her bedroom,—it
was never tidy, and she chewed a great deal of tobacco; but the children
were fond of her, and always carried her a Sunday dinner. Such simple
kindnesses went forth often from that thrifty home. Mrs. Child once
told me that always on the night before Thanksgiving, all the humble
friends of the household—"Ma'am Betty," the washerwoman, the berry-
woman, the wood-sawyer, the journeymen-bakers, and so on—some
twenty or thirty in all, were summoned to a preliminary entertainment.
They here partook of an immense chicken-pie, pumpkin-pies (made in
milk-pans), and heaps of doughnuts. They feasted in the large old-
fashioned kitchen, and went away loaded with crackers and bread by the
father, and with pies by the mother, not forgetting "turnovers" for their
children. Such homely applications of the doctrine "It is more blessed to
give than to receive" may have done more to mould the Lydia Maria
Child of maturer years than all the faithful labors of good Dr. Osgood,
to whom she and her brother used to repeat the Westminster Assembly's
Catechism once a month.

Apart from her brother's companionship, the young girl had, as was
then usual, a very subordinate share of educational opportunities; attending only the public schools, with one year at the private seminary of
Miss Swan, in Medford. Her mother died in 1814, after which the family
removed for a time to Maine. In 1819 Convers Francis was ordained over
the First Parish in Watertown, and there occurred in his study, in 1824,
an incident which was to determine the whole life of his sister.

Dr. J. G. Palfrey had written in the "North American Review" for April,
1821, a review of the now forgotten poem of "Yamoyden," in which he
had ably pointed out the use that might be made of early American history for the purposes of fictitious writing. Miss Francis read this article,
at her brother's house, one summer Sunday noon. Before attending the
afternoon service, she wrote the first chapter of a novel. It was soon fin-

ished, and was published that year,—a thin volume of two hundred pages, without her name, under the title of "Hobomok: a Tale of Early Times. By an American."

In judging of this little book, it is to be remembered that it marked the very dawn of American imaginative literature. Irving had printed only his "Sketch Book;" Cooper only "Precaution." This new production was the hasty work of a young woman of nineteen—an Indian tale by one who had scarcely even seen an Indian. Accordingly, "Hobomok" now seems very crude in execution, very improbable in plot; and is redeemed only by a certain earnestness which carries the reader along, and by a sincere attempt after local coloring. It is an Indian "Enoch Arden," with important modifications, which unfortunately all tend away from probability. Instead of the original lover who heroically yields his place, it is to him that the place is given up. The hero of this self-sacrifice is an Indian, a man of high and noble character, whose wife the heroine had consented to become, at a time when she had been almost stunned with the false tidings of her lover's death. The least artistic things in the book are these sudden nuptials, and the equally sudden resolution of Hobomok to abandon his wife and child on the reappearance of the original betrothed. As the first work whose scene was laid in Puritan days, "Hobomok" will always have a historic interest, but it must be read in very early youth to give it any other attraction.

The success of this first effort was at any rate such as to encourage the publication of a second tale in the following year. This was "The Rebels; or, Boston before the Revolution. By the author of 'Hobomok.'" It was a great advance on its predecessor, with more vigor, more variety, more picturesque grouping, and more animation of style. The historical point was well chosen, and the series of public and private events well combined, with something of that tendency to the over-tragic which is common with young authors,—it is so much easier to kill off superfluous characters than to do anything else with them. It compared not unfavorably with Cooper's revolutionary novels, and had in one respect a remarkable success. It contained an imaginary sermon by Whitefield and an imaginary speech by James Otis. Both of these were soon transplanted into "School Readers" and books of declamation, and the latter, at least, soon passed for a piece of genuine revolutionary eloquence. I remember learning it by heart, under that impression; and was really astonished, on recently reading "The Rebels" for the first time, to discover that the high-sounding periods which I had always attributed to Otis were really to be found in a young lady's romance.

This book has a motto from Bryant, and is "most respectfully inscribed" to George Ticknor. The closing paragraph states with some terseness the author's modest anxieties:—

"Many will complain that I have dwelt too much on political scenes, familiar to every one who reads our history; and others, on the contrary, will say that the character of the book is quite too tranquil for its title. I might mention many doubts and fears still more important; but I prefer silently to trust this humble volume to that futurity which no one can foresee and every one can read."

The fears must soon have seemed useless, for the young novelist early became almost a fashionable lion. She was an American Fanny Burney, with rather reduced copies of Burke and Johnson around her. Her personal qualities soon cemented some friendships, which lasted her life long, except where her later anti-slavery action interfered. She opened a private school in Watertown, which lasted from 1825 to 1828. She established, in 1827, the "Juvenile Miscellany," that delightful pioneer among children's magazines in America; and it was continued for eight years. In October, 1828, she was married to David Lee Child, a lawyer of Boston.

In those days it seemed to be held necessary for American women to work their passage into literature by first compiling some kind of cookery book. They must be perfect in that preliminary requisite before they could proceed to advanced standing. It was not quite as in Marvell's satire on Holland, "Invent a shovel and be a magistrate," but, as Charlotte Hawes has since written, "First this steak and then that stake." So Mrs. Child published in 1829 her "Frugal Housewife," a book which proved so popular that in 1836 it had reached its twentieth edition, and in 1855 its thirty-third.

The "Frugal Housewife" now lies before me, after a great many years of abstinence from its appetizing pages. The words seem as familiar as when we children used to study them beside the kitchen fire, poring over them as if their very descriptions had power to allay an unquenched appetite or prolong the delights of one satiated. There were the animals in the frontispiece, sternly divided by a dissecting knife of printer's ink, into sections whose culinary names seemed as complicated as those of surgical science,—chump and spring, sirloin and sperib,—for I faithfully follow the original spelling. There we read with profound acquiescence that "hard gingerbread is good to have in the family," but demurred at the reason given, "it keeps so well." It never kept well in ours! There we all learned that one should be governed in housekeeping by higher considerations than mere worldly vanity, knowing that "many people buy the upper part of the sparerib of pork, thinking it the most genteel; but the lower part is more sweet and juicy, and there is more meat in proportion to the bone."

Going beyond mere carnal desires, we read also the wholesome directions "to those who are not ashamed of economy." We were informed that "children could early learn to take care of their own clothes,"—a responsibility at which we shuddered; and also that it was a good thing for children to gather blackberries,—in which we heartily concurred. There, too, we were taught to pick up twine and paper, to write on the backs of old letters, like paper-sparing Pope, and if we had a dollar a day, which seemed a wild supposition, to live on seventy-five cents. We all read, too, with interest, the hints on the polishing of furniture and the education of daughters, and we got our first glimpses of political economy from the "Reasons for Hard Times." So varied and comprehensive was the good sense of the book that it surely would have seemed to our childish minds infallible, but for one fatal admission, which through life I have recalled with dismay,—the assertion, namely, that "economical people will seldom use preserves." "They are unhealthy, expensive, and useless to those who are well." This was a sumptuary law, against which the soul of youth revolted.

The wise counsels thus conveyed in this more-than-cookery book may naturally have led the way to a "Mother's Book," of more direct exhortation. This was published in 1831, and had a great success, reaching its eighth American edition in 1845, besides twelve English editions and a German translation. Doubtless it is now out of print, but one may still find at the antiquarian bookstores the "Girl's Own Book," by Mrs. Child, published during the same year. This is a capital manual of indoor games, and is worth owning by any one who has a houseful of children, or is liable to serve as the Lord of Misrule at Christmas parties. It is illustrated with vignettes by that wayward child of genius, Francis Graeter, a German, whom Mrs. Child afterwards described in the "Letters from New York." He was a personal friend of hers, and his pencil is also traceable in some of her later books. Indeed, the drollest games which he has delineated in the "Girl's Own Book" are not so amusing as the unintentional comedy of his attempts at a "Ladies' Sewing Circle," which illustrates American life in the "History of Woman." The fair laborers sit about a small round table, with a smirk of mistimed levity on their faces, and one feels an irresistible impulse to insert in their very curly hair the twisted papers employed in the game of "Genteel lady, always genteel," in the "Girl's Own Book."

The "History of Woman" appeared in 1832, as one of a series projected by Carter & Hendee, of which Mrs. Child was to be the editor, but which was interrupted at the fifth volume by the failure of the publishers. She compiled for this the "Biographies of Good Wives," the "Memoirs" of Madame De Staël and Madame Roland, those of Lady Russell and Madame Guion, and the two volumes of "Woman." All these aimed at a popular, not a profound, treatment. She was, perhaps, too good a compiler, showing in such work the traits of her brother's mind, and carefully excluding all those airy flights and bold speculations which afterwards seemed her favorite element. The "History of Woman," for instance, was a mere assemblage of facts, beginning and ending abruptly, and with no glimpse of any leading thought or general philosophy. It was, however, the first American storehouse of information upon that whole question, and no doubt helped the agitation along. Its author evidently looked with distrust, however, on that rising movement for the equality of the sexes, of which Frances Wright was then the rather formidable leader.

The "Biographies of Good Wives" reached a fifth edition in the course of time, as did the "History of Woman." I have a vague childish recollection of her next book, "The Coronal," published in 1833, which was of rather a fugitive description. The same year brought her to one of those bold steps which made successive eras in her literary life,—the publication of her "Appeal for that Class of Americans called Africans."

The name was rather cumbrous, like all attempts to include an epigram in the title-page, but the theme and the word "Appeal" were enough. It was under the form of an "Appeal" that the colored man, Alexander Walker, had thrown a firebrand into Southern society which had been followed by Nat Turner's insurrection; and now a literary lady, amid the cultivated circles of Boston, dared also to "appeal." Only two years before (1831), Garrison had begun the "Liberator," and only two years later (1835), he was dragged through Boston streets, with a rope around his body, by "gentlemen of property and standing," as the newspapers said next day. It was just at the very most dangerous moment of the rising storm that Mrs. Child appealed.

Miss Martineau in her article, "The Martyr Age in America,"—published in the "London and Westminster Review" in 1839, and at once reprinted in America,—gives by far the most graphic picture yet drawn of that perilous time. She describes Mrs. Child as "a lady of whom society was exceedingly proud before she published her Appeal, and to whom society has been extremely contemptuous ever since." She adds: "Her works were bought with avidity before, but fell into sudden oblivion as soon as she had done a greater deed than writing any of them."

It is evident that this result was not unexpected, for the preface to the book explicitly recognizes the probable dissatisfaction of the public. She says:

> I am fully aware of the unpopularity of the task I have undertaken; but though I expect ridicule and censure, I cannot fear them. A few years hence, the opinion of the world will be a matter in which I have not even the most transient interest; but this book will be abroad on its mission of humanity long after the hand that wrote it is mingling with the dust. Should it be the means of advancing, even one single hour, the inevitable progress of truth and justice, I would not exchange the consciousness for all Rothschild's wealth or Sir Walter's fame.

These words have in them a genuine ring; and the book is really worthy of them. In looking over its pages, after the lapse of many years, it seems incredible that it should have drawn upon her such hostility. The tone is calm and strong, the treatment systematic, the points well put, the statements well guarded. The successive chapters treat of the history of slavery, its comparative aspect in different ages and nations, its influence on politics, the profitableness of emancipation, the evils of the colonization scheme, the intellect of negroes, their morals, the feeling against them, and the duties of the community in their behalf. As it was the first anti-slavery work ever printed in America in book form, so I have always thought it the ablest; that is, it covered the whole ground better than any other. I know that, on reading it for the first time, nearly ten years after its first appearance, it had more formative influence on my mind in that direction than any other, although of course the eloquence of public meetings was a more exciting stimulus. It never surprised me to hear that even Dr. Channing attributed a part of his own anti-slavery awakening to this admirable book. He took pains to seek out its author immediately on its appearance, and there is in her biography an interesting account of their meeting. His own work on slavery did not appear until 1835.

Undaunted and perhaps stimulated by opposition, Mrs. Child followed up her self-appointed task. During the next year she published the "Oasis," a sort of anti-slavery annual, the precursor of Mrs. Chapman's "Liberty Bell," of later years. She also published, about this time, an "Anti-Slavery Catechism" and a small book called "Authentic Anecdotes of American Slavery." These I have never seen, but find them advertised on the cover of a third pamphlet, which, with them, went to a second edition in 1839. "The Evils of Slavery and the Cure of Slavery; the first proved by the opinions of Southerners themselves, the last shown by historical evidence." This is a compact and sensible little work.

While thus seemingly absorbed in reformatory work, she still kept an outlet in the direction of pure literature, and was employed for several years on "Philothea," which appeared in 1836. The scene of this novel was laid in ancient Greece. I well remember the admiration with which this romance was hailed; and for me personally it was one of those delights of boyhood which the criticism of maturity cannot disturb. What mattered it if she brought Anaxagoras and Plato on the stage together, whereas in truth the one died about the year when the other was born? What mattered it if in her book the classic themes were treated in a romantic spirit? That is the fate of almost all such attempts,—compare, for instance, the choruses of Swinburne's "Atalanta," which might have been written on the banks of the Rhine, and very likely were. But childhood never wishes to discriminate, only to combine; a period of life which likes to sugar its bread and butter prefers also to have its classic and romantic in one.

"Philothea" was Mrs. Child's first attempt to return, with her anti-slavery cross still upon her, into the ranks of literature. Mrs. S. J. Hale, who, in her "Woman's Record," reproves her sister writer for "wasting her soul's wealth" in radicalism, and "doing incalculable injury to humanity," seems to take a stern satisfaction in the fact that "the bitter feelings engendered by the strife have prevented the merits of this remarkable book from being appreciated as they deserve." This was perhaps true; nevertheless it went through three editions, and Mrs. Child, still keeping up the full circle of her labors, printed nothing but a rather short-lived "Family Nurse" (in 1837) before entering the anti-slavery arena again.

In 1841 Mr. and Mrs. Child were engaged by the American Anti-Slavery Society to edit the "Anti-Slavery Standard," a weekly newspaper published in New York. Mr. Child's health being impaired, his wife undertook the task alone, and conducted the newspaper in that manner for two years, after which she aided her husband in the work, remaining there for eight years in all. She was very successful as an editor, her management being brave and efficient, while her cultivated taste made the "Standard" attractive to many who were not attracted by the plainer fare of the "Liberator." The good judgment shown in her poetical and literary selections was always acknowledged with especial gratitude by those who read the "Standard" at that time.

During all this period she was a member of the family of the well-known Quaker philanthropist, Isaac T. Hopper, whose biographer she afterwards became. This must have been the most important and satisfactory time in Mrs. Child's whole life. She was placed where her sympathetic nature found abundant outlet and plenty of coöperation. Dwelling in a home where disinterestedness and noble labor were as daily breath, she had great opportunities. There was no mere almsgiving there, no mere secretaryship of benevolent societies; but sin and sorrow must be brought home to the fireside and to the heart; the fugitive slave, the drunkard, the outcast woman, must be the chosen guest of the abode,—must be taken and held and loved into reformation or hope. Since the stern tragedy of city life began, it has seen no more efficient organization for relief than when Isaac Hopper and Mrs. Child took up their abode beneath one roof in New York.

For a time she did no regular work in the cause of permanent literature,—though she edited an anti-slavery almanac in 1843,—but she found an opening for her best eloquence in writing letters to the "Boston Courier," then under the charge of Joseph T. Buckingham. This was the series of "Letters from New York" that afterwards became famous. They were the precursors of that modern school of newspaper correspondence in which women have so large a share, and which has something of the charm of women's private letters,—a style of writing where description preponderates over argument and statistics make way for fancy and enthusiasm. Many have since followed in this path, and perhaps Mrs. Child's letters would not now be hailed as they then were. Others may have equaled her, but she gave us a new sensation, and that epoch was perhaps the climax of her purely literary career.

Their tone also did much to promote the tendency, which was showing itself in those days, towards a fresh inquiry into the foundations of social science. The Brook Farm experiment was at its height; and though she did not call herself an Associationist, yet she quoted Fourier and Swedenborg, and other authors who were thought to mean mischief; and her highest rhapsodies about poetry and music were apt to end in some fervent appeal for some increase of harmony in daily life. She seemed always to be talking radicalism in a greenhouse; and there were many good people who held her all the more dangerous for her perfumes. There were young men and maidens, also, who looked to her as a teacher, and were influenced for life, perhaps, by what she wrote. I knew, for instance, a young lawyer, just entering on the practice of his profession under the most flattering auspices, who withdrew from the courts forever—wisely or unwisely,—because Mrs. Child's book had taught him to hate their contests and their injustice.

It was not long after this that James Russell Lowell, in his "Fable for Critics," gave himself up to one impulse of pure poetry in describing

Mrs. Child. It is by so many degrees the most charming sketch ever made of her that the best part of it must be inserted here:

> "There comes Philothea, her face all aglow,
> She has just been dividing some poor creature's woe,
> And can't tell which pleases her most, to relieve
> His want, or his story to hear and believe;
>
> "The pole, science tells us, the magnet controls,
> But she is a magnet to emigrant Poles,
> And folks with a mission that nobody knows
> Throng thickly about her as bees round a rose;
> She can fill up the *carets* in such, make their scope
> Converge to some focus of rational hope,
> And with sympathies fresh as the morning, their gall
> Can transmute into honey,—but this is not all;
> Not only for these she has solace, oh, say,
> Vice's desperate nursling adrift in Broadway,
> Who clingest with all that is left of thee human
> To the last slender spar from the wreck of the woman,
> Hast thou not found one shore where those tired drooping feet
> Could reach firm mother earth, one full heart on whose beat
> The soothed head in silence reposing could hear
> The chimes of far childhood throb back on the ear?
> Ah, there's many a beam from the fountain of day
> That, to reach us unclouded, must pass on its way
> Through the soul of a woman, and hers is wide ope
> To the influence of Heaven as the blue eyes of Hope;
> Yes, a great heart is hers, one that dares to go in
> To the prison, the slave-hut, the alleys of sin,
> And to bring into each, or to find there, some line
> Of the never completely out-trampled divine;
> If her heart at high floods swamps her brain now and then,
> 'T is but richer for that when the tide ebbs again,
> As after old Nile has subsided, his plain
> Overflows with a second broad deluge of grain;
> What a wealth would it bring to the narrow and sour,
> Could they be as a Child but for one little hour!"

The two series of "Letters from New York" appeared in 1843 and 1845, and went through seven or more editions. They were followed in 1846 by a collection of tales, mostly printed, entitled "Fact and Fiction." The book was dedicated to "Anna Loring, the Child of my Heart," and was a series of powerful and well-told narratives, some purely ideal, but mostly based upon the sins of great cities, especially those of man against woman. She might have sought more joyous themes, but none which at that time lay so near her heart. There was more sunshine in her next literary task, for, in 1852, she collected three small volumes of her stories from the "Juvenile Miscellany" and elsewhere, under the title of "Flowers for Children."

In 1853 she published her next book, entitled "Isaac T. Hopper; a True Life." This gave another new sensation to the public, for her books never seemed to repeat each other, and belonged to almost as many different departments as there were volumes. The critics complained that this memoir was a little fragmentary, a series of interesting stories without sufficient method or unity of conception. Perhaps it would have been hard to make it otherwise. Certainly, as the book stands, it seems like the department of "Benevolence" in the "Percy Anecdotes," and serves as an encyclopædia of daring and noble charities.

Her next book was the most arduous intellectual labor of her life, and, as often happens in such cases, the least profitable in the way of money. "The Progress of Religious Ideas through Successive Ages" was published in three large volumes in 1855. She had begun it long before in New York, with the aid of the Mercantile Library and the Commercial Library, then the best in the city. It was finished in Wayland, with the aid of her brother's store of books, and with his and Theodore Parker's counsel as to her course of reading. It seems, from the preface, that more than eight years elapsed between the planning and the printing, and for six years it was her main pursuit. For this great labor she had absolutely no pecuniary reward; the book paid its expenses and nothing more. It is now out of print and not easy to obtain.

This disappointment was no doubt due partly to the fact that the book set itself in decided opposition, unequivocal though gentle, to the prevailing religious impressions of the community. It may have been, also, that it was too learned for a popular book and too popular for a learned one. Learning, indeed, she distinctly disavowed. "If readers complain of want of profoundness, they may perchance be willing to accept simplicity and clearness in exchange for depth." . . . "Doubtless a learned person would have performed the task far better in many respects; but, on some accounts, my want of learning is an advantage. Thoughts do not range so freely when the storeroom of the brain is overloaded with furniture." And she gives at the end, with her usual frankness, a list of works consulted, all being in English except seven, which are in French. It was a bold thing to base a history of religious ideas on such books as Enfield's Philosophy and Taylor's Plato. The trouble was not so much that the learning was second-hand,—for such is most learning,—as that the authorities were second-rate. The stream could hardly go higher than its source; and a book based on such very inadequate researches could hardly be accepted, even when tried by that very accommodating standard, popular scholarship.

In 1857 Mrs. Child published a volume entitled "Autumnal Leaves; Tales and Sketches in Prose and Rhyme." It might seem from this title that she regarded her career of action as drawing to a close. If so she was soon undeceived, and the attack of Captain John Brown upon Harper's Ferry aroused her, like many others, from a dream of peace. Immediately on the arrest of Captain Brown she wrote him a brief letter, asking permission to go and nurse him, as he was wounded and among enemies, and as his wife was supposed to be beyond immediate reach. This letter she inclosed in one to Governor Wise. She then went home and packed her trunk, with her husband's full approval, but decided not to go until she heard from Captain Brown, not knowing what his precise wishes might be. She had heard that he had expressed a wish to have the aid of some lawyer not identified with the anti-slavery movement, and she thought he was entitled to the same considerations of policy in regard to a nurse. Meantime Mrs. Brown was sent for and promptly arrived, while Captain Brown wrote Mrs. Child one of his plain and characteristic letters, declining her offer, and asking her kind aid for his family, which was faithfully given.

But with this letter came one from Governor Wise,—courteous, but rather diplomatic,—and containing some reproof of her expressions of sympathy for the prisoner. To this she wrote an answer, well worded and quite effective, which, to her great surprise, soon appeared in the New York "Tribune." She wrote to the editor (November 10, 1859): "I was much surprised to see my correspondence with Governor Wise published in your columns. As I have never given any person a copy, I presume you must have obtained it from Virginia."

This correspondence soon led to another. Mrs. M. J. C. Mason wrote from "Alto, King George's County, Virginia," a formidable demonstration, beginning thus: "Do you read your Bible, Mrs. Child? If you do, read there, 'Woe unto you hypocrites,' and take to yourself, with twofold damnation, that terrible sentence; for, rest assured, in the day of judgment, it shall be more tolerable for those thus scathed by the awful denunciations of the Son of God than for you." This startling commencement—of which it must be calmly asserted that it comes very near swearing, for a lady—leads to something like bathos at the end, where Mrs. Mason adds in conclusion, "No Southerner ought, after your letters to Governor Wise, to read a line of your composition, or to touch a magazine which bears your name in its list of contributors." To begin with double-dyed future torments, and come gradually to the climax of "Stop my paper," admits of no other explanation than that Mrs. Mason had dabbled in literature herself, and knew how to pierce the soul of a sister in the trade.

But the great excitement of that period, and the general loss of temper that prevailed, may plead a little in vindication of Mrs. Mason's vehemence, and must certainly enhance the dignity of Mrs. Child's reply. It is one of the best things she ever wrote. She refuses to dwell on the invectives of her assailant, and only "wishes her well, both in this world and the next." Nor will she even debate the specific case of John Brown, whose body was in charge of the courts and his reputation sure to be in charge of posterity. "Men, however great they may be," she says, "are of small consequence in comparison with principles, and the principle for which John Brown died is the question at issue between us."

She accordingly proceeds to discuss this question, first scripturally (following the lead of her assailant), then on general principles; and gives one of her usual clear summaries of the whole argument. Now that the excitements of the hour have passed, the spirit of her whole statement must claim just praise. The series of letters was published in pamphlet form in 1860, and secured a wider circulation than anything she ever wrote, embracing some three hundred thousand copies. In return she received many private letters from the slave States, mostly anonymous, and often grossly insulting.

Having gained so good a hearing, she followed up her opportunity. During the same year she printed two small tracts, "The Patriarchal Institution" and "The Duty of Disobedience to the Fugitive Slave Law," and then one of her most elaborate compilations, entitled "The Right Way the Safe Way, proved by Emancipation in the British West Indies and Elsewhere." This shows the same systematic and thorough habit of mind with its predecessors; and this business-like way of dealing with facts is hard to reconcile with the dreamy and almost uncontrolled idealism which she elsewhere shows. In action, too, she has usually shown the same practical thoroughness, and in case of this very book forwarded copies at her own expense to fifteen hundred persons in the slave States.

In 1864 she published "Looking towards Sunset,"—a very agreeable collection of prose and verse, by various authors, all bearing upon the aspects of old age. This was another of those new directions of literary activity with which she so often surprised her friends. The next year brought still another in the "Freedmen's Book,"—a collection of short tales and sketches suited to the mental condition of the Southern freedmen, and published for their benefit. It was sold for that purpose at cost, and a good many copies were distributed through teachers and missionaries.

Her last publication, and perhaps (if one might venture to guess) her favorite among the whole series, appeared in 1867,—"A Romance of the Republic." It was received with great cordiality, and is in some respects her best fictitious work. The scenes are laid chiefly at the South, where she has given the local coloring in a way really remarkable for one who never visited that region, while the results of slavery are painted with the thorough knowledge of one who had devoted a lifetime to their study. The leading characters are of that type which has since become rather common in fiction, because American society affords none whose situation is so dramatic,—young quadroons educated to a high grade of culture, and sold as slaves after all. All the scenes are handled in a broad spirit of humanity, and betray no trace of that subtle sentiment of caste which runs through and through some novels written ostensibly to oppose caste. The characterization is good, and the events interesting and vigorously handled. The defect of the book is a common one,—too large a frame-work, too many *vertebræ* to the plot. Even the established climax of a wedding is a safer experiment than to prolong the history into the second generation, as here. The first two thirds of the story would have been more effective without the conclusion. But it will always possess value as one of the few really able delineations of slavery in fiction, and the author may well look back with pride on this final offering upon that altar of liberty where so much of her life had been already laid.

In later life Mrs. Child left not only the busy world of New York, but almost the world of society, and took up her abode (after a short residence at West Newton) in the house bequeathed to her by her father, at Wayland, Mass. In that quiet village she and her husband peacefully dwelt, avoiding even friendship's intrusion. Times of peace have no historian, and the later career of Mrs. Child had few of what the world calls events. Her domestic labors, her studies, her flowers, and her few guests kept her ever busy. She had never had children of her own,—though, as some one has said, she had a great many of other people's,— but more than one whom she had befriended came to dwell with her after her retirement, and she came forth sometimes to find new beneficiaries. But for many of her kindnesses she did not need to leave home, since they were given in the form least to be expected from a literary woman,—that of pecuniary bounty. Few households in the country contributed on a scale so very liberal, in proportion to their means.

One published letter, however, may serve as a sample of many. It was addressed to an Anti-Slavery Festival at Boston, and not only shows the mode of action adopted by Mr. and Mrs. Child, but their latest opinions as to public affairs:

WAYLAND, January 1, 1868.

DEAR FRIEND PHILLIPS,—We inclose fifty dollars as our subscription to the Anti-Slavery Society. If our means equaled our wishes, we would send a sum as large as the legacy Francis Jackson intended for that purpose, and of which the society was deprived, as we think, by an unjust legal decision. If our sensible and judicious friend could speak to us from the other side of Jordan, we doubt not he would say that the vigilance of the Anti-Slavery Society was never more needed than at the present crisis, and that, consequently, he was never more disposed to aid it liberally. . . .

The British Anti-Slavery Society deserted their post too soon. If they had been as watchful to protect the freed people of the West Indies as they were zealous to emancipate them, that horrid catastrophe in Jamaica might have been avoided. The state of things in those islands warns us how dangerous it is to trust those who have been slaveholders, and those who habitually sympathize with slaveholders, to frame laws and regulations for liberated slaves. As well might wolves be trusted to guard a sheepfold.

We thank God, friend Phillips, that you are preserved and strengthened to be a wakeful sentinel on the watch-tower, ever to warn a drowsy nation against selfish, timid politicians, and dawdling legislators, who manifest no trust either in God or the people.

YOURS FAITHFULLY,
DAVID L. CHILD,
L. MARIA CHILD.

Mrs. Child outlived her husband six years, and died at Wayland, October 20, 1880. She was one of those prominent instances in our literature of persons born for the pursuits of pure intellect, whose intellects were yet balanced by their hearts, both being absorbed in the great moral agitations of the age. "My natural inclinations," she once wrote to me, "drew me much more strongly towards literature and the arts than towards reform, and the weight of conscience was needed to turn the scale." In a community of artists, she would have belonged to that class, for she had that instinct in her soul. But she was placed where there was as yet no exacting literary standard; she wrote better than most of her contemporaries, and well enough for her public. She did not, therefore, win that intellectual immortality which only the very best writers command, and which few Americans have attained. But she won a meed which she would value more highly,—that warmth of sympathy, that mingled gratitude of intellect and heart which men give to those who have faithfully served their day and generation.

14

WILLIAM LLOYD GARRISON

William Lloyd Garrison was born at Newburyport, Mass., December 10, 1805, and died in New York City, May 24, 1879. There passed away in him the living centre of a remarkable group of men and women who have had no equals among us, in certain moral attributes, since the Revolutionary period and perhaps not then. The Earl of Carlisle said of them that they were "fighting a battle without parallel in the history of ancient or modern heroism;" and, without assuming to indorse this strong statement we may yet claim that there was some foundation for it. When we consider the single fact that the "Garrison mob" was composed, by the current assertion of leading journals, of "gentlemen of property and standing," and that the then mayor of the city, wishing to protect the victim, found it necessary to direct that the modest sign of the Ladies' Anti-Slavery Society should be torn down and given to this mob for destruction, we can form some distinct impression of the opposition through which the early abolitionists had to fight their way. Their period was a time when truth was called treason, and when a man who spoke it might be dragged through the streets with a rope round his body. We must remember that men thus decorated do not always find it easy to be tolerant or to exhibit their gentlest side in return. The so-called persecution of reformers is often a thing too trivial to be worth talking about, at least in English-speaking countries. Indeed, it is usually of that slight texture in these days, but in the early anti-slavery period it had something of the heroic quality.

A few years later, when the abolitionists had won the right to have meetings of their own, there could not be a moment's doubt, for any observer, as to the real centre of the gathering. In first looking in upon any old-time convention, any observing eye would promptly have selected Garrison as the leading figure on the platform. His firm and well-built person, his sonorous voice, and the grave and iron strength of his face would have at once indicated this. I never saw a countenance that could be compared to it in respect to moral strength and force; he seemed the visible embodiment of something deeper and more controlling than mere intellect. His utterance was like his face,—grave, powerful, with little variety or play; he had none of that rhetorical relief in which Phillips was so affluent; he was usually monotonous, sometimes fatiguing, but always controlling. His reason marched like an army *without* banners; his invective was scathing, but as it was almost always mainly scriptural, it did not carry an impression of personal anger, but simply seemed like a newly discovered chapter of Ezekiel. He constantly reiterated and intrenched his argument with ample details, and had a journalist's love for newspaper cuttings, which he inflicted without stint upon his audience, bearing down all reluctance with his commanding tones. For one, I cannot honestly say that I ever positively enjoyed one of his speeches, or that I ever failed to listen with a sense of deference and of moral leadership.

At some future period the historian of the anti-slavery movement may decide on the fit award of credit due to each of the various influences that brought about the abolition of slavery. The Garrisonian or Disunion Abolitionists represented the narrowest of the streams which made up the mighty river, but they undoubtedly represented the loftiest height and the greatest head of water. The Garrisonians were generally non-resistants, but those who believed in the physical rescue of fugitive slaves were nevertheless their pupils. The Garrisonians eschewed voting, yet many who voted drew strength from them. The Garrisonians took little part in raising troops for war, but the tradition of their influence did much to impel the army. The only great emotion in which they took no share was the instinct of national devotion to the Union; that sentiment had grown stronger in spite of them, and was largely due to Webster, who had, meanwhile, been led by it to make sacrifices which they had justly condemned. The forces at work during that great period of our nation's life were too complex to be held in any single hand, but it was to Garrison more than to any other man, that the great ultimate result was remotely due. Every other participant seemed to reflect, more or less, the current of popular progress around him; Garrison alone seemed an original and creative force. On this point the verdict of posterity will hardly appeal from the modest self-judgment of Abraham Lincoln when he said: "I have been only an instrument. The logic and moral power of

Garrison and the anti-slavery people of the country and the army have done all."[1]

It now seems, in looking back, as if the anti-slavery movement would have been a comparatively easy thing had the party which assailed slavery been united, and yet this is a drawback which it shared apparently with every great reform that was ever attempted. There raged within the anti-slavery ranks themselves a hostility, whose causes now seem very insufficient, but which vastly embarrassed the whole enterprise. The quarrel between "Old Organization" and "New Organization" certainly embittered for a time the lives of all concerned in it. Beginning partly in a generous protest by Garrison and others against the exclusion of women from a World's Anti-Slavery Convention, but partly also in his views on the Sabbath question and upon other side issues, it ended in the creation of two rival camps, with almost all the anti-slavery clergy and the voting abolitionists on one side, while Garrison and his Spartan band held the other. Some blame, as I always thought, was to be attached to both sides, and the over-vehemence of the contest may be judged from the fact that a leading "Garrisonian" once went so far as to insinuate a doubt whether the stainless Whittier—who was then counted in the other ranks—was "more knave or fool."

It is a very frequent experience of great reformers that they part company by degrees with some of the ablest and most devoted of their early adherents; but perhaps no man ever had so large an accumulation of this painful experience as had the recognized leader of the anti-slavery movement. The list of severed friendships included Benjamin Lundy, whom Garrison properly called "the pioneer" among abolitionists; and William Goodell, whom Garrison described as "a much older and a better soldier" than himself. It included Arthur Tappan, who had paid Garrison's fine when imprisoned at Baltimore; Lewis Tappan, whose house in New York had been sacked by a pro-slavery mob; James G. Birney, who had emancipated his own slaves; and Amos A. Phelps, who had defended Garrison against that Clerical Appeal which made so great a noise in its day. All these men were led by degrees into antagonism to their great leader; it was a permanent division and influenced the whole anti-slavery movement. For this alienation on their part that leader had no mercy; it was always attributed by him simply to "a mighty sectarian conspiracy" or a "jealous and envious spirit." Posterity, less easily satis-

---

[1]See "Lincoln's Conversation with Ex-Governor Chamberlain of South Carolina," in New York *Tribune*, November 4, 1883.

fied, quite disposed to honor the great anti-slavery warrior, but by no means inclined to give him exclusive laurels, will perhaps not wholly indorse this conclusion. I am ready to testify that, at the later period of the contest, and when his personal position was thoroughly established, he seemed wholly patient and considerate with younger recruits. He never demanded that they should see eye to eye with him, but only that they should have what abolitionists called "the root of the matter" in them. But I fear that the weight of testimony goes to show that he had not always been equally moderate in his demands.

The charge most commonly made against him by these early associates was that of manifesting a quality which the pioneer Benjamin Lundy called "arrogance," and the other pioneer, William Goodell, depicted in his article, "How to make a Pope." "You exalt yourself too much," wrote the plain-spoken Elizur Wright. "I pray to God that you may be brought to repent of it." Lewis Tappan at about the same time wrote,—"You speak of 'sedition' and 'chastising' Messrs. Fitch, Towne, and Woodbury: I do not like such language." The most fearless and formidable of all these indictments, because the gentlest and most unwilling, was that of Sarah Grimké. Speaking of the course pursued by Garrison and his immediate circle toward her and her sister, she says: "They wanted us to live out William Lloyd Garrison, not the convictions of our own souls; entirely unaware that they were exhibiting, in the high places of moral reform, the genuine spirit of slaveholding, by wishing to curtail the sacred privilege of conscience."[2]

This was the main complaint made against him from the inside, while the criticism from the outside was, and still is, that of excessive harshness of language. Here again it is to be observed that the charge does not rest on the testimony of enemies, but of friends. We find Harriet Martineau herself saying: "I do not pretend to like or to approve the tone of Garrison's pointed censures. I could not use such language myself toward any class of offenders, nor can I sympathize in its use by others." This was not said in her first book on America, but in her second more deliberate one; and when we consider the kind of language that Miss Martineau found herself able to use, this disclaimer becomes very forcible. What such critics overlooked and still overlook, is that the whole vocabulary of Garrison was the logical result of that stern school of old-fashioned Calvinism in which he had been trained. "The least of sins is infinite," says the Roman Catholic poet, Faber. This was the logical attitude of Calvinism, and apparently of the youthful reformer's mind. At twenty-

---

[2] *The Sisters Grimké*, p. 220.

three he wrote: "It is impossible to estimate the depravity and wickedness of those who, at the present day, reject the gospel of Jesus Christ." When a young man begins with such vehemence of epithet, in matters of abstract belief, is it to be supposed that when he is called upon to cope with an institution which even the milder Wesley called "The sum of all villanies," he will suddenly develop the habit of scrupulous moderation? "I will be harsh as truth," he said. The only question is, Was he never any harsher?

That there was such a thing possible as undue harshness in speaking of individual slaveholders the abolitionists themselves were compelled sometimes to admit. When Charles Remond, the eloquent colored orator, called George Washington a villain, Wendell Phillips replied, "Charles, the epithet is infelicitous." Yet if, as was constantly assumed by Garrison, the whole moral sin of slaveholding rested on the head of each individual participant, it is difficult to see why the epithet was not admirably appropriate. The point of doubt is whether it did so rest,—but if it did, Remond was right. Such extreme statements were not always thus rebuked. When a slaveholder was once speaking in an anti-slavery convention, he was flatly contradicted by Stephen Foster, who was, perhaps, next to Garrison, the hardest hitter among the abolitionists. "Do you think I would lie?" retorted the slaveholder. "Why not?" said Foster. "I know you steal." This Draconian inflexibility, finding the least of sins worthy of death, and having no higher penalty for the greatest, was a very common code upon the anti-slavery platform. It was a part of its power, but it brought also a certain weakness, as being really based upon an untruth.

Consider this matter for a moment. Men are not merely sometimes, but very often, better than the laws under which they live. Garrison wrote in one case:—

"For myself, I hold no fellowship with slave-owners. I will not make a truce with them even for a single hour. I blush for them as countrymen. I *know* that they are not *Christians;* and the higher they raise their professions of patriotism or piety, the stronger is my detestation of their hypocrisy. They are dishonest and cruel,—and God and the angels and devils and the universe know that *they are without excuse.*"[3]

"Without excuse!" Set aside all the facts of ignorance, of heredity, of environment, of all that makes excuse in charitable minds when judging sin, and look at this one point only,—the tremendous practical difficulties studiously accumulated by skillful lawgivers in the way of sundering

---

[3] *William Lloyd Garrison: The Story of his Life*, i. 208.

the relation between master and the slave. In all the great States of South Carolina, Georgia, Alabama, and Mississippi, a man becoming heir to human property was absolutely prohibited from emancipating it except by a special authority of the legislature, a permission usually impossible to get. In one of these States, Mississippi, it was also required that the legislature itself could grant freedom only for some special act of public or private service on the part of the individual slave, and the same restriction was made in North Carolina, with the substitution of the county court for the legislature as authority. In every one of these States the slave-owner, had he been Garrison himself, was as powerless to free his slaves without the formal consent of the state authorities as he would have been to swim the Atlantic with those slaves on his back; and yet these men were said to be "without excuse." Even in Virginia the converted slaveholder was met with the legal requirement that the freed slaves must be removed from the State within a certain time, in default of which they would be sold at auction to the highest bidder. Slavery itself had often impoverished the owner, so that he could not personally remove the slaves, and the auction-block was to all these poor people the last of all tragedies. Even Birney, it will be remembered, freed his slaves in Kentucky, while Palfrey freed his in Louisiana, the laws of both these States being exceptionally mild. The more we dwell on this complicated situation, the more impressed we become with the vast wrong of the institution and of its avowed propagandists; but the more charitable we become towards those exceptional slaveholders who had begun to open their eyes to its evils, yet found themselves bound hand and foot by its laws. In view of this class of facts, such general arraignments as that above cited from Garrison appear to me to have been too severe.[4]

The hostility of Garrison to the voting Abolitionists did not merely take the form of disapproval and distrust as being organized by men who had revolted from his immediate leadership, but he convinced himself that their political action was contemptible and even ludicrous. When an anti-slavery candidate was first nominated for the presidency, he called it "folly, presumption, almost unequaled infatuation," and if he varied from this attitude of contempt it was to "denounce it," in his own words, "as the worst form of pro-slavery." But when the Liberty party had expanded into the Free-Soil party, and that again into the Republican party, much of the old bitterness waned, and some of the political anti-slavery leaders, especially Sumner and Wilson, were in constant and hearty intercourse with the Garrisonian apostles. At this later period, at

---

[4]Stroud's *Slave Laws*, pp. 146–51.

least, as I have already said, there was visible none of that exacting or domineering spirit which had been earlier attributed to him.

Every candid estimate of Garrison's career must always end, it would seem, at substantially the same point. While not faultless, he kept far higher laws than he broke. He did the work of a man of iron in an iron age, so that even those who recognized his faults might well join, as they did, in the chorus of affectionate congratulations that marked his closing days. His fame is secure, and all the securer because time has enabled us to recognize, more clearly than at first, precisely what he did, and just what were the limitations of his temperament. It is a striking fact that in the Valhalla of contemporary statues in his own city, only two, those of Webster and Everett, commemorate those who stood for the party of conservatism in the great anti-slavery conflict; while all the rest, Lincoln, Quincy, Sumner, Andrew, Mann, Garrison, and Shaw represent the party of attack. It is the verdict of time, confirming in bronze and marble the great words of Emerson, "What forests of laurel we bring, and the tears of mankind, to those who stood firm against the opinion of their contemporaries!"

15

FOURTEEN YEARS LATER

Nothing in actual life can come so near the experience of Rip Van Winkle as to revisit war scenes after a dozen years of peace. Alice's adventures in Wonderland, when she finds herself dwarfed after eating the clover leaf, do not surpass the sense of insignificance that comes over any one who once wore uniform when he enters, as a temporary carpet-bagger, some city which he formerly ruled or helped to rule with absolute sway. An ex-commander of colored troops has this advantage, that the hackmen and longshore-men may remember him if nobody else does; and he at once possesses that immense practical convenience which comes only from a personal acquaintance with what are called the humbler classes. In a strange place, if one can establish relations with a black waiter or a newspaper correspondent, all doors fly open. The patronage of the great is powerless in comparison.

When I had last left Jacksonville, Florida, in March, 1864, the town was in flames: the streets were full of tongues of fire creeping from house to house; the air was dense with lurid smoke. Our steamers dropped rapidly down the river, laden to the gunwale with the goods of escaping inhabitants. The black soldiers, guiltless of all share in the flames, were yet excited by the occasion, recalled their favorite imagery of the Judgment Day, and sang and shouted without ceasing. I never saw a wilder scene. Fourteen years after, the steamboat came up to the same wharf, and I stepped quietly ashore into what seemed a summer watering-place: the roses were in bloom, the hotel verandas were full of guests, there were gay shops in the street, the wharves were covered with merchandise and with people. The delicious air was the same, the trees were the same; all else was changed. The earth-works we had built were leveled and overgrown; there was a bridge at the ford we used to picket; the church in whose steeple we built a lookout was still there, but it had a new tower, planned for peaceful purposes only. The very railroad along which we skirmished almost daily was now torn up, and a new track entered the town at a different point. I could not find even the wall which one of our men clambered over, loading and firing, with a captured goose between his legs. Only the blue sky and the soft air, the lovely atmosphere of Florida, remained; the distant line of woods had the same outlook, and when the noon guns began to be fired for Washington's birthday I could hardly convince myself that the roar was not that of our gunboats, still shelling the woods as they had done so many years before. Then the guns ceased; the past withdrew into yet deeper remoteness. It seemed as if I were the only man left on earth to recall it. An hour later, the warm grasp of some of my old soldiers dispelled the dream of oblivion.

I had a less vivid sense of change at Beaufort, South Carolina, so familiar to many during the war. The large white houses still look peacefully down the placid river, but there are repairs and paint everywhere, and many new houses or cabins have been built. There is a new village, called Port Royal, at the railroad terminus, about a mile from my first camp at Old Fort plantation; and there is also a station near Beaufort itself, approached by a fine shell-road. The fortifications on the old shell-road have almost disappeared; the freedmen's village near them, named after the present writer, blew away one day in a tornado, and returned no more. A great national cemetery is established near its site. There are changes enough, and yet the general effect of the town is unaltered; there is Northern energy there, and the discovery of valuable phosphates has opened a new branch of industry; but after all it is the same pleasant old sleepy Beaufort, and no military Rip Van Winkle need feel himself too rudely aroused.

However, I went South not to see places, but people. On the way from Washington I lingered for a day or two to visit some near kinsfolk in Virginia, formerly secessionists to a man, or, to be more emphatic, to a woman. Then I spent a Sunday in Richmond, traversed rapidly part of North Carolina and Georgia, spent a day and two nights in Charleston, two days at Beaufort, and visited various points in Florida, going as far as St. Augustine. I had not set foot in the Southern States for nearly fourteen years, but I remembered them vividly across that gap of time, and also recalled very distinctly a winter visit to Virginia during college days. With these memories ever present, it was to me a matter of great interest to observe the apparent influence of freedom on the colored people, and the relation between them and the whites.

And first, as to the material condition of the former slaves. Sydney Smith, revisiting Edinburgh in 1821, after ten years' absence, was struck with the "wonderful increase of shoes and stockings, streets and houses." The change as to the first item, in South Carolina, tells the story of social progress since emancipation. The very first of my old acquaintances whom I met in that region was the robust wife of one of my soldiers. I found her hoeing in a field, close beside our old camp-ground. I had seen that woman hoeing in the same field fifteen years before. The same sky was above her, the same soil beneath her feet; but the war was over, slavery was gone. The soil that had been her master's was now her own by purchase; and the substantial limbs that trod it were no longer bare and visibly black, but incased in red-striped stockings of the most conspicuous design. "Think of it!" I said to a clever Massachusetts damsel in Washington, "the whole world so changed, and yet that woman still hoes." "In hose," quoth the lively maiden; and I preserve for posterity the condensed epigram.

Besides the striped stockings, which are really so conspicuous that the St. Augustine light-house is painted to match them, one sees a marked, though moderate progress in all the comforts of life. Formerly the colored people of the sea islands, even in their first days of freedom, slept very generally on the floor; and when our regimental hospital was first fitted up, the surgeon found with dismay that the patients had regarded the beds as merely beautiful ornaments, and had unanimously laid themselves down in the intervening spaces. Now I noticed bedstead and bedding in every cabin I visited in South Carolina and Florida. Formerly the cabins often had no tables, and families rarely ate together, each taking food as was convenient; but now they seemed to have family meals, a step toward decent living. This progress they themselves recognized. Moreover, I often saw pictures from the illustrated papers on the wall, and the children's school-books on the shelf. I rarely met an ex-soldier who did not own his house and ground, the inclosures varying from five to two hundred acres; and I found one man on the St. John's who had been offered $3000 for his real estate. In many cases these homesteads had been bought within a few years, showing a steady progress in self-elevation.

I do not think the world could show a finer sample of self-respecting peasant life than a colored woman, with whom I came down the St. John's River to Jacksonville, from one of the little settlements along that magnificent stream. She was a freed slave, the wife of a former soldier, and was going to market, basket in hand, with her little boy by her side. She had the tall erect figure, clear black skin, thin features, fine teeth, and intelligent bearing that marked so many of my Florida soldiers. She was dressed very plainly, but with scrupulous cleanliness: a rather faded gingham dress, well-worn tweed sack, shoes and stockings, straw hat with plain black ribbon, and neat white collar and cuffs. She told me that she and her husband owned one hundred and sixty acres of land, bought and paid for by their own earnings, at $1.25 per acre; they had a log-house, and were going to build a frame-house; they raised for themselves all the food they needed, except meat and flour, which they bought in Jacksonville. They had a church within reach (Baptist); a school-house of forty pupils, taught by a colored teacher; her husband belonged to the Good Templars, as did all the men in their neighborhood. For miles along the St. John's, a little back from the river, such settlements are scattered; the men cultivating their own plots of ground, or working on the steam-boats, or fishing, or lumbering. What more could be expected of any race, after fifteen years of freedom? Are the Irish voters of New York their superiors in condition, or the factory operatives of Fall River?

I met perhaps a hundred men, in different places, who had been under my command, and whose statements I could trust. Only one of these complained of poverty; and he, as I found, earned good wages, had neither wife nor child to support, and was given to whisky. There were some singular instances of prosperity among these men. I was told in Jacksonville that I should find Corporal McGill "de most populous man in Beaufort." When I got there, I found him the proprietor of a livery stable populous with horses at any rate; he was worth $3000 or $4000, and was cordial and hospitable to the last degree. At parting, he drove me to the station with his best carriage and horses; and I regret to add that while he was refusing all compensation his young steeds ran away, and as the train whirled off I saw my "populous" corporal double-quick down the shell-road, to recapture his equipage. I found Sergeant Hodges a master carpenter at Jacksonville; Corporal Hicks was a preacher there, highly respected; and I heard of Corporal Sutton as a traveling minister farther up the river. Sergeant Shemeltella, a fine-looking half-Spaniard from St. Augustine, now patrols, with gun in hand, the woods which we once picketed at Port Royal Ferry, and supplies game to the markets of Charleston and Savannah. And without extending the list I may add that some of these men, before attaining prosperity, had to secure, by the severest experience, the necessary judgment in business affairs. It will hardly be believed that the men of my regiment alone sunk $30,000 in an impracticable building association, and in the purchase of a steam-boat which was lost uninsured. One of the shrewdest among them, after taking his share of this, resolved to be prudent, put $750 in the Freed-men's Bank, and lost that too. Their present prosperity must be judged in the light of such formidable calamities as these.

I did not hear a single charge of laziness made against the freed col-ored people in the States I visited. In Virginia it was admitted that they would work wherever they were paid, but that many were idle for want of employment. Rev. Dr. Pinckney, in a recent address before the Charleston Historical Society, declares that the negroes "do not refuse to work; all are planting;" and he only complains that they work unskill-fully. A rice-planter in Georgia told me that he got his work done more efficiently than under the slave system. Men and women worked well for seventy-five cents a day; many worked under contract, which at first they did not understand or like. On the other hand, he admitted, the planters did not at once learn how to manage them as freedmen, but had ac-quired the knowledge by degrees; so that even the strikes at harvest-time, which had at first embarrassed them, were now avoided. Another Georgia planter spoke with much interest of an effort now making by the colored people in Augusta to establish a cotton factory of their own, in emulation of the white factories which have there been so successful. He said that this proposed factory was to have a capital of fifty thousand dollars in fifty dollar shares, and that twenty-eight thousand dollars of it were already raised. The white business agent of one of the existing fac-tories was employed, he said, as the adviser of those organizing this. He spoke of it with interest as a proper outlet for the industry of the better class of colored people, who were educated rather above field labor. He also spoke with pride of the normal school for colored people at Atlanta.

The chief of police in Beaufort, South Carolina, a colored man, told me that the colored population there required but little public assis-tance, though two thousand of them had removed from the upper parts of the State within a year and a half, thinking they could find better wages at Beaufort. This removal struck me as being of itself a favorable indication, showing that they were now willing to migrate, whereas they were once hopelessly fixed to the soil, and therefore too much in the power of the land owners. The new industry of digging phosphates for exportation to England employs a good many in Beaufort County, and they earn by this from seventy-five cents to a dollar a day. Others are em-ployed in loading vessels at the new settlement of Port Royal; but the work is precarious and insufficient, and I was told that if they made two dollars a week they did well. But it must be remembered that they have mostly little patches of land of their own, and can raise for themselves the corn and vegetables on which they chiefly live. I asked an old man if he could supply his family from his own piece of ground. "Oh, yes, mars'r," he said (the younger men do not say "mars'r," but "boss"), and then he went on, with a curious accumulation of emphasis: "I raise plenty too, much more dan I destroy,"—meaning simply "very much more."

The price of cotton is now very low, and the sea-island cotton has lost forever, perhaps, its place in the English market. Yet Rev. Dr. Pinckney, in the address just quoted, while lamenting the ravages of war in the sea islands, admits that nearly half as much cotton was raised in them in 1875 as in 1860, and more than half as much corn, the population being about the same, and the area cultivated less than one third. To adopt his figures, the population in 1860 was 40,053; acres under cultivation, 274,015; corn, 618,959 bushels; cotton, 19,121 bales. In 1875 the population was 43,060; acres under cultivation, 86,449; corn, 314,271 bushels; cotton, 8199 bales.

When we consider the immense waste of war, the destruction of capital, the abandonment of estates by those who yet refuse to sell them, and the partial introduction of industry other than agricultural, this seems to me a promising exhibit. And when we observe how much more equitable than formerly is now the distribution of the products between capitalist and laborer, the case is still better. Dr. Pinckney's utmost complaint in regard to South Carolina is that the result of the war "has been injurious to the whites, and not beneficial to the blacks." Even he, a former slaveholder, does not claim that it has injured the blacks; and this, from his point of view, is quite a concession. Twenty years hence he may admit that whatever the result of war may have been, that of peace will be beneficial to both races.

In observing a lately emancipated race, it is always harder to judge as to the condition of the women than of the men, especially where the men alone have been enfranchised. My friend the judge, in Virginia, declared that the colored men and women were there so unlike that they seemed like different races: the men had behaved "admirably," he said; the women were almost hopelessly degraded. On the other hand, my white friends of both sexes at Beaufort took just the opposite view, and thought the women there quite superior to the men, especially in respect to whisky. Perhaps the influences of the two regions may have made the difference, as the sea islands have had the presence, ever since the beginning of the war, of self-devoted and well-educated teachers, mostly women, while such teachers have been much rarer in Virginia. They have also been rare in Florida; but then the Florida negroes are a superior class.

Certainly it was pleasant to me to hear favorable accounts of this and that particular colored woman of whom I had known something in war times. Almost the first old acquaintance named to me on the sea islands, for instance, was one Venus, whose marriage to a soldier of my regiment I chronicled in war times. "Now, cunnel," said that soldier in confidence, "I want for get me one good lady." And when I asked one of his friends about the success of the effort, he said triumphantly, "John's gwine for marry Venus." Now the record of Venus as a good lady was so very questionable in her earlier incarnations that the name was not encouraging; but I was delighted to hear of the goddess, fifteen years later, as a most virtuous wife and a very efficient teacher of sewing in Miss Botume's school. Her other sewing-teacher, by the way, is Juno.

I went into schools, here and there; the colored people seemed to value them very much, and to count upon their own votes as a means of securing these advantages, instead of depending, as formerly, on Northern aid. The schools I visited did not seem to me so good as those kept by Northern ladies during the war, at Port Royal; but the present schools form a part of a public system, and are in that respect better, while enough of the Northern teachers still remain to exert a beneficial influence, at least on the sea islands. I was sorry to be in Charleston only on Saturday, when the Shaw Memorial School was not in session. This is a large wooden building, erected on land bought with part of a fund collected in the colored regiments for a monument to Colonel Shaw. This school has an average attendance of five hundred and twenty, with twelve teachers, white and black. The Morris Street School for colored children, in Charleston, has fourteen hundred pupils. These two schools occupy nearly half of the four columns given by the Charleston News and Courier of April 12, 1878, to the annual exhibition of public schools. The full programme of exercises is given, with the names of the pupils receiving prizes and honors; and it seems almost incredible that the children whose successes are thus proudly recorded can be the sons and daughters of freed slaves. And I hold it utterly ungenerous, in view of such facts, to declare that the white people of the South have learned nothing by experience, and are "incapable of change."

Public officials at Beaufort told me that in that place most of the men could now sign their names,—certainly a great proof of progress since war times. I found some of my friends anxious lest school should unfit the young people for the hard work of the field; but I saw no real proof of this, nor did the parents confirm it. Miss Botume, however, said that the younger women now thought that, after marriage, they ought to be excused from field labor, if they took care of their homes and children; a proposal so directly in the line of advancing civilization that one can hardly object to it. The great solicitude of some of the teachers in that region relates to the passage of some congressional bill which shall set aside the tax sales under which much real estate is now held; but others think that there is no fear of this, even under a democratic administration.

This leads naturally to the question, What is to be the relation between the two races in those Southern States of which I speak? I remember that Corporal Simon Crier, one of the oddities of my regiment, used to declare that when the war was over, he should go to "Libery;" and, when pressed for a reason, used to say, "Dese yer secesh will neber be cibilized in my time." Yet Simon Crier's time is not ended, for I heard of him as peacefully dwelling near Charleston, and taking no part in that insignificant colonization movement of which we hear so much more at the North than at the South. Taking civilization in his sense,—a fair enough sense,—we shall find Virginia, South Carolina, and Florida holding an intermediate position; being probably behind North Carolina, West Virginia, and the border States, but decidedly in advance of Georgia, Alabama, and Mississippi.

It is certain that there is, in the States I visited, a condition of outward peace and no conspicuous outrages; and that this has now been the case for many months. All will admit that this state of things must be a blessing, unless there lies beneath it some covert plan for crushing or reënslaving the colored race. I know that a few good men at the North honestly believe in the existence of some such plan; I can only say that I thoroughly disbelieve in it. Taking the nature of the Southern whites as these very men describe it,—impulsive and ungoverned,—it is utterly inconceivable that such a plan, if formed, should not show itself in some personal ill usage of the blacks, in the withdrawal of privileges, in legislation endangering their rights. I can assert that, carrying with me the eyes of a tolerably suspicious abolitionist, I saw none of these indications. During the war, I could hardly go anywhere within the Union lines for twenty-four hours without being annoyed by some sign of race hostility, or being obliged to interfere for the protection of some abused man or woman. During this trip, I had absolutely no occasion for any such attitude. The change certainly has not resulted from any cringing demeanor on the part of the blacks, for they show much more manhood than they once did. I am satisfied that it results from the changed feeling created towards a race of freedmen and voters. How can we ask more of the States formerly in rebellion than that they should be abreast of New England in granting rights and privileges to the colored race? Yet this is now the case in the three States I name; or at least if they fall behind at some points, they lead at some points. Let us look at a few instances.

The republican legislature of Connecticut has just refused to incorporate a colored military company; but the colored militia regiment of Charleston was reviewed by General Hampton and his staff just before my visit. One of the colored officers told me that there was absolutely no difference in the treatment accorded this regiment and that shown toward the white militia, who were reviewed the day before; and Messrs. Whipper and Jones, the only dissatisfied republican leaders whom I saw, admitted that there was no opposition whatever to this arming of the blacks. I may add that while I was in Virginia a bill was reported favorably in the legislature for the creation of a colored militia company, called the State Guard, under control of their own officers, and reporting directly to the adjutant-general.

I do not know a Northern city which enrolls colored citizens in its police, though this may here and there have happened. I saw colored policemen in Charleston, Beaufort, and Jacksonville, though the former city is under democratic control; and I was told by a leading colored man that the number had lately been increased in Charleston, and that one lieutenant of police was of that race. The republican legislature of Rhode Island has just refused once more to repeal the bill prohibiting intermarriages, while the legislature of South Carolina has refused to pass such a bill. I can remember when Frederick Douglass was ejected from the railway cars in Massachusetts, because of his complexion; and it is not many years since one of the most cultivated and ladylike colored teachers in the nation was ejected from a street car in Philadelphia, her birthplace, for the same reason. But I rode with colored people in first-class cars throughout Virginia and South Carolina, and in street cars in Richmond and Charleston. I am told that this last is the case also in Savannah and New Orleans, but can testify only to what I have seen. In Georgia, I was told, the colored people were not allowed in first-class cars; but they had always a decent second-class car, opening from the smoking-car, with the door usually closed between.

All these things may be true, and still a great deal may remain to be done; but it is idle to declare that the sun has not risen because we do not yet see it in the zenith. Even the most extreme Southern newspapers constantly contain paragraphs that amaze us, not only in contrast to slavery times, but in contrast to the times immediately following the war. While I was in South Carolina the Charleston *News and Courier* published, with commendation, the report of a bill, passed by the Maryland legislature, admitting colored lawyers to practice, after the court of appeals had excluded them; and it copied with implied approval the re-mark of the Baltimore Gazette: "Raise the educational test, the rigidity of the examinations for admission, or the moral test as high as you please, but let us have done with the color test."

It is certain that every republican politician whom I saw in South Carolina, black or white, spoke well of Governor Hampton, with two exceptions,—Mr. W. J. Whipper, whom Governor Chamberlain refused to commission as judge, and Mr. Jones, who was clerk of the house of delegates through its most corrupt period. I give their dissent for what it is worth, but the opinion of others was as I have said. "We have no complaint to make of Governor Hampton; he has kept his pledges," was the general remark. For instance, a bill passed both houses by a party vote, requiring able-bodied male prisoners, under sentence in county jails, to work on the public roads and streets. The colored people remonstrated strongly, regarding it as aimed at them. Governor Hampton vetoed the bill, and the house, on reflection, sustained the veto by a vote of one hundred and two to ten. But he is not always so strong in influence: there is a minority of "fire-eaters" who resist him; he is denounced by the "upcountry people" as an aristocrat; and I was told that he might yet need the colored vote to sustain him against his own party. Grant that this assumes him to be governed by self-interest; that strengthens the value of this evidence. We do not expect that saints will have the monopoly of government at South or North; what we need is to know that the colored vote in South Carolina makes itself felt as a power, and secures its rightful ends.

The facts here stated are plain and unquestionable. When we come to consider the political condition of the former slaves, we find greater difficulties in taking in the precise position. First, it must be remembered that even at the North the practical antagonism towards colored voters lasted long after their actual enfranchisement, and has worn out only by degrees. Samuel Breck, in his very entertaining reminiscences, tells us that in Philadelphia, in the early part of this century, the colored voters seldom dared to come to the polls, for fear of ill usage. Then we must remember that in South Carolina, the State which has been most under discussion in this essay, the colored voters were practically massed, for years, under the banner of spoliation, and the antagonism created was hardly less intense than that created by the Tweed dynasty in New York. As far as I can judge, neither the "carpet-bag" frauds nor the "Ku-Klux" persecutions have been exaggerated, and they certainly kept each other alive, and have, at least temporarily, ceased together. No doubt the atrocities committed by the whites were the worst, inasmuch as murder is worse than robbery, but few in South Carolina will now deny that the provocation was simply enormous.

And it is moreover true that this state of things left bad blood behind it, which will long last. It has left jealousies which confound the innocent with the guilty. Judging the future by the past, the white South Carolinian finds it almost impossible to believe that a republican state administration can be decently honest. This is a feeling quite apart from any national attitude, and quite consistent with a fair degree of loyalty. Nor does it take the form of resistance to colored voters as such. The Southern whites accept them precisely as Northern men in cities accept the ignorant Irish vote,—not cheerfully, but with acquiescence in the inevitable; and when the strict color-line is once broken they are just as ready to conciliate the negro as the Northern politician to flatter the Irishman. Any powerful body of voters may be cajoled to-day and intimidated to-morrow and hated always, but it can never be left out of sight. At the South, politics are an absorbing interest: people are impetuous; they divide and subdivide on all local issues, and each faction needs votes. Two men are up for mayor or sheriff, or what not: each conciliates every voter he can reach, and each finds it for his interest to stand by those who help him. This has been long predicted by shrewd observers, and is beginning to happen all over the South. I heard of a dozen instances of it. Indeed, the vote of thanks passed by the Mississippi legislature to its colored senator, Mr. Bruce, for his vote on the silver bill was only the same thing on a larger scale. To praise him was to censure Mr. Lamar.

It may be said, "Ah, but the real test is, Will the black voters be allowed to vote for the republican party?" To assert this crowning right will undoubtedly demand a good deal of these voters; it will require courage, organization, intelligence, honesty, and leaders. Without these, any party, in any State, will sooner or later go to the wall. As to South Carolina, I can only say that one of the ablest republican lawyers in the State, a white man, unsuspected of corruption, said to me, "This is a republican State, and to prove it such we need only to bring out our voters. For this we do not need troops, but that half a dozen well-known Northern republicans should canvass the State, just as if it were a Northern State. The colored voters need to know that the party at the North has not, as they have been told, deserted them. With this and a perfectly clean list of nominees, we can carry the legislature, making no nominations against Hampton." "But," I asked, "would not these meetings be broken up?" "Not one of them," he said. "They will break up our local meetings, but not those held by speakers from other States. It would ruin them with the nation." And this remark was afterwards indorsed by others, white and black. When I asked one of the few educated colored leaders in the State, "Do you regret the withdrawal of the troops by President Hayes?" "No," he said; "the only misfortune was that they were not withdrawn two years earlier. That would have put us on our good behavior, obliged us to command respect, and made it easier to save the republican party. But it can still be saved."

There is no teacher so wholesome as personal necessity. In South Carolina a few men and many women cling absolutely to the past, learning nothing, forgetting nothing. But the bulk of thinking men see that the old Southern society is as absolutely annihilated as the feudal system, and that there is no other form of society now possible except such as prevails at the North and West. "The purse-proud Southerner," said Rev. Dr. Pinckney, in his address at Charleston, "is an institution which no longer exists. The race has passed away as completely as the Saurian tribes, whose bones we are now digging from the fossil beds of the Ashley." "The Yankees ought to be satisfied," said one gentleman to me: "every live man at the South is trying with all his might to be a Yankee." Business, money, financial prosperity,—these now form the absorbing Southern question. At the Exchange Hotel in Richmond, where I spent a Sunday, the members of the Assembly were talking all day about the debt,—how to escape bankruptcy. I did not overhear the slightest allusion to the negro or the North. It is likely enough that this may lead to claims on the national treasury, but it tends to nothing worse. The dream of reënslaving the negro, if it ever existed, is like the negro's dream, if he ever had it, of five acres and a mule from the government. Both races have long since come down to the stern reality of self-support. No sane Southerner would now take back as slaves, were they offered, a race of men who have been for a dozen years freemen and voters.

Every secessionist risked his all upon secession, and has received as the penalty of defeat only poverty. It is the mildest punishment ever inflicted after an unsuccessful civil war, and it proves in this case a blessing in disguise. Among Southern young men it has made energy and industry fashionable. Formerly, if a Southern planter wished to travel, he borrowed money on his coming crop, or sold a slave or two. Now he must learn what John Randolph, of Roanoke, once announced as the philosopher's stone, to "pay as you go." The Northern traveler asks himself, Where are the white people of the South? You meet few in public conveyances; you see no crowd in the streets. In the hotels of Washington you rarely hear the Southern accent, and, indeed, my Virginia friends declared that some of its more marked intonations were growing unfashionable. Out of one hundred and three Southern representatives in Congress, only twenty-three have their families with them. On one of the few day trains from Washington to Richmond, there was but one first-class car, and there were not twenty passengers, mostly from the Northern States. Among some fifty people on the steamboat from Savannah to Jacksonville, there were not six Southerners. Everywhere you hear immigration desired and emigration recognized as a fact. My friend the judge talked to me eloquently about the need of more Northern settlers, and the willingness of all to receive them; the plantations would readily be broken up to accommodate any purchaser who had money. But within an hour, his son, a young law student, told me that as soon as he was admitted to the bar he should go West.

The first essential to social progress at the South is that each State should possess local self-government. The States have been readmitted as States, and can no more be treated as Territories than you can replace a bird in the egg. They must now work out their own salvation, just as much as Connecticut and New Jersey. If any abuses exist, the remedy is not to be found in federal interference, except in case of actual insurrection, but in the voting power of the blacks, so far as they have strength or skill to assert it; and where that fails, in their power of locomotion. They must leave those counties or States which ill-use them for others which treat them better. If a man is dissatisfied with the laws of Massachusetts, and cannot get them mended, he can at least remove into Rhode Island or Connecticut, and the loss of valuable citizens will soon make itself felt.

This is the precise remedy possessed by the colored people at the South, with the great advantage that they have the monopoly of all the leading industries, and do not need the whites more, on the whole, than the whites need them. They have reached the point where civilized methods begin to prevail. When they have once enlisted the laws of political economy on their side, this silent ally will be worth more than an army with banners.

PART TWO

Colonel of the
First Black Regiment

The first man who organizes and commands a
successful black regiment will perform the most
important service in the history of the war.

MARY THACHER HIGGINSON, *Thomas Wentworth Higginson* (1914)

S outhern Barbarity: Lynching Outrages" (p. 136) had snuffed out the
hope Higginson had placed in the "better class" of white politicians
in the South. The triumph of white supremacy that was cause and consequence of these wrongs continued and had not been corrected by the
end of his life.

The reunion of the North and South had been achieved at the expense
of Americans of African ancestry. The "betrayal of the Negro," as the historian Rayford W. Logan called it in *The Negro in American Life and
Thought: The Nadir, 1877–1901* (The Dial Press, Inc., New York, 1954),
was being completed in the opening decade of the twentieth century.

Higginson's response to this situation after the war was to draw on his
recollections of his army service with the black regiment as recorded in
his book, and on his experience in the prewar abolitionist period as well.
Personal relations with men serving under him who had been slaves
only weeks, in some cases days, before they enlisted supplied evidence
that enabled him to object to the defamation of blacks as a class, as an
excuse for this betrayal of their rights.

"The Black Troops: Intensely Human" (Chapter 1) is a brief for a dissent from the majority—in the North as well as the South—who had

come to accept the existence of a two-caste society. Defying the racial views that dictated the outlawing of interracial marriage and segregation in schools and public transportation, and lent themselves as pretexts for lynchings at the ghastly average rate of one hundred per year as a form of social control, he concluded: "As the memories of the slave period fade away, the mere fetich [sic] of colorphobia will cease to control our society, and marriage may come to be founded, not upon the color of the skin, but on the common courtesies of life and upon genuine sympathies of heart and mind."

Even today, that point of view would be thought fairly progressive in many areas of the United States, radical in a few, and revolutionary in some backwaters. Deriving from his experience as an abolitionist and his service as an officer, the evidence in the book he was enabled to create, *Army Life in a Black Regiment* (Norton, 1984), would serve well in the patriotic "dialogue on race," currently aimed at bringing unity between African Americans and Americans of other ethnicities.

Higginson could have had the eventual utility of his experience in mind as he wrote the book that concluded with the words "It was their demeanor under arms that shamed the nation into recognizing them as men." Joy not only at fighting but also in anticipation of fighting would prove the entitlement to freedom that he had in mind when he said: "I had been an abolitionist too long, and had known and loved John Brown too well, not to feel a thrill of joy at last on finding myself in the position where he only wished to be."

He knew that he was on no romantic expedition, was aware that "the first man who organizes and commands a black regiment will perform the most important service in the history of the war."

The book's value as an aid to interracial understanding should not distract from appreciation of its literary value—in short, as a good read. "Negro Spirituals," "Camp Diary," and "The Negro as Soldier" (Chapters 2, 3, and 4) are included here.

The quality of Higginson's writing on his army experience has been unanimously affirmed by critics since it returned to print in 1962—and even before then. Peter Prescott, writing in *Newsweek* in 1955, when the book had been out of print for decades, called it a "forgotten masterpiece . . . almost a poem." Maxwell Geismar praised its "unusual literary poise and grace"; Edmund Wilson called Higginson's writing "elegant"; and *The New Republic* called it the "finest personal history to come out of the Civil War, but who knows anyone who ever heard of it?"

In an introduction to the Beacon Press edition of the book, edited by the noted historian John Hope Franklin, the equally noted sociologist E.

Franklin Frazier wrote of the "wide appeal" of the book, adding that "most important, it will appeal to the intelligent general reader because of the deep understanding of human nature and the broad sympathies of Higginson who represents one of the main intellectual and humanistic traditions in American society."

The question remains as to why the book remained a forgotten, neglected masterpiece for so long; this neglect seems especially curious in light of the prominent activities of so many Civil War buffs.

It was not easy to choose the three segments of *Army Life in a Black Regiment* among those available, but at least one can say that the selections do not disrupt a narrative. "Negro Spirituals" and "The Negro as Soldier"—like most of the book—were originally published quite independently as self-contained pieces.

It is worth adding that the piece on Negro spirituals was a pioneering first treatment of this subject in writing, which the knowledgeable in that branch of folk music treat as a classic.

More than one critic (but no African American) has offered the view that passages in parts of the book are "patronizing" or "condescending." Similar sentiment was voiced more than a score of years ago, in 1966, by a materials-recommendation committee of the New York City Board of Education—whose president, ironically, had informed the writer only a few years before that he "did not know" that "Negroes had fought for the Union in the Civil War."

A rejoinder came from Septima Clark, chief of the Citizen Education Program of Martin Luther King's Southern Leadership Conference. Herself the daughter of a slave, familiar with the dialect that still prevails among the inhabitants of the Sea Islands, she wrote: "The dialect is surely not exaggerated, and both black and white spoke it alike. There is no condescension, but a real spirit of understanding while working with a deprived group willing to protect its country."

1

THE BLACK TROOPS: "INTENSELY HUMAN"

When Major-General Rufus Saxton, then military governor of South Carolina, was solving triumphantly the original problem of the emancipated slaves, he was frequently interrupted by long lists of questions from Northern philanthropists as to the progress of his enterprise. They inquired especially as to the peculiar tastes, temptations, and perils of the newly emancipated race. After receiving one unusually elaborate catechism of this kind, he said rather impatiently to his secretary, "Draw a line across that whole list of questions about the freedmen, and write at the bottom, 'They are intensely human,'" which was done. In those four words is given, in my opinion, the whole key to that problem perennially reviving,—the so-called "negro question."

There prevailed, nearly sixty years ago, at the outset of the anti-slavery movement, a curious impression that the only people who understood the negro were those who had seen him in a state of subjection, and that those who advocated his cause at the North knew nothing about him. A similar delusion prevails at the present day, and not alone among those born and bred in the Southern states. I find in a book, otherwise admirable,—a recent Life of Whittier,—that the biographer not only speaks of the original anti-slavery movement as "extravagant and ill-informed," but says of Whittier and his associates, "Of the real negro, his capacities and limitations, he had, like his fellows, only a dim idea, based largely on theoretic speculation." But, as a matter of fact, the whole movement originated with men who had learned by personal observation that the negro was intensely human, and who believed all necessary knowledge to be included in that fact. They were men and women who had been born in the slave country, or had personally resided there for years, if not for life. Benjamin Lundy in Virginia, Rankin in Tennessee, Garrison in Maryland, Birney in Alabama, Channing in Virginia again, and the Grimké sisters in South Carolina, had gained on the spot that knowledge of slavery and slaves which made them Abolitionists. They had made observations, and some of them—acting on the poet Gray's maxim that memory is ten times worse than a lead pencil—had written them down.

Added to this, they were constantly in communication with those who had escaped from slavery, and the very closeness of contact into which the two classes were thrown gave them added knowledge of each other. Indeed, the very first anti-slavery book which attained wide attention, known as "Walker's Appeal," published in 1829, was not written by a Northern man, but by one born in Wilmington, South Carolina, of a free mother and a slave father, a man who had traveled widely through the South, expressly to study the degradation of his race, and had read what books of history he could procure bearing upon the subject. His book went through three editions; it advocated insurrection more and more directly. But it was based absolutely on the Declaration of Independence, and on the theory that the negro was a man.

It must be borne in mind that there never yet was an oppressed race which was not assumed by its oppressors to be incapable of freedom. In a late volume of diplomatic correspondence compiled from letters of an Englishman (Anthony B. North Peat), written in 1864–69 during the sway of Louis Napoleon, the letter-writer lays it down as a rule (p. 38) that "A Frenchman is not fit to be trusted with liberty. . . . A Frenchman is, more or less, born to be rode roughshod over, and he himself is positively happier when ruled with a rod of iron." Forty years have now passed since this was written, and who now predicts the extinction of the French Republic? It turned out just the same with those who predicted that the colored race in America was fitted only for slavery and would never attain freedom.

If I may refer to my own experience as one of the younger Abolitionists, I can truly say that my discovery of the negro's essential manhood first came, long before I had heard of the anti-slavery agitation, from a single remark of a slave made to my mother when she was traveling in Virginia in my childhood. After some efforts on her part to convince him that he was well off, he only replied, "Ah! Missis, free breath is good!" There spoke, even to my childish ear, the instinctive demand of the human being. To this were afterwards added my own observations when visiting in the same state during a college vacation, at the age of seventeen, and observing the actual slaves on a plantation; which experience was afterwards followed by years of intimate acquaintance with fugitive slaves in Massachusetts. It was the natural result of all this that, when called upon in maturer life to take military command of freed slaves, it never occurred to me to doubt that they would fight like any other men for their liberty, and so it proved. Yet I scarcely ever met a man or woman of Southern birth, during all that interval, who would not have laughed at the very thought of making them soldiers. They were feared as midnight plotters, as insurrectionists, disciples of Nat Turner, whose outbreak in 1831 filled the South with terror; but it was never believed, for a moment, that they would stand fire in the open field like men. Yet they proved themselves intensely human and did it.

Nor was their humanity recognized by the general public sentiment, even at the North, in earlier days. Even in Massachusetts, law or custom not only forbade any merchant or respectable mechanic to take a colored apprentice, but any common carrier by land or sea was expected to eject from his conveyance any negro on complaint of any white passenger; and I can myself remember when a case of this occurred in Cambridge in my childhood, within sight of the Washington Elm. Churches still had negro pews, these being sometimes boarded up in front, so that the occupants could only look out through peep-holes, as was once done in the old Baptist meeting-house at Hartford, Connecticut, where a negro had bought a pew and refused to leave it. Or the owner might be ejected by a constable, as happened in Park Street Church, Boston; or the floor be cut from under the negro's pew by the church authorities, as happened in Stoughton, Massachusetts. Even in places like the Quaker town of New Bedford, where pupils of both colors were admitted to the public schools, the black boys were seated by themselves, and white offenders were punished by being obliged to sit with them. So far was this carried that it excited the indignation of the European world, insomuch that Heine in his letters from Heligoland (July 1, 1830) gives it as an argument against emigrating to the United States, as Lieber and Follen had done: "Die eigentliche Sklaverei, die in den meisten nordamerikanischen Provinzen abgeschafft, empört mich nicht so sehr wie die Brutalität womit die freien Schwarzen und die Mulatten behandelt werden." The negro was still regarded, both in the Northern and in the Southern states, as being something imperfectly human. It was only the Abolitionists who saw him as he was. They never doubted that he would have human temptations—to idleness, folly, wastefulness, even sensuality. They knew that he would need, like any abused and neglected race, education, moral instruction, and, above all, high example. They knew, in short, all that we know about him now. They could have predicted the outcome of such half-freedom as has been given him,—a freedom tempered by chain-gangs, lynching, and the lash.

It may be assumed, therefore, that there is no charge more unfounded than that frequently made to the effect that the negro was best understood by his former masters. It would be more reasonable to say that the negro as a human being was really least comprehended by those to whom he represented merely a check for a thousand dollars, or less, from a slave auctioneer. This principle may be justly borne in mind in forming an opinion upon the very severest charges still brought against him. Thus a Southern negro has only to be suspected of any attempt at assault on a white woman, and the chances are that he will be put to death without trial, and perhaps with fiendish torture. Yet during my two years' service with colored troops, only one charge of such assault was brought against any soldier, and that was withdrawn in the end and admitted to be false by the very man who made the assertion; and this in a captured town. But even supposing him to have a tendency to such an offense, does any one suppose for a moment that the mob which burns him on suspicion of such a crime is doing it in defense of chastity? Not at all; it is in defense of caste. To decide its real character, we need only ask what would happen if the facts proved to be the reverse of those at first assumed,—if the woman had, after all, the slightest tinge of negro blood, and the offending man turned out to be a white man. Does anybody doubt that the case would be dismissed by acclamation in an instant, that the criminal would go free, and the victim be forgotten? If I err, then the books of evidence are all wrong, the tales of fugitives in the old days are all false. Was any white man ever lynched, either before or since emancipation, for insulting the modesty of a colored girl? Look in the autobiographies of slaves, dozens of which are in our public libraries! Look in the ante-bellum newspapers, or search the memories of those who, like the present writer, were employed on vigilance committees and underground railways before most of the present lynchers were born!

There were, again and again, women known to us who had fled to save their honor,—women so white that, like Ellen Craft, they passed in traveling for Caucasian. One such woman was under my observation for a whole winter in Worcester, who brought away with her the two children of her young master, whose mistress she had been, in spite of herself, and who was believed by many to have been her half-brother. So nearly white were she and her children that they were escorted up from Boston by a Worcester merchant, himself proslavery in sympathy, under whose care they had been skillfully put at the Boston station by the agent of the underground railway. They finally passed into the charge of an honorable man, a white mechanic, who married the woman with the full approval of the ladies who had her in charge. I never knew or wished to know his name, thinking it better that she and her children should disappear, as they easily could, in the white ranks. Another slave child, habitually passing for white, was known to the public as "Ida May," and was exhibited to audiences as a curiosity by Governor Andrew and others, until that injudicious practice was stopped. She, too, was under my care for a time, went to school, became clerk in a public office, and I willingly lost sight of her also for a very similar reason. It must never be forgotten that every instance of slaves almost white, in those days, was not the outcome of legal marriage, but of the ungoverned passion of some white man. The evil was also self-multiplying, since the fairer the complexion of every half-breed girl, the greater her attraction and her perils. Those who have read that remarkable volume of Southern stories, written in New Orleans by Grace King, under the inexpressive title of "Tales of a Time and Place," will remember the striking scene where a mob, which had utterly disregarded the danger run by a young girl who had passed for a mere octoroon, is lashed instantly into overpowering tumult when evidence is suddenly advanced at the last that she is not octoroon, but white.

Supposing, for the sake of argument, that there is to be found in the colored race, especially in the former slave states, a lower standard of chastity than among whites, it is hard to imagine any reasoning more grotesque than that which often comes from those who claim to represent the white race there. One recent writer from New Orleans in the Boston "Herald" describes the black race as being "in great part immoral in its sexual relations, whether from centuries of savagery or from nature, as some of the travelers insisted." This needs only to be compared with the testimony of another Southern witness to show its folly. In a little book entitled "Two Addresses on Negro Education in the South," Mr. A. A. Gunby of the Louisiana bar makes this simple statement: "Miscegenation in the South has always been and will always be confined to converse between white men and colored women, and the number of mulattoes in the future will depend absolutely on the extent to which white men restrain their immoral dealings with negro females." This same writer goes on to say, what would seem to be the obvious common sense of the matter, that "education is the best possible means to fortify negro women against the approaches of libertines."

For my own part, I have been for many years in the position to know the truth, even on its worst side, upon this subject. Apart from the knowledge derived in college days from Southern students, then very numerous at Harvard, with whom I happened to be very much thrown through a Southern relative, my classmate, I have evidence much beyond this. I have in my hands written evidence, unfit for publication, but discovered in a captured town during the Civil War,—evidence to show that Rome in its decline was not more utterly degraded, as to the relation between the sexes, than was the intercourse often existing between white men and colored women on American slave plantations. How could it be otherwise where one sex had all the power and the other had no means of escape? Rufus Choate, one of the most conservative Northern men of the time as to the slavery question, is said to have expressed the opinion, as the result of careful study, that he had no reason to think that the industrial condition of the slave, all things considered, was worse than that of the laboring population in most European countries, but that for the colored woman the condition of slavery was "simply hell." The race of mixed blood in America is the outcome of that condition; and that the colored race has emerged from such subjugation into the comparatively decent moral condition which it now holds proves conclusively that it is human in its virtues as well as in its sins. This I say as one who has been for nearly ten years trustee of a school for freedmen in the heart of the black district. The simple fact, admitted by all candid men and women, that no charges of immorality are ever brought against the graduates of these schools, and that, wherever they go, they are the centre of a healthy influence, is sufficient proof that what the whole nation needs is to deal with the negro race no longer as outcasts, but simply as men and women.

If thus dealt with, why should the very existence of such a race be regarded as an insuperable evil? The answer is that the tradition lies solely in the associations of slavery. Outside of this country, such insuperable aversion plainly does not exist; not even is it to be found in the land nearest to us in kindred, England. A relative of mine, a Boston lady distinguished in the last generation for beauty and bearing, was staying in London with her husband, fifty years ago, when they received a call at breakfast time from a mulatto of fine appearance, named Prince Sanders, whom they had known well as a steward, or head waiter, in Boston. She felt that she ought to ask him, as a fellow countryman, to sit down at table with them, but she shrank from doing it until he rose to go; and then, in a cowardly manner, as she frankly admitted, stammered out the invitation. To which his reply was, "Thank you, madam, but I am engaged to breakfast with the Prince of Wales this morning," which turned out to be true. No one can watch the carriages in Hyde Park, still less in Continental capitals, without recognizing the merely local quality of all distinct social antagonism between races. In a letter to the Boston "Herald," dated September 17, 1903, the writer, Bishop Douet of Jamaica, testifies that there is a large class of colored people who there fill important positions as ministers of religion, doctors, and lawyers. He says: "This element in our society that I have alluded to is the result of miscegenation, which the writers from the South seem to look upon with so much horror. We have not found that the mixing of the races has produced such dire results. I number among my friends many of this mixed race who are as accomplished and intelligent ladies and gentlemen as you can find in any society in Boston or the other great cities of America."

In connection with this, Bishop Douet claims that the masses of the colored population in all parts of the island are absolutely orderly, and that a white woman may travel from one end of the land to the other with perfect safety. All traces of the terrible period of the Maroon wars seem to have vanished, wars which lasted for nine years, during which martial law prevailed throughout the whole island, and high military authorities said of the Maroons that "their subjugation was more difficult than to obtain a victory over any army in Europe." These rebels, or their descendants, are the people who now live in a condition of entire peace and order, in spite of all the predicted perils of freedom. One of these perils, as we know, was supposed to be that of a mixture of blood between the races, but even that is found no longer a source of evil, this witness thinks, when concubinage has been replaced by legal marriage.

Among the ways in which the colored race shows itself intensely human are some faults which it certainly shares with the white race, besides the merely animal temptations. There is the love of fine clothes, for instance; the partiality for multiplying sects in religion, and secret societies in secular life; the tendency toward weakening forces by too much subdivision; the intolerance shown toward free individual action. It is only the last which takes just now a somewhat serious form. It is a positive calamity that a few indiscretions and exaggerations on each side have developed into a bitter hostility to Booker Washington on the part of some of the most intelligent and even cultivated of his race. Internal feuds among philanthropists are, alas, no new story, and few bodies of reformers have escaped this peril. When we consider the bitter contest fought between Charles Sumner and his opponents in the Prison Discipline Society; the conflicts in the early temperance meetings between

Total Abstainers and Teetotalers; those in the Woman Suffrage Movement between Mrs. Woodhull and her opponents, and in the anti-slavery movement itself between the voting and non-voting Abolitionists, we must not censure the warring negro reformer too severely. Nay, consider the subdivisions of the Garrison Abolitionists themselves, after slavery itself was abolished, at a period when I remember to have seen Edmund Quincy walk halfway up a stairway, and turn suddenly round to descend, merely to avoid Wendell Phillips, who was coming downstairs! Having worked side by side together through storm and through calm, having been denounced, threatened, and even mobbed side by side, the two men had yet separated in bitterness on the interpretation of a will made by a fellow laborer, Francis Jackson. When we look, indeed, beyond the circle of moral reformers, and consider simply the feuds of science, we see the same thing: Dr. Gould, the eminent astronomer, locking his own observatory against his own trustees to avoid interference; and Agassiz, in the height of the Darwinian controversy, denying that there was any division on the subject among scientific men, on the ground that any man who accepted the doctrine of evolution ceased thereby to be a man of science. If questions merely intellectual thus divide the leaders of thought, how can we expect points that divide men on the basis of conscience and moral service to be less potent in their influence? In the present case, as in most cases, the trouble seems chiefly due to the difficulty found by every energetic and enthusiastic person, absorbed in his own pursuits, in fully appreciating the equally important pursuits of others. Booker Washington, in urging the development of the industrial pursuits he represents, has surely gone no farther than Frederick Douglass, the acknowledged leader of his people, who said, "Every colored mechanic is by virtue of circumstances an elevator of his race." On the other hand, the critics of Mr. Washington are wholly right in holding that it is as important for this race to produce its own physicians, lawyers, preachers, and above all, teachers, as to rear mechanics; and he accordingly summoned the Harvard Class Orator of the year—Mr. Bruce—to be the head of the department of letters at Tuskegee. It is infinitely to be regretted that everybody cannot look at every matter all round, but this, unhappily, is a form of human weakness in which there is no distinction of color.

It must always be remembered that all forward movements have their experimental stage. In looking over, at this distance of time, the letters and printed editorials brought out by the enterprise of arming the blacks in our Civil War, I find that it was regarded by most people as a mere experiment. It now seems scarcely credible that I should have received, as I did, on first undertaking it, a letter from a sympathizer in Boston, recalling to my memory that Roman tradition of a body of rebellious slaves who were brought back to subjection, even after taking up arms, by a body of men armed with whips only. This correspondent anxiously warned me that the same method might be repeated. Yet it seems scarcely more credible that the young hero, Colonel Shaw, when I rode out to meet him, on his arrival with his Northern colored regiment, seriously asked me whether I felt perfectly sure that the negroes would stand fire in line of battle, and suggested that, at the worst, it would at least be possible to drive them forward by having a line of white soldiers advance in their rear, so that they would be between two fires. He admitted the mere matter of individual courage to have been already settled in their case, and only doubted whether they would do as well in line of battle as in skirmishing and on guard duty. Nor do I intend to imply that he had any serious doubt beyond this, but simply that the question had passed through his mind. He did not sufficiently consider that in this, as at all other points, they were simply men.

We must also remember that a common humanity does not by any means exclude individual variety, but rather protects it. At first glance, in a black regiment, the men usually looked to a newly arrived officer just alike, but it proved after a little experience that they varied as much in face as any soldiers. It was the same as to character. Yet at the same time they were on the whole more gregarious and cohesive than the whites; they preferred organization, whereas nothing pleased white American troops so much as to be out skirmishing, each on his own responsibility, without being bothered with officers. There was also a certain tropical element in black troops, a sort of fiery utterance when roused, which seemed more Celtic than Anglo-Saxon. The only point where I was doubtful, though I never had occasion to test it, was that they might show less endurance under prolonged and hopeless resistance, like Napoleon's men when during the retreat from Russia they simply drooped and died.

As to the general facts of courage and reliability, I think that no officer in my camp ever thought of there being any essential difference between black and white; and surely the judgment of these officers, who were risking their lives at every moment, month after month, on the fidelity of their men, was worth more than the opinion of the world besides. As the negroes were intensely human at these points, they were equally so in claiming that they had more to fight for than the white soldiers. They loved the United States flag, and I remember one zealous corporal, a man of natural eloquence, pointing to it during a meeting on the Fourth of July, and saying with more zeal than statistical accuracy, "Dar's dat flag, we hab lib under it for eighteen hundred and sixty-two years, and we'll lib and die for it now." But they could never forget that, besides the flag and the Union, they had home and wife and child to fight for. War was a very serious matter to them. They took a grim satisfaction when orders were issued that the officers of colored troops should be put to death on capture. It helped their *esprit de corps* immensely. Their officers, like themselves, were henceforward to fight with ropes around their necks. Even when the new black regiments began to come down from the North, the Southern soldiers pointed out this difference, that in case of ultimate defeat, the Northern troops, black or white, must sooner or later be exchanged and returned to their homes, whereas they themselves must fight it out or be reënslaved. All this was absolutely correct reasoning, and showed them human.

As all individuals differ, even in the same family, so there must doubtless be variations between different races. It is only that these differences balance one another so that all are human at last. Each race, like each individual, may have its strong point. Compare, for instance, the negroes and the Irish-Americans. So universal among negroes is the possession of a musical ear that I frequently had reason to be grateful for it as a blessing, were it only for the fact that those who saw colored soldiers for the first time always noticed it and exaggerated its importance. Because the negroes kept a better step, after forty-eight hours' training, than did most white regiments after three or four months, these observers expressed the conviction that the blacks would fight well; which seemed to me, perhaps, a hasty inference. As to the Irish-Americans, I could say truly that a single recruit of that race in my original white company had cost me more trouble in training him to keep step than all my black soldiers put together. On the other hand, it was generally agreed that it was impossible to conceive of an Irish coward; the Irish being, perhaps, as universally brave as any race existing. Now, I am not prepared to say that in the colored race cowardice would be totally impossible, nor could that be claimed, absolutely, for the Anglo-Saxon race. On the other hand, to extend the comparison, it would not have been conceivable to me that a black soldier should be a traitor to his own side, and it is unquestionable that there were sometimes Irish deserters. All this variety is according to the order of nature. The world would be very monotonous if all human beings had precisely the same combination of strong and weak points. It is enough that they should all be human.

In regard to warmth of heart and open demonstrativeness, the negroes and the Irish have much in common, and it is an attribute which makes them both attractive. The same may be held true of the religious element. No matter how reckless in bearing they might be, those negroes were almost fatalists in their confidence that God would watch over them; and if they died, it would be because their time had come. "If each one of us was a praying man," said one of my corporals in a speech, "it appears to me that we could fight as well with prayers as with bullets, for the Lord has said that if you have faith even as a grain of mustard seed cut into four parts, you can say to the sycamore tree 'Arise,' and it will come up." And though Corporal Long's botany may have got a little confused, his faith proved itself by works, for he volunteered to go many miles on a solitary scouting expedition into the enemy's country in Florida, and got back safe after he had been given up for lost. On the whole, it may be said that the colored and the Irish soldiers were a little nearer to one another than to the Anglo-Saxon type; and that both were nearer to the Western recruits, among Americans, than to the more reticent and self-controlled New England men. Each type had its characteristics, and all were intensely human.

All these judgments, formed in war, have thus far sustained themselves in peace. The enfranchisement of the negroes, once established, will of course never be undone. They have learned the art, if not of political self-defense, at least of migration from place to place, and those states which are most unjust to them will in time learn to prize their presence and regret their absence. The chances are that the mingling of races will diminish, but whether this is or is not the outcome, it is, of course, better for all that this result should be legal and voluntary, rather than illegal and perhaps forced. As the memories of the slave period fade away, the mere fetich of colorphobia will cease to control our society; and marriage may come to be founded, not on the color of the skin, but upon the common courtesies of life, and upon genuine sympathies of heart and mind. To show how high these sympathies might reach even in slavery, I turn back to a letter received by one of my soldiers from his wife,—a letter which I have just unearthed from a chaos of army papers where it has lain untouched for forty years. It is still inclosed in a quaint envelope of a pattern devised in Philadelphia at that day, and greatly in demand among the negroes. This shows a colored print of the tree of liberty bearing in the place of leaves little United States flags, each labeled with the name of some state, while the tree bears the date "1776" at its roots. The letter is addressed to "Solomon Steward, Company H., 1st S. C. Vols., Beaufort, S. C.," this being the name of a soldier in my regiment, who showed the letter to me and allowed me to keep it. He was one of the Florida men, who were, as a rule, better taught and more intelligent than the South Carolina negroes. They were therefore coveted as recruits by all my captains; and they had commonly been obliged on enlistment to leave their families behind them in Florida, not nearly so well cared for as those under General Saxton's immediate charge. The pay of my regiment being, moreover, for a long time delayed, these families often suffered in spite of all our efforts. I give the letter verbatim, and it requires no further explanation:

FERNANDINA, FLORIDA, Feb. the 8 [1864].
MY DEAR HUSBAND,—This Hour I Sit Me Down To write you In a Little world of sweet sounds The Choir In The Chapel near Here are Chanting at The organ and Thair Morning Hymn across The street are sounding and The Dear Little birds are joining Thair voices In Tones sweet and pure as angels whispers. but My Dear all The songs of The birds sounds sweet In My Ear but a sweeter song Than That I now Hear and That Is The song of a administing angel Has Come and borne My Dear Little babe To Join In Tones with Them sweet and pure as angels whispers. My babe only Live one day It was a Little Girl. Her name Is alice Gurtrude steward I am now sick In bed and have Got nothing To Live on The Rashion That They Give for six days I Can Make It Last but 2 days They dont send Me any wood They send The others wood and I Cant Get any I dont Get any Light at all You Must see To That as soon as possible for I am In in want of some Thing To Eat

I have nothing more to say to you but Give my Regards to all the friends all the family send thair love to you

NO MORE AT PRESSANT
EMMA STEWARD

Does it need any further commentary to prove that the writer of a letter like this was intensely human?

2

Negro Spirituals

The war brought to some of us, besides its direct experiences, many a strange fulfilment of dreams of other days. For instance, the present writer had been a faithful student of the Scottish ballads, and had always envied Sir Walter the delight of tracing them out amid their own heather, and of writing them down piecemeal from the lips of aged crones. It was a strange enjoyment, therefore, to be suddenly brought into the midst of a kindred world of unwritten songs, as simple and indigenous as the Border Minstrelsy, more uniformly plaintive, almost always more quaint, and often as essentially poetic.

This interest was rather increased by the fact that I had for many years heard of this class of songs under the name of "Negro Spirituals," and had even heard some of them sung by friends from South Carolina. I could now gather on their own soil these strange plants, which I had before seen as in museums alone. True, the individual songs rarely coincided; there was a line here, a chorus there,—just enough to fix the class, but this was unmistakable. It was not strange that they differed, for the range seemed almost endless, and South Carolina, Georgia, and Florida seemed to have nothing but the generic character in common, until all were mingled in the united stock of camp-melodies.

Often in the starlit evening, I have returned from some lonely ride by the swift river, or on the plover-haunted barrens, and, entering the camp, have silently approached some glimmering fire, round which the dusky figures moved in the rhythmical barbaric dance the negroes call a "shout," chanting, often harshly, but always in the most perfect time, some monotonous refrain. Writing down in the darkness, as I best could,—perhaps with my hand in the safe covert of my pocket,—the words of the song, I have afterwards carried it to my tent, like some cap-

tured bird or insect, and then, after examination, put it by. Or, sum-
moning one of the men at some period of leisure,—Corporal Robert
Sutton, for instance, whose iron memory held all the details of a song as
if it were a ford or a forest,—I have completed the new specimen by supplying the absent parts. The music I could only retain by ear, and though
the more common strains were repeated often enough to fix their impression, there were others that occurred only once or twice.

The words will be here given, as nearly as possible, in the original dialect; and if the spelling seems sometimes inconsistent, or the misspelling
insufficient, it is because I could get no nearer. I wished to avoid what
seems to me the only error of Lowell's "Biglow Papers" in respect to dialect,—the occasional use of an extreme misspelling, which merely confuses the eye, without taking us any closer to the peculiarity of sound.

The favorite song in camp was the following,—sung with no accom-
paniment but the measured clapping of hands and the clatter of many
feet. It was sung perhaps twice as often as any other. This was partly due
to the fact that it properly consisted of a chorus alone, with which the
verses of other songs might be combined at random.

I. Hold Your Light.

"Hold your light, Brudder Robert,—
Hold your light,
Hold your light on Canaan's shore.
"What make ole Satan for follow me so?
Satan ain't got notin' for do wid me.
Hold your light,
Hold your light,
Hold your light on Canaan's shore."

This would be sung for half an hour at a time, perhaps each person
present being named in turn. It seemed the simplest primitive type of
"spiritual." The next in popularity was almost as elementary, and, like
this, named successively each one of the circle. It was, however, much
more resounding and convivial in its music.

II. Bound to Go.

"Jordan River, I'm bound to go,
Bound to go, bound to go,—
Jordan River, I'm bound to go,
And bid 'em fare ye well.

"My Brudder Robert, I'm bound to go,
  Bound to go," &c.

"My Sister Lucy, I'm bound to go,
  Bound to go," &c.

Sometimes it was "tink 'em" (think them) "fare ye well." The *ye* was so detached that I thought at first it was "very" or "vary well."

Another picturesque song, which seemed immensely popular, was at first very bewildering to me. I could not make out the first words of the chorus, and called it the "Romandàr," being reminded of some Romaic song which I had formerly heard. That association quite fell in with the Orientalism of the new tent-life.

III. Room in There.
"O, my mudder is gone! my mudder is gone!
My mudder is gone into heaven, my Lord!
I can't stay behind!
Dere's room in dar, room in dar,
Room in dar, in de heaven, my Lord!
  I can't stay behind!
Can't stay behind, my dear,
  I can't stay behind!

"O, my fader is gone!" &c.

"O, de angels are gone!" &c.

"O, I'se been on de road! I'se been on de road!
I'se been on de road into heaven, my Lord!
  I can't stay behind!
O, room in dar, room in dar,
Room in dar, in de heaven, my Lord!
  I can't stay behind!"

By this time every man within hearing, from oldest to youngest, would be wriggling and shuffling, as if through some magic piper's bewitchment; for even those who at first affected contemptuous indifference would be drawn into the vortex erelong.

Next to these in popularity ranked a class of songs belonging emphatically to the Church Militant, and available for camp purposes with very little strain upon their symbolism. This, for instance, had a true companion-in-arms heartiness about it, not impaired by the feminine invocation at the end.

IV. Hail Mary.

"One more valiant soldier here,
One more valiant soldier here,
One more valiant soldier here,
To help me bear de cross.
O hail, Mary, hail!
Hail, Mary, hail!
Hail, Mary, hail!
To help me bear de cross."

I fancied that the original reading might have been "soul," instead of "soldier,"—with some other syllable inserted to fill out the metre,—and that the "Hail, Mary," might denote a Roman Catholic origin, as I had several men from St. Augustine who held in a dim way to that faith. It was a very ringing song, though not so grandly jubilant as the next, which was really impressive as the singers pealed it out, when marching or rowing or embarking.

V. My Army Cross Over.

"My army cross over,
My army cross over,
O, Pharaoh's army drownded!
My army cross over.

"We'll cross de mighty river,
My army cross over;
We'll cross de river Jordan,
My army cross over;
We'll cross de danger water,
My army cross over;
We'll cross de mighty Myo,
My army cross over. (Thrice.)
O, Pharaoh's army drownded!
My army cross over."

I could get no explanation of the "mighty Myo," except that one of the old men thought it meant the river of death. Perhaps it is an African word. In the Cameroon dialect, "Mawa" signifies "to die."

The next also has a military ring about it, and the first line is well matched by the music. The rest is conglomerate, and one or two lines show a more Northern origin. "Done" is a Virginia shibboleth, quite distinct from the "been" which replaces it in South Carolina. Yet one of their best choruses, without any fixed words, was, "De bell done ringing," for which, in proper South Carolina dialect, would have been substituted, "De bell been a-ring." This refrain may have gone South with our army.

VI. Ride In, Kind Saviour.

"Ride in, kind Saviour!
  No man can hinder me.
O, Jesus is a mighty man!
  No man, &c.
We're marching through Virginny fields.
  No man, &c.
O, Satan is a busy man,
  No man, &c.
And he has his sword and shield,
  No man, &c.
O, old Secesh done come and gone!
  No man can hinder me."

Sometimes they substituted "hinder *we*," which was more spicy to the ear, and more in keeping with the usual head-over-heels arrangement of their pronouns.

Almost all their songs were thoroughly religious in their tone, however quaint their expression, and were in a minor key, both as to words and music. The attitude is always the same, and, as a commentary on the life of the race, is infinitely pathetic. Nothing but patience for this life,—nothing but triumph in the next. Sometimes the present predominates, sometimes the future; but the combination is always implied. In the following, for instance, we hear simply the patience.

VII. This World Almost Done.

"Brudder, keep your lamp trimmin' and a-burnin',
Keep your lamp trimmin' and a-burnin',
Keep your lamp trimmin' and a-burnin',
  For dis world most done.
So keep your lamp, &c.
  Dis world most done."

But in the next, the final reward of patience is proclaimed as plaintively.

VIII. I Want to Go Home.
"Dere's no rain to wet you,
O, yes, I want to go home.
Dere's no sun to burn you,
O, yes, I want to go home;
O, push along, believers,
O, yes, &c.
Dere's no hard trials,
O, yes, &c.
Dere's no whips a-crackin',
O, yes, &c.
My brudder on de wayside,
O, yes, &c.
O, push along, my brudder,
O, yes, &c.
Where dere's no stormy weather,
O, yes, &c.
Dere's no tribulation,
O, yes," &c.

This next was a boat-song, and timed well with the tug of the oar.

IX. The Coming Day.
"I want to go to Canaan,
I want to go to Canaan,
I want to go to Canaan,
To meet 'em at de comin' day.
O, remember, let me go to Canaan, (Thrice.)
To meet 'em, &c.
O brudder, let me go to Canaan, (Thrice.)
To meet 'em, &c.
My brudder, you—oh!—remember, (Thrice.)
To meet 'em at de comin' day."

The following begins with a startling affirmation, yet the last line quite outdoes the first. This, too, was a capital boat-song.

X. One More River.
"O, Jordan bank was a great old bank,
Dere ain't but one more river to cross.
We have some valiant soldier here,
Dere ain't, &c.

> O, Jordan stream will never run dry,
>   Dere ain't, &c.
> Dere's a hill on my leff, and he catch on my right,
>   Dere ain't but one more river to cross."

I could get no explanation of this last riddle, except, "Dat mean, if you go on de leff, go to 'struction, and if you go on de right, go to God, for sure."

In others, more of spiritual conflict is implied, as in this next.

XI. O the Dying Lamb!

> "I wants to go where Moses trod,
>   O de dying Lamb!
> For Moses gone to de promised land,
>   O de dying Lamb!
> To drink from springs dat never run dry,
>   O, &c.
> Cry O my Lord!
>   O, &c.
> Before I'll stay in hell one day,
>   O, &c.
> I'm in hopes to pray my sins away,
>   O, &c.
> Cry O my Lord!
>   O, &c.
> Brudder Moses promised for be dar too,
>   O, &c.
> To drink from streams dat never run dry,
>   O de dying Lamb!"

In the next, the conflict is at its height, and the lurid imagery of the Apocalypse is brought to bear. This book, with the books of Moses, constituted their Bible; all that lay between, even the narratives of the life of Jesus, they hardly cared to read or to hear.

XII. Down in the Valley.

> "We'll run and never tire,
> We'll run and never tire,
> We'll run and never tire,
>   Jesus set poor sinners free.
> Way down in de valley,

Who will rise and go with me?
You've heern talk of Jesus,
  Who set poor sinners free.

"De lightnin' and de flashin'
De lightnin' and de flashin',
De lightnin' and de flashin',
Jesus set poor sinners free.
I can't stand the fire. (Thrice.)
  Jesus set poor sinners free,
De green trees a-flamin'. (Thrice.)
  Jesus set poor sinners free,
Way down in de valley,
  Who will rise and go with me?
You've heern talk of Jesus
  Who set poor sinners free."

"De valley" and "de lonesome valley" were familiar words in their religious experience. To descend into that region implied the same process with the "anxious-seat" of the camp-meeting. When a young girl was supposed to enter it, she bound a handkerchief by a peculiar knot over her head, and made it a point of honor not to change a single garment till the day of her baptism, so that she was sure of being in physical readiness for the cleansing rite, whatever her spiritual mood might be. More than once, in noticing a damsel thus mystically kerchiefed, I have asked some dusky attendant its meaning, and have received the unfailing answer,—framed with their usual indifference to the genders of pronouns—"He in de lonesome valley, sa."

The next gives the same dramatic conflict, while its detached and impersonal refrain gives it strikingly the character of the Scotch and Scandinavian ballads.

XIII. Cry Holy.

"Cry holy, holy!
  Look at de people dat is born of God.
And I run down de valley, and I run down to pray,
  Says, look at de people dat is born of God.
When I get dar, Cappen Satan was dar,
  Says, look at, &c.
Says, young man, young man, dere's no use for pray,
  Says, look at, &c.

For Jesus is dead, and God gone away,
   Says, look at, &c.
And I made him out a liar, and I went my way,
   Says, look at, &c.
      Sing holy, holy!

"O, Mary was a woman, and he had a one Son,
   Says, look at, &c.
And de Jews and de Romans had him hung,
   Says, look at, &c.
      Cry holy, holy!

"And I tell you, sinner, you had better had pray,
   Says, look at, &c.
For hell is a dark and dismal place,
   Says, look at, &c.
And I tell you, sinner, and I wouldn't go dar!
   Says, look at, &c.
      Cry holy, holy!"

Here is an infinitely quaint description of the length of the heavenly road:

XIV. O'er the Crossing.
"Yonder's my old mudder,
   Been a-waggin' at de hill so long.
It's about time she'll cross over;
   Get home bimeby.
Keep prayin', I do believe
   We're a long time waggin' o'er de crossin'.
Keep prayin', I do believe
   We'll get home to heaven bimeby.

"Hear dat mournful thunder
   Roll from door to door,
Calling home God's children;
   Get home bimeby.
Little chil'en, I do believe
   We're a long time, &c.
Little chil'en, I do believe
   We'll get home, &c.

"See dat forked lightnin'
 Flash from tree to tree,
Callin' home God's chil'en;
 Get home bimeby.
True believer, I do believe
 We're a long time, &c.
O brudders, I do believe,
 We'll get home to heaven bimeby."

One of the most singular pictures of future joys, and with a fine flavor of hospitality about it, was this:—

XV. Walk 'Em Easy.
"O, walk 'em easy round de heaven,
Walk 'em easy round de heaven,
Walk 'em easy round de heaven,
 Dat all de people may join de band.
Walk 'em easy round de heaven. (Thrice.)
 O, shout glory till 'em join dat band!"

The chorus was usually the greater part of the song, and often came in paradoxically, thus:—

XVI. O Yes, Lord.
"O, must I be like de foolish mans?
 O yes, Lord!
Will build de house on de sandy hill.
 O yes, Lord!
I'll build my house on Zion hill,
 O yes, Lord!
No wind nor rain can blow me down,
 O yes, Lord!"

The next is very graceful and lyrical, and with more variety of rhythm than usual:—

XVII. Bow Low, Mary.
"Bow low, Mary, bow low, Martha,
 For Jesus come and lock de door,
 And carry de keys away.
Sail, sail, over yonder,

> *And view de promised land.*
> 　　*For Jesus come, &c.*
> *Weep, O Mary, bow low, Martha,*
> 　　*For Jesus come, &c.*
> *Sail, sail, my true believer;*
> *Sail, sail, over yonder;*
> *Mary, bow low, Martha, bow low,*
> 　　*For Jesus come and lock de door*
> 　　*And carry de keys away."*

But of all the "spirituals" that which surprised me the most, I think,—perhaps because it was that in which external nature furnished the images most directly,—was this. With all my experience of their ideal ways of speech, I was startled when first I came on such a flower of poetry in that dark soil.

XVIII. I Know Moon-Rise.

> *"I know moon-rise, I know star-rise,*
> 　　*Lay dis body down.*
> *I walk in de moonlight, I walk in de starlight,*
> 　　*To lay dis body down.*
> *I'll walk in de graveyard, I'll walk through de graveyard,*
> 　　*To lay dis body down.*
> *I'll lie in de grave and stretch out my arms;*
> 　　*Lay dis body down.*
> *I go to de judgment in de evenin' of de day,*
> 　　*When I lay dis body down;*
> *And my soul and your soul will meet in de day*
> 　　*When I lay dis body down."*

"I'll lie in de grave and stretch out my arms." Never, it seems to me, since man first lived and suffered, was his infinite longing for peace uttered more plaintively than in that line.

The next is one of the wildest and most striking of the whole series: there is a mystical effect and a passionate striving throughout the whole. The Scriptural struggle between Jacob and the angel, which is only dimly expressed in the words, seems all uttered in the music. I think it impressed my imagination more powerfully than any other of these songs.

XIX. Wrestling Jacob.

> *"O wrestlin' Jacob, Jacob, day's a-breakin';*
> 　　*I will not let thee go!*

> *O wrestlin' Jacob, Jacob, day's a-breakin';*
>   *He will not let me go!*
> *O, I hold my brudder wid a tremblin' hand*
>   *I would not let him go!*
> *I hold my sister wid a tremblin' hand;*
>   *I would not let her go!*

> *"O, Jacob do hang from a tremblin' limb,*
>   *He would not let him go!*
> *O, Jacob do hang from a tremblin' limb;*
>   *De Lord will bless my soul.*
> *O wrestlin' Jacob, Jacob," &c.*

Of "occasional hymns," properly so called, I noticed but one, a funeral hymn for an infant, which is sung plaintively over and over, without variety of words.

XX. The Baby Gone Home.
> *"De little baby gone home,*
> *De little baby gone home,*
> *De little baby gone along,*
>   *For to climb up Jacob's ladder.*
> *And I wish I'd been dar,*
> *I wish I'd been dar,*
> *I wish I'd been dar, my Lord,*
>   *For to climb up Jacob's ladder."*

Still simpler is this, which is yet quite sweet and touching.

XXI. Jesus with Us.
> *"He have been wid us, Jesus,*
>   *He still wid us, Jesus,*
> *He will be wid us, Jesus,*
>   *Be wid us to the end."*

The next seemed to be a favorite about Christmas time, when meditations on "de rollin' year" were frequent among them.

XXII. Lord, Remember Me.
> *"O do, Lord, remember me!*
>   *O do, Lord, remember me!*

O, do remember me, until de year roll round!
  Do, Lord, remember me!

"If you want to die like Jesus died,
  Lay in de grave,
You would fold your arms and close your eyes
  And die wid a free good will.

"For Death is a simple ting,
  And he go from door to door,
And he knock down some, and he cripple up some,
  And he leave some here to pray.

"O do, Lord remember me!
  O do, Lord, remember me!
My old fader's gone till de year roll round;
  Do, Lord, remember me!"

The next was sung in such an operatic and rollicking way that it was quite hard to fancy it a religious performance, which, however, it was. I heard it but once.

XXIII. Early in the Morning.
"I meet little Rosa early in de mornin',
  O Jerusalem! early in de mornin';
And I ax her, How you do, my darter?
  O Jerusalem! early in de mornin'.

"I meet my mudder early in de mornin',
  O Jerusalem! &c.
And I ax her, How you do, my mudder?
  O Jerusalem! &c.

"I meet Brudder Robert early in de mornin',
  O Jerusalem! &c.
And I ax him, How you do, my sonny?
  O Jerusalem! &c.

"I meet Tittawisa early in de mornin',
  O Jerusalem! &c.
And I ax her, How you do, my darter?
  O Jerusalem!" &c.

"Tittawisa" means "Sister Louisa." In songs of this class the name of every person present successively appears.

Their best marching song, and one which was invaluable to lift their feet along, as they expressed it, was the following. There was a kind of spring and *lilt* to it, quite indescribable by words.

XXIV. Go in the Wilderness.

"Jesus call you. Go in de wilderness,
 Go in de wilderness, go in de wilderness,
Jesus call you. Go in de wilderness
 To wait upon de Lord.
Go wait upon de Lord,
Go wait upon de Lord,
Go wait upon de Lord, my God,
 He take away de sins of de world.

"Jesus a-waitin'. Go in de wilderness,
 Go, &c.
All dem chil'en go in de wilderness
 To wait upon de Lord."

The next was one of those which I had heard in boyish days, brought North from Charleston. But the chorus alone was identical; the words were mainly different, and those here given are quaint enough.

XXV. Blow Your Trumpet, Gabriel.

"O, blow your trumpet, Gabriel,
 Blow your trumpet louder;
And I want dat trumpet to blow me home
 To my new Jerusalem.

"De prettiest ting dat ever I done
Was to serve de Lord when I was young.
 So blow your trumpet, Gabriel, &c.

"O, Satan is a liar, and he conjure too,
And if you don't mind, he'll conjure you.
 So blow your trumpet, Gabriel, &c.

"O, I was lost in de wilderness.
King Jesus hand me de candle down.
 So blow your trumpet, Gabriel," &c.

The following contains one of those odd transformations of proper names with which their Scriptural citations were often enriched. It rivals their text, "Paul may plant, and may polish wid water," which I have elsewhere quoted, and in which the sainted Apollos would hardly have recognized himself.

XXVI. In the Morning.

"In de mornin',
In de mornin',
Chil'en? Yes, my Lord!
  Don't you hear de trumpet sound?
If I had a-died when I was young,
I never would had de race for run.
  Don't you hear de trumpet sound?

"O Sam and Peter was fishin' in de sea,
And dey drop de net and follow my Lord.
  Don't you hear de trumpet sound?
"Dere's a silver spade for to dig my grave
And a golden chain for to let me down.
Don't you hear de trumpet sound?
In de mornin',
In de mornin',
Chil'en? Yes, my Lord!
  Don't you hear de trumpet sound?"

These golden and silver fancies remind one of the King of Spain's daughter in "Mother Goose," and the golden apple, and the silver pear, which are doubtless themselves but the vestiges of some simple early composition like this. The next has a humbler and more domestic style of fancy.

XXVII. Fare Ye Well.

"My true believers, fare ye well,
Fare ye well, fare ye well,
Fare ye well, by de grace of God,
  For I'm going home.

"Massa Jesus give me a little broom
For to sweep my heart clean,
And I will try, by de grace of God,
  To win my way home."

Among the songs not available for marching, but requiring the concentrated enthusiasm of the camp, was "The Ship of Zion," of which
they had three wholly distinct versions, all quite exuberant and tumultuous.

XXVIII. The Ship of Zion.

"Come along, come along,
And let us go home,
O, glory, hallelujah!
Dis de ole ship o' Zion,
Halleloo! Halleloo!
Dis de ole ship o' Zion,
Hallelujah!
"She has landed many a tousand,
She can land as many more.
O, glory, hallelujah! &c.

"Do you think she will be able
For to take us all home?
O, glory, hallelujah! &c.

"You can tell 'em I'm a comin',
Halleloo! Halleloo!
You can tell 'em I'm a comin',
Hallelujah!
Come along, come along," &c.

XXIX. The Ship of Zion. (Second version.)

"Dis de good ole ship o' Zion,
Dis de good ole ship o' Zion,
Dis de good ole ship o' Zion,
And she's makin' for de Promise Land.
She hab angels for de sailors, (Thrice.)
And she's, &c.
And how you know dey's angels? (Thrice.)
And she's, &c.
Good Lord, Shall I be one? (Thrice.)
And she's, &c.

"Dat ship is out a-sailin', sailin', sailin',
And she's, &c.
She's a-sailin' mighty steady, steady, steady,

And she's, &c.
She'll neither reel nor totter, totter, totter,
And she's, &c.
She's a-sailin' away cold Jordan, Jordan, Jordan,
And she's, &c.
King Jesus is de captain, captain, captain,
And she's makin' for de Promise Land."

XXX. The Ship of Zion. (Third version.)
"De Gospel ship is sailin',
Hosann—sann.
O, Jesus is de captain,
Hosann—sann.
De angels are de sailors,
Hosann—sann.
O, is your bundle ready?
Hosann—sann.
O, have you got your ticket?
Hosann—sann."

This abbreviated chorus is given with unspeakable unction.

The three just given are modifications of an old camp-meeting melody; and the same may be true of the three following, although I cannot find them in the Methodist hymn-books. Each, however, has its characteristic modifications, which make it well worth giving. In the second verse of this next, for instance, "Saviour" evidently has become "soldier."

XXXI. Sweet Music.
"Sweet music in heaven,
Just beginning for to roll.
Don't you love God?
Glory, hallelujah!

"Yes, late I heard my soldier say,
Come, heavy soul, I am de way.
Don't you love God?
Glory, hallelujah!

"I'll go and tell to sinners round
What a kind Saviour I have found.
Don't you love God?

Glory, hallelujah!
"My grief my burden long has been,
Because I was not cease from sin.
    Don't you love God?
    Glory, hallelujah!"

XXXII. Good News.

"O, good news! O, good news!
De angels brought de tidings down,
    Just comin' from de trone.

"As grief from out my soul shall fly,
    Just comin' from de trone;
I'll shout salvation when I die,
    Good news, O, good news!
    Just comin' from de trone.

"Lord, I want to go to heaven when I die,
    Good news, O, good news! &c.

"De white folks call us a noisy crew,
    Good news, O, good news!
But dis I know, we are happy too,
    Just comin' from de trone."

XXXIII. The Heavenly Road.

"You may talk of my name as much as you please,
    And carry my name abroad,
But I really do believe I'm a child of God
    As I walk in de heavenly road.
O, won't you go wid me? (Thrice.)
    For to keep our garments clean.

"O Satan is a mighty busy ole man,
    And roll rocks in my way;
But Jesus is my bosom friend,
    And roll 'em out of de way.
O, won't you go wid me? (Thrice.)
    For to keep our garments clean.

"Come, my brudder, if you never did pray,
I hope you may pray to-night;
For I really believe I'm a child of God
As I walk in de heavenly road.
O, won't you," &c.

Some of the songs had played a historic part during the war. For singing the next, for instance, the negroes had been put in jail in Georgetown, S. C., at the outbreak of the Rebellion. "We'll soon be free" was too dangerous an assertion; and though the chant was an old one, it was no doubt sung with redoubled emphasis during the new events. "De Lord will call us home," was evidently thought to be a symbolical verse; for, as a little drummer-boy explained to me, showing all his white teeth as he sat in the moonlight by the door of my tent, "Dey tink *de Lord* mean for say *de Yankees.*"

XXXIV. We'll Soon Be Free.
"We'll soon be free,
We'll soon be free,
We'll soon be free,
When de Lord will call us home.
My brudder, how long,
My brudder, how long,
My brudder, how long,
'Fore we done sufferin' here?
It won't be long (Thrice.)
'Fore de Lord will call us home.
We'll walk de miry road (Thrice.)
Where pleasure never dies.
We'll walk de golden street (Thrice.)
Where pleasure never dies.
My brudder, how long (Thrice.)
'Fore we done sufferin' here?
We'll soon be free (Thrice.)
When Jesus sets me free.
We'll fight for liberty (Thrice.)
When de Lord will call us home."

The suspicion in this case was unfounded, but they had another song to which the Rebellion had actually given rise. This was composed by nobody knew whom,—though it was the most recent, doubtless, of all these "spirituals,"—and had been sung in secret to avoid detection. It is certainly plaintive enough. The peck of corn and pint of salt were slavery's rations.

XXXV. Many Thousand Go.

"No more peck o' corn for me,
  No more, no more,—
No more peck o' corn for me,
  Many tousand go.

"No more driver's lash for me, (Twice.)
  No more, &c.

"No more pint o' salt for me, (Twice.)
  No more, &c.

"No more hundred lash for me, (Twice.)
  No more, &c.

"No more mistress' call for me,
  No more, no more,—
No more mistress' call for me,
  Many tousand go."

Even of this last composition, however, we have only the approximate date and know nothing of the mode of composition. Allan Ramsay says of the Scotch songs, that, no matter who made them, they were soon attributed to the minister of the parish whence they sprang. And I always wondered, about these, whether they had always a conscious and definite origin in some leading mind, or whether they grew by gradual accretion, in an almost unconscious way. On this point I could get no information, though I asked many questions, until at last, one day when I was being rowed across from Beaufort to Ladies' Island, I found myself, with delight, on the actual trail of a song. One of the oarsmen, a brisk young fellow, not a soldier, on being asked for his theory of the matter, dropped out a coy confession. "Some good speriduals," he said, "are start jess out o' curiosity. I been a-raise a sing, myself, once."

My dream was fulfilled, and I had traced out, not the poem alone, but the poet. I implored him to proceed.

"Once we boys," he said, "went for tote some rice and de nigger-driver he keep a-callin' on us; and I say, 'O, de ole nigger-driver!' Den anudder

said, 'Fust ting my mammy tole me was, notin' so bad as nigger-driver.'
Den I made a sing, just puttin' a word, and den anudder word."

Then he began singing, and the men, after listening a moment, joined
in the chorus, as if it were an old acquaintance, though they evidently
had never heard it before. I saw how easily a new "sing" took root among
them.

XXXVI. The Driver.
"O, de ole nigger-driver!
O, gwine away!
Fust ting my mammy tell me,
O, gwine away!
Tell me 'bout de nigger-driver,
O, gwine away!
Nigger-driver second devil,
O, gwine away!
Best ting for do he driver,
O, gwine away!
Knock he down and spoil he labor,
O, gwine away!"

It will be observed that, although this song is quite secular in its character, yet its author called it a "spiritual." I heard but two songs among
them, at any time, to which they would not, perhaps, have given this
generic name. One of these consisted simply in the endless repetition—
after the manner of certain college songs—of the mysterious line,—

"Rain fall and wet Becky Lawton."

But who Becky Lawton was, and why she should or should not be wet,
and whether the dryness was a reward or a penalty, none could say. I got
the impression that, in either case, the event was posthumous, and that
there was some tradition of grass not growing over the grave of a sinner;
but even this was vague, and all else vaguer.

The other song I heard but once, on a morning when a squad of men
came in from picket duty, and chanted it in the most rousing way. It had
been a stormy and comfortless night, and the picket station was very exposed. It still rained in the morning when I strolled to the edge of the
camp, looking out for the men, and wondering how they had stood it.
Presently they came striding along the road, at a great pace, with their
shining rubber blankets worn as cloaks around them, the rain streaming

from these and from their equally shining faces, which were almost all upon the broad grin, as they pealed out this remarkable ditty:—

Hangman Johnny.

"O, dey call me Hangman Johnny!
O, ho! O, ho!
But I never hang nobody,
O, hang, boys, hang!

O dey, call me Hangman Johnny!
O, ho! O, ho!
But we'll all hang togedder,
O, hang, boys, hang!"

3

CAMP DIARY

November 27, 1862.

Thanksgiving-Day; it is the first moment I have had for writing during these three days, which have installed me into a new mode of life so thoroughly that they seem three years. Scarcely pausing in New York or in Beaufort, there seems to have been for me but one step from the camp of a Massachusetts regiment to this, and that step over leagues of waves.

It is a holiday wherever General Saxton's proclamation reaches. The chilly sunshine and the pale blue river seems like New England, but those alone. The air is full of noisy drumming, and of gunshots; for the prize-shooting is our great celebration of the day, and the drumming is chronic. My young barbarians are all at play. I look out from the broken windows of this forlorn plantation-house, through avenues of great live-oaks, with their hard, shining leaves, and their branches hung with a universal drapery of soft, long moss, like fringe-trees struck with grayness. Below, the sandy soil, scantly covered with coarse grass, bristles with sharp palmettoes and aloes; all the vegetation is stiff, shining, semi-tropical, with nothing soft or delicate in its texture. Numerous plantation-buildings totter around, all slovenly and unattractive, while the interspaces are filled with all manner of wreck and refuse, pigs, fowls, dogs, and omnipresent Ethiopian infancy. All this is the universal Southern panorama; but five minutes' walk beyond the hovels and the live-oaks will bring one to something so un-Southern that the whole Southern coast at this moment trembles at the suggestion of such a thing,—the camp of a regiment of freed slaves.

One adapts one's self so readily to new surroundings that already the full zest of the novelty seems passing away from my perceptions, and I write these lines in an eager effort to retain all I can. Already I am growing used to the experience, at first so novel, of living among five hundred men, and scarce a white face to be seen,—of seeing them go through all their daily processes, eating, frolicking, talking, just as if they were white. Each day at dress-parade I stand with the customary folding of the arms before a regimental line of countenances so black that I can hardly tell whether the men stand steadily or not; black is every hand which moves in ready cadence as I vociferate, "Battalion! Shoulder arms!" nor is it till the line of white officers moves forward, as parade is dismissed, that I am reminded that my own face is not the color of coal.

The first few days on duty with a new regiment must be devoted almost wholly to tightening reins; in this process one deals chiefly with the officers, and I have as yet had but little personal intercourse with the men. They concern me chiefly in bulk, as so many consumers of rations, wearers of uniforms, bearers of muskets. But as the machine comes into shape, I am beginning to decipher the individual parts. At first, of course, they all looked just alike; the variety comes afterwards, and they are just as distinguishable, the officers say, as so many whites. Most of them are wholly raw, but there are many who have already been for months in camp in the abortive "Hunter Regiment," yet in that loose kind of way which, like average militia training, is a doubtful advantage. I notice that some companies, too, look darker than others, though all are purer African than I expected. This is said to be partly a geographical difference between the South Carolina and Florida men. When the Rebels evacuated this region they probably took with them the house-servants, including most of the mixed blood, so that the residuum seems very black. But the men brought from Fernandina the other day average lighter in complexion, and look more intelligent, and they certainly take wonderfully to the drill.

It needs but a few days to show the absurdity of distrusting the military availability of these people. They have quite as much average comprehension as whites of the need of the thing, as much courage (I doubt not), as much previous knowledge of the gun, and, above all, a readiness of ear and of imitation, which, for purposes of drill, counterbalances any defect of mental training. To learn the drill, one does not want a set of college professors; one wants a squad of eager, active, pliant school-boys; and the more childlike these pupils are the better. There is no trouble about the drill; they will surpass whites in that. As to camp-life, they have little to sacrifice; they are better fed, housed, and clothed than ever in their lives before, and they appear to have few inconvenient vices. They are simple, docile, and affectionate almost to the point of absurdity. The same men who stood fire in open field with perfect coolness, on the late expedition, have come to me blubbering in the most irresistibly ludicrous manner on being transferred from one company in the regiment to another.

In noticing the squad-drills I perceive that the men learn less laboriously than whites that "double, double, toil and trouble," which is the elementary vexation of the drill-master,—that they more rarely mistake their left for their right,—and are more grave and sedate while under instruction. The extremes of jollity and sobriety, being greater with them, are less liable to be intermingled; these companies can be driven with a looser rein than my former one, for they restrain themselves; but the moment they are dismissed from drill every tongue is relaxed and every ivory tooth visible. This morning I wandered about where the different companies were target-shooting, and their glee was contagious. Such exulting shouts of "Ki! ole man," when some steady old turkey-shooter brought his gun down for an instant's aim, and then unerringly hit the mark; and then, when some unwary youth fired his piece into the ground at half-cock such guffawing and delight, such rolling over and over on the grass, such dances of ecstasy, as made the "Ethiopian minstrelsy" of the stage appear a feeble imitation.

Evening.—Better still was a scene on which I stumbled to-night. Strolling in the cool moonlight, I was attracted by a brilliant light beneath the trees, and cautiously approached it. A circle of thirty or forty soldiers sat around a roaring fire, while one old uncle, Cato by name, was narrating an interminable tale, to the insatiable delight of his audience. I came up into the dusky background, perceived only by a few, and he still continued. It was a narrative, dramatized to the last degree, of his adventures in escaping from his master to the Union vessels; and even I, who have heard the stories of Harriet Tubman, and such wonderful slave-comedians, never witnessed such a piece of acting. When I came upon the scene he had just come unexpectedly upon a plantation-house, and, putting a bold face upon it, had walked up to the door.

"Den I go up to de white man, berry humble, and say, would he please gib ole man a mouthful for eat?

"He say he must hab de valeration ob half a dollar.

"Den I look berry sorry, and turn for go away.

"Den he say I might gib him dat hatchet I had.

"Den I say" (this in a tragic vein) "dat I must hab dat hatchet for defend myself *from de dogs!*"

[Immense applause, and one appreciating auditor says, chuckling, "Dat was your *arms*, ole man," which brings down the house again.]

"Den he say de Yankee pickets was near by, and I must be very keerful.
  "Den I say, 'Good Lord, Mas'r, am dey?'"

Words cannot express the complete dissimulation with which these accents of terror were uttered,—this being precisely the piece of information he wished to obtain.

Then he narrated his devices to get into the house at night and obtain some food,—how a dog flew at him,—how the whole household, black and white, rose in pursuit,—how he scrambled under a hedge and over a high fence, etc.,—all in a style of which Gough alone among orators can give the faintest impression, so thoroughly dramatized was every syllable.

Then he described his reaching the river-side at last, and trying to decide whether certain vessels held friends or foes.

"Den I see guns on board, and sure sartin he Union boat, and I pop my head up. Den I been-a-tink [think] Seceshkey hab guns too, and my head go down again. Den I hide in de bush till morning. Den I open my bundle, and take ole white shirt and tie him on ole pole and wave him, and ebry time de wind blow, I been-a-tremble, and drap down in de bushes,"—because, being between two fires, he doubted whether friend or foe would see his signal first. And so on, with a succession of tricks beyond Molière, of acts of caution, foresight, patient cunning, which were listened to with infinite gusto and perfect comprehension by every listener.

And all this to a bivouac of negro soldiers, with the brilliant fire lighting up their red trousers and gleaming from their shining black faces,—eyes and teeth all white with tumultuous glee. Overhead, the mighty limbs of a great live-oak, with the weird moss swaying in the smoke, and the high moon gleaming faintly through.

Yet to-morrow strangers will remark on the hopeless, impenetrable stupidity in the daylight faces of many of these very men, the solid mask under which Nature has concealed all this wealth of mother-wit. This very comedian is one to whom one might point, as he hoed lazily in a cotton-field, as a being the light of whose brain had utterly gone out; and this scene seems like coming by night upon some conclave of black beetles, and finding them engaged, with green-room and foot-lights, in enacting "Poor Pillicoddy." This is their university; every young Sambo before me, as he turned over the sweet potatoes and peanuts which were roasting in the ashes, listened with reverence to the wiles of the ancient Ulysses, and meditated the same. It is Nature's compensation; oppression simply crushes the upper faculties of the head, and crowds everything into the perceptive organs. Cato, thou reasonest well! When I get into any serious scrape, in an enemy's country, may I be lucky enough to have you at my elbow, to pull me out of it!

The men seem to have enjoyed the novel event of Thanksgiving-Day; they have had company and regimental prize-shootings, a minimum of speeches and a maximum of dinner. Bill of fare: two beef-cattle and a thousand oranges. The oranges cost a cent apiece, and the cattle were Secesh, bestowed by General Saxby, as they all call him.

December 1, 1862.

How absurd is the impression bequeathed by Slavery in regard to these Southern blacks, that they are sluggish and inefficient in labor! Last night, after a hard day's work (our guns and the remainder of our tents being just issued), an order came from Beaufort that we should be ready in the evening to unload a steamboat's cargo of boards, being some of those captured by them a few weeks since, and now assigned for their use. I wondered if the men would grumble at the night-work; but the steamboat arrived by seven, and it was bright moonlight when they went at it. Never have I beheld such a jolly scene of labor. Tugging these wet and heavy boards over a bridge of boats ashore, then across the slimy beach at low tide, then up a steep bank, and all in one great uproar of merriment for two hours. Running most of the time, chattering all the time, snatching the boards from each other's backs as if they were some coveted treasure, getting up eager rivalries between different companies, pouring great choruses of ridicule on the heads of all shirkers, they made the whole scene so enlivening that I gladly stayed out in the moonlight for the whole time to watch it. And all this without any urging or any promised reward, but simply as the most natural way of doing the thing. The steamboat captain declared that they unloaded the ten thousand feet of boards quicker than any white gang could have done it; and they felt it so little, that, when, later in the night, I reproached one whom I found sitting by a campfire, cooking a surreptitious opossum, telling him that he ought to be asleep after such a job of work, he answered, with the broadest grin,—

"O no, Cunnel, da's no work at all, Cunnel; dat only jess enough *for stretch we.*"

December 2, 1862.

I believe I have not yet enumerated the probable drawbacks to the success of this regiment, if any. We are exposed to no direct annoyance from the white regiments, being out of their way; and we have as yet no discomforts or privations which we do not share with them. I do not as yet see the slightest obstacle, in the nature of the blacks, to making them good soldiers, but rather the contrary. They take readily to drill, and do not object to discipline; they are not especially dull or inattentive; they seem fully to understand the importance of the contest, and of their share in it. They show no jealousy or suspicion towards their officers.

They do show these feelings, however, towards the Government itself; and no one can wonder. Here lies the drawback to rapid recruiting. Were this a wholly new regiment, it would have been full to overflowing, I am satisfied, ere now. The trouble is in the legacy of bitter distrust bequeathed by the abortive regiment of General Hunter,—into which they were driven like cattle, kept for several months in camp, and then turned off without a shilling, by order of the War Department. The formation of that regiment was, on the whole, a great injury to this one; and the men who came from it, though the best soldiers we have in other respects, are the least sanguine and cheerful; while those who now refuse to enlist have a great influence in deterring others. Our soldiers are constantly twitted by their families and friends with their prospect of risking their lives in the service, and being paid nothing; and it is in vain that we read them the instructions of the Secretary of War to General Saxton, promising them the full pay of soldiers. They only half believe it.[1]

Another drawback is that some of the white soldiers delight in frightening the women on the plantations with doleful tales of plans for putting us in the front rank in all battles, and such silly talk,—the object being perhaps, to prevent our being employed on active service at all. All these considerations they feel precisely as white men would,—no less, no more; and it is the comparative freedom from such unfavorable influences which makes the Florida men seem more bold and manly, as they undoubtedly do. To-day General Saxton has returned from Fernandina with seventy-six recruits, and the eagerness of the captains to secure them was a sight to see. Yet they cannot deny that some of the very best men in the regiment are South Carolinians.

---

[1] With what utter humiliation were we, their officers, obliged to confess to them, eighteen months afterwards, that it was their distrust which was wise, and our faith in the pledges of the United States Government which was foolishness!

December 3, 1862.—7 P.M.

What a life is this I lead! It is a dark, mild, drizzling evening, and as the foggy air breeds sand-flies, so it calls out melodies and strange antics from this mysterious race of grown-up children with whom my lot is cast. All over the camp the lights glimmer in the tents, and as I sit at my desk in the open doorway, there come mingled sounds of stir and glee. Boys laugh and shout,—a feeble flute stirs somewhere in some tent, not an officer's,—a drum throbs far away in another,—wild kildeer-plover flit and wail above us, like the haunting souls of dead slave-masters,— and from a neighboring cook-fire comes the monotonous sound of that strange festival, half pow-wow, half prayer-meeting, which they know only as a "shout." These fires are usually enclosed in a little booth, made neatly of palm-leaves and covered in at top, a regular native African hut, in short, such as is pictured in books, and such as I once got up from dried palm-leaves for a fair at home. This hut is now crammed with men, singing at the top of their voices, in one of their quaint, monotonous, endless, negro-Methodist chants, with obscure syllables recurring constantly, and slight variations interwoven, all accompanied with a regular drumming of the feet and clapping of the hands, like castanets. Then the excitement spreads: inside and outside the enclosure men begin to quiver and dance, others join, a circle forms, winding monotonously round some one in the centre; some "heel and toe" tumultuously, others merely tremble and stagger on, others stoop and rise, others whirl, others caper sideways, all keep steadily circling like dervishes; spectators applaud special strokes of skill; my approach only enlivens the scene; the circle enlarges, louder grows the singing, rousing shouts of encouragement come in, half bacchanalian, half devout, "Wake 'em, brudder!" "Stan' up to 'em, brudder!"—and still the ceaseless drumming and clapping, in perfect cadence, goes steadily on. Suddenly there comes a sort of *snap*, and the spell breaks, amid general sighing and laughter. And this not rarely and occasionally, but night after night, while in other parts of the camp the soberest prayers and exhortations are proceeding sedately.

A simple and lovable people, whose graces seem to come by nature, and whose vices by training. Some of the best superintendents confirm the first tales of innocence, and Dr. Zachos told me last night that on his plantation, a sequestered one, "they had absolutely no vices." Nor have these men of mine yet shown any worth mentioning; since I took command I have heard of no man intoxicated, and there has been but one small quarrel. I suppose that scarcely a white regiment in the army shows so little swearing. Take the "Progressive Friends" and put them in red trousers, and I verily believe they would fill a guard-house sooner than these men. If camp regulations are violated, it seems to be usually through heedlessness. They love passionately three things besides their spiritual incantations; namely, sugar, home, and tobacco. This last affection brings tears to their eyes, almost, when they speak of their urgent need of pay; they speak of their last-remembered quid as if it were some deceased relative, too early lost, and to be mourned forever. As for sugar, no white man can drink coffee after they have sweetened it to their liking.

I see that the pride which military life creates may cause the plantation trickeries to diminish. For instance, these men make the most admirable sentinels. It is far harder to pass the camp lines at night than in the camp from which I came; and I have seen none of that disposition to connive at the offences of members of one's own company which is so troublesome among white soldiers. Nor are they lazy, either about work or drill; in all respects they seem better material for soldiers than I had dared to hope.

There is one company in particular, all Florida men, which I certainly think the finest-looking company I ever saw, white or black; they range admirably in size, have remarkable erectness and ease of carriage, and really march splendidly. Not a visitor but notices them; yet they have been under drill only a fortnight, and a part only two days. They have all been slaves, and very few are even mulattoes.

December 4, 1862.

"Dwelling in tents, with Abraham, Isaac, and Jacob." This condition is certainly mine,—and with a multitude of patriarchs beside, not to mention Cæsar and Pompey, Hercules and Bacchus.

A moving life, tented at night, this experience has been mine in civil society, if society be civil before the luxurious forest fires of Maine and the Adirondack, or upon the lonely prairies of Kansas. But a stationary tent life, deliberately going to housekeeping under canvas, I have never had before, though in our barrack life at "Camp Wool" I often wished for it.

The accommodations here are about as liberal as my quarters there, two wall-tents being placed end to end, for office and bedroom, and separated at will by a "fly" of canvas. There is a good board floor and mopboard, effectually excluding dampness and draughts, and everything but sand, which on windy days penetrates everywhere. The office furniture consists of a good desk or secretary, a very clumsy and disastrous settee, and a remarkable chair. The desk is a bequest of the slaveholders, and the settee of the slaves, being ecclesiastical in its origin, and appertaining to the little old church or "praise-house," now used for commissary purposes. The chair is a composite structure: I found a cane seat on a dust-heap, which a black sergeant combined with two legs from a broken bedstead and two more from an oak-bough. I sit on it with a pride of conscious invention, mitigated by profound insecurity. Bedroom furniture, a couch made of gun-boxes covered with condemned blankets, another settee, two pails, a tin cup, tin basin (we prize any tin or wooden ware as savages prize iron), and a valise, regulation size. Seriously considered, nothing more appears needful, unless ambition might crave another chair for company, and, perhaps, something for a wash-stand higher than a settee.

To-day it rains hard, and the wind quivers through the closed canvas, and makes one feel at sea. All the talk of the camp outside is fused into a cheerful and indistinguishable murmur, pierced through at every moment by the wail of the hovering plover. Sometimes a face, black or white, peers through the entrance with some message. Since the light readily penetrates, though the rain cannot, the tent conveys a feeling of charmed security, as if an invisible boundary checked the pattering drops and held the moaning wind. The front tent I share, as yet, with my adjutant; in the inner apartment I reign supreme, bounded in a nutshell, with no bad dreams.

In all pleasant weather the outer "fly" is open, and men pass and repass, a chattering throng. I think of Emerson's Saadi, "As thou sittest at thy door, on the desert's yellow floor,"—for these bare sand-plains, gray above, are always yellow when upturned, and there seems a tinge of Orientalism in all our life.

Thrice a day we go to the plantation-houses for our meals, camp-arrangements being yet very imperfect. The officers board in different messes, the adjutant and I still clinging to the household of William Washington,—William the quiet and the courteous, the pattern of house-servants, William the noiseless, the observing, the discriminating, who knows everything that can be got, and how to cook it. William and his tidy, lady-like little spouse Hetty—a pair of wedded lovers, if ever I saw one—set our table in their one room, half-way between an unglazed window and a large wood-fire, such as is often welcome. Thanks to the adjutant, we are provided with the social magnificence of napkins; while (lest pride take too high a flight) our table-cloth consists of two "New York Tribunes" and a "Leslie's Pictorial." Every steamer brings us a clean table-cloth. Here are we forever supplied with pork and oysters and sweet potatoes and rice and hominy and corn-bread and milk; also mysterious griddle-cakes of corn and pumpkin; also preserves made of pumpkin-chips, and other fanciful productions of Ethiop art. Mr. E. promised the plantation-superintendents who should come down here "all the luxuries of home," and we certainly have much apparent, if little real variety. Once William produced with some palpitation something fricasseed, which he boldly termed chicken; it was very small, and seemed in some undeveloped condition of ante-natal toughness. After the meal he frankly avowed it for a squirrel.

December 5, 1862.
Give these people their tongues, their feet, and their leisure, and they are happy. At every twilight the air is full of singing, talking, and clapping of hands in unison. One of their favorite songs is full of plaintive cadences; it is not, I think, a Methodist tune, and I wonder where they obtained a chant of such beauty.

> *"I can't stay behind, my Lord, I can't stay behind!*
> *O, my father is gone, my father is gone,*
> *My father is gone into heaven, my Lord!*
>   *I can't stay behind!*
> *Dere's room enough, room enough,*
> *Room enough in de heaven for de sojer:*
> *Can't stay behind!"*

It always excites them to have us looking on, yet they sing these songs at all times and seasons. I have heard this very song dimly droning on near midnight, and, tracing it into the recesses of a cook-house, have found an old fellow coiled away among the pots and provisions, chanting away with his "Can't stay behind, sinner," till I made him leave his song behind.

This evening, after working themselves up to the highest pitch, a party suddenly rushed off, got a barrel, and mounted some man upon it, who said, "Gib anoder song, boys, and I'se gib you a speech." After some hesitation and sundry shouts of "Rise de sing, somebody," and "Stan' up for Jesus, brudder," irreverently put in by the juveniles, they got upon the John Brown song, always a favorite, adding a jubilant verse which I had never before heard,—"We'll beat Beauregard on de clare battlefield." Then came the promised speech, and then no less than seven other speeches by as many men, on a variety of barrels, each orator being affectionately tugged to the pedestal and set on end by his special constituency. Every speech was good, without exception; with the queerest oddities of phrase and pronunciation, there was an invariable enthusiasm, a pungency of statement, and an understanding of the points at issue, which made them all rather thrilling. Those long-winded slaves in "Among the Pines" seemed rather fictitious and literary in comparison. The most eloquent, perhaps, was Corporal Price Lambkin, just arrived from Fernandina, who evidently had a previous reputation among them. His historical references were very interesting. He reminded them that he had predicted this war ever since Fremont's time, to which some of the crowd assented; he gave a very intelligent account of that Presidential campaign, and then described most impressively the secret anxiety of the slaves in Florida to know all about President Lincoln's election, and told how they all refused to work on the fourth of March, expecting their freedom to date from that day. He finally brought out one of the few really impressive appeals for the American flag that I have ever heard. "Our mas'rs dey hab lib under de flag, dey got dere wealth under it, and ebryting beautiful for dere chilen. Under it dey hab grind us up, and put us in dere pocket for money. But de fus' minute dey tink dat ole flag mean freedom for we colored people, dey pull it right down, and run up de rag ob dere own." (Immense applause). "But we'll neber desert de ole flag, boys, neber; we hab lib under it for *eighteen hundred sixty-two years*, and we'll die for it now." With which overpowering discharge of chronology-at-long-range, this most effective of stump-speeches closed. I see already with relief that there will be small demand in this regiment for harangues from the officers; give the men an empty barrel for a stump, and they will do their own exhortation.

December 11, 1862.

Haroun Alraschid, wandering in disguise through his imperial streets, scarcely happened upon a greater variety of groups than I, in my evening strolls among our own camp-fires.

Beside some of these fires the men are cleaning their guns or rehearsing their drill,—beside others, smoking in silence their very scanty supply of the beloved tobacco,—beside others, telling stories and shouting with laughter over the broadest mimicry, in which they excel, and in which the officers come in for a full share. The everlasting "shout" is always within hearing, with its mixture of piety and polka, and its castanet-like clapping of the hands. Then there are quieter prayer-meetings, with pious invocations and slow psalms, "deaconed out" from memory by the leader, two lines at a time, in a sort of wailing chant. Elsewhere, there are *conversazioni* around fires, with a woman for queen of the circle,—her Nubian face, gay headdress, gilt necklace, and white teeth, all resplendent in the glowing light. Sometimes the woman is spelling slow monosyllables out of a primer, a feat which always commands all ears,—they rightly recognizing a mighty spell, equal to the overthrowing of monarchs, in the magic assonance of *cat, hat, pat, bat,* and the rest of it. Elsewhere, it is some solitary old cook, some aged Uncle Tiff, with enormous spectacles, who is perusing a hymn-book by the light of a pine splinter, in his deserted cooking booth of palmetto leaves. By another fire there is an actual dance, red-legged soldiers doing right-and-left, and "now-lead-de-lady-ober," to the music of a violin which is rather artistically played, and which may have guided the steps, in other days, of Barnwells and Hugers. And yonder is a stump-orator perched on his barrel, pouring out his exhortations to fidelity in war and in religion. To-night for the first time I have heard a harangue in a different strain, quite saucy, sceptical, and defiant, appealing to them in a sort of French materialistic style, and claiming some personal experience of warfare. "You don't know notin' about it, boys. You tink you's brave enough; how you tink, if you stan' clar in de open field,—here you, and dar de Secesh? You's got to hab de right ting inside o' you. You must hab it 'served [preserved] in you, like dese yer sour plums dey 'serve in de barr'l; you's got to harden it down inside o' you, or it's notin'." Then he hit hard at the religionists: "When a man's got de sperit ob de Lord in him, it weakens him all out, can't hoe de corn." He had a great deal of broad sense in his speech; but presently some others began praying vociferously close by, as if to drown this free-thinker, when at last he exclaimed, "I mean to fight de war through, an' die a good sojer wid de last kick,—dat's *my* prayer!" and suddenly jumped off the barrel. I was quite interested at discovering this reverse side of the temperament, the devotional side preponderates so enormously, and the greatest scamps kneel and groan in their prayer-meetings with such entire zest. It shows that there is some individuality developed among them, and that they will not become too exclusively pietistic.

Their love of the spelling-book is perfectly inexhaustible,—they stumbling on by themselves, or the blind leading the blind, with the same pathetic patience which they carry into everything. The chaplain is getting up a schoolhouse, where he will soon teach them as regularly as he can. But the alphabet must always be a very incidental business in a camp.

January 1, 1863 (evening).

A happy New Year to civilized people,—mere white folks. Our festival has come and gone, with perfect success, and our good General has been altogether satisfied. Last night the great fires were kept smouldering in the pit, and the beeves were cooked more or less, chiefly more,—during which time they had to be carefully watched, and the great spits turned by main force. Happy were the merry fellows who were permitted to sit up all night, and watch the glimmering flames that threw a thousand fantastic shadows among the great gnarled oaks. And such a chattering as I was sure to hear whenever I awoke that night!

My first greeting to-day was from one of the most stylish sergeants, who approached me with the following little speech, evidently the result of some elaboration:—

"I tink myself happy, dis New Year's Day, for salute my own Cunnel. Dis day las' year I was servant to a Cunnel ob Secesh; but now I hab de privilege for salute my own Cunnel."

That officer, with the utmost sincerity, reciprocated the sentiment.

About ten o'clock the people began to collect by land, and also by water,—in steamers sent by General Saxton for the purpose; and from that time all the avenues of approach were thronged. The multitude were chiefly colored women, with gay handkerchiefs on their heads, and a sprinkling of men, with that peculiarly respectable look which these people always have on Sundays and holidays. There were many white visitors also,—ladies on horseback and in carriages, superintendents and teachers, officers, and cavalry-men. Our companies were marched to the neighborhood of the platform, and allowed to sit or stand, as at the Sunday services; the platform was occupied by ladies and dignitaries, and by the band of the Eighth Maine, which kindly volunteered for the occasion; the colored people filled up all the vacant openings in the beautiful grove around, and there was a cordon of mounted visitors beyond. Above, the great live-oak branches and their trailing moss; beyond the people, a glimpse of the blue river.

The services began at half past eleven o'clock, with prayer by our chaplain, Mr. Fowler, who is always, on such occasions, simple, reverential, and impressive. Then the President's Proclamation was read by Dr. W. H. Brisbane, a thing infinitely appropriate, a South Carolinian addressing South Carolinians; for he was reared among these very islands, and here long since emancipated his own slaves. Then the colors were presented to us by the Rev. Mr. French, a chaplain who brought them from the donors in New York. All this was according to the programme. Then followed an incident so simple, so touching, so utterly unexpected and startling, that I can scarcely believe it on recalling, though it gave the keynote to the whole day. The very moment the speaker had ceased, and just as I took and waved the flag, which now for the first time meant anything to these poor people, there suddenly arose, close beside the platform, a strong male voice (but rather cracked and elderly), into which two women's voices instantly blended, singing, as if by an impulse that could no more be repressed than the morning note of the song-sparrow.—

> *"My Country, 'tis of thee,*
> *Sweet land of liberty,*
> *Of thee I sing!"*

People looked at each other, and then at us on the platform, to see whence came this interruption, not set down in the bills. Firmly and irrepressibly the quavering voices sang on, verse after verse; others of the colored people joined in; some whites on the platform began, but I motioned them to silence. I never saw anything so electric; it made all other words cheap; it seemed the choked voice of a race at last unloosed. Nothing could be more wonderfully unconscious; art could not have dreamed of a tribute to the day of jubilee that should be so affecting; history will not believe it; and when I came to speak of it, after it was ended, tears were everywhere. If you could have heard how quaint and innocent it was! Old Tiff and his children might have sung it; and close before me was a little slave-boy, almost white, who seemed to belong to the party, and even he must join in. Just think of it!—the first day they had ever had a country, the first flag they had ever seen which promised anything to their people, and here, while mere spectators stood in silence, waiting for my stupid words, these simple souls burst out in their lay, as if they were by their own hearths at home! When they stopped, there was nothing to do for it but to speak, and I went on; but the life of the whole day was in those unknown people's song.

Receiving the flags, I gave them into the hands of two fine-looking men, jet black, as color-guard, and they also spoke, and very effectively,—Sergeant Prince Rivers and Corporal Robert Sutton. The regiment sang "Marching Along," and then General Saxton spoke, in his own simple, manly way, and Mrs. Francis D. Gage spoke very sensibly to the women, and Judge Stickney, from Florida, added something; then some gentleman sang an ode, and the regiment the John Brown song, and then they went to their beef and molasses. Everything was very orderly, and they seemed to have a very gay time. Most of the visitors had far to go, and so dispersed before dress-parade, though the band stayed to enliven it. In the evening we had letters from home, and General Saxton had a reception at his house, from which I excused myself; and so ended one of the most enthusiastic and happy gatherings I ever knew. The day was perfect, and there was nothing but success.

I forgot to say, that, in the midst of the services, it was announced that General Fremont was appointed Commander-in-Chief,—an announcement which was received with immense cheering, as would have been almost anything else, I verily believe, at that moment of high tide. It was shouted across by the pickets above,—a way in which we often receive news, but not always trustworthy.

January 12.

Many things glide by without time to narrate them. On Saturday we had a mail with the President's Second Message of Emancipation, and the next day it was read to the men. The words themselves did not stir them very much, because they have been often told that they were free, especially on New Year's Day, and, being unversed in politics, they do not understand, as well as we do, the importance of each additional guaranty. But the chaplain spoke to them afterwards very effectively, as usual; and then I proposed to them to hold up their hands and pledge themselves to be faithful to those still in bondage. They entered heartily into this, and the scene was quite impressive, beneath the great oak-branches. I heard afterwards that only one man refused to raise his hand, saying bluntly that his wife was out of slavery with him, and he did not care to fight. The other soldiers of his company were very indignant, and shoved him about among them while marching back to their quarters, calling him "Coward." I was glad of their exhibition of feeling, though it is very possible that the one who had thus the moral courage to stand alone among his comrades might be more reliable, on a pinch, than some who yielded a more ready assent. But the whole response, on their part, was very hearty, and will be a good thing to which to hold them hereafter, at any time of discouragement or demoralization,—which was my chief reason for proposing it. With their simple natures it is a great thing to tie them to some definite committal; they never forget a marked occurrence, and never seem disposed to evade a pledge.

It is this capacity of honor and fidelity which gives me such entire faith in them as soldiers. Without it all their religious demonstration would be mere sentimentality. For instance, every one who visits the camp is struck with their bearing as sentinels. They exhibit, in this capacity, not an upstart conceit, but a steady, conscientious devotion to duty. They would stop their idolized General Saxton, if he attempted to cross their beat contrary to orders: I have seen them. No feeble or incompetent race could do this. The officers tell many amusing instances of this fidelity, but I think mine the best.

It was very dark the other night,—an unusual thing here,—and the rain fell in torrents; so I put on my India-rubber suit, and went the rounds of the sentinels, incognito, to test them. I can only say that I shall never try such an experiment again and have cautioned my officers against it. 'Tis a wonder I escaped with life and limb,—such a charging of bayonets and clicking of gun-locks. Sometimes I tempted them by refusing to give any countersign, but offering them a piece of tobacco, which they could not accept without allowing me nearer than the prescribed bayonet's distance. Tobacco is more than gold to them, and it was touching to watch the struggle in their minds; but they always did their duty at last, and I never could persuade them. One man, as if wishing to crush all his inward vacillation at one fell stroke, told me stoutly that he never used tobacco, though I found next day that he loved it as much as any one of them. It seemed wrong thus to tamper with their fidelity; yet it was a vital matter to me to know how far it could be trusted, out of my sight. It was so intensely dark that not more than one or two knew me, even after I had talked with the very next sentinel, especially as they had never seen me in India-rubber clothing, and I can always disguise my voice. It was easy to distinguish those who did make the discovery; they were always conscious and simpering when their turn came; while the others were stout and irreverent till I revealed myself, and then rather cowed and anxious, fearing to have offended.

It rained harder and harder, and when I had nearly made the rounds I had had enough of it, and, simply giving the countersign to the challenging sentinel, undertook to pass within the lines.

"Halt!" exclaimed this dusky man and brother, bringing down his bayonet, "de countersign not correck."

Now the magic word, in this case, was "Vicksburg," in honor of a rumored victory. But as I knew that these hard names became quite transformed upon their lips, "Carthage" being familiarized into Cartridge, and "Concord" into Corncob, how could I possibly tell what shade of pronunciation my friend might prefer for this particular proper name?

"Vicksburg," I repeated, blandly, but authoritatively, endeavoring, as zealously as one of Christy's Minstrels, to assimilate my speech to any supposed predilection of the Ethiop vocal organs.

"Halt dar! Countersign not correck," was the only answer.

The bayonet still maintained a position which, in a military point of view, was impressive.

I tried persuasion, orthography, threats, tobacco, all in vain. I could not pass in. Of course my pride was up; for was I to defer to an untutored African on a point of pronunciation? Classic shades of Harvard, forbid! Affecting scornful indifference, I tried to edge away, proposing to myself to enter the camp at some other point, where my elocution would be better appreciated. Not a step could I stir.

"Halt!" shouted my gentleman again, still holding me at his bayonet's point, and I wincing and halting.

I explained to him the extreme absurdity of this proceeding, called his attention to the state of the weather, which, indeed, spoke for itself so loudly that we could hardly hear each other speak, and requested permission to withdraw. The bayonet, with mute eloquence, refused the application.

There flashed into my mind, with more enjoyment in the retrospect than I had experienced at the time, an adventure on a lecturing tour in other years, when I had spent an hour in trying to scramble into a country tavern, after bed-time, on the coldest night of winter. On that occasion I ultimately found myself stuck midway in the window, with my head in a temperature of 80°, and my heels in a temperature of –10°, with a heavy windowsash pinioning the small of my back. However, I had got safe out of that dilemma, and it was time to put an end to this one.

"Call the corporal of the guard," said I at last, with dignity, unwilling to make a night of it or to yield my incognito.

"Corporal ob de guard!" he shouted, lustily,—"Post Number Two!" while I could hear another sentinel chuckling with laughter. This last was a special guard, placed over a tent, with a prisoner in charge. Presently he broke silence.

"Who am dat?" he asked, in a stage whisper. "Am he a buckra [white man]?"

"Dunno whether he been a buckra or not," responded, doggedly, my Cerberus in uniform; "but I's bound to keep him here till de corporal ob de guard come."

Yet, when that dignitary arrived, and I revealed myself, poor Number Two appeared utterly transfixed with terror, and seemed to look for nothing less than immediate execution. Of course I praised his fidelity, and the next day complimented him before the guard, and mentioned him to his captain; and the whole affair was very good for them all. Hereafter, if Satan himself should approach them in darkness and storm, they will take him for "de Cunnel," and treat him with special severity.

January 13.

In many ways the childish nature of this people shows itself. I have just had to make a change of officers in a company which has constantly complained, and with good reason, of neglect and improper treatment. Two excellent officers have been assigned to them; and yet they sent a deputation to me in the evening, in a state of utter wretchedness. "We's bery grieved dis evening, Cunnel; 'pears like we couldn't bear it, to lose de Cap'n and de Lieutenant, all two togeder." Argument was useless; and I could only fall back on the general theory, that I knew what was best for them, which had much more effect; and I also could cite the instance of another company, which had been much improved by a new captain, as they readily admitted. So with the promise that the new officers should not be "savage to we," which was the one thing they deprecated, I assuaged their woes. Twenty-four hours have passed, and I hear them singing most merrily all down that company street.

I often notice how their griefs may be dispelled, like those of children, merely by permission to utter them: if they can tell their sorrows, they go away happy, even without asking to have anything done about them. I observe also a peculiar dislike of all *intermediate* control: they always wish to pass by the company officer, and deal with me personally for everything. General Saxton notices the same thing with the people on the plantations as regards himself. I suppose this proceeds partly from the old habit of appealing to the master against the overseer. Kind words would cost the master nothing, and he could easily put off any non-fulfilment upon the overseer. Moreover, the negroes have acquired such constitutional distrust of white people, that it is perhaps as much as they can do to trust more than one person at a time. Meanwhile this constant personal intercourse is out of the question in a well-ordered regiment; and the remedy for it is to introduce by degrees more and more of system, so that their immediate officers will become all-sufficient for the daily routine.

It is perfectly true (as I find everybody takes for granted) that the first essential for an officer of colored troops is to gain their confidence. But it is equally true, though many persons do not appreciate it, that the admirable methods and proprieties of the regular army are equally available for all troops, and that the sublimest philanthropist, if he does not appreciate this, is unfit to command them.

Another childlike attribute in these men, which is less agreeable, is a sort of blunt insensibility to giving physical pain. If they are cruel to animals, for instance, it always reminds me of children pulling off flies' legs, in a sort of pitiless, untaught, experimental way. Yet I should not fear any wanton outrage from them. After all their wrongs, they are not really revengeful; and I would far rather enter a captured city with them than with white troops, for they would be more subordinate. But for mere physical suffering they would have no fine sympathies. The cruel things they have seen and undergone have helped to blunt them; and if I ordered them to put to death a dozen prisoners, I think they would do it without remonstrance.

Yet their religious spirit grows more beautiful to me in living longer with them; it is certainly far more so than at first, when it seemed rather a matter of phrase and habit. It influences them both on the negative and the positive side. That is, it cultivates the feminine virtues first,— makes them patient, meek, resigned. This is very evident in the hospital; there is nothing of the restless, defiant habit of white invalids. Perhaps, if they had more of this, they would resist disease better. Imbued from childhood with the habit of submission, drinking in through every pore that other-world trust which is the one spirit of their songs, they can endure everything. This I expected; but I am relieved to find that their religion strengthens them on the positive side also,—gives zeal, energy, daring. They could easily be made fanatics, if I chose; but I do not choose. Their whole mood is essentially Mohammedan, perhaps, in its strength and its weakness; and I feel the same degree of sympathy that I should if I had a Turkish command,—that is, a sort of sympathetic admiration, not tending towards agreement, but towards co-operation. Their philosophizing is often the highest form of mysticism; and our dear surgeon declares that they are all natural transcendentalists. The white camps seem rough and secular, after this; and I hear our men talk about "a religious army," "a Gospel army," in their prayer-meetings. They are certainly evangelizing the chaplain, who was rather a heretic at the beginning; at least, this is his own admission. We have recruits on their way from St. Augustine, where the negroes are chiefly Roman Catholics; and it will be interesting to see how their type of character combines with that elder creed.

It is time for rest; and I have just looked out into the night, where the eternal stars shut down, in concave protection, over the yet glimmering camp, and Orion hangs above my tent-door, giving to me the sense of strength and assurance which these simple children obtain from their Moses and the Prophets. Yet external Nature does its share in their training; witness that most poetic of all their songs, which always reminds me of the "Lyke-Wake Dirge" in the "Scottish Border Minstrelsy,"—

> "I know moon-rise, I know star-rise;
>   Lay dis body down.
> I walk in de moonlight, I walk in de starlight,
>   To lay dis body down.

I'll walk in de graveyard, I'll walk through de graveyard,
  To lay dis body down.
I'll lie in de grave and stretch out my arms;
  Lay dis body down.
I go to de Judgment in de evening ob de day
  When I lay dis body down;
And my soul and your soul will meet in de day
  When I lay dis body down."

January 14.

In speaking of the military qualities of the blacks, I should add, that the only point where I am disappointed is one I have never seen raised by the most incredulous newspaper critics,—namely, their physical condition. To be sure they often look magnificently to my gymnasium-trained eye; and I always like to observe them when bathing,—such splendid muscular development, set off by that smooth coating of adipose tissue which makes them, like the South-Sea Islanders appear even more muscular than they are. Their skins are also of finer grain than those of whites, the surgeons say, and certainly are smoother and far more free from hair. But their weakness is pulmonary; pneumonia and pleurisy are their besetting ailments; they are easily made ill,—and easily cured, if promptly treated: childish organizations again. Guard-duty injures them more than whites, apparently; and double-quick movements, in choking dust, set them coughing badly. But then it is to be remembered that this is their sickly season, from January to March, and that their healthy season will come in summer, when the whites break down. Still my conviction of the physical superiority of more highly civilized races is strengthened on the whole, not weakened, by observing them. As to availability for military drill and duty in other respects, the only question I ever hear debated among the officers is, whether they are equal or superior to whites. I have never heard it suggested that they were inferior, although I expected frequently to hear such complaints from hasty or unsuccessful officers.

Of one thing I am sure, that their best qualities will be wasted by merely keeping them for garrison duty. They seem peculiarly fitted for offensive operations, and especially for partisan warfare; they have so much dash and such abundant resources, combined with such an Indian-like knowledge of the country and its ways. These traits have been often illustrated in expeditions sent after deserters. For instance, I despatched one of my best lieutenants and my best sergeant with a squad of men to search a certain plantation, where there were two separate negro villages. They went by night, and the force was divided. The lieutenant took one set of huts, the sergeant the other. Before the lieutenant had reached his first house, every man in the village was in the woods, innocent and guilty alike. But the sergeant's mode of operation was thus described by a corporal from a white regiment who happened to be in one of the negro houses. He said that not a sound was heard until suddenly a red leg appeared in the open doorway, and a voice outside said, "Rally." Going to the door, he observed a similar pair of red legs before every hut, and not a person was allowed to go out, until the quarters had been thoroughly searched, and the three deserters found. This was managed by Sergeant Prince Rivers, our color-sergeant, who is provost-sergeant also, and has entire charge of the prisoners and of the daily policing of the camp. He is a man of distinguished appearance, and in old times was the crack coachman of Beaufort, in which capacity he once drove Beauregard from this plantation to Charleston, I believe. They tell me that he was once allowed to present a petition to the Governor of South Carolina in behalf of slaves, for the redress of certain grievances; and that a placard, offering two thousand dollars for his recapture, is still to be seen by the wayside between here and Charleston. He was a sergeant in the old "Hunter Regiment," and was taken by General Hunter to New York last spring, where the *chevrons* on his arm brought a mob upon him in Broadway, whom he kept off till the police interfered. There is not a white officer in this regiment who has more administrative ability, or more absolute authority over the men; they do not love him, but his mere presence has controlling power over them. He writes well enough to prepare for me a daily report of his duties in the camp; if his education reached a higher point, I see no reason why he should not command the Army of the Potomac. He is jet-black, or rather, I should say, *wine-black;* his complexion, like that of others of my darkest men, having a sort of rich, clear depth, without a trace of sootiness, and to my eye very handsome. His features are tolerably regular, and full of command, and his figure superior to that of any of our white officers,—being six feet high, perfectly proportioned, and of apparently inexhaustible strength and activity. His gait is like a panther's; I never saw such a tread. No anti-slavery novel has described a man of such marked ability. He makes Toussaint perfectly intelligible; and if there should ever be a black monarchy in South Carolina, he will be its king.

4

THE NEGRO AS SOLDIER

There was in our regiment a very young recruit, named Sam Roberts, of whom Trowbridge used to tell this story. Early in the war Trowbridge had been once sent to Amelia Island with a squad of men, under direction of Commodore Goldsborough, to remove the negroes from the island. As the officers stood on the beach, talking to some of the older freedmen, they saw this urchin peeping at them from front and rear in a scrutinizing way for which his father at last called him to account, as thus:—

"Hi! Sammy, what you's doin', chile?"

"Daddy," said the inquisitive youth, "don't you know mas'r tell us Yankee hab tail? I don't see no tail, daddy!"

There were many who went to Port Royal during the war, in civil or military positions, whose previous impressions of the colored race were about as intelligent as Sam's view of themselves. But, for once, I had always had so much to do with fugitive slaves, and had studied the whole subject with such interest, that I found not much to learn or unlearn as to this one point. Their courage I had before seen tested; their docile and lovable qualities I had known; and the only real surprise that experience brought me was in finding them so little demoralized. I had not allowed for the extreme remoteness and seclusion of their lives, especially among the Sea Islands. Many of them had literally spent their whole existence on some lonely island or remote plantation, where the master never came, and the overseer only once or twice a week. With these exceptions, such persons had never seen a white face, and of the excitements or sins of larger communities they had not a conception. My friend Colonel Hallowell, of the Fifty-Fourth Massachusetts, told me that he had among his men some of the worst reprobates of Northern cities. While I had some men who were unprincipled and troublesome, there was not one whom I could call a hardened villain. I was constantly expecting to find male Topsies, with no notions of good and plenty of evil. But I never found one. Among the most ignorant there was very often a childlike absence of vices, which was rather to be classed as inexperience than as innocence, but which had some of the advantages of both.

Apart from this, they were very much like other men. General Saxton, examining with some impatience a long list of questions from some philanthropic Commission at the North, respecting the traits and habits of the freedmen, bade some staff-officer answer them all in two words,—"Intensely human." We all admitted that it was a striking and comprehensive description.

For instance, as to courage. So far as I have seen, the mass of men are naturally courageous up to a certain point. A man seldom runs away from danger which he ought to face, unless others run; each is apt to keep with the mass, and colored soldiers have more than usual of this gregariousness. In almost every regiment, black or white, there are a score or two of men who are naturally daring, who really hunger after dangerous adventures, and are happiest when allowed to seek them. Every commander gradually finds out who these men are, and habitually uses them; certainly I had such, and I remember with delight their bearing, their coolness, and their dash. Some of them were negroes, some mulattoes. One of them would have passed for white, with brown hair and blue eyes, while others were so black you could hardly see their features. These picked men varied in other respects too; some were neat and well-drilled soldiers, while others were slovenly, heedless fellows,— the despair of their officers at inspection, their pride on a raid. They were the natural scouts and rangers of the regiment; they had the two-o'clock-in-the-morning courage, which Napoleon thought so rare. The mass of the regiment rose to the same level under excitement, and were more excitable, I think, than whites, but neither more nor less courageous.

Perhaps the best proof of a good average of courage among them was in the readiness they always showed for any special enterprise. I do not remember ever to have had the slightest difficulty in obtaining volunteers, but rather in keeping down the number. The previous pages include many illustrations of this, as well as of their endurance of pain and discomfort. For instance, one of my lieutenants, a very daring Irishman, who had served for eight years as a sergeant of regular artillery in Texas, Utah, and South Carolina, said he had never been engaged in anything so risky as our raid up the St. Mary's. But in truth it seems to me a mere absurdity to deliberately argue the question of courage, as applied to men among whom I waked and slept, day and night, for so many months together. As well might he who has been wandering for years upon the desert, with a Bedouin escort, discuss the courage of the men whose tents have been his shelter and whose spears his guard. We, their officers, did not go there to teach lessons, but to receive them. There were more than a hundred men in the ranks who had voluntarily met more dangers in their escape from slavery than any of my young captains had incurred in all their lives.

There was a family named Wilson, I remember, of which we had several representatives. Three or four brothers had planned an escape from the interior to our lines; they finally decided that the youngest should stay and take care of the old mother; the rest, with their sister and her children, came in a "dug-out" down one of the rivers. They were fired upon, again and again, by the pickets along the banks, until finally every man on board was wounded; and still they got safely through. When the bullets began to fly about them, the woman shed tears, and her little girl of nine said to her, "Don't cry, mother, Jesus will help you," and then the child began praying as the wounded men still urged the boat along. This the mother told me, but I had previously heard it from an officer who was on the gunboat that picked them up,—a big, rough man, whose voice fairly broke as he described their appearance. He said that the mother and child had been hid for nine months in the woods before attempting their escape, and the child would speak to no one,—indeed, she hardly would when she came to our camp. She was almost white, and this officer wished to adopt her, but the mother said, "I would do anything but that for *oonah*,"—this being a sort of Indian formation of the second-person-plural, such as they sometimes use. This same officer afterwards saw a reward offered for this family in a Savannah paper.

I used to think that I should not care to read "Uncle Tom's Cabin" in our camp; it would have seemed tame. Any group of men in a tent would have had more exciting tales to tell. I needed no fiction when I had Fanny Wright, for instance, daily passing to and fro before my tent, with her shy little girl clinging to her skirts. Fanny was a modest little mulatto woman, a soldier's wife, and a company laundress. She had escaped from the main-land in a boat, with that child and another. Her baby was shot dead in her arms, and she reached our lines with one child safe on earth and the other in heaven. I never found it needful to give any elementary instructions in courage to Fanny's husband, you may be sure.

There was another family of brothers in the regiment named Miller. Their grandmother, a fine-looking old woman, nearly seventy, I should think, but erect as a pine-tree, used sometimes to come and visit them. She and her husband had once tried to escape from a plantation near Savannah. They had failed, and had been brought back; the husband had received five hundred lashes, and while the white men on the plantation were viewing the punishment, she was collecting her children and grandchildren, to the number of twenty-two, in a neighboring marsh, preparatory to another attempt that night. They found a flat-boat which had been rejected as unseaworthy, got on board,—still under the old woman's orders,—and drifted forty miles down the river to our lines. Trowbridge happened to be on board the gunboat which picked them up, and he said that when the "flat" touched the side of the vessel, the grandmother rose to her full height, with her youngest grandchild in her arms, and said only, "My God! are we free?" By one of those coincidences of which life is full, her husband escaped also, after his punishment, and was taken up by the same gunboat.

I hardly need point out that my young lieutenants did not have to teach the principles of courage to this woman's grandchildren.

I often asked myself why it was that, with this capacity of daring and endurance, they had not kept the land in a perpetual flame of insurrection; why, especially since the opening of the war, they had kept so still. The answer was to be found in the peculiar temperament of the races, in their religious faith, and in the habit of patience that centuries had fortified. The shrewder men all said substantially the same thing. What was the use of insurrection, where everything was against them? They had no knowledge, no money, no arms, no drill, no organization,—above all, no mutual confidence. It was the tradition among them that all insurrections were always betrayed by somebody. They had no mountain passes to defend like the Maroons of Jamaica,—no impenetrable swamps, like the Maroons of Surinam. Where they had these, even on a small scale, they had used them,—as in certain swamps round Savannah and in the everglades of Florida, where they united with the Indians, and would stand fire—so I was told by General Saxton, who had fought them there—when the Indians would retreat.

It always seemed to me that, had I been a slave, my life would have been one long scheme of insurrection. But I learned to respect the patient self-control of those who had waited till the course of events should open a better way. When it came they accepted it. Insurrection on their part would at once have divided the Northern sentiment; and a large part of our army would have joined with the Southern army to hunt them down. By their waiting till we needed them, their freedom was secured.

Two things chiefly surprised me in their feeling toward their former masters,—the absence of affection and the absence of revenge. I expected to find a good deal of the patriarchal feeling. It always seemed to me a very ill-applied emotion, as connected with the facts and laws of American slavery,—still I expected to find it. I suppose that my men and their families and visitors may have had as much of it as the mass of freed slaves; but certainly they had not a particle. I never could cajole one of them, in his most discontented moment, into regretting "ole mas'r time" for a single instant. I never heard one speak of the masters except as natural enemies. Yet they were perfectly discriminating as to individuals; many of them claimed to have had kind owners, and some expressed great gratitude to them for particular favors received. It was not the individuals, but the ownership, of which they complained. That they saw to be a wrong which no special kindnesses could right. On this, as on all points connected with slavery, they understood the matter as clearly as Garrison or Phillips; the wisest philosophy could teach them nothing as to that, nor could any false philosophy befog them. After all, personal experience is the best logician.

Certainly this indifference did not proceed from any want of personal affection, for they were the most affectionate people among whom I had ever lived. They attached themselves to every officer who deserved love, and to some who did not; and if they failed to show it to their masters, it proved the wrongfulness of the mastery. On the other hand, they rarely showed one gleam of revenge, and I shall never forget the self-control with which one of our best sergeants pointed out to me, at Jacksonville, the very place where one of his brothers had been hanged by the whites for leading a party of fugitive slaves. He spoke of it as a historic matter, without any bearing on the present issue.

But side by side with this faculty of patience, there was a certain tropical element in the men, a sort of fiery ecstasy when aroused, which seemed to link them by blood with the French Turcos, and made them really resemble their natural enemies, the Celts, far more than the Anglo-Saxon temperament. To balance this there were great individual resources when alone,—a sort of Indian wiliness and subtlety of resource. Their gregariousness and love of drill made them more easy to keep in hand than white American troops, who rather like to straggle or go in little squads, looking out for themselves, without being bothered with officers. The blacks prefer organization.

The point of inferiority that I always feared, though I never had occasion to prove it, was that they might show less fibre, less tough and dogged resistance, than whites, during a prolonged trial,—a long, disastrous march, for instance, or the hopeless defence of a besieged town. I should not be afraid of their mutinying or running away, but of their drooping and dying. It might not turn out so; but I mention it for the sake of fairness, and to avoid overstating the merits of these troops. As to the simple general fact of courage and reliability I think no officer in our camp ever thought of there being any difference between black and white. And certainly the opinions of these officers, who for years risked their lives every moment on the fidelity of their men, were worth more than those of all the world beside.

No doubt there were reasons why this particular war was an especially favorable test of the colored soldiers. They had more to fight for than the whites. Besides the flag and the Union, they had home and wife and child. They fought with ropes round their necks, and when orders were issued that the officers of colored troops should be put to death on capture, they took a grim satisfaction. It helped their *esprit de corps* immensely. With us, at least, there was to be no play-soldier. Though they had begun with a slight feeling of inferiority to the white troops, this compliment substituted a peculiar sense of self-respect. And even when the new colored regiments began to arrive from the North my men still pointed out this difference,—that in case of ultimate defeat, the Northern troops, black or white, would go home, while the First South Carolina must fight it out or be re-enslaved. This was one thing that made the St. John's River so attractive to them and even to me;—it was so much nearer the everglades. I used seriously to ponder, during the darker periods of the war, whether I might not end my days as an outlaw,—a leader of Maroons.

Meanwhile, I used to try to make some capital for the Northern troops, in their estimate, by pointing out that it was a disinterested thing in these men from the free States, to come down there and fight, that the slaves might be free. But they were apt keenly to reply, that many of the white soldiers disavowed this object, and said that that was not the object of the war, nor even likely to be its end. Some of them even repeated Mr. Seward's unfortunate words to Mr. Adams, which some general had been heard to quote. So, on the whole, I took nothing by the motion, as was apt to be the case with those who spoke a good word for our Government, in those vacillating and half proslavery days.

At any rate, this ungenerous discouragement had this good effect, that it touched their pride; they would deserve justice, even if they did not

obtain it. This pride was afterwards severely tested during the disgraceful period when the party of repudiation in Congress temporarily deprived them of their promised pay. In my regiment the men never mu-
tinied, nor even threatened mutiny; they seemed to make it a matter of
honor to do their part, even if the Government proved a defaulter; but
one third of them, including the best men in the regiment, quietly refused to take a dollar's pay, at the reduced price. "We'se gib our sogerin'
to de Guv'ment, Cunnel," they said, "but we won't 'spise ourselves so
much for take de seben dollar." They even made a contemptuous ballad,
of which I once caught a snatch.

> *"Ten dollar a month!*
> *Tree ob dat for clothin'!*
> *Go to Washington*
> *Fight for Linkum's darter!"*

This "Lincoln's daughter" stood for the Goddess of Liberty, it would
seem. They would be true to her, but they would not take the half-pay.
This was contrary to my advice, and to that of other officers; but I now
think it was wise. Nothing less than this would have called the attention
of the American people to this outrageous fraud.

The same slow forecast had often marked their action in other ways.
One of our ablest sergeants, Henry McIntyre, who had earned two dollars and a half per day as a master-carpenter in Florida, and paid one
dollar and a half to his master, told me that he had deliberately refrained
from learning to read, because that knowledge exposed the slaves to so
much more watching and suspicion. This man and a few others had
built on contract the greater part of the town of Micanopy in Florida,
and was a thriving man when his accustomed discretion failed for once,
and he lost all. He named his child William Lincoln, and it brought upon
him such suspicion that he had to make his escape.

I cannot conceive what people at the North mean by speaking of the negroes as a bestial or brutal race. Except in some insensibility to animal
pain, I never knew of an act in my regiment which I should call brutal. In
reading Kay's "Condition of the English Peasantry" I was constantly struck
with the unlikeness of my men to those therein described. This could not
proceed from my prejudices as an abolitionist, for they would have led me
the other way, and indeed I had once written a little essay to show the brutalizing influences of slavery. I learned to think that we abolitionists had
under-rated the suffering produced by slavery among the negroes, but had
overrated the demoralization. Or rather, we did not know how the reli-

gious temperament of the negroes had checked the demoralization. Yet again, it must be admitted that this temperament, born of sorrow and oppression, is far more marked in the slave than in the native African.

Theorize as we may, there was certainly in our camp an average tone of propriety which all visitors noticed, and which was not created, but only preserved by discipline. I was always struck, not merely by the courtesy of the men, but also by a certain sober decency of language. If a man had to report to me any disagreeable fact, for instance, he was sure to do it with gravity and decorum, and not blurt it out in an offensive way. And it certainly was a significant fact that the ladies of our camp, when we were so fortunate as to have such guests,—the young wives, especially, of the adjutant and quartermaster,—used to go among the tents when the men were off duty, in order to hear their big pupils read and spell, without the slightest fear of annoyance. I do not mean direct annoyance or insult, for no man who valued his life would have ventured that in presence of the others, but I mean the annoyance of accidentally seeing or hearing improprieties not intended for them. They both declared that they would not have moved about with anything like the same freedom in any white camp they had ever entered, and it always roused their indignation to hear the negro race called brutal or depraved.

This came partly from natural good manners, partly from the habit of deference, partly from ignorance of the refined and ingenious evil which is learned in large towns; but a large part came from their strongly religious temperament. Their comparative freedom from swearing, for instance,—an abstinence which I fear military life did not strengthen,—was partly a matter of principle. Once I heard one of them say to another, in a transport of indignation, "Ha-a-a, boy, s'pose I no be a Christian, I cuss you so!"—which was certainly drawing pretty hard upon the bridle. "Cuss," however, was a generic term for all manner of evil speaking; they would say, "He cuss me fool," or "He cuss me coward," as if the essence of propriety were in harsh and angry speech,—which I take to be good ethics. But certainly, if Uncle Toby could have recruited his army in Flanders from our ranks, their swearing would have ceased to be historic.

It used to seem to me that never, since Cromwell's time, had there been soldiers in whom the religious element held such a place. "A religious army," "a gospel army," were their frequent phrases. In their prayer-meetings there was always a mingling, often quaint enough, of the warlike and the pious. "If each one of us was a praying man," said

Corporal Thomas Long in a sermon, "it appears to me that we could fight as well with prayers as with bullets,—for the Lord has said that if you have faith even as a grain of mustard-seed cut into four parts, you can say to the sycamore-tree, Arise, and it will come up." And though Corporal Long may have got a little perplexed in his botany, his faith proved itself by works, for he volunteered and went many miles on a solitary scouting expedition into the enemy's country in Florida, and got back safe, after I had given him up for lost.

The extremes of religious enthusiasm I did not venture to encourage, for I could not do it honestly; neither did I discourage them, but simply treated them with respect, and let them have their way, so long as they did not interfere with discipline. In general they promoted it. The mischievous little drummer-boys, whose scrapes and quarrels were the torment of my existence, might be seen kneeling together in their tents to say their prayers at night, and I could hope that their slumbers were blessed by some spirit of peace, such as certainly did not rule over their waking. The most reckless and daring fellows in the regiment were perfect fatalists in their confidence that God would watch over them, and that if they died, it would be because their time had come. This almost excessive faith, and the love of freedom and of their families, all co-operated with their pride as soldiers to make them do their duty. I could not have spared any of these incentives. Those of our officers who were personally the least influenced by such considerations, still saw the need of encouraging them among the men.

I am bound to say that this strongly devotional turn was not always accompanied by the practical virtues; but neither was it strikingly divorced from them. A few men, I remember, who belonged to the ancient order of hypocrites, but not many. Old Jim Cushman was our favorite representative scamp. He used to vex his righteous soul over the admission of the unregenerate to prayer-meetings, and went off once shaking his head and muttering, "Too much goat shout wid de sheep." But he who objected to this profane admixture used to get our mess-funds far more hopelessly mixed with his own, when he went out to buy chickens. And I remember that, on being asked by our Major, in that semi-Ethiopian dialect into which we sometimes slid, "How much wife you got, Jim?" the veteran replied, with a sort of penitence for lost opportunities, "On'y but four, Sah!"

Another man of somewhat similar quality went among us by the name of Henry Ward Beecher, from a remarkable resemblance in face and figure to that sturdy divine. I always felt a sort of admiration for this worthy, because of the thoroughness with which he outwitted me, and the sublime impudence in which he culminated. He got a series of passes from me, every week or two, to go and see his wife on a neighboring plantation, and finally, when this resource seemed exhausted, he came boldly for one more pass, that he might go and be married.

We used to quote him a good deal, also, as a sample of a certain Shakespearian boldness of personification in which the men sometimes indulged. Once, I remember, his captain had given him a fowling-piece to clean. Henry Ward had left it in the captain's tent, and the latter, finding it, had transferred the job to some one else.

Then came a confession, in this precise form, with many dignified gesticulations:—

"Cappen! I took dat gun, and I put him in Cappen tent. Den I look, and de gun not dar! Den Conscience say, Cappen mus' hab gib dat gun to somebody else for clean. Den I say, Conscience, you reason correck."

Compare Lancelot Gobbo's soliloquy in the "Two Gentlemen of Verona"!

Still, I maintain that, as a whole, the men were remarkably free from inconvenient vices. There was no more lying and stealing than in average white regiments. The surgeon was not much troubled by shamming sickness, and there were not a great many complaints of theft. There was less quarrelling than among white soldiers, and scarcely ever an instance of drunkenness. Perhaps the influence of their officers had something to do with this; for not a ration of whiskey was ever issued to the men, nor did I ever touch it, while in the army, nor approve a requisition for any of the officers, without which it could not easily be obtained. In this respect our surgeons fortunately agreed with me, and we never had reason to regret it. I believe the use of ardent spirits to be as useless and injurious in the army as on board ship, and among the colored troops, especially, who had never been accustomed to it, I think that it did only harm.

The point of greatest laxity in their moral habits—the want of a high standard of chastity—was not one which affected their camp life to any great extent, and it therefore came less under my observation. But I found to my relief that, whatever their deficiency in this respect, it was modified by the general quality of their temperament, and indicated rather a softening and relaxation than a hardening and brutalizing of their moral natures. Any insult or violence in this direction was a thing unknown. I never heard of an instance. It was not uncommon for men to have two or three wives in different plantations,—the second, or remoter, partner being called a "'broad wife,'"—i.e. wife abroad. But the whole tendency was toward marriage, and this state of things was only regarded as a bequest from "mas'r time."

I knew a great deal about their marriages, for they often consulted me, and took my counsel as lovers are wont to do,—that is, when it pleased their fancy. Sometimes they would consult their captains first, and then come to me in despairing appeal. "Cap'n Scroby [Trowbridge] he acvise me not for marry dis lady, 'cause she hab seben chil'en. What for use? Cap'n Scroby can't lub for me. I mus' lub for myself, and I lub he." I remember that on this occasion "he" stood by, a most unattractive woman, jet black, with an old pink muslin dress, torn white cotton gloves, and a very flowery bonnet, that must have descended through generations of tawdry mistresses.

I felt myself compelled to reaffirm the decision of the inferior court. The result was as usual. They were married the next day, and I believe that she proved an excellent wife, though she had seven children, whose father was also in the regiment. If she did not, I know many others who did, and certainly I have never seen more faithful or more happy marriages than among that people.

The question was often asked, whether the Southern slaves or the Northern free blacks made the best soldiers. It was a compliment to both classes that each officer usually preferred those whom he had personally commanded. I preferred those who had been slaves, for their greater docility and affectionateness, for the powerful stimulus which their new freedom gave, and for the fact that they were fighting, in a manner, for their own homes and firesides. Every one of these considerations afforded a special aid to discipline, and cemented a peculiar tie of sympathy between them and their officers. They seemed like clansmen, and had a more confiding and filial relation to us than seemed to me to exist in the Northern colored regiments.

So far as the mere habits of slavery went, they were a poor preparation for military duty. Inexperienced officers often assumed that, because these men had been slaves before enlistment, they would bear to be treated as such afterwards. Experience proved the contrary. The more strongly we marked the difference between the slave and the soldier, the better for the regiment. One half of military duty lies in obedience, the other half in self-respect. A soldier without self-respect is worthless. Consequently there were no regiments in which it was so important to observe the courtesies and proprieties of military life as in these. I had to caution the officers to be more than usually particular in returning the salutations of the men; to be very careful in their dealings with those on picket or guard-duty; and on no account to omit the titles of the non-commissioned officers. So, in dealing out punishments, we had carefully to avoid all that was brutal and arbitrary, all that savored of the overseer. Any such dealing found them as obstinate and contemptuous as was Topsy when Miss Ophelia undertook to chastise her. A system of light punishments, rigidly administered according to the prescribed military forms, had more weight with them than any amount of angry severity. To make them feel as remote as possible from the plantation, this was essential. By adhering to this, and constantly appealing to their pride as soldiers and their sense of duty, we were able to maintain a high standard of discipline,—so, at least, the inspecting officers said,—and to get rid, almost entirely, of the more degrading class of punishments,—standing on barrels, tying up by the thumbs, and the ball and chain.

In all ways we had to educate their self-respect. For instance, at first they disliked to obey their own non-commissioned officers. "I don't want him to play de white man ober me," was a sincere objection. They had been so impressed with a sense of inferiority that the distinction extended to the very principles of honor. "I ain't got colored-man principles," said Corporal London Simmons, indignantly defending himself from some charge before me. "I'se got white-gemman principles. I'se do my best. If Cap'n tell me to take a man, s'pose de man be as big as a house, I'll clam hold on him till I die, inception [excepting] I'm sick."

But it was plain that this feeling was a bequest of slavery, which military life would wear off. We impressed it upon them that they did not obey their officers because they were white, but because they were their officers, just as the Captain must obey me, and I the General; that we were all subject to military law, and protected by it in turn. Then we taught them to take pride in having good material for non-commissioned officers among themselves, and in obeying them. On my arrival there was one white first sergeant, and it was a question whether to appoint others. This I prevented, but left that one, hoping the men themselves would at last petition for his removal, which at length they did. He was at once detailed on other duty. The picturesqueness of the regiment suffered, for he was very tall and fair, and I liked to see him step forward in the centre when the line of first sergeants came together at dress-parade. But it was a help to discipline to eliminate the Saxon, for it recognized a principle.

Afterwards I had excellent battalion-drills without a single white officer, by way of experiment; putting each company under a sergeant, and going through the most difficult movements, such as division-columns and oblique-squares. And as to actual discipline, it is doing no injustice to the line-officers of the regiment to say that none of them received from the men more implicit obedience than Color-Sergeant Rivers. I should have tried to obtain commissions for him and several others before I left the regiment, had their literary education been sufficient; and such an attempt was finally made by Lieutenant-Colonel Trowbridge, my successor in immediate command, but it proved unsuccessful. It always seemed to me an insult to those brave men to have novices put over their heads, on the ground of color alone; and the men felt it the more keenly as they remained longer in service. There were more than seven hundred enlisted men in the regiment, when mustered out after more than three years' service. The ranks had been kept full by enlistment, but there were only fourteen line-officers instead of the full thirty. The men who should have filled those vacancies were doing duty as sergeants in the ranks.

In what respect were the colored troops a source of disappointment? To me in one respect only,—that of health. Their health improved, indeed, as they grew more familiar with military life; but I think that neither their physical nor moral temperament gave them that toughness, that obstinate purpose of living, which sustains the more materialistic Anglo-Saxon. They had not, to be sure, the same predominant diseases, suffering in the pulmonary, not in the digestive organs; but they suffered a good deal. They felt malaria less, but they were more easily choked by dust and made ill by dampness. On the other hand, they submitted more readily to sanitary measures than whites, and, with efficient officers, were more easily kept clean. They were injured throughout the army by an undue share of fatigue duty, which is not only exhausting but demoralizing to a soldier; by the unsuitableness of the rations, which gave them salt meat instead of rice and hominy; and by the lack of good medical attendance. Their childlike constitutions peculiarly needed prompt and efficient surgical care; but almost all the colored troops were enlisted late in the war, when it was hard to get good surgeons for any regiments, and especially for these. In this respect I had nothing to complain of, since there were no surgeons in the army for whom I would have exchanged my own.

And this late arrival on the scene affected not only the medical supervision of the colored troops, but their opportunity for a career. It is not my province to write their history, nor to vindicate them, nor to follow them upon those larger fields compared with which the adventures of my regiment appear but a partisan warfare. Yet this, at least, may be said.

The operations on the South Atlantic coast, which long seemed a merely subordinate and incidental part of the great contest, proved to be one of the final pivots on which it turned. All now admit that the fate of the Confederacy was decided by Sherman's march to the sea. Port Royal was the objective point to which he marched, and he found the Department of the South, when he reached it, held almost exclusively by colored troops. Next to the merit of those who made the march was that of those who held open the door. That service will always remain among the laurels of the black regiments.

5

GRANT

When any great historical event is past, fame soon begins to concentrate itself on one or two leading figures, dropping inexorably all minor ones. How furious was the strife waged in England over West India emancipation, and then over the abolition of the corn-laws! Time, money, intellect, reputation, were freely bestowed for both these enterprises. Those great sacrifices are now forgotten; the very names of those who made them are lost; posterity associates only Wilberforce and Clarkson with the one agitation, Cobden and Bright with the other. When we turn to the war which saved the Union and brought emancipation, we find that the roll of fame is similarly narrowing. There is scarcely an American under thirty who is familiar with even the name of John P. Hale, whom Garrison called "the Abdiel of New Hampshire;" or of Henry Wilson, Vice-President of the United States, and historian of that slave power which he did so much toward over-throwing. The acute and decorous Seward, the stately Chase, the imperious Stanton, even the high-minded and commanding Sumner, with his reservoirs of knowledge,—all these are steadily fading from men's memories. Fifty years hence, perhaps, the mind of the nation will distinctly recognize only two figures as connected with all that great upheaval,—Lincoln and Grant.

Of these two, Grant will have one immeasurable advantage, in respect to fame,—that he wrote his own memoirs. A man who has done this can never become a myth; his individuality is as sure of preservation as is that of Cæsar. Something must of course depend upon the character of such an autobiography: it may by some mischance reveal new weaknesses only, or reaffirm and emphasize those previously known. Here again Grant is fortunate: his book is one of the greatest of his victories, and those who most criticised his two administrations may now be heard doubting whether they did, after all, any justice to the man. These memoirs have that first and highest quality both of literature and manhood, simplicity. Without a trace of attitudinizing or a suspicion of special pleading, written in a style so plain and terse that it suggests the reluctant conversation of a naturally reticent man, they would have a charm if the author had never emerged from obscurity except to write them. Considered as the records of the foremost soldier of his time, they are unique and of inestimable value.

This value is reinforced, at every point, by a certain typical quality which the book possesses. As with Lincoln, so with Grant, the reader hails with delight this exhibition of the resources of the Average American. It is not in the least necessary for the success of republican government that it should keep great men, so to speak, on tap all the time; it is rather our theory to be guided in public affairs by the general good sense of the community. What we need to know is whether leaders will be forthcoming for specific duties when needed; and in this the civil war confirmed the popular faith, and indeed developed it almost into fatalism. It is this representative character of the book which fascinates; the way in which destiny, looking about for material, took Grant and moulded him for a certain work. Apparently, there was not in him, during his boyhood, the slightest impulse towards a military life. He consented to go to West Point merely that he might visit New York and Philadelphia—that done, he would have been glad of any steamboat or railroad accident that should make it for a time impossible to enter the Academy. The things that he enjoyed were things that had scarcely the slightest reference to the career that lay unconsciously before him. Sydney Smith had a brother, known as Bobus, who bore through life this one distinction: that he had been thrashed as a boy by a schoolmate who subsequently became the Duke of Wellington. "He began with you," said Sydney Smith, "and ended with Napoleon." Grant began by breaking in a troublesome horse and ended with the Southern Confederacy.

There is always a certain piquant pleasure in the visible disproportion of means to ends. All Grant's early preparation or non-preparation for military life inspires the same feeling of gratified surprise with which we read that the young Napoleon, at the military school of St. Cyr, was simply reported as "very healthy." At West Point, Grant was at the foot of his class in the tactics, and he was dropped from sergeant to private in the junior year. A French or German officer would have looked with contempt on a military cadet who never had been a sportsman, and did not think he should ever have the courage to fight a duel. It would seem as if fate had the same perplexing problem in choosing its man for commander-in-chief that every war governor found in his choice of colonels and captains. Who could tell, how was any one to predict, what sort of soldier any citizen would be? Grant himself, when he came to appoint three men in Illinois as staff officers, failed, by his own statement, in two of the selections. What traits, what tendencies, shown in civil life, furnished the best guarantee for military abilities? None, perhaps, that could be definitely named, except habitual leadership in physical exercises. Of all positions, the captaincy of a college crew or a baseball club was surest to supply qualities available for military command. But even for athletic exercises, except so far as horses were concerned, Grant had no recorded taste.

Nor does his career in the Mexican war seem to have settled the point—and his animated sketch of that event, though one of the most graphic ever written, fails to give any signal proof of great attributes of leadership. This part of his book is especially interesting as showing the really small scale of the military events which then looked large. It is hard for us to believe that General Taylor invaded Mexico with three thousand men, a force no greater than was commanded at different times by dozens of mere colonels during the war for the Union. It is equally hard to believe that these men carried flint-lock muskets, and that their heaviest ordnance consisted of two eighteen-pound guns, while the Mexican artillery was easily evaded by simply stepping out of the way of the balls. It is difficult to convince ourselves that General Taylor never wore uniform, and habitually sat upon his horse with both feet hanging on the same side. Yet it was amid so little pomp and circumstance as this that Grant first practiced war. The experience developed in him sufficient moral insight to see, all along, that it was a contest in which his own country was wrong; and the knowledge he gained of the characters of his fellow officers was simply invaluable when he came to fight against some of them. At Fort Donelson he knew that with any force, however small, he could march within gunshot of General Pillow's intrenchments,—and when General Buckner said to him, after the surrender, that if he had been in command the Union army would not have got up to the fort so easily, Grant replied that if Buckner had been in command he should not have tried to do it in the way he did.

He was trained also by his Mexican campaign in that habit of simple and discriminating justice to an opponent which is so vital in war. The enormous advantages gained by the Americans over superior numbers during that contest have always been rather a puzzle to the reader. Grant makes it clear when he says that, though the Mexicans often "stood up as well as any troops ever did," they were a mere mob for want of trained supervision. He adds, with some humor, "The trouble seemed to be the lack of experience among the officers, which led them, after a certain period, to simply quit without being whipped, but because they had fought enough." He notes also that our losses in those battles were relatively far greater than theirs, and that for this reason, and because of the large indemnity paid at last, the Mexicans still celebrate Chapultepec and Molino del Rey as their victories, very much as Americans, under circumstances somewhat similar, celebrate the battle of Bunker Hill. Finally, Grant has the justice to see that, as Mexico has now a standing army and trained officers, the war of 1846–48 would be an impossibility in this generation.

When Grant comes to deal with the war for the Union itself, his prevailing note of simplicity gives a singularly quiet tone to the narrative. In his hands the tales of Shiloh and Donelson are told with far less of sound and fury than the boys' football game in "Tom Brown at Rugby." In reading the accounts of these victories, it seems as if anybody might have won them; just as the traveler, looking from Chamonix at the glittering slopes of Mont Blanc, feels as if there were nothing to do but to walk right up. Did any one in history ever accomplish so much as Grant with so little conscious expenditure of force, or meet dangers and worries so imperturbably? "I told them that I was not disturbed." "Why there should have been a panic I do not see." This is the sort of remark that occurs at intervals throughout the memoirs, and usually at the crisis of affairs; and this denotes the conquering temperament. Perhaps the climax of this expression is found when Grant says incidentally, "While a battle is raging, one can see his enemy mowed down by the thousand, or even the ten thousand, with great composure; but after the battle these scenes are distressing, and one is naturally disposed to do as much to alleviate the suffering of an enemy as [of] a friend." It is the word "composure" that is here characteristic; many men would share in the emotion, but very few would describe it by this placid phrase. Again, the same quality is shown when, in describing the siege of Vicksburg, after "the nearest approach to a council of war" he ever held, Grant pithily adds, "Against the general and almost unanimous judgment of the council, I sent the following letter,"—this containing essentially the terms that were accepted. Indeed, it is needless to point out how imperturbable must have been the character of the man who would take with him on a campaign his oldest son, a boy of twelve, and say of him at the end, "My son . . . caused no anxiety either to me or to his mother, who was at home. He looked out for himself, and was in every battle of the campaign."

This phlegmatic habit made General Grant in some respects uninteresting, as compared, for instance, with the impulsive and exuberant Sherman; but it gave him some solid and admirable minor qualities. "Our army," said Uncle Toby, "swore terribly in Flanders;" but the commander of the great Union army, by his own statement, was "not aware of ever having used a profane expletive" in his life. There is no more curious and inexplicable characteristic than the use of language. Lincoln impresses one as representing, on the whole, a higher type of character than Grant—more sympathetic, more sensitive, more poetic. Yet Lincoln would tell an indelicate story with the zest of a bar-room lounger, while Grant, by the general testimony of his staff officers, disliked and discouraged everything of the kind. There is a mediæval tale of a monk who was asked by a peasant to teach him a psalm, and he chose that beginning with the verse, "I will take heed to my ways that I offend not with my tongue." Having learned thus much, the peasant went away, saying that he would try and practice it before going farther; but he never returned, not having succeeded in living up to the first verse. Grant was apparently more successful.

Mere imperturbability would, however, be useless to a commander without that indefinable quality known as military instinct; and it was this which Grant possessed in a higher degree, probably, than any other man of his time. Like all instinct, it is a thing hard to distinguish from the exceedingly rapid putting of this and that together; as where Grant at Fort Donelson, finding that the knapsacks of the slain enemy were filled with rations, saw at once that they were trying to get away, and renewed the attack successfully. Again, when General Buell had some needless anxiety at Nashville and sent for large reinforcements, Grant told him, on arriving at the scene of action, that he was mistaken; the enemy was not advancing, but retreating. General Buell informed him that there was fighting in progress only ten or twelve miles away; upon which Grant said that this fighting was undoubtedly with the rear guard of the Confederates, who were trying to carry off with them all the stores they could,—and so it proved. Indeed, it was from an equally prompt recognition of what was really needed that he pressed on Vicksburg at all. Sherman, usually classed as daring and adventurous, dissuaded him, and wished him to hold fast to his base of supplies. Grant, usually esteemed cautious, insisted on going on, saying that the whole country needed a decisive victory just then, even if won at a great risk.

The very extent of Grant's military command has in one respect impaired his reputation; because he marshaled more men than his opponents, he has been assumed to be less great as a soldier than they were.

The "Saturday Review," for instance, forgetting that interior lines may make a small force practically equivalent to a large one, treats Grant's success, to this day, as merely the irresistible preponderance of greater numbers. But it was precisely here that Grant was tested as Lee was not. To say that it is easier to succeed with a larger force than a smaller one is like saying that it is easier to get across the country with a four-in-hand than in a pony phaeton: it is all very true if the road is smooth and straight and the team well broken; but if the horses are balky and the road a wilderness, the inexperienced driver will be safer with a single steed. The one thing that crushes a general of secondary ability is to have more men than he knows how to handle; his divisions simply get into one another's way, and his four-in-hand is in a hopeless tangle. Many a man has failed with a great force who would have been superb with a Spartan band. Garibaldi himself did not fit well into the complex mechanism of a German army. "Captain," said a bewildered volunteer naval lieutenant, accustomed to handling his own small crew upon the quarter-deck of his merchant vessel,—"captain, if you will just go below, and take two thirds of these men with you, I'll have this ship about in no time." It is possible that Lee might have commanded a million men as effectively as Grant did, but we shall never know, for that brilliant general had no opportunity to make the experiment. Meanwhile, it is a satisfaction to observe that the most willing European critic can impair the fame of one great American soldier only by setting up that of another.

Which is the more interesting matter of study for posterity in the career of a great general, the course of his campaigns or the development of his character? The latter half of Grant's life may be read from either of these points of view; but probably its greatest and most lasting interest will be from its elucidation of the personal traits that marked the man,—its biographical rather than its historical aspect. Behind the battles lay the genius or individual quality, whatever it was, which fought those battles; and which, in the tremendous competition of military selection, left this man above all his immediate competitors in his own field. Even in regard to the lives of Cæsar and Napoleon, we can observe that for one person who enters into the details of the strategy, there are ten who are interested in the evolution of the man. But in the case of Grant a new and peculiar interest is developed, for this reason, that he is the first great and conquering commander developed by modern republican institutions. This makes it almost certain that he will be one of the monumental men in history; and there is therefore no problem of the kind more interesting than to consider his character in the almost unerring light thrown by autobiography, and to comprehend what manner of man it is that has been added, in our own day, to those of whom Plutarch wrote.

It is noticeable, in Grant's Personal Memoirs, that the second volume has the same simplicity which was shown in the first. It would not have been strange if the habit of writing about himself—an exercise so wholly new to Grant—had by degrees impaired this quality as the book went on; but it really characterizes the later pages as much as the earlier, and the work might, so far as concerns this feature, have been struck off at a white heat. The author never poses nor attitudinizes—never wavers for an instant from his purpose to tell plain facts in the plainest possible way. The tremendous scenes through which he has passed never overwhelm or blur his statement; he tells of the manœuvring of hundreds of thousands of men as quietly as if he were narrating a contest of fishing-boats at Long Branch. When he describes that famous interview between himself and General Lee, in which was settled the permanent destiny of the American nation, the tale is told far more quietly than the ordinary reporter would describe the negotiations for a college rowing-match. Such a description, read in connection with Lincoln's Gettysburg address, shows that simplicity stands first among all literary gifts; that the greater the occasion, the more apt men are to be simple; and suggests that no time or place has ever surpassed, in this respect, the examples left behind by these two modern American men.

Next to the unconscious exhibition of character given by every man in writing about himself comes the light indirectly thrown upon his own nature by his way of judging of others. In this respect, also, Grant's quietness of tone places him at great advantage. He sometimes praises ardently, but he censures very moderately. Of Bragg's disastrous tactics at Chattanooga he only says, "I have never been able to see the wisdom of this move." Of Buell's refusal to accept a command under Sherman, on the ground that he had previously ranked Sherman, Grant says, "The worst excuse a soldier can give for declining service is that he once ranked the commander he is ordered to report." Again, when a question arose between Palmer and Schofield, as to whether the latter had a right to command the former, the comment is, "If he [Palmer] did raise this question while an action was going on, that act alone was exceedingly reprehensible."

That besetting sin of military commanders, the habit of throwing the responsibility for failure upon subordinates, never seems to tempt Grant. In speaking of Burnside's losing an important advantage at Spottsylvania, he says, "I attach no blame to Burnside for this, but I do to myself, for not having a staff officer with him to report to me his position." When we compare this guardedness of tone with the sweeping authoritativeness which marks many of our civilian critics of campaigns, the difference is certainly most gratifying. The only matters that rouse Grant to anything like wrath in the telling are those acts which imply crimes against humanity, like the massacre of colored troops at Fort Pillow; and in this case he simply characterizes Forrest's report of the affair as something "which shocks humanity to read." He does not even allow himself the luxury of vehemence against fate, or fortune, or inevitable destiny. Even when he describes his immense local obstacles in the country round Spottsylvania,—a heavily timbered region, full of little streams surrounded by wooded and marshy bottom lands,—he gently says, "It was a much better country to conduct a defensive campaign in than an offensive one." The man who can speak charitably of Virginia swamps may certainly lay claim to that virtue which is chief among the blessed three.

The severest test offered in Grant's memoirs, as to his judgment on men, is in his estimate of one whom he had allowed, in the opinion of many, to be most grievously wronged,—the late Major-General Gouverneur K. Warren. The great civil war caused a vast multitude of deaths, directly and indirectly, but among all these there was but one conspicuous and unquestionable instance of broken heart,—in the case of that high-minded and most estimable man who was removed by Sheridan from the command of an army corps just before the battle of Five Forks, and who spent the rest of his life in vainly endeavoring to secure even an investigation before a Court of Inquiry. All who remember General Warren's refined and melancholy face, with its permanent look of hopeless and crushing sorrow, must have turned eagerly to those pages of the Personal Memoirs in which his case was mentioned. Instead of evading the subject, Grant met it frankly. It has always been supposed among the friends of General Warren that the main objection to ordering a Court of Inquiry in his case was the known affection of the commander-in-chief for Sheridan, and his willingness to let Warren be sacrificed rather than expose his favorite officer to blame. Those who have read this book will be satisfied that no such theory will suffice. It is upon himself that Grant takes the main responsibility of Warren's displacement. He had made, as he avers, a careful study of Warren's peculiar temperament, long before this event occurred. He had at first felt in him a confidence so great that he would have put him in Meade's place had that officer fallen (ii. 216), but he came gradually to a very different opinion. He always regarded him as a "gallant soldier, an able man," and always thought him "thoroughly imbued with the solemnity and importance of the duty he had to perform." But he thus analyzes his character (ii. 214):—

"Warren's difficulty was twofold: when he received an order to do anything, it would at once occur to his mind how all the balance of the army should be engaged so as to properly coöperate with him. His ideas were generally good, but he would forget that the person giving him orders had thought of others at the time he had of him. In like manner, when he did get ready to execute an order, after giving most intelligent instructions to division commanders, he would go in with one division, holding the others in reserve, until he could superintend their movements in person also,—forgetting that division commanders could execute an order without his presence. His difficulty was constitutional and beyond his control. He was an officer of superior ability, quick perceptions, and personal courage to accomplish anything that could be done with a small command" (ii. 214–15).

This certainly gives a very clear analysis of a certain type of character; and whether the observer was correct or incorrect in his diagnosis, he was bound to act upon it. It further appears that Warren was again and again a source of solicitude to Grant. In some cases he did admirably, as at Cold Harbor. "The enemy charged Warren three separate times with vigor, but were repulsed each time with loss. There was no officer more capable, nor one more prompt in acting, than Warren, when the enemy forced him into it" (ii. 266). Again, at the siege of Petersburg, Warren obeyed orders perfectly, when Burnside paid no attention to him (ii. 313). Nevertheless Grant was "very much afraid,"—taking all things into consideration,—"that at the last moment he would fail Sheridan." He accordingly sent a staff officer to Sheridan to say that, although he personally liked Warren, it would not do to let personal feeling stand in the way of success, and "if his removal was necessary to success" Sheridan must not hesitate. On this authority the removal was made; and Grant only blames himself for not having assigned Warren, long before, to some other field of duty (ii. 445).

All this throws light not merely upon Grant's sustaining Sheridan in the removal of Warren, but on his uniform refusal afterwards to order any Court of Inquiry. This was the one thing for which Warren and his friends longed; and it was always assumed by them that it was refused merely in order to shield Sheridan. Yet it was the one thing which would have been, from Grant's point of view, utterly useless. When an officer is removed for an actual moral fault, as cowardice, drunkenness, or disobedience of orders, a formal investigation may settle the matter; for it is then a question of definite charges. But where a man of the highest char-

acter turns out to be, from mere peculiarities of temperament, unsuited
to a certain post, his displacement may be just as necessary; nor can war
be carried on in any other way. The stake is too tremendous, the interests
of the nation are too momentous for the matter to rest on any other
basis. Nor is it essential that the superior officer should be assumed as infallible; under these circumstances he must do the best he can. Had there
been a Court of Inquiry, nothing would have been established except that
Grant and Sheridan honestly believed that Warren was not the man for
the place, and that they therefore set him aside, as they might have done,
under like circumstances, with any other officer in himself estimable,—
as, for instance, Burnside. Grant may have sincerely thought that to say
this before a Court of Inquiry would really hurt Warren more than Sheridan, and that it was better for the sufferer himself to let the matter rest
where it lay. This was probably mistaken kindness, if kindness it was. A
man smarting under a real or supposed injustice always prefers an investigation, even if the result of that tribunal is sure to be against him. Nor
is it sure that it would have been technically against Warren. The considerations which influenced Grant and Sheridan were to some extent in-
tangible, and General Humphreys has shown that on some points they
were mistaken, and Warren had done rightly. But the real question is
whether Grant was also mistaken in his final analysis of Warren's character; and it is upon this, after all, that the whole thing turned.

This particular instance has been thus emphasized because it is, more
than any other, a test of Grant's habit of justice to his subordinates; a
quality in which, we are bound to say, he surpasses almost all writers of
military autobiographies. So far as justice to himself is concerned, he
could not have well helped doing it, had he tried, for any man shows
himself as he is, either willingly or unwillingly, when he tells his own
story. Nor is there any evidence that he sought to help it.

The latter part of his book bears literary marks of the tremendous
strain under which it was written, but it bears no moral marks of it; and
he keeps clear, from beginning to end, of all that ill-concealed enthusiasm about himself which is the common bane of autobiographies. He is
perfectly content to stand for what he was,—a combination of plain and
almost commonplace qualities, developed to a very high power, and becoming at length the equivalent of what we call military genius. This, at
least, is the inference to be drawn from his book. Whether he was or was
not, in the way of distinctive genius, a greater man than he thought himself must be left for the military historians of a future generation to determine. In any case the spectacle of an eminent commander who habitually underrates himself is rare enough to be very pleasing.

This process of self-development is never, of course, directly stated, or even intimated, by Grant himself. Had it been otherwise the quality of unconsciousness would have been wanting. But the adaptation of supreme good sense to the conditions and exigencies of army life may constantly be traced here, not merely between the lines, but in maxim after maxim, each an *obiter dictum,* given with a homely simplicity that half disguises its real wisdom. What Lincoln would have put into an anecdote or local proverb,—as when, for instance, he expressed his un-willingness to swap horses while crossing a stream or to cross Fox River before he reached it,—Grant condenses into some plain statement: "Ac-cident often decides the fate of battle" (ii. 212). "It would be bad to be defeated in two battles fought on the same day; but it would not be bad to win them" (ii. 20). "It is men who wait to be selected, and not those who seek, from whom we may always expect the most efficient service" (ii. 117). "The fact is, troops who have fought a few battles and won, and followed up their victories, improve upon what they were before to an extent that can hardly be reckoned by percentage" (ii. 109). "No man is so brave that he may not meet such defeats and disasters as to discour-age him and dampen his ardor for any cause, no matter how just he deems it" (ii. 419). "It had been my intention before this to remain at the West, even if I was made lieutenant-general; but when I got to Washing-ton, and saw the situation, it was plain that here was the point for the commanding-general to be. No one else could probably resist the pres-sure that would be brought to bear upon him to desist from his own plans and pursue others" (ii. 116).

In each passage we see clearly the working of Grant's mind. When once his convictions had taken shape in one of these simple formulæ, it was no more necessary for him to reconsider it than for a mathematician to go behind a preceding proposition. This clear and pellucid mental habit, joined with much reticence and a good deal of obstinacy, made a very powerful combination; kept him from being entangled by his own plans or confused by those of others; enabled him to form a policy, to hold to it, to overcome obstacles, to escape depression in defeat or undue excitement in victory. With all this—and here comes in the habit of mind generated by a republic—he never forgot that he was dealing with his own fellow countrymen, both as friends and foes, and that he must never leave their wishes and demands, nor even their whims and prejudices, out of sight. Many of his early risks were based upon the con-viction that the friends of the Union needed a victory or two, and must have it. All his strategy, during the closing campaign, was based upon the conviction—a conviction which Wellington or Von Moltke might very probably have missed—that the Confederates were thoroughly tired of the war, and were losing more men by desertion than they could possibly gain by impressment. Even in the terms at last given to Lee, the same quality of what we may call glorified common-sense came in; and there is no doubt that the whole process of reconstruction was facilitated when Grant decided that the vanquished Confederate soldiers had better keep their horses to help them in getting in their crops. All these considerations were precisely those we should expect a republican general to apply. It would be natural for him to recognize that the war in which he was engaged was not a mere competitive test of military machines, human or otherwise, but that it must be handled with constant reference to the instincts and habits that lay behind it. The absence of this ready comprehension helped to explain the curious failure, in our army, of many foreign officers who knew only the machine. The fact that Grant and Lincoln, however they might differ in other respects, had this mental habit in common was that which enabled them to work together so well. A striking instance of this was their common relation to the slavery question, which both had approached reluctantly, but which both accepted at last as the pivotal matter of the whole conflict. Both saw that it could be met in but one way, and both divined that the course of events was steadily abolitionizing all Union men. In general, Lincoln with sympathetic humor and Grant with strong sense kept always in mind the difference between a people's war and a mere contest of soldiers.

In other words, they were both representative Americans. So much stronger is the republican instinct among us than any professional feeling which even West Point can create that Grant, though trained to the pursuit of arms, never looked at things for a moment merely from the soldier's point of view. This was the key to his military successes,—the time, the place, the combatants being what they were,—and this was the key to the readiness with which, at last, both Grant and the soldiers under him laid down their arms. Here at last, Europe thought, was the crisis of danger; here was the "man on horseback," so often prophesied as the final instrument of Providence, surely destined to bring this turbulent republic back among the mass of nations that obey with ease. The moment of fancied peril came; and it turned out that old Israel Putnam, galloping in his shirt-sleeves to the battle of Bunker Hill, was not more harmless to the liberties of America than this later man-on-horseback, Grant.

The claims of Grant to permanent fame will lie first in the fact that he commanded the largest civilized armies the world ever saw; secondly, that with these armies he saved the integrity of the American nation;

thirdly, that he did all this by measures of his own initiating, rarely calling a council of war and commonly differing from it when called; fourthly, that he did all this for duty, not glory, and in the spirit of a citizen, not the military spirit, persisting to the last that he was, as he told Bismarck, more of a farmer than a soldier; then again, that when tested by the severest personal griefs and losses in the decline of life, he showed the same strong qualities still; and finally, that in writing his own memoirs he was simple as regards himself, candid towards opponents, and thus bequeathed to the world a book better worth reading than any military autobiography since Cæsar's Commentaries.

6

MEMO FROM
WAR OF THE REBELLION:
OFFICIAL RECORDS OF THE UNION AND
CONFEDERATE ARMIES

HEADQUARTERS THIRD MILITARY DISTRICT,
Pocotaligo, April 20, 1863.

Brig. Gen. THOMAS JORDAN, *Chief of Staff:*
GENERAL: I have the honor to report that Capt. James Lowndes, assistant
adjutant-general, and Lieut. George S. Worthington, aide-de camp, were
sent as bearers of a flag of truce to Port Royal Ferry, in compliance with
instructions from department headquarters. These officers were instructed by me to refuse to communicate with any officer of the negro
regiments, as they have been proclaimed outlaws and felons by the President of the Confederate States.

It is true that this outlawry extended to the general commanding, but I
could not but regard it as offensive and insulting that the immediate
agents engaged in these organizations should be sent to receive a flag of
truce dispatched from my headquarters.

In cases of necessity, where charity to the dead and wounded required
immediate action, I would feel forced to treat with any representative the
enemy might choose to send. But no such necessity now exists, and
among the considerable forces now assembled in our front their commanding officer should have chosen some one for the purpose of communication not obnoxious to the well-known sentiments of the authori-

ties of the Confederate Government. The enemy had been notified the day previous that a flag of truce would be sent with a communication for their commanding general. Captain Lowndes was met by an officer who announced himself as Colonel Higginson, of the First South Carolina Regiment. He was rowed to the bulkhead by a negro in the full uniform of a sergeant of infantry. His regiment is known from his special reports to be composed of negroes. Captain Lowndes informed him of the instructions from my headquarters, forbidding him to hold communication with any officer of a negro regiment, and returned. Colonel Higginson stated that he would communicate to the commanding general of the United States forces the refusal to communicate with him and the reasons assigned.

I have the honor to be, general, very respectfully, your obedient servant,

W. S. WALKER,
BRIGADIER-GENERAL, COMMANDING.

PART THREE

Crusader for Women's Rights

We men have been standing for years with our hands
crushing down the shoulders of woman, so that she
should not attain her true altitude; it is not so easy, after
we have cramped, dwarfed and crippled her, to get rid
of our responsibility by standing back and saying:
"There, we will let you go; stand up for yourself." If it is
true, as these women say, that we have wronged them
for centuries, we have got to do more than mere
negative duty. By as much as we have helped to wrong
them, we have got to help right them.

THOMAS WENTWORTH HIGGINSON,
ADDRESS TO THE 1856 WOMAN SUFFRAGE CONVENTION

Members of the modern media seem at regular intervals to redis-
cover that the post-1965 phase of the women's rights revolution
(whose leaders were Betty Friedan, Gloria Steinem, and others) was preceded by a long struggle usually said to have begun with the first
women's rights gathering in Seneca Falls in 1848. The general public
could be excused for thinking, as the leaders of this early phase of the
movement gain recognition via a major television show, the Ken
Burns/PBS documentary *Not for Ourselves Alone*, that no men were significant participants in this movement.

This was not the way it was seen by the editors of volume 6 of the *History of Woman Suffrage;* in respectfully noting Higginson's death in 1911,
the editors paid him this tribute:

He had been a champion of women's rights for more than sixty years. When a young minister he spoke for the cause. He signed the Call for the First National Women's Rights Convention in 1850. . . . He took part in organizing the American Woman Suffrage Association, was its President for a year. . . . For years he was a great power as a lecturer and writer and addressed suffrage conventions in many States. Beginning with 1870 he contributed a long series of brilliant editorials to the *Woman's Journal*.

Some of these editorials have been selected to appear in this section of Higginson's writings. They have more than historical value. Higginson dealt gracefully, forthrightly, and persuasively with myths and misconceptions still prevalent today—shibboleths and stereotypes that continue to plague us. A recent example of the kind of thinking decried by Higginson appeared as a feature piece in the *New York Times* (December 1, 1998). The writer of "Public Lives" deemed newsworthy and commented at length on a donor's funding of a "school where girls would be valued for their intelligence, not their sex appeal."

Such pieces as "Chances," "The Shadow of the Harem," and others included in this section can be read with profit by and to those still harboring old notions of male superiority.

"Ought Women to Learn the Alphabet?" was received as a truly major, nearly sensational, piece when it appeared in 1859. A prime example of an essay constructed to make a point, as an instance of satirical polemicizing it has few peers, being on a level with Jonathan Swift's "A Modest Proposal." "Ought Women to Learn the Alphabet?" was repeatedly reprinted in pamphlet form.

The essay on Margaret Fuller, "Who Was Margaret Fuller?"—like his full-length biography published fifteen years later—was designed to introduce to the public a woman whose life was of major significance; the essay dealt only cursorily with Fuller's writings. Even though he was a feminist, Higginson missed a point that has been made plain in recent studies: Fuller's writings of 1845 led directly to the organized and effective expression of the dissatisfaction felt but not often voiced by many American women before that time.

The authors M. V. Allen, in *The Achievement of Margaret Fuller* (Pennsylvania State University Press, 1979), and M. M. O. Urbanski, in *Margaret Fuller's "Women in the Nineteenth Century"* (Greenwood, 1980), document a point that is often ignored: that the very women who became leaders of the women's movement owed their own awakening to Fuller. Urbanski articulated this point when she cited the words of Paulina W. Davis, the president of the first national women's rights con-

vention at Worcester, Massachusetts, in 1850: "One great disappointment fell upon us. Margaret Fuller, to whom many eyes were turned as
the future leader in the movement, was not with us." Fuller had lost her
life in a shipwreck just a few a few weeks earlier.

Those who appreciate the revolutionary significance of Higginson's
many essays on the "woman question" and the still current relevance of
many points he made will be puzzled by a curious comment by a distinguished critic. The late Alfred Kazin, in his overview of American literary figures, *An American Procession* (1984), praised Higginson as "an advanced liberal for his time and place, a courageous, decent, limited
man."

The oddly subtracting word "limited" reflects negatively on Kazin
more than on its target; Kazin becomes outright snide in his footnote:
"It is amusing to read Higginson's smug little tract, 'Common Sense
About Women,' which Higginson probably considered the bravest word
on the subject." Such a view needs to be evaluated in light of a life of
work that was so loyal, of efforts so diligent, of writings so effective that
they won praise from Susan B. Anthony and Elizabeth Cady Stanton.

A perusal of selections that appeared in *Common Sense About Women*
(which is not a "tract"—itself a buzzword—but a collection of essays)
may raise questions about Kazin's intention in using the word "smug."
His ironic phrase "bravest word," implying that it was less than courageous in the world of the 1880s to denounce prevalent concepts tailored
to keep women in their place—for that is the common feature of the
pieces in the *Woman's Journal*—makes us wish that Kazin were here to
tell us what would have been braver.

1

Ought Women
to Learn the Alphabet?

Paris smiled, for an hour or two, in the year 1801, when, amidst Napoleon's mighty projects for remodelling the religion and government of his empire, the ironical satirist, Sylvain Maréchal, thrust in his "Plan for a Law prohibiting the Alphabet to Women."[1] Daring, keen, sarcastic, learned, the little tract retains to-day so much of its pungency, that we can hardly wonder at the honest simplicity of the author's friend and biographer, Madame Gacon Dufour, who declared that he must be insane, and soberly replied to him.

His proposed statute consists of eighty-two clauses, and is fortified by a "whereas" of a hundred and thirteen weighty reasons. He exhausts the range of history to show the frightful results which have followed this taste of fruit of the tree of knowledge; quotes from the Encyclopédie, to prove that the woman who knows the alphabet has already lost a portion of her innocence; cites the opinion of Molière, that any female who has unhappily learned anything in this line should affect ignorance, when possible; asserts that knowledge rarely makes men attractive, and females never; opines that women have no occasion to peruse Ovid's "Art of Love," since they know it all in advance; remarks that three quarters of female authors are no better than they should be; maintains that Madame Guion would have been far more useful had she been merely pretty and an ignoramus, such as Nature made her,—that Ruth and Naomi could not read, and Boaz probably would never have married into the family had they possessed that accomplishment,—that the

---

[1] *Projet d'une loi portant défense d'apprendre à live aux femmes.*

Spartan women did not know the alphabet, nor the Amazons, nor Penelope, nor Andromache, nor Lucretia, nor Joan of Arc, nor Petrarch's Laura, nor the daughters of Charlemagne, nor the three hundred and sixty-five wives of Mohammed; but that Sappho and Madame de Maintenon could read altogether too well; while the case of Saint Brigitta, who brought forth twelve children and twelve books, was clearly exceptional, and afforded no safe precedent.

It would seem that the brilliant Frenchman touched the root of the matter. Ought women to learn the alphabet? There the whole question lies. Concede this little fulcrum, and Archimedea will move the world before she has done with it: it becomes merely a question of time. Resistance must be made here or nowhere. *Obsta principiis.* Woman must be a subject or an equal: there is no middle ground. What if the Chinese proverb should turn out to be, after all, the summit of wisdom, "For men, to cultivate virtue is knowledge; for women, to renounce knowledge is virtue"?

No doubt, the progress of events is slow, like the working of the laws of gravitation generally. Certainly there has been but little change in the legal position of women since China was in its prime, until within the last half century. Lawyers admit that the fundamental theory of English and Oriental law is the same on this point: Man and wife are one, and that one is the husband. It is the oldest of legal traditions. When Blackstone declares that "the very being and existence of the woman is suspended during the marriage," and American Kent echoes that "her legal existence and authority are in a manner lost;" when Petersdorff asserts that "the husband has the right of imposing such corporeal restraints as he may deem necessary," and Bacon that "the husband hath, by law, power and dominion over his wife, and may keep her by force within the bounds of duty, and may beat her, but not in a violent or cruel manner;" when Mr. Justice Coleridge rules that the husband, in certain cases, "has a right to confine his wife in his own dwelling-house, and restrain her from liberty for an indefinite time," and Baron Alderson sums it all up tersely, "The wife is only the *servant* of her husband,"—these high authorities simply reaffirm the dogma of the Gentoo code, four thousand years old and more: "A man, both day and night, must keep his wife so much in subjection that she by no means be mistress of her own actions. If the wife have her own free will, notwithstanding she be of a superior caste, she will behave amiss."

Yet behind these unchanging institutions, a pressure has been for centuries becoming concentrated, which, now that it has begun to act, is threatening to overthrow them all. It has not yet operated very visibly in the Old World, where, even in England, the majority of women have not till lately mastered the alphabet sufficiently to sign their own names in the marriage register. But in this country the vast changes of the last few years are already a matter of history. No trumpet has been sounded, no earthquake has been felt, while State after State has ushered into legal existence one half of the population within its borders. Surely, here and now, might poor M. Maréchal exclaim, the bitter fruits of the original seed appear. The sad question recurs, Whether women ought ever to have tasted of the alphabet.

It is true that Eve ruined us all, according to theology, without knowing her letters. Still there is something to be said in defence of that venerable ancestress. The Veronese lady, Isotta Nogarola, five hundred and thirty-six of whose learned epistles were preserved by De Thou, composed a dialogue on the question, Whether Adam or Eve had committed the greater sin. But Ludovico Domenichi, in his "Dialogue on the Nobleness of Women," maintains that Eve did not sin at all, because she was not even created when Adam was told not to eat the apple. It was "in Adam all died," he shrewdly says; nobody died in Eve: which looks plausible. Be that as it may, Eve's daughters are in danger of swallowing a whole harvest of forbidden fruit, in these revolutionary days, unless something be done to cut off the supply.

It has been seriously asserted, that during the last half century more books have been written by women and about women than during all the previous uncounted ages. It may be true; although, when we think of the innumerable volumes of *Mémoires* by French women of the seventeenth and eighteenth centuries,—each justifying the existence of her own ten volumes by the remark, that all her contemporaries were writing as many,—we have our doubts. As to the increased multitude of general treatises on the female sex, however,—its education, life, health, diseases, charms, dress, deeds, sphere, rights, wrongs, work, wages, encroachments, and idiosyncrasies generally,—there can be no doubt whatever; and the poorest of these books recognizes a condition of public sentiment of which no other age ever dreamed.

Still, literary history preserves the names of some reformers before the Reformation, in this matter. There was Signora Moderata Fonte, the Venetian, who left a book to be published after her death, in 1592, "Dei Meriti delle Donne." There was her townswoman, Lucrezia Marinella, who followed, ten years after, with her essay, "La Nobilità e la Eccelenza delle Donne, con Difetti e Mancamenti degli Uomini,"—a comprehensive theme, truly! Then followed the all-accomplished Anna Maria

Schurman, in 1645, with her "Dissertatio de Ingenii Muliebris ad Doctrinam et meliores Literas Aptitudine," with a few miscellaneous letters appended in Greek and Hebrew. At last came boldly Jacquette Guillaume, in 1665, and threw down the gauntlet in her title-page, "Les Dames Illustres; où par bonnes et fortes Raisons il se prouve que le Sexe Feminin surpasse en toute Sorte de Genre le Sexe Masculin;" and with her came Margaret Boufflet and a host of others; and finally, in England, Mary Wollstonecraft, whose famous book, formidable in its day, would seem rather conservative now; and in America, that pious and worthy dame, Mrs. H. Mather Crocker, Cotton Mather's grandchild, who, in 1848, published the first book on the "Rights of Woman" ever written on this side the Atlantic.

Meanwhile there have never been wanting men, and strong men, to echo these appeals. From Cornelius Agrippa and his essay (1509) on the excellence of woman and her preëminence over man, down to the first youthful thesis of Agassiz, "Mens Feminæ Viri Animo Superior," there has been a succession of voices crying in the wilderness. In England, Anthony Gibson wrote a book, in 1599, called "A Woman's Woorth, defended against all the Men in the World, proving them to be more Perfect, Excellent, and Absolute in all Vertuous Actions than any Man of what Qualitie soever, *Interlarded with Poetry.*" *Per contra,* the learned Acidalius published a book in Latin, and afterwards in French, to prove that women are not reasonable creatures. Modern theologians are at worst merely sub-acid, and do not always say so, if they think so. Meanwhile most persons have been content to leave the world to go on its old course, in this matter as in others, and have thus acquiesced in that stern judicial decree with which Timon of Athens sums up all his curses upon womankind,—"If there sit twelve women at the table, let a dozen of them be—as they are."

Ancient or modern, nothing in any of these discussions is so valuable as the fact of the discussion itself. There is no discussion where there is no wrong. Nothing so indicates wrong as this morbid self-inspection. The complaints are a perpetual protest, the defences a perpetual confession. It is too late to ignore the question; and, once opened, it can be settled only on absolute and permanent principles. There is a wrong; but where? Does woman already know too much, or too little? Was she created for man's subject, or his equal? Shall she have the alphabet, or not?

Ancient mythology, which undertook to explain everything, easily accounted for the social and political disabilities of woman. Goguet quotes the story from Saint Augustine, who got it from Varro. Cecrops, building Athens, saw starting from the earth an olive-plant and a fountain, side by side. The Delphic oracle said that this indicated a strife between Minerva and Neptune for the honor of giving a name to the city, and that the people must decide between them. Cecrops thereupon assembled the men, and the women also, who then had a right to vote; and the result was that Minerva carried the election by a glorious majority of one. Then Attica was overflowed and laid waste: of course the citizens attributed the calamity to Neptune, and resolved to punish the women. It was therefore determined that in future they should not vote, nor should any child bear the name of its mother.

Thus easily did mythology explain all troublesome inconsistencies; but it is much that it should even have recognized them as needing explanation. The real solution is, however, more simple. The obstacle to the woman's sharing the alphabet, or indeed any other privilege, has been thought by some to be the fear of impairing her delicacy, or of destroying her domesticity, or of confounding the distinction between the sexes. These may have been plausible excuses. They have even been genuine, though minor, anxieties. But the whole thing, I take it, had always one simple, intelligible basis,—sheer contempt for the supposed intellectual inferiority of woman. She was not to be taught, because she was not worth teaching. The learned Acidalius aforesaid was in the majority. According to Aristotle and the Peripatetics, woman was *animal occasionatum,* as if a sort of monster and accidental production. Mediæval councils, charitably asserting her claims to the rank of humanity, still pronounced her unfit for instruction. In the Hindoo dramas she did not even speak the same language with her master, but used the dialect of slaves. When, in the sixteenth century, Françoise de Saintonges wished to establish girls' schools in France, she was hooted in the streets; and her father called together four doctors, learned in the law, to decide whether she was not possessed by demons, to think of educating women,—*pour s'assurer qu'instruire des femmes n'était pas un œuvre du démon.*

It was the same with political rights. The foundation of the Salic Law was not any sentimental anxiety to guard female delicacy and domesticity; it was, as stated by Froissart, a blunt, hearty contempt: "The kingdom of France being too noble to be ruled by a woman." And the same principle was reaffirmed for our own institutions, in rather softened language, by Theophilus Parsons, in his famous defence of the rights of Massachusetts men (the "Essex Result," in 1778): "Women, what age soever they are of, are not considered as having a sufficient acquired discretion [to exercise the franchise]."

In harmony with this are the various maxims and *bon-mots* of eminent men, in respect to women. Niebuhr thought he should not have educated a girl well,—he should have made her know too much. Lessing said, "The woman who thinks is like the man who puts on rouge, ridiculous." Voltaire said, "Ideas are like beards: women and young men have none." And witty Dr. Maginn carries to its extreme the atrocity, "We like to hear a few words of sense from a woman, as we do from a parrot, because they are so unexpected." Yet how can we wonder at these opinions, when the saints have been severer than the sages?—since the pious Fénelon taught that true virgin delicacy was almost as incompatible with learning as with vice; and Dr. Channing complained, in his "Essay on Exclusion and Denunciation," of "women forgetting the tenderness of their sex," and arguing on theology.

Now this impression of feminine inferiority may be right or wrong, but it obviously does a good deal towards explaining the facts it assumes. If contempt does not originally cause failure, it perpetuates it. Systematically discourage any individual, or class, from birth to death, and they learn, in nine cases out of ten, to acquiesce in their degradation, if not to claim it as a crown of glory. If the Abbé Choisi praised the Duchesse de Fontanges for being "beautiful as an angel and silly as a goose," it was natural that all the young ladies of the court should resolve to make up in folly what they wanted in charms. All generations of women having been bred under the shadow of intellectual contempt, they have, of course, done much to justify it. They have often used only for frivolous purposes even the poor opportunities allowed them. They have employed the alphabet, as Molière said, chiefly in spelling the verb *Amo.* Their use of science has been like that of Mlle. de Launay, who computed the decline in her lover's affection by his abbreviation of their evening walk in the public square, preferring to cross it rather than take the circuit; "from which I inferred," she says, "that his passion had diminished in the ratio between the diagonal of a rectangular parallelogram and the sum of two adjacent sides." And their conception, even of art, has been too often on the scale of Properzia de Rossi, who carved sixty-five heads on a walnut, the smallest of all recorded symbols of woman's sphere.

All this might, perhaps, be overcome, if the social prejudice which discourages women would only reward proportionately those who surmount the discouragement. The more obstacles, the more glory, if society would only pay in proportion to the labor; but it does not. Women being denied, not merely the training which prepares for great deeds, but the praise and compensation which follow them, have been weakened in both directions. The career of eminent men ordinarily begins with college and the memories of Miltiades, and ends with fortune and fame: woman begins under discouragement, and ends beneath the same. Single, she works with half preparation and half pay; married, she puts name and wages into the keeping of her husband, shrinks into John Smith's "lady" during life, and John Smith's "relict" on her tombstone; and still the world wonders that her deeds, like her opportunities, are inferior.

Evidently, then, the advocates of woman's claims—those who hold that "the virtues of the man and the woman are the same," with Antisthenes, or that "the talent of the man and the woman is the same," with Socrates in Xenophon's "Banquet"—must be cautious lest they attempt to prove too much. Of course, if women know as much as the men, without schools and colleges, there is no need of admitting them to those institutions. If they work as well on half pay, it diminishes the inducement to give them the other half. The safer position is, to claim that they have done just enough to show what they might have done under circumstances less discouraging. Take, for instance, the common remark, that women have invented nothing. It is a valid answer, that the only implements habitually used by woman have been the needle, the spindle, and the basket; and tradition reports that she herself invented all three. In the same way it may be shown that the departments in which women have equalled men have been the departments in which they have had equal training, equal encouragement, and equal compensation; as, for instance, the theatre. Madame Lagrange, the *prima donna,* after years of costly musical instruction, wins the zenith of professional success; she receives, the newspapers affirm, sixty thousand dollars a year, travelling expenses for ten persons, country-houses, stables, and liveries, besides an uncounted revenue of bracelets, bouquets, and *billets-doux.* Of course, every young *débutante* fancies the same thing within her own reach, with only a brief stage-vista between. On the stage there is no deduction for sex, and, therefore, woman has shown in that sphere an equal genius. But every female common-school teacher in the United States finds the enjoyment of her four hundred dollars a year to be secretly embittered by the knowledge that the young college stripling in the next schoolroom is paid twice that sum for work no harder or more responsible than her own, and that, too, after the whole pathway of education has been obstructed for her, and smoothed for him. These may be gross and carnal considerations; but Faith asks her daily bread, and fancy must be fed. We deny woman her fair share of training, of encouragement, of remuneration, and then talk fine nonsense about her instincts and intuitions. We say sentimentally with the Oriental proverbialist, "Every book of knowledge is implanted by nature in the heart of woman,"—and make the compliment a substitute for the alphabet.

Nothing can be more absurd than to impose entirely distinct standards, in this respect, on the two sexes, or to expect that woman, any more than man, will accomplish anything great without due preparation and adequate stimulus. Mrs. Patten, who navigated her husband's ship from Cape Horn to California, would have failed in the effort, for all her heroism, if she had not, unlike most of her sex, been taught to use her Bowditch's "Navigator." Florence Nightingale, when she heard of the distresses in the Crimea, did not, as most people imagine, rise up and say, "I am a woman, ignorant but intuitive, with very little sense and information, but exceedingly sublime aspirations; my strength lies in my weakness; I can do all things without knowing anything about them." Not at all: during ten years she had been in hard training for precisely such services; had visited all the hospitals in London, Edinburgh, Dublin, Paris, Lyons, Rome, Brussels, and Berlin; had studied under the Sisters of Charity, and been twice a nurse in the Protestant Institution at Kaiserswerth. Therefore she did not merely carry to the Crimea a woman's heart, as her stock in trade, but she knew the alphabet of her profession better than the men around her. Of course, genius and enthusiasm are, for both sexes, elements unforeseen and incalculable; but, as a general rule, great achievements imply great preparations and favorable conditions.

To disregard this truth is unreasonable in the abstract, and cruel in its consequences. If an extraordinary male gymnast can clear a height of ten feet with the aid of a springboard, it would be considered slightly absurd to ask a woman to leap eleven feet without one; yet this is precisely what society and the critics have always done. Training and wages and social approbation are very elastic springboards; and the whole course of history has seen these offered bounteously to one sex, and as sedulously withheld from the other. Let woman consent to be a doll, and there was no finery so gorgeous, no baby-house so costly, but she might aspire to share its lavish delights; let her ask simply for an equal chance to learn, to labor, and to live, and it was as if that same doll should open its lips, and propound Euclid's forty-seventh proposition. While we have all deplored the helpless position of indigent women, and lamented that they had no alternative beyond the needle, the wash-tub, the schoolroom, and the street, we have usually resisted their admission into every new occupation, denied them training, and cut their compensation down. Like Charles Lamb, who atoned for coming late to the office in the morning by going away early in the afternoon, we have, first, half educated women, and then, to restore the balance, only half paid them. What innumerable obstacles have been placed in their way as female physicians; what a complication of difficulties has been encountered by them, even as printers, engravers, and designers! In London, Mr. Bennett was once mobbed for lecturing to women on watchmaking. In this country, we have known grave professors refuse to address lyceums which thought fit to employ an occasional female lecturer. Mr. Comer stated that it was "in the face of ridicule and sneers" that he began to educate American women as bookkeepers many years ago; and it was a little contemptible in Miss Muloch to revive the same satire in "A Woman's Thoughts on Women," when she must have known that in half the retail shops in Paris her own sex rules the ledger, and Mammon knows no Salic law.

We find, on investigation, what these considerations would lead us to expect, that eminent women have commonly been exceptional in training and position, as well as in their genius. They have excelled the average of their own sex because they have shared the ordinary advantages of the other sex. Take any department of learning or skill; take, for instance, the knowledge of languages, the universal alphabet, philology. On the great stairway at Padua stands the statue of Elena Cornaro, professor of six languages in that once renowned university. But Elena Cornaro was educated like a boy, by her father. On the great door of the University of Bologna is inscribed the epitaph of Clotilda Tambroni, the honored correspondent of Porson, and the first Greek scholar of southern Europe in her day. But Clotilda Tambroni was educated like a boy, by Emanuele Aponte. How fine are those prefatory words, "by a Right Reverend Prelate," to that pioneer book in Anglo-Saxon lore, Elizabeth Elstob's grammar: "Our earthly possessions are indeed our patrimony, as derived to us by the industry of our fathers; but the language in which we speak is our mother tongue, and who so proper to play the critic in this as the females?" Yet this particular female obtained the rudiments of her rare education from her mother, before she was eight years old, in spite of much opposition from her right reverend guardians. Adelung declares that all modern philology is founded on the translation of a Russian vocabulary into two hundred different dialects by Catherine II. But Catherine shared, in childhood, the instructors of her brother, Prince Frederick, and was subject to some reproach for learning, though a girl, so much more rapidly than he did. Christina of Sweden ironically reproved Madame Dacier for her translation of Callimachus: "Such a pretty girl as you are, are you not ashamed to be so learned?" But Madame Dacier acquired Greek by contriving to do her embroidery in the room where her father was teaching her stupid brother; and her queenly critic had herself learned to read Thucydides, harder Greek than Callimachus, before she was fourteen. And so down to our own day, who knows how many mute, inglorious Minervas may have perished unenlightened, while Margaret Fuller Ossoli and Elizabeth Barrett Browning were being educated "like boys."

This expression simply means that they had the most solid training which the times afforded. Most persons would instantly take alarm at the very words; that is, they have so little faith in the distinctions which Nature has established, that they think, if you teach the alphabet, or anything else, indiscriminately to both sexes, you annul all difference between them. The common reasoning is thus: "Boys and girls are acknowledged to be very unlike. Now, boys study Greek and algebra, medicine and bookkeeping. Therefore girls should not." As if one should say: "Boys and girls are very unlike. Now, boys eat beef and potatoes. Therefore, obviously, girls should not."

The analogy between physical and spiritual food is precisely in point. The simple truth is, that, amid the vast range of human powers and properties, the fact of sex is but one item. Vital and momentous in itself, it does not constitute the whole organism, but only a part. The distinction of male and female is special, aimed at a certain end; and, apart from that end, it is, throughout all the kingdoms of Nature, of minor importance. With but trifling exceptions, from infusoria up to man, the female animal moves, breathes, looks, listens, runs, flies, swims, pursues its food, eats it, digests it, in precisely the same manner as the male: all instincts, all characteristics, are the same, except as to the one solitary fact of parentage. Mr. Ten Broeck's race-horses, Pryor and Prioress, were foaled alike, fed alike, trained alike, and finally ran side by side, competing for the same prize. The eagle is not checked in soaring by any consciousness of sex, nor asks the sex of the timid hare, its quarry. Nature, for high purposes, creates and guards the sexual distinction, but keeps it subordinate to those still more important.

Now all this bears directly upon the alphabet. What sort of philosophy is that which says, "John is a fool; Jane is a genius: nevertheless, John, being a man, shall learn, lead, make laws, make money; Jane, being a woman, shall be ignorant, dependent, disfranchised, underpaid"? Of course, the time is past when one would state this so frankly, though Comte comes quite near it, to say nothing of the Mormons; but this formula really lies at the bottom of the reasoning one hears every day. The answer is, Soul before sex. Give an equal chance, and let genius and industry do the rest. *La carrière ouverte aux talens!* Every man for himself, every woman for herself, and the alphabet for us all.

Thus far, my whole course of argument has been defensive and explanatory. I have shown that woman's inferiority in special achievements, so far as it exists, is a fact of small importance, because it is merely a corollary from her historic position of degradation. She has not excelled, because she has had no fair chance to excel. Man, placing his foot upon her shoulder, has taunted her with not rising. But the ulterior question remains behind. How came she into this attitude originally? Explain the explanation, the logician fairly demands. Granted that woman is weak because she has been systematically degraded: but why was she degraded? This is a far deeper question,—one to be met only by a profounder philosophy and a positive solution. We are coming on ground almost wholly untrod, and must do the best we can.

I venture to assert, then, that woman's social inferiority has been, to a great extent, in the past a legitimate thing. To all appearance, history would have been impossible without it, just as it would have been impossible without an epoch of war and slavery. It is simply a matter of social progress,—a part of the succession of civilizations. The past has been inevitably a period of ignorance, of engrossing physical necessities, and of brute force,—not of freedom, of philanthropy, and of culture. During that lower epoch, woman was necessarily an inferior, degraded by abject labor, even in time of peace,—degraded uniformly by war, chivalry to the contrary notwithstanding. Behind all the courtesies of Amadis and the Cid lay the stern fact,—woman a child or a toy. The flattering troubadours chanted her into a poet's paradise; but alas! that kingdom of heaven suffered violence, and the violent took it by force. The truth simply was, that her time had not come. Physical strength must rule for a time, and she was the weaker. She was very properly refused a feudal grant, by reason, say "Les Coustumes de Normandie," of her unfitness for war or policy: *C'est l'homme ki se bast et ki conseille.* Other authorities put it still more plainly: "A woman cannot serve the emperor or feudal lord in war, on account of the decorum of her sex; nor assist him with advice, because of her limited intellect; nor keep his counsel, owing to the infirmity of her disposition." All which was, no doubt, in the majority of cases, true; and the degradation of woman was simply a part of a system which has, indeed, had its day, but has bequeathed its associations.

From this reign of force, woman never freed herself by force. She could not fight, or would not. Bohemian annals, to be sure, record the legend of a literal war between the sexes, in which the women's army was led by Libussa and Wlasla, and which finally ended with the capture, by the army of men, of Castle Dziewin, Maiden's Tower, whose ruins are still visible near Prague. The armor of Libussa is still shown at Vienna; and the guide calls attention to the long-peaked toes of steel, with which, he avers, the tender princess was wont to pierce the hearts of her opponents, while careering through the battle. And there are abundant instances in which women have fought side by side with men, and on equal terms. The ancient British women mingled in the wars of their husbands, and their princesses were trained to the use of arms in the Maiden's Castle at Edinburgh, in the Isle of Skye. The Moorish wives and maidens fought in defence of their European peninsula; and the Portuguese women fought on the same soil, against the armies of Philip II. The king of Siam has, at present, a body-guard of four hundred women: they are armed with lance and rifle, are admirably disciplined, and their commander (appointed after saving the king's life at a tiger-hunt) ranks as one of the royal family, and has ten elephants at her service. When the all-conquering Dahomian army marched upon Abbeokuta, in 1851, they numbered ten thousand men and six thousand women. The women were, as usual, placed foremost in the assault, as being most reliable; and of the eighteen hundred bodies left dead before the walls, the vast majority were of women. The Hospital of the Invalides, in Paris, has sheltered, for half a century, a fine specimen of a female soldier, "Lieutenant Madame Bulan," who lived to be more than eighty years old, had been decorated by Napoleon's own hand with the cross of the Legion of Honor, and was credited on the hospital books with "seven years' service, seven campaigns, three wounds, several times distinguished, especially in Corsica, in defending a fort against the English." But these cases, though interesting to the historian, are still exceptional; and the instinctive repugnance they inspire is a condemnation, not of women, but of war.

The reason, then, for the long subjection of woman has been simply that humanity was passing through its first epoch, and her full career was to be reserved for the second. As the different races of man have appeared successively upon the stage of history, so there has been an order of succession of the sexes. Woman's appointed era, like that of the Teutonic races, was delayed, but not omitted. It is not merely true that the empire of the past has belonged to man, but that it has properly belonged to him; for it was an empire of the muscles, enlisting, at best, but the lower powers of the understanding. There can be no question that the present epoch is initiating an empire of the higher reason, of arts, affections, aspirations; and for that epoch the genius of woman has been reserved. The spirit of the age has always kept pace with the facts, and outstripped the statutes. Till the fulness of time came, woman was necessarily kept a slave to the spinning-wheel and the needle; now higher work is ready; peace has brought invention to her aid, and the mechanical means for her emancipation are ready also. No use in releasing her till man, with his strong arm, had worked out his preliminary share in civilization. "Earth waits for her queen" was a favorite motto of Margaret Fuller Ossoli; but it would be more correct to say that the queen has waited for her earth, till it could be smoothed and prepared for her occupancy. Now Cinderella may begin to think of putting on her royal robes.

Everybody sees that the times are altering the whole material position of woman; but most people do not appear to see the inevitable social and moral changes which are also involved. As has been already said, the woman of ancient history was a slave to physical necessities, both in war and peace. In war she could do too little; in peace she did too much, under the material compulsions which controlled the world. How could the Jews, for instance, elevate woman? They could not spare her from the wool and the flax, and the candle that goeth not out by night. In Rome, when the bride first stepped across her threshold, they did not ask her, Do you know the alphabet? they asked simply, Can you spin? There was no higher epitaph than Queen Amalasontha's,—*Domum servavit, lanam fecit.* In Bœotia, brides were conducted home in vehicles whose wheels were burned at the door, in token that they were never to leave the house again. Pythagoras instituted at Crotona an annual festival for the distaff; Confucius, in China, did the same for the spindle; and these celebrated not the freedom, but the serfdom, of woman.

And even into modern days this same tyrannical necessity has lingered. "Go spin, you jades! go spin!" was the only answer vouchsafed by the Earl of Pembroke to the twice-banished nuns of Wilton. Even now, travellers agree that throughout civilized Europe, with the partial exception of England and France, the profound absorption of the mass of women in household labors renders their general elevation impossible. But with us Americans, and in this age, when all these vast labors are being more and more transferred to arms of brass and iron; when Rochester grinds the flour and Lowell weaves the cloth, and the fire on the hearth has gone into black retirement and mourning; when the wiser a virgin is, the less she has to do with oil in her lamp; when the needle has made its last dying speech and confession in the "Song of the Shirt," and the sewing-machine has changed those doleful marches to delightful measures,—how is it possible for the blindest to help seeing that a new era is begun, and that the time has come for woman to learn the alphabet?

Nobody asks for any abolition of domestic labor for women, any more than of outdoor labor for men. Of course, most women will still continue to be mainly occupied with the indoor care of their families, and most men with their external support. All that is desirable for either sex is such an economy of labor, in this respect, as shall leave some spare time to be appropriated in other directions. The argument against each new emancipation of woman is precisely that always made against the liberation of serfs and the enfranchisement of plebeians,—that the new position will take them from their legitimate business. "How can he [or she] get wisdom that holdeth the plough [or the broom],—whose talk is of bullocks [or of babies]?" Yet the American farmer has already emancipated himself from these fancied incompatibilities; and so will the farmer's wife. In a nation where there is no leisure class and no peasantry, this whole theory of exclusion is an absurdity. We all have a little leisure, and we must all make the most of it. If we will confine large interests and duties to those who have nothing else to do, we must go back to monarchy at once. If otherwise, then the alphabet, and its consequences, must be open to woman as to man. Jean Paul says nobly, in his "Levana," that, "before and after being a mother, a woman is a human being, and neither maternal nor conjugal relation can supersede the human responsibility, but must become its means and instrument." And it is good to read the manly speech, on this subject, of John Quincy Adams, quoted at length in Quincy's life of him, in which, after fully defending the political petitions of the women of Plymouth, he declares that "the correct principle is that women are not only justified, but exhibit the most exalted virtue, when they do depart from the domestic circle, and enter on the concerns of their country, of humanity, and of their God."

There are duties devolving on every human being,—duties not small nor few, but vast and varied,—which spring from home and private life, and all their sweet relations. The support or care of the humblest household is a function worthy of men, women, and angels, so far as it goes. From these duties none must shrink, neither man nor woman; the loftiest genius cannot ignore them; the sublimest charity must begin with them. They are their own exceeding great reward; their self-sacrifice is infinite joy; and the selfishness which discards them is repaid by loneliness and a desolate old age. Yet these, though the most tender and intimate portion of human life, do not form its whole. It is given to noble souls to crave other interests also, added spheres, not necessarily alien from these; larger knowledge, larger action also; duties, responsibilities, anxieties, dangers, all the aliment that history has given to its heroes. Not home less, but humanity more. When the high-born English lady in the Crimean hospital, ordered to a post of almost certain death, only raised her hands to heaven, and said, "Thank God!" she did not renounce her true position as woman: she claimed it. When the queen of James I. of Scotland, already immortalized by him in stately verse, won a higher immortality by welcoming to her fair bosom the dagger aimed at his; when the Countess of Buchan hung confined in her iron cage, outside Berwick Castle, in penalty for crowning Robert the Bruce; when the stainless soul of Joan of Arc met God, like Moses, in a burning flame,—these things were as they should be. Man must not monopolize these privileges of peril, the birthright of great souls. Serenades and compliments must not replace the nobler hospitality which shares with woman the opportunity of martyrdom. Great administrative duties also, cares of state, for which one should be born gray-headed, how nobly do these sit upon a woman's brow! Each year adds to the storied renown of Elizabeth of England, greatest sovereign of the greatest of historic nations. Christina of Sweden, alone among the crowned heads of Europe (so says Voltaire), sustained the dignity of the throne against Richelieu and Mazarin. And these queens most assuredly did not sacrifice their womanhood in the process; for her Britannic Majesty's wardrobe included four thousand gowns; and Mlle. de Montpensier declares that when Christina had put on a wig of the latest fashion, "she really looked extremely pretty."

Les races se féminisent, said Buffon,—"The world is growing more feminine." It is a compliment, whether the naturalist intended it or not. Time has brought peace; peace, invention; and the poorest woman of to-day is born to an inheritance of which her ancestors never dreamed. Previous attempts to confer on women social and political equality,—as when Leopold, Grand Duke of Tuscany, made them magistrates; or when the Hungarian revolutionists made them voters; or when our own New Jersey tried the same experiment in a guarded fashion in early times, and then revoked the privilege, because (as in the ancient fable) the women voted the wrong way;—these things were premature, and valuable only as recognitions of a principle. But in view of the rapid changes now going on, he is a rash man who asserts the "Woman Question" to be anything but a mere question of time. The fulcrum has been already given in the alphabet, and we must simply watch, and see whether the earth does not move.

There is the plain fact: woman must be either a subject or an equal; there is no middle ground. Every concession to a supposed principle only involves the necessity of the next concession for which that principle calls. Once yield the alphabet, and we abandon the whole long theory of subjection and coverture: tradition is set aside, and we have nothing but reason to fall back upon. Reasoning abstractly, it must be admitted that the argument has been, thus far, entirely on the women's side, inasmuch as no man has yet seriously tried to meet them with argument. It is an alarming feature of this discussion, that it has reversed, very generally, the traditional positions of the sexes: the women have had all the logic; and the most intelligent men, when they have attempted the other side, have limited themselves to satire and gossip. What rational woman can be really convinced by the nonsense which is talked in ordinary society around her,—as, that it is right to admit girls to common schools, and equally right to exclude them from colleges; that it is proper for a woman to sing in public, but indelicate for her to speak in public; that a post-office box is an unexceptionable place to drop a bit of paper into, but a ballot-box terribly dangerous? No cause in the world can keep above water, sustained by such contradictions as these, too feeble and slight to be dignified by the name of fallacies. Some persons profess to think it impossible to reason with a woman, and such critics certainly show no disposition to try the experiment.

But we must remember that all our American institutions are based on consistency, or on nothing: all claim to be founded on the principles of natural right; and when they quit those, they are lost. In all European monarchies it is the theory that the mass of the people are children to be governed, not mature beings to govern themselves; this is clearly stated and consistently applied. In the United States we have formally abandoned this theory for one half of the human race, while for the other half it flourishes with little change. The moment the claims of woman are broached, the democrat becomes a monarchist. What Americans commonly criticise in English statesmen, namely, that they habitually evade all arguments based on natural right, and defend every legal wrong on the ground that it works well in practice, is the precise defect in our habitual view of woman. The perplexity must be resolved somehow. Most men admit that a strict adherence to our own principles would place both sexes in precisely equal positions before law and constitution, as well as in school and society. But each has his special quibble to apply, showing that in this case we must abandon all the general maxims to which we have pledged ourselves, and hold only by precedent. Nay, he construes even precedent with the most ingenious rigor; since the exclusion of women from all direct contact with affairs can be made far more perfect in a republic than is possible in a monarchy, where even sex is merged in rank, and the female patrician may have far more power than the male plebeian. But, as matters now stand among us, there is no aristocracy but of sex: all men are born patrician, all women are legally plebeian; all men are equal in having political power, and all women in having none. This is a paradox so evident, and such an anomaly in human progress, that it cannot last forever, without new discoveries in logic, or else a deliberate return to M. Maréchal's theory concerning the alphabet.

Meanwhile, as the newspapers say, we anxiously await further developments. According to present appearances, the final adjustment lies mainly in the hands of women themselves. Men can hardly be expected to concede either rights or privileges more rapidly than they are claimed, or to be truer to women than women are to each other. In fact, the worst effect of a condition of inferiority is the weakness it leaves behind; even when we say, "Hands off!" the sufferer does not rise. In such a case, there is but one counsel worth giving. More depends on determination than even on ability. Will, not talent, governs the world. Who believed that a poetess could ever be more than an Annot Lyle of the harp, to soothe with sweet melodies the leisure of her lord, until in Elizabeth Barrett Browning's hands the thing became a trumpet? Where are gone the sneers with which army surgeons and parliamentary orators opposed Mr. Sidney Herbert's first proposition to send Florence Nightingale to the Crimea? In how many towns was the current of popular prejudice against female orators reversed by one winning speech from Lucy Stone! Where no logic can prevail, success silences. First give woman, if you dare, the alphabet, then summon her to her career: and though men, ignorant and prejudiced, may oppose its beginnings, they will at last fling around her conquering footsteps more lavish praises than ever greeted the opera's idol,—more perfumed flowers than ever wooed, with intoxicating fragrance, the fairest butterfly of the ball-room.

2

WHO WAS
MARGARET FULLER?

Travelling by rail in Michigan, some ten years ago, I found myself
seated next to a young Western girl, with a very intelligent face,
who soon began to talk with me about literary subjects. She afterwards
gave me, as a reason for her confidence, that I "looked like one who
would enjoy Margaret Fuller's writings,"—these being, as I found, the
object of her special admiration. I certainly took the remark for a compliment; and it was, at any rate, a touching tribute to the woman whose
intellectual influence thus brought strangers together.

Margaret Fuller is connected, slightly but firmly, with my earliest recollections. We were born and bred in the same town (Cambridge, Massachusetts), and I was the playmate of her younger brothers. Their family
then lived at the old "Brattle House," which still stands behind its beautiful lindens, though the great buildings of the University Press now
cover the site of the old-fashioned garden, whose formal fish-ponds and
stone spring-house wore an air of European stateliness to our home-
bred eyes. There I dimly remember the discreet elder sister, book in
hand, watching over the gambols of the lovely little Ellen, who became,
long after, the wife of my near kinsman, Ellery Channing. This later connection cemented a new tie, and led to a few interviews in maturer years
with Margaret Fuller, and to much intercourse with others of the family.
It is well to mention even such slight ties of association as these, for they
unconsciously influence one's impressions; and, after all, it is the personal glimpses which make the best part of biography, great or small,
and indeed of all literature. How refreshing it is, amid the chaff of Aulus
Gellius, to come upon a reference to Virgil's own copy of the Æneid,

which the writer had once seen, *"quem ipsius Virgilii fuisse credebat;"* and nothing in all Lord Bacon's works ever stirred me like that one magic sentence, "When I was a child, and Queen Elizabeth was in the flower of her years." I can say that when I was a child, Margaret Fuller was the queen of Cambridge, though troubled with a large minority of rather unwilling and insurrectionary subjects.

Her mother I well remember as one of the sweetest and most sympathetic of women; she was tall and not unattractive in person, refined and gentle, but with a certain physical awkwardness, proceeding in part from extreme nearsightedness. Of the father I have no recollection, save that he was mentioned with a sort of respect, as being a lawyer and having been a congressman. But his daughter has described him, in her fragment of autobiography, with her accustomed frankness and precision:—

My father was a lawyer and a politician. He was a man largely endowed with that sagacious energy which the state of New England society for the last half century has been so well fitted to develop. His father was a clergyman, settled as pastor in Princeton, Massachusetts, within the bounds of whose parish farm was Wachusett. His means were small, and the great object of his ambition was to send his sons to college. As a boy, my father was taught to think only of preparing himself for Harvard University, and, when there, of preparing himself for the profession of law. As a lawyer, again, the ends constantly presented were to work for distinction in the community, and for the means of supporting a family. To be an honored citizen and to have a home on earth were made the great aims of existence. To open the deeper fountains of the soul, to regard life here as the prophetic entrance to immortality, to develop his spirit to perfection,— motives like these had never been suggested to him, either by fellow-beings or by outward circumstances. The result was a character, in its social aspect, of quite the common sort. A good son and brother, a kind neighbor, an active man of business,—in all these outward relations, he was but one of a class which surrounding conditions have made the majority among us. In the more delicate and individual relations he never approached but two mortals, my mother and myself.

"His love for my mother was the green spot on which he stood apart from the commonplaces of a mere bread-winning, bread-bestowing existence. She was one of those fair and flower-like natures which sometimes spring up even beside the most dusty highways of life,—a creature not to be shaped into a merely useful instrument, but bound by one law with the blue sky, the dew, and the frolic birds. Of all persons whom I have known she had in her most of the angelic,—of that spontaneous love for every living thing, for man, and beast, and tree, which restores the golden age.

Sarah Margaret Fuller was born May 23, 1810; the eldest child of Timothy Fuller and Margaret Crane. Her birthplace was a house on Cherry Street, in Cambridge, before whose door still stand the trees planted by her father on the year when she saw the light. The family afterwards removed to the "Dana House," which then crowned, in a stately way, the hill between Old Cambridge and Cambridgeport. It was later still that they resided in the "Brattle House," as I have described. This was Margaret Fuller's home until 1833, except that she spent a year or more at the school of the Misses Prescott, in Groton, Mass., where she went through that remarkable experience described by herself, under the assumed character of Mariana, in "Summer on the Lakes." In 1826 she returned to Cambridge.

The society of that University town had then, as it still has, great attractions for young people of talent. It offers something of that atmosphere of culture for which such persons yearn,—tinged, perhaps, with a little narrowness and constraint. She met there in girlhood the same persons who were afterwards to be her literary friends, colaborers, and even biographers. It was a stimulating and rather perilous position, for she found herself among a circle of highly cultivated young men, with no equal female companion; although she read Locke and Madame de Stael with Lydia Maria Francis, afterwards better known as Mrs. Child. Carlyle had just called attention to the rich stores of German literature; all her friends were exploring them, and some had just returned from the German universities. She had the college library at command, and she had that vast and omnivorous appetite for books which is the most common sign of literary talent in men, but is for some reason exceedingly rare among women. At least I have known but two young girls whose zeal in this respect was at all comparable to that reported of Margaret Fuller, these two being Harriet Prescott and the late Charlotte Hawes.

In 1833 her father removed to Groton, Mass., much to her regret. Yet her life there was probably a good change in training for one who had been living for several years in an atmosphere of mental excitement. In March, 1834, she wrote thus of her mode of life:—

March, 1834.—Four pupils are a serious and fatiguing charge for one of my somewhat ardent and impatient disposition. Five days in the week I have given daily lessons in three languages, in geography and history, besides many other exercises on alternate days. This has consumed often eight, always five hours of my day. There has been also a great deal of needle-work to do, which is now nearly finished, so that I shall not be obliged to pass my time about it when everything looks beautiful, as I did last summer. We have had very poor servants, and, for some time past, only one. My mother has been often ill. My grandmother, who passed the winter with us, has been ill. Thus you may imagine, as I am the only grown-up daughter, that my time has been considerably taxed.

But as, sad or merry, I must always be learning, I laid down a course of study at the beginning of winter, comprising certain subjects, about which I had always felt deficient. These were the History and Geography of modern Europe, beginning the former in the fourteenth century; the Elements of Architecture; the works of Alfieri, with his opinions on them; the historical and critical works of Goethe and Schiller, and the outlines of history of our own country.

I chose this time as one when I should have nothing to distract or dissipate my mind. I have nearly completed this course, in the style I proposed,—not minute or thorough, I confess,—though I have had only three evenings in the week, and chance hours in the day for it. I am very glad I have undertaken it, and feel the good effects already. Occasionally I try my hand at composition, but have not completed anything to my own satisfaction.

On September 23, 1835, her father was attacked by cholera, and died within three days. Great as must have been the blow to the whole family, it was greatest of all to Margaret. The tie between them had been very close, and this sudden death threw the weight of the whole household upon the eldest child. It came at what had seemed to her the golden moment of her whole life; for she was about to visit Europe with her constant friends, Professor and Mrs. Farrar, and with their friend Harriet Martineau, who was just returning home. But all this must be at once abandoned. Mr. Fuller had left barely property enough to support his widow, and to educate the younger children, with the aid of their elder sister. Mrs. Fuller was in delicate health, and of a more yielding nature than Margaret, who became virtually head of the house. Under her strong supervision, two out of the five boys went honorably through Harvard College,—a third having previously graduated,—while the young sister was sent to the best schools, where she showed the family talent.

In the autumn of 1836, Margaret Fuller went to Boston, where she taught Latin and French in Mr. Alcott's school, and had classes of young ladies in French, German, and Italian. She also devoted one evening in every week to translating German authors into English, for the gratification of Dr. Channing,—their chief reading being in De Wette and Herder. The following extract will show how absorbing were her occupations:—

And now let me try to tell you what has been done. To one class I taught the German language, and thought it good success, when, at the end of three months, they could read twenty pages of German at a lesson, and very well. This class, of course, was not interesting, except in the way of observation and analysis of language.

With more advanced pupils I read, in twenty-four weeks, Schiller's Don Carlos, Artists, and Song of the Bell, besides giving a sort of general lecture on Schiller; Goethe's Hermann and Dorothea; Goetz von Berlichingen; Iphigenia; first part of Faust,—three weeks of thorough study this, as valuable to me as to them; and Clavigo,—thus comprehending samples of all his efforts in poetry, and bringing forward some of his prominent opinions; Lessing's Nathan, Minna, Emilia Galeotti; parts of Tieck's Phantasus, and nearly the whole first volume of Richter's Titan.

With the Italian class, I read parts of Tasso, Petrarch,—whom they came to almost adore,—Ariosto, Alfieri, and the whole hundred cantos of the Divina Commedia, with the aid of the fine Athenæum copy, Flaxman's designs, and all the best commentaries. This last piece of work was and will be truly valuable to myself.

She was invited, in 1837, to become a teacher in a private school just organized, on Mr. Alcott's plan, in Providence, R. I. "The proposal is," she wrote, "that I shall teach the elder girls my favorite branches for four hours a day,—choosing my own hours and arranging the course,—for a thousand dollars a year, if upon trial I am well pleased enough to stay." This was a flattering offer, and certainly shows the intellectual reputation she had won. She accepted it, for the sake of her family, though it involved the necessity of leaving the friends and advantages which Boston had given. She had also to abandon her favorite literary project, the preparation of a Life of Goethe for Mr. Ripley's series of translations from foreign literature. It was perhaps as a substitute for this that she translated "Eckermann's Conversations with Goethe," though it did not appear till after her removal to Jamaica Plain, in 1839. It is an admirable version, and there is after all no book in English from which one has so vivid and familiar impression of Goethe. Her preface is clear, moderate, and full of good points, though less elaborate than her subsequent essay on the same subject. No one, I fancy, has ever compressed into one sentence a sharper analysis of this great writer than when she says of him in the preface, "I think he had the artist's eye and the artist's hand, but not the artist's love of structure."

She took a house in Jamaica Plain, on her own responsibility, in the spring of 1839, and removed thither the family, of which she was practically the head. The next year they returned once more to Cambridge, living in a small house near her birthplace.

In the autumn of 1839, she instituted that remarkable conversational class, which so stimulated the minds of the more cultivated women of Boston, that even now the leaders of thought and intellectual society date back their first enlightenment to her, and wish that their daughters might have such guidance. The very aim and motive of these meetings showed her clear judgment. She held that women were at a disadvantage as compared with men, because the former were not called on to test, apply, or reproduce what they learned; while the pursuits of life supplied this want to men. Systematic conversations, controlled by a leading mind, would train women to definite statement, and continuous thought; they would make blunders and gain by their mortification; they would seriously compare notes with each other, and discover where vague impression ended and clear knowledge began. She thus states, in her informal prospectus, her three especial aims:—

> To pass in review the departments of thought and knowledge, and endeavor to place them in due relation to one another in our minds. To systematize thought, and give a precision and clearness, in which our sex are so deficient,—chiefly, I think, because they have so few inducements to test and classify what they receive. To ascertain what pursuits are best suited to us, in our time and state of society, and how we may make best use of our means for building up the life of thought upon the life of action.

These conversations lasted during several successive winters, with much the same participants, numbering from twenty to thirty. These were all ladies. During one brief series, the experiment of admitting gentlemen was tried, and it seems singular that this should have failed, since many of her personal friends were of the other sex, and certainly men and women are apt to talk best when together. In this exceptional course, the subject was mythology, and it was thought that the presence of those trained in classical studies might be useful. But an exceedingly able historian of the enterprise adds, "All that depended on others entirely failed. . . . Even in the point of erudition on the subject, which Margaret did not profess, she proved the best informed of the party, while no one brought an idea, except herself. Take her as a whole," adds this lady, "she has the most to bestow upon others by conversation of any person I have ever known. I cannot conceive of any species of vanity living in her presence. She distances all who talk with her."

It is said by all her friends that no record of her conversation does it any justice. I have always fancied that the best impression now to be obtained of the way she talked when her classes called her "inspired," must be got by reading her sketch of the Roman and Greek characters, in her autobiographic fragment. That was written when her conversations most flourished, in 1840, and a marvellous thing it is. It is something to read and re-read, year after year, with ever new delight. Where else is there a statement, so vivid, so brilliant, so profound, of the total influence exerted on a thoughtful child by those two mighty teachers? No attempted report of her conversation gives such an impression of what it must have been, as this self-recorded reverie. If on the tritest of all subjects, she could so easily write something admirable, what must it have been when the restraints of the pen—to her most distasteful—were removed?

On the last day of these meetings—which were closed only by her departure for New York—she wrote thus:—

April 28, 1844. It was the last day with my class. How noble has been my experience of such relation now for six years, and with so many and so various minds! Life is worth living,—is it not? We had a most animated meeting. On bidding me good-by, they all and always show so much good-will and love that I feel I must really have become a friend to them. I was then loaded with beautiful gifts, accompanied with those little delicate poetic traits, which I should delight to tell you of, if you were near.

While thus serving women, she aided men also, by her editorship of the "Dial." This remarkable quarterly, established in 1840, by a circle of her friends, was under her exclusive charge for two years, and these the most characteristic years of its existence. It was a time of great seething in thought and many people had their one thing to say, which being said, they retired into the ranks of common men. The less instructed found their outlet in the radical conventions, then so abundant; the more cultivated uttered themselves in the "Dial." The contributors, who then thronged around Margaret Fuller,—Emerson, Alcott, Parker, Thoreau, Ripley, Hedge, Clarke, W. H. Channing,—were the true founders of American literature. They emancipated the thought of the nation, and also its culture, though their mode of utterance was often crude and cumbrous from excess of material. These writers are all now well known, and some are famous; but at that time not one of them was popular, save Theodore Parker, whose vigorous commonsense soon created for itself a wide public. It was his articles, as Mr. Emerson has since told me, that sold the numbers; that is, as far as they did sell, which was not very far. The editor was to have had two hundred dollars as her annual salary, but it hardly reached that sum, and I believe that the whole edition was but five hundred copies.

I can testify to the vast influence produced by this periodical, even upon those who came to it a year or two after its first appearance, and it seems to me, even now, that in spite of its obvious defects, no later periodical has had so fresh an aroma, or smacked so of the soil of spring. When the unwearied Theodore Parker attempted, half a dozen years after, to embody the maturer expression of the same phase of thought in the "Massachusetts Quarterly Review," he predicted that the new periodical would be "The Dial, with a beard." But the result was disappointment. It was all beard, and no "Dial."

During the first year of the "Dial's" existence, it contained but little from the editor,—four short articles, the "Essay on Critics," "Dialogue between Poet and Critic," "The Allston Exhibition," and "Menzel's View of Goethe,"—and two of what may be called fantasy-pieces, "Leila," and "The Magnolia of Lake Pontchartrain." The second volume was richer, containing four of her most elaborate critical articles,—"Goethe," "Lives of the Great Composers," "Festus," and "Bettine Brentano." Few American writers have ever published in one year so much of good criticism as is to be found in these four essays. She wrote also, during this period, the shorter critical notices, which were good, though unequal. She was one of the first to do hearty justice to Hawthorne, of whom she wrote, in 1840, "No one of all our imaginative writers has indicated a genius at once so fine and so rich." Hawthorne was at that time scarcely known, and it is singular to read in her diary, four years earlier, her account of reading one of his "Twice-told Tales," under the impression that it was written by "somebody in Salem," whom she took to be a lady.

I find that I underscored in my copy of the "Dial," with the zeal of eighteen, her sympathetic and wise remark on Lowell's first volume. "The proper critic of this book would be some youthful friend to whom it has been of real value as a stimulus. The exaggerated praise of such an one would be truer to the spiritual fact of its promise than accurate measure of its performance." This was received with delight by us ardent Lowellites in those days, and it still seems to me admirable.

In the third volume of the "Dial," she wrote of "Beethoven," "Sterling," "Romaie and Rhine Ballads," and other themes. In the fourth volume she published a remarkable article, entitled, "The Great Lawsuit; Man versus Men, Woman versus Women." It was a cumbrous name, for which even the vague title, "Woman in the Nineteenth Century," was hailed as a desirable substitute, when the essay was reprinted in book-form. In its original shape, it attracted so much attention that the number was soon out of print; and it is not uncommon to see sets of the "Dial" bound up without it.

She printed, in 1841, another small translation from the German,—a portion of that delightful book, the correspondence between Bettine Brentano and her friend Günderode. One-fourth of this was published in pamphlet form, by way of experiment; and it proved an unsuccessful one. Long after, her version was reprinted, the work being completed by a far inferior hand. Margaret Fuller was one of the best of translators, whether in reproducing the wise oracles of Goethe, or the girlish grace and daring originality of Bettine and her friend. She says of this last work, in a spirit worthy the subject: "I have followed as much as possible the idiom of the writer as well as her truly girlish punctuation. Commas and dashes are the only stops natural to girls; their sentences flow on in little minim ripples, unbroken as the brook in a green field unless by some slight waterfall or jet of Ohs and Ahs." I know of no other critic who has ever done exact justice to the wonderful Bettine, recognizing fully her genius and her charms, yet sternly pointing out the inevitable failure of such self-abandonment and the way in which the tree which defies the law mars its own growth.

During the summer of 1843, she made a tour to the West with her friends James Freeman Clarke and his artist-sister. The result of this was her first original work, "Summer on the Lakes,"—a book which, with all artistic defects upon its head, will yet always remain delightful to those who first read it in its freshness. To this day it is almost the only work which presents Western life in any thoughtful or ideal treatment,— which is anything more than a statistical almanac or a treatise on arithmetical progression. Though most of its statements of fact are long since superseded, it yet presents something which is truer than statistics,—the real aroma and spirit of Western life. It is almost the only book which makes that great region look attractive to any but the energetic and executive side of man's nature. In this point of view even her literary episodes seem in place; it is pleasant to think that such books as she describes could be read upon the prairies. In the narrative of most travellers it would seem inappropriate to say that they stopped in Chicago and read a poem. It would seem like being offered a New York "Tribune" at Pœstum. But when Margaret Fuller reads "Philip Van Artevelde," by the lake shore, just in the suburbs of the busy city, all seems appropriate and harmonized, and the moral that it yields her is fit to be remembered for years.

> In Chicago I read again "Philip Van Artevelde," and certain passages in it will always be in my mind associated with the deep sound of the lake, as heard in the night. I used to read a short time at night, and then open the blind to look out. The moon would be full upon the lake, and the calm breath, pure light, and the deep voice harmonized well with the thought of the Flemish hero. When will this country have such a man? *It is what she needs; no thin idealist, no coarse realist, but a man whose eye reads the heavens, while his feet step firmly on the ground, and his hands are strong and dexterous for the use of human implements.*

What was that power in Margaret Fuller which made her words barbed arrows, to remain in the hearts of young people forever? For one I know that for twenty years that sentence has haunted me, as being, more than any other, the true formula for the American man, the standard by which each should train himself in self-education. I fancy that the secret of my allegiance to this woman lies in the shaping influence of that one sentence. Others have acknowledged the same debt to other stray phrases she uses,—her "lyric glimpses," as Emerson called them. Thus William Hunt, the artist, acknowledged that a wholly new impulse of aspiration was aroused in him by a few stray words she had pencilled on the margin of a passage in Mrs. Jameson's "Italian Painters."

Even the narrative in this book, and its recorded conversations, show that she exerted on travelling acquaintances this stimulating and unlocking power. This showed itself with the Illinois farmers, "the large first product of the soil," and especially with that vanishing race, who can only be known through the sympathy of the imagination, the Indians. There is no book of travels, except, perhaps, Mrs. Jameson's, which gives more access to those finer traits of Indian character that are disappearing so fast amid persecution and demoralization. But the book as a whole, is very fragmentary and episodical, and in this respect, as well as in the wide range of merit and demerit in the verses here and there interspersed, it reminds one of Thoreau's "Week on the Concord and Merrimack Rivers." It is hardly possible, however, to regret these episodes, since one of them contains that rare piece of childish autobiography, "Mariana;" which is however separated from its context in her collected works.

In 1844 she removed to New York. It is not the least of Horace Greeley's services to the nation, that he was willing to entrust the literary criticisms of the "Tribune" to one whose standard of culture was so far above that of his readers or his own. Nevertheless, there she remained for nearly two years, making fearless use of her great opportunity of influence. She was dogmatic, egotistic, and liable to err; but in this she did not differ from her fellow-critics. The point of difference was in the thoroughness of training to which she had submitted,—at least in certain directions,—the elevation of her demands, her perfect independence, and her ready sympathy. With authors who demanded flattery on the one side, and a public on the other which demanded only intellectual substance, and was almost indifferent to literary form, she bravely asserted that literature was to be regarded as an art. Viewing it thus, she demanded the highest; reputations, popularity, cliques, to her were nothing; she might be whimsical, but she was always independent, and sought to try all by the loftiest standard. If she was ever biased by personal considerations,—and this rarely happened,—it was always on the chivalrous side.

Of all Americans thus far, she seems to me to have been born for a literary critic. One of her early associates said well "that she was no artist; she could never have written an epic, or romance, or drama; yet no one knew better the qualities which go to the making of these; and, though catholic as to kind, no one was more rigidly exacting as to quality." She puts this still better in her own journal: "How can I ever write, with this impatience of detail? I shall never be an artist. I have no patient love of execution. I am delighted with my sketch, but if I try to finish it, I am chilled. Never was there a great sculptor who did not love to chip the marble."

But the very fact that she was able to make this discrimination shows her critical discernment. There are not a dozen prose-writers in America who "love to chip the marble;" but so long as we do not discover the defect, we can neither do good work ourselves nor appreciate that of another. All Margaret Fuller's books are very defective as to form; but because she saw the fault, she was able to criticise the books of others.

She had also the rare quality of discerning both needs of the American mind,—originality and culture,—and no one, except Emerson, has done so much to bridge the passage from a tame and imitative epoch to a truly indigenous literature. Most of us are either effeminated by education, or are left crude and rough by the want of it. She who so exquisitely delineated the Greek and Roman culture in her fragment of autobiography, had yet the discernment to write in an essay, "It was a melancholy praise bestowed on the German Iphigenia, that it was an echo of the Greek mind. Oh, give us something rather than Greece more Grecian, so new, so universal, so individual!"

It was, therefore, an event in the history of our literature, when a woman thus eminently gifted became the literary critic of the New York "Tribune,"—then, and perhaps still, the journal possessing the most formative influence over the most active class of American minds. There were, of course, drawbacks upon her fitness. She was sometimes fantastic in her likings; so are most fastidious people; so is Emerson. She might be egotistical and overbearing. But she was honest and true. It was apt to be the strong, not the weak, whom she assailed. Her greatest errors were committed in vindicating those whom others attacked, or in dethroning popular favorites to make room for obscurer merit. A different course would have made her life smoother and her memory less noble.

In her day, as now, there were few well-trained writers in the country, and they had little leisure for criticism; so that work was chiefly left to boys. The few exceptions were cynics, like Poe, or universal flatterers, like Willis and Griswold. Into the midst of these came a woman with no gifts for conciliation, with no personal attractions, with a habit of saying things very explicitly and of using the first person singular a good deal too much. In her volume of "Papers on Literature and Art," published in 1846, there is a preface of three pages in which this unpleasant grammatical form occurs just fifty times. This is very characteristic; she puts the worst side foremost. The preface once ended, the rest of the book seems wise and gentle, and only egotistic here and there.

Or at least, nothing need be excepted from this claim, except the article on "American Literature"—the only essay in the book which had not been previously published. Gentle this was not always, nor could it be; and she furthermore apologized for it in the preface (wisely or unwisely), as prepared too hastily for a theme so difficult, and claimed only that it was "written with sincere and earnest feelings, and from a mind that cares for nothing but what is permanent and essential." "It should, then," she adds, "have some merit, if only in the power of suggestion." It certainly has such merit. It is remarkable, after twenty years, to see how many of her judgments have been confirmed by the public mind. How well, for instance, she brought forth from obscurity the then forgotten genius of Charles Brockden Brown; how just were her delineations of Bryant, Willis, Dana, Halleck; how well she described Prescott, then at his culmination,—his industry, his wealth of material, his clear and elegant arrangement, and his polished tameness! So much the public could endure. It was when she touched Longfellow and Lowell that her audience, or that portion of it which dwelt round Boston, grew clamorously indignant.

In reverting, after twenty years, to these criticisms, one perceives that the community must have grown more frank or less sensitive. There seems no good reason why they should have made so much stir. There is no improper personality in them, and, though they may be incorrect, they are not unfair. She frankly confesses to "a coolness towards Mr. Longfellow, in consequence of the exaggerated praise bestowed upon him. When we see a person of moderate powers receive honors which should be reserved for the highest, we feel somewhat like assailing him and taking from him the crown which should be reserved for grander brows. *And yet this is perhaps ungenerous.*" She then goes on to point out the atmosphere of overpraise which has always surrounded this poet,— says that this is not justly chargeable on himself, but on his admirers, publishers, and portrait-painters; and adds in illustration that the likeness of him in the illustrated edition of his works suggests the impression of a "dandy Pindar." This phrase, I remember, gave great offence at the time; yet, on inspection of that rather smirking portrait, it proves to be a fair description; and she expressly disclaims all application of the phrase to the poet himself. She defends him from Poe's charges of specific plagiarism, and points out, very justly, that these accusations only proceed from something imitative and foreign in many of his images and in the atmosphere of much of his verse. She says, as many have felt, that he sees nature, whether human or external, too much through the windows of literature, and finally assigns him his place as "a man of cultivated taste, delicate though not deep feeling, and some, though not much, poetic force." This may not be an adequate statement of the literary claims of Longfellow; but it certainly does not differ so widely from the probable final award as to give just ground for complaint against the critic. It is also recorded by Mr. Greeley that she only consented to review Longfellow's poems with the greatest reluctance, and at the editor's particular request, "assigning the wide divergence of her views of poetry from those of the author and his school as the reason."

Towards Lowell she showed more asperity. Yet there was nothing personal in her remarks, even here; there was simply an adverse literary criticism, conveyed with a slight air of arrogance. To preface an opinion with "We must declare it, though to the grief of some friends and the disgust of more," was undoubtedly meant for a deprecatory and regretful expression; but it had a sort of pompous effect that did not soften the subsequent brief verdict. She declared him "absolutely wanting in the true spirit and tone of poesy," with the addition that "his interest in the

moral questions of the day had supplied the want of vitality in himself."
Even this last statement was far too strong, no doubt. Yet it will now be
admitted by Lowell's warmest admirers that his poetic phases have been
singularly coincident with his phases of moral enthusiasm. His early development of genius was united with extreme radicalism of position;
then followed many years, comprising the prime of his life, when both
his genius and his enthusiasm seemed quiescent. It was the unforeseen
stimulus of the war which made him again put on his singing robes, for
that "Commemoration Ode," which is incomparably the greatest of his
poems. All this vindicated in some degree the discernment, though it
could not justify the sweeping manner of Margaret Fuller's criticism;
and her tone of arrogance is more than counter-balanced by the fierce
personalities with which the poet retaliated upon her in the "Fable for
Critics."

The criticisms on English poets in this collection seem to me singularly admirable; they take rank with those of Elizabeth Barrett Browning, in her "Essays on the Poets." There are many single phrases that are
unsurpassed in insight and expression, as where she speaks of the
"strange, bleak fidelity of Crabbe." "Give Coleridge a canvas," she says,
"and he will paint a picture as if his colors were made of the mind's own
atoms." "The rush, the flow, the delicacy of vibration in Shelley's verse
can only be paralleled by the waterfall, the rivulet, the notes of the bird
and of the insect world." "It is as yet impossible to estimate duly the effect which the balm of his [Wordsworth's] meditations has had in allay-
ing the fever of the public heart, as exhibited in Byron and Shelley." This
is a rare series of condensed criticisms, on authors about whom so much
has been written, and her remarks on the new men—Sterling, Henry
Taylor, and Browning—were almost as good. She was one of the first in
America to recognize the genius of Browning, and, while his "Bells and
Pomegranates" was yet in course of publication, she placed him at the
head of contemporary English poets.

There is much beside, in these rich volumes; a brief criticism on
"Hamlet," for instance, in one of the dialogues, which is worthy to take
rank with those of Mrs. Jameson; and an essay on "Sir James Mackin-
tosh," which, in calm completeness and thorough workmanship, was her
best work, as it was one of her latest. Indeed, the "Papers on Literature
and Art" always seemed to me her best book; far superior to the
"Woman in the Nineteenth Century" (published two years previously),
which was perhaps framed on too large a scale for one who had so little
constructive power. It was noble in tone, enlightened in its statements,
and full of suggestion; yet after all it was crude and disconnected in its

execution. But the "Papers" have been delightful reading, to me at least, for twenty years, and I could quote many a sentence which has passed into my bone and marrow, as have those of Emerson. "Tragedy is always a mistake." "The difference between heartlessness and the want of a deep heart." "We need to hear the excuses men make to themselves for their worthlessness." "It needs not that one of deeply thoughtful mind be passionate, to divine all the secrets of passion. Thought is a bee that cannot miss those flowers." And so on.

The only complaint I should make in regard to this book is founded on its title, "Papers on Literature and Art." With art, save as included in literature, she should not have meddled. At least, she should have dealt only with the biography and personal traits of artists,—not with their work. One of her early friends said that the god Terminus presided over her intellect; but to me it seems that she did not always recognize her own limits. A French wit said that there were three things he had loved very much, without knowing anything about them,—music, painting, and women. Margaret Fuller loved all three, and understood the last.

If, however, she was thus tempted beyond her sphere, it was less perhaps from vanity than because she yielded to the demand popularly made on all our intellectual laborers, that they should scatter themselves as much as possible. Literary work being as yet crude and unorganized in America, the public takes a vague delight in seeing one person do a great many different things. It is like hearing a street musician perform on six instruments at once; he plays them all ill, but it is so remarkable that he should play them together. If we have a stirring pulpit orator, he must try his hand on a novel; if a popular editor, he must write a history of the rebellion. Margaret Fuller, under the same influence, wrote on painting and music, and of course wrote badly.

As to this whole charge of vanity, indeed, there have certainly been great exaggerations. She had by inheritance certain unpleasant tricks of manner, which gave the impression, as Emerson said, of "a rather mountainous Me." She was accustomed to finding herself among inferiors, and lorded it a little in her talk. She was also obliged, as a woman, to fight harder than others, first for an education and then for a career. All these influences marred her, in some degree; and those whom her criticisms wounded, made the most of the result. But though her most private diaries and letters have been set before the public, I do not see that anything has been produced which shows a petty or conceited disposition, while she has certainly left on record many noble disclaimers. A woman who could calmly set aside all the applauses she received for her wonderful conversation by pointing out to herself that this faculty "bespoke a second-rate mind," could not have had her head turned by vanity. At another time she wrote in her diary, "When I look at my papers, I feel as if I had never had a thought that was worthy the attention of any but myself; and 'tis only when, on talking with people, I find I tell them what they did not know, that my confidence at all returns."

In truth, she was not made of pure intellect; if that quality marks men (which I have never discovered), then she was essentially a woman. "Of all whom I have known," wrote one of her female friends, "she was the largest woman, and not a woman who wished to be a man." And one of her friends of the other sex wrote of her, "The *dry light* which Lord Bacon loved she never knew; her light was life, was love, was warm with sympathy, and a boundless energy of affection and hope." The self-devotion of her closing years brought no surprise to those who remembered how she had sacrificed her most cherished plans for the sake of educating her brothers; and how she had through all her life been ready to spend money and toil for those around her, when she had little money and no health. She gave to the community, also, the better boon of moral courage; it showed itself most conspicuously in the telling of unwelcome truth; but it was manifested also in heroic endurance, since she was, as Mr. Emerson has testified, "all her life the victim of disease and pain."

Her life thus did more for the intellectual enfranchisement of American women than was done by even her book on the subject, though that doubtless did much, exerting a permanent influence on many minds. No one has ever given so compact a formula for the requirements of woman. She claims for her sex "not only equal power with man,—for of that omnipotent nature will never permit her to be defrauded,—but a *chartered* power, too fully recognized to be abused." Never were there ten words which put the whole principle of impartial suffrage so plainly as these. And even where her statements are less clear, they always rest on wise reflection, not on any one-sided view. Thus, for instance, she showed better than most her faith in the eternal laws which make woman unlike man,—for she was ready to trust these laws instead of legislating to sustain them. She knew that there was no fear of woman's unsexing herself. "Nature has pointed out her ordinary sphere by the circumstances of her physical existence. She cannot wander far. . . . Achilles had long plied the distaff as a princess, yet at first sight of a sword, he seized it. So with woman,—one hour of love would teach her more of her proper relations than all your formulas."

After twenty months of happy life and labor in New York, she sailed for Europe, thus fulfilling the design abandoned eleven years before, when her home duties demanded the sacrifice. She published in the

"Tribune" (Aug. 1, 1846), a cordial and almost enthusiastic "Farewell to New York," thanking the great city for all it had been to her. She had found no more of evil there than elsewhere, she said, and more of sympathy, and there was at least nothing petty or provincial. Perhaps, after visiting Europe, she thought differently. New York does not at first seem provincial to a Bostonian, nor Paris to a New Yorker; but all great cities soon show themselves provincial, by their disproportioned self-estimate, their tiresome local gossip, and their inability to tolerate real independence. Still it was good for one, who lived her life as strongly as Margaret Fuller, to seek the largest atmosphere she could find, and win her own emancipation at last.

Over the tragic remainder of her life I shall pass but lightly, for I have preferred to reverse the proverb and be the historian of her times of peace alone. It is because they were not really her times of peace, but only her training for final action; besides, it was during those years that she was most misconstrued and maligned; and it is more interesting to dwell on this period than to add a garland where all men praise. Enough to say that in that later epoch all the undue self-culture of her earlier life was corrected, and all its self-devotion found a surer outlet. That "hour of love" of which she had written came to her, and all succeeding hours were enriched and ennobled. Throwing herself into the struggle for a nation's life, blending this great interest with the devotion due to her Italian husband, she lived a career that then seemed unexampled for an American woman, though our war has since afforded many parallels. During the siege of Rome, in 1848, the greater part of her time was passed in the hospital *"dei Pellegrini,"* which was put under her special direction. "The weather was intensely hot; her health was feeble and delicate; the dead and dying were around her in every stage of pain and horror; but she never shrank from the duty she had assumed." "I have seen," wrote the American consul, Mr. Cass, "the eyes of the dying, as she moved among them, extended on opposite beds, meet in commendation of her universal kindness."

She was married in Italy, during the year 1847, to Giovanni Angelo, Marquis Ossoli,—a man younger than herself, and of less intellectual culture, but of simple and noble nature. He had given up rank and station in the cause of the Roman Republic, while all the rest of his family had espoused the other side; and it was this bond of sympathy which first united them. Their child, Angelo Philip Eugene Ossoli, was born at Rieti, September 5th, 1848. After the fall of the republic it was necessary for them to leave Rome, and this fact, joined with her desire to print in America her history of the Italian struggle, formed the main reasons for their return to this country. They sailed from Leghorn, May 17th, 1850, in the barque Elizabeth, Captain Hasty.

Singular anticipations of danger seem to have hung over their departure. "Beware of the sea" had been a warning given Ossoli by a fortune-teller, in his youth, and he had never before been on board a ship. "Various omens have combined," wrote his wife, "to give me a dark feeling." "In case of mishap, however, I shall perish with my husband and child." Again she wrote, "It seems to me that my future on earth will soon close." "I have a vague expectation of some crisis, I know not what. But it has long seemed that in the year 1850 I should stand on a plateau in the ascent of life, where I should be allowed to pause for a while and take a more clear and commanding view than ever before. Yet my life proceeds as regularly as the fates of a Greek tragedy, and I can but accept the pages as they turn."

As they were leaving Florence at the last moment, letters arrived which would probably have led them to remain in Italy, had not all preparations been made. And on the very day of sailing, in Leghorn, Margaret lingered for a final hour on shore, almost unable to force herself to embark. It seemed as if there were conflicting currents in their destiny, which held them back while they urged them forward.

Their voyage was very long, and the same shadow still appeared to hang over them. The captain of the barque, in whom they had placed the greatest confidence, soon sickened and died of malignant small-pox, and was buried off Gibraltar. They sailed thence on June 9th. Two days after, the little Angelo was attacked with the same fearful disease, and only recovered after an illness that long seemed hopeless. On July 15th, they made the New Jersey coast at noon, and stood to the north-east, the weather being thick, and the wind south-east. The passengers packed their trunks, assured that they should be landed at New York the next morning. By nine o'clock the wind had risen to a gale, and this, with the current, swept them much farther to the north than was supposed. At two and a half, A. M., the mate in command took soundings, found twenty-one fathoms of water, pronounced all safe, and retired to his berth. One hour afterwards, the bark struck on Fire Island beach, just off Long Island.

The main and mizen masts were at once cut away, but the ship held by the bow, and careened towards the land, every wave sweeping over her, and carrying away every boat. She was heavily laden with marble and soon bilged. The passengers hastily left their berths and collected in the cabin, which was already half full of water. They braced themselves as well as they could, against the windward side. Little Angelo cried, the survivors say, until his mother sang him to sleep, while Ossoli quieted the rest with prayer. The crew were at the forward end of the vessel; and when the wreck seemed ready to go to pieces, the second mate, Mr. Davis, came aft to the cabin with two sailors, and helped the passengers to a safer place. This transfer was made terribly dangerous by the breaking surf. The captain's wife, who went first, was once swept away, and was caught only by her hair. Little Angelo was carried in a canvas bag, hung round the neck of a sailor.

Passengers and crew were now crowded round the foremast, as the part likely to last longest. Here they remained for several hours. Men were seen collecting on the beach, but there was no life-boat. After a time, two sailors succeeded in reaching the shore, the one with a life-preserver, the other with a spar. Then Mr. Davis, the courageous mate, bound the captain's wife to a plank, and swam with her to the shore, where she arrived almost lifeless. The distance was less than a hundred yards, but the surf was fearful. Madame Ossoli was urged to attempt the passage as Mrs. Hasty had done, but steadily refused to be separated from her husband and child. Time was passing; the tide was out; the sea grew for the time a little calmer. It was impossible to build a raft, and there was but this one chance of escape before the tide returned. Still the husband and wife declined to be parted; and, seeing them resolute, the first mate ordered the crew to save themselves, and most of them leaped overboard. It was now past three o'clock; they had been there twelve hours. At length the tide turned, and the gale rose higher.

The after part of the vessel broke away, and the foremast shook with every wave. From this point the accounts vary, as is inevitable. It seems however to be agreed, that the few remaining sailors had again advised the Ossolis to leave the wreck; and that the steward had just taken little Angelo in his arms to try to bear him ashore, when a more powerful sea swept over, and the mast fell, carrying with it the deck, and all on board. Ossoli was seen to catch for a moment at the rigging, and then to sink. The last recorded glimpse of Margaret was when she was seated at the foot of the mast, in her white night-dress, with her hair fallen loose about her shoulders.

Their bodies were never found; but that of the little Angelo was cast upon the beach twenty minutes after, and was reverently buried among the sand-hills by the sailors, one of whom gave his chest for a coffin. The remains were afterwards transferred to Mount Auburn cemetery, near Boston, and there reinterred in presence of weeping kinsfolk, who had never looked upon the living beauty of the child.

It was the expressed opinion of one who visited the scene, a few days after, that seven resolute men could have saved all on board the "Elizabeth." The life-boat from Fire Island light-house, three miles off, was not brought to the beach till noon, and was not launched at all. For a time the journals were full of the tragedy that had taken away a life whose preciousness had not been fully felt till then. But now, looking through the vista of nearly twenty years, even this great grief appears softened by time. The very forebodings which preceded it seem now to sanctify that doom of a household, and take from its remembrance the sting. Three months before, in planning her departure, this wife and mother had thus unconsciously accepted her coming fate: "Safety is not to be secured by the wisest foresight. I shall embark more composedly in our merchant-ship, praying fervently, indeed, that it may not be my lot to lose my boy at sea, either by unsolaced illness or amid the howling waves; or, if so, that Ossoli, Angelo, and I may go together, and that the anguish may be brief." Her prayer was fulfilled.

The precious manuscript, for whose publication her friends and the friends of Italy had looked with eagerness, was lost in the shipwreck. Her remaining works were reprinted in Boston, a few years later, under the careful editorship of her brother Arthur;—that "Chaplain Fuller," who had been educated by her self-sacrifice, and who afterwards gained a place beside hers, in the heart of the nation, by his heroic death at Fredericksburg, during the late rebellion. Her biography has also been amply written by the friends whom she would most readily have selected for the task, Messrs. Emerson, Clarke, and Channing.

Since her day, American literature has greatly widened its base, but has raised its summit no higher. There is a multiplicity of books and magazines, and a vast increase of untrained literary activity. Yet, not only has she had no successor among women, but we still miss throughout our criticism her culture, her insight, her fearlessness, her generous sympathies, and her resolute purpose to apply the highest artistic standard to the facts of American life. It is this sense of loss that is her true epitaph. It was said to have been Fontenelle's funeral oration, when the most brilliant woman in France, having uttered after his death a witticism too delicate for her audience, exclaimed sadly, "Fontenelle! where are you?" And so every American author, who has a higher aim than to amuse, or a nobler test to merit than his publishers' account, must feel that something is wanting while Margaret Fuller's place remains unfilled.

3

THE SHADOW OF THE HAREM

We sometimes hear surprise expressed that woman has contributed so little to the masterpieces of the world in science, art, literature. To me the wonder is always the other way—that she has produced anything in that direction at all; and this for the plain reason that the shadow of repression, which is the bequest of the Oriental harem, still hangs over her. That she has always been at a great disadvantage in training or education is also true, but it is a secondary matter. The real disadvantage of women has lain in being systematically taught from childhood up that it is their highest duty to efface themselves, or at least keep out of sight. One can overcome great obstacles as to education, but to do anything remarkable without running the risk of being conspicuous—this would puzzle the most skilful. Fame is the shadow of great action. Now nobody but Peter Schlemihl ever succeeded in living without his shadow, and it is not recorded that even he enjoyed that situation.

It would be easy to show by a long series of examples the eager desire of men, especially the mediocre ones, that women should remain invisible. It was the Latin epitaph upon the model woman that she stayed at home and spun—*Domum servavit, lanam fecit.* It is a motto which Mr. Newell, the scientific explorer of nursery rhymes, would perhaps find preserved in Mrs. Mouse's answer to the "frog who would a-wooing go:"

"'Pray, Mistress Mouse, are you within?'—
—Heigho! says Rowley.
'Oh yes, kind sir; I'm sitting to spin'—
—With a Rowley, Powley," etc.

But as no amount of spinning saved that excellent matron from the terrible cat, so Harriet Martineau and other literary women might be as good housekeepers as they pleased without clearing themselves from reproach. Indeed, it is rather pathetic to notice how the pioneer women authors in America, such as Mrs. Child and Miss Leslie, endeavored to disarm public judgment by printing some "Frugal Housewife" or "Seventy-five Receipts" before showing their heads as writers. Even now the practice is not discontinued, and Marion Harland, with all her wide popularity, has to wind up with a practical work on "Breakfast, Dinner, and Supper" to demonstrate that, though an author, she still has the virtues of her sex. We have not yet outgrown that profound remark of Fredrika Bremer that a woman may do almost anything she pleases with a man if she always has something nice to pop into his mouth.

From the days of that Roman epitaph onward the theory of suppression has been pretty well sustained. It would be easy to fill pages with the sayings of wise men to the general effect that women should, as far as possible, be kept in some place that has a lid to it. The favorite German novelist Auerbach, for instance, puts this with a praiseworthy directness: "The best woman is she of whom men speak least. I understand it so that where a man speaks of a woman he should content himself with a few words. He should say, 'She is an intelligent, a good, a domestic, or a noble woman.' Qualify these words, and the strength of the comment is lost." It is certain that in saying this Auerbach speaks the spirit of his nation. He says it gravely too, and does nothing inconsistent with it, being in this respect more fortunate than the English Archdeacon Trench, who thoroughly approves the Latin motto as applied to women, *Bene vixit qui bene latuit* ("She has lived well who has kept well concealed"), and quotes it with pride in a preface to a very thick octavo volume containing several hundred of his mother's most private letters.

There is one way alone in which men have been willing to see any amount of literary or artistic genius developed in women—when these ladies have consented to attribute their work to a husband or brother, and say nothing about it. This is the self-effacement, the *bene latuit*, at its most delightful point, when the woman does the work and the man gets the fame. The Mendelssohn family had not the slightest objection to their gifted Fanny's composing as much music as she pleased, provided it appeared under the name of her brother Felix. Nobody knows, the recent biographers tell us, how many of his "songs without words" the sister contributed; but the moment she proposed to publish anything under her own name the whole household was aroused, and the shadow of the harem was invoked; it was improper, unwomanly, indelicate, for her to publish music—except to swell her brother's fame. Mademoiselle De Scudéry, whose interminable novels delighted all good society in France and England two centuries and a half ago, printed most of her fifty volumes under the name of her brother. Charles De Scudéry undoubtedly wrote part of the books, and he certainly may be said to have encouraged his sister in writing them, inasmuch as he used to lock her up in her room to keep her at it. But he never seems to have doubted as to his fraternal right to claim them all; and he once drew his sword on a personal friend for doubting his authorship of "Le Grand Cyrus," a novel of nearly 13,000 pages, of which it is now pretty well established that the sister wrote the whole.

In short, the repressing influence has not consisted in this or that trivial disadvantage, but in the Oriental theory itself. If women have less natural gift than men, they need more encouragement and not more hinderance; if a young man of puny appearance comes into a gymnasium, he is not invited to exercise with his hands tied. At all events, for what work a woman does she is entitled to credit, and not to have the shadow of the harem invoked to hush up her existence as much as possible, letting the credit go to some one else. I know a lady who, when a child, was once coaxed by her elder brothers to climb through the sliding-door of the pantry, which she alone was small enough to enter, and to bring them out an apronful of apples. The elder accomplices then carried them off into the orchard and devoured them without leaving her a single one. If art and authorship in women be crimes, like stealing apples, men have certainly adjusted the rewards and penalties somewhat in this way.

4

THE PLEASING ART OF
SELF-EXTINCTION

All admit the great change in the position of woman—legal, social, and educational—within a hundred years. The most conservative woman cannot if she would withdraw herself within the shell of the old protection and privacy. The shell is not there to receive her; laws and usages are all changed. If she must, like the mass of women, toil for her own support, she can no longer stay at home and spin, for nobody wishes the result of her spinning; she must go out into that vast Babel known as the labor market. If she is protected from this necessity, the protection goes little further; law and custom all assume that she should know something for herself, should do something for others. The married woman is no longer a *femme covert,* an irresponsible agent, but in many respects stands alone. What we do not always recognize is that all these changes imply further changes, and that every woman must adapt herself, as Emerson said of all of us, to "the new works of the new days."

She must, for instance, learn to keep her own accounts, and know something of what is comprehensively called "business"—as if it were, what in some respects it is, the essential business of life. Formerly it was not so; indeed, the less she knew of all this, the better. "A Woman ought to handle Money," wrote Don Francisco Manocl, two centuries ago, "with as much caution as she would a Sword or Fire or anything else she ought to be afraid of. Money in the hands of a Woman is as unbecoming as a Weapon." But surely this is more consistent and intelligible than to put her in a state of society where she is responsible for her own debts, can make her own contracts, can transact business independently of her husband—and yet leave her wholly ignorant of prices, stocks, and profits, and thus absolutely dependent on some man to do all this for her. I have always remembered how admirably a Boston merchant of the last generation discoursed in public on the propriety of explaining business affairs to women; but when this was mentioned years after to one of his daughters, she said, "I only wish he had applied it in his own family." A rich heiress, the daughter of an eminent financier, told me that she was herself absolutely ignorant of all money matters; after her father's death, her brothers had managed her affairs; then, "of course," her husband; but she herself knew absolutely nothing. It reminded me of another heiress I had known, who was twice married; the first husband lost two-thirds of her property; the second made away with the rest of it; and she supported herself and her child for the rest of her life—there being nothing left to tempt a third fortune-hunter—by giving public readings. One of the minor achievements of an eminent financier now under arrest in New York is stated to be that of sweeping in among his vast losses the whole property ($14,000) of two ladies, who had assigned to him certain stocks or certificates to be transferred for their benefit. Perhaps it would be unjust to call him a swindler, in this case, or to call those other men fortune-hunters; they may have expected better results; but certainly the absolute ignorance, absolute trust, and, one might almost say, absolute folly of many confiding women presents a combined temptation which sometimes demoralizes the very elect.

Again, another necessary sacrifice now asked of women—outside of convents at least—is that of the bliss of entire self-surrender. The time is past when women can indulge the great pleasure—if pleasure it be—of absolute self-extinction and complete merging of themselves in another. The simple and comprehensive phrase used in the old Russian marriage ceremony, "Here wolf, take thy lamb," is no longer practicable: no matter how ready the lamb may be to be devoured, the laws and practices of society are no longer constructed that way; and even the lingering "obey" is very likely to be construed by the very clergyman who administers it, that there is left only the most remote and shadowy significance. "Why should brides object to it?" said to me the most amiable of clergymen's wives last summer. "I promised to obey, and I am sure I have never done it once yet;" while her equally amiable husband looked on and smiled. Compare this with the period when the Princess de la Roche Suryon could say, in France ("who was a most discreet woman, and unhappy in a husband"), that of three faculties of the soul which she had when she was married, her husband had taken two and left her but one, which she would willingly give him, "for that she now neither had will nor understanding, and only retained the memory that she had once possessed them, which served only more to grieve her for the loss." This was more than two centuries ago, and about that time wrote Don Francisco Manoel, whose delightful hand-book—already quoted—*The Government of a Wife,* being rendered into English by Captain John Stevens (1697), was for a long time held a good model of vigorous domestic discipline, wrote as follows: "Singing," he says, "is a Heavenly Perfection, if a Woman has discretion to know when to use and when to forbear it; it is always commendable for her to divert herself, to please her Husband, to be sociable among other Women; but to be heard to Sing in the company of other Men, without the express Command of her Husband, is not only vain, foolish, and undecent, but savors much of Impudence" (p. 61). The whole condition of things has changed. A woman cannot, if she would, lead the life which would two centuries ago, and in Europe, have been the only life recognized as commendable and proper.

And she must, finally, sacrifice something of her privacy. If she works in the world, she must do it in her own name and be known in the world. Dr. Lynes, president of the Middle Georgia Military and Agricultural College, has lately been describing in a lecture how one of the most momentous inventions in all history, that of the cotton-gin, was really the work of a woman. It has been long known that Eli Whitney, its recognized inventor, was encouraged and aided by Mrs. Greene, the widow of General Greene, with whom he was then living. But Dr. Lynes shows that the scheme really originated with her; that it failed at first, because wooden teeth were used, and Whitney was then ready to abandon it, when she proposed iron wire, which was adopted; the machine then worked perfectly, and has been ever since used in very much the same form. It was then an unheard-of thing for a woman to take out a patent, and the result was that Eli Whitney, whose share was merely mechanical, has ever since had the fame of the invention. These are the things that are destined to disappear. The pleasing art of self-extinction is one of the delights which the women of the future will have to sacrifice.

5

REPRESSION AT LONG RANGE

The critic of poetry in the New York *Nation*, while showing himself quite ready to do justice to the work of women, feels bound to admit that few women have reached in poetry the white-heat of passion. He cites Helen Jackson's "Vintage" and Saxe Holm's "Three Kisses of Farewell" as examples of this white-heat; and names others who have at least reached the red-heat, while he thinks that several American "poet-esses of passion" fail to reach any real heat at all, but offer only an obtrusive burning of unseemly stubble. Be this as it may, it must be remembered that it is only lately that women have even begun to compete with men, on a large scale, in artistic expression of any kind; it is a part of the later evolution of the sex, and must, as with all great processes, proceed slowly. Lateness of arrival on the scene is not only no discredit, but, by the analogies of nature, rather creditable; else would man have preceded the *mylodon*. With more of poetic sympathy, woman has as yet produced less of high poetry than man; with more of musical feeling, she has been little known as a composer; and so of various other spheres in science and art. In accounting for this it is not enough to take into account the special disadvantages, as when Mary Somerville met only universal ridicule in her early mathematical studies, and wrote of herself, "I was very sad and forlorn; not a hand held out to help me;" or when Fanny Mendelssohn was required by her family to publish her musical compositions as her brother's. But beyond all these discouragements of the individual there was the collective discouragement of the sex. There was the fact pressing on all society around them, the universal tradition of the human race, disturbed even now only in two or three of the more advanced countries, that women have, to all intents and purposes, no brains.

An eminent teacher has lately written a paper directed against certain extreme theories of teaching, and entitled "The Presumption of Brains." What has weighed down woman, and still weighs her down, is not so much any temporary or local inconvenience as the great collective tradition still held against her—"The Presumption of No Brains." There is a solidarity of the human race, and the total soil and atmosphere of the planet, socially speaking, is to be taken into account in her case. The most gifted woman, struggling for intellectual progress in the most favorable surroundings, is still like a single plant or little group of plants trying to sustain itself where the soil as a whole is not yet fitted for its reception, and it is only in some favored nook that it manages to exist at all. The traditions of Turkey still keep down Europe; the vast East, with its solid and unbroken prejudice, discourages our little England and America. When we consider that out of the 1,877,942 pupils in the schools of British India in 1877–78 less than 100,000 were girls, we have a fact which makes it seem as if this planet, taken as a whole, was still intellectually uninhabitable for women. Then we must take further into view that in the Presidency of Bombay the prize books distributed to deserving girls in the government-aided schools have such passages as the following: "If the husband of a virtuous woman be ugly, of good or bad disposition, diseased, fiendish, irascible, a drunkard, old, stupid, dumb, blind, deaf, hot-tempered, poor, extremely covetous, a slanderer, cowardly, perfidious, and immoral, nevertheless she ought to worship him as a god with mind, speech, and person. The wife who gives an angry answer to her husband will become a village pariah dog; she will also become a female jackal, and live in an uninhabited desert. . . . The woman who speaks disrespectfully to her husband will be dumb in the next incarnation. The woman who hates her husband's relations will become from birth to birth a muskrat living in ordure and filth." We must remember that the marriages for which this code is provided are mostly child marriages, made without the consent of the poor little bride; we must remember that these prize books are distributed virtually at the expense of the British Government—and how vast is the abyss of ignorance and degradation in which these things show women as plunged! But that abyss comprises the greater part of the human race, and the teeming millions of China, Africa, and Oceanica would show nothing much better.

The moral is that any intellectual opportunities given to woman, even in the most enlightened countries, are but exceptional and recent things. She enters every competition burdened with the world-wide discouragement and repression of her sex. The obstacles with which she has to contend are not merely the obvious and local ones, but have the vast super-incumbent weight of a cosmic tradition behind them. The local obstacles are often quite enough. An accomplished German woman, long resident in England, told me that she once went back to her native land to live, but found the intellectual position of women so humiliating, compared with England, that she could not remain. Yet about the same time a brilliant American woman told me that it took her a whole year in England to get accustomed to the subordinate position of women there, as compared with America. As to France, Mr. John D. Philbrick told me at the Exposition of 1878, where he had charge of our educational exhibit, that he spent a large part of his time in trying to convince incredulous Frenchmen that there were actually institutions in the United States where girls studied Greek. They went away, he said, bowing courteously, but evidently unconvinced. Yet these are the foremost countries of the world in their recognition of brains in women, and even these, it seems, are backward and reluctant. But behind these lies, it must always be remembered, the vast, hopeless, impenetrable incredulity of India, China, and the Dark Continent. This dense resistance may not affect, directly and obviously, the more enlightened sentiment of more favored regions, but it affects it indirectly and unconsciously: the status of woman is determined by the condition of mind of the human race. The wonder will one day be not that she did not accomplish more in the nineteenth century, but that she accomplished what she has. For many years, or perhaps centuries, she will still work at disadvantage; she will still find herself surrounded, nearer or farther off, by an atmosphere of distrust and disparagement. There are obstacles enough, under all circumstances, to the rearing of first-class genius. It certainly is not easy for it to raise itself when it has the weight of the globe on its shoulders.

6

THE FACT OF SEX

I t is constantly said that the advocates of woman suffrage ignore the fact of sex. On the contrary, they seem to me to be the only people who do not ignore it.

Were there no such thing as sexual difference, the wrong done to woman by disfranchisement would be far less. It is precisely because her traits, habits, needs, and probable demands are distinct from those of man, that she is not, never was, never can, and never will be, justly represented by him. It is not merely that a vast number of human individuals are disfranchised; it is not even because in many of our States the disfranchisement extends to a majority, that the evil is so great; it is not merely that we disfranchise so many units and tens: but we exclude a special element, a peculiar power, a distinct interest,—in a word, a sex.

Whether this sex is more or less wise, more or less important, than the other sex, does not affect the argument: it is a sex, and, being such, is more absolutely distinct from the other than is any mere race from any other race. The more you emphasize the fact of sex, the more you strengthen our argument. If the white man cannot justly represent the negro,—although the two races are now so amalgamated that not even the microscope can always decide to which race one belongs,—how impossible that one sex should stand in legislation for the other sex!

This is so clear that, so soon as it is stated, there is a shifting of the ground. "But consider the danger of introducing the sexual influence into legislation!" . . . Then we are sure to be confronted with the case of Miss Vinnie Ream, the sculptor. See how that beguiling damsel cajoled all Congress into buying poor statues! they say. If one woman could do so much, how would it be with one hundred? Precisely the Irishman's argument against the use of pillows: he had put one feather on a rock, and found it a very uncomfortable support. Grant, for the sake of argument, that Miss Ream gave us poor art; but what gave her so much power? Plainly that she was but a single feather. Congress being composed exclusively of men, the mere fact of her sex gave her an exceptional and dangerous influence. Fill a dozen of the seats in Congress with women, and that danger at least will be cancelled. The taste in art may be no better; but an artist will no more be selected for being a pretty girl than now for being a pretty boy. So in all such cases. Here, as everywhere, it is the advocate of woman suffrage who wishes to recognize the fact of sex, and guard against its perils.

It is precisely so in education. Believing boys and girls to be unlike, and yet seeing them to be placed by the Creator on the same planet and in the same family, we hold it safer to follow his method. As they are born to interest each other, to stimulate each other, to excite each other, it seems better to let this impulse work itself off in a natural way,—to let in upon it the fresh air and the daylight, instead of attempting to suppress and destroy it. In a mixed school, as in a family, the fact of sex presents itself as an unconscious, healthy, mutual stimulus. It is in the separate schools that the healthy relation vanishes, and the thought of sex becomes a morbid and diseased thing. This observation first occurred to me when a pupil and a teacher in boys' boarding-schools years ago: there was such marked superiority as to sexual refinement in the day-scholars, who saw their sisters and the friends of their sisters every day. All later experience of our public-school system has confirmed this opinion. It is because I believe the distinction of sex to be momentous, that I dread to see the sexes educated apart.

The truth of the whole matter is that Nature will have her rights—innocently if she can, guiltily if she must; and it is a little amusing that the writer of an ingenious paper on the other side, called "Sex in Politics," in an able New York journal, puts our case better than I can put it, before he gets through, only that he is then speaking of wealth, not women: "Anybody who considers seriously what is meant by the conflict between labor and capital, of which we are only just witnessing the beginning, and what is to be done *to give money legitimately that influence on legislation which it now exercises illegitimately,* must acknowledge at once that the next generation will have a thorny path to travel." The italics are my own. Precisely what this writer wishes to secure for money, we claim for the disfranchised half of the human race,—open instead of secret influence; the English tradition instead of the French; women as rulers, not as kings' mistresses; women as legislators, not merely as lobbyists; women employing in legitimate form that power which they will otherwise illegitimately wield. This is all our demand.

7

WOMANHOOD AND MOTHERHOOD

I always groan in spirit when any advocate of woman suffrage, carried away by zeal, says anything disrespectful about the nursery. It is contrary to the general tone of feeling among reformers, I am sure, to speak of this priceless institution as a trivial or degrading sphere, unworthy the emancipated woman. It is rarely that anybody speaks in this way; but a single such utterance hinders progress more than any arguments of the enemy. For every thoughtful person sees that the cares of motherhood, though not the whole duty of woman, are an essential part of that duty, wherever they occur; and that no theory of womanly life is good for anything which undertakes to leave out the cradle. Even her school education is based on this fact, were it only on Stendhal's theory that the sons of a woman who reads Gibbon and Schiller will be more likely to show talent than those of one who only tells her beads and reads Mme. de Genlis. And so clearly is this understood among us, that, when we ask for suffrage for woman, it is almost always claimed that she needs it for the sake of her children. To secure her in her right to them; to give her a voice in their education; to give her a vote in the government beneath which they are to live,—these points are seldom omitted in our statement of her claims. Anything else would be an error.

But there is an error at the other extreme, which is still greater. A woman should no more merge herself in her child than in her husband. Yet we often hear that she should do just this. What is all the public sphere of woman, it is said,—what good can she do by all her speaking and writing and action,—compared with that she does by properly training the soul of one child? It is not easy to see the logic of this claim.

For what service is that child to render in the universe, except that he, too, may write and speak and act for that which is good and true? And if the mother foregoes all this that the child, in growing up, may simply do what the mother has left undone, the world gains nothing. In sacrificing her own work to her child's, moreover, she exchanges a present good for a prospective and merely possible one. If she does this through over-whelming love, we can hardly blame her; but she cannot justify it before reason and truth. Her child may die, and the service to mankind be done by neither. Her child may grow up with talents unlike hers, or with none at all; as the son of Howard was selfish, the son of Chesterfield a boor, and the son of Wordsworth in the last degree prosaic.

Or the special occasion when she might have done great good may have passed before her boy or girl grows up to do it. If Mrs. Child had re-fused to write "An Appeal for that Class of Americans called Africans," or Mrs. Stowe had laid aside "Uncle Tom's Cabin," or Florence Nightingale had declined to go to the Crimea, on the ground that a woman's true work was through the nursery, and they must all wait for that, the con-sequence would be that these things would have remained undone. The brave acts of the world must be performed when occasion offers, by the first brave soul who feels moved to do them, man or woman. If all the children in all the nurseries are thereby helped to do other brave deeds when their turn comes, so much the better. But when a great opportu-nity offers for direct aid to the world, we have no right to transfer that work to other hands—not even to the hands of our own children. We must do the work, and train the children besides.

I am willing to admit, therefore, that the work of education, in any form, is as great as any other work; but I fail to see why it should be greater. Usefulness is usefulness: there is no reason why it should be postponed from generation to generation, or why it is better to rear a serviceable human being than to be one in person. Carry the theory consistently out: if each mother must simply rear her daughter that she in turn may rear somebody else, then from each generation the work will devolve upon a succeeding generation, so that it will be only the last woman who will personally do any service, except that of motherhood; and when her time comes it will be too late for any service at all.

If it be said, "But some of these children will be men, who are neces-sarily of more use than women," I deny the necessity. If it be said, "The children may be many, and the mother, who is but one, may well be sac-rificed," it might be replied that, as one great act may be worth many smaller ones, so all the numerous children and grandchildren of a woman like Lucretia Mott may not collectively equal the usefulness of herself alone. If she, like many women, had held it her duty to renounce all other duties and interests from the time her motherhood began, I think that the world, and even her children, would have lost more than could ever have been gained by her more complete absorption in the nursery.

The true theory seems a very simple one. The very fact that during one half the years of a woman's average life she is made incapable of child-bearing shows that there are, even for the most prolific and devoted mothers, duties other than the maternal. Even during the most absorbing years of motherhood, the wisest women still try to keep up their interest in society, in literature, in the world's affairs—were it only for their children's sake. Multitudes of women will never be mothers; and those more fortunate may find even the usefulness of their motherhood surpassed by what they do in other ways. If maternal duties interfere in some degree with all other functions, the same is true, though in a far less degree, of those of a father. But there are those who combine both spheres. The German poet Wieland claimed to be the parent of fourteen children and forty books; and who knows by which parentage he served the world the best?

8

"Chances"

The head of a great collegiate institution for women once told me of receiving a visit from a titled Englishman, who examined with much interest all the departments. Finally, taking her aside with an air of mystery, he said that there was one question which he greatly desired to ask her. On her assenting, he said, "This is all very interesting, but I really want to know what influence it is found to have upon their future lives, don't you know." She was pleased at the question, and at once proceeded to give statistics as to how many of the graduates were now teachers, how many were missionaries, and the like. This evidently did not satisfy him. "Ah! that's very interesting," he said—"very interesting indeed; but that isn't just it. What effect does this higher education have upon—upon their *chances*?" "Upon their chances?" she näively said—"chances of what?" "Why, of course," he said, "their chances of getting a husband."

Being a lady of some humor, she found it difficult at first to answer, but presently explained that she had not tabulated any statistics on that point, although, judging from the frequency with which wedding-cards came through the post-office, the graduates were in a fair way to be married quite as fast as was desirable, possibly faster. And Sir John was apparently a little relieved when, on exhibiting to him the gymnasium, she pointed out the use of various articles of apparatus for physical improvement. "Ah!" he said, "that, now, is very interesting indeed; that is excellent. After all, don't you know, nothing improves a girl's chances like a good carriage of the person!"

Why is it that nobody ever speaks of a man's "chances" in a sense wholly matrimonial? Perhaps they do in England, where, I must say, one grows accustomed to hearing the worldly side of marriage presented in a way that rather disgusts an American; but even a travelling Englishman would hardly, I fancy, go through Harvard or Yale asking himself whether the lecture-rooms and the gymnasium were likely to hinder or help the young men's chances of marriage. Yet he—and possibly some of our own countrymen also—would use this odd phrase about women without thinking of its oddity. The assumption is, of course, that marriage is the one momentous event of a woman's life, and a very subordinate matter in a man's; and, moreover, that in a woman's case it is a matter of chance, and in a man's of certainty. Let us consider all this a little.

We may well grant that marriage must hold a more controlling share in a woman's life than in a man's, because she is anchored by her children as a man is not. Yet when we look round us and see the enormous number of cases where a woman either is never married, or is childless, or is left widowed, it is quite evident that there are for her in life other opportunities and duties, and therefore "chances," besides those determined by marriage alone. And as to the risk involved in marriage, the more we reduce it to a minimum by care and judgment and good sense, the better. There is no surer preparation for misery, one would think, than to accustom a young girl to think of every offer of marriage as a "chance," to be eagerly seized as a fish swallows the bait, without knowing who or what is at the other end of the fishing-rod.

So long as it is the custom of society for men to ask the momentous question and for women only to answer it—and this custom will probably last, in spite of certain philosophers, forever—so long there will be a little more element of chance in the marriage relations of women than of men. A ballroom is in this respect a mimic world, and it is perfectly clear that the young lady who must sit still behind her bouquet and be asked has less control of her own destiny than the young man who can try every girl in the room in succession until he finds a partner. But we certainly cannot say that chance entirely controls either sex, in real life, when we consider how many men die unmarried through inability to find or win the woman they want; and when we reflect, on the other hand, that there are probably very few women who do not have first or last an opportunity of marriage, if they were only as easy to satisfy as men sometimes seem. Perhaps nobody will ever frame a philosophical theory of the law that brings together certain men and certain women as lovers. The brilliant author of "Counterparts" tried her hand at it, and while she produced a remarkable novel, she did not establish her theory very firmly after all. But whatever the true philosophy may be, it is pretty certain that the element of chance is distributed between man and woman, and that a good deal of it exists for both in that formidable practical problem we call marriage.

But why, oh why, if Sir John and his fellow-worldlings are so anxious about a girl's "chances" at all, do they not carry their solicitude far beyond marriage, and make it include the whole life? Up to the wedding-day it is comparatively easy to ward off the storms of fate; indeed, the only serious storm to young people in love consists in the possible putting off of that day of bliss. But it is in later life that perils begin—perils which neither the presence of geometrical knowledge nor its absence, nor even a genteel carriage of the person, can very seriously affect. "Ah, sir!" said a pretty young Irish "second-girl" to me the other day, "my aunt is always at me to be a Sister [of Charity], and not be married at all; and indade, sir, when I think of the girls that I went to school with, and see some of them married already, and maybe with children, and maybe a husband that drinks, I think that if their example doesn't make a Sister of me, nothing of my aunt's taching will ever do it." Here is a glimpse, given with the stern realism of humble life, of the really formidable chances of a woman's career—chances that begin after the orange blossoms are faded, and the handfuls of rice thrown, and the guests gone home. Let us, if possible, Sir John, give to our daughters a training in character and purpose which shall enable them, with or without geometry and gymnastics, to do true women's work in the world, and make their usefulness, and even their happiness, something more than things of chance.

PART FOUR

The Essayist as Activist

> We all need action. This is shown by the way it
> transforms us just as the water of a brook that glides
> turgid and dull along its common bed becomes radiant
> and of a sunny purity when compelled to find its way
> over a cascade of rocks.
>
> THOMAS WENTWORTH HIGGINSON,
> LETTERS AND JOURNALS (BOSTON, 1921)

Higginson once compared himself to "a horse that had never won a race, but was prized as having gained second place more than any other." At another time he told his diary, "My great intellectual difficulty is having too many irons in the fire."

The many causes Higginson wrote about in the essays presented in this part suggest that he was at least partially correct in his self-assessment. "The Clergy and Reform" was delivered as a sort of "test sermon" at Visitation Day, some weeks before graduation from Harvard Divinity School. The audience was not a church congregation but a select group who were almost all academics and clergy. A dozen sermons were delivered that day, but the others were more conventional than Higginson's.

One of the audience called it the best Visitation Day sermon he had ever heard. Others who heard it were impressed and said so. This positive response thrilled the young speaker. Perhaps overreacting, Higginson wrote his mother: "Like Byron I have waked up & found myself famous—it bewilders me."

"A New Counterblast," an attack on the dangers of tobacco, was perhaps too temperate to have lasting effect. Reading it today we can't help wondering, "What did we know and when did we know it?" Higginson wrote that many cases of cancer attributable to tobacco had been noted by French surgeons and reported in the British medical journal *Lancet*. Higginson's early observations and anecdotal evidence make even blacker the comedy played out by tobacco tycoons and televised to the nation as they took an oath denying their awareness of tobacco's addictiveness.

There was no follow-up to Higginson's pioneering essay. Abuse of alcohol was a greater social evil in those days and commanded commensurately greater attention. But in a number of other articles dealing with health issues Higginson argued for the recognition of the importance of healthy habits and for ending the neglect of physical well-being as a personal and social aim.

Numerous letters and diaries stemming from this historical period tell us he influenced the conduct of quite a few Americans. Evidence of this comes from a 1932 *Atlantic Monthly* essay, "Our Sporting Grandfathers" (and, from the evidence, a good many grandmothers), whose author called Higginson "a strenuous young champion of the cause of health and happiness."

Scholarly confirmation of the value of Higginson's efforts in this field came in 1971 from John A. Lucas, professor of physical education at Pennsylvania State University and a historian of sport. In an article (supported with dozens of footnotes) in the *Journal of Health, Physical Education and Recreation* titled "Early Apostle of Health and Fitness," Lucas told of Higginson's effort's to improve Americans' health, and included words paying respect to Higginson's ahead-of-its-time critique of tobacco and its pernicious effects.

In "Scripture Idolatry" (Chapter 3) Higginson takes an early stand against Christian fundamentalism. "The Sympathy of Religions" (Chapter 4) joins with it as the statement of a cause that came to be called "free religion" and that culminated in 1893 in the formation of the World Parliament of Religions, but did not continue independently (lately there has been a revival of interest in the idea). Elements of Higginson's ideas on this score survive in the philosophies of Unitarian Universalism and the Ethical Culture Society.

"The Sympathy of Religions" is something more than advocacy of "free religion" in the land of the free. It is a presentation of points of similarity in the traditions, the myths, and the doctrines of every system of organized religion, East and West. It suggests an approach that is insufficiently, if ever, used to counter the preaching of hatred and sectarian violence—intergroup assassination—in the name of a deity.

Other essays included here make points that became for a period majority opinion concerning poverty, immigration, and the socialism called "nationalism" that was promulgated in the socialist Edward Bellamy's book, *Looking Backward: 2000–1887.*

At age seventy-five Higginson was one of the principal leaders of a new cause, anti-imperialism; in one of the selections in this section, "Where Liberty Is *Not,* There Is My Country," he explains his position. It developed as the war against Spain, ostensibly pursued with the aim of freeing Cuba of Spanish colonial rule, was drawing to a close.

Former abolitionists and younger Americans of conscience united to oppose the military subjugation of the native movement for Philippine freedom that had initially aided Americans in ousting the Spanish colonial rulers. The old abolitionists and a new generation whose members revered them thought the issues were similar to those of the earlier cause. They persuasively argued that conquest in order to rule darker peoples differed little from the slavery that they had fought to end in our land. The anti-imperialist cause failed in its day, only to succeed on a global scale half a century later.

"Higginson Answers Captain Mahan," remarks made at a meeting in 1900, concerns Higginson's reaction to the views of the influential naval historian Admiral Alfred Thayer Mahan on the U.S. role in the Philippine Islands. Readers will ask themselves, How many present-day militarists and navalists remember and revere Admiral Mahan; and how many present-day pacifists know of Higginson the ex-colonel who protested the use of American soldiers in what he saw as an imperialist cause?

1

The Clergy and Reform

*An Essay Read at the Annual Visitation of
the Camb. Theol. School, July 15, 1847*

It is one of the brilliant aphorisms of Novalis that there exists an eternal antagonism between a priesthood or clerical order and the progressive, thinking or literary class—inasmuch as they strive after the same position—namely the moral and intellectual government of the people. He speaks particularly of the literary class—but the identity of that with the reforming class has been often pointed out and was never more apparent than today.

Nor did any period ever show more clearly the progress of this division. The same old ground is taken—The same old parties drawn out. Nothing can save the clerical order from the vulnerable point laid bare by its very position. If any possess zeal and courage, it may admit new views—but it is not by right of them that it hold its place, even in the most lax of our congregational bodies; it inherits an established station and acts from this:—and hence an eternal jealousy on the part of those who have no established station, no outward aid for their assistance and take their stand on zeal, courage and new views alone.

Again in another way, as society moves forward and existing institutions are brought up one by one for judgment, we see a striking analogy in the positions always taken in regard to them by different parties. It is not alone that the Conservative party is always the same—but even the party disposed to Reform opens always into the same two subdivisions—which judge from different points of view and come to different conclusions. The moderate or prudential Reformers refer all to a comparative standard, point to an undeniable past and applaud the Present, the thorough or ultra Reformers refer all to an *absolute* standard, point to a possible Future and condemn the Present. One party is delighted with the improvement already made, while the other will never be satisfied that there is no [word missing]. Neither appreciates the other's view; each is sincerely alarmed for the cause of human progress; and the one is driven into a position more antagonistic than is any way necessary— the other slides back into conservatism.

And thus stands among us the question between the Clergy and the Reformers.

On the one side there are many who are perplexed by these repeated attacks on the Clergy, unable to see why they should be selected as the particular object of assault. "All they tried is all that is to be done," they ask, "and do they not do as much as other men now? Certainly there has been great progress in their position as regards practical action in the world and a general reformatory tendency—and are they not now coming to take quite a satisfactory position?"

But all this does not touch the impatient Reformer, who obstinately persists in seeing these matters from his quite different point of view. "The case is plain," he says, "between the Clergy and the People. We set them apart, a privileged body of authorized Teachers. We give them education, we give them support, we give them an immense opportunity for influence, an opportunity far above that conferred by its mere external position on any other class of men, and in return put into their hands the work of guiding, reforming and regenerating the world—or at least of leading in that work. But lo! the work is not done—the world is not reformed, it is not regenerated—and it seems to us that so far as it is so, they are left behind; it is done in spite of them, instead of by their actions. "Is there no balm in Gilead, is there no physician there?" Then why is not the health of the daughter of my people restored?

And thus we have the case narrowed down to the simple condition among us at the present day. The question has been plainly asked, "Do you not demand too much of the Clergy?" and as distinctly answered, "*No*, not too much, *when we consider the position they occupy.*" It is felt that if they take that, they must take the full responsibility that comes with it, that if those demands are unreasonable, then that position is unreasonable and thus the individual can only be excused by condoning the institution.

That was a grand thought of Gregory VII—his theory of the Catholic priesthood; "Quod romanus pontifex efficitur omnio sanctus"—"Not every Pope should be a saint!" Let such a theory be carried out in action and the gigantic claims of that church will be an insufficient tribute for the grateful race to grant it. What sacrifice is too great to make, what prerogative too vast to concede *to a dynasty of saints?* But see the terrible responsibility imposed by this position. A single error, a single weakness, a single folly in one of this dynasty vitiates the whole theory and instantly converts the magnificent institution into a stupendous fraud. The slightest shortcoming gives the humblest man of the race a right, nay makes it his duty, to expose the outrage; what is it to him if they did as well as other men could in their place; that place was granted of their being *incomparably more*—if they do not, let them abandon it forever! Well, says the eloquent Quinet, "Ask us not of the unreasonableness of our demand upon the Romish Clergy;—how reasonable are their demands upon us then? When they claim to occupy the throne of God—and to do nothing then, or to do evil?"

The position of those who arraign the clergy today is substantially this same. "We admit," they say, "that your claims are smaller, your position far inferior and consequently our rightful demand on you you have as yet scarcely begun to fulfill—and concerning which when we sometimes ask you to account, you put us off with the assurance that we ask too much and no man can be expected to fulfill it. We wait around to see how this insolvency is to end. The burden of proof always lies with the clergy. *They are liable to be called upon at every instant to justify their own existence.* Carlyle truly said: The one question in regard to any organized clerical order is "Does this Clergy lead and teach the people or not? If not, its doom is stated."

To examine the justice of this representation,—to see if there be no exaggeration in the statement first in the position trust and opportunities of the clergy and second of their shortcomings, we must glance at the Past. It is undeniable that thus far in the world's history a priesthood of some sort has always existed as the necessary companion of Forms and Doctrine. The connection is inseparable: there must be a distinct class to fulfill forms and to teach doctrine: and in proportion to the religious importance attached to these will be the weight given in society to this body. The Catholic Church laid some stress on the former, the Protestant on the latter. It used to be said after the Reformation, "The Catholics go to Mass, the Protestants to Sermon." Then the Mass was formed and demanded for its administration at most an apostolical succession of the regular inductees into office. The sermon was doctrinal and demanded of its ministers at least an able Theology. And so long as religion was Form and Doctrine, alone or mainly, then ministers had their place and were also doubtless well filled.

Even under Protestantism when Doctrine was the main thing the Clergy had a claim to existence, for their office was Theological Teachers. They were duly qualified for this by a regular professional training and thus had a fair claim to remain in power amply in virtue of their clerical position, quite apart from their individual claims as men—just such as a lawyer has by his knowledge of law or a physician by his knowledge of physics. A proportionate authority was given them in all ethical and theological matters—the annals of Congregationalism are full of instances of the individual power wielded by ministers seemingly in virtue of their professional position and though that power be diminishing now it will be years before the clergy of any denomination will lose the prestige afforded by the associations of the Past.

But this artificial aid is not necessary to give a peculiar character to this process. There cannot be a clerical order without this great responsibility (growing out of a great opportunity) which is made the ground of the demand on them. Reformers may be disposed to exaggerate this, as well as the extent of their shortcomings—but not perhaps much. Any class of men that has as this does, constant and regular access to the minds of the people, in public and in private, under the very most favorable circumstance for influence and in any sense disproportionate to the claims of the individuals composing it, must incur a tremendous responsibility. This responsibility may be met or it may not. But so far as it is not, it is just as much the absolute duty of each man who discovers the defect to proclaim and instantly do his utmost to annul the influence of the clergy as it was in the Roman Catholic Church.

Can we dare to say that it has been met—that the duty has been fulfilled? Long enough has it been tempted to evade the charge by attacking the character of those who can make it; since it is on the contrary coming to be more and more evident that if they were wrong in everything they were right in this. Sadly I [words missing] are more and more among the clergy themselves (of all bodies) coming to own that the duty has *not* been fulfilled. It has been admitted again and again that we owe these great philanthropic movements in which the Christianity of our day has concentrated itself, mainly to *laymen;* and that there are far more cases of clergymen who have resolutely opposed these movements than of clergymen who have helped them on. Are we aware what a fatal admission is this? There are social evils against which we know that Christ if alive would have protested with the whole strength of his soul—evils which only require the Christlike spirit of love and moral indignation to put them down; and yet those who fill the office of minis-

ters of Christ (I speak not of particular denominations) have not only
left them untouched and even unmentioned but actually have lent their
influence by threatening, by slander, and even by satire, against those
who would touch them. How do they justify this? They have fallen back
(and here, here they have acted consistently) upon the principles of the
Past—the false principles upon which their order has been based. For
they have said, "Our business is to conduct public worship and to preach
the abstract gospel, not to excite individual minds by a specific application of it—in other words our *Priesthood is built for Form and Doctrine,
not on practical life!*"

But what can become of a priesthood so founded, of an influence so
founded, in the presence of the new movements which our times are be-
holding? He is blind who sees not that the reign of mere Form and Doctrine is gone forever, that a new religious movement such as the world
has never seen is taking possession of man's mind, the triple religion of
Christ's two great commandments—a love to God irrespective of all
doctrinal opinions, a love to Man equally liberal. The new church announced by Swedenborg is rising up as he predicted in the new spirit of
Liberty, Fellowship and Love in the world. The universal movement for
freedom within the existing churches everywhere—the universal philanthropic movements without them—these are the uprising of the church
of the future. But what has that Church, that new Union, whose very
foundation is the subordination of Form and Doctrine alone. *It knows
them not.* It says to all, "Ye are unprofitable servants, except so far as any
principles reign in you—and the position which you have assumed on
any other ground is an utterly false one. The Ministry of Form and Doctrine is *past forever* and only insofar as the present institution can convert itself into a ministry of light and love can it be suffered to remain.
Its only salvation is that. Thenceforth a Clergy which suffers any new
thought to originate elsewhere, which permits any true Reform to lead it
instead of itself taking the lead—hath the mischief in itself and is condemned already!"

These thoughts are not novel. Good men are everywhere pointing out
the new life of these times. We hear everywhere rejoicings at the substitution of practical Christianity for doctrinal and formal Christianity.
They see or should see also that such change must instantly affect the
Clergy—that whereas they before needed to be better formalists and
wiser theologians than others, they need now to be better and wiser
men—that there is a spiritual democracy in this practical Christianity,
and that a body of paid Teachers will not be tolerated unless they are

truly leaders! That they have not been in this sense leaders it is utterly too late now to deny—and ask that it is left to the future.

Brothers—all that I have said is only matter of right, what we may *see* if we will; it is not *acting*. But we need to see before we act. To see this appears very plain. But it were foolhardy to deny that the practical application of its moral is full of difficulties. God forbid that we should begin our career by aspersing others or boasting of ourselves. But God forbid that we should *not* begin by seeing clearly and owning candidly the state of the times in which we are called on to work. There is no boastfulness, there is no irreverence in humble aspirations. We are faithless to our fathers if we do not begin where they left off instead of stopping there. We are faithless to ourselves if we do not look with our own eyes, speak our own thoughts and act our own life.

Meanwhile many still tell us we have fallen upon evil days. There never were days that were not evil, if imperfection be evil. But if to see a new hope lighting up the eyes of youth and reinvigorating the mature strength of a liberal age—if to see reconstruction beginning after years of destruction—if to see old errors tottering and a sudden birth of good movements looking every one toward heaven on earth—if this be good and glorious to behold; then is this age of all ages most blessed to dwell in. True, it is at best imperfect—nay evil if you will, when viewed in the light of that ever advancing Ideal which floods on before every [words missing] shrink from being called Good—but we are utterly faithless if we are blind to the great Drama that God is working out in this troubled world. The Race, like the individual, passes from ignorant innocence through trial and sin to assured peace and love and righteousness and we feel varying hope and fear, for we dwell in its stirring and passionate youth. But it is not, like the fabled Orion, blinded by sin and sensual indulgence, but now climbing up to fix its desolate eyes upon the sun again, and receive its light. Oh! there was never such a time to live!

We would not be enthusiasts, we would not be fanatics. Great is the enthusiast—his burning words sink through us and open before us a range of possible duty whose vastness bids us almost despair. Gladly do we yield ourselves to the potent magic of his flashing eyes and ask to become his followers and give ourselves to the seconding of the great crusades that we never could have originated—but when the moments of brief intoxication have passed we sink back from our stimulated state into exhaustion and a dreary lethargy, we feel no native strength and our best efforts are nervousness and agitation. For calmness is always the highest defense most great whose action is as peaceful and strong—who is part of no movement but makes every good movement part of him, who is love, courage and who has that ocean-like repose from which alone ocean-like power can come. To what purpose have we studied Christ, if we have not learned that he who would move the world must have already overcome the world—must be able to ignore failure and discouragement—must never feel alone since his Father is with him and must work his highest miracles of faith as easily as he breathes the common air.

Oh let never our interest or our shortcomings deter us from yearning after this Ideal. There is hopeless mediocrity in a low aim—but there is endless hope in adopting for ourselves a standard higher than the most exacting venture to impose on us. They that wait upon the Lord in this aim shall renew their strength. They shall shrink from claiming the humblet merit, yet rejoice to attribute each to the [word missing] of spirit. They shall be sheltered from fatigue and fear and discomfort. They shall work while it is day and await placidly the new dawning lights and new falling shadows of the mysterious and inevitable future.

2

A NEW COUNTERBLAST

"He that taketh tobacco saith he cannot leave it, it doth
bewitch him."

—KING JAMES'S *Counterblast to Tobacco*

A merica is especially responsible to the whole world for tobacco,
since the two are twin-sisters, born to the globe in a day. The sailors
first sent on shore by Columbus came back with news of a new continent and a new condiment. There was solid land, and there was a novel
perfume, which rolled in clouds from the lips of the natives. The fame of
the two great discoveries instantly began to overspread the world; but
the smoke travelled fastest, as is its nature. There are many races which
have not yet heard of America: there are very few which have not yet
tasted of tobacco. A plant which was originally the amusement of a few
savage tribes has become in a few centuries the fancied necessary of life
to the most enlightened nations of the earth, and it is probable that there
is nothing cultivated by man which is now so universally employed.

And the plant owes this width of celebrity to a combination of natural
qualities so remarkable as to yield great diversities of good and evil fame.
It was first heralded as a medical panacea, "the most sovereign and precious weed that ever the earth tendered to the use of man," and was seldom mentioned, in the sixteenth century, without some reverential epithet. It was a plant divine, a canonized vegetable. Each nation had its
own pious name to bestow upon it. The French called it *herbe sainte,
herbe sacrée, herbe propre à tous maux, panacée antarctique,*—the Italians, *herba santa croce,*—the Germans, *heilig wundkraut.* Botanists
soberly classified it as *herba panacea* and *herba sancta,* and Gerard in his

"Herbal" fixed its name finally as *sana sancta Indorum*, by which title it commonly appears in the professional recipes of the time. Spenser, in his "Faërie Queene," bids the lovely Belphœbe gather it as "divine tobacco," and Lilly the Euphuist calls it "our holy herb Nicotian," ranking it between violets and honey. It was cultivated in France for medicinal purposes solely, for half a century before any one there used it for pleasure, and till within the last hundred years it was familiarly prescribed, all over Europe, for asthma, gout, catarrh, consumption, headache; and, in short, was credited with curing more diseases than even the eighty-seven which Dr. Shew now charges it with producing.

So vast were the results of all this sanitary enthusiasm, that the use of tobacco in Europe probably reached its climax in a century or two, and has since rather diminished than increased, in proportion to the population. It probably appeared in England in 1586, being first used in the Indian fashion, by handing one pipe from man to man throughout the company; the medium of communication being a silver tube for the higher classes, and a straw and walnut-shell for the baser sort. Paul Hentzner, who travelled in England in 1598, and Monsieur Misson, who wrote precisely a century later, note almost in the same words "a perpetual use of tobacco"; and the latter suspects that this is what makes "the generality of Englishmen so taciturn, so thoughtful, and so melancholy." In Queen Elizabeth's time, the ladies of the court "would not scruple to blow a pipe together very socially." In 1614 it was asserted that tobacco was sold openly in more than seven thousand places in London, some of these being already attended by that patient Indian who still stands seductive at tobacconists' doors. It was also estimated that the annual receipts of these establishments amounted to more than three hundred thousand pounds. Elegant ladies had their pictures painted, at least one in 1650 did, with pipe and box in hand. Rochefort, a rather apocryphal French traveller in 1672, reported it to be the general custom in English homes to set pipes on the table in the evening for the females as well as males of the family, and to provide children's luncheon-baskets with a well-filled pipe, to be smoked at school, under the directing eye of the master. In 1703, Lawrence Spooner wrote that "the sin of the kingdom in the intemperate use of tobacco swelleth and increaseth so daily, that I can compare it to nothing but the waters of Noah, that swelled fifteen cubits above the highest mountains." The deluge reached its height in England—so thinks the amusing and indefatigable Mr. Fairholt, author of "Tobacco and its Associations"—in the reign of Queen Anne. Steele, in the "Spectator," (1711,) describes the snuff-box as a rival to the fan among ladies; and Goldsmith pictures the

belles at Bath as entering the water in full bathing costume, each provided with a small floating basket, to hold a snuff-box, a kerchief, and a
nosegay. And finally, in 1797, Dr. Clarke complains of the handing
about of the snuff-box in churches during worship, "to the great scandal of religious people,"—adding, that kneeling in prayer was prevented
by the large quantity of saliva ejected in all directions. In view of such
formidable statements as these, it is hardly possible to believe that the
present generation surpasses or even equals the past in the consumption of tobacco.

And all this sudden popularity was in spite of a vast persecution which
sought to unite all Europe against this indulgence, in the seventeenth
century. In Russia, its use was punishable with amputation of the nose;
in Berne, it ranked next to adultery among offences; Sandys, the traveller, saw a Turk led through the streets of Constantinople mounted
backward on an ass with a tobacco-pipe thrust through his nose. Pope
Urban VIII., in 1624, excommunicated those who should use it in
churches, and Innocent XII., in 1690, echoed the same anathema. Yet
within a few years afterwards travellers reported that same free use of
snuff in Romish worship which still astonishes spectators. To see a
priest, during the momentous ceremonial of High Mass, enliven the occasion by a voluptuous pinch, is a sight even more astonishing, though
perhaps less disagreeable, than the well-used spittoon which decorates
so many Protestant pulpits.

But the Protestant pulpits did their full share in fighting the habit, for
a time at least. Among the Puritans, no man could use tobacco publicly,
on penalty of a fine of two and sixpence, or in a private dwelling, if
strangers were present; and no two could use it together. That iron pipe
of Miles Standish, still preserved at Plymouth, must have been smoked
in solitude, or not at all. This strictness was gradually relaxed, however,
as the clergy took up the habit of smoking; and I have seen an old painting, on the panels of an ancient parsonage in Newburyport, representing
a jovial circle of portly divines sitting pipe in hand around a table, with
the Latin motto, "In essentials unity, in non-essentials liberty, in all
things charity." Apparently the tobacco was one of the essentials, since
there was unity respecting that. Furthermore, Captain Underhill, hero of
the Pequot War, boasted to the saints of having received his assurance of
salvation "while enjoying a pipe of that good creature, tobacco," "since
when he had never doubted it, though he should fall into sin." But it is
melancholy to relate that this fall did presently take place, in a very fla-
grant manner, and brought discredit upon tobacco conversions, as being
liable to end in smoke.

Indeed, some of the most royal wills that ever lived in the world have measured themselves against the tobacco-plant and been defeated. Charles I attempted to banish it, and in return the soldiers of Cromwell puffed their smoke contemptuously in his face, as he sat a prisoner in the guard-chamber. Cromwell himself undertook it, and Evelyn says that the troopers smoked in triumph at his funeral. Wellington tried it, and the artists caricatured him on a pipe's head with a soldier behind him defying with a whiff that imperial nose. Louis Napoleon is said to be now attempting it, and probably finds his subjects more ready to surrender the freedom of the press than of the pipe.

The more recent efforts against tobacco, like most arguments in which morals and physiology are mingled, have lost much of their effect through exaggeration. On both sides there has been enlisted much loose statement, with some bad logic. It is, for instance, unreasonable to hold up the tobacco-plant to general indignation because Linnæus classed it with the natural order *Luridæ*,—since he attributed the luridness only to the color of those plants, not to their character. It is absurd to denounce it as belonging to the poisonous nightshade tribe, when the potato and the tomato also appertain to that perilous domestic circle. It is hardly fair even to complain of it for yielding a poisonous oil, when these two virtuous plants—to say nothing of the peach and the almond—will, under sufficient chemical provocation, do the same thing. Two drops of nicotine will, indeed, kill a rabbit; but so, it is said, will two drops of solanine. Great are the resources of chemistry, and a well-regulated scientific mind can detect something deadly almost anywhere.

Nor is it safe to assume, as many do, that tobacco predisposes very powerfully to more dangerous dissipations. The non-smoking Saxons were probably far more intemperate in drinking than the modern English; and Lane, the best authority, points out that wine is now far less used by the Orientals than at the time of the "Arabian Nights," when tobacco had not been introduced. And in respect to yet more perilous sensual excesses, tobacco is now admitted, both by friends and foes, to be quite as much a sedative as a stimulant.

The point of objection on the ground of inordinate expense is doubtless better taken, and can be met only by substantial proof that the enormous outlay is a wise one. Tobacco may be "the anodyne of poverty," as somebody has said, but it certainly promotes poverty. This narcotic lulls to sleep all pecuniary economy. Every pipe may not, indeed, cost so much as that jewelled one seen by Dibdin in Vienna, which was valued at a thousand pounds; or even as the German meerschaum which was passed from mouth to mouth through a whole regiment of soldiers till it was colored to perfection, having never been allowed to cool,—a bill of one hundred pounds being ultimately rendered for the tobacco consumed. But how heedlessly men squander money on this pet luxury! By the report of the English University Commissioners, some ten years ago, a student's annual tobacco-bill often amounts to forty pounds. Dr. Solly puts thirty pounds as the lowest annual expenditure of an English smoker, and knows many who spend one hundred and twenty pounds, and one three hundred pounds a year, on tobacco alone. In this country the facts are hard to obtain, but many a man smokes twelve four-cent cigars a day, and many a man four twelve-cent cigars,—spending in either case about half a dollar a day and not far from two hundred dollars per annum. An industrious mechanic earns his two dollars and fifty cents a day, or a clerk his eight hundred dollars a year, spends a quarter of it on tobacco, and *the rest* on his wife, children, and miscellaneous expenses.

But the impotency which marks some of the stock arguments against tobacco extends to most of those in favor of it. My friend assures me that every one needs some narcotic, that the American brain is too active, and that the influence of tobacco is quieting,—great is the enjoyment of a comfortable pipe after dinner. I grant, on observing him at that period, that it appears so. But I also observe, that, when the placid hour has passed away, his nervous system is more susceptible, his hand more tremulous, his temper more irritable on slight occasions, than during the days when the comfortable pipe chances to be omitted. The only effect of the narcotic appears, therefore, to be a demand for another narcotic; and there seems no decided advantage over the life of the birds and bees, who appear to keep their nervous systems in tolerably healthy condition with no narcotic at all.

The argument drawn from a comparison of races is no better. Germans are vigorous and Turks are long-lived, and they are all great smokers. But certainly the Germans do not appear so vivacious, nor the Turks so energetic, as to afford triumphant demonstrations in behalf of the sacred weed. Moreover, the Eastern tobacco is as much milder than ours, as are the Continental wines than even those semi-alcoholic mixtures which prevail at scrupulous communion-tables. And as for German health, Dr. Schneider declares, in the London "Lancet," that it is because of smoke that all his educated countrymen wear spectacles, that an immense amount of consumption is produced in Germany by tobacco, and that English insurance companies are proverbially cautious in insuring German lives. Dr. Carlyon gives much the same as his observation in Holland. These facts may be overstated, but they are at least as good as those which they answer.

Not much better is the excuse alleged in the social and genial influences of tobacco. It certainly seems a singular way of opening the lips for conversation by closing them on a pipe-stem, and it would rather appear as if Fate designed to gag the smokers and let the non-smokers talk. But supposing it otherwise, does it not mark a condition of extreme juvenility in our social development, if no resources of intellect can enable a half-dozen intelligent men to be agreeable to each other, without applying the forcing process, by turning the room into an imperfectly organized chimney? Brilliant women can be brilliant without either wine or tobacco, and Napoleon always maintained that without an admixture of feminine wit conversation grew tame. Are all male beings so much stupider by nature than the other sex, that men require stimulants and narcotics to make them mutually endurable?

And as the conversational superiorities of woman disprove the supposed social inspirations of tobacco, so do her more refined perceptions yet more emphatically pronounce its doom. Though belles of the less mature description, eulogistic of sophomores, may stoutly profess that they dote on the Virginian perfume, yet cultivated womanhood barely tolerates the choicest tobacco-smoke, even in its freshness, and utterly recoils from the stale suggestions of yesterday. By whatever enthusiasm misled, she finds something abhorrent in the very nature of the thing. In vain did loyal Frenchmen baptize the weed as the queen's own favorite, *Herba Catherinæ Medicæ;* it is easier to admit that Catherine de' Medici was not feminine than that tobacco is. Man also recognizes the antagonism; there is scarcely a husband in America who would not be converted from smoking, if his wife resolutely demanded her right of moiety in the cigar-box. No Lady Mary, no loveliest Marquise, could make snuff-taking beauty otherwise than repugnant to this generation. Rustic females who habitually chew even pitch or spruce-gum are rendered thereby so repulsive that the fancy refuses to pursue the horror farther and imagine it tobacco; and all the charms of the veil and the fan can scarcely reconcile the most fumacious American to the *cigarrito* of the Spanish fair. How strange seems Parton's picture of General Jackson puffing his long clay pipe on one side of the fireplace and Mrs. Jackson puffing hers on the other! No doubt, to the heart of the chivalrous backwoodsman those smoke-dried lips were yet the altar of early passion,— as that rather ungrammatical tongue was still the music of the spheres; but the unattractiveness of that conjugal counterblast is Nature's own protest against smoking.

The use of tobacco must, therefore, be held to mark a rather coarse and childish epoch in our civilization, if nothing worse. Its most ardent admirer hardly paints it into his picture of the Golden Age. It is difficult to associate it with one's fancies of the noblest manhood, and Miss Muloch reasonably defies the human imagination to portray Shakespeare or Dante with pipe in mouth. Goethe detested it; so did Napoleon, save in the form of snuff, which he apparently used on Talleyrand's principle, that diplomacy was impossible without it. Bacon said, "Tobacco-smoking is a secret delight, serving only to steal away men's brains." Newton abstained from it: the contrary is often claimed, but thus says his biographer, Brewster,—saying that "he would make no necessities to himself." Franklin says he never used it, and never met with one of its votaries who advised him to follow the example. John Quincy Adams used it in early youth, and after thirty years of abstinence said, that, if every one would try abstinence for three months, it would annihilate the practice, and add five years to the average length of human life.

In attempting to go beyond these general charges of waste and foolishness, and to examine the physiological results of the use of tobacco, one is met by the contradictions and perplexities which haunt all such inquiries. Doctors, of course, disagree, and the special cases cited triumphantly by either side are ruled out as exceptional by the other. It is like the question of the precise degree of injury done by alcoholic drinks. To-day's newspaper writes the eulogy of A. B., who recently died at the age of ninety-nine, without ever tasting ardent spirits; to-morrow's will add the epitaph of C. D., aged one hundred, who has imbibed a quart of rum a day since reaching the age of indiscretion; and yet, after all, both editors have to admit that the drinking usages of society are growing decidedly more decent. It is the same with the tobacco argument. Individual cases prove nothing either way; there is such a range of vital vigor in different individuals, that one may withstand a life of error, and another perish in spite of prudence. The question is of the general tendency. It is not enough to know that Dr. Parr smoked twenty pipes in an evening, and lived to be seventy-eight; that Thomas Hobbes smoked thirteen, and survived to ninety-two; that Brissiac of Trieste died at one hundred and sixteen, with a pipe in his mouth; and that Henry Hartz of Schleswig used tobacco steadily from the age of sixteen to one hundred and forty-two; nor would any accumulation of such healthy old sinners prove anything satisfactory. It seems rather overwhelming, to be sure, when Mr. Fairholt assures us that his respected father "died at the age of seventy-two: he had been twelve hours a day in a tobacco-manufactory for nearly fifty years; and he both smoked and chewed while busy in the labors of the workshop, sometimes in a dense cloud of steam from drying the damp tobacco over the stoves; and his health and appetite were perfect to the day of his death: he was a model of muscular and stomachic energy; in which his son, who neither smokes, snuffs, nor chews, by no means rivals him." But until we know precisely what capital of health the venerable tobacconist inherited from his fathers, and in what condition he transmitted it to his sons, the statement certainly has two edges.

For there are facts equally notorious on the other side. It is not denied that it is found necessary to exclude tobacco, as a general rule, from insane asylums, or that it produces, in extreme cases, among perfectly sober persons, effects akin to delirium tremens. Nor is it denied that terrible local diseases follow it,—as, for instance, cancer of the mouth, which has become, according to the eminent surgeon, Brouisson, the disease most dreaded in the French hospitals. He has performed sixty-eight operations for this, within fourteen years, in the Hospital St. Eloi, and traces it entirely to the use of tobacco. Such facts are chiefly valuable as showing the tendency of the thing. Where the evils of excess are so glaring, the advantages of even moderate use are questionable. Where weak persons are made insane, there is room for suspicion that the strong may suffer unconsciously. You may say that the victims must have been constitutionally nervous; but where is the native-born American who is not?

In France and England the recent inquiries into the effects of tobacco seem to have been a little more systematic than our own. In the former country, the newspapers state, the attention of the Emperor was called to the fact that those pupils of the Polytechnic School who used this indulgence were decidedly inferior in average attainments to the rest. This is stated to have led to its prohibition in the school, and to the forming of an anti-tobacco organization, which is said to be making great progress in France. I cannot, however, obtain from any of our medical libraries any satisfactory information as to the French agitation, and am led by private advices to believe that even these general statements are hardly trustworthy. The recent English discussions are, however, more easy of access.

"The Great Tobacco Question," as the controversy in England was called, originated in a Clinical Lecture on Paralysis, by Mr. Solly, Surgeon of St. Thomas's Hospital, which was published in the "Lancet," December 13, 1856. He incidentally spoke of tobacco as an important source of this disease, and went on to say: "I know of no single vice which does so much harm as smoking. It is a snare and a delusion. It soothes the excited nervous system at the time, to render it more irritable and feeble ultimately. It is like opium in this respect; and if you want to know all the wretchedness which this drug can produce, you should read the

'Confessions of an English Opium-Eater.'" This statement was presently echoed by J. Ranald Martin, an eminent surgeon, "whose Eastern experience rendered his opinion of immense value," and who used language almost identical with that of Mr. Solly:—"'I can state of my own observation, that the miseries, mental and bodily, which I have witnessed from the abuse of cigar-smoking, far exceed anything detailed in the 'Confessions of an Opium-Eater.'"

This led off a controversy, which continued for several months, in the columns of the "Lancet,"—a controversy conducted in a wonderfully good-natured spirit, considering that more than fifty physicians took part in it, and that these were almost equally divided. The debate took a wide range, and some interesting facts were elicited: as that Lord Raglan, General Markham, and Admirals Dundas and Napier always abandoned tobacco from the moment when they were ordered on actual service; that nine tenths of the first-class men at the Universities were non-smokers; that two Indian chiefs told Power, the actor, that "those Indians who smoked gave out soonest in the chase"; and so on. There were also American examples, rather loosely gathered: thus, a remark of the venerable Dr. Waterhouse, made many years ago, was cited as the contemporary opinion of "the Medical Professor in Harvard University"; also it was mentioned, as an acknowledged fact, that the American *physique* was rapidly deteriorating because of tobacco, and that coroners' verdicts were constantly being thus pronounced on American youths: "Died of excessive smoking." On the other hand, that eminent citizen of our Union, General Thomas Thumb, was about that time professionally examined in London, and his verdict on tobacco was quoted to be, that it was "one of his chief comforts"; also mention was made of a hapless quack who announced himself as coming from Boston, and who, to keep up the Yankee reputation, issued a combined advertisement of "medical advice gratis" and "prime cigars."

But these stray American instances were of course quite outnumbered by the English, and there is scarcely an ill which was not in this controversy charged upon tobacco by its enemies, nor a physical or moral benefit which was not claimed for it by its friends. According to these, it prevents dissension and dyspnœa, inflammation and insanity, saves the waste of tissue and of time, blunts the edge of grief, and lightens pain. "No man was ever in a passion with a pipe in his mouth." There are more female lunatics chiefly because the fumigatory education of the fair sex has been neglected. Yet it is important to notice that these same advocates almost outdo its opponents in admitting its liability to misuse, and the perilous consequences. "The injurious effects of excessive smok-

ing,"—"there is no more pitiable object than the inveterate smoker,"—
"sedentary life is incompatible with smoking,"—highly pernicious,—
general debility,—secretions all wrong,—cerebral softening,—partial
paralysis,—trembling of the hand,—enervation and depression,—great
irritability,—neuralgia,—narcotism of the heart: this Chamber of Horrors forms a part of the very Temple of Tobacco, as builded, not by foes,
but by worshippers. "All men of observation and experience," they
admit, "must be able to point to instances of disease and derangement
from the abuse of this luxury." Yet they advocate it, as the same men advocate intoxicating drinks; not meeting the question, in either case,
whether it be wise, or even generous, for the strong to continue an indulgence which is thus confessedly ruinous to the weak.

The controversy had its course, and ended, like most controversies,
without establishing anything. The editor of the "Lancet," to be sure,
summed up the evidence very fairly, and it is worth while to quote him:
"It is almost unnecessary to make a separate inquiry into the pathological conditions which follow upon excessive smoking. Abundant evidence has been adduced of the gigantic evils which attend the abuse of
tobacco. Let it be granted at once that there is such a thing as moderate
smoking, and let it be admitted that we cannot accuse tobacco of being
guilty of the whole of Cullen's 'Nosology'; it still remains that there is a
long catalogue of frightful penalties attached to its abuse." He then proceeds to consider what is to be called abuse: as, for instance, smoking
more than one or two cigars or pipes daily,—smoking too early in the
day or too early in life,—and in general, the use of tobacco by those with
whom it does not agree,—which rather reminds one of the early temperance pledges, which bound a man to drink no more rum than he
found to be good for him. But the Chief Justice of the Medical Court finally instructs his jury of readers that young men should give up a dubious pleasure for a certain good, and abandon tobacco altogether: "Shun
the habit of smoking as you would shun self-destruction. As you value
your physical and moral well-being, avoid a habit which for you can
offer no advantage to compare with the dangers you incur."

Yet, after all, neither he nor his witnesses seem fairly to have hit upon
what seem to this present writer the two incontrovertible arguments
against tobacco; one being drawn from theory, and the other from practice.

First, as to the theory of the thing. The laws of Nature warn every man
who uses tobacco for the first time, that he is dealing with a poison. Nobody denies this attribute of the plant; it is "a narcotic poison of the
most active class." It is not merely that a poison can by chemical process

be extracted from it, but it is a poison in its simplest form. Its mere application to the skin has often produced uncontrollable nausea and prostration. Children have in several cases been killed by the mere application of tobacco ointment to the head. Soldiers have simulated sickness by placing it beneath the armpits,—though in most cases our regiments would probably consider this a mistaken application of the treasure. Tobacco, then, is simply and absolutely a poison.

Now to say that a substance is a poison, is not to say that it inevitably kills; it may be apparently innocuous, if not incidentally beneficial. King Mithridates, it is said, learned habitually to consume these dangerous commodities; and the scarcely less mythical Du Chaillu, after the fatigues of his gorilla warfare, found decided benefit from two ounces of arsenic. But to say that a substance is a poison, is to say at least that it is a noxious drug,—that it is a medicine, not an aliment,—that its effects are pathological, not physiological,—and that its use should therefore be exceptional, not habitual. Not tending to the preservation of a normal state, but at best to the correction of some abnormal one, its whole value, if it have any, lies in the rarity of its application. To apply a powerful drug at a certain hour every day, is like a schoolmaster's whipping his pupil at a certain hour every day: the victim may become inured, but undoubtedly the specific value of the remedy must vanish with the repetition.

Thus much would be true, were it proved that tobacco is in some cases apparently beneficial. No drug is beneficial, when constantly employed. But, furthermore, if not beneficial, it then is injurious. As Dr. Holmes has so forcibly expounded, every medicine is in itself hurtful. All noxious agents, according to him, cost a patient, on an average, five per cent of his vital power; that is, twenty times as much would kill him. It is believed that they are sometimes indirectly useful; it is known that they are always directly hurtful. That is, I have a neighbor on one side who takes tobacco to cure his dyspepsia, and a neighbor on the other side who takes blue pills for his infirmities generally. The profit of the operation may be sure or doubtful; the outlay is certain, and to be deducted in any event. I have no doubt, my dear Madam, that your interesting son has learned to smoke, as he states, in order to check that very distressing toothache which so hindered his studies; but I sincerely think it would be better to have the affliction removed by a dentist at a cost of fifty cents, than by a drug at an expense of five per cent of vital power.

Fortunately, when it comes to the practical test, the whole position is conceded to our hands, and the very devotees of tobacco are false to their idol. It is not merely that the most fumigatory parent dissuades his sons from the practice; but there is a more remarkable instance. If any two classes can be singled out in the community as the largest habitual consumers of tobacco, it must be the college students and the city "roughs" or "rowdies," or whatever the latest slang name is,—for these roysterers, like oysters, incline to names with an *r* in. Now the "rough," when brought to a physical climax, becomes the prize-fighter; and the college student is seen in his highest condition as the prize-oarsman; and both these representative men, under such circumstances of ambition, straightway abandon tobacco. Such a concession, from such a quarter, is worth all the denunciations of good Mr. Trask. Appeal, O anxious mother! from Philip smoking to Philip training. What your progeny will not do for any considerations of ethics or economy,—to save his sisters' olfactories or the atmosphere of the family altar,—that he does unflinchingly at one word from the stroke-oar or the commodore. In so doing, he surrenders every inch of the ground, and owns unequivocally that he is in better condition without tobacco. The old traditions of training are in some other respects being softened: strawberries are no longer contraband, and the last agonies of thirst are no longer a part of the prescription; but training and tobacco are still incompatible. There is not a regatta or a prize-fight in which the betting would not be seriously affected by the discovery that either party used the beguiling weed.

The argument is irresistible,—or rather, it is not so much an argument as a plea of guilty under the indictment. The prime devotees of tobacco voluntarily abstain from it, like Lord Raglan and Admiral Napier, when they wish to be in their best condition. But are we ever, any of us, in too good condition? Have all the sanitary conventions yet succeeded in detecting one man, in our high-pressure America, who finds himself too well? If a man goes into training for the mimic contest, why not for the actual one? If he needs steady nerves and a cool head for the play of life,—and even prize-fighting is called "sporting,"—why not for its earnest? Here we are all croaking that we are not in the health in which our twentieth birthday found us, and yet we will not condescend to the wise abstinence which even twenty practises. Moderate training is simply a rational and healthful life.

So palpable is this, that there is strong reason to believe that the increased attention to physical training is operating against tobacco. If we may trust literature, as has been shown, its use is not now so great as formerly, in spite of the vague guesses of alarmists. "It is estimated," says Mr. Coles, "that the consumption of tobacco in this country is eight times as great as in France and three times as great as in England, in proportion to the population"; but there is nothing in the world more uncertain than "It is estimated." It is frequently estimated, for instance, that nine out of ten of our college students use tobacco; and yet, by the statistics of the last graduating class at Cambridge, it appears that it is used by only thirty-one out of seventy-six. I am satisfied that the extent of the practice is often exaggerated. In a gymnastic club of young men, for instance, where I have had opportunity to take the statistics, it is found that less than one quarter use it, though there has never been any agitation or discussion of the matter. These things indicate that it can no longer be claimed, as Molière asserted two centuries ago, that he who lives without tobacco is not worthy to live.

And as there has been some exaggeration in describing the extent to which Tobacco is King, so there has doubtless been some overstatement as to the cruelty of his despotism. Enough, however, remains to condemn him. The present writer, at least, has the firmest conviction, from personal observation and experience, that the imagined benefits of tobacco-using (which have never, perhaps, been better stated than in an essay which appeared in the Atlantic Monthly, in August, 1860) are ordinarily an illusion, and its evils a far more solid reality,—that it stimulates only to enervate, soothes only to depress,—that it neither permanently calms the nerves nor softens the temper nor enlightens the brain, but that in the end its tendencies are precisely the opposites of these, beside the undoubted incidental objections of costliness and uncleanness. When men can find any other instance of a poisonous drug which is suitable for daily consumption, they will be more consistent in using this. When it is admitted to be innocuous to those who are training for athletic feats, it may be possible to suppose it beneficial to those who are out of training. Meanwhile there seems no ground for its supporters except that to which the famous Robert Hall was reduced, as he says, by "the Society of Doctors of Divinity." He sent a message to Dr. Clarke, in return for a pamphlet against tobacco, that he could not possibly refute his arguments and could not possibly give up smoking.

SCRIPTURE IDOLATRY

'The corner-stone of our Fabric is the *Light Within,* as
God's gift for man's salvation. This is Emmanuel or God
with us, and this admits not any book or judge to come
between this voice of God in the soul, as its rule of faith
and practice.'

—Wm. Penn. *'Rise and Progress of the People called Quakers'*

'The demand of intellect and reason must be met, in
order to satisfy a reasonable being. . . . If there is any
book in all the world addressed to the sober reason and
judgment of men, that book is the Bible. It is written by
men, addressed to men, and designed for men.'

—Prof. Stuart on the Old Testament

'The intuitive convictions of the minds of created beings,
as to honour and dishonour, right and wrong, are the
most important in the universe. They are the voice of
God himself in the soul. On them all just views of God
depend. On them, as a basis, his universal and eternal
government must ever rest. Shake them, and you shake
the very foundations of his kingdom; for righteousness
and judgment are the habitation of his throne.'

—Edward Beecher, *'Conflict of Ages'*

'Why even of yourselves judge ye not that which is right?' says the
Scripture. Every thoughtful mind pauses at last before this problem—
What is the final basis of authority? Some say our church, some our

creed, some our book or Bible, some our own conscience and reason, such as they are, revealing to us the laws of God. It is a hard question to settle, and the saddest history of the world has turned upon it. Men have been killed, for instance, for being Protestants instead of Catholics—that is, for settling it in one way. Four women have been imprisoned at Stockholm for becoming Catholics instead of Protestants—that is, for settling it in another way. Men have been killed for asserting almost every creed, and killed for denying it; killed for undervaluing the Bible, and killed for overvaluing it: it is as hard to test the merits of sects by martyrdoms as in any other way; as hard to tell which has had most martyrs, as which has had most arguments.

I have tried, in a series of discourses, to begin at the outside of the popular creed, and come gradually to the inside. We have reached the centre at length. All sects in this country claim to rest upon the Bible. Even the Catholic church, oldest, grandest, and most consistent of sects, must rest its infallibility here at last. These various bodies may not succeed in proving their doctrines from Scripture, but they do not commonly pretend to prove them from any thing else. 'To the Law and the Testimony,' they all say; from firm, bold, consistent Roman Catholics, to weak, timid, and inconsistent Unitarians. Surely, then, we must first settle what is Law and what is Testimony.

Our subject has been, I may say, Ecclesiastical Architecture; we have traversed stately halls and lowly chapels of the church, studied its arches and its columns and its storied windows—the wonderous achievements of wondrous men. But our task is not done. The superstructure can never be firmer than the foundation. 'We must at last go down and strike upon the underpinning stones of this great fabric, and see if they are sound, able to stand the tests of time and the shocks of eternity.'

Has this yet been done? It has been done by theologians, and for theologians; not by the mass of the people or for them. Yet, even among American theologians (the pious Neander complains) few have learned 'to distinguish between the divine and human in the sacred writings,' while of their parishioners, many have learned the lesson without their aid. Strange that the clergy should not see that the time for exoteric and esoteric philosophies has passed away, as popular education has advanced. 'Speak what will not shock the people (says the cautious elderly professor to the young theological student)—but you may do your own thinking in your study.' 'But suppose that my parishioners do their own thinking also (pleads the young candidate), and that the thing which shocks them most is to see me act a lie?'

O that men could learn that the salvation of mankind does not need shelter behind their refuges of lies; that doubt is not dangerous, except to that which is dubious. It does not endanger the solid pillars of the earth to bring man's utmost strength to bear against them; why should it peril the pillars of any true authority?

The question of Scripture authority is the great popular question of the age—the point in progress at which we stand hesitating now. We have thought and protested, till we have got back to first principles; now let us not shrink from grappling with those. It is a great question that we have to deal with; let us begin at the beginning.

First let us notice the theory of the matter. Nothing can be the final basis of authority which has itself to be sustained by another authority. You know the Hindoo theory of the earth—that it rests on an elephant, and the elephant on a tortoise. But where does the tortoise rest? The mind pertinaciously demands to reach the foundation of things. In the case of an infallible book, it is hard to get there. To know that any book is infallible, we must know, first, that we have it in the original language, or in an infallible translation. Then we must be sure that we have the original manuscript, or an infallible copy of it. Then we must be sure that the authors knew infallibly that of which they wrote; and lastly, that they wrote infallibly that which they knew—all these infallibilities being unique in history and belonging to no other book.

Now, these things are either probable or improbable. But, observe! What does 'probable' mean? It means *susceptible of proof.* These things, then, are not self-evident; nobody pretends that they are self-evident; they must be *proved* before some other tribunal. Below your supposed authority you must, then, have some other authority; below your foundations, other foundations. As the most solid courses of stone that ever mason laid must, after all, rest upon the earth, and take the risk of its upheavals; so your supposed infallibility must rest upon conscience and reason at last, and if these are not infallible, nothing else is. Is an authority to be established, they must establish it. This argument, long used as conclusive against an infallible church, weighs with the same irresistible power against an infallible book. You must trust your own reason and conscience at last, for you have nothing else to trust to.

Moses and Jesus, you say, spoke the truth. How know you this? Only through your own reason and conscience, which lead you to trust the words or the men. If these powers are not infallible, there is no infallibility. Plainly, then, there is none; for these very powers are imperfect, and need educating. Just so, our senses are not infallible. They say, for instance, that a straight stick, when thrust in the water, becomes crooked;

half the conclusions of science (said Herschel) seem opposed to the direct evidence of the senses; and yet science itself is but a larger application of the senses, and rests upon their observation at last. And so we
have to trust them, imperfect as they are, and improve them as fast as we
can. And just so it is with our conscience and reason. They are not infallible; but every authority which rests upon them must partake of their
weakness: no building can be firmer than its own foundations.

There is no reproach to the building, if it claims no more than this;
and, fortunately, the Bible does not profess to be infallible. The claim is
of later origin; and its sole meagre scriptural support is found in the
text, 'All Scripture is given by inspiration of God, and is profitable,' &c.
But even this says nothing of infallibility. And some translate the passage, 'All Scripture *which* is given by inspiration of God, is profitable!'
and old Tertullian translated it, 'All Scripture which is profitable is given
by inspiration of God.' So that the text decides nothing, except the impossibility of deciding anything by a text. The mere necessity of translation is itself an insuperable obstacle. Every man may translate as he
wishes. Unitarians may have their version, Presbyterians theirs, Episco-
palians theirs, Baptists theirs, and so on indefinitely. A child has been excluded from a public school, in this free city, because his father would
not permit him to read in the Protestant translation of the Bible!

But the whole difficulty does not lie in matters of translation. Of all
the uncertain tribunals ever adopted by fallible mortals, the Bible appears to be the most uncertain. Composed of the writings of a hundred
different authors, an argument can be drawn from it to support either
side of every question. War, Slavery, Capital Punishment, Polygamy, the
use of Intoxicating Drinks—it is far easier to decide whether these
things are right or wrong, than whether they are scriptural or unscriptural. Every one who has travelled at the South knows that the strong-
hold of Slavery is the Bible; and I have heard a clergyman in a public assembly denounce Total Abstinence as utterly unscriptural, and declare
that those who defend it ought to become Mohammedans instantly.
Once begin to argue a question on Scripture grounds, and it is like fighting a battle in the everglades of Florida; the wilderness of texts is denser
than the wilderness of trees and you may manœuvre a whole day in one
part of the forest, without coming in sight of your opponent, who,
meanwhile, has the field to himself in another part.

Thus, there is no end to the inconsistencies between the different interpretations of the Scripture, or to the strange and sad practices
founded upon these. Yet, strange to say, men have selected this very
charge to bring against those who try to walk by the Inner Light. Your

natural religion (say they) is one thing in one place, and another in another. Under its guidance, the Hindoos have burned widows, and the Puritans burned witches. But the illustration is as injudicious as the charge. For both Hindoo and Puritan got from their *sacred books* the coals with which to kindle the fire around their victims, and the 'Inner Light' might have taught them better. Many a gentle heart among the Puritans thrilled in horror at the torments which those gloomy saints inflicted: some men said, 'There were no such things as witches or devils, except the Puritan ministers, and such as they.' But there stood the priest, with his stern 'Thus saith the Lord,' and the terrible tragedy went on. The worst cruelty the world has ever seen has grown out of alleged revelations which displaced the light of Nature. All the bloodshed of the French Revolution was slight, compared with the bloodshed of the Inquisition; and, indeed, the Revolution itself was in part a reaction from the Inquisition.

Yet we actually find men, sometimes, in the community, who seriously suppose all ideas of right and wrong to come from the Bible. Strange perversion of the truest impulses of our nature! Whence came the blush and the downcast look of shame upon the cheek of your little child, my friend, the first time he disobeyed or deceived you? Not, surely, from any outward oracle, but from within; that glowing tint was reflected from the 'trailing cloud of glory' which came with the young spirit from the world unseen. We know the difference between right and wrong, as we know the difference between light and darkness; and the peculiarities of men's mental temperaments are not greater (so naturalists say) than the peculiarities of their eyes in judging colour. Take away the Bible from the world, and you do not take away conscience; and the distinction between right and wrong is a plant of universal growth.

But you say that this natural conscience is at first dim, variable, and deceptive. Undoubtedly; and so are the senses of a child, who grasps at the setting sun as if it were an orange.—And the Bible enlightens Conscience? Pause there; the Bible *helps* to enlighten it. It co-operates with all other good influences, schools, laws, science, and everything else which strengthens or elevates mankind. It is but one influence among many, which mutually interact and sustain each other.

This is shown by the fact that there are sins hardly named in the Bible, about which the moral sentiment of the community is yet clearer, than about many which are there condemned. Take, for instance, *suicide*. Think how strong has been the conscience of the world in its protest against this crime. It has been ranked upon the statute-books with murder, but as the law could not re-murder the poor sinner, it merely murdered his reputation, and forbade him a grave. I know of no more universal, popular sentiment in civilised countries; and yet, where is the condemnation of suicide in the Bible?

There is a singular fact in regard to the sin of *lying*. You all think it wrong to lie; a much worse offence, I should hope, than the man-made crime, Sabbath-breaking—or than coveting the goods of a neighbour, while shrinking from actual theft. Yet the Ten Commandments, while condemning these things, do not regard lying as worth mentioning, unless malice be superadded. And while vehemently denounced by David and Solomon, it is nowhere explicitly condemned by Jesus. Of course, the omission is accidental; it is no ground of complaint against the Bible writers. I only quote these things to show that men really judge independently of scriptural authority; and I think that, in condemning sin as sin, men commonly decide the question first, and then look for Bible arguments, if at all.

Then there is that further difficulty, that, when they do look, they commonly find what they wish for, right or wrong. One man wishes to find arguments for Capital Punishment, and so he reads, 'Whoso sheddeth man's blood, by man shall his blood be shed'—construes 'shall' to be a command, not a prediction (though he never studied Hebrew), and clings to the gallows as if it were the fairest altar of God. Yet that same man, if he likes fresh meat, will have it, though it is expressly prohibited in the same chapter. Another man frowns on all attempts to remove poverty, because Jesus said, 'The poor ye have always with you,' and he resists it as if there were danger of abolishing poverty too soon. Yet take that same man's coat, and demand his cloak also; smite him on one cheek, and ask access to the other; compel him to walk a reluctant mile, and then show him the unimpeachable text which requires a second mile—and see if the most literal Scripture means anything to him when it goes against his own inclination.

It is past the power of language to express a thought so plainly, but that an unwilling devotee will convince himself that it means something else. It is in vain that the unknown writer of the first chapter of Genesis describes the firmament as a solid body, holding the rain above (with windows to let the showers through), and the sun and stars hung like lamps in it, after the great earth is made; it is in vain that the evangelists represent insane persons as possessed by devils, who may be transferred into the doomed bodies of swine; it is in vain that Jesus says explicitly, 'This is my body' of the sacramental bread; it is in vain that he predicts his own visible return, in the clouds of heaven, during the lifetime of his disciples—a prediction worked up into that sublimest of dramas, the Apocalypse. All these things are vain; 'he who runs may read,' but he who clings to his creed will not, and he will torture all etymology and all syntax, rather than find in the Bible what he does not choose to find.

There are darker things than these in the Bible; things which I should not be willing to read to you here; passages which shock my conscience and reason by their utter indelicacy, terrible cruelty, or entire improbability. And yet persons of the most admirable character have dwelt on those things with enjoyment. To be sure, Professor Stuart is half disposed to doubt the edifying character of Solomon's Song to the young people of the present day; and yet that heroic orthodox saint, Mary Lyon, was accustomed to peruse it with delight in her later years.

Men read in the Bible what they wish to read; they find what they carry to it. The Puritans thought, when the fashion of wearing wigs first came into use, that the practice was 'clean contrary to the light of nature and to express Scripture' (1 Cor. xi., 14–6); Increase Mather wrote a sermon to show that it was the anger of God, at this new vanity, which kindled the great Boston fire; yet the new vanity soon became customary among the clergy, and was finally almost confined to these, and we hear no more of the 'Express Scripture.' The same men who at first condemned witches because the book said 'Thou shalt not suffer a witch to live,' abandoned the practice when they found it made witchcraft increase; and the same transformation seems to be beginning among the clerical supporters of capital punishment now.

If you wish to make the decision of a moral question hopeless, refer it to scriptural authority. The Bible Society has made the best of books accessible to every nation of the earth (with the exception of one-sixth of our own native population); but in all that accumulation of oracles, you cannot make a man read one text which he does not wish to read. He will pass unmoved over the golden rule, but he will find an eternal ordinance of God in 'Cursed be Canaan,' and can tell you the precise quantity and quality of the wine which Jesus is said to have made at Cana. I have heard a clergyman make the estimate. Thus he erects both Cana and Canaan into solid fortresses to defend his favourite sins; and he will find materials for as many more as he may chance to need.

It is pathetic to read the predictions of the good French missionaries, that 'so soon as they shall have taught the Mongols to say, "Our Father who art in heaven," slavery will fall in Tartary;' for in every episcopal church of our Southern States, the touching words of the Lord's Prayer are repeated every Sunday; but I have never heard that those consecrated altars could thereby afford a refuge to one hunted slave.

It is vain to make a man's familiarity with the Bible the index of his moral condition. I know very profligate and worldly men, who are 'mighty in the Scriptures,' and very pure and noble men who scarcely read them at all. And so various are their contents, that there is room for a wide diversity of tastes, even among those who do read. One enjoys the beautiful piety of the 107th Psalm, and another the horrible curses of the 109th; one the noble heroism of Jewish history, and another its narrow cruelty; one reads the voluptuousness of the Song of Solomon, one the Epicurean philosophy of Ecclesiastes; one seeks the beatitudes of Jesus, one the metaphysics of Paul, one the romance of Revelation. And their characters may be utterly unaffected by this, for though books have an influence, it is only one influence among many.

A man really forms his moral judgment, in the perplexities of life, not upon the basis of scriptural authority, but of his own temperament, education, and circumstances. 'As a man thinketh in his heart, so is he.' What he thinketh is the result of a thousand influences; his inherited qualities, his mother's prayers, and tears, and counsels; his father's advice and guidance; the moral atmosphere of the town he lived in; the boys he played with, the school he went to, the books he read; his choice of an occupation, and the example of elder persons in the same pursuit. The net result of all is—A. B., aged twenty-five, with such or such qualities, good or bad. He then judges or acts, at each moment, according to his personal character and the immediate circumstances; and afterwards, perhaps, if asked for a reason, he quotes scriptural authority.

The whole position of the Bible was well enough stated by Edmund Burke. 'It is,' he says, 'no one summary of doctrine, regularly digested, in which a man could not miss his way; it is a most venerable, but a most multifarious collection of the records of divine economy—a collection of an infinite variety of cosmogony, theology, history, prophecy, psalmody, morality, apologue, allegory, legislation, ethics, carried through different books by different authors, at different ages, for different ends and purposes. It is necessary to sort out what was intended for example, what only as narrative; what to be understood literally, what figuratively; where one precept is to be controlled and modified by another; what is used directly, and what used as an *argumentum ad hominum;* what is temporary and what of perpetual obligation; what appropriated to one state and set of men, and what the general duty of men in all ages.'

To speak yet more plainly, it should be clearly understood that the Old Testament is simply an arbitrary collection of the best early Hebrew literature, and the New Testament of the best early Christian literature.

The selection depended on the discretion of certain individuals; and individuals may still differ as to the comparative value of the books inserted and those excluded. When they asked a famous and facetious clergyman of the last century why the Song of Solomon got into the Bible, while the wisdom of Solomon was left out, he could only reply, that 'men had always preferred songs to wisdom.' It is an accidental collection, whose arrangement is best represented by some school reader or volume of elegant extracts in our own day. Suppose all the libraries to be burnt, and nothing left of English and American literature but one such book. What a strange miscellany! Here we might find a hymn of Milton, and there a passage from Whewell or Herschel—a section of the revised statutes, a heroic appeal from Garrison or Giddings, a voluptuous love song by Byron, an extract from Mather's 'Magnalia' (full of witches and devils), some memorials of the life of Howard or Fenelon, a metaphysical argument of Jonathan Edwards, closing with a vision by Andrew Jackson Davis. A book like this would have in it so much that was noble and glorious, that one might well overlook all that was incredible or objectionable. But to take this work and try to make out of it an unerring standard of faith, to quote texts from it—Mather, Milton, Byron, all the same—to try to find some common ground of sweetest harmony in all that variety—this would be delusion beyond the wildest dream of Roman Catholic or Mormon.

Yet, if we had been brought up to revere this same volume from infancy, our hearts would still cling to it, with a love fondly sensitive to the idlest breath of reproach; there would be sentences blotted with youth's passionate tears, and pages which a mother had folded down; there would be maxims intertwined with our loftiest aspirations and intensest struggles; the earthly stains upon the book had never been noticed, perhaps, by us—how could they have injured others? How could we bid those dear associations farewell? We should cling to them as the nun clings to her cloister.

Ah, but the advancing progress of thought does not leave the nun in her sanctuary, but leads her out beneath the fresh and blessed air of heaven; and you thank God for that. Will our sanctuary be any more permanent, or its loss any more real? Who wishes to destroy any man's love for the Bible? God forbid! but only to make it a more reasonable love, a love like that which a man feels for his parents, which yet does not bind him to be a bigot because his sainted mother was narrow-minded, or to drink wine, because his father lived before the days of total abstinence.

Moreover, the stern fact confronts us, that, with advancing knowledge, this support is doomed to fail; the confidence in scriptural infallibility must perish; and I wish to help to prepare the way for that inevitable event—no more. Test the case for yourself. Let any man begin at the beginning, and read his Bible attentively through, noting in the margin the statements which seem to him contradictory or incredible, profane or impure, and he will be astonished in a day to see the work his pencil has done. I mean by this to throw no especial discredit on the Bible, for I say only what is equally true of all equally ancient collections. And human reverence has for years testified, that no other volume contains an equally large proportion of eloquence, of piety, and of wisdom.

Therefore, I say, men need to be warned in time, so that when their confidence in Bible infallibility goes, their confidence in God may not go also. As you see a vine growing on a tottering wall; it is fair to look at— why disturb it, even to substitute another prop? men ask. And then a wind arises, and it falls with a crash, and the fruit perishes—and who knows what fair child may be overwhelmed among those ruins?

The soul needs some other support also; it must find this within—in the cultivation of the Inward Light; in personal experience of religion; in the life of God in the human soul; in faith in God and love to man; in the reverent study of the vast and simple laws of nature. All these are different names for the same things, as seen variously by various temperaments. But in these, and nowhere else, lies the real foundation of all authority; build your faith here, and churches and Bibles may come or go, and leave it undisturbed.

I do not know if it be true, as old writers assert, that 'the body of man is magnetical, and if it be placed in a boat in still water, the head of the boat will gradually float round to the north;' but the whole course of history shows that the soul of man, at least, has a magnet in it, and slowly and surely comes round to the reception of all truth.

4

THE SYMPATHY OF RELIGIONS

Our true religious life begins when we discover that there is an Inner Light, not infallible but invaluable, which "lighteth every man that cometh into the world." Then we have something to steer by; and it is chiefly this, and not an anchor, that we need. The human soul, like any other noble vessel, was not built to be anchored, but to sail. An anchorage may, indeed, be at times a temporary need, in order to make some special repairs, or to take fresh cargo in; yet the natural destiny of both ship and soul is not the harbor, but the ocean; to cut with even keel the vast and beautiful expanse; to pass from island on to island of more than Indian balm, or to continents fairer than Columbus won; or, best of all, steering close to the wind, to extract motive power from the greatest obstacles. Men forget the eternity through which they have yet to sail, when they talk of anchoring here upon this bank and shoal of time. It would be a tragedy to see the shipping of the world whitening the seas no more, and idly riding at anchor in Atlantic ports; but it would be more tragic to see a world of souls fascinated into a fatal repose and renouncing their destiny of motion.

And as with individuals, so with communities. The great historic religions of the world are not so many stranded hulks left to perish. The

---

This essay was originally written during a winter spent on the island of Fayal, 1855–56, being then intended as a chapter in a larger work, which was never completed. It was read as a lecture some years later in a course conducted by the Free Religious Association in Boston; and was then printed, with some additions, in pamphlet form. It has since gone through various editions, in America and England, and is still doing service as a tract in the "Unity Mission" series, published in Chicago. A special edition was also printed for the "Parliament of Religions" held at Chicago, in September, 1893. A French translation, by Mrs. Maria E. McKaye, appeared at Paris in 1898.

most conspicuous among them are yet full of life and activity. All over the world the divine influence moves men. There is a sympathy in religions, and this sympathy is shown alike in their origin, their records, and their career. I have worshipped in an evangelical church when thousands rose to their feet at the motion of one hand. I have worshipped in a Roman Catholic church when the lifting of one finger broke the motionless multitude into twinkling motion, till the magic sign was made, and all was still. But I never for an instant have supposed that this concentrated moment of devotion was more holy or more beautiful than when one cry from a minaret hushes a Mohammedan city to prayer; or, when, at sunset, the low invocation, "Oh! the gem in the lotus—oh! the gem in the lotus," goes murmuring, like the cooing of many doves, across the vast surface of Thibet. True, "the gem in the lotus" means nothing to us, but it has for those who use it a meaning as significant as "the Lamb of God," for it is a symbol of aspiration.

Every year brings new knowledge of the religions of the world, and every step in knowledge brings out the sympathy between them. They all show similar aims, symbols, forms, weaknesses, and aspirations. Looking at these points of unity, we might say that under many forms there is but one religion, whose essential creed is the Fatherhood of God and the Brotherhood of Man,—disguised by corruptions, symbolized by mythologies, ennobled by virtues, degraded by vices, but still the same. Or if, passing to a closer analysis, we dwell rather on the shades of difference, we shall find in these varying faiths the several instruments which perform what Cudworth calls "the Symphony of Religions." And though some may stir like drums, and others soothe like flutes, and others like violins command the whole range of softness and of strength, yet they are all alike instruments, and nothing in any one of them is so wondrous as the great laws of sound which control them all.

"Amid so much war and contest and variety of opinion," said Maximus Tyrius, "you will find one consenting conviction in every land, that there is one God, the King and Father of all." "God being one," said Aristotle, "only receives various names from the various manifestations we perceive." "Sovereign God," said Cleanthes, in that sublime prayer which Paul quoted, "whom men invoke under many names, and who rulest alone, . . . it is to thee that all nations should address themselves, for we are all thy children." "It is of little consequence," says Seneca, "by what name you call the first Nature, the divine Reason that presides over the universe and fills all parts of it. He is still the same God. We Stoics sometimes call him Father Bacchus, because he is the Universal Life that animates Nature; sometimes Mercury, because he is the Eternal Reason, Order, and Wisdom. You may give him as many names as you please, provided you allow but one sole principle universally." St. Augustine readily accepts these interpretations. "It was one God," he says, "the universal Creator and Sustainer, who in the ethereal spaces was called Jupiter; in the sea, Neptune; in the sun, Phœbus; in the fire, Vulcan; in the vintage, Bacchus; in the harvest, Ceres; in the forests, Diana; in the sciences, Minerva." So Origen, the Christian Father, frankly says that no man can be blamed for calling God's name in Egyptian, or in Scythian, or in such other language as he best knows.[1]

To say that different races worship different Gods is like saying that they are warmed by different suns. The names differ, but the sun is the same, and so is God. As there is but one source of light and warmth, so there is but one source of religion. To this all nations testify alike. We have yet but a part of our Holy Bible. The time will come when, as in the Middle Ages, all pious books will be called sacred scriptures, *Scripturæ Sacræ*. From the most remote portions of the earth, from the Vedas and the Sagas, from Plato and Zoroaster, Confucius and Mohammed, from the Emperor Marcus Antoninus and the slave Epictetus, from learned Alexandrians and the ignorant Galla negroes, there will be gathered hymns and prayers and maxims in which every religious soul may unite,—the magnificent liturgy of the human race.

Alexander von Humboldt asserted in middle life, and repeated the assertion in old age, that "all positive religions contain three distinct parts. First, a code of morals, very fine, and nearly the same in all. Second, a geological dream, and, third, a myth or historical novelette, which last becomes the most important of all." And though his observation may be somewhat roughly stated, its essential truth is seen when we compare the religions of the world, side by side. With such startling points of similarity, where is the difference? The main difference lies here, that each fills some blank space in its creed with the name of a diferent teacher. For instance, the oriental Parsee wears a fine white garment, bound around him with a certain knot; and whenever this knot is undone, he repeats the four main points of his creed, which are as follows:—

---

[1]This is Cudworth's interpretation, but he has rather strained the passage, which must be that beginning, Οὐδὲν οὖν οἶμαι διαφέρειν (*Adv. Celsum*, v.). The passages from Aristotle and Cleanthes are in Stobæus. See, also, Maximus Tyrius, *Diss.* i.: Θεὸς εἶς πάντων βασιλεὺς καὶ πατὴρ; Seneca, *De Beneficiis*, bk. iv. c. 7–8; Augustine, *De Civ. Dei*, bk. iv. c. 2.

"To believe in one God, and hope for mercy from him only."

"To believe in a future state of existence."

"To do as you would be done by."

Thus far the Parsee keeps on the universal ground of religion. Then he drops into the language of his sect and adds:—

"To believe in Zoroaster as lawgiver, and to hold his writings sacred."

The creed thus furnishes a formula for all faiths. It might be printed in blank like a circular, leaving only the closing name to be filled in.[2] For Zoroaster read Christ, and you have Christianity; read Buddha, and you have Buddhism; read Mohammed, and you have Mohammedanism. Each of these, in short, is Natural Religion *plus* an individual name. It is by insisting on that *plus* that each religion stops short of being universal.

In this religion of the human race, thus variously disguised, we meet constantly the same leading features. The same great doctrines, good or bad,—regeneration, predestination, atonement, the future life, the final judgment, the Divine Reason or Logos, and the Trinity. The same religious institutions,—monks, missionaries, priests, and pilgrims. The same ritual,—prayers, liturgies, sacrifices, sermons, hymns. The same implements,—frankincense, candles, holy water, relics, amulets, votive offerings. The same symbols,—the cross, the ball, the triangle, the serpent, the all-seeing eye, the halo of rays, the tree of life. The same saints, angels, and martyrs. The same holiness attached to particular cities, rivers, and mountains. The same prophecies and miracles,—the dead restored and evil spirits cast out. The self-same holy days; for Easter and Christmas were kept as spring and autumn festivals, centuries before our era, by Egyptians, Persians, Saxons, Romans. The same artistic designs; for the mother and child stand depicted, not only in the temples of Europe, but in those of Etruria and Arabia, Egypt and Thibet. In ancient Christian art, the evangelists were represented as bearing the heads of birds and quadrupeds, like those upon which we gaze with amazement in Egyptian tombs. Nay, the very sects and subdivisions of all historic religions have been the same, and each supplies us with mystic and rationalist, formalist and philanthropist, ascetic and epicurean. The simple fact is that all these things are as indigenous as grass and mosses; they

---

[2]Compare Augustine, *De Vera Relig.*, c. iv.: "Paucis mutatis verbis atque sententiis Christiani fierent." The Parsee creed is given as above in a valuable article in Martin's *Colonial Magazine*, No. 18.

spring up in every soil, and often the miscroscope alone can distinguish the varieties.

And, as all these inevitably recur, so comes back again and again the idea of incarnation,—the Divine Man. Here, too, all religions sympathize, and, with slight modifications, each is the copy of the other. As in the dim robing-rooms of foreign churches are kept rich stores of sacred vestments, ready to be thrown over every successive generation of priests, so the world has kept in memory the same stately traditions to decorate each new Messiah. He is predicted by prophecy, hailed by sages, born of a virgin, attended by miracle, borne to heaven without tasting death, and with promise of return. Zoroaster and Confucius have no human father. Osiris is the Son of God, he is called the Revealer of Life and Light; he first teaches one chosen race; he then goes with his apostles to teach the Gentiles, conquering the world by peace; he is slain by evil powers; after death he descends into hell, then rises again, and presides at the last judgment of all mankind: those who call upon his name shall be saved. Buddha is born of a virgin; his name means the Word, the Logos, but he is known more tenderly as the Saviour of Man; he embarrasses his teachers, when a child, by his understanding and his answers; he is tempted in the wilderness, when older; he goes with his apostles to redeem the world; he abolishes caste and cruelty, and teaches forgiveness; he receives among his followers outcasts whom Pharisaic pride despises, and he says, "My law is a law of mercy to all."

These are the recognized properties of religious tradition; the beautiful garments belong not to the individual, but to the race. It is the drawback on all human greatness that it makes itself deified. Even of Jesus it was said sincerely by the Platonic philosopher Porphyry, "That noble soul, who has ascended into heaven, has by a certain fatality become an occasion of error." The inequality of gifts is a problem not yet solved, and there is always a craving for some miracle to explain it. Men set up their sublime representatives as so many spiritual athletes, and measure them. "See, this one is six inches taller; those six inches prove him divine." But because men surpass us, or surpass everybody, shall we hold them separate from the race? Construct the race as you will, somebody must stand at the head, in virtue as in intellect. Shall we deify Shakespeare? Because we may begin upon his treasury of wisdom almost before we enjoy any other book, and can hold to it longer, and read it all our lives, from those earnest moments when we demand the very core of thought, down to moments of sickness and sadness when nothing else captivates; because we may go the rounds of all literature, and grow surfeited with every other great author, and learn a dozen languages and a score of philosophical systems, and travel the wide world over, and come back to Shakespeare at length, fresh as ever, and begin at the beginning of his infinite meanings once more,—are we therefore to consider him as separated from mortality? Are we to raise him to the heavens, as in the magnificent eulogium of Keats, who heads creation with "things real, as sun, stars, and passages of Shakespeare"? Or are we to erect into a creed the bold words I once heard an enthusiast soberly say, "that it is impossible to think of Shakespeare as a man"? Or shall we reverently own, that, as man's humility first bids him separate himself from these his great superiors, so his faith and hope bring him back to them and renew the tie. It paralyzes my intellect if I doubt whether Shakespeare was a man; it paralyzes my whole spiritual nature if I doubt whether Jesus was.

Therefore I believe that all religion is natural, all revealed. What faith in humanity springs up, what trust in God, when one recognizes the sympathy of religions! Every race has some conception of a Creator and Governor of the world, in whom devout souls recognize a Father also. Even where, as among the Buddhists, the reported teachings of the founder seem to ignore the existence of a Deity, the popular instinct is too strong for the teacher, so that the Buddhist races are not atheistic. Every race has some conception of an existence after death. Every race in some way recognizes by its religious precepts the brotherhood of man. The whole gigantic system of caste in Hindostan has grown up in defiance of the Vedas, which are now being invoked to abolish it.[3] The Hitopadesa of Vishnu Sarman forbids caste. "Is this one of our tribe or a stranger? is the calculation of the narrow-minded; but, to those of a noble disposition, the earth itself is but one family." "What is religion?" says elsewhere the same book, and answers, "Tenderness toward all creatures." "He is my beloved of whom mankind are not afraid and who of mankind is not afraid," says the Bhagvat Geeta. "Kesava is pleased with him who does

---

[3]See the discourses of Keshub Chunder Sen in England, as reported by Sophia Dobson Collet. The speaker said of the Brahmo Somaj, or Hindoo reformers, "They were in the beginning a body of Vedantists. They based their teaching upon the national books of the Hindoos; they accepted those books as the word of God, and tried to fling away all the later superstition and idolatry of their countrymen" (p. 530). "You must also admit that the subject of caste distinction was not known to my ancestors. It is said—This is my friend, that is not; so counteth a man of narrow heart; but to the man of large heart all mankind are kinsmen" (p. 493). "With regard to caste, this passage occurs in the sacred writings—This man is my friend; that man is not my friend; so counteth he whose heart is narrow; but he who has a catholic heart looketh upon all mankind as his kinsmen" (p. 299). Again, at Glasgow, "he referred to what these earlier writings revealed in respect to the formerly elevated condition of female society, the doctrine of the divine unity, and the feeling of human brotherhood as opposed to caste" (p. 516). Also pp. 34, 587.

good to others . . . who is always desirous of the welfare of all creatures," says the Vishnu Purana. The traditional greeting of the Buddhist Tartars is, "All men are brethren and should help one another." When a disciple asked Confucius about benevolence, he said, "It is to love *all* men;" and he elsewhere said, "My doctrine is simple and easy to understand;" and his chief disciple adds, "It consists only in having the heart right and in loving one's neighbor as one's self." When he was asked, "Is there one word which may serve as a rule of practice for all one's life?" he answered, "Is not 'Reciprocity' such a word? What you wish done to yourself, do to others." By some translators the rule is given in a negative form, in which it is also found in the Jewish Talmud (Rabbi Hillel), "Do not to another what thou wouldst not he should do to thee; this is the sum of the law." So Thales, when asked for a rule of life, taught, "That which thou blamest in another, do not thyself." "Thou shalt love thy neighbor as thyself," said the Hebrew book of Leviticus. "None of you can be called a true believer," says the Koran, "till he loves for his brother what he loves for himself." Iamblichus tells us that Pythagoras taught "the love of all to all," and Plutarch that Zeno taught us "to look upon all men in general to be our fellow-countrymen and citizens . . . like a flock feeding together with equal right in a common pasture." "To live is not to live for one's self alone," said the Greek dramatist Menander; and the Roman dramatist Terence, following him, brought down the applause of the whole theatre by the saying, "I am a man; I count nothing human foreign to me." "Give bread to a stranger," said Quintilian, "in the name of the universal brotherhood which binds together all men under the common father of nature." "What good man will look on any suffering as foreign to himself?" said the Latin satirist Juvenal. "This sympathy is what distinguishes us from brutes," he adds. Plutarch consoles Apollonius for the death of his son by praising the youth as "a lover of mankind." The poet Lucan predicted a time when warlike weapons should be laid aside, and all men love one another. "Nature has inclined us to love men," said Cicero, "and this is the foundation of the law." He also described his favorite virtue of justice as "devoting itself wholly to the good of others." "Love mankind," wrote Marcus Antoninus, summing it all up in two words; while the loving soul of Epictetus extended the sphere of mutual affection beyond this earth, holding that "the universe is but one great city, full of beloved ones, divine and human, by nature endeared to each other."[4]

This sympathy of religions extends even to the loftiest virtues,—the forgiveness of injuries, the love of enemies, and the overcoming of evil

---

[4]The passages above cited will be found as follows: *Vishnu Sarman* (tr. by Johnson), pp. 16, 28; *Bhagvat Geeta* (tr. by Wilkins), ch. 12; *Vishnu Purana* (tr. by Wilson), p. 291; Huc's *Travels in Thibet, passim.*

with good. "It is declared in our Ved and Codes of Law," says Ram Mohun Roy, "that mercy is the root of virtue." Buddha said, "A man who foolishly does me wrong, I will return to him the protection of my ungrudging love; the more evil comes from him, the more good shall go from me." "Hatred," says the Buddhist Dhammapada, or "Path of Virtue," "does not cease by hatred at any time; hatred ceases by love; this is an old rule." "To overwhelm evil with good is good, and to resist evil by evil is evil," says a Mohammedan manual of ethics. "Turn not away from a sinner, but look on him with compassion," says Sadi's "Gulistan." "If thine enemy hunger, give him bread to eat; if he thirst, give him water to drink," said the Hebrew proverb. "He who commits injustice is ever made more wretched than he who suffers it," said Plato, and adds, "It is never right to return an injury." "No one will dare maintain," said Aristotle, "that it is better to do injustice than to bear it." "We should do good to our enemy," said Cleobulus, "and make him our friend." "Speak not evil to a friend, nor even to an enemy," said Pittacus, one of the Seven Wise Men. "It is more beautiful," said Valerius Maximus, "to overcome injury by the power of kindness than to oppose to it the obstinacy of hatred." Maximus Tyrius has a

---

Confucius, in Legge's *Confucian Analects,* bk. xii. c. 22, and bk. xv. c. 23. Also, *Lun-yu* (tr. by Pauthier), c. iv. § 16; Davis's *Chinese,* ii. 50. Compare the exhaustive essay of Ezra Abbot (*Proceedings Am. Orient. Soc. for* 1870, p. ix.).

Thales, in *Diogenes Laertius,* bk. i. § 36. Πῶς ἂν ἄριστα καὶ δικαιότατα βιώσαιμεν; ἐάω ἃ τοῖς ἄλλοιζ ἐπιτιμῶμεν, αὐτοὶ μὴ δρῶμεν. Stobæus reads instead (c. 43), ὅσα νεμεσεῖς τὸν πλησίον αὐτὸς μὴ ποίει. Leviticus xix. 18. Koran, quoted in *Akhlak-i-Jalaly,* p. 78. Iamblichus, *De Pythag. vita,* cc. 16, 33: Φιλίαν δὲ διαφανέστατα πάντων πρὸς ἅπαντας Πυθαγόρας παρέωκε. Plutarch, *De Alex. seu Virt., seu Fort.,* bk. i. § 68: Ἀλλὰ πάντας ἀνθρώπους ἡγώμεθα δημότας καὶ πολίτας ... ὥσπερ ἀγέλης ὁυννόμου νόμῳ συντρεφόμενης. Menander (ed. Dübner), *Incert. Fab. Fragm.,* 257: Τοῦτ' ἐστι τὸ ζῆν οὐχ ἑαυτῷ ζῆν μόον.

Terence, *Heaut.,* i. 1, 25: "Homo sum, humani nihil a me alienum puto." Quintilian, *Declamations,* quoted by Denis. Juvenal, *Sat.* xv. 140–142:—

> "Quis enim bonus . . .
> Ulla aliena sibi credat mala?"

Plutarch, *Consol. ad Apollon.,* § 34: Φιλοπάτωρ γενόμενος καὶ φιλομήτωρ, καὶ Φιλοίκειος καὶ Φιλόσοφος, τὸ δὲ σύμαν εἰπεῖν Φιλάνθρωπος.

Lucan, *Pharsalia,* i. 60, 61:—

> "Tunc genus humanum positis sibi consulat armis
> Inque vicem gens omnis amet."

Cicero, *De Legibus,* i. 15: "Nam hæc nascuntur ex eo, quia natura propensi sumus ad diligendos homines, quod fundamentum juris est." Also *De Republica,* iii. 7, 7 (fragment): "Quæ virtus, præter ceteras, tota se ad alienas porrigit utilitates et explicat." Marcus Antoninus, vii. 31: Φίλησον τὸν ἀνθρώπινον γένος. Epictetus, bk. iii. c. xxiv. : Οτι ὁ κόσμος οὗτος μία πόλις ἐστὶ ... πάντα δὲ φίλων μεστὰ, πρῶτον μὲν Θεῶν εἶτα καὶ ἀνθρώπων, φύσει πρὸς ἀλλχλοις ψκειωμένων. Compare Cicero, *De Nat. Deorum* (ii. § lxii.): "Est enim mundus quasi communis Deorum, atque hominum domus, aut urbs utrorumque."

special chapter on the treatment of injuries, and concludes, "If he who injures does wrong, he who returns the injury does equally wrong." Plutarch, in his essay, "How to profit by our enemies," bids us sympathize with them in affliction and aid their needs. "A philosopher, when smitten, must love those who smite him, as if he were the father, the brother, of all men," said Epictetus. "It is peculiar to man," said Marcus Antoninus, "to even love those who do wrong. . . . Ask thyself daily to how many ill-minded persons thou hast shown a kind disposition." He compares the wise and humane soul to a spring of pure water which blesses even him who curses it; as the Oriental story likens such a soul to the sandalwood tree, which imparts its fragrance even to the axe that cuts it down.[5]

How it cheers and enlarges us to hear of these great thoughts and know that the Divine has never been without a witness on earth! How it must sadden the soul to disbelieve them! Worse yet, to be in a position where it is necessary to hope that they may not be correctly reported,— that one by one they may be explained away. A prosecuting attorney once told me that the most painful part of his position was that he had to hope that every man he prosecuted would be proved a villain. But what is this to the position of those who are bound to hope that the character of humanity will be blackened by wholesale,—who are compelled to resist every new gleam of light that the study of ancient history reveals. For instance, as the great character of Buddha has come out from the darkness, within fifty years, how these reluctant people have struggled against it, still desiring to escape. "Save us, O God!" they have seemed to say, "from the distress of believing that so many years ago

---

[5]Ram Mohun Roy, *Conference on Burning Widows* (Calcutta, 1818), p. 27; Beal's *Buddhist Scriptures from the Chinese,* p. 193; *Dhammapada* (tr. by Max Müller), in Roger's *Buddhagosha's Parables,* also in Max Müller's *Lectures on the Science of Religion* (Am. ed.), p. 194; *Akhlak-i-Jalaly* (tr. by Thompson), p. 441; Sadi's *Gulistan* (tr. by Ross), p. 240; (tr. by Gladwin, Am. ed.), p. 209; Proverbs xxv. 21. Plato, *Gorgias,* § 35: ᾽Αεὶ τὸν ἀδικοῦντα τοῦ ἀδικουμένου ἀθλιώτερον εἶναι. *Crito,* § 10: ῾Ως οὐδέποτε ὀρθῶς ἔχοντος οὔτε τοῦ ἀδικεῖν οὔτε τοῦ ἀνταδικεῖν. (Plato devotes much of the first book of his *Republic* to refuting with great elaboration those who allege that it is right to injure an enemy.) Cleobulus, in *Diog. Laertius,* bk. i. § 91: ῎Ελεγέ τε τὸν φίλον δεῖν εὐεργετεῖν, ὅπως ᾖ μᾶλλον φίλος. τὸν δὲ ἐχθρὸν, φίλον ποιεῖν. Pittacus in *Diog. Laertius,* bk. i. § 78: Φίλον μὴ λέγειν κακῶς, ἀλλὰ μηδὲ ἐχθρόν. Val. Maximus, iv. 2, 4: "Quia speciosius aliquanto injuriæ beneficiis vincuntur quam mutui odii pertinacia pensantur." Max. Tyrius, *Diss.* xviii.: Καὶ μὴν εἰ ὁ ἀδικῶν κακῶς ποιεῖ, ὁ ἀντιποιῶν κακῶς οὐδὲν ἧττον ποιεῖ κακῶς καν ἀμύνηται. Plutarch's *Morals* (tr. by Goodwin, i. 293). Epictetus, bk. vii. c. 22: Δαίρεσθαι δεῖ αὐτον, ὡς ὄνον, καὶ δαιρόμενον φιλεῖν αὐτούς δαίπροντας, ὡς πατέρα πάντων, ὡς ἀδελφόν. Marcus Antoninus, *Medit.,* v. 31: Εἰς ὅσους δὲ ἀγνώμονας εὐγνώμων εγένου. vii. 22: ῎Ιδιον ἀνθρώπου φιλεῖν χαὶ τοὺς πταίοντας.

there was a sublime human life." Show such persons that the great religious ideas and maxims are as old as literature; and how they resist the knowledge! "Surely it is not so bad as that," they seem to say. "Is there no possibility of a mistranslation! Let us see the text, explore the lexicon; is there no labor, no device, by which we can convince ourselves that there is a mistake?" Anything rather than believe that there is a light which lighteth every man that cometh into the world.

For this purpose the very facts of history must be suppressed or explained away. Sir George Mackenzie, in his "Travels in Iceland," says that the clergy prevented till 1630, with "mistaken zeal," the publication of the Scandinavian Eddas. Huc, the Roman Catholic missionary, described in such truthful colors the religious influence of Buddhism in Thibet that his book was put in the *Index Expurgatorius* at Rome. Balmes, a learned Roman Catholic writer, declares that "Christianity is stripped of a portion of its honors" if we trace back any high standard of female purity to the ancient Germans; and so he coolly sets aside as "poetical" the plain statements of the accurate Tacitus. If we are to believe the accounts given of the Jewish Essenes by Josephus, De Quincey thinks, the claims made by Christianity are annihilated. "If Essenism could make good its pretensions, there, at one blow, would be an end of Christianity, which, in that case, is not only superseded as an idle repetition of a religious system already published, but as a criminal plagiarism. Nor can the wit of man evade the conclusion." He accordingly attempts to explain away the unequivocal testimony of Josephus.[6]

And what makes this exclusiveness the more replusive is its modern origin. Paul himself quoted from the sublime hymn of Cleanthes to prove to the Greeks that they too recognized the Fatherhood of God. The early Christian apologists, living face to face with the elder religions, made no exclusive claims. Tertullian declared the soul to be an older authority than prophecy, and its voice the gift of God from the beginning. Justin Martyr said, "Those who live according to Reason are Christians, though you may call them atheists. . . . Such among the Greeks were Socrates and Heraclitus and the rest. They who have made or do make Reason (Logos) their rule of life are Christians, and men without fear and trembling." "The same God," said Clement, "to whom we owe the Old and New Testaments gave also to the Greeks their Greek philosophy by which the Almighty is glorified among the Greeks." Lactantius declared that the ancient philosophers "attained the full truth and the whole mystery of reli-

---

[6]Balmes, *Protestantism and Catholicity,* c. xxvii. and note; Mackenzie's *Iceland,* p. 26; De Quincey, *Autobiographical Sketches* (Am. ed.), p. 17, and *Essay on the Essenes.* The condemnation of Huc's book is mentioned by Max Müller, *Chips,* etc. (Am. ed.), i. 187.

gion." "One would suppose," said Minucius Felix, "either that the Christians were philosophers, or the philosophers Christians." "What is now called the Christian religion," said Augustine, "has existed among the ancients, and was not absent from the beginning of the human race, until Christ came in the flesh; from which time the true religion, which existed already, began to be called Christian." Jerome said that "the knowledge of God was present by nature in all, nor was there any one born without God, or who had not in himself the seeds of all virtues."[7]

There is undoubtedly an increasing willingness among Christian theologians to express views like these. Yet there are many who still shrink from the admission that any such sympathy exists between religions. "There never was a time," says a distinguished European preacher, "when there did not exist an infinite gulf between the ideas of the ancients and the ideas of Christianity. There is an end of Christianity if men agree in thinking the contrary." And an eminent American clergyman says, "If the truths of Christianity are intuitive and self-evident, how is it that they formed no part of any man's consciousness till the advent of Christ?" But how can any one look history in the face, how can any man open even the dictionary of any ancient language, and yet say this? What word sums up the highest Christian virtue if not *philanthropy*? And yet the word is a Greek word, and was used in the same sense before Christendom existed.[8]

Some of the ablest Christian writers have honestly disclaimed any such monopoly of the truth. In William Penn's "No Cross, No Crown," one half the pages are devoted to the religious testimony of Christians, and one half to that of the non-Christian world. The pious Scougal, in his discourse "On the indispensable duty of loving our enemies," admits that it was taught also by "the more sober of the heathen." "If," says Dean

---

[7]"Nec hoc ullis Mosis libris debent. Ante anima quam prophetia. Animæ enim a primordio conscientia Dei dos est." Tertullian, *Adv. Marcion,* 1, 10.

Οἱ μετὰ Λόγου βιώσαντες χριστιανοί εἰσι, κἄν ἄθεοι ἐνομσίθησαν, οἷον ἐν Ἕλλησι μὲν Σωκράτης καὶ Ἡράκλειτος καὶ οἱ ὁμοῖοι αὐτοῖς, κ. τ.λ. Justin Martyr, *Apol.,* i. 46

Ππὸς δὲ καὶ ὅτι ὁ αὐτὸς θεὸς ἀμφοῖν ταῖν διαθήκαιν χορηγὸς ὁ καὶ τῆς Ἑλληνικῆς φιλοσοφίας δοτὴρ τοῖς Ἕλληοιν, δι᾽ ἧς ὁ παντοκράτωρ παρ᾽ Ἕλλησι δοξάζεται, παρέστησεν, δῆλον δὲ κἀνθένδε. Clem. Alex., *Strom.,* vi. v. 42.

"Totam igitur veritatem et omne divinæ religionis arcanum philosophi attigerunt." Lactantius, *Inst.,* viii. 7.

"Ut quivis arbitretur, aut nunc Christianos philosophos esse, aut philosophos fuisse jam tunc Christianos." Minucius Felix, *Octavius,* c. xx.

Milman, "we were to glean from the later Jewish writings, from the beautiful aphorisms of other Oriental nations, which we cannot fairly trace to Christian sources, and from the Platonic and Stoic philosophy, their more striking precepts, we might find, perhaps, a counterpart to almost all the moral sayings of Jesus." The writings of the most learned of English Catholics, Digby, are a treasure-house of ancient religion, and the conflict between the churchman and the scholar makes him deliciously inconsistent. He states a doctrine, illustrates it from the schoolmen or the fathers, proudly claims it as being monopolized by the Christian church, and ends by citing a parallel passage from Plato or Æschylus! "The ancient poets," he declares, "seem never to have conceived the idea of a spirit of resignation which would sanctify calamity;" and accordingly he quotes Aristotle's assertion, that "suffering becomes beautiful when any one bears great calamities with cheerfulness, not through insensibility, but through greatness of mind." "There is not a passage in the classics," he declares, "which recognizes the beauty of holiness and Christian mildness;" and in the next breath he remarks that Homer's description of Patroclus furnishes "language which might convey an idea of that mildness of manner which belonged to men in Christian ages." And he closes his eloquent picture of the faith of the Middle Ages in immortality by attributing to the monks and friars the opinion uttered by the dying Socrates, that "a man who has spent his life in the study of philosophy ought to take courage in his death, and to be full of hope that he is about to possess the greatest good that can be obtained, which will be in his possession as soon as he dies." Yet all this is done in a manner so absolutely free from sophistry, the conflict between the two attitudes is so innocent and transparent, that one almost loves it in Digby. In many writers on these subjects there is greater bigotry, without the amiability and the learning.[9]

"Res ipsa, quæ nunc religio Christiana nuncupatur, erat apud antiquos, nec defuit ab initio generis humani, quousque Christus veniret in carnem, unde vera religio, quæ jam erat, cœpit appellari Christiana." Augustine, *Retr.,* i. 13.

"Natura omnibus Dei inesse notitiam, nec quemquam sine Deo nasci, et non habere in se semina sapientiæ et justitiæ reliquarumque virtutum." Hieron., *Comm. in Gal.,* i. 1, 15.

[8] Ἐγὼ δὲ φοβοῦμαι μὴ ὑπὸ φιλανθρωπίας δοκῶ αὐτοῖς ὅτε περ ἔχω ἐκκεχυμένως παντὶ ἀνιδρὶ λέγειν. Plato, *Euthyphron,* § 3.

"Quodque a Græcis φιλανθρωπία dicitur, et significat dexteritatem quandam benevolentiamque erga omnes homines promiscuam." Aulus Gellius, bk. xiii. c. xvi. I.

See, further, an essay "On the word Philanthropy," by the present writer, which follows the present essay in this volume.

And, if it is thus hard to do historical justice, it is far harder to look with fairness upon contemporary religions. Thus the Jesuit Father Ripa thought that Satan had created the Buddhist religion on purpose to bewilder the Christian church. There we see a creed possessing more votaries than any other in the world, numbering nearly one third of the human race. Its traditions go back to a founder whose record is stainless and sublime. It has the doctrine of the Real Presence, the Madonna and Child, the invocation of the dead, monasteries and pilgrimages, celibacy and tonsure, relics, rosaries, and holy water. Wherever it has spread, it has broken down the barrier of caste. It teaches that all men are brethren, and makes them prove it by their acts; it diffuses gentleness and self-sacrificing benevolence. "It has become," as Neander admits, "to many tribes of people a means of transition from the wildest barbarism to semi-civilization." Tennent, living amid the lowest form of it in Ceylon, says that its code of morals is second only to that of Christianity itself," and enjoins "every conceivable virtue and excellence." Shall we not rejoice in this consoling discovery? "Yes," said the simple-hearted Abbé Huc: so he published his account of Buddhism, and saw the book excommunicated. "No!" said Father Ripa, "it is the invention of the devil!"[10]

With a steady wave of progress Mohammedanism is sweeping through Africa, where Christianity scarcely advances a step. Wherever Mohammedanism reaches, schools and libraries are established, gambling and drunkenness cease, theft and falsehood diminish, polygamy is limited, woman begins to be elevated and has property rights guaranteed; and, instead of witnessing human sacrifices, you see the cottager reading the Koran at her door, like the Christian cottager in Cowper's description. "Its gradual extension," says an eye-witness, "is gradually but surely modifying the negro. . . . Within the last half century the humanizing influence of the Koran is acknowledged by all who are acquainted with the interior tribes." So in India, Mohammedanism makes

---

[9]Milman's *Hist. Christianity,* bk. i. c. iv. § 3. (Compare Merivale's *Conversion of the Roman Empire,* Note F, § 4.) Digby's *Ages of Faith* (Am. ed.), ii. 174, 178, 287–289, etc. Digby's inconsistent method has ample precedent in the early Christian apologists. Tertullian, for instance, glorifies the Christian martyrs, and then, to show that they are not foolish or desperate men, cites the precedents of Regulus, Zeno, Mutius Scævola, and many others! *Apol.,* c. 50.

[10]Compare *Neander* (Am. tr.), i. 450; Huc's *Thibet,* ii. 50; Tennent's *Christianity in Ceylon,* pp. 219, 220.

[11]Capt. Canot, pp. 153, 180, 181; Wilson's *Western Africa,* 75, 79, 92; Richardson's *Great Desert,* ii. 63, 129; Johnston's *Abyssinia,* i. 267; Allen's *Niger Expedition,* i. 383; Du Chaillu, *Ashango Land,* xiii. 129. Barth, *passim,* especially (i. 310, Am. ed.): "That continual struggle, which always continuing further and further, seems destined to overpower the nations

converts by thousands, according to Colonel Sleeman, where Christianity makes but a handful; and this, he testifies, because in Mohammedanism there is no spirit of caste, while Christians have a caste of their own, and will not put converts on an equality with themselves. Do we rejoice in this great work of progress? No! one would think we were still in the time of the crusades by the way we ignore the providential value of Mohammedanism.[11]

The one unpardonable sin is exclusiveness. Any form of religion is endangered when we bring it to the test of practical results, for none can yet bear that test. There never existed a person, a book, or an institution, which did not share, however distantly, the merits and the drawbacks of its rivals. Granting all that can be established as to the debt of the world to the very best dispensation, the fact still remains, that there is not a single maxim, or idea, or application, or triumph, that any one religion can claim as exclusively its own. Neither faith, nor love, nor truth, nor disinterestedness, nor forgiveness, nor patience, nor peace, nor equality, nor education, nor missionary effort, nor prayer, nor honesty, nor the sentiment of brotherhood, nor reverence for woman, nor the spirit of humility, nor the fact of martyrdom, nor any other good thing, is monopolized by any form of faith. All religions recognize, more or less remotely, these principles; all do something to exemplify, something to dishonor them. Travelers find that virtue is in a seeming minority in all other countries, and forget that they have left it in a minority at home. A Hin-

---

at the very equator, if Christianity does not presently step in to dispute the ground with it." He says "that a great part of the Berbers of the desert were once Christians, and that they afterwards changed their religion and adopted Islam" (i. 197, 198). He represents the slave merchants of the interior as complaining that the Mohammedans of Tunis have abolished slavery, but that Christians still continue it (i. 465). "It is difficult to decide how a Christian government is to deal with these countries, where none but Mohammedans maintain any sort of government" (ii. 196). "There is a vital principle in Islam, which has only to be brought out by a reformer to accomplish great things" (i. 164).

Reade, in his *Savage Africa,* discusses the subject fully in a closing chapter, and concludes thus: "Mohammed, a servant of God, redeemed the eastern world. His followers are now redeeming Africa. . . . Let us aid the Mohammedans in their great work, the redemption of Africa. . . . In every Mohammedan town there is a public school and a public library." He complains that Christianity utterly fails to check theft, but Mohammedanism stops it entirely (pp. 135, 579, English ed.).

For Asiatic Mohammedanism, see *Sleeman's Recollections,* ii. 164, and compare Tennent's *Christianity in Ceylon,* p. 330, and Max Müller's *Chips from a German Workshop,* ii. 351.

Since the above note was written, this whole subject has been exhaustively treated by R. Bosworth Smith, M. A., Assistant Master in Harrow School, in the first of his admirable *Lectures before the Royal Institution of Great Britain,* on "Mohammed and Mohammedanism" (pp. 49–66, Am. ed.).

doo girl, astonished at the humanity of a British officer toward her father, declared her surprise that any one could display so much kindness who did not believe in the God Vishnu. Rev. J. R. Wolf, an English missionary, met a Buddhist who readily offered to believe in Jesus Christ if the missionary would believe in Buddha. Gladwin, in his "Persian Classics," narrates a scene which occurred in his presence between a Jew and a Mohammedan. The Mohammedan said in wrath, "If this deed of conveyance is not authentic, may God cause me to die a Jew." The Jew said, "I make my oath on the Pentateuch, and if I swear falsely I am a Mohammedan like you."

What religion stands highest in its moral results, if not Christianity? Yet Christendom has produced the slave-trader as well as the saint. If we say that Christendom was not truly represented by the slaves in the hold of John Newton's slave-ship, but only by his pious meditations in the cabin, then we must admit that Buddhism is not be judged merely by its prostrations before Fo, but by the learning of its lamaseries and the beneficence of its people. Keshub Chunder Sen goes from India to England, and implores Christians to cease demoralizing the young Hindoos by teaching them the use of strong drink. "Man after man dies," he says, "and people sometimes compute the results of English education by the number of deaths that actually take place, every month and year, through intemperance." The greater humanity of Hindoos towards animals has been, according to Dr. Hedge, a serious embarrassment to our missionaries. Men interrupt the missionaries in China, Coffin tells us, by asking them why, if their doctrines are true, Christian nations forced opium on an unwilling emperor, who refused to the last to receive money from the traffic; and it is well known that Gutzlaff, a missionary, accompanied the English ships, as interpreter, on that occasion.[12]

What a history has been our treatment of the American Indians! "Instead of virtues," said Cadwallader Colden, writing as early as 1727, "we have taught them vices that they were entirely free from before that time." The delegation from the Society of Friends reported, in 1869, that an Indian chief brought a young Indian before a white commissioner to

---

[12]*Keshub Chunder Sen in England,* by S. D. Collett, p. 265, also pp. 152, 221, etc.; Hedge's *Primeval World of Hebrew Tradition,* p. 83; Coffin's *New Way round the World,* pp. 270, 308, 361; Williams's *Middle Kingdom,* ii. 529, 544. Mr. Williams states that the Chinese emperor caused to be destroyed 20,291 chests of opium, and calls the act "a solitary instance in the history of the world of a pagan monarch preferring to destroy what would injure his own subjects, than to fill his pockets with its sale." Dr. Jeffreys was told by a Mussulman in India, speaking of a certain tribe, that he knew they were Christians "from their being nearly all drunkards." *British Army in India,* by Jeffreys, p. 19.

give evidence, and the commissioner hesitated a little in receiving a part of the testimony, when the chief said with great emphasis, "Oh! you may believe what he says: he tells the truth: he has never seen a white man before!" In Southey's "Wesley" there is an account of an Indian whom Wesley met in Georgia, and who thus summed up his objections to Christianity: "Christian much drunk! Christian beat man! Christian tell lies! Devil Christian! Me no Christian!"[13] What then? All other religions show the same discrepancy between belief and practice, and each is safe till it begins to traduce the rest. Test each sect by its best or its worst as you will, by its high-water mark of virtue or its low-water mark of vice. But falsehood begins when you measure the ebb of any other religion against the flood-tide of your own.

There is a noble and a base side to every history. The same religion varies in different soils. Christianity is not the same in England and Italy; in Armenia and in Ethiopia; in the Protestant and Catholic cantons of Switzerland; in Massachusetts and in Utah. Neither is Buddhism the same in China, in Thibet, and in Ceylon; nor Mohammedanism in Turkey and in Persia. We have no right to pluck the best fruit from one tree, the worst from another, and then say that the tree is known by its fruits. I say again, Christianity has, on the whole, produced the highest results of all, in manners, in arts, in virtue. Yet when Christianity had been five centuries in the world, the world's only hope seemed to be in the superior strength and purity of Pagan races. "Can we wonder," wrote Salvian (A. D. 400), "if our lands have been given over to the barbarians by God? since that which we

---

[13]Colden's *History of the Five Indian Nations* (dedication). He says also, "We have reason to be ashamed that those infidels, by our conversation and neighborhood, are become worse than they were before they knew us." It appears from this book (as from other witnesses), that one of the worst crimes now practised by Indians has sprung up since that day, being certainly countenanced by the brutalities practised by whites towards Indian women. Colden says: "I have been assured that there is not an instance of their offering the least violence to the chastity of any woman that was their captive." Vol. i. p. 9, 3d ed. [It is probable, however, that different tribes have always differed in this respect. Compare Parkman's *Pontiac*, ii. 236; Southey's *Wesley*, chap. iii.; Report of Joint Delegation of the Society of Friends, 1869.] The Indians whom Catlin took with him to England could not be made to understand why missionaries were sent from London to convert the red men, when there was so much more vice and suffering in London than in the Indian country. They said: "The people around us can all read the good book, and they can understand all the black coats say; and still we find they are not so honest and so good people as ours; this we are sure of. . . . We believe that the Great Spirit has made our religion for us and white man's religion for white men. Their sins we believe are much greater than ours; and perhaps the Great Spirit has thought it best to give them a different religion." Catlin's *Indians in Europe*, i. 164; ii. 40; also ii. 61, 71.

have polluted by our profligacy the barbarians have cleansed by their chastity."[14] At the end of its first thousand years, Christianity could only show Europe at its lowest ebb of civilization, in a state which Guizot calls "death by the extinction of every faculty." The barbarians had only deteriorated since their conversion; the great empires were falling to pieces; and the only bright spot in Europe was Mohammedan Spain, whose universities taught all Christendom science, as its knights taught chivalry. Even at the end of fifteen hundred years, the Turks, having conquered successively Jerusalem and Constantinople, seemed altogether the most powerful nation of the world; their empire was compared to the Roman empire; they were gaining all the time. You will find everywhere—in Luther's "Tabletalk," for instance—how weak Christendom seemed against them in the middle of the sixteenth century; and Lord Bacon, yet later, describes them in his "Essays" as the only warlike nation in Europe except the Spaniards. But the art of printing had been discovered, and that other new world, America; the study of Greek literature was reviving the intellect of Europe, and the tide had begun to turn. For four hundred years it has been safe for Christendom to be boastful, but if at any time during the fifteen hundred years previous the comparison had been made, the boasting would have been the other way. It is unsafe to claim a monopoly of merit on the basis of facts that cover four centuries out of nineteen. Let us not be misled by a hasty vanity, lest some new incursion of barbarians teach us, as it taught the early Christians, to be humble.

We see what Christianity has done for Europe; but we do not remember how much Europe has done for Christianity."[15] Take away the influence of race and climate; take away Greek literature and Mohammedan chivalry and the art of printing; set the decline of Christianity in Asia and Africa against its gain in Europe and America,—and, whatever superiority may be left, it affords no basis for any exclusive claims.[16] The recent scientific advances of the age are a brilliant theme for the rhetori-

---

[14]"Cum ea quæ Romani polluerant fornicatione, nunc mundent barbari castitate." Salvian, *De Gubern. Dei*, ed. 1623, p. 254, quoted in Gilly's *Vigilantius*, p. 360.

[15]"Neither history nor more recent experience can furnish any example of the long retention of pure Christianity by a people themselves rude and unenlightened. In all the nations of Europe, embracing every period since the second century, Christianity must be regarded as having taken the hue and complexion of the social state with which it was incorporated, presenting itself unsullied, contaminated, or corrupted, in sympathy with the enlightenment or ignorance or debasement of those by whom it had been originally embraced. The rapid and universal degeneracy of the early Asiatic churches is associated with the decline of education and the intellectual decay of the communities among whom they were established." Tennent's *Christianity in Ceylon*, p. 273.

cian; but those who make these advances appear very little disposed to ascribe them to the influence of any form of religion.

Indeed it is only very lately that the claim of superiority in civilization and the arts of life has been made in behalf of Christianity. Down to the time of the Reformation it was usual to contrast the intellectual and practical superiority of the heathen with the purely spiritual claims of the church. Ruskin complains that in Raphael's decorations of the Vatican he concedes Philosophy and Poetry to the ancients, and claims only Theology for the moderns. "From the beginning of the world," said Luther, "there have always been among the heathens higher and rarer people, of greater and more exalted understanding, more excellent diligence and skill in all arts, than among Christians, or the people of God." "Do we excel in intellect, in learning, in decency of morals?" said Melanchthon. "By no means. But we excel in the true knowledge and worship and adoration of God." "The church has always been accustomed," says the Roman Catholic Digby, "to see genius and learning in the ranks opposed to her."[17]

Historically, of course, we are Christians, and can enjoy the advantage which that better training has given, just as the favored son of a king may enjoy his special advantages and yet admit that the less favored are also sons. The name of Christianity only ceases to excite respect when it is used to represent any false or exclusive claims, or when it takes the place of the older and grander words, "Religion" and "Virtue." When we fully comprehend the sympathy of religions we shall deal with other faiths on fairer terms. We shall cease trying to free men from one superstition by inviting them into another. The true missionaries are men inside each religion who have outgrown its limitations. But no Christian missionary has ever yet consented to meet the man of other religions upon the common ground of Theism. In Bishop Heber's time, the Hindoo reformer Swamee Narain was teaching purity and peace, the unity of God, and the abolition of caste. Many thousands of men followed his teachings, and whole villages and districts were raised from the worst immorality by his

---

[16]For the influence of Mohammedanism on the revival of letters in Europe, see Andres, *Origine di ogni litteratura;* Jourdain, *Recherches critiques sur les traductions latines d'Aristote;* Schmölders, *Ecoles Philosophiques entre les Arabes;* Forster, *Mohammedanism Unveiled;* Urquhart, *Phillars of Hercules;* Lecky's *Rationalism,* ii. 284; Humboldt's *Cosmos,* ii. xvii. 579, 584, 594; Neander's *Church History* (Am. tr.), iv. 301.

[17]"Quid igitur nos antecellimus? Num ingenio, doctrina, morum moderatione illos superamus? Nequaqum. Sed vera Dei agnitione, invocatione et celebratione præstamus." Melanchthon, quoted by Feuerbach, *Essence of Christianity,* (Eng. tr.), p. 284. He also cites the passage from Luther. Digby's *Ages of Faith* (Am. ed.), ii. 84.

labors, as the Bishop himself bears witness. But the good Bishop seems to have despaired of him as soon as Swamee Narain refused conversion to Christianity, making the objection that God was not incarnated in one man, but in many. Then there was Ram Mohun Roy, sixty years ago, who argued from the Vedas against idolatry, caste, and the burning of widows. He also refused to be called a Christian, and the missionaries denounced him. Now comes Keshub Chunder Sen, with his generous utterances: "We profess the universal and absolute religion, whose cardinal doctrines are the Fatherhood of God and the Brotherhood of Man, and which accepts the truths of all scriptures, and honors the prophets of all nations." The movement reaches thousands whom no foreign influence could touch; yet the Methodist missionaries denounce it in the name of Christ. It is the same with our treatment of the Jews. According to Bayard Taylor, Christendom converts annually three of four Jews in Jerusalem, at a cost of $20,000 each; and yet the reformed Jews in America have already gone in advance of the most liberal Christian sects in their width of religious sympathy. "The happiness of man," says Rabbi Wise, speaking for them, "depends on no creed and no book; it depends on the dominion of truth, which is the Redeemer and Saviour, the Messiah and the King of Glory."[18]

It is our happiness to live in a time when all religions are at last outgrowing their mythologies, and emancipated men are stretching out their hands to share together "the luxury of a religion that does not degrade." The progressive Brahmoes of India, the Mohammedan students in London, the Jewish radicals in America, are teaching essentially the same principles, seeking the same ends, with the most enlightened Christian reformers. The Jewish congregations in Baltimore were the first to contribute for the education of the freedmen; the Buddhist temple, in San Francisco, was the first edifice of that city draped in mourning after the murder of President Lincoln; the Parsees of the East sent contributions to the Sanitary Commission. The great religions of the world are but larger sects; they come together, like the lesser sects, for works of benevolence; they share the same aspirations, and every step in

---

[18]Rabbi Wise's remarks may be found in the Report of the Free Religious Association for 1869, p. 118. For Swamee Narain, see Heber's *Journal*, ii. 109–121 (Am. ed.). For Ram Mohun Roy, see his translation of the Sama Veda (Calcutta, 1816), his two tracts on the burning of widows (Calcutta, 1818, 1820), and other pamphlets. Victor Jacquemont wrote of him from Calcutta in 1830, "Il n'est pas Chrétien quoi qu'on en dise. . . . Les honnêtes Anglais l'exècrent parce que, disent ils, c'est un affreux déiste." *Lettres*, i. 288. Keshub Chunder Sen complains of his own treatment by the missionaries (Collet, 302, 375).

the progress of each brings it nearer to all the rest. For most of us in America, the door out of superstition and sin may be called Christianity; that is our historical name for it; it is the accident of a birthplace. But other nations find other outlets; they must pass through their own doors, not through ours; and all will come at last upon the broad ground of God's providing, which bears no man's name. The reign of heaven on earth will not be called the Kingdom of Christ or of Buddha,—it will be called the Church of God, or the Commonwealth of Man. I do not wish to belong to a religion only, but to *the* religion; it must not include less than the piety of the world.

If one insists on being exclusive, where shall he find a home? What hold has any Protestant sect among us on a thoughtful mind? They are too little, too new, too inconsistent, too feeble. What are these children of a day compared with that magnificent Church of Rome, which counts its years by centuries, and its votaries by millions, and its martyrs by myriads; with kings for confessors and nations for converts; carrying to all the earth one Lord, one faith, one baptism, and claiming for itself no less title than the Catholic, the Universal? Yet in conversing with Catholics one is again repelled by the comparative juvenility, and modernness, and scanty numbers of their church. It claims to be elder brother of our little sects, doubtless, and seems to have most of the family fortune. But the whole fortune is so small! and even the elder brother is so young! The Romanist himself ignores traditions more vast than his own, antiquity more remote, a literature of piety more grand. His temple suffocates: give us a shrine still wider; something than this Catholicism more catholic; not the Church of Rome, but of God and Man; a Pantheon, not a Parthenon; the true *semper, ubique, et ab omnibus;* the Religion of the Ages, Natural Religion.

I was once in a Portuguese cathedral when, after the three days of mourning, in Holy Week, came the final day of Hallelujah. The great church had looked dim and sad, with the innumerable windows closely curtained, since the moment when the symbolical bier of Jesus was borne to its symbolical tomb beneath the High Altar, while the three mystic candles blazed above it. There had been agony and beating of cheeks in the darkness, while ghostly processions moved through the aisles, and fearful transparencies were unrolled from the pulpit. The priests kneeled in gorgeous robes, chanting, with their heads resting on the altar steps; the multitude hung expectant on their words. Suddenly burst forth a new chant, "Gloria in Excelsis!" In that instant every curtain was rolled aside, the cathedral was bathed in glory, the organs clashed, the bells chimed, flowers were thrown from the galleries, little birds were let loose, friends embraced and greeted one another, and we looked down upon a tumultuous sea of faces, all floating in a sunlit haze. And yet, I thought, the whole of this sublime transformation consisted in letting in the light of day! These priests and attendants, each stationed at his post, had only removed the darkness they themselves had made. Unveil these darkened windows, but remove also these darkening walls; the temple itself is but a lingering shadow of that gloom. Instead of its stifling incense, give us God's pure air, and teach us that the broadest religion is the best.

5

PUBLIC AND PRIVATE VIRTUES

When the civil war broke out, Governor John A. Andrew found himself suddenly called upon to organize a large number of regiments of soldiers and to select for each regiment thirty-seven commissioned officers. This last was a very serious undertaking, for a man who was utterly inexperienced in that sort of selection, and who was himself a civilian of civilians. He told me more than once that he found great guidance in a saying of Emerson's that everything should do after its own kind, whether it be a milch-cow or a rattle-snake. As he interpreted this, he must select his officers solely with a view to their probable military efficiency. A man might be a good son or brother, and yet not have the qualities for an officer; and on the other hand a man might have shown serious faults in civil life and yet have the making of a first-class soldier. Upon this system Governor Andrew endeavored to act, and, though he was an impulsive man and not always consistent, he made exceedingly good selections, on the whole.

The principle he recognized was one which we all recognize in emergencies. If a shipwrecked mother, like Margaret Fuller Ossoli, had to entrust her child to a sailor, she would choose that man whom she believed to be bravest and most faithful for that particular duty; and if she was told that that same man, when on shore, was vicious and profligate, it would make no difference. What she needed of him, at sea, would be the virtues of a sailor, and if the same man had the vices of a sailor also—as, in the inconsistency of human nature, is perfectly supposable—this would not deter her. But put her on shore and let her be

375

selecting a teacher or guardian for that child, the case would be very different. The sailor-virtues of courage and self-devotion would not then be what she most needed; but another class of virtues would come uppermost. Of course, it would be very desirable to combine all these virtues in every person, but since this is sometimes impossible, we often have to choose between two different types of character, each defective. This selection has to be determined, mainly, by the particular service we need. We must consider what it is that we chiefly want of a man; and whether he has the qualities we need for that particular place; whether the place be that of the head of an army or of a Sunday school.

Now I am perfectly willing to admit that the Presidency of the United States is a position which demands both the public and private virtues. The occupant of the White House should set a good example to the whole nation, by his personal habits; and this not merely through the pressure of public opinion but as a matter of principle. The chances are that he will do this, simply from the glare of publicity in which he lives; but he should do it from inclination. It is even desirable if possible that he should never have sinned in his life, never tasted whiskey, never had an unchaste thought, never sworn an oath. But after all, when it comes to being the ruler of a great nation, these virtues, however important, are secondary, not primary. To be absolutely honest in public office; to have the courage to act as one thinks right; these are the primary virtues. These are the virtues on which nations rest; it is upon these that our republic is founded. It exists because Franklin and Hamilton and Jefferson, whatever their private delinquencies, were impregnable in public virtue. To come to our own day, the fact that Abraham Lincoln told indecent stories with the relish of a frontier lawyer did not prevent him from being the pilot for our storm.

I am not undervaluing any class of virtues, only showing that when we have to choose, there is a gradation, according to the duty to be done. To have been once self-convicted of endeavoring to employ high office for personal ends is in my opinion incompatible with public employment thenceforward. To have once fallen before what may be, under some circumstances, one of the strongest of human temptations, does not necessarily so disqualify a man. This in reference to the presidential office. Were the question in regard to the superintendency of a girls' school, my reasoning would be just the other way. There the question of chastity would rank first and all else would be secondary. But the one thing now needful in the presidential chair is a man who will have the courage to be absolutely honest and to break up the spoils system. If the unchaste men can manifest the public virtue to do this, and the chaste men cannot, it would seem a very crushing argument against chastity. I do not accept the alternative, any more than I believe Grover Cleveland to be habitually unchaste. But to this subject I shall recur again.

6

"TELL THE TRUTH"

The readers of the WOMAN'S JOURNAL will testify that, while I am well known to take an interest in the coming Presidential election, I have carefully avoided all allusion to it in my editorial articles. All the leading candidates being understood to favor Woman Suffrage, I have seen no reason for making the election an issue in these columns. Some friends of Woman Suffrage will naturally incline to the Republican candidate, others to the Democratic; some will be Independents and others will see nothing in such a movement but hatred and ill-temper. In other words, women and reformers will show a great deal of human nature, in the usual variety; and, whatever they say, somebody who writes mild platitudes over the signature "A Woman" in the *Daily Advertiser* will be quite horrified and say "There! I told you so." So I see no object in entering on the Presidential question, in this place. But as the charges against one particular candidate have already occupied much space in the WOMAN'S JOURNAL, I must, for the sake of justice, have something to say about these.

It does not need much experience of human life to prove that the most damaging of all charges to make, against man or woman, are those in respect to the virtue of chastity. This proceeds not only from the seriousness of the matter, but from the fact that such charges, once made, are sure to be remembered and are almost impossible to disprove. Even legal investigation—as has been shown in very conspicuous cases—is powerless, and however prolonged, is apt to leave the matter just where it was before. Again there is no charge so capable of exaggeration. Let a man or woman once swerve from virtue, and no life of stainless propriety thenceforward can convince the harsh critic that all is well. In one respect this is creditable to the community, for it shows the high value placed on this virtue. In another respect it is discreditable, for it shows a love of gossip, and of prurient gossip. In the late statements about Governor Cleveland there is mingled a worse element than these; the element of political antagonism. Does any one suppose that the Boston *Journal* would have sent a special reporter to interview people in Maine in regard to the personal offences of the Republican nominee? Does any one attribute a lofty moral purpose to the editor of the obscure little sheet in Buffalo that has suddenly leaped into national fame as the savior of the Republican party? Of course truth is truth, from whatever source it comes, but calm and judicial truth, in a difficult question of private action, rarely comes from the heat of politics. Political debate can deal, though imperfectly, with public acts, because these are matters of public record, accessible to all. But facts of private life, whose evidence lies mainly in rumor and gossip, are rarely to be found justly or even decently handled by political editors or committees.

Mr. Cleveland is, in the opinion of many reformers, including myself, a man of such admirable public career as to leave no comparison in this respect between him and his leading rival. Were men to be supported in public life for public services alone—as was the case in what we call "the better days of the republic"—the case would be clear. Franklin, Jefferson, Hamilton were thus supported, in spite of just censure on the very point now concerned; Washington himself did not escape aspersion, which history has not sustained. But I am ready to admit that in this respect times have changed for the better. A man habitually and openly profligate could not, now, probably, be elected to high office. To carry the claim farther and say that any man who has once in his life, even in early youth, sinned against chastity, should be forever after excluded from public service, would be urging the scruple, in my opinion, much too far. It this view is correct, the question in regard to Mr. Cleveland is greatly simplified. All the mass of indecent trash that is now being circulated by political committees really bears upon a single transaction—enormously exaggerated, as far as I can find out, but still highly culpable—which took place some fifteen years ago, when he was thirty-three years old. Deeply as I deplore that transaction, I must distinctly decline to abandon, for that reason only, a candidate whose public record is so admirable. It must be proved to my satisfaction, not merely that he committed one such culpable act at that time, but that he habitually commits such acts to-day. Of this, I am bound to say, I have not yet seen one ray of positive evidence. Against it there stands the manly telegraphic message sent by him to his friend, in respect to these charges, "Tell the truth"; an answer which will be quoted and remembered, if I mistake not, when falsehoods and exaggerations are forgotten

No evidence has been brought forward,—and it is a wonder that some alleged proof, real or fictions, has not been forthcoming—to show that Governor Cleveland's present habits are anything but correct, in private as in public. There are clergymen in Buffalo who think ill of him, and others who are as strongly in his favor. Experience teaches that even clergymen are not infallible. I know some very worthy men in that profession who regard every one who drinks lager beer as a drunkard; and who are unable to conceive of a single lapse from virtue as not staining a person forever. But there lies before me a private letter from a Buffalo clergyman, who says to me, after quoting the opinions of men of high character, "My own personal acquaintance with Mr. Cleveland confirms the statements above made, and I am sure that the sin of his early manhood is the only one, and that his professional and private life since has been and is correct. His fellow-citizens in Buffalo so estimate him, for he is honored and respected by all classes." Who shall decide when Doctors—of Divinity—disagree? Legal investigation is impossible, and would, as experience has shown, be worthless if applied. Public character is a thing of which all can judge, and which is often judged more correctly at a distance than near home. But the test of private character is in the concurrence of opinion among a man's own neighbors—the unconscious verdict of the community where he dwells. What that verdict is in regard to Grover Cleveland, the citizens of Buffalo, without regard to party, have shown.

MORE MINGLED RACES

When we see in New York city a group of stolid Russian Jews just landed, or notice a newly arrived party of gayly attired Italian women who are being conducted behind a shed by their friends that they may exchange their picturesque attire for second-hand American gowns, we are apt to be thankful that we are not such as they. Or when we hear of an arrival of Finnish stone-cutters at Gloucester, Massachusetts, or of Armenian iron-workers at Worcester, we reflect that the landing of the Pilgrims of 1620 was not just like theirs. But, after all, the Pilgrims landed; that is the essential point. They were not the indigenous race. They were poor; they were sometimes ignorant; some of their women could only make their mark instead of signing their names. At the best it is not very long since they landed, for what is two or three centuries in the history of the human race? Tried by the standard of ancient races, we are all new-comers together; we are still pilgrims and sojourners, as our fathers were. Those of us who are of English blood represent a race so mingled and combined, so swept over by successive invasions and conquests, that it can claim no purity of strain, but only the strength of composite structure. Trace back the origin of the Dutch or the French Huguenot element, and it is much the same. The French Canadians who are now pouring in upon us, or the Jews from whatever quarter, have probably a less mingled descent than most of those who deprecate their arrival. If this be the standard, it is for them to criticise us, not for us to criticise them.

Whatever may be the right policy as to restricting immigration, it is always to be remembered that it is immigration, not natural increase, which has made the material greatness of this country. It is not the seventy persons residing in Chicago in 1830 who were the progenitors of the two million claimed by that city to-day. In a remarkable book, called *The New Rome, or the United States of the World,* published in New York fifty years ago, the authors, both Germans, described the mission of the United States to be "the fusion of all nations—not of this continent alone, but of all continents—into one people." But as there can proverbially be no omelet without the breaking of eggs, so there can be no fusing of all nations except by bringing the nations here to be fused. If the patricians of those races will not come—and why should they, since they have more exclusive privileges at home?—we must accept the plebeians, in the knowledge that they may provide us with patricians in their grandchildren a century hence. Inasmuch as the ancestors of most of our present patricians were plebeians, why not? At any given moment the "society" of any American city or town looks like something fixed and permanent; people talk of "getting into it," as if it were a definite enclosure; but in reality it is about as fixed and definite as the waves of the sea. Any social upheaval sweeps through it as a heavy sea sweeps through the carefully laid seines and stake-nets of the fishermen along our coasts, sending into the nets a great deal which the fishermen never expected to find there. Of all nations this is the last where we can regard newcomers as anything but American in the making—a new supply of eggs, fresh or stale, to be broken for our omelet.

No test, no classification, can do very much to limit this supply. We have already laws to sift out criminals and paupers. But the most dangerous criminals are those who are not yet publicly known as such; and the most perilous paupers are those who arrive with no money of their own, but with some that has been plundered from other people. Moreover, those who are appalled by the aspect of the latest arrivals are apt to forget the looks of some that preceded them. Those early squalid crowds have simply vanished in their descendants. Who that sees the vast and well-dressed congregations that come and go to our Roman Catholic churches can recall the advance-guard of the Irish immigration as it came among us sixty years ago—"poor Paddy, whose country is his wheelbarrow," as Emerson says, whose first act on arrival was to dig himself an earthen shanty, and live in it? Who that sees the equally prosperous French Canadian congregations pouring out of the great Roman Catholic churches of Fall River, Massachusetts, or Woonsocket, Rhode Island, can recall the Canadian families that used to cross the frontier forty or fifty years ago—a man, a woman, twelve children, and a large bundle? Each of those early migrations was a step in progress; as De Tocqueville pointed out in his day, a log hut in America was not a home, but a halting-place on the way to something better. Each type of new arrivals brought qualities of its own; the French Canadian was less energetic than the Irish, but less turbulent; the Irish more original and aggressive, but less temperate. All our Civil War scarcely brought to light such a phenomenon as an Irish coward; but when it came to the statistics of the guard-house the report was less favorable.

We err in assuming that any one race monopolizes all the virtues, or that the community only suffers with each new importation. The late Rev. Horatio Wood, who was for more than half a century city missionary at Lowell, and who watched the whole change from American to Irish factory girls, told me that in one respect it brought a distinct moral improvement: the ignorant Irish girls were more uniformly chaste than the Protestant farmers' daughters whom they superseded. Now the French Canadians have replaced the Irish; but a Protestant physician of great experience, whose practice included several large manufacturing villages, almost wholly French, told me that he had never known an illegitimate birth to occur there. At the old "North End" of Boston, where Irish superseded Americans, and have now given place to Italians and Russian Jews, a city missionary has testified to a moral improvement from the change; the Italians, though quarrelsome, are temperate, and he says that he never saw a Jew intoxicated. No doubt the prisons show a larger proportion of foreigners than of natives, because the foreigners represent the poorer class and the less befriended class. But the eminent scoundrels, who are rich and shrewd enough to keep out of prison, are rarely foreigners; they are more often the native product, and use the others as their tools; one such successful swindler doing more real harm in the community than twenty men convicted of drunkenness or petty larceny. Even as to crimes of violence, it is not among the vehement Italians that lynchings occur, but in those portions of the Union least touched by foreign immigration. Let us make laws, then, to regulate those landing on our shores; but let us not forget that the ancestors of our lawmakers also landed here.

8

EDWARD BELLAMY'S
NATIONALISM

GROWTH OF MONOPOLIES AND TRUSTS

It is now ascertained, Mr. Chairman, and ladies, and gentlemen, that two thousand capitalists own more than all the rest of the 65,000,000 of our population. Two hundred and fifty thousand rich men control seventy-five per cent of the national wealth. The American republic, therefore, is practically owned by less than a quarter of a million persons. If present causes which bring about a concentration of capital keep up their operation, the republic will soon be owned by less than fifty thousand men.

Lazarus and Dives in America have no hereditary positions. We have no hereditary wealthy class, and therefore the concentration of capital is not with us as great a peril as it would be if connected with an aristocratic organization of society. Two thousand men own more than all the rest of us, but this does not mean that they own *us*. [Laughter and applause.] Some of the rest of us may yet have places among the two thousand, and we all have votes. The wealthy in America are not a close corporation, class, clan, or clique. Andrew Carnegie says that between poverty, up the curve of the wheel of fortune, past the summit and back to poverty again, only about three generations, or at most five, usually intervene. His vivid phrase is that not more than five generations lie between shirt sleeves and shirt sleeves again in the roll of the wheel. Millionaires multiply in Congress and out of it, but their sons, or their grandsons, very rarely occupy their fathers' places. You are a rich man; what care you for a poor man? Your sons may be poor. You are a poor man; what care you for a rich man? Your sons may be rich. Therefore I maintain that in America the cause of the poor man is every man's cause [Applause]; and that for the same reason the cause of the rich man is every man's cause also. [Laughter and applause.]

It is said, however, that capitalists, although not as yet closely banded together, are rapidly forming syndicates and are really becoming a class, or clique. Giant monopolies, colossal trusts, begin to have power to control government, and to tax people indirectly without their consent. It must be admitted that the possible growth of trusts is a menace to republican institutions. Our great staples, oil, sugar, coal, iron, cotton, are all very likely soon to be largely controlled by combinations of capitalists. More than one great trust already has power to crack the domes of legislative halls like egg-shells. It may become necessary to curb trusts by national power. It may ultimately be thought best to take certain great staples out of the hands of trusts and syndicates and monopolies and put them under national control.

The moment we begin to think of doing this, however, we find ourselves standing on uncertain ground, for the question arises, How far under national control of great industries we can keep the workshop out of polities? Shall we not open the way to prodigious political corruption if, besides political parties, we have political land, political coal, political cotton, political sugar, political oil? Will this make the wheels of government and of society run more easily? The political grab-bag is now as wide as the continent; will it be safe to make it wider and deeper?

The rich, it is said, are growing richer, and the poor, poorer. But I suppose the fact carefully stated is that wages in the recent history of both America and England have risen in purchasing power faster than capital has increased its average gains. So Mr. Gladstone and Mr. Blaine both affirm. It is fifteen years since I began to discuss this subject, and the conclusion to which I have come after looking at many sides of it is, that as a rule the rich are growing richer, but that the poor are the better for this on the whole and on the average. The rich slowly, but the poor less slowly, improve their condition. As capital increases, the capitalist has a smaller, and the laborer a larger, proportional share of the product. I believe this to be the truth ascertainable by the broadest induction from the statistics of Germany, England, and the United States. Cary and Bastiat affirm this; so do Atkinson and the Hon. Carroll D. Wright.

The poor grow more intelligent. Their wants, therefore, increase; and the poor have ballots. There is a giant significance in the question, Is nationalism or socialism a necessary or probable result of the growth of intelligence among the masses who have votes? What relations will the twentieth century establish between capital and far more fully educated labor than now exists? Shall society be Christian or canine, human or wolfish? Shall the organizing principle of business be coöperation or competition? Or, to put the whole question in the words of the Nationalists, Shall industry be placed under public control for the public advantage, or under corporate control for corporate advantage?

No doubt this question is a burning one, liable to excite passion among the masses, and capable of causing great mischief in certain directions, but that mischief can be put down in this country only by fair, open, Christian discussion. For one, I wish, with all courtesy to the Nationalists, to recognize the importance of this question, its timeliness, and the necessity of some answer to it. It is time that all that anybody knows on this subject everybody should know. If you dam up the stream of labor reform, you prepare an era when it will burst forth with havoc. Are we not wise enough to answer this question in America for Americans, and here at the close of the nineteenth century for the opening of the twentieth?

Mr. Bellamy's answer to this question has been given to the world in a novel which has attained an almost unprecedented circulation at home and abroad. Since "Uncle Tom's Cabin" was published, no novel on reform has had as wide a reading. My attention was first called to this book by Mr. Moody, with whom for the moment I was laboring in Chicago. He said to me at a dinner-table in the Grand Pacific Hotel, "I have had thrust into my hands lately, a book entitled 'Looking Backward.' The workingmen say I must read it; they affirm that that is what is coming. You cannot reach them unless you know what is in that book. I haven't read it," said he, "but you must." [Laughter.] So when I went up to my summer residence at Lake George I read that book as I rolled over the Green Mountains, and I confess that I have since read the whole of it the second time.

Mr. Bellamy is descended from a ministerial family of great eminence. Among his ancestors was Joseph Bellamy, one of the most eloquent preachers of the early days of New England. He was a worthy coadjutor of Jonathan Edwards. He was also a preceptor of Aaron Burr. Edward Bellamy's father was a preacher. Our author and reformer was born at Chicopee Falls, in one of the busiest factory centres of Massachusetts, in 1850. After a partial course at Union College, he spent a year in Germany. He became a member of the Hampden County Bar, but developed a taste for journalism, and was connected for a time with the "New York Evening Post." Since 1876 he has devoted himself to literature. (See the "New England Magazine" for September, 1889.) Edward Bellamy is a man of literary genius, as his book shows. And if I criticise somewhat pointedly certain details of his plan of reform, this will by no means be considered as indicating anything but high personal regard for him, and for the distinguished scholars who have more or less directly indorsed his scheme.

DEFECTS OF MR. BELLAMY'S SCHEME OF NATIONALISM.

What is to be said of Edward Bellamy's nationalism, taken as a whole?

1. Mr. Bellamy's plan, as exhibited in his novel, is very complicated, very revolutionary, very optimistic, very self-contradictory, and, as I think, very visionary [laughter]; but
2. It has in it elements that are very Christian [applause]; but
3. The Christianity is in the voluntary coöperation, and not in the compulsory nationalism. [Applause.]

Where, then, does the line of cleavage lie between the sense and non-sense of this book? Between voluntary progressive, general coöperation, combined with competition, all this on the one side, and compulsory, universal, almost immediate nationalism, with total abolition of competition, all this on the other side. Mr. Bellamy hopes that his plans can all be carried out within fifty years.

I venture to think that most of the scholars, men of letters, and re-formers, who have dignified Mr. Bellamy's scheme by their approval, are really coöperationists and not nationalists. I call myself, I have always called myself, a progressive coöperationist. I am not a nationalist in the strict meaning of that word, but I do wish to see the sphere of coöpera-tion gradually, and, if necessary, rapidly broadened. I am not a national-ist because I do not believe in the schemes which reduce labor reform to a single wheel. In my opinion the driving wheels of labor reform ought to be four,—self-help, state help, school help, church help. [Applause.] But Nationalism, instead of this locomotive with four driving wheels, re-duces labor reform to a wheel-barrow with one wheel, Nationalism [laughter], and it is an exceedingly difficult vehicle to manage. [Laugh-ter and applause.]

Mrs. Hunt tells us that twenty-seven States of the American Union, besides all the schools under the control of the national government, are now under laws making scientific temperance education compul-sory. Great publishing houses, like Appleton & Co., Ivison, Blakeman &

Co., Van Antwerp & Co., compete with each other in furnishing graded text-books for these schools. All these text-books, as I happen to know, and as one or two gentlemen on this platform know very well from prolonged attention to them, inculcate total abstinence from alcoholics and all other narcotics, including tobacco. A teacher should bring his example up to the level of his precept. His precept now must be brought up to the level of total abstinence. If, therefore, a school-teacher should not set a bad example, then for stronger reasons a minister should not. [Applause.] According to Mr. Bellamy's book, society in the year 2000 has not learned what is now taught in the name of science. Even in the twentieth century ladies have to leave dining-rooms in order that gentlemen may fill the apartments with smudge. [Laughter.] I am deliberate in thus criticising one or two evils in Mr. Bellamy's social code. I suppose he is deliberate, also, in calling the evils merits. He says that in the society of the year 2000 the people will not permit government to tell them what they shall eat, wear, or drink, and so I suppose saloons are to be nationalized. That will make this wheelbarrow a very dizzy affair. [Laughter.] This is an integral part of the scheme of Mr. Bellamy's book.

Nationalism, as outlined in Mr. Bellamy's novel, is a statue, with feet of clay and limbs of iron, and forehead of brass, and crutches of splintered reeds—I mean by the crutches, the political parties that are to rule under his scheme—and with a cigar in its lips and a wine-cup in its right hand. Is this the angel that is to lead us into the millennium? I think not. [Applause and laughter.] But because the figure has a golden heart and philanthropic motives, I mean to speak of it with adequate respect. [Laughter.]

The brotherhood of men is a great idea, a divine reality, but only in divine fellowship can human fellowship be consummated. The priesthood of the people must mean the priesthood of believers, otherwise theocracy will never be consistent with democracy. There are two rules in the Bible, the Golden Rule and the iron rule—do as you would be done by; and if any man will not work, neither shall he eat. The angel who is to bring in the millennium will come through a door of which the sides are those two rules. Mr. Bellamy does not seem to me to be as severe as the Scriptures are upon the drones. He is severe to a certain extent, for he feeds them on bread and water and cuts them off from human society, but he has almost no criminal class and makes provision for almost none.

What are some of the special defects in Mr. Bellamy's scheme of Nationalism?

1. It changes republican into class government. It concentrates national power of colossal extent in the hands of probably less than half of what is now the voting population.

Everybody, according to the scheme of Nationalism, has to go to school until twenty-one, then everybody has to be a member of the industrial army till the age of forty-five, and nobody is to vote until he is graduated from the industrial army. The graduates of that army are to manage the nation. I think this concentration of power in the hands of men over forty-five years of age—or of men and women, for I believe female suffrage prevails; and, therefore, I suppose there is involved in the scheme a cure for the cigar and the wine-cup—this limitation of political power to a fraction of the people appears to me to be contrary to the trend of modern political reform. Most Americans would call this practically an aristocracy. My first count against Nationalism is, not that it limits universal suffrage, for I would be glad to limit it by the reading and writing test, but that it limits it savagely, with a broad slash into approved ideas as to freedom. It institutes government by a class less in numbers than a majority of the mature part of the people. We believe, most of us, I suppose, that if a man can read and write he ought to have a voice at the ballot-box after he is twenty-one. But, according to Mr. Bellamy's scheme, you cannot vote, any of you, till you are forty-five, and by that time many of you will have lost interest in politics. [Laughter.]

2. It is a defect of Mr. Bellamy's scheme that it opens the way to prodigious political corruption.

The more we concentrate the management of industry in the hands of a class, the wider and deeper we make the grab-bag for national parties. The wider and deeper the grab-bag the greater will be the dangers from partisan greed and fraud. The remedy for the concentration of wealth in the hands of capitalists is not its concentration in the hands of political parties, and especially not in the hands of parties made up exclusively of citizens over forty-five years of age.

3. Nationalism can be reached only by processes that are at once untried and revolutionary.

The parallel which Mr. Bellamy draws between the operations of trusts and the operations of the national government proposed under his scheme has in it much obscurity.

It is difficult to understand how we are to make the transition from trusts which are governed by unadulterated selfishness, to Mr. Bellamy's scheme, which cannot work unless governed by unadulterated unselfishness. What is a trust? It is a combination of capitalists. Its leaders come together in a parlor in New York, and, as General Walker has told us in the "Atlantic Monthly," they agree that they will raise the prices of certain staples they have to sell; they will not compete with each other, but, in order to divide profits, they agree upon a certain price. They tax sixty millions of us much as they please. This means the crushing of competition outside the ring, and millions of gain inside it. They have the whole public to plunder; they have their inner ring to enrich. Now, in Mr. Bellamy's scheme of Nationalism there is no inner ring to enrich, and there is no people to plunder. How, therefore, can there be a close parallel between trusts and the scheme of Nationalism? How can the former develop into the latter? I do not see how the transition is to be made from our present arrangements to the scheme of Nationalism along the line of the operations of trusts, because the cases are by no means parallel. There is no inner ring left in the nation, after Mr. Bellamy's scheme is put on foot. The conditions under which a trust enriches itself no longer exist; and so the motives which give vigor to a trust are lacking.

4.   It is not made clear by his book how Mr. Bellamy's theory provides for the purchase of property now in private hands.

There is to be no property of a private sort, or almost none, except individual belongings, under Mr. Bellamy's scheme. The land is to be nationalized. How is it to be obtained? Is private property to be confiscated? Are you to abolish inheritance? Is the scheme to be purchase or spoliation? This question always arises when nationalistic schemes are brought forward, and I do not find a clear answer to it in the book, or even in the speeches of its distinguished author. When private property is to become public property, are the private owners to be compensated? Are the minority to be forced to accept the will of the majority in this matter? Are we to subject everybody to compulsory Nationalism? These are all fair questions and very old ones, for the topic is not new. The objection to most of these schemes is that they mean the abolition of the right of inheritance, or the abolition of the right of private property. They mean spoliation, forced loans, forced sales. Where is the money to come from to pay private owners? Money is to be abolished, and men are to live on credit cards. The scheme is said to be simple. In the field that I am now traversing, the scheme appears to me to be dangerously complex.

5. The scheme cuts the nerve of personal ownership and destroys individual initiative in industry. It does not provide motives sufficient to induce men to work without votes in the manner proposed. The driving-wheels of the whole plan are simply pap and prizes.

All men are paid alike. One of the grand ideas in this book is that all that do their best do the same. Of course that epigram needs a little qualification. If it is to be stated in plain prose you must make a distinction, as General Walker suggests, between moral merit and economic merit. The moral merit of all people who do their best is the same; the economic merit is not. Mr. Bellamy says if a horse and a goat draw loads of different weight, their merit is the same; each does his best. Yes, the moral merit is the same, if you can speak of it in connection with a brute, but the economic merit is not the same, and the proof is that the horse sells for more than the goat. When skilled and swift laborers are paid only as much as unskilled and slow laborers, except that the former have more honor and better chances of promotion, how are you to prove that the skilled laborers will keep up their enthusiasm? There is to be no appeal to the love of gain. If the shiftless are to be paid as much as the industrious, if all are guaranteed an ample sustenance, provided they perform a certain small amount of labor, how do you know that the industrious will keep up their activity, and how can you be sure that it may not ultimately be worse even with the shiftless than it was before?

6. Nationalism attempts to reform men chiefly by mere political machinery, not by moral and industrial motives.

Where are the motives to come from that will drive this engine of Nationalism with a speed sufficient to support the physical wants of the people? Very true, there is a saving by massing your industries; the larger the establishment, the less, other things being equal, is the cost of running it, in proportion to what it turns out. That is a fixed law of manufactures, and Mr. Bellamy shows with great clearness how much saving at certain points would be effected by his plan. But I am not yet convinced that, when all expenses are taken into view, men between twenty-one and forty-five can produce enough, even under the nationalistic scheme, to feed us all. Skilled workingmen would be somewhat influenced by badges and ribbons, but where have we any example in history of average populations being held to courses of laborious toil through all the middle portion of their life by no other motive than the love of promotion, honor among their fellows, badges, governmental prizes, without the spur of hunger, or the incitement of personal ownership? You say that in the army there is such a case. Yes, but that is where life and death are plainly at stake; that is where national existence may be at stake; that is where men work, not under the lash merely, but at the point of the bayonet. Retreat, and you will be shot by your own sergeant. There are quite other motives than those of badges and prizes and promotions at work on the battlefield, as old soldiers here know. The parallel between the industrial army and a military organization is very loose at a multitude of points, but Mr. Bellamy seems to have been carried away with the parallel.

7. The scheme does not provide for early development of special tastes, and so represses individual genius.

Suppose a man has a divine call to be an author; he is a member of this industrial army. He may publish a book at his own expense, and if the book succeeds he may use the funds flowing from it to purchase exemption from his duties in the army, and at thirty-five such a man may begin a career as an author. That is ten years too late at least. Mr. Bellamy says that the real, serious, important, alluring business of life does not begin until after one is forty-five. Well, in most cases a man is beyond the most powerful youthful enthusiasms at that age. He may be matured, and if he has had a long training before in his chosen profession he may then be worth more than he was in his department, and may be worth that for twenty years, but if he is not to engage in special work in his adopted profession until after he is forty-five, how can he be expected to become a specialist or an expert in it before the time when he will be superannuated by the advance of years? I think this is one of the worst things in Mr. Bellamy's scheme of Nationalism, that in most cases he holds back men from their special pursuits, whatever tastes and endowments they have for them, until they are forty-five years of age.

8. This scheme makes itself responsible for the maintenance not only of all the present generation, but also of all that they may choose to bring into the world.

John Stuart Mill has said that the human family ought to support itself; we are all brethren, and so long as there is a loaf left it should be divided. Very true. But John Stuart Mill himself says that humanity is not responsible for all that humanity may choose to bring into the world. We now afford sustenance to the poorest of the poor, even though they cannot labor. Germany insists upon a scheme of compulsory insurance which provides for a pension for workingmen after they have attained a certain age. We already have governmental provision for cases of extreme need. But to make sustenance for all of us precisely alike, and guarantee it not only for those who are now on the stage, but for all who may come after, is a guarantee that seems to me to be a premium on shiftlessness.[1]

9. The scheme makes no adequate provision for eliminating drones and the criminal class from the industrial army.
10. It forgets, or makes far too little, of the necessity of personal regeneration to social regeneration.
11. It fails to remember that other ways exist of throttling dangerous trusts than by national control of all industry.
12. It encourages Socialism and Communism by exaggerating the infelicities of the working class and stimulating the hopes of the shiftless and the unscrupulous.
13. Nationalism does not remember with sufficient distinctness that a nationalized branch of industry may succeed only because other branches are not nationalized.

Our army, navy, and post office are now conducted by the nation. Germany puts her railroads under national control. I am not sure but that

---

[1]In the *North American Review* for February, Mr. Bellamy makes this candid admission: "The nationalist plan is even so elastic that it will permit a man to loaf the rest of his life after a very brief service, if he shall consent to accept a quarter or half the rate of support of other citizens" (p. 357). "Some have said that Nationalism requires a change in human nature; but men on becoming soldiers do not become better men, do not experience a change of heart. They are merely placed under the influence of different incentives. Make industry a public service as war now is and you will win for work the inspiration of war."

But how can work thrive when men at forty-five may cease to be industrial soldiers and become permanent loafers on half-pay?

"Confiscation," Mr. Bellamy says (p. 362), "is not a method of Nationalism." He proposes not only free schools and compulsory education, but that the poorest of the poor shall be paid for sending their children to school.

we shall ultimately do so. If the railroads should come into the possession of a syndicate or a trust, I should be in favor of putting them under
governmental control. [Applause.] I am not averse to Mr. Bellamy's suggestion that we should put the telegraph into the hands of the postal authorities and let it be governed from Washington. But I would experiment very cautiously in this direction, for political corruption might be
increased after all our effort to keep these things out of politics. But your
army, your post-office, your navy, or anything else you have nationalized
thus far would not be a success if you had not the principle of competition at work side by side with it to stimulate individual effort in the ac-
quisition of wealth.

REMEDIES FOR INDUSTRIAL PERILS.

What, then, are the remedies that we are to offer for the industrial perils
of our time?

1. Let coöperation be brought into action on a wide scale among
   workingmen.
2. Let profit-sharing between employers and employed be tried.
   [Applause.] Very loud voices of experience now call us to this
   field of labor reform.
3. Let there be governmental restraint of trusts and monopolies
   within the bounds of their charters. [Applause.]
4. Let cautious enlargement of national control of a few great staples and industries be undertaken, whenever the aggressions of
   trusts make such control necessary.
5. Let labor bureaus, state and national, have an extension of their
   present advisory powers. Pour out into the lap of your government the funds needed to support these bureaus, which have
   done as much as any other one cause in recent years to create a
   sound public sentiment concerning labor reform.
6. Experiment slowly, cautiously, along the line followed by Germany, that is, in the direction of state ownership of railroads
   and telegraphs, compulsory insurance for workingmen, and
   state aid to the poorest of the poor.
7. Insist first on compulsory education, and afterwards on the
   reading test for the suffrage, on ballot reform and on compulsory voting, such as prevails in some of the Swiss cantons and

such as even David Dudley Field, with all his legal learning and caution, now advocates.

8. Make the liquor traffic an outlaw by both state and national constitutional enactments.

9. Let there be a glorious American church, enlightened, aggressive, omnipresent, in order that there may be a glorious American republic, united, progressive, incorruptible.

10. And above all seek a combination of competition and coöperation, a balanced scheme, self-help, state help, school help, church help,—the four wheels of your locomotive; and the Golden Rule and the iron rule, the two rails of the track on which it runs. [Applause.]

> Some day, by laws as fixed and fair
> As guide the planets in their sweep,
> The children of each outcast heir
> The harvest-fruits of time shall reap.
>
> The peasant brain shall yet be wise,
> The untamed purse grow calm and still;
> The blind shall see, the lowly rise,
> And work in peace Time's wondrous will.
>
> Some day, without a trumpet's call,
> This news will o'er the world be blown:
> "The heritage comes back to all!
> The myriad monarchs take their own!"

9

The Complaint of
the Poor

I t is impossible for a prosperous and comfortable person to understand the point of view of the dissatisfied—whether in the case of the
ordinary socialist or of Mr. Howells—without keeping in mind such
facts as the following, which the writer happens to know pretty directly:
A poor cobbler was troubled, as many men are, with an insatiable love of
mechanical invention; and this was finally concentrated on a mechanism
for "tying and binding" in connection with a "reaper." It was for a need
then very imperfectly filled, and promised great rewards if successful. He
worked at it for years, impoverishing his family for it, until his wife implored him to give it up altogether. Getting it at last, however, into final
shape, he carried it to one of the chief establishments which manufactured reapers, and offered it for inspection and sale. After a little examination it was rejected decisively as being too complicated; the inventor
went home in despair, put his model away under his bench, and
promised his wife to abstain from inventions thenceforward. A few
weeks or months passed, and a shabby man one day came to the door
asking to see it, and saying that he himself had invented a reaper, and it
might be worth while for them to join forces. Pulling out the rejected
model from under the bench, the inventor showed it, and finally sold it
for a small sum to the visitor. It turned out afterwards that the shabby
man was an employé of the great establishment which had nominally rejected the invention, and had taken this mean way to buy it for a song. It
has since proved immensely profitable. If taxed with the trick, those concerned would simply reply that business was business, and each man
must look out for himself.

This precise story may not be true, though it rests on good authority. That it might be true there is no question. It is the possibility of its being true which vitiates all theories of the dignity of wealth. If wealth were, as is sometimes asserted, simply the cumulative result of industry, patience, and honesty, it would not be hard to treat it with a certain reverence. Where one man has grown rich by economy, energy, and skill, and another has grown or remained poor by indolence or incapacity, there wealth seems to denote qualities that claim respect, and men do not grudge the deference shown to it. It is because men of any experience all know instances to the contrary, and have watched the many examples of tricks like that applied to this poor cobbler, that they denounce all wealth as a fraud upon the community. Sow a victim, and you reap a socialist.

Yet it is so difficult to resist the prestige of success, and so easy to believe the great man to be also good, that people are not, in the individual case, very critical. It is easy to convince one's self that gossip is malicious, that one does not know all the details. At any rate, in the next generation the facts grow wholly vague; they represent old scandal; they no more vitiate the inheritor of a fortune than the nobleman or noble lady of today, in England or Austria, is vitiated in reputation by the fact that the original dukedom or earldom may have been bought by the dishonor of an ancestor. But all this, or even the fact that the privileged position is well used, does not usually propitiate the mind of the socialist or even of the philosophic critic. His question is whether the money of the so-called benefactor is to be regarded as an actual gift or as an act of restitution—giving back to the community its rightful share hitherto withheld. If these benefactors were really public-spirited—thus the malcontents reason—they would not object to an income-tax, for instance, which would put the gift in a more unequivocal form. Probably there never was a time or place where more money was spent than is devoted here and now, by rich men, for the benefit of the community. The trouble is that the wealth increases in spite of it, and so does poverty. Moreover, the wealth does not get the credit of what it really does. Its occasional follies and extravagances and titled marriages are before all men's eyes; its acts of benevolence are less advertised, and not so interesting for purposes of gossip. Many men of profuse generosity are really simple and retiring in personal habits, but these are usually ignored. The only American millionaire whom one finds habitually reverenced in the more radical newspapers is Peter Cooper, and this not so much for the money he spent as for the way he spent it; and, in part, from his greenback and other theories.

It is impossible not to recognize that much of the distrust of wealth on the part of the poor has come from the mere increase of the figures employed to describe it; that we count by millions instead of by thousands, and that the word multi-millionaire has become necessary. Greville records, fifty years ago, the registering of a will bequeathing the largest fortune ever known in England—over a million pounds, or five million dollars. Only that! It is a great step from this to the period when all the newspapers condoled with the daughters of a single American family for being limited by their father's will to ten million dollars apiece. There was such a general expression of sympathy that one expected to see a proposal to take up collections for them in Sunday-schools or by penny-in-a-slot boxes. Since then, moreover, the maximum figure of wealth has increased so rapidly that it haunts the imagination, especially of the poor. All the old theories, as that wealth would be limited, in this country, by the absence of primogeniture, or checked by cutting off the old sources of supply, such as the India trade—all these have vanished. Then the question recurs, for those who are poor and philosophers at the same time, what is the outcome to be? It is almost as difficult to reconcile the principles of republican society with the existence of billionaires as of dukes. Meanwhile, as to the question of outcome, the most courageous theorizers differ fundamentally. Henry George and Edward Bellamy agree as to the disease, but prescribe remedies almost absolutely opposite. It is perhaps fortunate that it is so, for it gives people time to open their eyes and to think.

The remaining three chapters in Part IV of this book constitute a subsection on the subject of the "Anti-imperialist."

10

WHERE LIBERTY IS *NOT*, THERE IS MY COUNTRY

When the great French Revolution broke out, Thomas Paine felt an immediate wish to take a hand in it. His book, "Common Sense," had probably done more than any other book to bring the American Revolution to a point, and his other publication, "The Crisis," to carry it safely through. He had retired with honor. Congress voted him $3,000 for his services, and the State of New York gave him five hundred acres of land, but he was not content to live on these comforts when he could help the cause of freedom elsewhere. When his friends urged him to stay at home, and quoted to him the Latin motto, "Where liberty is, there is my country" (*ubi libertas ibi patria*), he said that this was a motto for a coward. The true motto for a brave man was, he said, "Where liberty is *not*, there is my country"; and so he went to Paris and took a hand in the French Revolution. When he opposed the killing of the king, he was shut up in the Bastile, and only escaped the guillotine because, when the doors of those prisoners ordered to execution for the next day were marked with chalk, it happened that his door was open and was marked on the wrong side, being afterwards closed again, so that he escaped. Thus he followed up his motto, "Where liberty is *not*, there is my country."

For a century since his time the American nation has habitually acted on this motto and given its sympathy to the under side. Greece, Holland, Hungary, Italy, Ireland, Mexico, Cuba, the South American republics, have all called forth the national sympathy, because they were or seemed to be oppressed. No one has asked whether their heroes were all Washingtons and their generals all Grants. Probably they were not. No doubt the prominent insurgent leaders, Bozzaris, Kossuth, Garibaldi, called forth plenty of criticism. Bolivar was called more than once a braggart and a traitor, yet it was practically due to him that South America is now republican and not monarchial, and it is for this that his statue adorns American parks. So much for the leaders; and as for the people, there were always plenty who doubted, while the struggle lasted, whether the insurgents were worthy of freedom or could ever sustain a government of their own. Vincennes, the great French minister, who sent Rochambeau and his army to save us at Yorktown, always expected that the new American States would soon go to pieces. Sir George Trevelyan, in the best history of the American Revolution yet written, tells us that, when the war began, George III., his ministers, and his army agreed in the opinion that "no population was every composed of worse men or poorer creatures than the rebellious town of Boston. Probably there never was an insurrection, large or small, in which the party apparently stronger did not honestly believe the weaker party to be utterly incapable of self-government.

The flaw in the whole reasoning in such cases is in leaving out the principle of liberty. When a nation, or even a family, once enters on the project of managing the affairs of its neighbors, it is on the wrong track. It is as if a farmer assumed the right of confiscating the adjoining farm because he can raise better crops than its owner; or a shopkeeper should seize his neighbor's stock of goods on the ground that he can make more money out of it than the owner can.

There is such a thing as personal ownership; freedom is freedom; and it is not for a nation born and reared on this theory to ignore it in judging the affairs of others. What would become of the neighborhood if Mrs. Jones, who manages her family rather ill, should come home and find that Mrs. Smith, her neighbor, has carried off the baby, on the ground that she can do better by it, and has therefore a natural right to it? No doubt there are extreme cases where the law must interfere and do this, but it is too great a responsibility to intrust to Mrs. Jones herself. The whole early history of free states usually consists in rebellion against the interference of other states who think themselves wiser and stronger. But the men who are remembered in history the longest are sometimes those who raise their voices against such aggressions, even when their own government commits them. Probably the thing by which the great Lord Chatham will be longest remembered will be his exclamation in Parliament, on November 18, 1777, "If I were an American, as I am an

Englishman, while a foreign troop was landed in my country I would never lay down my arms—never, never, never!"

Twice in history has the North American republic won just gratitude from the human race when it might have forfeited it by a policy less advanced. To this day, to be sure, Mr. Cecil Rhodes, engaged in his career of empire-making, has never ceased to blame this nation for letting Mexico go, when she lay conquered in our hands—for taking down that flag which once waved in "the halls of the Montezumas,"' and contenting ourselves with a slice of territory when we might have plundered the whole. But the world has judged differently. More striking still is the case of Japan. There is in the public park at Newport, R. I., the statue of a naval hero whose greatness lay not merely in what he did, but in what he abstained from doing; so that, having for the first time opened Japan to modern civilization, Commodore Perry left it to work out its own destiny, and become one of the great free nations of the world. Can any one doubt that Mexico and Japan are now far higher in condition than if they had been reduced to subject or tributary states, as Clive and Hastings reduced British India? There is no proof that the Japanese are intrinsically superior to the Hindoos, but the one race was left free by the Americans, and the other subjugated by Englishmen. So there is no proof that the Filipinos are not, as Admiral Dewey said, as well fitted for freedom as the Cubans, or, one may add, as the Mexicans. This nation has never needed to vindicate its power of fighting. In two instances. Japan and Mexico, it has also proved its power of self-control. Can it be possible that we shall fail to exercise the same self-control in dealing with the Filipinos? If we succeed, if we trust the principle of liberty, we may see them stand where the Japanese stand: if we pursue the policy of conquest, they can never rise above the humbler condition of the Hindoos. There appears to be no human being for whom the British government has less use than for an educated Hindoo, unless he has a taste for the game of cricket.

11

How Should a
Colored Man Vote in 1900?

A few suggestions to the Colored People of the United States of America:

We, the undersigned, address you at one of the most important points in your history. If there ever was a war of races in this world, the war now going on in the Philippines is precisely that. Yet, if there is anything which the colored race in this country have to dread, and the white race also, it is just such a war. Every day in the Philippines is already training our young Caucasian soldiers to the habit of thinking that the white man, as such, is the rightful ruler of all other men.

This is seen, for instance, in the fact that these very soldiers, in writing home letters from the seat of war, describe the inhabitants of the Philippines more and more constantly as "niggers," thus giving a new lease of life to a word which was previously dying out among us.

Every defender of the war in Congress sustains the contest on the assumed ground that the Filippinos are unfit for freedom, although Admiral Dewey described them as more fit for it than the Cubans, and Senator Hoar describes them to be probably better fitted than any race in the two American Continents south of ourselves.

In other words, freedom is to become, for the new Republican Party, a matter of complexion. If this doctrine is to prevail, what hope is there for the colored race in the United States? The answer is clearly, there is, in that case, no hope at all. In the name of the old anti-slavery sentiment, we call on you to resist this great danger, even if you have for that purpose to turn your back on the party you once had reason to love.

This danger can evidently not be resisted by any further voting for the Republican Party. In other days that party freed the slaves and passed amendments to the United States Constitution for the protection of those who had been slaves. These amendments are now being steadily set aside, and the Republican Party shows no signs of raising a finger in their defense. There have been far more outrages on the American negro during one term of McKinley than under two terms of Cleveland. On the other hand, the South's Democrats are at least doing the colored man this service, that they, as a rule, oppose the national policy of imperialism.

This may be seen as incorrect, but it is really very simple. The very fact of their unwillingness to give equal political right to the American negro makes them unfit to undertake the government of 10,000,000 more belonging to the colored race. This much, at least, of their experience has taught this. Thus far, at any rate, they are on your side.

The undersigned, trained from youth in the strictest school of anti-slavery convictions, are following out the same early opinion when they now write to you. We wish to warn you that the imperialistic Republican Party of today is not the liberty-loving party of that name which set the American negro free forty years ago.

The time is past when you can safely give to them as heretofore your implicit support. We warn you that the American negro must henceforth think for himself and must cut adrift from any organization which wars on the dark races as such and begins to talk again of the natural supremacy of the Anglo-Saxon. We went through a four-year war to get rid of that doctrine and enlisted nearly 200,000 black soldiers for the purpose. It is too soon to see such a thing brought up again. It rests with you to make it impossible.

THOMAS WENTWORTH HIGGINSON
WILLIAM LLOYD GARRISON
GEORGE S. BOUTWELL

12

HIGGINSON ANSWERS CAPTAIN MAHAN

The subject of the address of Colonel Thomas Wentworth Higginson before the Twentieth Century Club last night was "Freedom," and its chief feature was a reply to the recent letter of Captain Mahan to the New York Independent. Colonel Higginson took as the text of his remarks the Declaration of Independence, and cited as an antithetic utterance the arguments advanced by Captain Mahan for imperial treatment of such peoples as those who have been resisting the American forces in the Philippine Islands. The captain had held that these people had not the right to administer uncontrolled the country they were occupying, such right in his view depending even in the future upon conditions of political fitness, and a fair probability of political propriety of action.

The speaker took up this view and showed some of the absurd results which would be reached if the Mahan, the imperial, the Napoleonic theory were applied generally. Colonel Higginson characterized Captain Mahan's idea as "the Naval Board of Prize Money Theory." "It disposes of every man's right to his own earnings and every mother's right to her own child. Not a farm in New England, not a set of carpenter tools, not a block of telephone stock could be held by its owner under this theory unless he used it with propriety.

"How superbly would President Eliot provide for Harvard should he take possession of all the property even of Cambridge people who were using it injudiciously. The result would be a final swallowing up of nations until only two English-speaking nations remained with the necessity of one swallowing the other." Illustrating further the idea Colonel

Higginson read from Rob Roy who said: "They should take who have the power and those should keep who can."

"We may assume the founders of our Government assumed that the right of the human being to self-government or to be governed by laws of their own making only, was not a thing requiring an elaborate course of argument, but it settled itself. If we go no further than that we come at once to the point made clear by so many successive writers on liberty and on principles of government from the larger point of view, that the essential difference between despotism and freedom in the working is that freedom is an educational force and despotism is not; so that while despotism may give you a thousand things better than the average free institutions give you, it leaves the people in no way advanced; things remain as they were, and the next despot may be, as a certain Czar of Russia once said, only a happy accident, and the whole thing may be reversed.

"The difference is that every point gained by freedom is gained forever. Every one who works for the carrying out of laws, then for the making of them works to make the whole community more intelligent and the whole law better. It is very easy—it used to be peculiarly easy in the time of Louis Napoleon, for instance—to point to the good effects of imperialism as exemplified by him. I remember that in his time, thirty years ago, I stayed in Paris for a time as the guest of an artist family, consisting of the father and mother and one daughter. The father, it appeared on investigation, was a Republican, the mother was a Bonapartist, a Legitimist, and the daughter was in favor of the empire. Why was she in favor of the empire? Because, as she maintained and justly demonstrated by approved facts, the streets of Paris were better kept under the empire than they had been before. It is a simple mode of solution, and you generalize easily from that, only you leave the people out. You leave all popular education out, all progress, all the knowledge that not only makes the streets better under one accident of imperialism, but makes them better for all coming time. And no one brought this so clearly before us, and lodged it—I had always supposed until lately—in the American mind as a Frenchman, De Tocqueville. De Tocqueville brought out the principle very simply and very strongly. He said:

"'It is incontestable that the people frequently conduct public business very ill; but it is impossible that the lower order should take a part in public business without extending the circle of their ideas and without quitting the ordinary routine of their mental acquirements; the humblest individual who is called upon to coöperate in the government of society acquires a certain degree of self-respect; and, as he possesses authority, he can command the services of minds much more enlightened than his own. He is canvassed by a multitude of applicants, who seek to deceive him in a thousand different ways, but who instruct him by their deceit. . . . Democracy does not confer the most skillful kind of government upon the people; but it produces that which the most skillful governments are frequently unable to awaken, namely, an all-pervading and restless activity, a superabundant force, and an energy which is inseparable from it, and which may, under favorable circumstances, beget the most amazing benefits. These are the true advantages of democracy.'

"In another place in his book he quotes some American who had pointed out to him the perfection of the business department of the French Government, the accurate way in which everything is done in every part of France, because it is all done from one centre, and the French minister of education boasts that in any given moment he has only to look at his watch to know with precision what every child in every school in France is doing at that moment. De Tocqueville knows all that, De Tocqueville recognizes all that, but he says, 'Side by side with all that there exists the greatest sluggishness and the greatest ignorance, because the people have nothing to do with their own Government.' And there is where De Tocqueville cleared up our average American mind on the question of self-government for years and years.

"I must do justice to many others, and to one in particular who has said the same thing most admirably. He was criticising several years ago—I will tell you his name presently, unless you can guess it for yourself—he was criticising Carlyle's idea of liberty, which was absolutely the Louis Napoleon idea. Carlyle had said: 'The true liberty of a man you would say consisted in his finding out, or being forced to find out, the right path and to walk therein; to learn, or to be taught, what work he is actually able to do, and then by permission, persuasion, or even compulsion, to be set about doing the same. Oh, if thou really art my senior, my elder, or priest,—if thou art in any way wiser—may a beneficent instinct lead and impel thee to conquer and command me! If thou do know better than I what is good and right, I conjure you, in the name of God, force me to do it; were it never by such brass collars, whips and handcuffs, leave me not to walk over precipices.'

"That was Carlyle. And this little book, published a few years ago, entitled 'Christianity and Social Problems,' gives this answer to Carlyle: 'No,' the author says, 'no, this is not liberty; it is servitude. Servitude may be better than walking over precipices; but it is not liberty. Liberty is ability to do as one pleases. Freedom is the exemption from the power and control of another: this is liberty. It assumes not that every man can safely govern himself, but first that it is safer to leave every man to govern himself than to put any man under the government of another man, or any class of men under the government of any other class; and, secondly, that there is such potentiality of self-governing power in every man, such capacity to learn by his blunders, that he will acquire a wisdom and a self-restraint through the very perils of self-government, which he will never acquire under the protecting government of others wiser and better than himself.'

"Do you recognise, any of you, the author of that fine and exhaustive statement of the principle of free government? The author's name is Lyman Abbott. I know of no one who is doing a finer work than Rev. Dr. Lyman Abbott at this moment for the religious emancipation of men's minds. I only wish, when he deals with human freedom, human political freedom, that he had stayed where he was when he wrote that fine sentence."

"It is easy for the English to believe they are doing the will of God," the speaker continued. "Despotism calls itself benevolent. The other side is not heard. A subject nation is declared unfit for self-government and then despotism tries to keep it so."

Colonel Higginson gave an illustration of England's encouragement of the liquor traffic in India, and said that while famine kills thousands there it is not such a gigantic evil as intemperance. He referred also to the virtual enslavement of the black races in South Africa, many of whom are actually prisoners in the mines. One ground of complaint, he said, had been that the Boers enslaved the natives. Yet the British themselves were weaving a net around the blacks such as was introducing them, if not to the name, certainly to the substance of slavery. The Africans disliked to work in the mines. But emissaries were being sent farther and farther into the country to persuade whole tribes by liberal offers to give their labor. When once they consented, on however small a scale, to work in the mines, they became actual prisoners. The ground on which they lived belonged to the mine-owners. Once there they were there practically for life, unless they escaped and left their families to starve.

Wherever, in fact, it was applied imperial reign did injustice to the people with whom it dealt. If tyranny, continued Colonel Higginson, was a power which works in the dark, freedom was a power which worked in the light as an educational force to increase the intelligence of men and to promote law-abiding in the community. History showed, moreover, that imperialism, being tyrannical and against freedom, had always worked to destroy itself, and that in the development of the race the principles embodied in the Declaration of Independence had always triumphed and would always triumph.

"Therefore," said the colonel, "I would simply say as between freedom and imperialism, not speaking of any particular freedom or imperialism, not speaking of mere expansion, but of imperialism enforced by power upon the unwilling, and in defence of our Declaration of Independence, imperialism has these fatal objections to it: That it is opposed to the self-evident propositions of the Declaration of Independence; that it is a thing superficial in its methods and not educating the people as every step in freedom does, and then again as doing injustice to the people it deals with, in not knowing what the real condition of those people is.

"Still less does it know what the condition of those people might be without it. There is no reason to suppose that the Japanese are superior by nature to the Hindooes. We see what the Hindooes are under subjection; we see what the Japanese are today. There is no reason to suppose—so the admiral who conquered them said—that the Filipinos are less fit for self-government than the Cubans. There is no reason to suppose that the Cubans are less fit for it than the Mexicans; but see what the Philippines and Cuba have been made by the long Spanish domination, and see where Mexico is today. We assume, because nations are crushed by imperialism, that they never could be otherwise. The only comparison which you can make is by placing them side by side with some unconquered nation of the same blood, and see what that nation has done.

"People often say, and mention it as a remarkable thing, that the strongest sentiments against imperialism come today from the older men. It is because the older men were brought up in the period when the revolutionary traditions still lingered among us. I am very glad that we are too old to lay aside the memory of those refreshing days. I only wish that we could transfer them more effectually than others. All imperialism is self-destructive, I firmly believe; even the imperial crown with which the vanity of a Jewish sycophant tempted the good Queen Victoria. I believe it is a transitory thing. The word freedom and the word empire, as Mr. Morley said in England, have nothing in common; they never can be reconciled. The greatest of Englishmen have recognized that. Who was the greatest among her public men? Cowper calls it

Praise enough
To fill the ambition of a private man,
That Chatham's language was his mother tongue.

"What was Chatham's language? The phrase of it which will be longest remembered is that in which he said in the very House of Lords, 'America has resisted! I rejoice, my lords!' It is something, perhaps, to fill the ambition of one State of the Union, that she has as her representative in the American House of Lords a man who in an equal exigency spoke as Chatham might have spoken."

Other speakers were Dr. James, Joseph Lee and Rev. C. G. Ames. Referring to the attitude of this Government toward the Philippines, Mr. Ames said: "We have thrown all the power into the executive hands, which has resulted in Cæsarism, pure and simple, with a Senate behind him." He regretted that this Government has abandoned the principles upon which it was founded.

PART FIVE

Naturalist

The eternal youthfulness of nature answers to my own
feeling of youth and preserves it. As I turn from those
men and women around me, whom I watch gradually
submerged under the tide of gray hairs, it seems a bliss I
have not earned to find bird and insect, and flower
renewing itself every year in fresh and eternal beauty the
same as in my earliest childhood.

THOMAS WENTWORTH HIGGINSON,
LETTERS AND JOURNALS (BOSTON, 1921)

On surveying the range of Higginson's activism, one is tempted to
think that the causes he espoused eclipsed his vocation as a writer.
Two paragraphs at the end of the essay "The Procession of the Flowers"
furnish an appropriate commentary on that thought. There he says: "In
after years the memory of books seems barren or valueless, compared
with the immortal bequest of hours like this [spent immersed in a natural setting]. . . . There is no conceivable beauty of blossom so beautiful
as words—none so graceful, none so perfumed."

At first, the two ideas seem inconsistent. Which predominated, the
naturalist or the writer? But after some reflection and further reading of
the nature studies he wrote, one may agree that for Higginson, paradoxically, both statements are true.

Higginson's individual nature essays need no introduction. There is
no need to supply context, describe setting or the other participants, or
supply a time frame. Each speaks for itself.

The term "nature studies" may be too narrow for the essays in which
Higginson demonstrated his talent for the observation and description
of what most of us miss. As in "Oldport Wharves," his interest in his en-

vironment is not limited to botany or biology. Higginson had an ability to describe with new eyes much that most people find ordinary.

Higginson's talent for writing interesting as well as accurate descriptions of the outdoors and his surroundings was not employed solely in essays on the observation of nature. Readers of *Army Life in a Black Regiment* frequently encounter a variety of passages that express appreciation for and introduce us seductively to the non-Yankee setting in which he found himself, such as "avenues of great live oaks, with their hard shining leaves, and their branches heavy with a universal drapery of soft long moss, like fringe trees struck with grayness. Below, the sandy soil covered with coarse gray bristles with sharp palmetto and aloes, all of the vegetation is stiff, shining, subtropical, with nothing soft or delicate in its texture."

The diverse directions taken by his advocacy could well be said to include another cause, one not usually attributed to him; implicit in his writings on the outdoors is support for a cause not yet named until a century later: environmentalism. Indeed, the title of an essay that appeared in the *New England Quarterly,* by the Higginson scholar Frank Rashid (his primary concern is the life and work of Emily Dickinson), is "Higginson the Entomologist."

He describes Higginson's undergraduate years, when he had extracurricular employment as curator of entomology for the Harvard Natural History Society. He also served as aide to Thaddeus William Harris, a faculty member who was a Linnaean scholar, an expert in classification of fauna. Harris called the young bug expert "preceptor," literally "teacher," implying that Higginson had attained a high level of knowledge in entomology.

Rashid then explores the essays, emphasizing the skill and care with which Higginson demonstrated his entitlement to the title "entomologist." He finds it to be more than a coincidence that in some of her letters Emily Dickinson addressed Higginson as "Dear Preceptor." We also find the phrase used as the title of a biography by Anna Mary Wells that focuses on the poet's indebtedness to Higginson. Rashid proceeds to present examples of Dickinson's poetry that show an unusually frequent use of insect-related metaphors or other allusions to insects, insect life, and the insect-sized world, including bees, butterflies, crickets, spiders, and flies. No more can be said about this in the way of evidence that Dickinson's use of these images had a connection with Higginson's preceptorship: he preserved her letters to him, but the many letters that he sent to her disappeared, probably destroyed by her.

Higginson's death in 1911 was followed by a sudden diminution of his renown as a writer and reputation as an activist. This is not surprising in view of the wretched state his prime causes had come to by the time he passed on. Civil rights were at a very low ebb: when the racist film *Birth of a Nation* was released in 1915 it was accepted as a historically accurate account. In 1913 President Wilson gave the order for segregation in government employment. Women's right to equality in every respect but suffrage seemed to recede after the vote was won in 1920. From 1911 to 1962, Higginson became a forgotten man, his many books all out of print.

Then with the simultaneous independent publication of three editions of *Army Life in a Black Regiment* (edited by John Hope Franklin, Howard Mumford Jones, and the writer Howard N. Meyer, respectively), there was a minirevival. Certainly there had been references to Higginson in footnotes when his writings were credited (sometimes they were not) as the source of biographical information on his contemporaries, or historic information of his era. Nevertheless, in the half century until his Civil War memoir reappeared he was virtually a nonperson, practically unknown in all respects, with two exceptions. One was the Dickinson connection, albeit often with distortion. Also, there was recognition of the superb quality of Higginson's writings on nature and natural history, his illumination of the value and joy of an intimate relation with the natural world.

1

WATER-LILIES

The inconstant April mornings drop showers or sun-beams over the glistening lake, while far beneath its surface a murky mass disengages itself from the muddy bottom, and rises slowly through the waves. The tasselled alder-branches droop above it; the last year's blackbird's nest swings over it in the grape-vine; the newly-opened Hepaticas and Epigæas on the neighboring bank peer down modestly to look for it; the water-skater (Gerris) pauses on the surface near it, casting on the shallow bottom the odd shadow of his feet, like three pairs of boxing-gloves; the Notonecta, or water-boatman, rows round and round it, sometimes on his breast, sometimes on his back; queer caddis-worms trail their self-made homesteads of leaves or twigs beside it; the Dytiscus, dorbug of the water, blunders clumsily against it; the tadpole wriggles his stupid way to it, and rests upon it, meditating of future frogdom; the passing wild-duck dives and nibbles at it; the mink and muskrat brush it with their soft fur; the spotted turtle slides over it; the slow larvae of gauzy dragon-flies cling sleepily to its sides and await their changes: all these fair or uncouth creatures feel, through the dim waves, the blessed longing of spring; and yet not one of them dreams that within that murky mass there lies a treasure too white and beautiful to be yet intrusted to the waves, and that for many a day the bud must yearn toward the surface, before, aspiring above it, as mortals to heaven, it meets the sunshine with the answering beauty of the Water-Lily.

Days and weeks have passed away; the wild-duck has flown onward, to dive for his luncheon in some remoter lake; the tadpoles have made themselves legs, with which they have vanished; the caddis-worms have sealed themselves up in their cylinders, and emerged again as winged insects; the dragon-flies have crawled up the water-reeds, and, clinging with heads upturned, have undergone the change which symbolizes immortality; the world is transformed from spring to summer; the lily-buds are opened into glossy leaf and radiant flower, and we have come for the harvest.

We visitors lodged, last night, in the old English phrase, "at the sign of the Oak and Star." Wishing, not, indeed, like the ancient magicians, to gather magic berry and bud before sunrise, but at least to see these treasures of the lake in their morning hour, we camped last night on a little island, which one tall tree almost covers with it branches, while a dense undergrowth of young chestnuts and birches fills all the intervening space, touching the water all around the circular, shelving shore. Yesterday was hot, but the night was cool, and we kindled a gypsy fire of twigs, less for warmth than for society. The first gleam made the dark, lonely islet into a cheering home, turned the protecting tree to a starlit roof, and the chestnut-sprays to illuminated walls. To us, lying beneath their shelter, every fresh flickering of the fire kindled the leaves into brightness and banished into dark interstices the lake and sky; then the fire died into embers, the leaves faded into solid darkness in their turn, and water and heavens showed light and close and near, until fresh twigs caught fire and the blaze came up again. Rising to look forth, at intervals, during the peaceful hours,—for it is the worst feature of a night out-doors, that sleeping seems such a waste of time,—we watched the hilly and wooded shores of the lake sink into gloom and glimmer into dawn again, amid the low plash of waters and the noises of the night.

Precisely at half past three, a song-sparrow above our heads gave one liquid trill, so inexpressibly sudden and delicious, that it seemed to set to music every atom of freshness and fragrance that Nature held; then the spell was broken, and the whole shore and lake were vocal with song. Joining in this jubilee of morning, we were early in motion; bathing and breakfast, though they seemed indisputably in accordance with the instincts of the Universe, yet did not detain us long, and we were promptly on our way to Lily Pond. Will the reader join us?

It is one of those summer days when a veil of mist gradually burns away before the intense sunshine, and the sultry morning only plays at coolness, and that with its earliest visitors alone. But we are before the sunlight, though not before the sunrise, and can watch the pretty game of alternating mist and shine. Stray gleams of glory lend their trailing magnificence to the tops of chestnut-trees, floating vapors raise the outlines of the hills and make mystery of the wooded islands, and, as we glide through the placid water, we can sing, with the Chorus in the "Ion" of Euripides, "O immense and brilliant air, resound with our cries of joy!"

Almost every town has its Lily Pond, dear to boys and maidens, and partially equalizing, by its annual delights, the presence or absence of other geographical advantages. Ours is accessible from the larger lake only by taking the skiff over a narrow embankment, which protects our fairy-land by its presence, and eight distant factories by its dam. Once beyond it, we are in a realm of dark Lethean water, utterly unlike the sunny depths of the main lake. Hither the water-lilies have retreated, to a domain of their own. In the bosom of these shallow waves, there stand hundreds of submerged and dismasted roots, still upright, spreading their vast, uncouth limbs like enormous spiders beneath the surface. They are remnants of border wars with the axe, vegetable Witheringtons, still fighting on their stumps, but gradually sinking into the soft ooze, and ready, perhaps, when a score of centuries has piled two more strata of similar remains in mud above them, to furnish foundations for a newer New Orleans; that city having been lately discovered to be thus supported.

The present decline in the manufacturing business is clear revenue to the water-lilies, and these ponds are higher than usual, because the idle mills do not draw them off. But we may notice, in observing the shores, that peculiar charm of water, that, whether its quantity be greater or less, its grace is the same; it makes its own boundary in lake or river, and where its edge is, there seems the natural and permanent margin. And the same natural fitness, without reference to mere quantity, extends to its flowery children. Before us lie islands and continents of lilies, acres of charms, whole, vast, unbroken surfaces of stainless whiteness. And yet, as we approach them, every islanded cup that floats in lonely dignity, apart from the multitude, appears as perfect in itself, couched in white expanded perfection, its reflection taking a faint glory of pink that is scarcely perceptible in the flower. As we glide gently among them, the air grows fragrant, and a stray breeze flaps the leaves, as if to welcome us. Each floating flower becomes suddenly a ship at anchor, or rather seems beating up against the summer wind, in a regatta of blossoms.

Early as it is in the day, the greater part of the flowers are already ex-panded. Indeed, that experience of Thoreau's, of watching them open in the first sunbeams, rank by rank, is not easily obtained, unless perhaps in a narrow stream, where the beautiful slumberers are more regularly marshalled. In our lake, at least, they open irregularly, though rapidly. But, this morning, many linger as buds, while others peer up, in half-expanded beauty, beneath the lifted leaves, frolicsome as Pucks or baby-nymphs. As you raise the leaf, in such cases, it is impossible not to imagine that a pair of tiny hands have upheld it, and that the pretty head will dip down again, and disappear. Others, again, have expanded all but the inmost pair of white petals, and these spring apart at the first touch of the finger on the stem. Some spread vast vases of fragrance, six or seven inches in diameter, while others are small and delicate, with petals like fine lace-work. Smaller still, we sometimes pass a flotilla of infant leaves, an inch in diameter. All these grow from the dark water,—and the blacker it is, the fairer their whiteness shows. But your eye follows the stem often vainly into those sombre depths, and vainly seeks to behold Sabrina fair, sitting with her twisted braids of lilies, beneath the glassy, cool, but not translucent wave. Do not start, when, in such an effort, only your own dreamy face looks back upon you, beyond the gunwale of the reflected boat, and you find that you float double, self and shadow.

Let us rest our paddles, and look round us, while the idle motion sways our light skiff onward, now half embayed among the lily-pads, now lazily gliding over intervening gulfs. There is a great deal going on in these waters and their fringing woods and meadows. All the summer long, the pond is bordered with successive walls of flowers. In early spring emerge the yellow catkins of the swamp-willow, first; then the long tassels of the graceful alders expand and droop, till they weep their yellow dust upon the water; then come the birch-blossoms, more tardily; then the downy leaves and white clusters of the medlar or shad-bush (*Amelanchier Canadensis* of Gray); these dropping, the roseate chalices of the mountain-laurel open; as they fade into melancholy brown, the sweet Azalea uncloses; and before its last honeyed blossom has trailed down, dying, from the stem, the more fragrant Clethra starts out above, the button-bush thrusts forth its merry face amid wild roses, and the Clematis waves its sprays of beauty. Mingled with these grow, lower, the spiræas, white and pink, yellow touch-me-not, fresh white arrowhead, bright blue vervain and skullcap, dull snake-head, gay monkey-flower, coarse eupatoriums, milkweeds, golden-rods, asters, thistles, and a host beside. Beneath, the brilliant scarlet cardinal-flower begins to palisade the moist shores; and after its superb reflection has passed away from the waters, the grotesque witch-hazel flares out its narrow yellow petals amidst the October leaves, and so ends the floral year. There is not a week during all these months, when one cannot stand in the boat and wreathe garlands of blossoms from the shores.

These all crowd around the brink, and watch, day and night, the opening and closing of the water-lilies. Meanwhile, upon the waters, our queen keeps her chosen court, nor can one of these mere land-loving blossoms touch the hem of her garment. In truth, she bears no sister near her throne. There is but this one species among us, *Nymphœa odorata.* The beautiful little rose-colored *Nymphœa sanguinea,* which once adorned the Botanic Garden at Cambridge, was merely an occasional variety of costume. She has, indeed, an English half-sister, *Nymphœa alba,* less beautiful, less fragrant, but keeping more fashionable hours,— not opening (according to Linnæus) till seven, nor closing till four. And she has a humble cousin, the yellow Nuphar, who keeps commonly aloof, as becomes a poor relation, though created from the self-same mud,—a fact which Hawthorne has beautifully moralized. The prouder Nelumbium, a second-cousin, lineal descendant of the sacred bean of Pythagoras, has fallen to an obscurer position, and dwells, like a sturdy democrat, in the Far West.

But, undisturbed, the water-lily reigns on, with her retinue around her. The tall pickerel-weed (Pontederia) is her gentleman-usher, gorgeous in blue and gold through July, somewhat rusty in August. The water-shield (Hydropeltis) is chief maid-of-honor; a high-born lady she, not without royal blood indeed, but with rather a bend sinister; not precisely beautiful, but very fastidious; encased over her whole person with a gelatinous covering, literally a starched duenna. Sometimes she is suspected of conspiring to drive her mistress from the throne; for we have observed certain slow watercourses where the leaves of the water-lily have been almost wholly replaced, in a series of years, by the similar, but smaller, leaves of the water-shield. More rarely seen is the slender Utricularia, a dainty maiden, whose light feet scarce touch the water,—with the still more delicate floating white Water-Ranunculus, and the shy Villarsia, whose submerged flowers merely peep one day above the surface and then close again forever. Then there are many humbler attendants, Potamogetons or pond-weeds. And here float little emissaries from the dominions of land; for the fallen florets of the Viburnum drift among the lily-pads, with mast-like stamens erect, sprinkling the water with a strange beauty, and cheating us with the promise of a new aquatic flower.

These are the still life of this sequestered nook; but it is in fact a crowded thoroughfare. No tropic jungle more swarms with busy existence than these midsummer waters and their bushy banks. The warm and humming air is filled with insect sounds, ranging from the murmur of invisible gnats and midges, to the impetuous whirring of the great Libellulæ, large almost as swallows, and hawking high in air for their food. Swift butterflies glance by, moths flutter, flies buzz, grasshoppers and katydids pipe their shrill notes, sharp as the edges of the sunbeams. Busy bees go humming past, straight as arrows, express-freight-trains from one blossoming copse to another. Showy wasps of many species fume uselessly about, in gallant uniforms, wasting an immense deal of unnecessary anger on the sultry universe. Graceful, stingless Sphexes and Ichneumon flies emulate their bustle, without their weapons. Delicate ladybirds come and go to the milkweeds, spotted almost as regularly as if Nature had decided to number the species, like policemen or hack-drivers, from one to twenty. Elegant little Lepturæ fly with them, so gay and airy, they hardly seem like beetles. Phryganeæ (*nés* caddis-worms), lace-flies, and long-tailed Ephemeræ flutter more heavily by. On the large alder-flowers clings the superb *Desmocerus palliatus,* beautiful as a tropical insect, with his steel-blue armor and his golden cloak (*pallium*) above his shoulders, grandest knight on this Field of the Cloth of Gold. The countless fire-flies which spangled the evening mist now only crawl sleepily, daylight creatures, with the lustre buried in their milky bodies. More wholly children of night, the soft, luxurious Sphinxes (or hawk-moths) come not here; fine ladies of the insect world, their home is among gardens and green-houses, late and languid by day, but all night long upon the wing, dancing in the air with unwearied muscles till long past midnight, and supping on honey at last. They come not; but the nobler butterflies soar above us, stoop a moment to the water, and then with a few lazy wavings of their sumptuous wings float far over the oak-trees to the woods they love.

All these hover near the water-lily; but its special parasites are an enamelled beetle (*Donacia metallica*) which keeps house permanently in the flower, and a few smaller ones which tenant the surface of the leaves,—larva, pupa, and perfect insect, forty feeding like one, and each leading its whole earthly career on this floating island of perishable verdure. The "beautiful blue damsel-flies" alight also in multitudes among them, so fearless that they perch with equal readiness on our boat or paddle, and so various that two adjacent ponds will sometimes be haunted by two distinct sets of species. In the water, among the leaves, little shining whirlwigs wheel round and round, fifty joining in the dance, till, at the slightest alarm, they whirl away to some safer ball-room, and renew the merriment. On every floating log, as we approach it, there is a convention of turtles, sitting in calm debate, like mailed barons, till, as we draw near, they plump into the water, and paddle away for some subaqueous Runnymede. Beneath, the shy and stately pickerel vanishes at a glance, shoals of minnows glide, black and bearded pouts frisk aimlessly, soft water-newts hang poised without motion, and slender pickerel-frogs cease occasionally their submerged croaking, and, darting to the surface with swift vertical strokes, gulp a mouthful of fresh air, and down again to renew the moist soliloquy.

Time would fail us to tell of the feathered life around us,—the blackbirds that build securely in these thickets, the stray swallows that dip their wings in the quiet waters, and the kingfishers that still bring, as the ancients fabled, halcyon days. Yonder stands, against the shore, a bittern, motionless in that wreath of mist which makes his long-legged person almost as dim as his far-off booming by night. There poises a hawk, before sweeping down to some chosen bough in the dense forest; and there fly a pair of blue-jays, screaming, from tree to tree. As for wild quadrupeds, the race is almost passed away. Far to the north, indeed, the great moose still browses on the lily-pads, and the shy beaver nibbles them; but here the few lingering four-footed creatures only haunt, but do not graze upon, these floating pastures. Eyes more favored than ours may yet chance to spy an otter in this still place; there by the shore are the small footprints of a mink; that dark thing disappearing in the waters yonder, a soft mass of drowned fur, is a "musquash." Later in the season, a mound of earth will be his winter dwelling-place; and those myriad muscle-shells at the water's edge are the remnant of his banquets,—once banquets for the Indians, too.

But we must return to our lilies. There is no sense of wealth like floating in this archipelago of white and green. The emotions of avarice become almost demoralizing. Every flower bears a fragrant California in its bosom, and you feel impoverished at the thought of leaving one behind. But after the first half-hour of eager grasping, one becomes fastidious, rather avoids those on which the wasps and flies have alighted, and seeks only the stainless. But handle them tenderly, as if you loved them. Do not grasp at the open flower as if it were a peony or a hollyhock, for then it will come off, stalkless, in your hand, and you will cast it blighted upon the water; but coil your thumb and second finger affectionately around it, press the extended forefinger firmly to the stem below, and, with one steady pull, you will secure a long and delicate stalk, fit to twine around the graceful head of your beloved, as the Hindoo goddess of beauty encircled with a Lotus the brow of Rama.

Consider the lilies. All over our rural watercourses, at midsummer, float these cups of snow. They are Nature's symbols of coolness. They suggest to us the white garments of their Oriental worshippers. They come with the white roses, and prepare the way for the white lilies of the garden. The white doe of Rylstone and Andrew Marvell's fawn might fitly bathe amid their beauties. Yonder steep bank slopes down to the lake-side, one solid mass of pale pink laurel, but, once upon the water, a purer tint prevails. The pink fades into a lingering flush, and the white creature floats peerless, set in green without and gold within. That bright circle of stamens is the very ring with which Doges once wedded the Adriatic; Venice has lost it, but it dropped into the water-lily's bosom, and there it rests forever. So perfect in form, so redundant in beauty, so delicate, so spotless, so fragrant,—what presumptuous lover ever dared, in his most enamored hour, to liken his mistress to a water-lily? No human Blanche or Lilian was ever so fair as that.

The water-lily comes of an ancient and sacred family of white-robed priests. They assisted at the most momentous religious ceremonies, from the beginning of recorded time. The Egyptian Lotus was a sacred plant; it was dedicated to Harpocrates and to the god Nofr Atmoo,—*Nofr* meaning *good*, whence the name of our yellow lily, Nuphar. But the true Egyptian flower was *Nymphœa Lotus*, though *Nymphœa cœrulea*, Moore's "blue water-lilies," can be traced on the sculptures also. It was cultivated in tanks in the gardens; it was the chief material for festal wreaths; a single bud hung over the forehead of many a queenly dame; and the sculptures represent the weary flowers as dropping from the heated hands of belles, in the later hours of the feast. Rock softly on the waters, fair lilies! your Eastern kindred have rocked on the stormier bosom of Cleopatra. The Egyptian Lotus was, moreover, the emblem of the sacred Nile,—as the Hindoo species, of the sacred Ganges; and each was held the symbol of the creation of the world from the waters. The sacred bull Apis was wreathed with its garlands; there were niches for water, to place it among tombs; it was carved in the capitals of columns; it was represented on plates and vases; the sculptures show it in many sacred uses, even as a burnt-offering; Isis holds it; and the god Nilus still binds a wreath of water-lilies around the throne of Memnon.

From Egypt the Lotus was carried to Assyria, and Layard found it among fir-cones and honeysuckles on the later sculptures of Nineveh. The Greeks dedicated it to the nymphs, whence the name *Nymphœa*. Nor did the Romans disregard it, though the Lotus to which Ovid's nymph Lotis was changed, *servato nomine*, was a tree, and not a flower. Still different a thing was the enchanted stem of the Lotus-eaters of Herodotus, which prosaic botanists have reduced to the *Zizyphus Lotus* found by Mungo Park, translating also the yellow Lotus-dust into a mere "farina, tasting like sweet gingerbread."

But in the Lotus of Hindostan we find our flower again, and the Oriental sacred books are cool with water-lilies. Open the Vishnu Purana at any page, and it is a *Sortes Lilianœ*. The orb of the earth is Lotus-shaped, and is upborne by the tusks of Vesava, as if he had been sporting in a lake where the leaves and blossoms float. Brahma, first incarnation of Vishnu, creator of the world, was born from a Lotus; so was Sri or Lakshmu, the Hindoo Venus, goddess of beauty and prosperity, protectress of womanhood, whose worship guards the house from all danger. "Seated on a full-blown Lotus, and holding a Lotus in her hand, the goddess Sri, radiant with beauty, rose from the waves." The Lotus is the chief ornament of the subterranean Eden, Patala, and the holy mountain Meru is thought to be shaped like its seed-vessel, larger at summit than at base. When the heavenly Urvasi fled from her earthly spouse, Purúvavas, he found her sporting with four nymphs of heaven, in a lake beautified with the Lotus. When the virtuous Prahlada was burned at the stake, he cried to his cruel father, "The fire burneth me not, and all around I behold the face of the sky, cool and fragrant with beds of Lotus-flowers!" Above all, the graceful history of the transformations of Krishna is everywhere hung with these fresh chaplets. Every successive maiden whom the deity wooes is Lotus-eyed, Lotus-mouthed, or Lotus-cheeked, and the youthful here wears always a Lotus-wreath. Also "the clear sky was bright with the autumnal moon, and the air fragrant with the perfume of the wild water-lily, in whose buds the clustering bees were murmuring their song."

Elsewhere we find fuller details. "In the primordial state of the world, the rudimental universe, submerged in water, reposed on the bosom of the Eternal. Brahma, the architect of the world, poised on a Lotus-leaf, floated upon the waters, and all that he was able to discern with his eight eyes was water and darkness. Amid scenes so ungenial and dismal, the god sank into a profound reverie, when he thus soliloquized: 'Who am I? Whence am I?' In this state of abstraction Brahma continued during the period of a century and a half of the gods, without apparent benefit or a solution of his inquiries,—a circumstance which caused him great uneasiness of mind." It is a comfort, however, to know that subsequently a voice came to him, on which he rose, "seated himself upon the Lotus in an attitude of contemplation, and reflected upon the Eternal, who soon appeared to him in the form of a man with a thousand heads,"—a questionable exchange for his Lotus-solitude.

This is Brahminism; but the other great form of Oriental religion has carried the same fair symbol with it. One of the Bibles of the Buddhists is named "The White Lotus of the Good Law." A pious Nepaulese bowed in reverence before a vase of lilies which perfumed the study of Sir William Jones. At sunset in Thibet, the French missionaries tell us, every inhabitant of every village prostrates himself in the public square, and the holy invocation, "O, the gem in the Lotus!" goes murmuring over hill and valley, like the sound of many bees. It is no unmeaning phrase, but an utterance of ardent desire to be absorbed into that Brahma whose emblem is the sacred flower. This mystic formula or "mani" is imprinted on the pavement of the streets, it floats on flags from the temples, and the wealthy Buddhists maintain sculptor-missionaries, Old Mortalities of the water-lily, who, wandering to distant lands, carve the blessed words upon cliff and stone.

Having got thus far into Orientalism, we can hardly expect to get out again without some slight entanglement in philology. Lily-pads. Whence *pads?* No other leaf is identified with that singular monosyllable. Has our floating Lotus-leaf any connection with padding, or with a footpad? with the ambling pad of an abbot, or a paddle, or a paddock, or a pad-lock? with many-doméd Padua proud, or with St. Patrick? Is the name derived from the Anglo-Saxon *paad* or *petthian,* or the Greek πατέω? All the etymologists are silent; Tooke and Richardson ignore the problem; and of the innumerable pamphlets in the Worcester and Webster Controversy, loading the tables of school-committee-men, not one ventures to grapple with the lily-pad.

But was there ever a philological trouble for which the Sanscrit could not afford at least a conjectural cure? A dictionary of that extremely venerable tongue is an ostrich's stomach, which can crack the hardest etymological nut. The Sanscrit name for the Lotus is simply *Padma.* The learned Brahmins call the Egyptian deities Padma Devi, or Lotus-Gods; the second of the eighteen Hindoo Puranas is styled the Padma Purana, because it treats of the "epoch when the world was a golden Lotus"; and the sacred incantation which goes murmuring through Thibet is "Om mani padme houm." It would be singular, if upon these delicate floating leaves a fragment of our earliest vernacular has been borne down to us, so that here the school-boy is more learned than the *savans.*

This lets us down easily to the more familiar uses of this plant divine. By the Nile, in early days, the water-lily was good not merely for devotion, but for diet. "From the seeds of the Lotus," said Pliny, "the Egyptians make bread." The Hindoos still eat the seeds, roasted in sand; also the stalks and roots. In South America, from the seeds of the Victoria (*Nymphœa Victoria,* now *Victoria Regia*) a farina is made, preferred to that of the finest wheat,—Bonpland even suggesting to our reluctant imagination Victoria-pies. But the European species are used, so far as is reported, only in dyeing, and as food (if the truth be told) of swine. Our own water-lily is rather more powerful in its uses; the root contains tannin and gallic acid, and a decoction of it "gives a black precipitate, with sulphate of iron." It graciously consents to become an astringent, and a styptic, and a poultice, and, banished from all other temples, still lingers in those of Æsculapius.

The botanist also finds his special satisfactions in the flower. It has some strange peculiarities of structure. So loose is the internal distribution of its tissues, that it was for some time held doubtful to which of the two great vegetable divisions, exogenous or endogenous, it belonged. Its petals, moreover, furnish the best example of the gradual transition of petals into stamens,—illustrating that wonderful law of identity which is the great discovery of modern science. Every child knows this peculiarity of the water-lily, but the extent of it seems to vary with season and locality, and sometimes one finds a succession of flowers almost entirely free from this confusion of organs.

The reader may not care to learn that the order of Nymphæaceæ "differs from Ranunculaceæ in the consolidation of its carpels, from Papaveraceæ in the placentation not being parietal, and from Nelumbiaceæ in the want of a large truncated disc containing monospermous achenia"; but they may like to know that the water-lily has relations on land, in all gradations of society, from poppy to magnolia, and yet does not conform its habits precisely to those of any of them. Its great black roots, sometimes as large as a man's arm, form a network at the bottom of the water. Its stem floats, an airy four-celled tube, adapting itself to the depth, and stiff in shallows, like the stalk of the yellow lily: and it contracts and curves downward when seed-time approaches. The leaves show beneath the magnifier beautiful adaptations of structure. They are not, like those of land-plants, constructed with deep veins to receive the rain and conduct it to the stem, but are smooth and glossy, and of even surface. The leaves of land-vegetation have also thousands of little breathing-pores, principally on the under side: the apple-leaf, for instance, has twenty-four thousand to a square inch. But here they are fewer; they are wholly on the upper side, and, whereas in other cases they open or shut according to the moisture of the atmosphere, here the greedy leaves, secure of moisture, scarcely deign to close them. Nevertheless, even these give some recognition of hygrometric necessities, and, though living on the water, and not merely christened with dewdrops like other leaves, but baptized by immersion all the time, they are yet known to suffer in drought and to take pleasure in the rain.

After speaking of the various kindred of the water-lily, it would be wrong to leave our fragrant subject without due mention of its most magnificent, most lovely relative, at first claimed even as its twin sister, and classed as a Nymphæa. I once lived near neighbor to a Victoria Regia. Nothing in the world of vegetable existence has such a human interest. The charm is not in the mere size of the plant, which disappoints everybody, as Niagara does, when tried by that sole standard. The leaves of the Victoria, indeed, attain a diameter of six feet; the largest flowers, of twenty-three inches,—four times the size of the largest of our water-lilies. But it is not the measurements of the Victoria, it is its life which fascinates. It is not a thing merely of dimensions, nor merely of beauty, but a creature of vitality and motion. Those vast leaves expand and change almost visibly. They have been known to grow half an inch an hour, eight inches a day. Rising one day from the water, a mere clenched mass of yellow prickles, a leaf is transformed the next day to a crimson salver, gorgeously tinted on its upturned rim. Then it spreads into a raft of green, armed with long thorns, and supported by a framework of ribs and cross-pieces, an inch thick, and so substantial, that the Brazil Indians, while gathering the seed-vessels, place their young children on the leaves;—*yrupe*, or water-platter, they call the accommodating plant. But even these expanding leaves are not the glory of the Victoria; the glory is in the opening of the flower.

I have sometimes looked in, for a passing moment, at the green-house, its dwelling-place, during the period of flowering,—and then stayed for more than an hour, unable to leave the fascinating scene. After the strange flower-bud has reared its dark head from the placid tank, moving it a little, uneasily, like some imprisoned water-creature, it pauses for a moment in a sort of dumb despair. Then trembling again, and collecting all its powers, it thrusts open, with an indignant jerk, the rough calyx-leaves, and the beautiful disrobing begins. The firm, white, central cone, first so closely infolded, quivers a little, and swiftly, before your eyes, the first of the hundred petals detaches its delicate edges, and springs back, opening towards the water, while its white reflection opens to meet it from below. Many moments of repose follow,—you watch,— another petal trembles, detaches, springs open, and is still. Then another, and another, and another. Each movement is so quiet, yet so decided, so living, so human, that the radiant creature seems a Musidora of the water, and you almost blush with a sense of guilt, in gazing on that peerless privacy. As petal by petal slowly opens, there still stands the central cone of snow, a glacier, an alp, a jungfrau, while each avalanche of whiteness seems the last. Meanwhile a strange rich odor fills the air, and Nature seems to concentrate all fascinations and claim all senses for this jubilee of her darling.

So pass the enchanted moments of the evening, till the fair thing pauses at last, and remains for hours unchanged. In the morning, one by one, those white petals close again, shutting all their beauty in, and you watch through the short sleep for the period of waking. Can this bright transfigured creature appear again, in the same chaste loveliness? Your fancy can scarcely trust it, fearing some disastrous change; and your fancy is too true a prophet. Come again, after the second day's opening, and you start at the transformation which one hour has secretly produced. Can this be the virgin Victoria,—this thing of crimson passion, this pile of pink and yellow, relaxed, expanded, voluptuous, lolling languidly upon the water, never to rise again? In this short time every tint of every petal is transformed; it is gorgeous in beauty, but it is "Hebe turned to Magdalen."

Such is the Victoria Regia. But our rustic water-lily, our innocent Nymphæa, never claiming such a hot-house glory, never drooping into such a blush, blooms on placidly in the quiet waters, till she modestly folds her leaves for the last time, and bows her head beneath the surface forever. Next year she lives for us only in her children, fair and pure as herself.

Nay, not alone in them, but also in memory. The fair vision will not fade from us, though the paddle has dipped its last crystal drop from the waves, and the boat is drawn upon the shore. We may yet visit many lovely and lonely places,—meadows thick with violet, or the homes of the shy Rhodora, or those sloping forest-haunts where the slight Linnæa hangs its twin-born heads,—but no scene will linger on our vision like this annual Feast of the Lilies. On scorching mountains, amid raw prairie-winds, or upon the regal ocean, the white pageant shall come back to memory again, with all the luxury of summer heats, and all the fragrant coolness that can relieve them. We shall fancy ourselves again among these fleets of anchored lilies,—again, like Urvasi, sporting amid the Lake of Lotuses.

For that which is remembered is often more vivid than that which is seen. The eye paints better in the presence, the heart in the absence, of the object most dear. "He who longs after beautiful Nature can best describe her," said Bettine; "he who is in the midst of her loveliness can only lie down and enjoy." It enhances the truth of the poet's verses, that he writes them in his study. Absence is the very air of passion, and all the best description is *in memoriam*. As with our human beloved, when the graceful presence is with us, we cannot analyze or describe, but merely possess, and only after its departure can it be portrayed by our yearning desires; so is it with Nature: only in losing her do we gain the power to describe her, and we are introduced to Art, as we are to Eternity, by the dropping away of our companions.

2

SNOW

All through the long hours of yesterday the low clouds hung close above our heads, to pour with more unswerving aim their constant storm of sleet and snow,—sometimes working in soft silence, sometimes with impatient gusty breaths, but always busily at work. Darkness brought no rest to these laborious warriors of the air, but only fiercer strife: the wild winds rose; noisy recruits, they howled beneath the eaves, or swept around the walls, like hungry wolves, now here, now there, howling at opposite doors. Thus, through the anxious and wakeful night, the storm went on. The household lay vexed by broken dreams, with changing fancies of lost children on solitary moors, of sleighs hopelessly overturned in drifted and pathless gorges, or of icy cordage upon disabled vessels in Arctic seas; until a softer warmth, as of sheltering snow-wreaths, lulled all into deeper rest till morning.

And what a morning! The sun, a young conqueror, sends in his glorious rays, like heralds, to rouse us for the inspection of his trophies. The baffled foe, retiring, has left far and near the high-heaped spoils behind. The glittering plains own the new victor. Over all these level and wide-swept meadows, over all these drifted, spotless slopes, he is proclaimed undisputed monarch. On the wooded hillsides the startled shadows are in motion; they flee like young fawns, bounding upward and downward over rock and dell, as through the long gleaming arches the king comes marching to his throne. But shade yet lingers undisturbed in the valleys, mingled with timid smoke from household chimneys; blue as the smoke, a gauzy haze is twined around the brow of every distant hill; and the same soft azure confuses the outlines of the nearer trees, to whose branches snowy wreaths are clinging, far up among the boughs, like strange new flowers. Everywhere the unstained surface glistens in the sunbeams. In the curves and wreaths and turrets of the drifts a blue tinge nestles. The fresh pure sky answers to it; every cloud has vanished, save one or two which linger near the horizon, pardoned offenders, seeming far too innocent for mischief, although their dark and sullen brothers, banished ignominiously below the horizon's verge, may be plotting nameless treachery there. The brook still flows visibly through the valley, and the myriad rocks that check its course are all rounded with fleecy surfaces, till they seem like flocks of tranquil sheep that drink the shallow flood.

The day is one of moderate cold, but clear and bracing; the air sparkles like the snow; everything seems dry and resonant, like the wood of a violin. All sounds are musical,—the voices of children, the cooing of doves, the crowing of cocks, the chopping of wood, the creaking of country sleds, the sweet jangle of sleigh-bells. The snow has fallen under a cold temperature, and the flakes are perfectly crystallized; every shrub we pass bears wreaths which glitter as gorgeously as the nebula in the constellation Perseus; but in another hour of sunshine every one of those fragile outlines will disappear, and the white surface glitter no longer with stars, but with star-dust. On such a day, the universe seems to hold but three pure tints,—blue, white, and green. The loveliness of the universe seems simplified to its last extreme of refined delicacy. That sensation we poor mortals often have, of being just on the edge of infinite beauty, yet with always a lingering film between, never presses down more closely than on days like this. Everything seems perfectly prepared to satiate the soul with inexpressible felicity, if we could only, by one infinitesimal step farther, reach the mood to dwell in it.

Leaving behind us the sleighs and snow-shovels of the street, we turn noiselessly toward the radiant margin of the sunlit woods. The yellow willows on the causeway burn like flame against the darker background, and will burn on until they burst into April. Yonder pines and hemlocks stand motionless and dark against the sky. The statelier trees have already shaken all the snow from their summits, but it still clothes the lower ones with a white covering that looks solid as marble. Yet see how lightly it escapes!—a slight gust shakes a single tree, there is a *Staub-bach* for a moment, and the branches stand free as in summer, a pyramid of green amid the whiteness of the yet imprisoned forest. Each branch raises itself when emancipated, thus changing the whole outline of the growth; and the snow beneath is punctured with a thousand little depressions, where the petty avalanches have just buried themselves and disappeared.

In crossing this white level, we have been tracking our way across an invisible pond, which was alive last week with five hundred skaters. Now there is a foot of snow upon it, through which there is a boyish excitement in making the first path. Looking back upon our track, it proves to be like all other human paths, straight in intention, but slightly devious in deed. We have gay companions on our way; for a breeze overtakes us, and a hundred little simooms of drift whirl along beside us, and whelm in miniature burial whole caravans of dry leaves. Here, too, our track intersects with that of some previous passer; he has but just gone on, judging by the freshness of the trail, and we can study his character and purposes. The large boots betoken a woodman or iceman; yet such a one would hardly have stepped so irresolutely where a little film of water has spread between the ice and snow and given a look of insecurity; and here again he has stopped to observe the wreaths on this pendent bough, and this snow-filled bird's-nest. And there the footsteps of the lover of beauty turn abruptly to the road again, and he vanishes from us forever.

As we wander on through the wood, all the labyrinths of summer are buried beneath one white inviting pathway, and the pledge of perfect loneliness is given by the unbroken surface of the all-revealing snow. There appears nothing living except a downy woodpecker, whirling round and round upon a young beech-stem, and a few sparrows, plump with grass-seed and hurrying with jerking flight down the sunny glade. But the trees furnish society enough. What a congress of ermined kings is this circle of hemlocks, which stand, white in their soft raiment, around the dais of this woodland pond! Are they held here, like the sovereigns in the palace of the Sleeping Beauty, till some mortal breaks their spell? What sage counsels must be theirs, as they nod their weary heads and whisper ghostly memories and old men's tales to each other, while the red leaves dance on the snowy sward below, or a fox or squirrel steals hurriedly through the wild and wintry night! Here and there is some discrowned Lear, who has thrown off his regal mantle, and stands in faded russet, misplaced among the monarchs.

What a simple and stately hospitality is that of Nature in winter! The season which the residents of cities think an obstruction is in the country an extension of intercourse: it opens every forest from here to Labrador, free of entrance; the most tangled thicket, the most treacherous marsh, becomes passable; and the lumberer or moose-hunter, mounted on his snow-shoes, has the world before him. He says "good snow-shoeing," as we say "good sleighing"; and it gives a sensation like a first visit to the sea-side and the shipping, when one first sees exhibited for sale, in the streets of Bangor or Montreal, these delicate Indian conveyances. It seems as if a new element were suddenly opened for travel, and all due facilities provided. One expects to go a little farther, and see in the shop-windows, "Wings for sale,—gentlemen's and ladies' sizes." The snow-shoe and the birch canoe,—what other dying race ever left behind it two memorials so perfect and so graceful.

The shadows thrown by the trees upon the snow are blue and soft, sharply defined, and so contrasted with the gleaming white as to appear narrower than the boughs which cast them. There is something subtle and fantastic about these shadows. Here is a leafless larch-sapling, eight feet high. The image of the lower boughs is traced upon the snow, distinct and firm as cordage, while the higher ones grow dimmer by fine gradations, until the slender topmost twig is blurred, and almost effaced. But the denser upper spire of the young spruce by its side throws almost as distinct a shadow as its base, and the whole figure looks of a more solid texture, as if you could feel it with your hand. More beautiful than either is the fine image of this baby hemlock: each delicate leaf droops above as delicate a copy, and here and there the shadow and the substance kiss and frolic with each other in the downy snow.

The larger larches have a different plaything: on the bare branches, thickly studded with buds, cling airily the small, light cones of last year's growth, each crowned with a little ball of soft snow, four times taller than itself,—save where some have drooped sideways, so that each carries, poor weary Atlas, a sphere upon its back. Thus the coy creatures play cup and ball, and one has lost its plaything yonder, as the branch slightly stirs, and the whole vanishes in a whirl of snow. Meanwhile a fragment of low arbor-vitæ hedge, poor outpost of a neighboring plantation, is so covered and packed with solid drift, inside and out, that it seems as if no power of sunshine could ever steal in among its twigs and disentangle it.

In winter each separate object interests us; in summer, the mass. Natural beauty in winter is a poor man's luxury, infinitely enhanced in quality by the diminution in quantity. Winter, with fewer and simpler methods, yet seems to give all her works a finish even more delicate than that of summer, working, as Emerson says of English agriculture, with a pencil, instead of a plough. Or rather, the ploughshare is but concealed; since a pithy old English preacher has said that "the frost is God's plough, which he drives through every inch of ground in the world, opening each clod, and pulverizing the whole."

Coming out upon a high hillside, more exposed to the direct fury of the sleet, we find Nature wearing a wilder look. Every white-birch clump around us is bent divergingly to the ground, each white form prostrated in mute despair upon the whiter bank. The bare, writhing branches of yonder sombre oak-grove are steeped in snow, and in the misty air they look so remote and foreign that there is not a wild creature of the Norse mythology who might not stalk from beneath their haunted branches. Buried races, Teutons and Cimbri, might tramp solemnly forth from those weird arcades. The soft pines on this nearer knoll seem separated from them by ages and generations. On the farther hills spread woods of smaller growth, like forests of spun glass, jewelry by the acre provided for this coronation of winter.

We descend a steep bank, little pellets of snow rolling hastily beside us, and leaving enamelled furrows behind. Entering the sheltered and sunny glade, we are assailed by a sudden warmth whose languor is almost oppressive. Wherever the sun strikes upon the pines and hemlocks, there is a household gleam which gives a more vivid sensation than the diffused brilliancy of summer. The sunbeams maintain a thousand secondary fires in the reflection of light from every tree and stalk, for the preservation of animal life and ultimate melting of these accumulated drifts. Around each trunk or stone the snow has melted and fallen back. It is a singular fact, established beyond doubt by science, that the snow is absolutely less influenced by the direct rays of the sun than by these reflections. "If a blackened card is placed upon the snow or ice in the sunshine, the frozen mass underneath it will be gradually thawed, while that by which it is surrounded, though exposed to the full power of solar heat, is but little disturbed. If, however, we reflect the sun's rays from a metal surface, an exactly contrary result takes place: the uncovered parts are the first to melt, and the blackened card stands high above the surrounding portion." Look round upon this buried meadow, and you will see emerging through the white surface a thousand stalks of grass, sedge, osmunda, golden-rod, mullein, Saint-John's-wort, plaintain, and eupatorium,—an allied army of the sun, keeping up a perpetual volley of innumerable rays upon the yielding snow.

It is their last dying service. We misplace our tenderness in winter, and look with pity upon the leafless trees. But there is no tragedy in the trees: each is not dead, but sleepeth; and each bears a future summer of buds safe nestled on its bosom, as a mother reposes with her baby at her breast. The same security of life pervades every woody shrub: the alder and the birch have their catkins all ready for the first day of spring, and the sweet-fern has even now filled with fragrance its folded blossom. Winter is no such solid bar between season and season as we fancy, but only a slight check and interruption: one may at any time produce these March blossoms by bringing the buds into the warm house; and the petals of the May-flower sometimes show their pink and white edges in autumn. But every grass-blade and flower-stalk is a mausoleum of vanished summer, itself crumbling to dust, never to rise again. Each child of June, scarce distinguishable in November against the background of moss and rocks and bushes, is brought into final prominence in December by the white snow which imbeds it. The delicate flakes collapse and fall back around it, but retain their inexorable hold. Thus delicate is the action of Nature,—a finger of air, and a grasp of iron.

We pass the old red foundry, banked in with snow and its low eaves draped with icicles, and come to the brook which turns its resounding wheel. The musical motion of the water seems almost unnatural amidst the general stillness: brooks, like men, must keep themselves warm by exercise. The overhanging rushes and alder-sprays, weary of winter's sameness, have made for themselves playthings,—each dangling a crystal knob of ice, which sways gently in the water and gleams ruddy in the sunlight. As we approach the foaming cascade, the toys become larger and more glittering, movable stalactites, which the water tosses merrily upon their flexible stems. The torrent pours down beneath an enamelled mask of ice, wreathed and convoluted like a brain, and sparkling with gorgeous glow. Tremulous motions and glimmerings go through the translucent veil, as if it throbbed with the throbbing wave beneath. It holds in its mazes stray bits of color,—scarlet berries, evergreen sprigs, blue raspberry-stems, and sprays of yellow willow; glittering necklaces and wreaths and tiaras of brilliant ice-work cling and trail around its edges, and no regal palace shines with such carcanets of jewels as this winter ball-room of the dancing drops.

Above, the brook becomes a smooth black canal between two steep white banks; and the glassy water seems momentarily stiffening into the solider blackness of ice. Here and there thin films are already formed over it, and are being constantly broken apart by the treacherous current; a flake a foot square is jerked away and goes sliding beneath the slight transparent surface till it reappears below. The same thing, on a larger scale, helps to form the mighty ice-pack of the Northern seas. Nothing except ice is capable of combining, on the largest scale, bulk with mobility, and this imparts a dignity to its motions even on the smallest scale. I do not believe that anything in Behring's Straits could impress me with a grander sense of desolation or of power, than when in boyhood I watched the ice break up in the winding channel of Charles River.

Amidst so much that seems like death, let us turn and study the life. There is much more to be seen in winter than most of us have ever noticed. Far in the North the "moose-yards" are crowded and trampled, at this season, and the wolf and the deer run noiselessly a deadly race, as I have heard the hunters describe, upon the white surface of the gleaming lake. But the pond beneath our feet keeps its stores of life chiefly below its level platform, as the bright fishes in the basket of yon heavy-booted fisherman can tell. Yet the scattered tracks of mink and muskrat beside the banks, of meadow-mice around the hay-stacks, of squirrels under the trees, of rabbits and partridges in the wood, show the warm life that is beating unseen, beneath fur or feathers, close beside us. The chickadees are chattering merrily in the upland grove, the blue-jays scream in the hemlock glade, the snow-bird mates the snow with its whiteness, and the robin contrasts with it his still ruddy breast. The weird and impenetrable crows, most talkative of birds and most uncommunicative, their very food at this season a mystery, are almost as numerous now as in summer. They always seem like some race of banished goblins, doing penance for some primeval and inscrutable transgression, and if any bird have a history, it is they. In the Spanish version of the tradition of King Arthur, it is said that he fled from the weeping queens and the island valley of Avilion in the form of a crow; and hence it is said in "Don Quixote" that no Englishman will ever kill one.

The traces of the insects in the winter are prophetic,—from the delicate cocoon of some infinitesimal feathery thing which hangs upon the dry, starry calyx of the aster, to the large brown-paper parcel which hides in peasant garb the costly beauty of some gorgeous moth. But the hints of birds are retrospective. In each tree of this pasture, the very pasture where last spring we looked for nests and found them not among the deceitful foliage, the fragile domiciles now stand revealed. But where are the birds that filled them? Could the airy creatures nurtured in those nests have left permanently traced upon the air behind them their own bright summer flight, the whole atmosphere would be filled with interlacing lines and curves of gorgeous coloring, the centre of all being this forsaken bird's-nest filled with snow.

Among the many birds which winter here, and the many insects which are called forth by a few days of thaw, not a few must die of cold or of fatigue amid the storms. Yet how few traces one sees of this mortality! Provision is made for it. Yonder a dead wasp has fallen on the snow, and the warmth of its body, or its power of reflecting a few small rays of light, is melting its little grave beneath it. With what a cleanly purity does Nature strive to withdraw all unsightly objects into her cemetery! Their own weight and lingering warmth take them through air or water, snow or ice, to the level of the earth, and there with spring comes an army of burying-insects, *Necrophagi,* in a livery of red and black, to dig a grave beneath every one, and not a sparrow falleth to the ground without knowledge. The tiny remains thus disappear from the surface, and the dry leaves are soon spread above these Children in the Wood.

Thus varied and benignant are the aspects of winter on these sunny days. But it is impossible to claim this weather as the only type of our winter climate. There occasionally come days which, though perfectly still and serene, suggest more terror than any tempest,—terrible, clear, glaring days of pitiless cold,—when the sun seems powerless or only a brighter moon, when the windows remain ground-glass at high noon-tide, and when, on going out of doors, one is dazzled by the brightness, and fancies for a moment that it cannot be so cold as has been reported, but presently discovers that the severity is only more deadly for being so still. Exercise on such days seems to produce no warmth; one's limbs appear ready to break on any sudden motion, like icy boughs. Stage-drivers and draymen are transformed to mere human buffaloes by their fur coats; the patient oxen are frost-covered; the horse that goes racing by waves a wreath of steam from his tossing head. On such days life becomes a battle to all householders, the ordinary apparatus for defence is insufficient, and the price of caloric is continual vigilance. In innumerable armies the frost besieges the portal, creeps in beneath it and above it, and on every latch and key-handle lodges an advanced guard of white rime. Leave the door ajar never so slightly, and a chill creeps in cat-like; we are conscious by the warmest fireside of the near vicinity of cold, its fingers are feeling after us, and even if they do not clutch us, we know that they are there. The sensations of such days almost make us associate their clearness and whiteness with something malignant and evil. Charles Lamb asserts of snow, "It glares too much for an innocent color, methinks." Why does popular mythology associate the infernal regions with a high temperature instead of a low one? El Aishi, the Arab writer, says of the bleak wind of the Desert, (so writes Richardson, the African traveller,) "The north wind blows with an intensity equalling *the cold of hell;* language fails me to describe its rigorous temperature." Some have thought that there is a similar allusion in the phrase, "weeping and gnashing of teeth,"—the teeth chattering from frost. Milton also enumerates cold as one of the torments of the lost,—

"O'er many a frozen, many a fiery Alp";

and one may sup full of horrors on the exceedingly cold collation provided for the next world by the Norse Edda.

But, after all, there are but few such terrific periods in our Massachusetts winters, and the appointed exit from their frigidity is usually through a snow-storm. After a day of this severe sunshine there comes commonly a darker day of cloud, still hard and forbidding, though milder in promise, with a sky of lead, deepening near the horizon into darker films of iron. Then, while all the nerves of the universe seem rigid and tense, the first reluctant flake steals slowly down, like a tear. In a few hours the whole atmosphere begins to relax once more, and in our astonishing climate very possibly the snow changes to rain in twenty-four hours, and a thaw sets in. It is not strange, therefore, that snow, which to Southern races is typical of cold and terror, brings associations of warmth and shelter to the children of the North.

Snow, indeed, actually nourishes animal life. It holds in its bosom numerous animalcules: you may have a glass of water, perfectly free from *infusoria*, which yet, after your dissolving in it a handful of snow, will show itself full of microscopic creatures, shrimp-like and swift; and the famous red snow of the Arctic regions is only an exhibition of the same property. It has sometimes been fancied that persons buried under the snow have received sustenance through the pores of the skin, like reptiles imbedded in rock. Elizabeth Woodcock lived eight days beneath a snow-drift, in 1799, without eating a morsel; and a Swiss family were buried beneath an avalanche, in a manger, for five months, in 1755, with no food but a trifling store of chestnuts and a small daily supply of milk from a goat which was buried with them. In neither case was there extreme suffering from cold, and it is unquestionable that the interior of a drift is far warmer than the surface. On the 23d of December, 1860, at 9 P.M., I was surprised to observe drops falling from the under side of a heavy bank of snow at the eaves, at a distance from any chimney, while the mercury on the same side was only fifteen degrees above zero, not having indeed risen above the point of freezing during the whole day.

Dr. Kane pays ample tribute to these kindly properties. "Few of us at home can recognize the protecting value of this warm coverlet of snow. No eider-down in the cradle of an infant is tucked in more kindly than the sleeping-dress of winter about this feeble flower-life. The first warm snows of August and September, falling on a thickly pleached carpet of grasses, heaths, and willows, enshrine the flowery growths which nestle round them in a non-conducting air-chamber; and as each successive snow increases the thickness of the cover, we have, before the intense cold of winter sets in, a light cellular bed covered by drift, six, eight, or ten feet deep, in which the plant retains its vitality. . . . . . I have found in midwinter, in this high latitude of 78° 50′, the surface so nearly moist as to be friable to the touch; and upon the ice-floes, commencing with a surface-temperature of $-30°$, I found at two feet deep a temperature of $-8°$, at four feet $+2°$, and at eight feet $+26°$. . . . . . The glacier which we became so familiar with afterwards at Etah yields an uninterrupted stream throughout the year." And he afterwards shows that even the varying texture and quality of the snow deposited during the earlier and later portions of the Arctic winter have their special adaptations to the welfare of the vegetation they protect.

The process of crystallization seems a microcosm of the universe. Radiata, mollusea, feathers, flowers, ferns, mosses, palms, pines, grain-fields, leaves of cedar, chestnut, elm, acanthus: these and multitudes of other objects are figured on your frosty window; on sixteen different panes I have counted sixteen patterns strikingly distinct, and it appeared like a show-case for the globe. What can seem remoter relatives than the star, the star-fish, the star-flower, and the starry snow-flake which clings this moment to your sleeve?—yet some philosophers hold that one day their law of existence will be found precisely the same. The connection with the primeval star, especially, seems far and fanciful enough, but there are yet unexplored affinities between light and crystallization: some crystals have a tendency to grow toward the light, and others develop electricity and give out flashes of light during their formation. Slight foundations for scientific fancies, indeed, but slight is all our knowledge.

More than a hundred different figures of snow-flakes, all regular and kaleidoscopic, have been drawn by Scoresby, Lowe, and Glaisher, and may be found pictured in the encyclopædias and elsewhere, ranging from the simplest stellar shapes to the most complicated ramifications. Professor Tyndall, in his delightful book on "The Glaciers of the Alps," gives drawings of a few of these snow-blossoms, which he watched falling for hours, the whole air being filled with them, and drifts of several inches being accumulated while he watched. "Let us imagine the eye gifted with microscopic power sufficient to enable it to see the molecules which composed these starry crystals; to observe the solid nucleus formed and floating in the air; to see it drawing towards it its allied atoms, and these arranging themselves as if they moved to music, and ended with rendering that music concrete." Thus do the Alpine winds, like Orpheus, build their walls by harmony.

In some of these frost-flowers the rare and delicate blossom of our wild *Mitella diphylla* is beautifully figured. Snow-flakes have been also found in the form of regular hexagons and other plane figures, as well as in cylinders and spheres. As a general rule, the intenser the cold the more perfect the formation, and the most perfect specimens are Arctic or Alpine in their locality. In this climate the snow seldom falls when the mercury is much below zero; but the slightest atmospheric changes may alter the whole condition of the deposit, and decide whether it shall sparkle like Italian marble, or be dead-white like the statuary marble of Vermont,—whether it shall be a fine powder which can sift through wherever dust can, or descend in large woolly masses, tossed like mouthfuls to the hungry earth.

The most remarkable display of crystallization which I have ever seen was on the 13th of January, 1859. There had been three days of unusual cold, but during the night the weather had moderated, and the mercury in the morning stood at +14°. About two inches of snow had fallen, and the trees appeared densely coated with it. It proved, on examination, that every twig had on the leeward side a dense row of miniature fronds or fern-leaves executed in snow, with a sharply defined central nerve, or midrib, and perfect ramification, tapering to a point, and varying in length from half an inch to three inches. On every post, every rail, and the corners of every building, the same spectacle was seen; and where the snow had accumulated in deep drifts, it was still made up of the ruins of these fairy structures. The white, enamelled landscape was beautiful, but a close view of the details was far more so. The crystallizations were somewhat uniform in structure, yet suggested a variety of natural objects, as feathermosses, birds' feathers, and the most delicate lace-corals, but the predominant analogy was with ferns. Yet they seemed to assume a sort of fantastic kindred with the objects to which they adhered: thus, on the leaves of spruce-trees and on delicate lichens they seemed like reduplications of the original growth, and they made the broad, flat leaves of the arbor-vitæ fully twice as wide as before. But this fringe was always on one side only, except when gathered upon dangling fragments of spider's web, or bits of stray thread: these they entirely encircled, probably because these objects had twirled in the light wind while the crystals were forming. Singular disguises were produced: a bit of ragged rope appeared a piece of twisted lace-work; a knot-hole in a board was adorned with a deep antechamber of snowy wreaths; and the frozen body of a hairy caterpillar became its own well-plumed hearse. The most peculiar circumstance was the fact that single flakes never showed any regular crystallization: the magic was in the combination; the under sides of rails and boards exhibited it as unequivocally as the upper sides, indicating that the phenomenon was created in the lower atmosphere, and was more akin to frost than snow; and yet the largest snow-banks were composed of nothing else, and seemed like heaps of blanched iron-filings.

Interesting observations have been made on the relations between ice and snow. The difference seems to lie only in the more or less compacted arrangement of the frozen particles. Water and air, each being transparent when separate, become opaque when intimately mingled; the reason being that the inequalities of refraction break up and scatter every ray of light. Thus, clouds cast a shadow; so does steam; so does foam: and the same elements take a still denser texture when combined as snow. Every snow-flake is permeated with minute airy chambers, among which the light is bewildered and lost; while from perfectly hard and transparent ice every trace of air disappears, and the transmission of light is unbroken. Yet that same ice becomes white and opaque when pulverized, its fragments being then intermingled with air again,—just as colorless glass may be crushed into white powder. On the other hand, Professor Tyndall has converted slabs of snow to ice by regular pressure, and has shown that every Alpine glacier begins as a snow-drift at its summit, and ends in a transparent ice-cavern below. "The blue blocks which span the sources of the Arveiron were once powdery snow upon the slopes of the Col du Géant."

The varied and wonderful shapes assumed by snow and ice have been best portrayed, perhaps, by Dr. Kane in his two works; but their resources of color have been so explored by no one as by this same favored Professor Tyndall, among his Alps. It appears that the tints which in temperate regions are seen feebly and occasionally, in hollows or angles of fresh drifts, become brilliant and constant above the line of perpetual snow, and the higher the altitude the more lustrous the display. When a staff was struck into the new-fallen drift, the hollow seemed instantly to fill with a soft blue liquid, while the snow adhering to the staff took a complementary color of pinkish yellow, and on moving it up and down it was hard to resist the impression that a pink flame was rising and sinking in the hole. The little natural furrows in the drifts appeared faintly blue, the ridges were gray, while the parts most exposed to view seemed least illuminated, and as if a light brown dust had been sprinkled over them. The fresher the snow, the more marked the colors, and it made no difference whether the sky were cloudless or foggy. Thus was every white peak decked upon its brow with this tiara of ineffable beauty.

The impression is very general that the average quantity of snow has greatly diminished in America; but it must be remembered that very severe storms occur only at considerable intervals, and the Puritans did not always, as boys fancy, step out of the upper windows upon the snow.

In 1717, the ground was covered from ten to twenty feet, indeed; but during January, 1861, the snow was six feet on a level in many parts of Maine and New Hampshire, and was probably drifted three times that depth in particular spots. The greatest storm recorded in England, I believe, is that of 1814, in which for forty-eight hours the snow fell so furiously that drifts of sixteen, twenty, and even twenty-four feet were recorded in various places. An inch an hour is thought to be the average rate of deposit, though four inches are said to have fallen during the severe storm of January 3d, 1859. When thus intensified, the "beautiful meteor of the snow" begins to give a sensation of something formidable; and when the mercury suddenly falls meanwhile, and the wind rises, there are sometimes suggestions of such terror in a snow-storm as no summer thunders can rival. The brief and singular tempest of February 7th, 1861, was a thing to be forever remembered by those who saw it, as I did, over a wide plain. The sky suddenly appeared to open and let down whole solid snow-banks at once, which were caught and torn to pieces by the ravenous winds, and the traveller was instantaneously enveloped in a whirling mass far denser than any fog; it was a tornado with snow stirred into it. Standing in the middle of the road, with houses close on every side, one could see absolutely nothing in any direction, one could hear no sound but the storm. Every landmark vanished, and it was no more possible to guess the points of the compass than in mid-ocean. It was easy to conceive of being bewildered and overwhelmed within a rod of one's own door. The tempest lasted only an hour; but if it had lasted a week, we should have had such a storm as occurred on the steppes of Kirgheez in Siberia, in 1827, destroying two hundred and eighty thousand five hundred horses, thirty thousand four hundred cattle, a million sheep, and ten thousand camels,—or as "the thirteen drifty days," in 1620, which killed nine tenths of all the sheep in the South of Scotland. On Eskdale Moor, out of twenty thousand only forty-five were left alive, and the shepherds everywhere built up huge semicircular walls of the dead creatures, to afford shelter to the living, till the gale should end. But the most remarkable narrative of a snow-storm which I have ever seen was that written by James Hogg, the Ettrick Shepherd, in record of one which took place January 24th, 1790.

James Hogg at this time belonged to a sort of literary society of young shepherds, and had set out, the day previous, to walk twenty miles over the hills to the place of meeting; but so formidable was the look of the sky that he felt anxious for his sheep, and finally turned back again. There was at that time only a slight fall of snow, in thin flakes which seemed uncertain whether to go up or down; the hills were covered with deep folds of frost-fog, and in the valleys the same fog seemed dark, dense, and as it were crushed together. An old shepherd, predicting a storm, bade him watch for a sudden opening through this fog, and expect a wind from that quarter; yet when he saw such an opening suddenly form at midnight, (having then reached his own home,) he thought it all a delusion, as the weather had grown milder and a thaw seemed setting in. He therefore went to bed, and felt no more anxiety for his sheep; yet he lay awake in spite of himself, and at two o'clock he heard the storm begin. It smote the house suddenly, like a great peal of thunder,—something utterly unlike any storm he had ever before heard. On his rising and thrusting his bare arm through a hole in the roof, it seemed precisely as if he had thrust it into a snow-bank, so densely was the air filled with falling and driving particles. He lay still for an hour, while the house rocked with the tempest, hoping it might prove only a hurricane; but as there was no abatement, he wakened his companion-shepherd, telling him "it was come on such a night or morning as never blew from the heavens." The other at once arose, and, opening the door of the shed where they slept, found a drift as high as the farm-house already heaped between them and its walls, a distance of only fourteen yards. He floundered through, Hogg soon following, and, finding all the family up, they agreed that they must reach the sheep as soon as possible, especially eight hundred ewes that were in one lot together, at the farthest end of the farm. So, after family-prayers and breakfast, four of them stuffed their pockets with bread and cheese, sewed their plaids about them, tied down their hats, and, taking each his staff, set out on their tremendous undertaking, two hours before day.

Day dawned before they got three hundred yards from the house. They could not see each other, and kept together with the greatest difficulty. They had to make paths with their staves, rolled themselves over drifts otherwise impassable, and every three or four minutes had to hold their heads down between their knees to recover breath. They went in single file, taking the lead by turns. The master soon gave out, and was speechless and semi-conscious for more than an hour, though he afterwards recovered and held out with the rest. Two of them lost their headgear, and Hogg himself fell over a high precipice; but they reached the flock at half past ten. They found the ewes huddled together in a dense body, under ten feet of snow,—packed so closely, that, to the amazement of the shepherds, when they had extricated the first, the whole flock walked out one after another, in a body, through the hole.

How they got them home it is almost impossible to tell. It was now noon, and they sometimes could see through the storm for twenty yards, but they had only one momentary glimpse of the hills through all that terrible day. Yet Hogg persisted in going by himself afterwards to rescue some flocks of his own, barely escaping with life from the expedition; his eyes were sealed up with the storm, and he crossed a formidable torrent, without knowing it, on a wreath of snow. Two of the others lost themselves in a deep valley, and would have perished but for being accidentally heard by a neighboring shepherd, who guided them home, where the female portion of the family had abandoned all hope of ever seeing them again.

The next day was clear, with a cold wind, and they set forth again at daybreak to seek the remainder of the flock. The face of the country was perfectly transformed: not a hill was the same, not a brook or lake could be recognized. Deep glens were filled in with snow, covering the very tops of the trees; and over a hundred acres of ground, under an average depth of six or eight feet, they were to look for four or five hundred sheep. The attempt would have been hopeless but for a dog that accompanied them: seeing their perplexity, he began snuffing about, and presently scratching in the snow at a certain point, and then looking round at his master: digging at this spot, they found a sheep beneath. And so the dog led them all day, bounding eagerly from one place to another, much faster than they could dig the creatures out, so that he sometimes had twenty or thirty holes marked beforehand. In this way, within a week, they got out every sheep on the farm except four, these last being buried under a mountain of snow fifty feet deep, on the top of which the dog had marked their places again and again. In every case the sheep proved to be alive and warm, though half suffocated; on being taken out, they usually bounded away swiftly, and then fell helplessly in a few moments, overcome by the change of atmosphere; some then died almost instantly, and others were carried home and with difficulty preserved, only about sixty being lost in all. Marvellous to tell, the country-people unanimously agreed afterwards to refer the whole terrific storm to some secret incantations of poor Hogg's literary society aforesaid; it was generally maintained that a club of young dare-devils had raised the Fiend himself among them in the likeness of a black dog, the night preceding the storm, and the young students actually did not dare to show themselves at fairs or at markets for a year afterwards.

Snow-scenes less exciting, but more wild and dreary, may be found in Alexander Henry's Travels with the Indians, in the last century. In the winter of 1776, for instance, they wandered for many hundred miles over the farthest northwestern prairies, where scarcely a white man had before trodden. The snow lay from four to six feet deep. They went on snow-shoes, drawing their stores on sleds. The mercury was sometimes −32°; no fire could keep them warm at night, and often they had no fire, being scarcely able to find wood enough to melt the snow for drink. They lay beneath buffalo-skins and the stripped bark of trees: a foot of snow sometimes fell on them before morning. The sun rose at half past nine and set at half past two. "The country was one uninterrupted plain, in many parts of which no wood, nor even the smallest shrub, was to be seen: a frozen sea, of which the little coppices were the islands. That behind which we had encamped the night before soon sank in the horizon, and the eye had nothing left save only the sky and snow." Fancy them encamped by night, seeking shelter in a scanty grove from a wild tempest of snow; then suddenly charged upon by a herd of buffaloes, thronging in from all sides of the wood to take shelter likewise,—the dogs barking, the Indians firing, and still the bewildered beasts rushing madly in, blinded by the storm, fearing the guns within less than the fury without, crashing through the trees, trampling over the tents, and falling about in the deep and dreary snow! No other writer has ever given us the full desolation of Indian winter-life. Whole families, Henry said, frequently perished together in such storms. No wonder that the aboriginal legends are full of "mighty Peboan, the Winter," and of Kabibonokka in his lodge of snow-drifts.

The interest inspired by these simple narratives suggests the reflection, that literature, which has thus far portrayed so few aspects of external Nature, has described almost nothing of winter beauty. In English books, especially, this season is simply forlorn and disagreeable, dark and dismal.

> "And foul and fierce
> All winter drives along the darkened air."

> "When dark December shrouds the transient day,
>   And stormy winds are howling in their ire,
> Why com'st not thou?. . . . O, haste to pay
>   The cordial visit sullen hours require!"

> "Winter will oft at eve resume the breeze,
> Chill the pale morn, and bid his driving blasts
> Deform the day delightless."

> "Now that the fields are dank and ways are mire,
> With whom you might converse, and by the fire
> Help waste the sullen day."

But our prevalent association with winter, in the Northern United States, is with something white and dazzling and brilliant; and it is time to paint our own pictures, and cease to borrow these gloomy alien tints. One must turn eagerly every season to the few glimpses of American winter aspects: to Emerson's "Snow-Storm," every word a sculpture; to the admirable storm in "Margaret"; to Thoreau's "Winter Walk," in the "Dial"; and to Lowell's "First Snow-Flake." These are fresh and real pictures, which carry us back to the Greek Anthology, where the herds come wandering down from the wooded mountains, covered with snow, and to Homer's aged Ulysses, his wise words falling like the snows of winter.

Let me add to this scanty gallery of snow-pictures the quaint lore contained in one of the multitudinous sermons of Increase Mather, printed in 1704, entitled "A Brief Discourse concerning the Prayse due to God for His Mercy in giving Snow like Wool." One can fancy the delight of the oppressed Puritan boys in the days of the nineteenthlies, driven to the place of worship by the tithing-men, and cooped up on the pulpit and gallery stairs under charge of the constables, at hearing for once a discourse which they could understand,—snowballing spiritualized. This was not one of Emerson's terrible examples,—"the storm real, and the preacher only phenomenal"; but this setting of snow-drifts, which in our winters lends such grace to every stern rock and rugged tree, throws a charm even around the grim theology of the Mathers. Three main propositions, seven subdivisions, four applications, and four uses, but the wreaths and the gracefulness are cast about them all,—while the wonderful commonplace-books of those days, which held everything, had accumulated scraps of winter learning which cannot be spared from these less abstruse pages.

Beginning first at the foundation, the preacher must prove, "Prop. I. *That the Snow is fitly resembled to Wool.* Snow like Wool, sayes the Psalmist. And not only the Sacred Writers, but others make use of this Comparison. The Grecians of old were wont to call the Snow ERIODES HUDOR, *Wooly Water*, or wet Wool. The Latin word *Floccus* signifies both a Lock of Wool and a Flake of Snow, in that they resemble one another. The aptness of the similitude appears in three things." "1. In respect of the Whiteness thereof." "2. In respect of Softness." "3. In respect of that Warming Vertue that does attend the Snow." [Here the reasoning must not be omitted.] "Wool is warm. We say, *As warm as Wool.* Woolen-cloth has a greater warmth than other Cloathing has. The wool on Sheep keeps them warm in the Winter season. So when the back of the Ground is covered with Snow, it keeps it warm. Some mention it as one of the wonders of the Snow, that tho' it is itself cold, yet it makes the Earth warm. But Naturalists observe that there is a saline spirit in it, which is hot, by means whereof Plants under the Snow are kept from freezing. Ice under the Snow is sooner melted and broken than other Ice. In some Northern Climates, the wild barbarous People use to cover themselves over with it to keep them warm. When the sharp Air has begun to freeze a man's Limbs, Snow will bring heat into them again. If persons Eat much Snow, or drink immoderately of Snow-water, it will burn their Bowels and make them black. So that it has a warming vertue in it, and is therefore fitly compared to Wool."

Snow has many merits. "In *Lapland,* where there is little or no light of the sun in the depth of Winter, there are great Snows continually on the ground, and by the Light of that they are able to Travel from one place to another. . . . . . At this day in some hot Countreys, they have their Snow-cellars, where it is kept in Summer, and if moderately used, is known to be both refreshing and healthful. There are also Medicinal Vertues in the snow. A late Learned Physician has found that a *Salt* extracted out of snow is a sovereign Remedy against both putrid and pestilential Feavors. Therefore Men should Praise God, who giveth Snow like Wool." But there is an account against the snow, also. "Not only the disease called *Bulimia,* but others more fatal have come out of the Snow. *Geographers* give us to understand that in some Countries Vapours from the Snow have killed multitudes in less than a Quarter of an Hour. Sometimes both Men and Beasts have been destroyed thereby. Writers speak of no less than Forty Thousand men killed by a great Snow in one Day."

It gives a touching sense of human sympathy, to find that we may look at Orion and the Pleiades through the grave eyes of a Puritan divine. "The *Seven Stars* are the Summer Constellation: they bring on the spring and summer; and *Orion* is a Winter Constellation, which is attended with snow and cold, as at this Day. . . . . . Moreover, Late *Philosophers* by the help of the *Microscope* have observed the wonderful Wisdom of God in the Figure of the Snow; each flake is usually of a *Stellate* Form, and of six Angles of exact equal length from the Center. It is *like a little Star.* A great man speaks of it with admiration, that in a Body so familiar as the Snow is, no Philosopher should for many Ages take notice of a thing so obvious as the Figure of it. The learned *Kepler,* who lived in this last Age, is acknowledged to be the first that acquainted the world with the Sexangular Figure of the Snow."

Then come the devout applications. "There is not a Flake of Snow that falls on the Ground without the hand of God, Mat. 10. 29. 30. Not a

Sparrow falls to the Ground, without the Will of your Heavenly Father, all the Hairs of your head are numbred. So the Great God has numbred all the Flakes of Snow that covers the Earth. Altho' no man can number them, that God that tells the number of the Stars has numbred them all. . . . We often see it, when the Ground is bare, if God speaks the word, the Earth is covered with snow in a few Minutes' time. Here is the power of the Great God. If all the Princes and Great Ones of the Earth should send their Commands to the Clouds, not a Flake of snow would come from thence."

Then follow the "uses," at last,—the little boys in the congregation having grown uneasy long since, at hearing so much theorizing about snow-drifts, with so little opportunity of personal practice. "Use I. If we should Praise God for His giving Snow, surely then we ought to Praise Him for Spiritual Blessings much more." "Use II. We should Humble our selves under the Hand of God, when Snow in the season of it is witheld from us." "Use III. Hence all Atheists will be left Eternally Inexcusable." "Use IV. We should hence Learn to make a Spiritual Improvement of the Snow." And then with a closing volley of every text which figures under the head of "Snow" in the Concordance, the discourse comes to an end; and every liberated urchin goes home with his head full of devout fancies of building a snow-fort, after sunset, from which to propel conse-crated missiles against imaginary or traditional Pequots.

And the patient reader, too long snow-bound, must be liberated also. After the winters of deepest drifts the spring often comes most suddenly; there is little frost in the ground, and the liberated waters, free without the expected freshet, are filtered into the earth, or climb on ladders of sunbeams to the sky. The beautiful crystals all melt away, and the places where they lay are silently made ready to be submerged in new drifts of summer verdure. These also will be transmuted in their turn, and so the eternal cycle of the season glides along.

Near my house there is a garden, beneath whose stately sycamores a fountain plays. Three sculptured girls lift forever upward a chalice which distils unceasingly a fine and plashing rain; in summer the spray holds the maidens in a glittering veil, but winter takes the radiant drops and slowly builds them up into a shroud of ice which creeps gradually about the three slight figures: the feet vanish, the waist is encircled, the head is covered, the piteous uplifted arms disappear, as if each were a Vestal Virgin entombed alive for her transgression. They vanishing entirely, the fountain yet plays on unseen; all winter the pile of ice grows larger, glit-tering organ-pipes of congelation add themselves outside, and by Febru-ary a great glacier is formed, at whose buried centre stand immovably the patient girls. Spring comes at last, the fated prince, to free with glittering spear these enchanted beauties; the waning glacier, slowly receding, lies conquered before their liberated feet; and still the fountain plays. Who can despair before the iciest human life, when its unconscious symbols are so beautiful?

3

OLDPORT WHARVES

Every one who comes to a wharf feels an impulse to follow it down, and look from the end. It is the point of contact between land and sea. A bridge evades the water, and unites land with land, as if there were no obstacle. But a wharf seeks the water, and grasps it with a solid hand. It is the sign of a lasting friendship; once extended, there it remains; the water embraces it, takes it into its tumultuous bosom at high tide, leaves it in peace at ebb, rushes back to it eagerly again, plays with it in sunshine, surges round it in storm, almost crushing the massive thing. But the pledge once given is never withdrawn. Buildings may rise and fall, but a solid wharf is almost indestructible. Even if it seems destroyed, its materials are all there. This shore might be swept away, these piers be submerged or dashed asunder, still every brick and stone would remain. Half the wharves of Oldport were ruined in the great storm of 1815. Yet not one of them has stirred from the place where it lay; its foundations have only spread more widely and firmly; they are a part of the very pavement of the harbor, submarine mountain ranges, on one of which yonder schooner now lies aground. Thus the wild ocean only punished itself, and has been embarrassed for half a century, like many another mad profligate, by the wrecks of what it ruined.

Yet the surges are wont to deal very tenderly with these wharves. In summer the sea decks them with floating weeds, and studs them with an armor of shells. In the winter it surrounds them with a smoother mail of ice, and the detached piles stand white and gleaming, like the outdoor palace of a Russian queen. How softly and eagerly this coming tide swirls round them! All day the fishes haunt their shadows; all night the phosphorescent water glimmers by them, and washes with long, refluent waves along their sides, decking their blackness with a spray of stars.

Water seems the natural outlet and discharge for every landscape, and when we have followed down this artificial promontory, a wharf, and have seen the waves on three sides of us, we have taken the first step toward circumnavigating the globe. This is our last *terra firma*. One step farther, and there is no possible foothold but a deck, which tilts and totters beneath our feet. A wharf, therefore, is properly neutral ground for all. It is a silent hospitality, understood by all nations. It is in some sort a thing of universal ownership. Having once built it, you must grant its use to every one; it is no trespass to land upon any man's wharf.

The sea, like other beautiful savage creatures, derives most of its charm from its reserves of untamed power. When a wild animal is subdued to abjectness, all its interest is gone. The ocean is never thus humiliated. So slight an advance of its waves would overwhelm us, if only the water should keep on rising! Even here, in these safe haunts of commerce, we deal with the same salt tide which I myself have seen ascend above these piers, and which within half a century drowned a whole family in their home upon our Long Wharf. It is still the same ungoverned ocean which twice in every twenty-four hours reasserts its right of way, and stops only where it will. At Monckton, on the Bay of Fundy, the wharves are built forty feet high, and at ebb-tide you may look down on the schooners lying aground upon the mud below. In six hours they will be floating at your side. But the motions of the tide are as resistless whether its rise be six feet or forty; as in the lazy stretching of the caged lion's paw you can see all the terrors of his spring.

Our principal wharf, the oldest in the town, has lately been doubled in size, and quite transformed in shape, by an importation of broad acres from the country. It is now what is called "made land,"—a manufacture which has grown so easy that I daily expect to see some enterprising contractor set up endwise a bar of railroad iron, and construct a new planet at its summit, which shall presently go spinning off into space and be called an asteroid. There are some people whom it would be pleasant to colonize in that way; but meanwhile the unchanged southern side of the pier seems pleasanter, with its boat-builders' shops, all facing sunward,—a cheerful haunt upon a winter's day. On the early maps this wharf appears as "Queen-Hithe," a name more graceful than its present cognomen. "Hithe" or "Hythe" signifies a small harbor, and is the final syllable of many English names, as of Lambeth. Hythe is also one of those Cinque Ports of which the Duke of Wellington was warden. This wharf was probably still familiarly called Queen-Hithe in 1781, when Washington and Rochambeau walked its length bareheaded between the ranks of French soldiers; and it doubtless bore that name when Dean

Berkeley arrived in 1729, and the Rev. Mr. Honyman and all his flock closed hastily their prayer-books, and hastened to the landing to receive their guest. But it had lost this name ere the days, yet remembered by aged men, when the Long Wharf became a market. Beeves were then driven thither and tethered, while each hungry applicant marked with a piece of chalk upon the creature's side the desired cut; when a sufficient portion had been thus secured, the sentence of death was issued. Fancy the chalk a live coal, or the beast endowed with human consciousness, and no Indian or Inquisitorial tortures could have been more fearful.

It is like visiting the houses at Pompeii, to enter the strange little black warehouses which cover some of our smaller wharves. They are so old and so small it seems as if some race of pygmies must have built them. Though they are two or three stories high, with steep gambrel-roofs, and heavily timbered, their rooms are yet so low that a man six feet high can hardly stand upright beneath the great cross-beams. There is a row of these structures, for instance, described on a map of 1762 as "the old buildings on Lopez' Wharf," and to these another century has probably brought very little change. Lopez was a Portuguese Jew, who came to this place, with several hundred others, after the Lisbon earthquake of 1755. He is said to have owned eighty square-rigged vessels in this port, from which not one such craft now sails. His little counting-room is in the second story of the building; its wall-timbers are of oak, and are still sound; the few remaining planks are grained to resemble rosewood and mahogany; the fragments of wallpaper are of English make. In the cross-beam, just above your head, are the pigeon-holes once devoted to different vessels, whose names are still recorded above them on faded paper,—"Ship Cleopatra," "Brig Juno," and the like. Many of these vessels measured less than two hundred tons, and it seems as if their owner had built his ships to match the size of his counting-room.

A sterner tradition clings around an old building on a remoter wharf; for men have but lately died who had seen slaves pass within its doors for confinement. The wharf in those days appertained to a distillery, an establishment then constantly connected with the slave trade, rum being sent to Africa, and human beings brought back. Occasionally a cargo was landed here, instead of being sent to the West Indies or to South Carolina, and this building was fitted up for their temporary quarters. It is but some twenty-five feet square, and must be less than thirty feet in height, yet it is divided into three stories, of which the lowest was used for other purposes, and the two upper were reserved for slaves. There are still to be seen the barred partitions and latticed door, making half the second floor into a sort of cage, while the agent's room appears to have occupied the other half. A similar latticed door—just such as I have seen in Southern slave-pens—secures the foot of the upper stairway. The whole small attic constitutes a single room, with a couple of windows, and two additional breathing-holes, two feet square, opening on the yard. It makes one sick to think of the poor creatures who may once have gripped those bars with their hands, or have glared with eager eyes between them; and it makes me recall with delight the day when I once wrenched away the stocks and chains from the floor of a pen like this, on the St. Mary's River in Florida. It is almost forty years since this distillery became a mill, and sixty since the slave trade was abolished. The date "1803" is scrawled upon the door of the cage,—the very year when the port of Charleston was reopened for slaves, just before the traffic ceased. A few years more, and such horrors will seem as remote a memory in South Carolina, thank God! as in Rhode Island.

Other wharves are occupied by mast-yards, places that seem like play-rooms for grown men, crammed fuller than any old garret with those odds and ends in which the youthful soul delights. There are planks and spars and timber, broken rudders, rusty anchors, coils of rope, bales of sail-cloth, heaps of blocks, piles of chain cable, great iron tar-kettles like antique helmets, strange machines for steaming planks, inexplicable little chimneys, engines that seem like dwarf locomotives, windlasses that apparently turn nothing, and incipient canals that lead nowhere. For in these yards there seems no particular difference between land and water; the tide comes and goes anywhere, and nobody minds it; boats are drawn up among burdocks and ambrosia, and the platform on which you stand suddenly proves to be something afloat. Vessels are hauled upon the ways, each side of the wharf, their poor ribs pitiably unclothed, ready for a cumbrous mantua-making of oak and iron. On one side, within a floating boom, lies a fleet of masts and unhewn logs, tethered uneasily, like a herd of captive sea monsters, rocking in the ripples. A vast shed, that has doubtless looked ready to fall for these dozen years, spreads over half the entrance to the wharf, and is filled with spars, knee-timber, and planks of fragrant wood; its uprights are festooned with all manner of great hawsers and smaller ropes, and its dim loft is piled with empty casks and idle sails. The sun always seems to shine in a shipyard; there are apt to be more loungers than laborers, and this gives a pleasant air of repose; the neighboring water softens all harsher sounds, the foot treads upon an elastic carpet of embedded chips, and pleasant resinous odors are in the air.

Then there are wharves quite abandoned by commerce, and given over to small tenements, filled with families so abundant that they might dispel the fears of those alarmists who suspect that children are ceasing to be born. Shrill voices resound there—American or Irish, as the case may be—through the summer noon-tides; and the domestic clothes-line forever stretches across the paths where imported slaves once trod, or rich merchandise lay piled. Some of these abodes are nestled in the corners of houses once stately, with large windows and carven doorways. Others occupy separate buildings, almost always of black, unpainted wood, sometimes with the long, sloping roof of Massachusetts, oftener with the quaint "gambrel" of Rhode Island. From the busiest point of our main street I can show you a single cottage, with low gables, projecting eaves, and sheltering sweetbrier, that seems as if it must have strayed hither, a century or two ago, out of some English lane.

Some of the more secluded wharves appear wholly deserted by men and women, and are tenanted alone by rats and boys,—two amphibious races; either can swim anywhere, or scramble and penetrate everywhere. The boys launch some abandoned skiff, and, with an oar for a sail and another for a rudder, pass from wharf to wharf; nor would it be surprising if the bright-eyed rats were to take similar passage on a shingle. Yet, after all, the human juveniles are the more sagacious brood. It is strange that people should go to Europe, and seek the society of potentates less imposing, when home can endow them with the occasional privilege of a nod from an American boy. In these sequestered haunts I frequently meet some urchin three feet high who carries with him an air of consummate worldly experience that completely overpowers me, and I seem to shrink to the dimensions of Tom Thumb. Before his calm and terrible glance all disguises fail. You may put on a bold and careless air, and affect to overlook him as you pass; but it is like assuming to ignore the existence of the Pope of Rome, or of the London "Times." He knows better. Grown men are never very formidable; they are shy and shamefaced themselves, usually preoccupied, and not very observing. If they see a man loitering about, without visible aim, they class him as a mild imbecile, and let him go; but boys are nature's detectives, and one does not so easily evade their scrutinizing eyes. I know full well that, while I study their ways, they are noting mine through a clearer lens, and are probably taking my measure far better than I take theirs. One instinctively shrinks from making a sketch or memorandum while they are by; and if caught in the act, one fondly hopes to pass for some harmless speculator in real estate, whose pencillings may be only a matter of habit, like those casual sums in compound interest which are usually to be found scrawled on the margins of the daily papers in Boston reading-rooms.

Our wharves are almost all connected by intricate byways among the buildings; and one almost wishes to be a pirate or a smuggler, for the pleasure of eluding the officers of justice through such seductive paths. It is, perhaps, to counteract this perilous fascination that our new police-office has been established on a wharf. You will see its brick tower rising not ungracefully, as you enter the inner harbor; it looks the better for being almost windowless, though beauty was not the aim of the omission. A curious stranger is said to have asked one of our city fathers the reason of this peculiarity. "No use in windows," said the experienced official sadly; "the boys would only break 'em." It seems very unjust to assert that there is no subordination in our American society; the citizens show deference to the police, and the police to the boys.

The ancient aspect of these wharves extends itself sometimes to the vessels which lie moored beside them. At yonder pier, for instance, has lain for thirteen years a decaying bark, which was suspected of being engaged in the slave trade. She was run ashore and abandoned on Block Island, in the winter of 1854, and was afterwards brought in here. Her purchaser was offered eight thousand dollars for his bargain, but refused it; and here the vessel has remained, paying annual wharf dues and charges, till she is worthless. She lies chained at the wharf, and the tide rises and falls within her, thus furnishing a convenient bathing-house for the children, who also find a perpetual gymnasium in the broken shrouds that dangle from her masts. Turner, when he painted his "Slave Ship," could have asked no better model. There is no name upon the stern, and it exhibits merely a carved eagle, with the wings clipped and the head knocked off. Only the lower masts remain, which are of a dismal black, as are the tops and mizzen cross-trees. Within the bulwarks, on each side, stand rows of black blocks, to which the shrouds were once attached; these blocks are called by sailors "dead-eyes," and each stands in weird mockery, with its three ominous holes, like so many human skulls before some palace in Dahomey. Other blocks like these swing more ominously yet at the ends of the shrouds, that still hang suspended, waving and creaking and jostling in the wind. Each year the ropes decay, and soon the repulsive pendants will be gone. Not so with the iron belaying-pins, a few of which still stand around the mast, so rusted into the iron fife-rail that even the persevering industry of the children cannot wrench them out. It seems as if some guilty stain must cling to their sides, and hold them in. By one of those fitnesses which fortune often adjusts, but which seem incredible in art, the wharf is now used on one side for the storage of slate, and the hulk is approached through an avenue of gravestones. I never find myself in that neighborhood but my steps instinctively seek that condemned vessel, whether by day, when she makes a dark foreground for the white yachts and the summer waves, or by night, when the storm breaks over her desolate deck.

If we follow northward from "Queen-Hithe" along the shore, we pass into a region where the ancient wharves of commerce, ruined in 1815, have never been rebuilt; and only slender pathways for pleasure voyagers now stretch above the submerged foundations. Once the court end of the town, then its commercial centre, it is now divided between the tenements of fishermen and the summer homes of city households. Still the great old houses remain, with mahogany stairways, carved wainscoting, and painted tiles; the sea has encroached upon their gardens, and only boats like mine approach where English dukes and French courtiers once landed. At the head of yonder private wharf, in that spacious and still cheerful abode, dwelt the beautiful Robinson sisterhood,—the three Quaker belles of Revolutionary days, the memory of whose loves might lend romance to this neighborhood forever. One of these maidens was asked in marriage by a captain in the English army, and was banished by her family to the Narragansett shore, under a flag of truce, to avoid him; her lover was afterward killed by a cannon-ball, in his tent, and she died unwedded. Another was sought by two aspirants, who came in the same ship to woo her, the one from Philadelphia, the other from New York. She refused them both, and they sailed southward together; but, the wind proving adverse, they returned, and one lingered till he won her hand. Still another lover was forced into a vessel by his friends, to tear him from the enchanted neighborhood; while sailing past the house, he suddenly threw himself into the water,—it must have been about where the end of the wharf now rests,—that he might be rescued, and carried, a passive Leander, into yonder door. The house was first the headquarters of the English commander, then of the French; and the sentinels of De Noailles once trod where now croquet balls form the heaviest ordnance. Peaceful and untitled guests now throng in summer where St. Vincents and Northumberlands once rustled and glittered; and there is nothing to recall those brilliant days except the painted tiles on the chimney, where there is a choice society of coquettes and beaux, priests and conjurers, beggars and dancers, and every wig and hoop dates back to the days of Queen Anne.

Sometimes when I stand upon this pier by night, and look across the calm black water, so still, perhaps, that the starry reflections seem to drop through it in prolonged javelins of light instead of resting on the surface, and the opposite lighthouse spreads its cloth of gold across the bay,—I can imagine that I discern the French and English vessels just weighing anchor; I see De Lauzun and De Noailles embarking, and catch the last sheen upon their lace, the last glitter of their swords. It vanishes, and I see only the lighthouse gleam, and the dark masts of a sunken ship across the neighboring island. Those motionless spars have, after all, a nearer interest, and, as I saw them sink, I will tell their tale.

That vessel came in here one day last August, a stately, full-sailed bark; nor was it known, till she had anchored, that she was a mass of imprisoned fire below. She was the Trajan, from Rockland, bound to New Orleans with a cargo of lime, which took fire in a gale of wind, being wet with sea-water as the vessel rolled. The captain and crew retreated to the deck, and made the hatches fast, leaving even their clothing and provisions below. They remained on deck, after reaching this harbor, till the planks grew too hot beneath their feet, and the water came boiling from the pumps. Then the vessel was towed into a depth of five fathoms, to be scuttled and sunk. I watched her go down. Early impressions from "Peter Parley" had portrayed the sinking of a vessel as a frightful plunge, endangering all around, like a maelstrom. The actual process was merely a subsidence so calm and gentle that a child might have stood upon the deck till it sank beneath him, and then might have floated away. Instead of a convulsion, it was something stately and very pathetic to the imagination. The bark remained almost level, the bows a little higher than the stern; and her breath appeared to be surrendered in a series of pulsations, as if every gasp of the lungs admitted more of the suffocating wave. After each long heave, she went visibly a few inches deeper, and then paused. The face of the benign Emperor, her namesake, was on the stern; first sank the carven beard, then the rather mutilated nose, then the white and staring eyes, that gazed blankly over the engulfing waves. The figure-head was Trajan again, at full length, with the costume of an Indian hunter, and the face of a Roman sage; this image lingered longer, and then vanished, like Victor Hugo's Gilliatt, by cruel gradations. Meanwhile the gilded name upon the taffrail had slowly disappeared also; but even when the ripples began to meet across her deck, still her descent was calm. As the water gained, the hidden fire was extinguished, and the smoke, at first densely rising, grew rapidly less. Yet when it had stopped altogether, and all but the top of the cabin had disappeared, there came a new ebullition of steam, like a hot spring, throwing itself several feet in air, and then ceasing.

As the vessel went down, several beams and planks came springing endwise up the hatchway, like liberated men. But nothing had a stranger look to me than some great black casks which had been left on deck.

These, as the water floated them, seemed to stir and wake, and to become gifted with life, and then got into motion and wallowed heavily
about, like hippopotami or any unwieldy and bewildered beasts. At last
the most enterprising of them slid somehow to the bulwark, and, after
several clumsy efforts, shouldered itself over; then others bounced out,
eagerly following, as sheep leap a wall, and then they all went bobbing
away, over the dancing waves. For the wind blew fresh meanwhile, and
there were some twenty sailboats lying-to with reefed sails by the wreck,
like so many sea-birds; and when the loose stuff began to be washed
from the deck, they all took wing at once, to save whatever could be
picked up,—since at such times, as at a conflagration on land, every little thing seems to assume a value,—and at last one young fellow steered
boldly up to the sinking ship itself, sprang upon the vanishing taffrail for
one instant, as if resolved to be the last on board, and then pushed off
again. I never saw anything seem so extinguished out of the universe as
that great vessel, which had towered so colossal above my little boat; it
was impossible to imagine that she was all there yet, beneath the foaming and indifferent waves. No effort has yet been made to raise her; and
a dead eagle seems to have more in common with the living bird than
has now this submerged and decaying hulk with the white and winged
creature that came sailing into our harbor on that summer day.

It shows what conversational resources are always at hand in a seaport
town, that the boatman with whom I first happened to visit this burning
vessel had been thrice at sea on ships similarly destroyed, and could give
all the particulars of their fate. I know no class of uneducated men
whose talk is so apt to be worth hearing as that of sailors. Even apart
from their personal adventures and their glimpses at foreign lands, they
have made observations of nature which are far more careful and
minute than those of farmers, because the very lives of sailors are always
at risk. Their voyages have also made them sociable and fond of talk,
while the pursuits of most men tend to make them silent; and their constant changes of scene, though not touching them very deeply, have really given a certain enlargement to their minds. A quiet demeanor in a
seaport town proves nothing; the most inconspicuous man may have the
most thrilling career to look back upon. With what a superb familiarity
do these men treat this habitable globe! Cape Horn and the Cape of
Good Hope are in their phrase but the West Cape and the East Cape,
merely two familiar portals of their wonted home. With what undis-
guised contempt they speak of the enthusiasm displayed over the ocean
yacht-race! That any man should boast of crossing the Atlantic in a
schooner of two hundred tons, in presence of those who have more than

once reached the Indian Ocean in a fishing-smack of fifty, and have beaten in the homeward race the ships in whose company they sailed! It is not many years since there was here a fishing-skipper, whose surname was "Daredevil," and who sailed from this port to all parts of the world, on sealing voyages, in a sloop so small that she was popularly said to go under water when she got outside the lights, and never to reappear until she reached her port.

And not only those who sail on long voyages, but even our local pilots and fishermen, still lead an adventurous and untamed life, less softened than any other by the appliances of modern days. In their undecked boats they hover day and night along these stormy coasts, and at any hour the beating of the long roll upon the beach may call their full manhood into action. Cowardice is sifted and crushed out from among them by a pressure so constant; and they are withal truthful and steady in their ways, with few vices and many virtues. They are born poor, and remain poor, for their work is hard, with more blanks than prizes; but their life is a life for a man, and though it makes them prematurely old, yet their old age comes peacefully and well. In almost all pursuits the advance of years brings something forlorn. It is not merely that the body decays, but that men grow isolated and are pushed aside; there is no common interest between age and youth. The old farmer leads a lonely existence, and ceases to meet his compeers except on Sunday; nobody consults him; his experience has been monotonous, and his age is apt to grow unsocial. The old mechanic finds his tools and his methods superseded by those of younger men. But the superannuated fisherman graduates into an oracle; the longer he lives, the greater the dignity of his experience; he remembers the great storm, the great tide, the great catch, the great shipwreck; and on all emergencies his counsel has weight. He still busies himself about the boats too, and still sails on sunny days to show the youngsters the best fishing-ground. When too infirm for even this, he can at least sun himself beside the landing, and, dreaming over inexhaustible memories, watch the bark of his own life go down.

4

The Life of Birds

When one thinks of a bird, one fancies a soft, swift, aimless, joyous thing, full of nervous energy and arrowy motions,—a song with wings. So remote from ours their mode of existence, they seem accidental exiles from an unknown globe, banished where none can understand their language; and men only stare at their darting, inexplicable ways, as at the gyrations of the circus. Watch their little traits for hours, and it only tantalizes curiosity. Every man's secret is penetrable, if his neighbor be sharp-sighted. Dickens, for instance, can take a poor condemned wretch, like Fagin, whose emotions neither he nor his reader has experienced, and can paint him in colors that seem made of the soul's own atoms, so that each beholder feels as if he, personally, had been the man. But this bird that hovers and alights beside me, peers up at me, takes its food, then looks again, attitudinizing, jerking, flirting its tail, with a thousand inquisitive and fantastic motions,—although I have power to grasp it in my hand and crush its life out, yet I cannot gain its secret thus, and the centre of its consciousness is really farther from mine than the remotest planetary orbit. "We do not steadily bear in mind," says Darwin, with a noble scientific humility, "how profoundly ignorant we are of the condition of existence of every animal."

What "sympathetic penetration" can fathom the life, for instance, of yonder mysterious, almost voiceless, Humming-Bird, smallest of feathery things, and loneliest, whirring among birds, insect-like, and among insects, bird-like, his path untraceable, his home unseen? An image of airy motion, yet it sometimes seems as if there were nothing joyous in him. He seems like some exiled pygmy prince, banished, but still regal, and doomed to wings. Did gems turn to flowers, flowers to feathers, in that long-past dynasty of the Humming-Birds? It is strange to come upon his tiny nest, in some gray and tangled swamp, with this brilliant atom perched disconsolately near it, upon some mossy twig; it is like visiting Cinderella among her ashes. And from Humming-Bird to Eagle, the daily existence of every bird is a remote and bewitching mystery.

Pythagoras has been charged, both before and since the days of Malvolio, with holding that "the soul of our grandam might haply inhabit a fowl,"—that delinquent men must revisit earth as women, and delinquent women as birds. Malvolio thought nobly of the soul, and in no way approved his opinion; but I remember that Harriet Rohan, in her school-days, accepted this, her destiny, with glee. "When I saw the Oriole," she wrote to me, "from his nest among the plum-trees in the garden, sail over the air and high above the Gothic arches of the elm, a stream of flashing light, or watched him swinging silently on pendent twigs, I did not dream how near akin we were. Or when a Humming-Bird, a winged drop of gorgeous sheen and gloss, a living gem, poising on his wings, thrust his dark, slender, honey-seeking bill into the white blossoms of a little bush beside my window, I should have thought it no such bad thing to be a bird, even if one next became a bat, like the colony in our eaves, that dart and drop and skim and skurry, all the length of moonless nights, in such ecstasies of dusky joy." Was this weird creature, the bat, in very truth a bird, in some far primeval time? and does he fancy, in unquiet dreams at night-fall, that he is one still? I wonder whether he can enjoy the winged brotherhood into which he has thrust himself,—victim, perhaps, of some rash quadruped-ambition,—an Icarus doomed forever *not* to fall.

I think, that, if required, on pain of death, to name instantly the most perfect thing in the universe, I should risk my fate on a bird's egg. There is, first, its exquisite fragility of material, strong only by the mathematical precision of that form so daintily moulded. There is its absolute purity from external stain, since that thin barrier remains impassable until the whole is in ruins,—a purity recognized in the household proverb of "An apple, an egg, and a nut." Then, its range of tints, so varied, so subdued, and so beautiful,—whether of pure white, like the Martin's, or pure green, like the Robin's, or dotted and mottled into the loveliest of browns, like the Red Thrush's, or aqua-marine, with stains of moss-agate, like the Chipping-Sparrow's, or blotched with long weird ink-marks on a pale ground, like the Oriole's, as if it bore inscribed some magic clew to the bird's darting flight and pensile nest. Above all, the associations and predictions of this little wonder,—that one may bear home between his fingers all that winged splendor, all that celestial melody, coiled in mystery within these tiny walls! Even the chrysalis is less amazing, for its form always preserves some trace, however fantastic, of the perfect insect, and it is but moulting a skin; but this egg appears to the eye like a separate unit from some other kingdom of Nature, claiming more kindred with the very stones than with feathery existence; and it is as if a pearl opened and an angel sang.

The nest which is to contain these fair things is a wondrous study also, from the coarse masonry of the Robin to the soft structure of the Humming-Bird, a baby-house among nests. Among all created things, the birds come nearest to man in their domesticity. Their unions are usually in pairs, and for life; and with them, unlike the practice of most quadrupeds, the male labors for the young. He chooses the locality of the nest, aids in its construction, and fights for it, if needful. He sometimes assists in hatching the eggs. He feeds the brood with exhausting labor, like yonder Robin, whose winged picturesque day is spent in putting worms into insatiable beaks, at the rate of one morsel in every three minutes. He has to teach them to fly, as among the Swallows, or even to hunt, as among the Hawks. His life is anchored to his home. Yonder Oriole fills with light and melody the thousand branches of a neighborhood; and yet the centre for all this divergent splendor is always that one drooping dome upon one chosen tree. This he helped to build in May, confiscating cotton as if he were a Union provost-marshal, and singing many songs, with his mouth full of plunder; and there he watches over his household, all through the leafy June, perched often upon the airy cradle-edge, and swaying with it in the summer wind. And from this deep nest, after the pretty eggs are hatched, will he and his mate extract every fragment of the shell, leaving it, like all other nests, save those of birds of prey, clean and pure, when the young are flown. This they do chiefly from an instinct of delicacy; since wood-birds are not wont to use the same nest a second time, even if they rear several broods in a season.

The subdued tints and notes which almost always mark the female sex, among birds,—unlike insects and human beings, of which the female is often more showy than the male,—seem designed to secure their safety while sitting on the nest, while the brighter colors and louder song of the male enable his domestic circle to detect his whereabouts more easily. It is commonly noticed, in the same way, that ground-birds have more neutral tints than those which build out of reach. With the aid of these advantages, it is astonishing how well these roving creatures keep their secrets, and what sharp eyes are needed to spy out their habitations,—while it always seems as if the empty last-year's nests were very plenty. Some, indeed, are very elaborately concealed, as of the Golden-

Crowned Thrush, called, for this reason, the Oven-Bird,—the Meadow-Lark, with its burrowed gallery among the grass,—and the Kingfisher, which mines four feet into the earth. But most of the rarer nests would hardly be discovered, only that the maternal instinct seems sometimes so overloaded by Nature as to defeat itself, and the bird flies and chirps in agony, when she might pass unnoticed by keeping still. The most marked exception which I have noticed is the Red Thrush, which, in this respect, as in others, has the most high-bred manners among all our birds: both male and female sometimes flit in perfect silence through the bushes, and show solicitude only in a sob which is scarcely audible.

Passing along the shore-path by our lake, one day in June, I heard a great sound of scuffling and yelping before me, as if dogs were hunting rabbits or woodchucks. On approaching, I saw no sign of such disturbances, and presently a Partridge came running at me through the trees, with ruff and tail expanded, bill wide open, and hissing like a Goose,—then turned suddenly, and with ruff and tail furled, but with no pretence of lameness, scudded off through the woods in a circle,—then at me again fiercely, approaching within two yards, and spreading all her furbelows, to intimidate, as before,—then, taking in sail, went off again, always at the same rate of speed, yelping like an angry squirrel, squealing like a pig, occasionally clucking like a hen, and, in general, so filling the woods with bustle and disturbance that there seemed no room for anything else. Quite overawed by the display, I stood watching her for some time, then entered the underbrush, where the little invisible brood had been unceasingly piping, in their baby way. So motionless were they, that, for all their noise, I stood with my feet among them, for some minutes, without finding it possible to detect them. When found and taken from the ground, which they so closely resembled, they made no attempt to escape; but when replaced, they presently ran away fast, as if conscious that the first policy had failed, and that their mother had retreated. Such is the summer life of these little things; but come again in the fall, when the wild autumnal winds go marching through the woods, and a dozen pairs of strong wings will thrill like thunder through the arches of the trees, as the full-grown brood whirrs away around you.

Not only have we scarcely any species of birds which are thoroughly and unquestionably identical with European species, but there are certain general variations of habit. For instance, in regard to migration. This is, of course, a universal instinct, since even tropical birds migrate for short distances from the equator, so essential to their existence do these wanderings seem. But in New England, among birds as among men, the roving habit seems unusually strong, and abodes are shifted very rapidly. The whole number of species observed in Massachusetts is about the same as in England,—some three hundred in all. But of this number, in England, about a hundred habitually winter on the island, and half that number even in the Hebrides, some birds actually breeding in Scotland during January and February, incredible as it may seem. Their habits can, therefore, be observed through a long period of the year; while with us the bright army comes and encamps for a month or two and then vanishes. You must attend their dress-parades, while they last; for you will have but few opportunities, and their domestic life must commonly be studied during a few weeks of the season, or not at all.

Wonderful as the instinct of migration seems, it is not, perhaps, so altogether amazing in itself as in some of its attendant details. To a great extent, birds follow the opening foliage northward, and flee from its fading, south; they must keep near the food on which they live, and secure due shelter for their eggs. Our earliest visitors shrink from trusting the bare trees with their nests; the Song-Sparrow seeks the ground; the Blue-Bird finds a box or a hole somewhere; the Red-Wing haunts the marshy thickets, safer in spring than at any other season; and even the sociable Robin prefers a pine-tree to an apple-tree, if resolved to begin housekeeping prematurely. The movements of birds are chiefly timed by the advance of vegetation; and the thing most thoroughly surprising about them is not the general fact of the change of latitude, but their accuracy in hitting the precise locality. That the same Cat-Bird should find its way back, every spring, to almost the same branch of yonder larch-tree,— that is the thing astonishing to me. In England, a lame Redstart was observed in the same garden for sixteen successive years; and the astonishing precision of course which enables some birds of small size to fly from Australia to New-Zealand in a day—probably the longest single flight ever taken—is only a part of the same mysterious instinct of direction.

In comparing modes of flight, the most surprising, of course, is that of the Swallow tribe, remarkable not merely for its velocity, but for the amazing boldness and instantaneousness of the angles it makes; so that eminent European mechanicians have speculated in vain upon the methods used in its locomotion, and prizes have been offered, by mechanical exhibitions, to him who could best explain it. With impetuous dash, they sweep through our perilous streets, these wild hunters of the air, "so near, and yet so far"; they bathe flying, and flying they feed their young. In my immediate vicinity, the Chimney-Swallow is not now common, nor the Sand-Swallow; but the Cliff-Swallow, that strange emigrant from the Far West, the Barn-Swallow, and the white-breasted species, are abundant, together with the Purple Martin. I know no prettier sight than a bevy of these bright little creatures, met from a dozen different farm-houses to picnic at a wayside pool, splashing and fluttering, with their long wings expanded like butterflies, keeping poised by a constant hovering motion, just tilting upon their feet, which scarcely touch the moist ground. You will seldom see them actually perch on anything less airy than some telegraphic wire; but when they do alight, each will make chatter enough for a dozen, as if all the rushing hurry of the wings had passed into the tongue.

Between the swiftness of the Swallow and the stateliness of the birds of prey, the whole range of bird-motion seems included. The long wave of a Hawk's wings seems almost to send a slow vibration through the atmosphere, tolling upon the eye as yon distant bell upon the ear. I never was more impressed with the superior dignity of these soarings than in observing a bloodless contest in the air, last April. Standing beside a little grove, on a rocky hillside, I heard Crows cawing near by, and then a sound like great flies buzzing, which I really attributed, for a moment, to some early insect. Turning, I saw two Crows flapping their heavy wings among the trees, and observed that they were teasing a Hawk about as large as themselves, which was also on the wing. Presently all three had risen above the branches, and were circling higher and higher in a slow spiral. The Crows kept constantly swooping at their enemy, with the same angry buzz, one of the two taking decidedly the lead. They seldom struck at him with their beaks, but kept lumbering against him, and flapping him with their wings, as if in a fruitless effort to capsize him; while the Hawk kept carelessly eluding the assaults, now inclining on one side, now on the other, with a stately grace, never retaliating, but seeming rather to enjoy the novel amusement, as if it were a skirmish in balloons. During all this, indeed, he scarcely seemed once to wave his wings; yet he soared steadily aloft, till the Crows refused to follow, though already higher than I ever saw Crows before, dim against the fleecy sky; then the Hawk flew northward, but soon after he sailed over us once again, with loud, scornful *chirr,* and they only cawed, and left him undisturbed.

When we hear the tumult of music from these various artists of the air, it seems as if the symphony never could be analyzed into its different instruments. But with time and patience it is not so difficult; nor can we really enjoy the performance, so long as it is only a confused chorus to our ears. It is not merely the highest form of animal language, but, in strictness of etymology, the only form, if it be true, as is claimed, that no other animal employs its tongue, *lingua,* in producing sound. In the

Middle Ages, the song of birds was called their Latin, as was any other foreign dialect. It was the old German superstition, that any one who should eat the heart of a bird would thenceforth comprehend its language; and one modern philologist of the same nation (Masius declares) has so far studied the sounds produced by domestic fowls as to announce a Goose-Lexicon. Dupont de Nemours asserted that he understood eleven words of the Pigeon language, the same number of that of Fowls, fourteen of the Cat tongue, twenty-two of that of Cattle, thirty of that of Dogs, and the Raven language he understood completely. But the ordinary observer seldom attains farther than to comprehend some of the cries of anxiety and fear around him, often so unlike the accustomed carol of the bird,—as the mew of the Cat-Bird, the lamb-like bleating of the Veery and his impatient *yeoick*, the *chaip* of the Meadow-Lark, the *towyee* of the Chewink, the petulant *psit* and *tsee* of the Red-Winged Blackbird, and the hoarse cooing of the Bobolink. And with some of our most familiar birds the variety of notes is so great as really to promise difficulties in the American department of the bird-lexicon. I have watched two Song-Sparrows, perched near each other, in whom the spyglass could show not the slightest difference of marking, even in the characteristic stains upon the breast, who yet chanted to each other, for fifteen minutes, over and over, two elaborate songs which had nothing in common. I have observed a similar thing in two Wood-Sparrows, with their sweet, distinct, accelerating lay; nor can I find it stated that the difference is sexual. Who can claim to have heard the whole song of the Robin? Taking shelter from a shower beneath an oak-tree, the other day, I caught a few of the notes which one of those cheery creatures, who love to sing in wet weather, tossed down to me through the drops.

(Before noticing me,)	*chirrup, cheerup;*
(pausing in alarm, at my approach,)	*che, che, che;*
(broken presently by a thoughtful strain,)	*caw, caw;*
(then softer and more confiding,)	*see, see, see;*
(then the original note, in a whisper,)	*chirrup, cheerup;*
(often broken by a soft note,)	*see, wee;*
(and an odder one,)	*squeal;*
(and a mellow note,)	*tweedle.*

And all these were mingled with more complex combinations, and with half-imitations, as of the Blue-Bird, so that it seemed almost impossible to doubt that there was some specific meaning, to him and his peers, in this endless vocabulary. Yet other birds, as quick-witted as the Robins, possess but one or two chirping notes, to which they seem unable to give more than the very rudest variation of accent.

The controversy between the singing-birds of Europe and America has had various phases and influential disputants. Buffon easily convinced himself that our Thrushes had no songs, because the voices of all birds grew harsh in savage countries, such as he naturally held this continent to be. Audubon, on the other hand, relates that even in his childhood he was assured by his father that the American songsters were the best, though neither Americans nor Europeans could be convinced of it. MacGillivray, the Scottish naturalist, reports that Audubon himself, in conversation, arranged our vocalists in the following order:—first, the Mocking-Bird, as unrivalled; then, the Wood-Thrush, Cat-Bird, and Red Thrush; the Rose-Breasted, Pine, and Blue Grosbeak; the Orchard and Golden Oriole; the Tawny and Hermit Thrushes; several Finches,— Bachmann's, the White-Crowned, the Indigo, and the Nonpareil; and finally, the Bobolink.

Among those birds of this list which frequent Massachusetts, Audubon might well put the Wood-Thrush at the head. As I sat the other day in the deep woods beside a black brook which dropped from stone to stone beneath the shadow of our Rattlesnake Rocks, the air seemed at first as silent above me as the earth below. The buzz of summer sounds had not begun. Sometimes a bee hummed by with a long swift thrill like a chord of music; sometimes a breeze came resounding up the forest like an approaching locomotive, and then died utterly away. Then, at length, a Veery's delicious note rose in a fountain of liquid melody from beneath me; and when it was ended, the clear, calm, interrupted chant of the Wood-Thrush fell like solemn water-drops from some source above. I am acquainted with no sound in Nature so sweet, so elevated, so serene. Flutes and flageolets are Art's poor efforts to recall that softer sound. It is simple, and seems all prelude; but the music to which it is the overture belongs to other spheres. It might be the *Angelus* of some lost convent. It might be the meditation of some maiden-hermit, saying over to herself in solitude, with recurrent tuneful pauses, the only song she knows. Beside this soliloquy of seraphs, the carol of the Veery seems a familiar and almost domestic thing; yet it is so charming that Audubon must have designed to include it among the Thrushes whose merits he proclaims.

But the range of musical perfection is a wide one; and if the standard of excellence be that wondrous brilliancy and variety of execution suggested by the Mocking-Bird, then the palm belongs, among our New-England songsters, to the Red Thrush, otherwise called the Mavis or

Brown Thrasher. I have never heard the Mocking-Bird sing at liberty; and while the caged bird may surpass the Red Thrush in volume of voice and in quaintness of direct imitation, he gives me no such impression of depth and magnificence. I know not how to describe the voluble and fantastic notes which fall like pearls and diamonds from the beak of our Mavis, while his stately attitudes and high-born bearing are in full harmony with the song. I recall the steep, bare hillside, and the two great boulders which guard the lonely grove, where I first fully learned the wonder of this lay, as if I had met Saint Cecilia there. A thoroughly happy song, overflowing with life, it gives even its most familiar phrases an air of gracious condescension, as when some great violinist stoops to the "Carnival of Venice." The Red Thrush does not, however, consent to any parrot-like mimiery, though every note of wood or field—Oriole, Bobolink, Crow, Jay, Robin, Whippoorwill—appears to pass in veiled procession through the song.

Retain the execution of the Red Thrush, but hopelessly impair his organ, and you have the Cat-Bird. This accustomed visitor would seem a gifted vocalist, but for the inevitable comparison between his thinner note and the gushing melodies of the lordlier bird. Is it some hopeless consciousness of this disadvantage which leads him to pursue that peculiar habit of singing softly to himself very often, in a fancied seclusion? When other birds are cheerily out-of-doors, on some bright morning of May or June, one will often discover a solitary Cat-Bird sitting concealed in the middle of a dense bush, and twittering busily, in subdued rehearsal, the whole copious variety of his lay, practising trills and preparing half-imitations, which, at some other time, sitting on the topmost twig, he shall hilariously seem to improvise before all the world. Can it be that he is really in some slight disgrace with Nature, with that demi-mourning garb of his,—and that his feline cry of terror, which makes his opprobrium with boys, is part of some hidden doom decreed? No, the lovely color of the eggs which his companion watches on that laboriously builded staging of twigs shall vindicate this familiar companion from any suspicion of original sin. Indeed, it is well demonstrated by our American oölogist, Dr. Brewer, that the eggs of the Cat-Bird affiliate him with the Robin and the Wood-Thrush, all three being widely separated in this respect from the Red Thrush. The Red Thrush builds on the ground, and has mottled eggs; while the whole household establishment of the Wood-Thrush is scarcely distinguishable from that of the Robin, and the Cat-Bird differs chiefly in being more of a carpenter and less of a mason.

The Rose-Breasted Grosbeak, which Audubon places so high on his list of minstrels, comes annually to one region in this vicinity, but I am not sure of having heard it. The young Pine Grosbeaks come to our woods in winter, and have then but a subdued twitter. Every one knows the Bobolink; and almost all recognize the Oriole, by sight at least, even if unfamiliar with all the notes of his cheery and resounding song. The Red-Eyed Flycatcher, heard even more constantly, is less generally identified by name; but his note sounds all day among the elms of our streets, and seems a sort of piano-adaptation, popularized for the million, of the rich notes of the Thrushes. He is not mentioned by Audubon among his favorites, and has no right to complain of the exclusion. Yet the birds which most endear summer are not necessarily the finest performers; and certainly there is none whose note I could spare less easily than the little Chipping-Sparrow, called hereabouts the Hair-Bird. To lie half awake on a warm morning in June, and hear that soft insect-like chirp draw in and out with long melodious pulsations, like the rising and falling of the human breath, condenses for my ear the whole luxury of summer. Later in the day, among the multiplicity of noises, the chirping becomes louder and more detached, losing that faint and dream-like thrill.

The bird-notes which have the most familiar fascination are perhaps simply those most intimately associated with other rural things. This applies especially to the earliest spring songsters. Listening to these delicious prophets upon some of those still and moist days which slip in between the rough winds of March, and fill our lives for a moment with anticipated delights, it has seemed to me that their varied notes were sent to symbolize all the different elements of spring association. The Blue-Bird seems to represent simply spring's faint, tremulous, liquid sweetness, the Song-Sparrow its changing pulsations of more positive and varied joy, and the Robin its cheery and superabundant vitality. The later birds of the season, suggesting no such fine-drawn sensations, yet identify themselves with their chosen haunts, so that we cannot think of the one without the other. In the meadows, we hear the languid and tender drawl of the Meadow-Lark,—one of the most peculiar of notes, almost amounting to affectation in its excess of laborious sweetness. When we reach the thickets and wooded streams, there is no affectation in the Maryland Yellow-Throat, that little restless busybody, with his eternal *which-is-it, which-is-it, which-is-it,* emphasizing each syllable at will, in despair of response. Passing into the loftier woods, we find them resounding with the loud proclamation of the Golden-Crowned Thrush,— *scheat, scheat, scheat, scheat,*—rising and growing louder in a vigorous way that rather suggests some great Woodpecker than such a tiny thing. And penetrating to some yet lonelier place, we find it consecrated to that life-long sorrow, whatever it may be, which is made immortal in the plaintive cadence of the Pewee.

There is one favorite bird,—the Chewink, or Ground-Robin,—which, I always fancied, must have been known to Keats when he wrote those few words of perfect descriptiveness,—

"If an innocent bird
Before my heedless footsteps *stirred and stirred*
In little journeys."

What restless spirit is in this creature, that, while so shy in its own personal habits, it yet watches every visitor with a Paul-Pry curiosity, follows him in the woods, peers out among the underbrush, scratches upon the leaves with a pretty pretence of important business there, and presently, when disregarded, ascends some small tree and begins to carol its monotonous song, as if there were no such thing as man in the universe? There is something irregular and fantastic in the coloring, also, of the Chewink: unlike the generality of ground-birds, it is a showy thing, with black, white, and bay intermingled, and it is one of the most unmistakable of all our feathery creatures, in its aspect and its ways.

Another of my favorites, perhaps from our sympathy as to localities, since we meet freely every summer at a favorite lake, is the King-Bird or Tyrant-Flycatcher. The habits of royalty or tyranny I have never been able to perceive,—only a democratic habit of resistance to tyrants; but this bird always impresses me as a perfectly well-dressed and well-mannered person, who amid a very talkative society prefers to listen, and shows his character by action only. So long as he sits silently on some stake or bush in the neighborhood of his family circle, you notice only his glossy black cap and the white feathers in his handsome tail; but let a Hawk or a Crow come near, and you find that he is something more than a mere lazy listener to the Bobolink: far up in the air, determined to be thorough in his chastisements, you will see him, with a comrade or two, driving the bulky intruder away into the distance, till you wonder how he ever expects to find his own way back again. He speaks with emphasis on these occasions, and then reverts, more sedately than ever, to his accustomed silence.

After all the great labors of Audubon and Wilson, it is certain that the recent visible progress of American ornithology has by no means equalled that of several other departments of Natural History. The older books are now out of print, and there is actually no popular treatise on the subject to be had: a destitution singularly contrasted with the variety of excellent botanical works which the last twenty years have produced. Nuttall's fascinating volumes, and Brewer's edition of Wilson, are equally inaccessible; and the most valuable contributions since their time, so far as I know, are that portion of Dr. Brewer's work on eggs printed in the eleventh volume of the "Smithsonian Contributions," and four admirable articles in the Atlantic Monthly.[1] But the most important observations are locked up in the desks or exhibited in the cabinets of private observers, who have little opportunity of comparing facts with other students, or with reliable printed authorities. What do we know, for instance, of the local distribution of our birds? I remember that in my latest conversation with Thoreau, last December, he mentioned most remarkable facts in this department, which had fallen under his unerring eyes. The Hawk most common at Concord, the Red-Tailed species, is not known near the sea-shore, twenty miles off,—as at Boston or Plymouth. The White-Breasted Sparrow is rare in Concord; but the Ashburnham woods, thirty miles away, are full of it. The Scarlet Tanager's is the commonest note in Concord, except the Red-Eyed Flycatcher's; yet one of the best field-ornithologists in Boston had never heard it. The Rose-Breasted Grosbeak is seen not infrequently at Concord, though its nest is rarely found; but in Minnesota Thoreau found it more abundant than any other bird, far more so than the Robin. But his most interesting statement, to my fancy, was, that, during a stay of ten weeks on Monadnock, he found that the Snow-Bird built its nest on the top of the mountain, and probably never came down through the season. That was its Arctic; and it would probably yet be found, he predicted, on Wachusett and other Massachusetts peaks. It is known that the Snow-Bird, or "Snow-Flake," as it is called in England, was reported by Audubon as having only once been proved to build in the United States, namely, among the White Mountains, though Wilson found its nests among the Alleghanies; and in New England it used to be the rural belief that the Snow-Bird and the Chipping-Sparrow were the same.

After July, most of our birds grow silent, and, but for the insects, August would be almost the stillest month in the year,—stiller than the winter, when the woods are often vocal with the Crow, the Jay, and the Chickadee. But with patient attention one may hear, even far into the autumn, the accustomed notes. As I sat in my boat, one sunny afternoon

---

[1]"Our Birds and their Ways" (December, 1857); "The Singing-Birds and their Songs" (August, 1858); "The Birds of the Garden and Orchard" (October, 1858); "The Birds of the Pasture and Forest" (December, 1858);—the first by J. Elliot Cabot, and the last three by Wilson Flagg.

of last September, beneath the shady western shore of our quiet lake, with the low sunlight striking almost level across the wooded banks, it seemed as if the last hoarded drops of summer's sweetness were being poured over all the world. The air was full of quiet sounds. Turtles rustled beside the brink and slid into the water,—cows plashed in the shallows,—fishes leaped from the placid depths,—a squirrel sobbed and fretted on a neighboring stump,—a katydid across the lake maintained its hard, dry croak,—the crickets chirped pertinaciously, but with little fatigued pauses, as if glad that their work was almost done,—the grasshoppers kept up their continual chant, which seemed thoroughly melted and amalgamated into the summer, as if it would go on indefinitely, though the body of the little creature were dried into dust. All this time the birds were silent and invisible, as if they would take no more part in the symphony of the year. Then, seemingly by preconcerted signal, they joined in: Crows cawed anxiously afar; Jays screamed in the woods; a Partridge clucked to its brood, like the gurgle of water from a bottle; a King-fisher wound his rattle, more briefly than in spring, as if we now knew all about it and the merest hint ought to suffice; a Fish-Hawk flapped into the water, with a great rude splash, and then flew heavily away; a flock of Wild Ducks went southward overhead, and a smaller party returned beneath them, flying low and anxiously, as if to pick up some lost baggage; and, at last, a Loon laughed loud from behind a distant island, and it was pleasant to people these woods and waters with that wild shouting, linking them with Katahdin Lake and Amperzand.

But the later the birds linger in the autumn, the more their aspect differs from that of spring. In spring, they come, jubilant, noisy, triumphant, from the South, the winter conquered and the long journey done. In autumn, they come timidly from the North, and, pausing on their anxious retreat, lurk within the fading copses and twitter snatches of song as fading. Others fly as openly as ever, but gather in flocks, as the Robins, most piteous of all birds at this season,—thin, faded, ragged, their bold note sunk to a feeble quaver, and their manner a mere caricature of that inexpressible military smartness with which they held up their heads in May.

Yet I cannot really find anything sad even in November. When I think of the thrilling beauty of the season past, the birds that came and went, the insects that took up the choral song as the birds grew silent, the procession of the flowers, the glory of autumn,—and when I think that, this also ended, a new gallery of wonder is opening, almost more beautiful, in the magnificence of frost and snow,—there comes an impression of affluence and liberality in the universe which seasons of changeless and uneventful verdure would never give. The catkins already formed on the alder, quite prepared to droop into April's beauty,—the white edges of the May-flower's petals, already visible through the bud, show in advance that winter is but a slight and temporary retardation of the life of Nature, and that the barrier which separates November from March is not really more solid than that which parts the sunset from the sunrise.

5

THE PROCESSION OF
THE FLOWERS

In Cuba there is a blossoming shrub whose multitudinous crimson flowers are so seductive to the humming-birds that they hover all day around it, buried in its blossoms until petal and wing seem one. At first upright, the gorgeous bells droop downward, and fall unwithered to the ground, and are thence called by the Creoles "Cupid's Tears." Fredrika Bremer relates that daily she brought home handfuls of these blossoms to her chamber, and nightly they all disappeared. One morning she looked toward the wall of the apartment, and there, in a long crimson line, the delicate flowers went ascending one by one to the ceiling, and passed from sight. She found that each was borne laboriously onward by a little colorless ant much smaller than itself: the bearer was invisible, but the lovely burdens festooned the wall with beauty.

To a watcher from the sky, the march of the flowers of any zone across the year would seem as beautiful as that West-Indian pageant. These frail creatures, rooted where they stand, a part of the "still life" of Nature, yet share her ceaseless motion. In the most sultry silence of summer noons, the vital current is coursing with desperate speed through the innumerable veins of every leaflet; and the apparent stillness, like the sleeping of a child's top, is in truth the very ecstasy of perfected motion.

Not in the tropics only, but even in England, whence most of our floral associations and traditions come, the march of the flowers is in an endless circle, and, unlike our experience, something is always in bloom. In the Northern United States, it is said, the active growth of most plants is condensed into ten weeks, while in the mother country the full activity is maintained through sixteen. But even the English winter does not seem to be a winter, in the same sense as ours, appearing more like a chilly and comfortless autumn. There is no month in the year when some special plant does not bloom: the Colts-foot there opens its fragrant flowers from December to February; the yellow-flowered Hellebore, and its cousin, the sacred Christmas Rose of Glastonbury, extend from January to March; and the Snowdrop and Primrose often come before the first of February. Something may be gained, much lost, by that perennial succession; those links, however slight, must make the floral period continuous to the imagination; while our year gives a pause and an interval to its children, and after exhausted October has effloresced into Witch-Hazel, there is an absolute reserve of blossom, until the Alders wave again.

No symbol could so well represent Nature's first yielding in spring-time as this blossoming of the Alder, this drooping of the tresses of these tender things. Before the frost is gone, and while the new-born season is yet too weak to assert itself by actually uplifting anything, it can at least let fall these blossoms, one by one, till they wave defiance to the winter on a thousand boughs. How patiently they have waited! Men are perplexed with anxieties about their own immortality; but these catkins, which hang, almost full-formed, above the ice all winter, show no such solicitude, but when March wooes them they are ready. Once relaxing, their pollen is so prompt to fall that it sprinkles your hand as you gather them; then, for one day, they are the perfection of grace upon your table, and next day they are weary and emaciated, and their little contribution to the spring is done.

Then many eyes watch for the opening of the May-flower, day by day, and a few for the Hepatica. So marked and fantastic are the local preferences of all our plants, that, with miles of woods and meadows open to their choice, each selects only some few spots for its accustomed abodes, and some one among them all for its very earliest blossoming. There is always some single chosen nook, which you might almost cover with your handkerchief, where each flower seems to bloom earliest, without variation, year by year. I know one such place for Hepatica a mile north-east,—another for May-flower two miles southwest; and each year the whimsical creature is in bloom on that little spot, when not another flower can be found open through the whole country round. Accidental as the choice may appear, it is undoubtedly based on laws more eternal than the stars; yet why all subtle influences conspire to bless that undistinguishable knoll no man can say. Another and similar puzzle offers itself in the distribution of the tints of flowers,—in these two species among the rest. There are certain localities, near by, where the Hepatica is all but white, and others where the May-flower is sumptuous in pink; yet it is not traceable to wet or dry, sun or shadow, and no agricultural chemistry can disclose the secret. Is it by some Darwinian law of selection that the white Hepatica has utterly overpowered the blue, in our Cascade Woods, for instance, while yet in the very midst of this pale plantation a single clump will sometimes bloom with all heaven on its petals? Why can one recognize the Plymouth May-flower, as soon as seen, by its wondrous depth of color? Does it blush with triumph to see how Nature has outwitted the Pilgrims, and even succeeded in preserving her deer like an English duke, still maintaining the deepest woods in Massachusetts precisely where those sturdy immigrants first began their clearings?

The Hepatica (called also Liverwort, Squirrel-Cup, or Blue Anemone) has been found in Worcester as early as March seventeenth, and in Danvers on March twelfth,—dates which appear almost the extreme of credibility.

Our next wild-flower in this region is the Claytonia, or Spring-Beauty, which is common in the Middle States, but here found in only a few localities. It is the Indian *Miskodeed,* and was said to have been left behind when mighty Peboan, the Winter, was melted by the breath of Spring. It is an exquisitely delicate little creature, bears its blossoms in clusters, unlike most of the early species, and opens in gradual succession each white and pink-veined bell. It grows in moist places on the sunny edges of woods, and prolongs its shy career from about the tenth of April until almost the end of May.

A week farther into April, and the Bloodroot opens,—a name of guilt, and a type of innocence. This fresh and lovely thing appears to concentrate all its stains within its ensanguined root, that it may condense all purity in the peculiar whiteness of its petals. It emerges from the ground with each shy blossom wrapt in its own pale-green leaf, then doffs the cloak and spreads its long petals round a group of yellow stamens. The flower falls apart so easily, that when in full bloom it will hardly bear transportation, but with a touch the stem stands naked, a bare gold-tipped sceptre amid drifts of snow. And the contradiction of its hues seems carried into its habits. One of the most shy of wild plants, easily banished from its locality by any invasion, it yet takes to the garden with unpardonable readiness, doubles its size, blossoms earlier, repudiates its love of water, and flaunts its great leaves in the unnatural confinement, until it elbows out the exotics. Its charm is gone, unless one find it in its native haunts, beside some cascade which streams over rocks that are dark with moisture, green with moss, and snowy with white bubbles. Each spray of dripping feather-moss exudes a tiny torrent of its own, or braided with some tiny neighbor, above the little water-fonts which sleep sunless in ever-verdant caves. Sometimes along these emerald canals there comes a sudden rush and hurry, as if some anxious housekeeper upon the hill above were afraid that things were not stirring fast enough,—and then again the waving and sinuous lines of water are quieted to a serener flow. The delicious red thrush and the busy little yellow-throat are not yet come to this their summer haunt; but all day long the answering field-sparrows trill out their sweet, shy, accelerating lay.

In the same localities with the Bloodroot, though some days later, grows the Dog-Tooth Violet,—a name hopelessly inappropriate, but likely never to be changed. These hardy and prolific creatures have also many localities of their own; for, though they do not acquiesce in cultivation, like the sycophantic Bloodroot, yet they are hard to banish from their native haunts, but linger after the woods are cleared and the meadow drained. The bright flowers blaze back all the yellow light of noonday, as the gay petals curl and spread themselves above their beds of mottled leaves; but it is always a disappointment to gather them, for indoors they miss the full ardor of the sunbeams, and are apt to go to sleep and nod expressionless from the stalk.

And almost on the same day with this bright apparition one may greet a multitude of concurrent visitors, arriving so accurately together that it is almost a matter of accident which of the party shall first report himself. Perhaps the Dandelion should have the earliest place; indeed, I once found it in Brookline on the seventh of April. But it cannot ordinarily be expected before the twentieth, in Eastern Massachusetts, and rather later in the interior; while by the same date I have also found near Boston the Cowslip or Marsh-Marigold, the Spring-Saxifrage, the Anemones, the Violets, the Bellwort, the Houstonia, the Cinquefoil, and the Strawberry-blossom. Varying, of course, in different spots and years, the arrival of this coterie is yet nearly simultaneous, and they may all be expected hereabouts before May-day at the very latest. After all, in spite of the croakers, this festival could not have been much better timed, the delicate blossoms which mark the period are usually in perfection on this day, and it is not long before they are past their prime.

Some early plants which have now almost disappeared from Eastern Massachusetts are still found near Worcester in the greatest abundance,—as the larger Yellow Violet, the Red Trillium, the Dwarf Ginseng, the Clintonia or Wild Lily-of-the-Valley, and the pretty fringed Polygala, which Miss Cooper christened "Gay-Wings." Others again are now rare in this vicinity, and growing rarer, though still abundant a hundred miles farther inland. In several bits of old swampy wood one may still find, usually close together, the Hobble-Bush and the Painted Trillium, the Mitella, or Bishop's-Cap, and the snowy Tiarella. Others again have entirely vanished within ten years, and that in some cases without any adequate explanation. The dainty white Corydalis, profanely called "Dutchman's Breeches," and the quaint woolly Ledum, or Labrador Tea, have disappeared within that time. The beautiful Linnæa is still found annually, but flowers no more; as is also the case, in all but one distant locality, with the once abundant Rhododendron. Nothing in Nature has for me a more fascinating interest than these secret movements of vegetation,—the sweet blind instinct with which flowers cling to old domains until absolutely compelled to forsake them. How touching is the fact, now well known, that salt-water plants still flower beside the Great Lakes, yet dreaming of the time when those waters were briny as the sea! Nothing in the demonstrations of Geology seems grander than the light lately thrown by Professor Gray, from the analogies between the flora of Japan and of North America, upon the successive epochs of heat which led the wandering flowers along the Arctic lands, and of cold which isolated them once more. Yet doubtless these humble movements of our local plants may be laying up results as important, and may hereafter supply evidence of earth's changes upon some smaller scale.

May expands to its prime of beauty; the summer birds come with the fruit-blossoms, the gardens are deluged with bloom, and the air with melody, while in the woods the timid spring flowers fold themselves away in silence and give place to a brighter splendor. On the margin of some quiet swamp a myriad of bare twigs seem suddenly overspread with purple butterflies, and we know that the Rhodora is in bloom. Wordsworth never immortalized a flower more surely than Emerson this, and it needs no weaker words; there is nothing else in which the change from nakedness to beauty is so sudden, and when you bring home the great mass of blossoms they appear all ready to flutter away again from your hands and leave you disenchanted.

At the same time the beautiful Cornel-tree is in perfection; startling as a tree of the tropics, it flaunts its great flowers high up among the forest-branches, intermingling its long slender twigs with theirs, and garnishing them with alien blooms. It is very available for household decoration, with its four great creamy petals,—flowers they are not, but floral involucres,—each with a fantastic curl and stain at its tip, as if the fireflies had alighted on them and scorched them; and yet I like it best as it peers out in barbaric splendor from the delicate green of young Maples. And beneath it grows often its more abundant kinsman, the Dwarf Cornel, with the same four great petals enveloping its floral cluster, but lingering low upon the ground,—an herb whose blossoms mimic the statelier tree.

The same rich creamy hue and texture show themselves in the Wild Calla, which grows at this season in dark, sequestered water-courses, and sometimes well rivals, in all but size, that superb whiteness out of a land of darkness, the Ethiopic Calla of the conservatory. At this season, too, we seek another semi-aquatic rarity, whose homely name cannot deprive it of a certain garden-like elegance, the Buckbean. This is one of the shy plants which yet grow in profusion within their own domain. I have found it of old in Cambridge, and then upon the pleasant shallows of the Artichoke, that loveliest tributary of the Merrimack, and I have never seen it where it occupied a patch more than a few yards square, while yet within that space the multitudinous spikes grow always tall and close, reminding one of hyacinths, when in perfection, but more delicate and beautiful. The only locality I know for it in this vicinity lies seven miles away, where a little inlet from the lower winding bays of Lake Quinsigamond goes stealing up among a farmer's hay-fields, and there, close beside the public road and in full view of the farm-house, this rare creature fills the water. But to reach it we commonly row down the lake to a sheltered lagoon, separated from the main lake by a long island which is gradually forming itself like the coral isles, growing each year denser with alder thickets where the king-birds build;—there leave the boat among the lily-leaves, and take a lane which winds among the meadows and gives a fitting avenue for the pretty thing we seek. But it is not safe to vary many days from the twentieth of May, for the plant is not long in perfection, and is past its prime when the lower blossoms begin to wither on the stem.

But should we miss this delicate adjustment of time, it is easy to console ourselves with bright armfuls of Lupine, which bounteously flowers for six weeks along our lakeside, ranging from the twenty-third of May to the sixth of July. The Lupine is one of our most travelled plants; for, though never seen off the American continent, it stretches to the Pacific, and is found upon the Arctic coast. On these banks of Lake Quinsigamond it grows in great families, and should be gathered in masses and placed in a vase by itself; for it needs no relief from other flowers, its own soft leaves afford background enough, and though the white variety rarely occurs, yet the varying tints of blue upon the same stalk are a perpetual gratification to the eye. I know not why shaded blues should be so beautiful in flowers, and yet avoided as distasteful in ladies' fancy-work; but it is a mystery like that which repudiates blue-and-green from all well-regulated costumes, while Nature yet evidently prefers it to any other combination in her wardrobe.

Another constant ornament of the end of May is the large pink Lady's-Slipper, or Moccason-Flower, the "Cypripedium not due till to-morrow" which Emerson attributes to the note-book of Thoreau,—to-morrow, in these parts, meaning about the twentieth of May. It belongs to the family of Orchids, a high-bred race, fastidious in habits, sensitive as to abodes. Of the ten species named as rarest among American en-dogenous plants by Dr. Gray, in his valuable essay on the statistics of our Northern Flora, all but one are Orchids. And even an abundant species, like the present, retains the family traits in its person, and never loses its high-born air and its delicate veining. I know a grove where it can be gathered by the hundreds within a half-acre, and yet I never can divest myself of the feeling that each specimen is a choice novelty. But the ac-tual rarity occurs, at least in this region, when one finds the smaller and more beautiful Yellow Moccason-Flower,—*parviflorum,*—which accepts only our very choicest botanical locality, the "Rattlesnake Ledge" on Tatessit Hill,—and may, for aught I know, have been the very plant which Elsie Venner laid upon her schoolmistress's desk.

June is an intermediate month between the spring and summer flow-ers. Of the more delicate early blossoms, the Dwarf Cornel, the Solomon's-Seal, and the Yellow Violet still linger in the woods, but rapidly make way for larger masses and more conspicuous hues. The meadows are gorgeous with Clover, Buttercups, and Wild Geranium; but Nature is a little chary for a week or two, maturing a more abundant show. Meanwhile one may afford to take some pains to search for an-other rarity, almost disappearing from this region,—the lovely Pink Azalea. It still grows plentifully in a few sequestered places, selecting woody swamps to hide itself; and certainly no shrub suggests, when found, more tropical associations. Those great, nodding, airy, fragrant clusters, tossing far above one's head their slender cups of honey, seem searcely to belong to our sober zone, any more than the searlet tanager which sometimes builds its nest beside them. They appear bright ex-otics, which have wandered into our woods, and seem too happy to feel any wish for exit. And just as they fade, their humbler sister in white be-gins to bloom, and carries on through the summer the same intoxicat-ing fragrance.

But when June is at its height, the sculptured chalices of the Mountain Laurel begin to unfold, and thenceforward, for more than a month, ex-tends the reign of this our woodland queen. I know not why one should sigh after the blossoming gorges of the Himalaya, when our forests are all so crowded with this glowing magnificence,—rounding the tangled swamps into smoothness, lighting up the underwoods, overtopping the pastures, lining the rural lanes, and rearing its great pinkish masses till they meet overhead. The color ranges from the purest white to a perfect rose-pink, and there is an inexhaustible vegetable vigor about the whole thing, which puts to shame those tenderer shrubs that shrink before the progress of cultivation. There is the Rhododendron, for instance, a plant of the same natural family with the Laurel and the Azalea, and looking more robust and woody than either: it once grew in many localities in this region, and still lingers in a few, without consenting either to die or to blossom, and there is only one remote place from which any one now brings into our streets those large luxuriant flowers, waving white above the dark green leaves, and bearing "just a dream of sunset on their edges, and just a breath from the green sea in their hearts." But the Laurel, on the other hand, maintains its ground, imperturbable and almost impassable, on every hillside, takes no hints, suspects no danger, and nothing but the most unmistakable onset from spade or axe can diminish its profusion. Gathering it on the most lavish scale seems only to serve as wholesome pruning; nor can I conceive that the Indians, who once ruled over this whole county from Wigwam Hill, could ever have found it more inconveniently abundant than now. We have perhaps no single spot where it grows in such perfect picturesqueness as at "The Laurels," on the Merrimack, just above Newburyport,—a whole hillside scooped out and the hollow piled solidly with flowers, the pines curving around it above, and the river encircling it below, on which your boat glides along, and you look up through glimmering arcades of bloom. But for the last half of June it monopolizes everything in the Worcester woods,—no one picks anything else; and it fades so slowly that I have found a perfect blossom on the last day of July.

At the same time with this royalty of the woods, the queen of the water ascends her throne, for a reign as undisputed and far more prolonged. The extremes of the Water-Lily in this vicinity, so far as I have known, are the eighteenth of June and the thirteenth of October,—a longer range than belongs to any other conspicuous wild-flower, unless we except the Dandelion and Houstonia. It is not only the most fascinating of all flowers to gather, but more available for decorative purposes than almost any other, if it can only be kept fresh. The best method for this purpose, I believe, is to cut the stalk very short before placing in the vase; then, at night, the lily will close and the stalk curl upward;—refresh them by changing the water, and in the morning the stalk will be straight and the flower open.

From this time forth Summer has it all her own way. After the first of July the yellow flowers begin to watch the yellow fire-flies; Hawkweeds, Loosestrifes, Primroses bloom, and the bushy Wild Indigo. The variety of hues increases; delicate purple Orchises bloom in their chosen haunts, and Wild Roses blush over hill and dale. On peat-meadows the Adder's-Tongue Arethusa (now called *Pogonia*) flowers profusely, with a faint, delicious perfume,—and its more elegant cousin, the Calopogon, by its side. In this vicinity we miss the blue Harebell, the identical harebell of Ellen Douglas, which I remember waving its exquisite flowers along the banks of the Merrimack, and again at Brattleboro', below the cascade in the village, where it has climbed the precipitous sides of old buildings, and nods inaccessibly from their crevices, in that picturesque spot, looking down on the hurrying river. But with this exception, there is nothing wanting here of the flowers of early summer.

The more closely one studies Nature, the finer her adaptations grow. For instance, the change of seasons is analogous to a change of zones, and summer assimilates our vegetation to that of the tropics. In those lands, Humboldt has remarked, one misses the beauty of wild-flowers in the grass, because the luxuriance of vegetation develops everything into shrubs. The form and color are beautiful, "but, being too high above the soil, they disturb that harmonious proportion which characterizes the plants of our European meadows. Nature has, in every zone, stamped on the landscape the peculiar type of beauty proper to the locality." But every midsummer reveals the same tendency. In early spring, when all is bare, and small objects are easily made prominent, the wild-flowers are generally delicate. Later, when all verdure is profusely expanded, these miniature strokes would be lost, and Nature then practises landscape-gardening in large, lights up the copses with great masses of White Alder, makes the roadsides gay with Aster and Golden-Rod, and tops the tall coarse Meadow-Grass with nodding Lilies and tufted Spiræa. One instinctively follows these plain hints, and gathers bouquets sparingly in spring and exuberantly in summer.

The use of wild-flowers for decorative purposes merits a word in passing, for it is unquestionably a branch of high art in favored hands. It is true that we are bidden, on high authority, to love the wood-rose and leave it on its stalk; but against this may be set the saying of Bettine, that "all flowers which are broken become immortal in the sacrifice"; and certainly the secret harmonies of these fair creatures are so marked and delicate that we do not understand them till we try to group floral decorations for ourselves. The most successful artists will not, for instance, consent to put those together which do not grow together; Nature understands her business, and distributes her masses and backgrounds un-erringly. Yonder soft and feathery Meadow-Sweet longs to be combined with Wild Roses: it yearns towards them in the field, and, after withering in the hand most readily, it revives in water as if to be with them in the vase. In the same way the White Spiræa serves as natural background for the Field-Lilies. These lilies, by the way, are the brightest adornment of our meadows during the short period of their perfection. We have two species: one slender, erect, solitary, scarlet, looking up to heaven with all its blushes on; the other clustered, drooping, pale-yellow. I never saw the former in such profusion as last week, on the bare summit of Wachusett. The granite ribs have there a thin covering of crispest moss, spangled with the white starry blossoms of the Mountain Cinquefoil; and as I lay and watched the red lilies that waved their innumerable urns around me, it needed but little imagination to see a thousand altars, sending vis-ible flames forever upward to the answering sun.

August comes: the Thistles are out, beloved of butterflies; deeper and deeper tints, more passionate intensities of color, prepare the way for the year's decline. A wealth of gorgeous Golden-Rod waves over all the hills, and enriches every bouquet one gathers; its bright colors command the eye, and it is graceful as an elm. Fitly arranged, it gives a bright relief to the superb beauty of the Cardinal-Flowers, the brilliant blue-purple of the Vervain, the pearl-white of the Life-Everlasting, the delicate lilac of the Monkey-Flower, the soft pink and white of the Spiræas,—for the white yet lingers,—all surrounded by trailing wreaths of blossoming Clematis.

But the Cardinal-Flower is best seen by itself, and, indeed, needs the surroundings of its native haunts to display its fullest beauty. It favorite abode is along the dank mossy stones of some black and winding brook, shaded with overarching bushes, and running one long stream of scarlet with these superb occupants. It seems amazing how anything so brilliant can mature in such a darkness. When a ray of sunlight strays in upon it, the wondrous creature seems to hover on the stalk, ready to take flight, like some lost tropic bird. There is a spot whence I have in ten minutes brought away as many as I could hold in both arms, some bearing fifty blossoms on a single stalk; and I could not believe that there was such another mass of color in the world. Nothing cultivated is comparable to them; and, with all the talent lately lavished on wild-flower painting, I have never seen the peculiar sheen of these petals in the least degree de-lineated. It seems some new and separate tint, equally distinct from scar-let and from crimson, a splendor for which there is as yet no name, but only the reality.

It seems the signal of autumn, when September exhibits the first Barrel-Gentian by the roadside; and there is a pretty insect in the meadows—the Mourning-Cloak Moth it might be called—which gives coincident warning. The innumerable Asters mark this period with their varied and wide-spread beauty; the meadows are full of rose-colored Polygala, of the white spiral spikes of the Ladies'-Tresses, and of the fringed loveliness of the Gentian. This flower, always unique and beautiful, opening its delicate eyelashes every morning to the sunlight, closing them again each night, has also a thoughtful charm about it as the last of the year's especial darlings. It lingers long, each remaining blossom growing larger and more deep in color, as with many other flowers; and after it there is nothing for which to look forward, save the fantastic Witch-Hazel.

On the water, meanwhile, the last White Lilies are sinking beneath the surface, the last gay Pickerel-Weed is gone, though the rootless plants of the delicate Bladder-Wort, spreading over acres of shallows, still impurple the wide, smooth surface. Harriet Prescott says that some souls are like the Water-Lilies, fixed, yet floating. But others are like this graceful purple blossom, floating unfixed, kept in place only by its fellows around it, until perhaps a breeze comes, and, breaking the accidental cohesion, sweeps them all away.

The season reluctantly yields its reign, and over the quiet autumnal landscape everywhere, even after the glory of the trees is past, there are tints and fascinations of minor beauty. Last October, for instance, in walking, I found myself on a little knoll, looking northward. Overhead was a bower of climbing Waxwork, with its yellowish pods scarce disclosing their scarlet berries,—a wild Grape-vine, with its fruit withered by the frost into still purple raisins,—and yellow Beech-leaves, detaching themselves with an effort audible to the ear. In the foreground were blue Raspberry-stems, yet bearing greenish leaves,—pale-yellow Witch-Hazel, almost leafless,—purple Viburnum-berries,—the silky cocoons of the Milkweed,—and, amid the underbrush, a few lingering Asters and Golden-Rods, Ferns still green, and Maidenhair bleached white. In the background were hazy hills, white Birches bare and snow-like, and a Maple half-way up a sheltered hillside, one mass of canary-color, its fallen leaves making an apparent reflection on the earth at its foot,—and then a real reflection, fused into a glassy light intenser than itself, upon the smooth, dark stream below.

The beautiful disrobing suggested the persistent and unconquerable delicacy of Nature, who shrinks from nakedness and is always seeking to veil her graceful boughs,—if not with leaves, then with feathery hoar-frost, ermined snow, or transparent icy armor.

But, after all, the fascination of summer lies not in any details, however perfect, but in the sense of total wealth which summer gives. Wholly to enjoy this, one must give one's self passively to it, and not expect to reproduce it in words. We strive to picture heaven, when we are barely at the threshold of the inconceivable beauty of earth. Perhaps the truant boy who simply bathes himself in the lake and then basks in the sunshine, dimly conscious of the exquisite loveliness around him, is wiser, because humbler, than is he who with presumptuous phrases tries to utter it. There are multitudes of moments when the atmosphere is so surcharged with luxury that every pore of the body becomes an ample gate for sensation to flow in, and one has simply to sit still and be filled. In after years the memory of books seems barren or vanishing, compared with the immortal bequest of hours like these. Other sources of illumination seem cisterns only; these are fountains. They may not increase the mere quantity of available thought, but they impart to it a quality which is priceless. No man can measure what a single hour with Nature may have contributed to the moulding of his mind. The influence is self-renewing, and if for a long time it baffles expression by reason of its fineness, so much the better in the end.

The soul is like a musical instrument: it is not enough that it be framed for the very most delicate vibration, but it must vibrate long and often before the fibres grow mellow to the finest waves of sympathy. I perceive that in the veery's carolling, the clover's scent, the glistening of the water, the waving wings of butterflies, the sunset tints, the floating clouds, there are attainable infinitely more subtle modulations of delight than I can yet reach the sensibility to discriminate, much less describe. If, in the simple process of writing, one could physically impart to this page the fragrance of this spray of azalea beside me, what a wonder would it seem!—and yet one ought to be able, by the mere use of language, to supply to every reader the total of that white, honeyed, trailing sweetness, which summer insects haunt and the Spirit of the Universe loves. The defect is not in language, but in men. There is no conceivable beauty of blossom so beautiful as words,—none so graceful, none so perfumed. It is possible to dream of combinations of syllables so delicious that all the dawning and decay of summer cannot rival their perfection, nor winter's stainless white and azure match their purity and their charm. To write them, were it possible, would be to take rank with Nature; nor is there any other method, even by music, for human art to reach so high.

PART SIX

Critic as Essayist

Literary fame is, then, by no means a fixed increment
but a series of vibrations of the pendulum. Happy is the
author who comes to be benefited by an actual return of
reputation—as athletes get beyond their period of
breathlessness and come to their "second wind."

THOMAS WENTWORTH HIGGINSON, "THE LITERARY PENDULUM," 1892

L etter to a Young Contributor" and "Emily Dickinson," two of this
section's essays, bracket the period from the first encounter of the
ex-colonel and the poet until her death. Both are notable as examples of
the art of the essay. Together they so well illuminate what Anna Mary
Wells has called the "most important literary work in Higginson's life,"
his support of Dickinson while she lived and sponsorship of her work
after her death.

That appraisal is complemented by Dickinson's foremost editor and
biographer, Thomas H. Johnson. In his brief preface to *The Complete
Poems* (1960), he calls April 19, 1862, the day when Higginson received a
letter from Dickinson with four of her poems enclosed, one of "three
significant dates in [nineteenth-century] American literary history."
(The other two were the day in 1837 that Emerson delivered his Phi Beta
Kappa address at Harvard, "The American Scholar," and the day in 1857
when Walt Whitman began to circulate privately printed copies of
Leaves of Grass.)

Perhaps Higginson's open "Letter to a Young Contributor" had
prompted the bold (for its day and from its writer) letter to ask the older
writer whether he was "too deeply occupied to say if my verse is alive."
He must have received many replies to its message to aspiring writers
who remained unpublished. Her response was the only one he ever

thought worth telling about. It appears in the memoir "Emily Dickinson," which was published three decades later (see Chapter 6).

The open "Letter to a Young Contributor" that she was moved to answer has merit quite independent of its importance to us as an overture to study of their relationship. Within its text are compressed the basic elements that are generally accepted as useful to any writer as she develops her craft and shapes her conduct and work to improve the chances of gaining publication. Its precepts have been restated in whole or in part, in one form or another, in the handbooks and magazines targeted for sale to writers ever since.

It is the source of a number of striking phrases—two of them so striking that they have become accepted aphorisms and are quite often repeated as such (without identification of the author): "There may be years of crowded passion in a word and half a lifetime in a sentence"; and "Many great writers have created the taste by which they were enjoyed." Thus he began an association that gave such sustenance to a reclusive "isolato" that, as she said in a later letter, "You were not aware that you saved my life."

That estimate, perhaps only slightly hyperbolic, of Higginson's value to her has been treated as without significance—and often ignored—by scholars and other writers discussing her life and work. His indispensable role in securing publication of poetry so revolutionary in form and content could not be ignored—but it has been muddled by exaggerating the significance of the minor tampering that he (or his coeditor, Mabel Todd, who wisely turned to him for assistance when she found herself unable to find a willing publisher) thought was needed to assure acceptance of the work when published.

"Sappho" is a readable essay of enormous contemporary interest. It shows us why the poet Sappho's role as daughter of the island of Lesbos should win the respect of us all. Few men possess the easy familiarity with classical culture and sensitivity to the justice of the woman's movement to have written it.

A few of Higginson's essays originated as lectures that were prepared for the Lyceum circuit. There they were tried out, their content edited and delivery honed with the help of audience response. But the first draft of "Sappho" was initially shared with a more sophisticated audience made up of "members" (there was no truly formal membership) of the Radical Club of Chestnut Street, in Boston, which Higginson helped found and participated in during the Newport years.

The club had its origins in the movement known as Transcendentalism, which itself sparked the movement of radical reform. Transcendentalism as a reform movement did not survive the Civil War, but a few aging survivors did carry on, as members of discussion groups; one of these groups chose to celebrate its members' radicalism in the name of their club.

In addition to Higginson, membership in the Radical Club of Chestnut Street included the basic group of Emerson himself (considered by some to be the founding father of Transcendentalism), John Greenleaf Whittier, Julia Ward Howe, Elizabeth Peabody, Henry James (the father of the writer Henry James), and Dr. Oliver Wendell Holmes (the father of the Supreme Court justice). At the meetings one member would read a paper that was then the subject of discussion. Henry James, Sr., read a paper at two, and Higginson at one, of the forty-five meetings for which records survive.

In the early days of the club, the radicalism related to questions of religion and theology; later, it extended to matters of education and philosophy. In her biography of her husband, Mary Thacher Higginson (Higginson's second wife) described his participation in the discussions as usually speaking up for the underdog.

The subject he chose when his turn came to read a paper was Sappho, the Greek poet who lived on the island of Lesbos in the sixth century B.C. Historically, the Lesbians of both sexes were subjugated when the Athenians raided the island during the Pelopponnesian War; the Athenians were said to have justified their action partly on the basis of their distaste for Sappho's cultural leadership, including sexual love among women— though this was no different than the affinity among men in Athens itself.

The reader will find the essay not merely informative on a subject little known, but also tingling with the enthusiasm that Higginson felt for his subject. Written in mid-Victorian times, it is a refutation of the claim, thoughtlessly made by some critics, that Higginson is irrelevant by dint of being a member of the "genteel" tradition.

The writer Henry James did not share the viewpoint that his father had heard with sympathy at the Radical Club. He was badly stung around the time that the "Sappho" paper was read, by the essay "Henry James," in which Higginson critically reviewed his work. James felt Higginson's criticisms keenly. Reading "Henry James" may suggest an explanation not hitherto offered for the vitriolic fashion, the "malice behind the satire," as the critic Maxwell Geismar termed it, with which James, in *The Bostonians*, treated everything that he felt Higginson stood for.

In the overview of James's early novels Higginson's essay offered a certain amount of faint praise. Interlarded were expressions of distaste or displeasure such as "We miss the contact with the mass of mankind." (What modern readers would not agree that the work, the milieu, the problems of people they know are not to be found in James's writings?) Or, "[H]is life has been so far transatlantic that one hardly knows whether he would wish to be counted as an American writer." As the years passed, we know, James's preference for life as an expatriate became ever more confirmed. When we read in the essay such comments as "vulgar horror," we can speculate how James felt on reading this critique by his father's comrade.

Higginson's essay on Henry James was published November 22, 1879, in *The Literary World*. On January 31 of the following year, James wrote their mutual friend William Dean Howells, then editor of the *Atlantic Monthly*, telling of his concern that the "Higginsonian Fangs" might again strike and hoping that the editor would protect him, since "there is no reason for the decent public to be bespattered with my gore."

James's novel *The Bostonians*, which paints a negative—in a sense, derogatory—portrait of the feminist movement, was begun soon after. The scholar Marcia Jacobson has written, "That James chose to write about the feminist movement is somewhat puzzling at first glance." James's choice might be more understandable to some had he written about the feminist movement with sympathy or used it as a neutral backdrop for a study of some aspect of human relations.

His explanation for his choice of subject matter was that he wished to write a "very *American* novel," and that "the most salient and peculiar point" in American life at the time was "the situation of women, the agitation on their behalf." Throughout, the novel is a multiple satire on that agitation, its attitude peaking in James's depiction of Miss Birdseye, a character clearly intended to represent the feminist and Radical Club member Elizabeth Peabody. Of Miss Birdseye James said: "[S]he belonged to any and every league that had been founded for almost any purpose whatever"; she was "confused, inconsequent, discursive. . . . [S]he had gone into the field to testify against the iniquity of most arrangements"; "She looked as if she had spent her life on platforms, in audiences, in conventions."

And that only skims the surface. There was a central theme with another target, the love of woman for woman, shown in the relationship of Olive Chancellor and Verena Tarrant. This was viciously unkind; to top it off the younger woman loses her heart to an unreconstructed Confederate army veteran, Basil Ransome. This man from Mississippi appears throughout the story and is the voice through whom James projects his contempt and cynicism toward Boston and its mores. "Beneath the satire, farce and parody, the animating spirit of the novel was James's own . . . anger at Boston itself," wrote Maxwell Geismar in his 1964 book *Henry James and the Jacobites.* Or was the anger directed at Higginson, as earlier suggested?

In the century and a quarter since the essay "The Word Philanthropy" was published, "philanthropy" has come to have a decidedly narrower meaning than it did in Higginson's circle.

We think of philanthropy in terms of money only: charity for the needy, or grants, usually from foundations, in aid of a project or purpose acceptable to those who write the checks. But we always mean money.

The concept, the behavior associated with the word "philanthropy" was not so limited in Higginson's view. Beginning as a seeming exercise in philology, his discussion is a meditation on the history and the prior use of a word that has a far broader and nobler connotation than giving a handout. His view is based on the literal meaning of the Greek terms for "love" and "mankind" that are embedded in the English word "philanthropy," thus, "love of mankind."

In the process of explaining this word, he quite unself-consciously, without making any claims in his own behalf, tells us what his enduring motivation has been as he has joined, advocated, and fought for all the causes with which he has been identified.

Most revealing are the references to Epictetus, the Greek philosopher and former slave whose work Higginson translated for publication immediately after the war that terminated American slavery's legal status. He quotes affectionately the Greek's aphoristic assertion, "Nothing is meaner than love of pleasure, the love of gain, and insolence; nothing nobler than magnanimity, meekness and philanthropy." And Higginson tells us the ex-slave's explanation for so believing: "The universe is one great city, full of beloved ones divine and human, by nature endeared to each other."

Whatever one may think of Higginson's review of the work of Henry James, it would seem that it had no hostile motivation. In 1866, when the author of *The Bostonians,* the novel hostile to everything that Higginson stood for, was a very young man, he was assigned by the *North American Review* to write a review of Higginson's translation of *The Works of Epictetus* (Boston, 1866). He reviewed it very favorably, asserting, "[W]e agree with the editor, then, that the teachings of Epictetus possess a permanent value—that they may properly form at least a department in a modern handbook of morals."

"The Sunny Side of the Transcendental Period" needs no introduction or commentary beyond that offered by its title and opening anecdote: the little English lady who asked Higginson, late in the century, "Don't you think it rather a pity that all the really interesting Americans are dead?"

"The Literary Pendulum" is but one of Higginson's discussions in essay form of a problem that seemed to haunt him—or perhaps not a "problem" but rather an intriguing phenomenon, the frequently inexplicable posthumous fate of an author's work. Some work neglected during the author's life gains remarkable glory; other authors who were greatly successful when alive are nearly forgotten soon after their deaths.

That Higginson proved to be one of the latter category has been, his writings show, a loss to succeeding generations of Americans. He deserves to make a comeback.

1

SAPPHO

The voyager in the Ægean Sea, who has grown weary of the prevailing barrenness of the Grecian Isles, finds at length, when in sight of Lesbos, something that fulfils his dreams of beauty. The village of Mitylene, which now gives its name to the island, is built upon a rocky promontory, with a harbor on either hand. Behind it there are softly wooded hills, swelling to meet the abrupt bases of the loftier mountains. These hills are clothed in one dense forest of silvery olive and darker pomegranate, and as you ascend their paths, the myrtle, covered with delicate white blossoms, and exhaling a sweet perfume, forms a continuous arch above your head. The upper mountain heights rise above vegetation, but their ravines are dyed crimson with fringing oleanders. From the summits of their passes you look eastward upon the pale distances of Asia Minor, or down upon the calm Ægean, intensely blue, amid which the island rests as if inlaid in *lapis lazuli.*

This decaying Turkish village of Mitylene marks the site of what was, twenty-five centuries ago, one of the great centres of Greek civilization. The city then covered the whole breadth of the peninsula, and the grand canal, that separated it from the mainland, was crossed by bridges of white marble. The great theatre of Mitylene was such a masterpiece of architecture, that the Roman Pompey wished to copy it in the metropolis of the world. The city was classed by Horace with Rhodes, Ephesus, and Corinth. Yet each of those places we now remember as famous in itself, while we think of Lesbos only as the home of Sappho.

It was in the city of Mitylene that she lived and taught and sung. But to find her birth-place you must traverse nearly the length of the island, till you come to Ereso or Eresus, a yet smaller village, and Greek instead of Turkish. To reach it you must penetrate aromatic pine forests, where the deer lurk, and must ascend mountain paths like rocky ladders, where the mule alone can climb. But as you approach the village, you find pastoral beauty all around you; though the Æolian lyric music is heard no more, yet the hillsides echo with sheep-bells and with the shepherds' cries. Among the villagers you find manners more simple and hospitable than elsewhere in the Greek islands; there are more traces of the ancient beauty of the race; and the women on festal days wear long white veils edged with a crimson border, and look, as they follow one another to church, like processional figures on an antique urn. These women are permitted to share the meals of their husbands, contrary to the usual practice of rural Greece; and as a compensation, they make for their husbands such admirable bread, that it has preserved its reputation for two thousand years. The old Greek poet Archestratus, who wrote a work on the art of cookery, said that if the gods were to eat bread, they would send Hermes to Eresus to buy it; and the only modern traveller, so far as I know, who has visited the village, reports the same excellent recipe to be still in vogue.[1]

It was among these well-trained women that the most eminent poetess of the world was born. Let us now turn and look upon her in her later abode of Mitylene; either in some garden of orange and myrtle, such as once skirted the city, or in that marble house which she called the dwelling of the Muses.[2] Let us call around her, in fancy, the maidens who have come from different parts of Greece to learn of her. Anactoria is here from Miletus, Eunica from Salamis, Gongyla from Colophon, and others from Pamphylia and the isle of Telos. Erinna and Damophyla study together the complex Sapphic metres; Atthis learns how to strike the harp with the plectron, Sappho's invention; Mnasidica embroiders a sacred robe for the temple. The teacher meanwhile corrects the measures of one, the notes of another, the stitches of a third, then summons all from their work to rehearse together some sacred chorus or temple ritual; then stops to read a verse of her own, or—must I say it?—to denounce a rival preceptress. For if the too fascinating Andromeda has beguiled away some favorite pupil to one of those rival feminine academies that not only exist in Lesbos, but have spread as far as illiterate Sparta, then Sappho may at least wish to remark that Andromeda does not know how to dress herself. "And what woman ever charmed thy mind," she says to the vacillating pupil, "who wore a vulgar and tasteless dress, or did not know how to draw her garments close about her ankles?"

---

[1] *Travels and Discoveries in the Levant*, by C. T. Newton, i. 99. London, 1865.
[2] Μονσοπόλω οἰκίαν.

Out of a long list of Greek poetesses there were seven women who were, as a poem in the Greek Anthology says, "divinely tongued" or "spoke like gods."[3] Of these Sappho was the admitted chief. Among the Greeks "the poet" meant Homer, and "the poetess" equally designated her. "There flourished in those days," said Strabo, writing a little before our era, "Sappho, a wondrous creature; for we know not any woman to have appeared, within recorded time, who was in the least to be compared with her in respect to poesy."

The dates of her birth and death are alike uncertain, but she lived somewhere between the years 628 and 572 B. C.: thus flourishing three or four centuries after Homer, and less than two centuries before Pericles. Her father's name is variously given, and we can only hope, in charity, that it was not Scamandronimus. We have no better authority than that of Ovid for saying that he died when his daughter was six years old. Her mother's name was Cleis, and Sappho had a daughter of the same name. The husband of the poetess was probably named Cercolas, and there is a faint suspicion that he was a man of property. It is supposed that she became early a widow, and won most of her poetic fame while in that condition. She had at least two brothers: one being Larichus, whom she praises for his graceful demeanor as cup-bearer in the public banquets,—an office which belonged only to beautiful youths of noble birth; the other was Charaxus, whom Sappho had occasion to reproach, according to Herodotus,[4] for buying and marrying a slave of disreputable antecedents.

Of the actual events of Sappho's life almost nothing is known, except that she once had to flee for safety from Lesbos to Sicily, perhaps to escape the political persecutions that prevailed in the island. It is not necessary to assume that she had reached an advanced age when she spoke of herself as "one of the elders,"[5] inasmuch as people are quite as likely to use that term of mild self-reproach while young enough for somebody to contradict them. It is hard to ascertain whether she possessed beauty even in her prime. Tradition represents her as having been "little and dark," but tradition describes Cleopatra in the same way; and we should clearly lose much from history by ignoring all the execution done by small brunettes. The Greek Anthology describes her as "the pride of the lovely haired Lesbians;" Plato calls her "the beautiful Sappho" or "the

---

[3]Θεογλώσσους. Brunck, ii. 114.

[4]ii. 153.

[5]Γεραίτερα.

fair Sappho,"[6]—as you please to render the phrase more or less ardently,—and Plutarch and Athenæus use similar epithets. But when Professor Felton finds evidence of her charms in her portraits on the Lesbian coins, as engraved by Wolf, I must think that he is too easily pleased with the outside of the lady's head, however it may have been with the inside.

The most interesting intellectual fact in Sappho's life was doubtless her relation to her great townsman Alcæus. These two will always be united in fame as the joint founders of the lyric poetry of Greece, and therefore of the world. Anacreon was a child, or perhaps unborn, when they died; and Pindar was a pupil of women who seem to have been Sappho's imitators, Myrtis and Corinna. The Latin poets Horace and Catullus, five or six centuries after, drew avowedly from these Æolian models, to whom nearly all their metres have been traced back. Horace wrote of Alcæus: "The Lesbian poet sang of war amid the din of arms, or when he had bound the storm-tossed ship to the moist shore, he sang of Bacchus, and the Muses, of Venus and the boy who clings forever by her side, and of Lycus, beautiful with his black hair and black eyes."[7] But the name of the Greek singer is still better preserved to Anglo-Saxons through an imitation of a single fragment by Sir William Jones,—the noble poem beginning "What constitutes a state?" It is worth while to remember that we owe these fine lines to the lover of Sappho. And indeed the poems of Alcæus, so far as they remain, show much of the grace and elegance of Horace, joined with a far more heroic tone. His life was spent amid political convulsions, in which he was prominent, and, in spite of his fine verses, it is suspected, from the evidence remaining, that he was a good deal of a fop and not much of a soldier; and it is perhaps as well that the lady did not smile upon him, even in verse.

Their loves rest, after all, rather on tradition than on direct evidence; for there remain to us only two verses which Alcæus addressed to Sappho. The one is a compliment, the other an apology. The compliment is found in one graceful line, which is perhaps her best description:—

"Violet-crowned, pure, sweetly smiling Sappho."

The freshness of those violets, the charm of that smile, the assurance of that purity, all rest upon this one line, and securely rest. If every lover,

---

[6] Σαπφοῦς τῆς καλῆς. *Phædr.*, 24. Homer celebrates the beauty of the Lesbian women in his day. *Iliad*, ix. 129, 271.

[7] *Carm.*, i. 32, 5.

having thus said in three epithets the whole story about his mistress, would be content to retire into oblivion, and add no more, what a comfort it would be! Alcæus unhappily went one phrase further, and therefore goes down to future ages, not only as an ardent lover, but as an unsuccessful one. For Aristotle, in his "Rhetoric,"[8] records that this poet once addressed Sappho as follows:—

"I wish to speak, but shame restrains my tongue."

Now this apology may have had the simplest possible occasion. Alcæus may have undertaken to amend a verse of Sappho's and have spoiled it; or he may have breakfasted in the garden, with her and her maidens, and may have spilled some honey from Hymettus on a crimson-bordered veil from Eresus. But it is recorded by Aristotle that the violet-crowned thus answered: "If thy wishes were fair and noble, and thy tongue designed not to utter what is base, shame would not cloud thine eyes, but thou wouldst freely speak thy just desires." Never was reproof more exquisitely uttered than is this in the Greek; and if we take it for serious, as we probably should, there is all the dignity of womanhood in the reply, so that Sappho comes well out of the dialogue, however it may be with her wooer. Yet if, as is also possible, the occasion was but trivial, it is rather refreshing to find these gifted lovers, in the very morning of civilization, simply rehearsing just the dialogue that goes on between every village schoolgirl and her awkward swain, when he falters and "fears to speak," and says finally the wrong thing, and she blushingly answers, "I should think you would be ashamed."

But whether the admiration of Alcæus was more or less ardent, it certainly was not peculiar to him. There were hardly any limits to the enthusiasm habitually expressed in ancient times for the poetry of Sappho. In respect to the abundance of laurels, she stands unapproached among women, even to the present day. Ælian preserves the tradition that the recitation of one of her poems so affected the great lawgiver Solon, that he expressed the wish that he might not die till he had learned it by heart. Plato called her the tenth Muse. Others described her as uniting in herself the qualities of Muse and Aphrodite; and others again as the joint foster-child of Aphrodite, Cupid, and the Graces. Grammarians lectured on her poems and wrote essays on her metres; and her image appeared on at least six different coins of her native land. And it has generally been admitted by modern critics that "the loss of her poems is the greatest

---

[8]*Carm.*, i. 9.

over which we have to mourn in the whole range of Greek literature, at least of the imaginative species."

Now why is it that, in case of a woman thus famous, some cloud of reproach has always mingled with the incense? In part, perhaps, because she was a woman, and thus subject to harsher criticism in coarse periods of the world's career. More, no doubt, because she stood in a transition period of history, and, in a contest between two social systems, represented an unsuccessful effort to combine the merits of both. In the Homeric period the position of the Greek woman was simple and free. In the Iliad and Odyssey she is always treated with respect; unlike most of the great poems of modern Europe, they do not contain an indelicate line. But with the advancing culture of the Ionian colonies, represented by Athens, there inevitably arose the question, what to do with the women. Should they be admitted to share this culture, or be excluded? Athens, under the influence of Asiatic models, decided to exclude them. Sparta and the Dorian colonies, on the other hand, preferred to exclude the culture. It was only the Æolian colonies, such as Lesbos, that undertook to admit the culture and the women also. Nowhere else in Greece did women occupy what we should call a modern position. The attempt was premature, and the reputation of Lesbos was crushed in the process.

Among the Ionians of Asia, according to Herodotus, the wife did not share the table of her husband; she dared not call him by his name, but addressed him with the title of "Lord"; and this was hardly an exaggeration of the social habits of Athens itself. But among the Dorians of Sparta, and probably among the Æolians as well, the husband called his wife "mistress," not in subserviency, but after the English peasant fashion; Spartan mothers preserved a power over their adult sons such as was nowhere else seen; the dignity of maidenhood was celebrated in public songs called "Parthenia," which were peculiar to Sparta; and the women took so free a part in the conversation, that Socrates, in a half-sarcastic passage in the "Protagoras," compares their quickness of wit to that of the men.[9] The Spartan women, in short, were free, though ignorant, and this freedom the Athenians thought bad enough. But when the Æolians of Lesbos carried the equality a step further, and to freedom added culture, the Athenians found it intolerable. Such an innovation was equivalent to setting up the Protestant theory of woman's position as against the Roman Catholic, or the English against the French.

---

[9]The best authority in regard to the Spartan women is K. O. Müller's *Dorier*, book iv. c. iv., also book v. c. viii. § 5 (Eng. tr. vol. ii. pp. 290–300; also p. 311). For his view of the women of Lesbos see his *Literature of Greece* (Eng. tr.), c. xiii.

It is perhaps fortunate for historic justice that we have within our reach an illustration so obvious, showing the way in which a whole race of women may be misconstrued. If a Frenchman visits America and sees a young girl walking or riding with a young man, unchaperoned, he is apt to assume that she is of doubtful character. Should he hear a married woman talk about "emancipation," he will infer either that her marriage is not legal, or that her husband has good reason to wish it were not. Precisely thus did an Athenian view a Lesbian woman; and if she collected round her a class of young pupils for instruction, so much the worse. He could no more imagine any difference between Sappho and Aspasia, than could a Frenchman between Margaret Fuller and George Sand. To claim any high moral standard in either case would merely strengthen the indictment by the additional count of hypocrisy. Better Aspasia than a learned woman who had the effrontery to set up for the domestic virtues. The stories that thus gradually came to be told about Sappho in later years—scandal at longer and longer range—were simply inevitable from the point of view of Athens. If Aristophanes spared neither Socrates nor Euripides, why should his successors spare Sappho?

Therefore the reckless comic authors of that luxurious city, those Pre-Bohemians of literature, made the most of their game. Ameipsias, Amphis, Antiphanes, Diphilus, Ephippus, Timocles, all wrote farces bearing the name of a woman who had died in excellent repute, so far as appears, two centuries before. With what utter recklessness they did their work is shown by their naming as her lovers Archilochus, who died before she was born, and Hipponax, who was born after she died. Then came, in later literature, the Roman Ovid, who had learned from licentious princesses to regard womanly virtue as only a pretty fable. He took up the tale of Sappho, conjured up a certain Phaon, with whom she might be enamored, and left her memory covered with stains such as even the Leucadian leap could not purge. Finally, since Sappho was a heathen, a theologian was found at last to make an end of her; the Church put an apostolic sanction upon these corrupt reveries of the Roman profligate, and Tatian, the Christian Father, fixed her name in ecclesiastical tradition as that of "an impure and lovesick woman who sings her own shame."[10]

The process has, alas! plenty of parallels in history. Worse, for instance, than the malice of the Greek comedians or of Ovid—since they possibly believed their own stories—was the attempt made by Voltaire to pollute, through twenty-one books of an epic poem, the stainless fame

---

[10]Tatian, *Adv. Græcos,* c. 33. Ovid, *Heroid.,* xv. 61–70.

of his own virgin countrywoman, Joan of Arc. In that work he revels in a series of impurities so loathsome that the worst of them are omitted from the common editions, and only lurk in appendices, here and there, as if even the shameless printing-presses of Paris were ashamed of them. Suppose, now, that the art of printing had remained undiscovered, that all contemporary memorials of this maiden had vanished, and posterity had possessed no record of her except Voltaire's "Pucelle." In place of that heroic image there would have remained to us only a monster of profligacy, unless some possible Welcker had appeared, long centuries after, to right the wrong.

The remarkable essay of Welcker,[11] from which all modern estimates of Sappho date, was first published in 1816, under the title, "Sappho vindicated from a prevailing Prejudice." It was a remarkable instance of the power of a single exhaustive investigation to change the verdict of scholars. Bishop Thirlwall, for instance, says of it: "The tenderness of Sappho, whose character has been rescued, by one of the happiest efforts of modern criticism, from the unmerited reproach under which it had labored for so many centuries, appears to have been no less pure than glowing." And Felton, who is usually not more inclined than becomes a man and a professor to put a high estimate on literary women, declares of her that "she has shared the fortunes of others of her sex, endowed like her with God's richest gifts of intellect and heart, who have been the victims of remorseless calumny for asserting the prerogatives of genius, and daring to compete with men in the struggle for fame and glory." Indeed, I know of no writer since Welcker who has seriously attempted to impugn his conclusions, except Colonel Mure, an Edinburgh advocate, whose onslaught upon Sappho is so vehement that Felton compares it to that of John Knox on Mary Stuart, and finds in it proof of a constitutional hostility between Scotch Presbyterians and handsome women.

But Mure's scholarship is not high, when tried by the German standard, whatever it may be according to the English or American. His book is also somewhat vitiated in this respect by being obviously written under a theory, namely, that love, as a theme for poetry, is a rather low and debasing thing; that the subordinate part it plays in Homer is one reason why Homer is great; and that the decline of literature began with lyric poetry. "A ready subjection," he says, "to the fascinations of the in-

---

[11]"Sappho von einem herrschenden Vorurtheil befreit," Welcker, *Kleine Schriften*, ii. 80. See, also, his "Sappho," a review of Neue's edition of her works, first published in 1828 (*K. S.*, i. 110), and "Sappho und Phaon," published in 1863, a review of Mure and Theodor Kock (*K. S.*, v. 228).

ferior order of their species can hardly be a solid basis of renown for kings or heroes." Such a critic could hardly be expected to look with favor upon one who not only chose an inferior order of themes, but had the temerity to belong to an inferior order herself.

Apart from this, I am unable to see that this writer brings forward anything to disturb the verdict of abler scholars. He does not indeed claim to produce any direct evidence of his proposition that Sappho was a corrupt woman, and her school at Lesbos a nursery of sins; but he seeks to show this indirectly, through a minute criticism of her writings. Into this he carries, I regret to say, an essential coarseness of mind, like that of Voltaire, which delights to torture the most innocent phrases till they yield a double meaning. He reads these graceful fragments as the sailors in some forecastle might read Juliet's soliloquies, or as a criminal lawyer reads in court the letters of some warm-hearted woman; the shame lying not in the words, but in the tongue. The manner in which he gloats over the scattered lines of a wedding song, for instance, weaving together the phrases and supplying the innuendoes, is enough to rule him out of the class of pure-minded men. But besides this quality of coarseness, he shows a serious want of candor. For though he admits that Sappho first introduced into literature—in her Epithalamia—a dramatic movement, yet he never gives her the benefit of this dramatic attitude except where it suits his own argument. It is as if one were to cite Browning into court and undertake to convict him, on his own confession, of sharing every mental condition he describes.

What, then, was this Lesbian school that assembled around Sappho? Mure pronounces it to have been a school of vice. The German professors see in it a school of science. Professor Felton thinks that it may have resembled the Courts of Love in the Middle Ages. But a more reasonable parallel, nearer home, must occur to the minds of those of us who remember Margaret Fuller Ossoli and her classes. If Sappho, in addition to all that the American gave her pupils, undertook the duty of instruction in the most difficult music, the most complex metres, and the profoundest religious rites, then she had on her hands quite too much work to be exclusively a troubadour or a *savante* or a sinner. And if such ardent attachments as Margaret Fuller Ossoli inspired among her own sex were habitually expressed by Sappho's maiden lovers, in the language of Lesbos instead of Boston, we can easily conceive of sentimental ardors which Attic comedians would find ludicrous and Scotch advocates nothing less than a scandal.

Fortunately we can come within six centuries of the real Lesbian society in the reports of Maximus Tyrius, whom Felton strangely calls "a tedious writer of the time of the Antonines," but who seems to me often to rival Epictetus and Plutarch in eloquence and nobleness of tone. In his eighth dissertation he draws a parallel between the instruction given by Socrates to men and that afforded by Sappho to women. "Each," he says, "appears to me to deal with the same kind of love, the one as subsisting among males, the other among females." "What Alcibiades and Charmides and Phædrus are with Socrates, that Gyrinna and Atthis and Anactoria are with the Lesbian. And what those rivals Prodicus, Gorgias, Thrasymachus, and Protagoras are to Socrates, that Gorgo and Androméda are to Sappho. At one time she reproves, at another she confutes these, and addresses them in the same ironical language with Socrates." Then he draws parallels between the writings of the two. "Diotima says to Socrates that love flourishes in abundance, but dies in want. Sappho conveys the same meaning when she calls love 'sweetly bitter' and 'a painful gift.' Socrates calls love 'a sophist,' Sappho 'a ringlet of words.' Socrates says that he is agitated with Bacchic fury through the love of Phædrus; but she that 'love shakes her mind as the wind when it falls on mountain-oaks.' Socrates reproves Xantippe when she laments that he must die, and Sappho writes to her daughter, 'Grief is not lawful in the residence of the Muse, nor does it become us.'"

Thus far Maximus Tyrius. But that a high intellectual standard prevailed in this academy of Sappho's may be inferred from a fragment of her verse, in which she utters her disappointment over an uncultivated woman, whom she had, perhaps, tried in vain to influence. This imaginary epitaph warns this pupil that she is in danger of being forgotten through forgetfulness of those Pierian roses which are the Muses' symbol. This version retains the brevity of the original lines, and though rhymed, is literal, except that it changes the second person to the third:—

> Dying she reposes;
> Oblivion grasps her now;
> Since never Pierian roses
> Were wreathed round her empty brow;
> She goeth unwept and lonely
> To Hades' dusky homes,
> And bodiless shadows only
> Bid her welcome as she comes.

To show how differently Sappho lamented her favorites, I give Elton's version of another epitaph on a maiden, whom we may fancy lying robed for the grave, while her companions sever their tresses around her, that something of themselves may be entombed with her.

> "This dust was Timas'; ere her bridal hour
> She lies in Proserpina's gloomy bower;
> Her virgin playmates from each lovely head
> Cut with sharp steel their locks, the strewments for the dead."

These are only fragments; but of the single complete poem that remains to us from Sappho, I shall venture on a translation, which can claim only to be tolerably literal, and to keep, in some degree, to the Sapphic metre. Yet I am cheered by the remark of an old grammarian, Demetrius Phalereus, that "Sappho's whole poetry is so perfectly musical and harmonious, that even the harshest voice or most awkward recital can hardly render it unpleasing to the ear." Let us hope that the Muses may extend some such grace, even to a translation.

Hymn to Aphrodite

Beautiful-throned, immortal Aphrodite!
Daughter of Zeus, beguiler, I implore thee,
Weigh me not down with weariness and anguish,
O thou most holy!

Come to me now! if ever thou in kindness
Hearkenedst my words,—and often hast thou hearkened,
Heeding, and coming from the mansions golden
Of thy great Father,

Yoking thy chariot, borne by thy most lovely
Consecrated birds, with dusky-tinted pinions,
Waving swift wings from utmost heights of heaven
Through the mid-ether:

Swiftly they vanished; leaving thee, O goddess,
Smiling, with face immortal in its beauty,
Asking why I grieved, and why in utter longing
I had dared call thee;

Asking what I sought, thus hopeless in desiring,
'Wildered in brain, and spreading nets of passion
Alas, for whom? and saidst thou, "Who has harmed thee?
O my poor Sappho!"

"Though now he flies, erelong he shall pursue thee;
Fearing thy gifts, he too in turn shall bring them;
Loveless to-day, to-morrow he shall woo thee,
Though thou shouldst spurn him."

Thus seek me now, O holy Aphrodite!
Save me from anguish, give me all I ask for,
Gifts at thy hand; and thine shall be the glory,
Sacred protector!

It is safe to say that there is not a lyrical poem in Greek literature, nor in any other, which has, by its artistic structure, inspired more enthusiasm than this. Is it autobiographical? The German critics, true to their national instincts, hint that she may have written some of her verses in her character of pedagogue, as exercises in different forms of verse. It is as if Shakespeare had written his sonnet, "Shall I compare thee to a summer's day?" only to show young Southampton where the rhymes came in. Still more difficult is it to determine the same question—autobiographical or dramatic?—in case of the fragment next in length to this poem. It has been well engrafted into English literature through the translation of Ambrose Philips, as follows:—

To a Beloved Woman
"Blest as the immortal gods is he,
The youth who fondly sits by thee,
And hears and sees thee, all the while,
Softly speak and sweetly smile.

"'T was that deprived my soul of rest,
And raised such tumult in my breast;
For while I gazed, in transport tost,
My breath was gone, my voice was lost.

"My bosom glowed; the subtile flame
Ran quick through all my vital frame;
On my dim eyes a darkness hung;
My ears with hollow murmurs rung.

"With dewy damps my limbs were chilled;
My blood with gentle horrors thrilled;
My feeble pulse forgot to play;
I fainted, sunk, and died away."

The translation would give the impression that this is a complete poem; but it is not. A fragment of the next verse brings some revival from this desperate condition, but what exit is finally provided does not appear. The existing lines are preserved by Longinus in the eighth chapter of his famous book, "On the Sublime;" and his commentary is almost as impassioned as the poem. "Is it not wonderful how she calls at once on soul, body, ears, tongue, eyes, color,—as on so many separate deaths,—and how in self-contradiction and simultaneously she freezes, she glows, she raves, she returns to reason, she is terrified, she is at the brink of death? It is not a single passion that she exhibits, but a whole congress of passions." The poem thus described, while its grammatical formations show it to have been addressed by a woman to a woman, is quite as likely to have been dramatic as autobiographical in its motive. It became so famous, at any rate, as a diagnosis of passion, that a Greek physician is said to have "copied it bodily into his book, and to have regulated his prescriptions accordingly."

All that remains to us of Sappho, besides, is a chaos of short fragments, which have been assiduously collected and edited by Wolf, Blomfield, Neue, and others. Among the spirited translations by our own poet Percival, there are several of these fragments; one of which I quote for its exceeding grace, though it consists of only two lines:—

"Sweet mother, I can weave the web no more;
So much I love the youth, so much I lingering love."

But this last adjective, so effective to the ear, is, after all, an interpolation. It should be:—

So much I love the youth, by Aphrodite's charm.

Percival also translates one striking fragment whose few short lines seem to toll like a bell, mourning the dreariness of a forgotten tryst, on which the moon and stars look down. I should render it thus:—

The moon is down;
And I've watched the dying
Of the Pleiades;
'T is the middle night,
The hour glides by,
And alone I'm sighing.

Percival puts it in blank verse, more smoothly:

"The moon is set; the Pleiades are gone;
'T is the midnoon of night; the hour is by,
And yet I watch alone."

There are some little fragments of verse addressed by Sappho to the evening star, which are supposed to have suggested the celebrated lines of Byron; she says,—

"O Hesperus, thou bringest all things,
Thou bringest wine, thou bringest [home] the goat,
To the mother thou bringest the child."

Again she says, with a touch of higher imagination,—

"Hesperus, bringing home all that the light-giving morning has scattered."

Grammarians have quoted this line to illustrate the derivation of the word Hesperus;[12] and the passage may be meant to denote, not merely the assembling of the household at night, but the more spiritual reuniting of the thoughts and dreams that draw round us with the shadows and vanish with the dawn.

Achilles Tatius, in the fifth century, gave in prose the substance of one of Sappho's poems, not otherwise preserved. It may be called "The Song of the Rose."

"If Zeus had wished to appoint a sovereign over the flowers, he would have made the rose their king. It is the ornament of the earth, the glory of plants, the eye of the flowers, the blush of the meadows, a flash of beauty. It breathes of love, welcomes Aphrodite, adorns itself with fragrant leaves, and is decked with tremulous petals, that laugh in the zephyr."

Indeed, that love of external nature, which is so often mistakenly said to have been wanting among the Greeks, is strongly marked in Sappho. She observes "the vernal swallow and the melodious nightingale, Spring's herald." "The moon," she elsewhere says, "was at the full, and they [the stars] stood round her, as round an altar." And again, "The stars around the lovely moon withdraw their splendor when, in her fulness, she most illumines earth."

Of herself Sappho speaks but little in the fragments left to us. In one place she asserts that she is "not of malignant nature, but has a placid

---

[12]Εσπέρα ἀπὸ του ἔσω ποιεῖν περᾶν τὰ ζῶα, κ. τ. λ.

mind," and again that her desire is for "a mode of life that shall be elegant and at the same time honest," the first wish doing credit to her taste, and the other to her conscience. In several places she confesses to a love of luxury, yet she is described by a later Greek author, Aristides, as having rebuked certain vain and showy women for their ostentation, while pointing out that the pursuits of intellect afford a surer joy. It is hardly needful to add that not a line remains of her writings which can be charged with indelicacy; and had any such existed, they would hardly have passed unnoticed or been forgotten.

It is odd that the most direct report left to us of Sappho's familiar conversation should have enrolled her among those enemies of the human race who give out conundrums. Or rather it is in this case a riddle of the old Greek fashion, such as the Sphinx set the example of propounding to men, before devouring them in any other manner. I will render it in plain prose.

Sappho's Riddle.

There is a feminine creature who bears in her bosom a voiceless brood; yet they send forth a clear voice, over sea and land, to whatsoever mortals they will; the absent hear it; so do the deaf.

This is the riddle, as recorded by Antiphanes, and preserved by Athenæus. It appears that somebody tried to guess it. The feminine creature, he thought, was the state. The brood must be the orators, to be sure, whose voices reached beyond the seas, as far as Asia and Thrace, and brought back thence something to their own advantage; while the community sat dumb and deaf amid their railings. This seemed plausible, but somebody else objected to the solution; for who ever knew an orator to be silent, he said, until he was put down by force? All which sounds quite American and modern; but he gave it up, at last, and appealed to Sappho, who thus replied:—

Sappho's Solution.

A *letter* is a thing essentially feminine in its character. It bears a brood in its bosom named the alphabet. They are voiceless, yet speak to whom they will; and if any man shall stand next to him who reads, will he not hear?

It is not an exciting species of wit. Yet this kind of riddle was in immense demand in Greek society, and "if you make believe very hard, it's quite nice." But it seems rather a pity that this memorial of Sappho should be preserved, while her solemn hymns and her Epithalamia, or marriage-songs, which were, as has been said, almost the first Greek effort toward dramatic poetry, are lost to us forever.

And thus we might go on through the literature of Greece, peering after little grains of Sappho among the rubbish of voluminous authors. But perhaps these specimens are enough. It remains to say that the name of Phaon, who is represented by Ovid as having been her lover, is not once mentioned in these fragments, and the general tendency of modern criticism is to deny his existence. Some suppose him to have been a merely mythical being, based upon the supposed loves of Aphrodite and Adonis, who was called by the Greeks Phæthon or Phaon. It is said that this Phaon was a ferryman at Mitylene, who was growing old and ugly till he rowed Aphrodite in his boat, and then refused payment; on which she gave him for recompense youth, beauty, and Sappho. This was certainly, "Take, O boatman, thrice thy fee," as in Uhland's ballad; but the Greek passengers have long since grown as shadowy as the German, and we shall never know whether this oarsman really ferried himself into the favor of goddess or of dame. It is of little consequence; Sappho doubtless had lovers, and one of them may as well have been named Phaon as anything else.

But to lose her fabled leap from the Leucadian promontory would doubtless be a greater sacrifice; it formed so much more effective a termination for her life than any novelist could have contrived. It is certain that the leap itself, as a Greek practice, was no fable; sometimes it was a form of suicide, sometimes a religious incantation, and sometimes again an expiation of crime. But it was also used often as a figure of speech by comfortable poets who would have been sorry to find in it anything more. Anacreon, for instance, says in an ode, "Again casting myself from the Leucadian rock, I plunge into the gray sea, drunk with love;" though it is clear that he was not a man to drown his cares in anything larger than a punch-bowl. It is certainly hard to suppose that the most lovelorn lady, residing on an island whose every shore was a precipice, and where her lover was at hand to feel the anguish of her fate, would take ship and sail for weary days over five hundred miles of water to seek a more sensational rock. Theodor Kock, the latest German writer on Sappho, thinks it is as if a lover should travel from the Rhine to Niagara to drown himself. "Are not Abana and Pharpar rivers of Damascus?" More solid, negative proof is found in the fact that Ptolemy Hephæstion, the author who has collected the most numerous notices of the Leucadian leap, entirely omits the conspicuous name of Sappho from his record. Even Colonel Mure, who is as anxious to prove this deed against her as if it were a violation of all the ten commandments, is staggered for a moment by this omission; but soon recovering himself, with an ingenuity that does him credit as attorney for the prosecution, he points out that the reason Ptolemy omitted Sappho's name was undoubtedly because it was so well known already; a use of negative evidence to which there can be no objection, except that under it any one of us might be convicted of having died last year, on the plea that his death was a fact too notorious to be mentioned in the newspapers.

But whether by way of the Leucadian cliff or otherwise, Sappho is gone, with her music and her pupils and most of the words she wrote, and the very city where she dwelt, and all but the island she loved. It is something to be able to record that, twenty-five centuries ago, in that remote nook among the Grecian Isles, a woman's genius could play such a part in moulding the great literature that has moulded the world. Colonel Mure thinks that a hundred such women might have demoralized all Greece. But it grew demoralized at any rate; and even the island where Sappho taught took its share in the degradation. If, on the other hand, the view taken of her by more careful criticism be correct, a hundred such women might have done much to save it. Modern nations must take up again the problem where Athens failed and Lesbos only pointed the way to the solution,—to create a civilization where the highest culture shall be extended to woman also. It is not enough that we should dream, with Plato, of a republic where man is free and woman but a serf. The aspirations of modern life culminate, like the greatest of modern poems, in the elevation of womanhood. *Das ewige Weibliche zieht uns hinan.*

2

THE WORD PHILANTHROPY

Some writer on philology has said that there is more to be learned from language itself than from all that has been written by its aid. It is often possible to reconstruct some part of the moral attitude of a race, through a single word of its language; and this essay will simply offer an illustration of that process.

In the natural sciences, the method is familiar. For instance, it was long supposed that the mammoth and the cave-bear had perished from the earth before man appeared. No argument from the occasional intermixture of their bones with man's was quite conclusive. But when there was dug up a drawing of the cave-bear on slate, and a rude carving of the living mammoth, mane and all, on a tusk of the animal itself, then doubt vanished, and the question was settled. Thoreau has remarked that "some circumstantial evidence may be very strong, as where you find a live trout in the milk-pan." These discoveries in palæontology were quite as conclusive.

Now what is true in palæontology is true in philology as well. When a word comes into existence, its meaning is carved on the language that holds it; if you find the name of a certain virtue written in a certain tongue, then the race which framed that language knew that virtue. This may be briefly illustrated by the history of the word "Philanthropy."

This word, it is known, came rather late into the English tongue. When the Pilgrim Fathers stepped on Plymouth Rock, in 1620, though they may have been practising what the word meant, there were few among them to whom its sound was familiar, and perhaps none who habitually used it. It is not in Chaucer, Spenser, or Shakespeare. It is not even in the English

---

This essay appeared originally in a volume called *Freedom and Fellowship in Religion* published by the Free Religious Association.

Bible, first published in 1611; and the corresponding Greek word, occuring three times in the original, is rendered in each case by a circumlocution. It does not appear in that pioneer English Dictionary, Minsheu's "Guide to the Tongues," as first published in 1617. It does not appear in the Spanish Dictionary of the same Minsheu, in 1623. But two years later than this, in the second edition of his "Guide to the Tongues" (1625), it appears as follows, among the new words distinguished by a dagger:—

"Philanthropie; Humanitie, a loving of men."

Then follow the Greek and Latin words, as sources of derivation.

This is the first appearance in print, so far as my knowledge goes, of the word "Philanthropie." But Lord Bacon, publishing in the same year (1625) his essay on "Goodness, and Goodness of Heart,"—the thirteenth of the series of his essays, as now constituted, and occupying the place of an essay on "Friendship," which stood thirteenth in the previous editions,—uses the word in its Greek form only, and in a way that would seem to indicate, but for the evidence of Minsheu, that it had not yet been Anglicized. His essay opens thus: "I take goodness in this sense, the affecting of the weal of men, which is what the Greeks call *Philanthropia;* and the word *Humanity,* as it is used, is a little too light to express it."

The next author who uses the word is Jeremy Taylor. It is true that in his "Holy Dying" (1651), when translating the dying words of Cyrus from Xenophon's "Cyropædia," he renders the word φιλάνθρωπος "a lover of mankind," citing the original Greek in the margin.[1] But in Taylor's sermons, published two years later (1653), there occur the first instances known to me, after Minsheu, of the use of the Anglicized word. Jeremy Taylor speaks of "that godlike excellency, a philanthropy and love to all mankind;" and again, of "the philanthropy of God."[2] The inference would seem to be that while this word had now become familiar, at least among men of learning, the corresponding words "philanthropic" and "philanthropist" were not equally well known. If they had been, Jeremy Taylor would probably have used either the one or the other, in translating the words attributed to Cyrus.

So slowly did the word take root, indeed, that when so learned a writer as Dryden used it, nearly seventy years after Minsheu, he still did it with an apology, and with especial reference to the Greek author on whom he was commenting. For when, in 1693, Sir Henry Steere published a poor

---

[1] Xen., *Cyrop.,* viii. 7. 25. Taylor's *Holy Dying,* c. ii. § 3, par. 2.

[2] Taylor's *Sermons,* vol. iii. Sermons I and II. (Cited in Richardson's Dictionary.) In his sermon entitled *Via Intelligentæ,* he quotes the Greek adjective, translating it "gentle."

translation of Polybius and Dryden was employed to write the preface, he said:—

"This philanthropy (which we have not a proper word in English to express) is everywhere manifest in our author, and from hence proceeded that divine rule which he gave to Scipio, that whensoever he went abroad he should take care not to return to his house before he had acquired a friend by some new obligement."

We have, then, three leading English writers of the seventeenth century—Bacon, Taylor, Dryden—as milestones to show how gradually this word "philanthropy" became established in our language. To recapitulate briefly: Bacon uses the original Greek word, spelled in Roman characters, and attributes it to "the Grecians," saying that there is no English equivalent; Taylor, twenty-eight years later, uses it in Anglicized form, without apology or explanation, although when quoting and translating the Greek word φιλάθρωπος, he does not use the equivalent word in his translation. Dryden, forty years later, commenting on a Greek author, makes a sort of apology for the use of the word, as representing something "which we have not a proper word in English to express," although he uses the English form. It is therefore clear that the word "philanthropy" was taken directly and consciously from the Greek, for want of a satisfactory English word. Men do not take the trouble to borrow a word, any more than an umbrella, if they already possess one that will answer the purpose.

Let us now consider the original word φιλανθρωπία. It has an illustrious position in Greek literature and history. It affords the keynote to the greatest dramatic poem preserved to us; and also to the sublimest life of Greece, that of Socrates. It was first used, however, in neither of these connections, but by an obscurer writer, Epicharmus, whose fragments have a peculiar historical value, as he was born about 540 B. C., and his authority thus carries back the word nearly to the First Olympiad, 776 B. C., which is commonly recognized as the beginning of authentic history. Setting these fragments aside, however, the first conspicuous appearance of the word in literature is in that astonishing poem, the "Prometheus Bound" of Æschylus, which was probably represented about 460 B. C., as the central play of a "trilogy," the theme being an ideal hero, on whom the vengeance of Zeus has fallen for his love of man. The word we seek occurs in the first two speeches of the drama, where Strength and Hephaistos (Vulcan) in turn inform Prometheus that he is to be bound to the desert rock in punishment for his philanthropy, φιλανθρώπου τρόπου; and it is repeated later, in the most magnificent soliloquy in ancient literature, where Prometheus accepts the charge, and glories in his offence, of too much love for man, τὴν λίαν φιλότητα βροτῶν. He admits that when Zeus had resolved to destroy the human race, and had withdrawn from men the use of fire, he himself had reconveyed fire to them, and thus saved them from destruction; that he had afterwards taught them to tame animals, to build ships, to observe the stars, to mine for metals, to heal diseases. For this he was punished by Zeus; for this he defies Zeus, and predicts that his tyranny must end, and justice be done. On this the three tragedies turn; the first showing Prometheus as carrying the sacred gift of fire to men; the second as chained to Caucasus; the third as delivered from his chains. If we had the first play, we should have the virtue of philanthropy exhibited in its details; if we had the last, we should see its triumph; but in the remaining tragedy we see what is, perhaps, nobler than either,—the philanthropic man under torment for his self-devotion, but refusing to regret what he has done. There is not a play in modern literature, I should say, which turns so directly and completely, from beginning to end, upon the word and the thing "philanthropy."

Seeking, now, another instance of the early use of the Greek word, and turning from the ideal to the actual, we have Socrates, in the "Euthyphron" of Plato,—composed probably about 400 B. C.,—questioned as to how it is that he has called upon himself the vengeance of those in power by telling unwelcome truths. And when his opponent hints that he himself has never got into any serious trouble, Socrates answers, in that half-jesting way which he never wholly lays aside—I quote Jowett's translation:—

"I dare say that you don't make yourself common, and are not apt to impart your wisdom. But I have a benevolent habit of pouring myself out to everybody, and would even pay for a listener, and I am afraid that the Athenians know this." The phrase rendered "benevolent habit" is ἀπὸ φιλανθρωπίας;[3] that is, "through philanthropy;" and I know nowhere a franker glimpse of the real man Socrates.

Coming down to later authors, we find the use of the word in Greek to be always such as to bring out distinctly that meaning for which it has been imported into English. How apt we are to say that the Greeks thought only of the state, not of individuals, nor of the world outside! Yet the great orator Isocrates (born 436 B. C.) heaps praises upon a certain person as being one who loved man and Athens and wisdom,— φιλανθρωπίος καὶ φιλαθηναῖος καὶ φιλόσφος,—a noble epitaph.

---

[3]Plato, *Euthyph.*, § 3. Jowett's *Plato*, i. 286.

So the orator Demosthenes (born 385 B.C.) uses the word φιλανθρωπία in contrast to φθόνος, hate, and to ὠμότης, cruelty; and speaks of employing philanthropy towards any one φιλανθρωπίαν τινὶ χρῆσθαι. So Xenophon, as we have seen, makes Cyrus describe himself on his deathbed as "philanthropic."

So Epictetus, at a later period, said, "Nothing is meaner than the love of pleasure, the love of gain, and insolence; nothing nobler than magnanimity, meekness, and philanthropy." So Plutarch, addressing his "Consolations to Apollonius" on the death of his son, sums up the praises of the youth by calling him "philanthropic,"—φιλάνθρωπος. In his life of Solon, also, he uses the word φιλανθραώπευμα,—a philanthropic act. So Diodorus speaks of a desert country as ἐστερημένη πάσης φιλανθρωπίας,—destitute of all philanthropy, or, as we should say, "pitiless,"—as if wherever man might be there would also be the love of man.[4]

We have, then, a virtue called philanthropy, which dates back nearly six hundred years before our era, and within about two centuries of the beginning of authentic history,—a virtue which inspired the self-devotion of Prometheus in the great tragedy of antiquity; which prompted the manner of life of Socrates; to which Demosthenes appealed, in opposition to hate and cruelty; to which Isocrates gave precedence before the love of country and the love of knowledge; which Polybius admired, when shown toward captives; which Epictetus classed as the noblest of all things; and which Plutarch inscribed as the highest praise upon the epitaph of a noble youth. Thus thoroughly was the word "philanthropy" rooted in the Greek language, and recognized by the Greek heart; and it is clear that we, speaking a language in which this word was unknown for centuries,—being introduced at last, according to Dryden, because there was no English word to express the same idea,—cannot claim the virtue it expresses as an exclusively modern possession.

It is worth noticing that there is another use of the word "philanthropy," which prevailed among the Greeks, and was employed for a time in English. The word was used to express an attribute of Deity, as, for instance, when Aristophanes applies it to Hermes, Ω φιλΩνθρωόπε, "O! most philanthropic"—that is, loving towards man. Paul uses the Greek word but once, and then in this same sense; and the Greek Father Athanasius uses it as a term of courtesy, Ἡ σή φιλανθρωπία, "Your philanthropy," as we say to republican governors,

---

[4]Isoc., *Epist.*, v. 2; Dem., *Adv. Leptines*, § 165; Xen., *Cyrop.*, viii. 7. 25; Epict., *Frag.*, 46; Plut., *Cons.*, § 34, *Solon*, § 15; Diod., xvii. 50.

"Your Excellency." Young, in his "Night Thoughts," addresses the Deity, "Thou great Philanthropist;" Jeremy Taylor speaks of "the philanthropy of God;" and Barrow, speaking of the goodness of God, says, "Commonly also it is by the most obliging and endearing name called love and philanthropy."[5] But I do not recall any recent instances of this use of the word.

And the use of this word, in this sense, by the Greeks, reminds us that the Greek religion, even if deficient in the loveliest spiritual results, had on the other hand little that was gloomy or terrifying. Thus the Greek funeral inscriptions, though never so triumphant as the Christian, were yet almost always marked, as Milman has pointed out, by a "quiet beauty." And this word "philanthropy" thus did a double duty, including in its range two thoughts, familiar to modern times in separate phrases,—the Fatherhood of God and the Brotherhood of Man.

It is to this consideration, I fancy, that we owe those glimpses not merely of general philanthropy, but of a recognized unity in the human race, that we find from time to time in ancient literature. It is hardly strange that in Greece, with its isolated position, its exceptional cultivation and refinement, and its scanty communications, this feeling should have been less prominent than in a world girdled with railways and encircled by telegraphic wires. In those days the great majority of men, and women almost without exception, spent their lives within the limit of some narrow state; and it was hard for the most enlightened to think of those beyond their borders except as we think even now of the vast populations of South America or Africa,—whom we regard as human beings, no doubt, but as having few habits or interests in common with our own. But every great conquest by Greece or Rome tended to familiarize men with the thought of a community of nations, even before a special stimulus was at last added by Christianity. It does not seem to me just, therefore, in Max Müller to say that "humanity is a word for which you look in vain in Plato or Aristotle," without pointing out that later Greek writers, utterly uninfluenced by Christianity, made the same criticism on these authors. Thus, in an essay attributed to Plutarch on the Fortune of Alexander, he makes this remarkable statement:—

"Alexander did not hearken to his preceptor Aristotle, who advised him to bear himself as a prince among the Greeks, his own people, but as a master among the Barbarians; to treat the one as friends and kins-

---

[5] Aristoph., *Peace*, 394; Paul, Titus iii. 4; Athanasius, cited in Sophocles's Lexicon; Young, Night Fourth; Taylor, vol. iii. sermon II (Richardson); Barrow, vol. ii. p. 356 (ed. 1700).

men, the others as animals or chattels. . . . But, conceiving that he was sent by God to be an umpire between all and to unite all together, he reduced by arms those whom he could not conquer by persuasion, and formed of a hundred diverse nations one single universal body, mingling, as it were, in one cup of friendship the customs, the marriages, and the laws of all. He desired that all should regard the whole world as their common country, the good as fellow-citizens and brethren, the bad as aliens and enemies; that the Greeks should no longer be distinguished from the foreigner by arms or costume, but that every good man should be esteemed an Hellene, every evil man a barbarian."[6]

Here we have not a piece of vague sentimentalism, but the plan attributed by tradition to one of the great generals of the world's history; and whether this was Alexander's real thought, or something invented for him by biographers, it is equally a recognition of the brotherhood of man. And the same Plutarch tells us that "the so much admired commonwealth of Zeno, first author of the Stoic sect, aims singly at this, that neither in cities nor in towns we should live under laws distinct from one another, but that we should look on all men in general to be our fellow-countrymen and citizens, observing one manner of living and one kind of order, like a flock feeding together with equal right in one common pasture."[7] So Jamblichus reports that Pythagoras, five centuries before our era, taught "the love of all to all;"[8] and Menander the dramatist said, "to live is not to live for one's self alone; let us help one another;"[9] and later, Epictetus maintained that "the universe is but one great city, full of beloved ones, divine and human, by nature endeared to each other;"[10] and Marcus Antoninus taught that we must "love mankind."[11] In none of these passages do we find the Greek word φιλανθρωπία; but in all we find the noble feeling indicated by that word; while Aulus Gellius quotes the word itself, and attaches to it the self-same meaning borne by the English word.[12]

And it is well known that the same chain of tradition runs through the Latin writers, as when Terence brought down the applause of the theatre

---

[6]Merivale's translation: *Conversion of the Roman Empire*, p. 64. He also gives the original, p. 203. Compare Goodwin's *Plutarch*, i. 481.

[7]Plutarch's *Morals*. Goodwin's translation, i. 481.

[8]*Jamblichi de Pythag. vita*, cc. 16, 33. Φιλίαν δὲ διαφανέστατα πάντων πρὸς ἅπαντας Πυθαγόρας παρέδωκε.

[9]Meineke, *Fragmenta Com. Græc.*

[10]Epictetus, iii. 24.

[11]Marcus Antoninus, vii. 31. Φίλησου τὸν ἀνθρώπινον γένος.

[12]Aulus Gellius, xiii. xvi, 1. "Quodque a Græcis φιλανθρωπέα dicitur, et significat dexteritatem quandam benevolentiamque erga omnes homines promiscuam."

by saying, "Homo sum; humani nihil a me alienum puto;"[13] and Cicero says, "we are framed by nature to love mankind (naturâ propensi sumus ad diligendos homines); this is the foundation of law;" and Lucan predicts a time when all laws shall cease and nations disarm and all men love one another (inque vicem gens omnis amet); and Quintilian teaches that we should "give heed to a stranger in the name of the universal brotherhood which binds together all men under the common father of Nature;" and Seneca says that "we are members of one great body," and "born for the good of the whole;" and Juvenal, that "mutual sympathy is what distinguishes us from brutes."

Shall we think the better or the worse of the Greeks for having no noun substantive just corresponding to our word "philanthropist," whether as a term of praise or reproach? With us, while it should be the noblest of all epithets, it is felt in some quarters to carry with it a certain slight tinge of suspicion, as is alleged of the word "deacon" or "Christian statesman." There is a peril in the habit of doing good; I do not mean merely in case of hypocrisy; but I have noticed that when a man feels that he is serving his fellow-men, he sometimes takes great liberties in the process. It was of this style of philanthropists that old Count Gurowski spoke, when he cautioned a young lady of my acquaintance, above all things, against marrying one of that class. "Marry thief!" he said, "Marry murderer! But marry *philantrope* never-r-r!"

It is a singular fact that while the generous word "philanthropy" was thus widely used in Greek and widely spread in English, there should have been no such widespread word for the answering sin, self-love. The word φιλαντία was known to the Greeks, and a word, "philauty," was made from it, in English; and φιλαντος is used once in the New Testament by Paul;[14] but in neither language did it become classic or familiar. Minsheu has "philautie" in his second edition, and Beaumont, in his poem of "Psyche;" and Holinshed, in his "Chronicle" (1577), speaks of "philautie" or "self-love, which rageth in men so preposterouslie." But the word is omitted from most English dictionaries, and we will hope that the sin rages less "preposterouslie" now. I once heard a mother say that if she could teach her little boy good words one half as easily as he could learn the bad ones for himself, she should be quite satisfied. Here is the human race, on the other hand, seizing eagerly on the good word,

---

[13]Terence, *Heaut.*, i. 1. 25; Cicero, *De Legibus*, i. 15, and *De Repub.*, iii. 7. 7 (fragm.); Lucan, *Pharsalia*, i. 60, 61; Quintilian, *Declamations*, quoted by Denis; Seneca, *Ep.*, 95-Juvenal, *Sat.*, xv. 140–142.

[14]2 Timothy iii. 2.

transplanting it and keeping it alive in the new soil, while the bad word dies out, unregretted. In view of this, we may well claim that our debt to the Greek race is not merely scientific or æsthetic, but, in some degree, moral and spiritual also. However vast may be the spread of human kindliness in Christendom, we should yet give to the Greeks some credit for the spirit of philanthropy, as we are compelled, at any rate, to give them full credit for the word.

3

UNCONSCIOUS SUCCESSES

No better social maxim has been uttered in our times than that laid down fifty years ago by the veteran English reformer, John Jacob Holyoke, in his newspaper, *The Reasoner*, namely this: "The unconscious progress of fifty years is equivalent to a revolution." The older one grows, the more the truth of this doctrine is felt. Another English reformer, on a somewhat higher social plane, the late Honorable Mrs. William Grey—to whom was largely due, with Lady Stanley of Alderley, the establishment of Girton College in England—told me some thirty years ago, that when she looked back on her youth and counted over the reforms for which she and her friends had then labored, and saw how large a part of them had triumphed, it almost seemed as if there were nothing left to be done. It is the same with many Americans who suddenly have the thought come over them anew that, no matter what happens, negro slavery is dead on our soil. In movements that affect whole nations, we hardly appreciate the changes that have come until we look back and wonder what brought them about. When we reflect that Pope Alexander VI once divided the unexplored portions of the globe between the Spaniards and the Portuguese, as the two controlling nations of the earth; that Lord Bacon spoke of the Turks and Spaniards as the only nations of Europe which could claim real military greatness; that the Dutch admiral, Van Tromp, once cruised with a broom at the masthead to show that he had swept the British forever from the seas; it sometimes impresses us as being something almost as remote as the days of the Plesiosaurus or the Mylodon in zoölogy.

Later still, we saw before our eyes, the utter vanishing of the French military prestige. There was a time when merely to be French was to be formidable, even though Napoleon was gone. The tradition lasted really unbroken down to the Crimean war, during which the French still seemed, compared with the English, like trained men beside brave but clumsy schoolboys. In 1859, Matthew Arnold wrote from Strasburg, then still French, "He [Lord Cowley] entirely shared my conviction as to the French always beating any number of Germans who came into the field against them. They will never be beaten by any other nation but the English." When our American Civil War began, every tradition of our army, every text-book, every evolution was French. The technical words were often of that language —*échelon, glacis, barbette.* There sprung up everywhere zouave companies with gaiters. A few years later this whole illusion suddenly broke and subsided almost instantly like a wave on the beach. Since the Civil War our entire system of tactics has been modified and simplified, our young officers are sent to Germany to study the maneuvers, and our militia men are trained by German rules. Then came our easy victory over Spain; in short, there has passed before our eyes a change of position as astonishing as that under which Turkey and Holland had previously become insignificant powers. It is to be further noticed in such cases, that our eyes are kept veiled up to the very moment when the thing occurs. At the outbreak of the Franco-Prussian War, a deluge of war maps suddenly appeared, both in London and in Paris. They were invariably, however, maps of North Germany and the Rhine provinces and were, of course, utterly useless. No one had dreamed for an instant that the war would take place wholly on French soil.

Lord Shelburne, chief of the English ministry, predicted that with the loss of the American colonies "the sun of England would set and her glories be eclipsed forever." Edmund Burke, whom Macaulay declares to have probably ranked above all others in foresight, pronounced France to be in 1790 "not politically existing" and "expunged out of the map of Europe." Mr. Gladstone thought that Jefferson Davis had created not merely an army but a nation. An acute English book, Pearson's "National Life and Character," after mentioning these and other instances of the blindness of statesmen, goes on to add to them two equally striking of the author's own. Writing in 1893, and therefore before the war between China and Japan, he predicts that China is likely to be organized into a great power, her flag floating on every sea, but that she will gradually acquire new dominion, and that we cannot imagine such a thing as a foreign conquest of China. Thus much in respect to the history of nations, but his prediction in regard to science goes even beyond this in its failures. It is his favorite conclusion that human life is destined to grow in the end more comfortable but less enjoyable, since all the fine thoughts will have been thought, and all the really interesting discoveries made:

"Even if the epoch of great discovery is not exhausted, the new results are almost certain to be less simple, less sensational than the first revelations of astronomy and geology have been." Thus wrote Mr. Pearson in 1893, and three years later came the x-rays and wireless telegraphy. The wit of man could not have devised a greater anticlimax, whatever we may think of the deserts and alleged canals of Mars.

When we turn to social progress, we find similar high expectations, not always proved true by direct results, while the aims and ideas represented often reappear in some higher form. Fourier, having announced that he would remain at home every noon to receive offers of a million francs to carry out his vast designs, kept faithfully the tryst for twelve years, without a single visitor. Robert Owen, disappointed at the failure of Parliament to take up his suggestions for prompt action, said sadly, "What! postpone the happiness of the whole human race to the next session?" The late Thomas Hughes admitted that when Maurice and the Christian Socialists first formulated their plans, they all believed that the results would develop very quickly. The American Socialists of the Brook Farm period confidently believed, as one of their leaders assured me, that the national workshops of the French Revolution of 1848 would be a complete success, although Louis Blanc, who had charge of them, told me in later years that he personally had never shared this belief. Brook Farm was in some ideal and social ways so attractive, that I never met any one who did not look back with enjoyment on the life there; and all the faithful believed that such experiments would be multiplied on a larger and larger scale, until they molded society. Every succeeding effort in the same line has broken down with great regularity, after a period of promise; and yet who can deny that the vast development of organization among workingmen, the growth of public ownership and of philosophic thought, has come indirectly as the fulfillment of what Fourier and Owen and Maurice dreamed?

4

LONGFELLOW AS A POET

The great literary lesson of Longfellow's life is to be found, after all, in this, that while he was the first among American poets to create for himself a world-wide fame, he was guided from youth to age by a strong national feeling, or at any rate by the desire to stand for the life and the associations by which he was actually surrounded. Such a tendency has been traced in this volume from his first childish poetry through his chosen theme for a college debate, his commencement oration, his plans formed during a first foreign trip, and the appeal made in his first really original paper in the "North American Review." All these elements of aim and doctrine were directly and explicitly American, and his most conspicuous poems, "Evangeline," "The Courtship of Miles Standish," "Hiawatha," and "The Wayside Inn," were unequivocally American also. In the group of poets to which he belonged, he was the most travelled and the most cultivated, in the ordinary sense, while Whittier was the least so; and yet they are, as we have seen, the two who—in the English-speaking world, at least—hold their own best; the line between them being drawn only where foreign languages are in question, and there Longfellow has of course the advantage. In neither case, it is to be observed, was this Americanism trivial, boastful, or ignoble in its tone. It would be idle to say that this alone constitutes, for an American, the basis of fame; for the high imaginative powers of Poe, with his especial gift of melody, though absolutely without national flavor, have achieved for him European fame, at least in France, this being due, however, mainly to his prose rather than to his poetry, and perhaps also the result, more largely than we recognize, of the assiduous discipleship of a single Frenchman, just as Carlyle's influence in America was due largely to Emerson. Be this as it may, it is certain that the hold of both Longfellow and Whittier is a thing absolutely due, first, to the elevated tone of their works, and secondly, that they have made themselves the poets of the people. No one can attend popular meetings in England without being struck with the readiness with which quotations from these two poets are heard from the lips of speakers, and this, while not affording the highest test of poetic art, still yields the highest secondary test, and one on which both these authors would doubtless have been willing to rest their final appeal for remembrance.

In looking back over Longfellow's whole career, it is certain that the early criticisms upon him, especially those of Margaret Fuller, had an immediate and temporary justification, but found ultimate refutation. The most commonplace man can be better comprehended at the end of his career than he can be analyzed at its beginning; and of men possessed of the poetic temperament, this is eminently true. We now know that at the very time when "Hyperion" and the "Voices of the Night" seemed largely European in their atmosphere, the author himself, in his diaries, was expressing that longing for American subjects which afterwards predominated in his career. Though the citizen among us best known in Europe, most sought after by foreign visitors, he yet gravitated naturally to American themes, American friends, home interests, plans, and improvements. He always voted at elections, and generally with the same party, took an interest in all local affairs and public improvements, headed subscription papers, was known by sight among children, and answered readily to their salutations. The same quality of citizenship was visible in his literary work. Lowell, who was regarded in England as an almost defiant American, yet had a distinct liking, which was not especially shared by Longfellow, for English ways. If people were ever misled on this point, which perhaps was not the case, it grew out of his unvarying hospitality and courtesy, and out of the fact vaguely recognized by all, but best stated by that keen critic, the late Mr. Horace E. Scudder, when he says of Longfellow: "He gave of himself freely to his intimate friends, but he dwelt, nevertheless, in a charmed circle, beyond the lines of which men could not penetrate. . . . It is rare that one in our time has been the centre of so much admiration, and still rarer that one has preserved in the midst of it all that integrity of nature which never abdicates."[1]

It is an obvious truth in regard to the literary works of Longfellow, that while they would have been of value at any time and place, their

---

[1]Scudder's *Men and Letters,* p. 68.

worth to a new and unformed literature was priceless. The first need of such a literature was no doubt a great original thinker, such as was afforded us in Emerson. But for him we should perhaps have been still provincial in thought and imitative in theme and illustration; our poets would have gone on writing about the skylark and the nightingale, which they might never have seen or heard anywhere, rather than about the bobolink and the humble-bee, which they knew. It was Emerson and the so-called Transcendentalists who really set our literature free; yet Longfellow rendered a service only secondary, in enriching and refining it and giving it a cosmopolitan culture, and an unquestioned standing in the literary courts of the civilized world. It was a great advantage, too, that in his more moderate and level standard of execution there was afforded no room for reaction. The same attributes that keep Longfellow from being the greatest of poets will make him also one of the most permanent. There will be no extreme ups and downs in his fame, as in that of those great poets of whom Ruskin writes, "Cast Coleridge at once aside, as sickly and useless; and Shelley as shallow and verbose." The finished excellence of his average execution will sustain it against that of profounder thinkers and more daring sons of song. His range of measures is not great, but his workmanship is perfect; he has always "the inimitable grace of not too much;" he has tested all literatures, all poetic motives, and all the simpler forms of versification, and he can never be taken unprepared. He will never be read for the profoundest stirring, or for the unlocking of the deepest mysteries; he will always be read for invigoration, for comfort, for content.

No man is always consistent, and it is not to be claimed that Longfellow was always ready to reaffirm his early attitude in respect to a national literature. It is not strange that after he had fairly begun to create one, he should sometimes be repelled by the class which has always existed who think that mere nationality should rank first and an artistic standard afterwards. He writes on July 24, 1844, to an unknown correspondent:—

"I dislike as much as any one can the tone of English criticism in reference to our literature. But when you say, 'It is a lamentable fact that as yet our country has taken no decided steps towards establishing a national literature,' it seems to me that you are repeating one of the most fallacious assertions of the English critics. Upon this point I differ entirely from you in opinion. A national literature is the expression of national character and thought; and as our character and modes of thought do not differ essentially from those of England, our literature cannot. Vast forests, lakes, and prairies cannot make great poets. They are but the scenery of the play, and have much less to do with the poetic character than has been imagined. Neither Mexico nor Switzerland has produced any remarkable poet.

"I do not think a 'Poets' Convention' would help the matter. In fact, the matter needs no helping."[2]

In the same way he speaks with regret, three years later, November 5, 1847, of "The prospectus of a new magazine in Philadelphia to build up 'a national literature worthy of the country of Niagara—of the land of forests and eagles.'"

One feels an inexhaustible curiosity as to the precise manner in which each favorite poem by a favorite author comes into existence. In the case of Longfellow we find this illustrated only here and there. We know that "The Arrow and the Song," for instance, came into his mind instantaneously; that "My Lost Youth" occurred to him in the night, after a day of pain, and was written the next morning; that on December 17, 1839, he read of shipwrecks reported in the papers and of bodies washed ashore near Gloucester, one lashed to a piece of the wreck, and that he wrote, "There is a reef called Norman's Woe where many of these took place; among others the schooner Hesperus. Also the Sea-Flower on Black Rock. I must write a ballad upon this; also two others,—'The Skeleton in Armor' and 'Sir Humphrey Gilbert.'" A fortnight later he sat at twelve o'clock by his fire, smoking, when suddenly it came into his mind to write the Ballad of the Schooner Hesperus, which he says, "I accordingly did. Then I went to bed, but could not sleep. New thoughts were running in my mind, and I got up to add them to the ballad. It was three by the clock. I then went to bed and fell asleep. I feel pleased with the ballad. It hardly cost me an effort. It did not come into my mind by lines, but by stanzas." A few weeks before, taking up a volume of Scott's "Border Minstrelsy," he had received in a similar way the suggestion of "The Beleaguered City" and of "The Luck of Edenhall."

We know by Longfellow's own statement to Mr. W. C. Lawton,[3] that it was his rule to do his best in polishing a poem before printing it, but afterwards to leave it untouched, on the principle that "the readers of a poem acquired a right to the poet's work in the form they had learned to love." He thought also that Bryant and Whittier hardly seemed happy in these belated revisions, and mentioned especially Bryant's "Water-Fowl,"

---

[2]*Life,* ii. 19, 20.
[3]*The New England Poets,* p. 141.

"As darkly limned upon the ethereal sky,"

where Longfellow preferred the original reading "painted on." It is, however, rare to find a poet who can carry out this principle of abstinence, at least in his own verse, and we know too surely that Longfellow was no exception; thus we learn that he had made important alterations in the "Golden Legend" within a few weeks of publication. These things show that his remark to Mr. Lawton does not tell quite the whole story. As with most poets, his alterations were not always improvements. Thus, in "The Wreck of the Hesperus," he made the fourth verse much more vigorous to the ear as it was originally written,—

"Then up and spoke an old sailór
Had sailed the Spanish Main,"

than when he made the latter line read

"Sailed to the Spanish Main,"

as in all recent editions. The explanation doubtless was that he at first supposed the "Spanish Main" to mean the Caribbean Sea; whereas it actually referred only to the southern shore of it. Still more curious is the history of a line in one of his favorite poems, "To a Child." Speaking of this, he says in his diary,[4] "Some years ago, writing an 'Ode to a Child,' I spoke of

The buried treasures of the miser, Time.'

What was my astonishment to-day, in reading for the first time in my life Wordsworth's ode 'On the Power of Sound,' to read

'All treasures hoarded by the miser, Time.'"

As a matter of fact, this was not the original form of the Longfellow passage, which was,—

"The buried treasures of dead centuries,"

followed by

---

[4]*Life*, ii. 189.

"The burning tropic skies."

More than this, the very word "miser" was not invariably used in this passage by the poet, as during an intermediate period it had been changed to "pirate," a phrase in some sense more appropriate and better satisfying the ear. The curious analogy to Wordsworth's line did not therefore lie in the original form of his own poem, but was an afterthought. It is fortunate that this curious combination of facts, all utterly unconscious on his part, did not attract the attention of Poe during his vindictive period.

It is to be noticed, however, that Longfellow apparently made all these changes to satisfy his own judgment, and did not make them, as Whittier and even Browning often did, in deference to the judgment of dull or incompetent critics. It is to be remembered that even the academic commentators on Longfellow still leave children to suppose that the Berserk's tale in "The Skeleton in Armor" refers to a supposed story that the Berserk was telling; although the word "tale" is unquestionably used in the sense of "tally" or "reckoning," to indicate how much ale the Norse hero could drink. Readers of Milton often misinterpret his line,

"And every shepherd tells his tale,"

in a similar manner, and the shepherd is supposed by many young readers to be pouring out a story of love or of adventure, whereas he is merely counting up the number of his sheep.

It will always remain uncertain how far Poe influenced the New England poets, whether by example or avoidance. That he sometimes touched Lowell, and not for good, is unquestionable, in respect to rhythm; but it will always remain a question whether his influence did not work in the other direction with Longfellow in making him limit himself more strictly to a narrow range of metrical structure. It was an admirable remark of Tennyson's that "every short poem should have a definite shape like the curve, sometimes a single, sometimes a double one, assumed by a severed tress, or the rind of an apple when flung to the floor."[5] This type of verse was rarely attempted by Longfellow, but he chose it most appropriately for "Seaweed" and in some degree succeeded. Poe himself in his waywardness could not adhere to it when he reached it, and after giving us in the original form of "Lenore," as published in "The Pioneer," perhaps the finest piece of lyric measure in our

[5]Tennyson's *Life*, by his son, i. 507.

literature, made it over into a form of mere jingling and hackneyed rhythm, adding even the final commonplaceness of his tiresome "repetend." Lowell did something of the same in cutting down the original fine strain of the verses beginning "Pine in the distance," but Longfellow showed absolutely no trace of Poe, unless as a warning against multiplying such rhythmic experiments as he once tried successfully in "Seaweed." On the other hand, with all his love for Lowell, his native good taste kept him from the confused metaphors and occasional over-familiarities into which Lowell was sometimes tempted.

Perhaps the most penetrating remark made about Longfellow's art is that of Horace Scudder: "He was first of all a composer, and he saw his subjects in their relations, rather than in their essence." As a translator, he was generally admitted to have no superior in the English tongue, his skill was unvarying and absolutely reliable. Even here it might be doubted whether he ever attained the wonderful success sometimes achieved in single instances, as, for instance, in Mrs. Sarah Austen's "Many a Year is in its Grave," which, under the guise of a perfect translation, yet gives a higher and finer touch than that of the original poem of Rückert. But taking Longfellow's great gift in this direction as it was, we can see that it was somewhat akin to this quality of "composition," rather than of inspiration, which marked his poems.

He could find it delightful

"To lie
And gaze into a summer sky
And watch the trailing clouds go by
Like ships upon the sea."

But it is a vast step from this to Browning's mountain picture

"Toward it tilting cloudlets prest
Like Persian ships to Salamis."

In Browning everything is vigorous and individualized. We see the ships, we know the nationality, we recall the very battle, and over these we see in imagination the very shape and movements of the clouds; but there is no conceivable reason why Longfellow's lines should not have been written by a blind man who knew clouds merely by the descriptions of others. The limitation of Longfellow's poems reveals his temperament. He was in his perceptions essentially of poetic mind, but always in touch with the common mind; as individual lives grow deeper, students are apt to leave Longfellow for Tennyson, just as they forsake Tennyson for Browning. As to action, the tonic of life, so far as he had it, was supplied to him through friends,—Sumner in America; Freiligrath in Europe,— and yet it must be remembered that he would not, but for a corresponding quality in his own nature, have had just such friends as these. He was not led by his own convictions to leave his study like Emerson and take direct part as a contestant in the struggles of the time. It is a curious fact that Lowell should have censured Thoreau for not doing in this respect just the thing which Thoreau ultimately did and Longfellow did not. It was, however, essentially a difference of temperament, and it must be remembered that Longfellow wrote in his diary under date of December 2, 1859, "This will be a great day in our history; the date of a new Revolution,—quite as much needed as the old one. Even now as I write, they are leading old John Brown to execution in Virginia, for attempting to rescue slaves! This is sowing the wind to reap the whirlwind, which will come soon."

His relations with Whittier remained always kindly and unbroken. They dined together at the Atlantic Club and Saturday Club, and Longfellow wrote of him in 1857, "He grows milder and mellower, as does his poetry." He went to Concord sometimes to dine with Emerson, "and meet his philosophers, Alcott, Thoreau, and Channing." Or Emerson came to Cambridge, "to take tea," giving a lecture at the Lyceum, of which Longfellow says, "The lecture good, but not of his richest and rarest. His subject 'Eloquence.' By turns he was grave and jocose, and had some striking views and passages. He lets in a thousand new lights, sidelights, and cross-lights, into every subject." When Emerson's collected poems are sent him, Longfellow has the book read to him all the evening and until late at night, and writes of it in his diary: "Throughout the volume, through the golden mist and sublimation of fancy, gleam bright veins of purest poetry, like rivers running through meadows. Truly, a rare volume; with many exquisite poems in it, among which I should single out 'Monadnoc,' 'Threnody,' 'The Humble-Bee,' as containing much of the quintessence of poetry." Emerson's was one of the five portraits drawn in crayon by Eastman Johnson, and always kept hanging in the library at Craigie House; the others being those of Hawthorne, Sumner, Felton, and Longfellow himself. No one can deny to our poet the merits of absolute freedom from all jealousy and of an invariable readiness to appreciate those classified by many critics as greater than himself. He was one of the first students of Browning in America, when the latter was known chiefly by his "Bells and Pomegranates," and instinctively selected the "Blot in the 'Scutcheon" as "a play of great power and beauty," as the critics would say, and as every one must say who reads it. He is an extraordinary genius, Browning, with dramatic power of the first order. "Paracelsus" he describes, with some justice, as "very lofty, but very diffuse." Of Browning's "Christmas Eve" he later writes, "A wonderful man is Browning, but too obscure," and later makes a similar remark on "The Ring and the Book." Of Tennyson he writes, as to "The Princess," calling it "a gentle satire, in the easiest and most flowing blank verse, with two delicious unrhymed songs, and many exquisite passages. I went to bed after it, with delightful music ringing in my ears; yet half disappointed in the poem, though not knowing why. There is a discordant note somewhere."

One very uncertain test of a man of genius is his "table-talk." Surrounded by a group of men who were such masters of this gift as Lowell, Holmes, and T. G. Appleton, Longfellow might well be excused from developing it to the highest extent, and he also "being rather a silent man," as he says of himself, escaped thereby the tendency to monologue, which was sometimes a subject of complaint in regard to the other three. Longfellow's reticence and self-control saved him from all such perils; but it must be admitted, on the other hand, that when his brother collects a dozen pages of his "table-talk" at the end of his memoirs, or when one reads his own list of them in "Kavanagh," the reader feels a slight inadequacy, as of things good enough to be said, but not quite worth the printing. Yet at their best, they are sometimes pungent and telling, as where he says, "When looking for anything lost, begin by looking where you think it is not;" or, "Silence is a great peace-maker;" or, "In youth all doors open outward; in old age they all open inward," or, more thoughtfully, "Amusements are like specie payments. We do not much care for them, if we know we can have them; but we like to know they may be had," or more profoundly still, "How often it happens that after we know a man personally, we cease to read his writings. Is it that we exhaust him by a look? Is it that his personality gives us all of him we desire?" There are also included among these passages some thoroughly poetic touches, as where he says, "The spring came suddenly, bursting upon the world as a child bursts into a room, with a laugh and a shout, and hands full of flowers." Or this, "How sudden and sweet are the visitations of our happiest thoughts; what delightful surprises! In the midst of life's most trivial occupations,—as when we are reading a newspaper, or lighting a bed-candle, or waiting for our horses to drive round,—the lovely face appears, and thoughts more precious than gold are whispered in our ear."

The test of popularity in a poet is nowhere more visible than in the demand for autographs. Longfellow writes in his own diary that on November 25, 1856, he has more than sixty such requests lying on his table; and again on January 9, "Yesterday I wrote, sealed, and directed seventy autographs. To-day I added five or six more and mailed them." It does not appear whether the later seventy applications included the earlier sixty, but it is, in view of the weakness of human nature, very probable. This number must have gone on increasing. I remember that in 1875 I saw in his study a pile which must have numbered more than seventy, and which had come in a single day from a single high school in a Western city, to congratulate him on his birthday, and each hinting at an autograph, which I think he was about to supply.

At the time of his seventy-fourth birthday, 1881, a lady in Ohio sent him a hundred blank cards, with the request that he would write his name on each, that she might distribute them among her guests at a party she was to give on that day. The same day was celebrated by some forty different schools in the Western States, all writing him letters and requesting answers. He sent to each school, his brother tells us, some stanza with signature and good wishes. He was patient even with the gentleman who wrote to him to request that he would send his autograph in his "own handwriting." As a matter of fact, he had to leave many letters unanswered, even by a secretary, in his latest years.

It is a most tantalizing thing to know, through the revelations of Mr. William Winter, that Longfellow left certain poems unpublished. Mr. Winter says: "He said also that he sometimes wrote poems that were for himself alone, that he should not care ever to publish, because they were too delicate for publication."[6] Quite akin to this was another remark made by him to the same friend, that "the desire of the young poet is not for applause, but for recognition." The two remarks limit one another; the desire for recognition only begins when the longing for mere expression is satisfied. Thoroughly practical and methodical and industrious, Longfellow yet needed some self-expression first of all. It is impossible to imagine him as writing puffs of himself, like Poe, or volunteering reports of receptions given to him, like Whitman. He said to Mr. Winter, again and again, "What you desire will come, if you will but wait for it." The question is not whether this is the only form of the poetic temperament, but it was clearly his form of it. Thoreau well says that there is no definition of poetry which the poet will not instantly set aside by defying all its limitations, and it is the same with the poetic temperament itself.

---

[6]*Life*, iii. 356.

5

A LETTER TO A YOUNG
CONTRIBUTOR

My dear young gentleman or young lady,—for many are the Cecil Dreemes of literature who superscribe their offered manuscripts with very masculine names in very feminine handwriting,—it seems wrong not to meet your accumulated and urgent epistles with one comprehensive reply, thus condensing many private letters into a printed one. And so many of those who read the "Atlantic Monthly" have at times the impulse to write for it also, that this epistle will be sure of perusal, though Mrs. Stowe remain uncut and the Autocrat go for an hour without readers.

Far from me be the wild expectation that every author will not habitually measure the merits of a periodical by its appreciation of his or her last manuscript. I should as soon ask a young lady not to estimate the management of a ball by her own private luck in respect to partners. But it is worth while at least to point out that in the treatment of every contribution the real interests of editor and writer are absolutely the same, and any antagonism is merely traditional, like the supposed hostility between France and England, or between England and Slavery. No editor can ever afford the rejection of a good thing, and no author the publication of a bad one. The only difficulty lies in drawing the line. Were all offered manuscripts unequivocally good or bad, there would be no great trouble; it is the vast range of mediocrity which perplexes: the majority are too bad for blessing and too good for banning; so that no conceivable reason can be given for either fate, save that upon the destiny of any single one may hang that of a hundred others just like it. But whatever be the standard fixed, it is equally for the interest of all concerned that it be enforced without flinching.

Nor is there the slightest foundation for the supposed editorial prejudice against new or obscure contributors. On the contrary, every editor is always hungering and thirsting after novelties. To take the lead in bringing forward a new genius is as fascinating a privilege as that of the physician who boasted to Sir Henry Halford of having been the first man to discover the Asiatic cholera and to communicate it to the public. It is only stern necessity which compels the magazine to fall back so constantly on the regular old staff of contributors, whose average product has been gauged already; just as every country lyceum attempts annually to arrange an entirely new list of lecturers, and ends with no bolder experiment than to substitute Gough and Beecher in place of last year's Beecher and Gough.

Of course no editor is infallible, and the best magazine contains an occasional poor article. Do not blame the unfortunate conductor. He knows it as well as you do,—after the deed is done. The newspapers kindly pass it over, still preparing their accustomed opiate of sweet praises, so much for each contributor, so much for the magazine collectively,—like a hostess with her tea-making, a spoonful for each person and one for the pot. But I can tell you that there is an official person who meditates and groans, meanwhile, in the night-watches, to think that in some atrocious moment of good-nature or sleepiness he left the door open and let that ungainly intruder in. Do you expect him to acknowledge the blunder, when you tax him with it? Never,—he feels it too keenly. He will rather stand up stoutly for the surpassing merits of the misshapen thing, as a mother for her deformed child; and as the mother is nevertheless inwardly imploring that there may never be such another born to her, so be sure that it is not by reminding the editor of this calamity that you can allure him into risking a repetition.

An editor thus shows himself to be but human; and it is well enough to remember this fact, when you approach him. He is not a gloomy despot, no Nemesis or Rhadamanthus, but a bland and virtuous man, exceedingly anxious to secure plenty of good subscribers and contributors, and very ready to perform any acts of kindness not inconsistent with this grand design. Draw near him, therefore, with soft approaches and mild persuasions. Do not treat him like an enemy, and insist on reading your whole manuscript aloud to him, with appropriate gestures. His time has some value, if yours has not; and he has therefore educated his eye till it has become microscopic, like a naturalist's, and can classify nine out of ten specimens by one glance at a scale or a feather. Fancy an ambitious echinoderm claiming a private interview with Agassiz, to demonstrate by verbal arguments that he is a mollusk! Besides, do you expect to administer the thing orally to each of the two hundred thousand, more or less, who turn the leaves of the magazine? You are writing for the average eye, and must submit to its verdict. "Do not trouble yourself about the light on your statue; it is the light of the public square which must test its value."

Therefore do not despise any honest propitiation, however small, in dealing with your editor. Look to the physical aspect of your manuscript, and prepare your page so neatly that it shall allure instead of repelling. Use good pens, black ink, nice white paper and plenty of it. Do not emulate "paper-sparing Pope," whose chaotic manuscript of the "Iliad," written chiefly on the backs of old letters, still remains in the British Museum. If your document be slovenly, the presumption is that its literary execution is the same, Pope to the contrary not withstanding. An editor's eye becomes carnal, and is easily attracted by a comely outside. If you really wish to obtain his good-will for your production, do not first tax his time for deciphering it, any more than in visiting a millionaire to solicit a loan you would begin by asking him to pay for the hire of the carriage which takes you to his door.

On the same principle, send your composition in such a shape that it shall not need the slightest literary revision before printing. Many a bright production dies discarded which might have been made thoroughly presentable by a single day's labor of a competent scholar, in shaping, smoothing, dovetailing, and retrenching. The revision seems so slight an affair that the aspirant cannot conceive why there should be so much fuss about it.

> "The piece, you think, is incorrect; why, take it;
> I'm all submission; what you'd have it, make it."

But to discharge that friendly office no universal genius is salaried; and for intellect in the rough there is no market.

Rules for style, as for manners, must be chiefly negative: a positively good style indicates certain natural powers in the individual, but a merely unexceptionable style is only a matter of culture and good models. Dr. Channing established in New England a standard of style which really attained almost the perfection of the pure and the colorless, and the disciplinary value of such a literary influence, in a raw and crude nation, has been very great; but the defect of this standard is that it ends in utterly renouncing all the great traditions of literature, and ignoring the magnificent mystery of words. Human language may be polite and prosaic in itself, uplifted with difficulty into expression by the high thoughts it utters, or it may in itself become so saturated with warm life and delicious association that every sentence shall palpitate and thrill with the mere fascination of the syllables. The statue is not more surely included in the block of marble than is all conceivable splendor of utterance in "Worcester's Unabridged." And as Ruskin says of painting that it is in the perfection and precision of the instantaneous line that the claim to immortality is made, so it is easy to see that a phrase may outweigh a library. Keats heads the catalogue of things real with "sun, moon, and passages of Shakespeare"; and Keats himself has left behind him winged wonders of expression that were not surpassed by Shakespeare, nor by any one else who ever dared touch the English tongue. There may be phrases which shall be palaces to dwell in, treasure-houses to explore; a single word may be a window from which one may perceive all the kingdoms of the earth and the glory of them. Oftentimes a word shall speak what accumulated volumes have labored in vain to utter: there may be years of crowded passion in a word, and half a life in a sentence.

Such being the majesty of the art you seek to practise, you can at least take time and deliberation before dishonoring it. Disabuse yourself especially of the belief that any grace or flow of style can come from writing rapidly. Haste can make you slipshod, but it can never make you graceful. With what dismay one reads of the wonderful fellows in fashionable novels, who can easily dash off a brilliant essay in a single night! When I think how slowly my poor thoughts come in, how tardily they connect themselves, what a delicious prolonged perplexity it is to cut and contrive a decent clothing of words for them, as a little girl does for her doll,—nay, how many new outfits a single sentence sometimes costs before it is presentable, till it seems at last, like our army on the Potomac, as if it never could be thoroughly clothed,—I certainly should never dare to venture into print, but for the confirmed suspicion that the greatest writers have done even thus. Do you know, my dear neophyte, how Balzac used to compose? As a specimen of the labor that sometimes goes to make an effective style, the process is worth recording. When Balzac had a new work in view, he first spent weeks in studying from real life for it, haunting the streets of Paris by day and night, note-book in hand. His materials gained, he shut himself up till the book was written, perhaps two months, absolutely excluding everybody but his publisher. He emerged pale and thin, with the complete manuscript in his hand,— not only written, but almost rewritten, so thoroughly was the original copy altered, interlined, and rearranged. This strange production, almost illegible, was sent to the unfortunate printers; with infinite difficulty a proof-sheet was obtained, which, being sent to the author, was presently returned in a condition almost as hopeless as that of the manuscript. Whole sentences were erased, others transposed, everything modified. A second and a third proof followed, alike torn to pieces by the ravenous pen of Balzac. The despairing printers labored by turns, only the picked men of the office being equal to the task, and they relieving each other at hourly intervals, as beyond that time no one could endure the fatigue. At last, by the fourth proof-sheet, the author too was wearied out, though not contented. "I work ten hours out of the twenty-four," said he, "over the elaboration of my unhappy style, and I am never satisfied, myself, when all is done."

Do not complain that this scrupulousness is probably wasted, after all, and that nobody knows. The public knows. People criticise far beyond what they can attain. When the Athenian audience hissed a public speaker for a mispronunciation, it did not follow that any one of the malcontents could pronounce as well as the orator. In our own lyceum-audiences there may not be a man who does not yield to his own private eccentricities of dialect, but see if they do not appreciate good English from Sumner or Phillips! Men talk of writing down to the public taste who have never yet written up to that standard. "There never yet was a good tongue," said old Fuller, "that wanted ears to hear it." If one were expecting to be judged by a few scholars only, one might hope somehow to cajole them; but it is this vast, unimpassioned, unconscious tribunal, this average judgment of intelligent minds, which is truly formidable. It is something more undying than senates and more omnipotent than courts, something which rapidly cancels all transitory reputations, and at last becomes the organ of eternal justice and awards posthumous fame.

The first demand made by the public upon every composition is, of course, that it should be attractive. In addressing a miscellaneous audience, whether through eye or ear, it is certain that no man living has a right to be tedious. Every editor is therefore compelled to insist that his contributors should make themselves agreeable, whatever else they may do. To be agreeable, it is not necessary to be amusing; an essay may be thoroughly delightful without a single witticism, while a monotone of jokes soon grows tedious. Charge your style with life; and the public will not ask for conundrums. But the profounder your discourse, the greater must necessarily be the effort to refresh and diversify. I have observed, in addressing audiences of children in schools and elsewhere, that there is no fact so grave, no thought so abstract, but you can make it very interesting to the small people, if you will only put in plenty of detail and illustration; and I have not observed that in this respect grown men are so very different. If, therefore, in writing, you find it your mission to be abstruse, fight to render your statement clear and attractive, as if your life depended on it: your literary life does depend on it, and, if you fail, relapses into a dead language, and becomes, like that of Coleridge, only a *Biographia Literaria*. Labor, therefore, not in thought alone, but in utterance; clothe and reclothe your grand conception twenty times, if need be, until you find some phrase that with its grandeur shall be lucid also. It is this unwearied literary patience that has enabled Emerson not merely to introduce, but even to popularize, thoughts of such a quality as never reached the popular mind before. And when a writer, thus laborious to do his utmost for his disciples, becomes after all incomprehensible, we can try to believe that it is only that inevitable obscurity of depth which Coleridge calls a compliment to the reader.

In learning to write availably, a newspaper-office is a capital preparatory school. Nothing is so good to teach the use of materials, and to compel to pungency of style. Being always at close quarters with his readers, a journalist must shorten and sharpen his sentences, or he is doomed. Yet this mental alertness is bought at a severe price; such living from hand to mouth cheapens the whole mode of intellectual existence, and it would seem that no successful journalist could ever get the newspaper out of his blood, or achieve any high literary success.

For purposes of illustration and elucidation, and even for amplitude of vocabulary, wealth of accumulated materials is essential; and whether this wealth be won by reading or by experience makes no great difference. Coleridge attended Davy's chemical lectures to acquire new metaphors, and it is of no consequence whether one comes to literature from a library, a machine-shop, or a forecastle, provided he has learned to work with thoroughness the soil he knows. Remember, however, that copious preparation has its perils also, in the crude display to which it tempts. The object of high culture is not to exhibit culture, but its results. You do not put guano on your garden that your garden may blossom guano. Indeed, even for the proper subordination of one's own thoughts the same self-control is needed; and there is no severer test of literary training than in the power to prune out your most cherished sentence, when you find that the sacrifice will help the symmetry or vigor of the whole.

Be noble both in the affluence and the economy of your diction; spare no wealth that you can put in, and tolerate no superfluity that can be struck out. Remember the Lacedemonian who was fined for saying that in three words which might as well have been expressed in two. Do not throw a dozen vague epithets at a thing, in the hope that some one of them will fit; but study each phrase so carefully that the most ingenious critic cannot alter it without spoiling the whole passage for everybody but himself. For the same reason do not take refuge, as was the practice a few years since, in German combinations, heart-utterances, soul-sentiments, and hyphenized phrases generally; but roll your thought into one good English word. There is no fault which seems so hopeless as commonplaceness, but it is really easier to elevate the commonplace than to reduce the turgid. How few men in all the pride of culture can emulate the easy grace of a bright woman's letter!

Have faith enough in your own individuality to keep it resolutely down for a year or two. A man has not much intellectual capital who cannot allow himself a brief interval of modesty. Premature individualism commonly ends either in a reaction against the original whims, or in a mannerism which perpetuates them. For mannerism no one is great enough, because, though in the hands of a strong man it imprisons us in novel fascination, yet we soon grow weary, and then hate our prison forever. How sparkling was Reade's crisp brilliancy in "Peg Woffington!"— but into what disagreeable affectations it has since degenerated! Carlyle was a boon to the human race, amid the tameness into which English style was declining; but who is not tired of him and his catchwords now? Now the age has outgrown him, and is approaching a mode of writing which unites the smoothness of the eighteenth century with the vital vigor of the seventeenth, so that Sir Thomas Browne and Andrew Marvell seem quite as near to us as Pope or Addison,—a style penetrated with the best spirit of Carlyle, without a trace of Carlylism.

Be neither too lax nor too precise in your use of language: the one fault ends in stiffness, the other in slang. Some one told the Emperor Tiberius that he might give citizenship to men, but not to words. To be sure, Louis XIV in childhood, wishing for a carriage, called for *mon carrosse,* and made the former feminine a masculine to all future Frenchmen. But do not undertake to exercise these prerogatives of royalty until you are quite sure of being crowned. The only thing I remember in our college text-book of Rhetoric is one admirable verse of caution which it quoted:—

"In words, as fashions, the same rule will hold,
Alike fantastic, if too new or old;
Be not the first by whom the new are tried,
Nor yet the last to lay the old aside."

Especially do not indulge any fantastic preference for either Latin or Anglo-Saxon, the two great wings on which our magnificent English soars and sings; we can spare neither. The combination gives us an affluence of synonymes and a delicacy of discrimination such as no unmixed idiom can show.

While you utterly shun slang, whether native or foreign born,—at present, by the way, our popular writers use far less slang than the English,—yet do not shrink from Americanisms, so they be good ones. American literature is now thoroughly out of leading-strings; and the nation which supplied the first appreciative audience for Carlyle, Tennyson, and the Brownings, can certainly trust its own literary instincts to create the new words it needs. To be sure, the inelegancies with which we are chiefly reproached are not distinctively American: Burke uses "pretty considerable"; Miss Burney says, "I trembled a few"; the English Bible says "reckon," Locke has "guess," and Southey "realize," in the exact sense in which one sometimes hears them used colloquially here. Nevertheless, such improprieties are of course to be avoided; but whatever good Americanisms exist, let us hold to them by all means. The diction of Emerson alone is a sufficient proof, by its unequalled range and precision, that no people in the world ever had access to a vocabulary so rich and copious as we are acquiring. To the previous traditions and associations of the English tongue we add resources of contemporary life such as England cannot rival. Political freedom makes every man an individual; a vast industrial activity makes every man an inventor, not merely of labor-saving machines, but of labor-saving words; universal schooling popularizes all thought and sharpens the edge of all language. We unconsciously demand of our writers the same dash and the same accuracy that we demand in railroading or dry-goods jobbing. The mixture of nationalities is constantly coining and exchanging new felicities of dialect: Ireland, Scotland, Germany, Africa, are present everywhere with their various contributions of wit and shrewdness, thought and geniality; in New York and elsewhere one finds whole thoroughfares of France, Italy, Spain, Portugal; on our Western railways there are placards printed in Swedish; even China is creeping in. The colonies of England are too far and too provincial to have had much reflex influence on her literature, but how our phraseology is already amplified by our relations with Spanish America! The life-blood of Mexico flowed into our newspapers while the Mexican war was in progress; and the gold of California glitters in our primers. Many foreign cities may show a greater variety of more national costumes, but the representative value of our immigrant tribes is far greater from the very fact that they merge their mental costume in ours. Thus the American writer finds himself among his phrases like an American sea-captain amid his crew: a medley of all nations, waiting for some organizing mind to mould them into a unit of force.

There are certain minor matters, subsidiary to elegance, if not elegancies, and therefore worth attention. Do not habitually prop your sentences on crutches, such as Italics and exclamation-points, but make them stand without aid; if they cannot emphasize themselves, these devices are commonly but a confession of helplessness. Do not leave loose ends as you go on, straggling things, to be caught up and dragged along uneasily in foot-notes, but work them all in neatly, as Biddy at her bread-pan gradually kneads in all the outlying bits of dough, till she has one round and comely mass. Reduce yourself to short allowance of parentheses and dashes; if you employ them merely from clumsiness, they will lose all their proper power in your hands. Economize quotation-marks also, clear that dust from your pages, assume your readers to be acquainted with the current jokes and the stock epithets: all persons like the compliment of having it presumed that they know something, and prefer to discover the wit or beauty of your allusion without a guide-board.

The same principle applies to learned citations and the results of study. Knead these thoroughly in, supplying the maximum of desired information with a minimum of visible schoolmaster. It requires no pedantic mention of Euclid to indicate a mathematical mind, but only the habitual use of clear terms and close connections. To employ in argument the forms of Whately's Logic would render it probable that you are juvenile and certain that you are tedious; wreathe the chain with roses. The more you have studied foreign languages, the more you will be disposed to keep Ollendorff in the background: the proper result of such acquirements is visible in a finer ear for words; so that Goethe said, the man who had studied but one language could not know that one. But spare the raw material; deal as cautiously in Latin as did General Jackson when Jack Downing was out of the way; and avoid French as some fashionable novelists avoid English.

Thus far, these are elementary and rather technical suggestions, fitted for the very opening of your literary career. Supposing you fairly in print, there are needed some further counsels.

Do not waste a minute, not a second, in trying to demonstrate to others the merit of your own performance. If your work does not vindicate itself, you cannot vindicate it, but you can labor steadily on to something which needs no advocate but itself. It was said of Haydon, the English artist, that, if he had taken half the pains to paint great pictures that he took to persuade the public he had painted them, his fame would have been secure. Like his was the career of poor Horne, who wrote the far-thing epic of "Orion" with one grand line in it, and a prose work (without any), on "The False Medium excluding Men of Genius from the Public." He spent years in ineffectually trying to repeal the exclusion in his own case, and has since manfully gone to the grazing regions in Australia, hoping there at least to find the sheep and the goats better discriminated. Do not emulate these tragedies. Remember how many great writers have created the taste by which they were enjoyed, and do not be in a hurry. Toughen yourself a little, and accomplish something better. Inscribe above your desk the words of Rivarol, "Genius is only great patience." It takes less time to build an avenue of shingle palaces than to hide away unseen, block by block, the vast foundation-stones of an observatory. Most bygone literary fames have been very short-lived in America, because they have lasted no longer than they deserved. Happening the other day to recur to a list of Cambridge lyceum-lecturers in my boyish days, I find with dismay that the only name now popularly remembered is that of Emerson; death, oblivion, or a professorship has closed over each of the others, while the whole standard of American literature has been vastly raised meanwhile, and no doubt partly through their labors. To this day, some of our most gifted writers are being dwarfed by the unkind friendliness of too early praise. It was Keats, the most precocious of all great poets, who declared that "nothing is finer for purposes of production than a very gradual ripening of the intellectual powers."

Yet do not be made conceited by obscurity, any more than by notoriety. Many fine geniuses have been long neglected; but what would become of us, if all the neglected were to turn out geniuses? It is unsafe reasoning from either extreme. You are not necessarily writing like Holmes because your reputation for talent began in college, nor like Hawthorne because you have been before the public ten years without an admirer. Above all, do not seek to encourage yourself by dwelling on the defects of your rivals: strength comes only from what is above you. Northcote, the painter, said, that, in observing an inferior picture, he always felt his spirits droop, with the suspicion that perhaps he deceived himself and his own paintings might be no better than that; but the works of the mighty masters always gave him renewed strength, in the hope that perhaps his own had in their smaller way something of the same divine quality.

Do not complacently imagine, because your first literary attempt proved good and successful, that your second will doubtless improve upon it. The very contrary sometimes happens. A man dreams for years over one projected composition, all his reading converges to it, all his experience stands related to it, it is the net result of his existence up to a certain time, it is the cistern into which he pours his accumulated life. Emboldened by success, he mistakes the cistern for a fountain, and instantly taps his brain again. The second production, as compared with the first, costs but half the pains and attains but a quarter part of the merit; a little more of fluency and facility perhaps,—but the vigor, the wealth, the originality, the head of water, in short, are wanting. One would think that almost any intelligent man might write one good thing in a lifetime, by reserving himself long enough: it is the effort after quantity which proves destructive. The greatest man has passed his zenith, when he once begins to cheapen his style of work and sink into a bookmaker: after that, though the newspapers may never hint at it, nor his admirers own it, the decline of his career has begun.

Yet the author is not alone to blame for this, but also the world which first tempts and then reproves him. Goethe says, that, if a person once does a good thing, society forms a league to prevent his doing another. His seclusion is gone, and therefore his unconsciousness and his leisure; luxuries tempt him from his frugality, and soon he must toil for luxuries; then, because he has done one thing well, he is urged to squander himself and do a thousand things badly. In this country especially, if one can learn languages, he must go to Congress; if he can argue a law-case, he must become agent of a factory: out of this comes a variety of training which is very valuable, but a wise man must have strength to call in his resources before middle life, prune off divergent activities, and concentrate himself on the main work, be it what it may. It is shameful to see the indeterminate lives of many of our gifted men, unable to resist the temptations of a busy land, and so losing themselves in an aimless and miscellaneous career.

Yet it is unjust and unworthy in Marsh to disfigure his fine work on the English language by traducing all who now write that tongue. "None seek the audience, fit, though few, which contented the ambition of Milton, and all writers for the press now measure their glory by their gains," and so indefinitely onward,—which is simply cant. Does a man who honestly earns his annual ten thousand dollars by writing "dime novels," take rank as head of American literature by virtue of his salary? Because the profits of true literature are rising,—trivial as they still are beside those of commerce or the professions,—its merits do not necessarily decrease, but the contrary is more likely to happen; for in this pursuit, as in all others, cheap work is usually poor work. None but gentlemen of fortune can enjoy the bliss of writing for nothing and paying their own printer. Nor does the practice of compensation by the page work the injury that has often been ignorantly predicted. No contributor need hope to cover two pages of a magazine with what might be adequately said in one, unless he assumes his editor to be as foolish as himself. The Spartans exiled Ctesiphon for bragging that he could speak the whole day on any subject selected; and a modern periodical is of little value, unless it has a Spartan at its head.

Strive always to remember—though it does not seem the plan of the universe that we should quite bring it home to ourselves—that "To-Day is a king in disguise," and that this American literature of ours will be just as classic a thing, if we do our part, as any which the past has treasured. There is a mirage over all literary associations. Keats and Lamb seem to our young people to be existences as remote and legendary as Homer, yet it is not an old man's life since Keats was an awkward boy at the door of Hazlitt's lecture-room, and Lamb was introducing Talfourd to Wordsworth as his own only admirer. In reading Spence's "Anecdotes," Pope and Addison appear no further off; and wherever I open Bacon's "Essays," I am sure to end at last with that one magical sentence, annihilating centuries, "When I was a child, and Queen Elizabeth was in the flower of her years."

And this imperceptible transformation of the commonplace present into the storied past applies equally to the pursuits of war and to the serenest works of peace. Be not misled by the excitements of the moment[1] into overrating the charms of military life. In this chaos of uniforms, we seem to be approaching times such as existed in England after Waterloo, when the splenetic Byron declared that the only distinction was to be a little undistinguished. No doubt, war brings out grand and unexpected qualities, and there is a perennial fascination in the Elizabethan Raleighs and Sidneys, heroes of pen and sword. But the fact is patent, that there is scarcely any art whose rudiments are so easy to acquire as the military; the manuals of tactics have no difficulties comparable to those of the ordinary professional text-books; and any one who can drill a boat's crew or a ball club can learn in a very few weeks to drill a company or even a regiment. Given in addition the power to command, to organize, and to execute,—high qualities, though not rare in this community,—and you have a man needing but time and experience to make a general. More than this can be acquired only by an exclusive absorption in this one art; as Napoleon said, that, to have good soldiers, a nation must be always at war.

---

[1]Written early in 1862.

If, therefore, duty and opportunity call, count it a privilege to obtain your share in the new career; throw yourself into it as resolutely and joyously as if it were a summer campaign in the Adirondack, but never fancy for a moment that you have discovered any grander or manlier life than you should have been leading every day at home. It is not needful here to decide which is intrinsically the better thing, a column of a newspaper or a column of attack, Wordsworth's "Lines on Immortality" or Wellington's Lines of Torres Vedras; each is noble, if nobly done, though posterity seems to remember literature the longest. The writer is not celebrated for having been the favorite of the conqueror, but sometimes the conqueror only for having favored or even for having spurned the writer. "When the great Sultan died, his power and glory departed from him, and nothing remained but this one fact, that he knew not the worth of Ferdousi." There is a slight delusion in this dazzling glory. What a fantastic whim the young lieutenants thought it, when General Wolfe, on the eve of battle, said of Gray's "Elegy," "Gentlemen, I would rather have written that poem than have taken Quebec." Yet, no doubt, it is by the memory of that remark that Wolfe will live the longest,—aided by the stray line of another poet, still reminding us, not needlessly, that "Wolfe's great name's cotemporal with our own."

Once the poets and the sages were held to be pleasing triflers, fit for hours of relaxation in the lulls of war. Now the pursuits of peace are recognized as the real, and war as the accidental. It interrupts all higher avocations, as does the cry of fire: when the fire is extinguished, the important affairs of life are resumed. A few years ago the London "Times" was bewailing that all thought and culture in England were suspended by the Crimean War. "We want no more books. Give us good recruits, at least five feet seven, a good model for a floating-battery, and a gun to take effect at five thousand yards,—and Whigs and Tories, High and Low Church, the poets, astronomers, and critics, may settle it among themselves." How remote seems that epoch now! and how remote will the present erelong appear! while art and science will resume their sway serene, beneath skies eternal. Yesterday I turned from treatises on gunnery and fortification to open Milton's Latin Poems, which I had never read, and there, in the "Sylvarum Liber," I came upon a passage as grand as anything in "Paradise Lost,"—his description of Plato's archetypal man, the vast ideal of the human race, eternal, incorrupt, coeval with the stars, dwelling either in the sidereal spaces, or among the Lethean mansions of souls unborn, or pacing the unexplored confines of the habitable globe. There stood the majestic image, veiled in a dead language, yet still visible; and it was as if one of the poet's own sylvan groves had been suddenly cut down, and opened a view of Olympus. Then all these present fascinating trivialities of war and diplomacy ebbed away, like Greece and Rome before them, and there seemed nothing real in the universe but Plato's archetypal man.

Indeed, it is the same with all contemporary notorieties. In all free governments, especially, it is the habit to over-rate the *dramatis personœ* of the hour. How empty to us are now the names of the great American politicians of the last generation, as Crawford and Lowndes!—yet it is but a few years since these men filled in the public ear as large a space as Clay or Calhoun afterwards, and when they died, the race of the giants seemed ended. The path to oblivion of these later idols is just as sure; even Webster will be to the next age but a mighty tradition, and all that he has left will appear no more commensurate with his fame than is his statue by Powers. If anything is to give longer life to the statesmen of today, it is only because we are engaged in a contest of more vital principles, which may better embalm the men. Of all gifts, eloquence is the most short-lived. The most accomplished orator fades forgotten, and his laurels pass to some hoarse, inaudible Burke, accounted rather a bore during his lifetime, and possessed of a faculty of scattering, not convincing, the members of the House. "After all," said the brilliant Choate, with melancholy foreboding, "a book is the only immortality."

So few men in any age are born with a marked gift for literary expression, so few of this number have access to high culture, so few even of these have the personal nobleness to use their powers well, and this small band is finally so decimated by disease and manifold disaster, that it makes one shudder to observe how little of the embodied intellect of any age is left behind. Literature is attar of roses, one distilled drop from a million blossoms. Think how Spain and Portugal once divided the globe between them in a treaty, when England was a petty kingdom of illiterate tribes!—and now all Spain is condensed for us into Cervantes, and all Portugal into the fading fame of the unread Camoens. The long magnificence of Italian culture has left us only *I Quattro Poeti*, the Four Poets. The difference between Shakespeare and his contemporaries is not that he is read twice, ten times, a hundred times as much as they: it is an absolute difference; he is read, and they are only printed.

Yet, if our life be immortal, this temporary distinction is of little moment, and we may learn humility, without learning despair, from earth's evanescent glories. Who cannot bear a few disappointments, if the vista be so wide that the mute inglorious Miltons of this sphere may in some other sing their Paradise as Found? War or peace, fame or forgetfulness, can bring no real injury to one who has formed the fixed purpose to live nobly day by day. I fancy that in some other realm of existence we may look back with a kindly interest on this scene of our earlier life, and say to one another, "Do you remember yonder planet, where once we went to school"? And whether our elective study here lay chiefly in the fields of action or of thought will matter little to us then, when other schools shall have led us through other disciplines.

6

EMILY DICKINSON

F ew events in American literary history have been more curious than the sudden rise of Emily Dickinson many years since into a posthumous fame only more accentuated by the utterly recluse character of her life. The lines which formed a prelude to the first volume of her poems are the only ones that have yet come to light which indicate even a temporary desire to come in contact with the great world of readers; for she seems to have had no reference, in all the rest, to anything but her own thought and a few friends. But for her only sister, it is very doubtful if her poems would ever have been printed at all; and when published, they were launched quietly and without any expectation of a wide audience. Yet the outcome of it was that six editions of the volume were sold within six months, a suddenness of success almost without a parallel in American literature.

On April 16, 1862, I took from the post-office the following letter:—

MR. HIGGINSON,

—Are you too deeply occupied to say if my verse is alive?

The mind is so near itself it cannot see distinctly, and I have none to ask.

Should you think it breathed, and had you the leisure to tell me, I should feel quick gratitude.

If I make the mistake, that you dared to tell me would give me sincerer honor toward you.

I inclose my name, asking you, if you please, sir, to tell me what is true?

That you will not betray me it is needless to ask, since honor is its own pawn.

The letter was postmarked "Amherst," and it was in a handwriting so peculiar that it seemed as if the writer might have taken her first lessons by studying the famous fossil bird-tracks in the museum of that college town. Yet it was not in the slightest degree illiterate, but cultivated, quaint, and wholly unique. Of punctuation there was little; she used chiefly dashes, and it has been thought better, in printing these letters, as with her poems, to give them the benefit in this respect of the ordinary usages; and so with her habit as to capitalization, as the printers call it, in which she followed the Old English and present German method of thus distinguishing every noun substantive. But the most curious thing about the letter was the total absence of a signature. It proved, however, that she had written her name on a card, and put it under the shelter of a smaller envelope inclosed in the larger; and even this name was written—as if the shy writer wished to recede as far as possible from view—in pencil, not in ink. The name was Emily Dickinson. Inclosed with the letter were four poems, two of which have since been separately printed,—"Safe in their alabaster chambers" and "I'll tell you how the sun rose," besides the two that here follow. The first comprises in its eight lines a truth so searching that it seems a condensed summary of the whole experience of a long life:—

> "We play at paste
> Till qualified for pearl;
> Then drop the paste
> And deem ourself a fool.
>
> "The shapes, though, were similar
> And our new hands
> Learned gem-tactics,
> Practicing sands."

Then came one which I have always classed among the most exquisite of her productions, with a singular felicity of phrase and an aerial lift that bears the ear upward with the bee it traces:—

> "The nearest dream recedes unrealized.
> The heaven we chase,
> Like the June bee
> Before the schoolboy,
> Invites the race,
> Stoops to an easy clover,

Dips—evades—teases—deploys—
Then to the royal clouds
Lifts his light pinnace,
Heedless of the boy
Staring, bewildered, at the mocking sky.

"Homesick for steadfast honey,—
Ah! the bee flies not
Which brews that rare variety."

The impression of a wholly new and original poetic genius was as distinct on my mind at the first reading of these four poems as it is now,
after half a century of further knowledge; and with it came the problem
never yet solved, what place ought to be assigned in literature to what is
so remarkable, yet so elusive of criticism. The bee himself did not evade
the schoolboy more than she evaded me; and even at this day I still stand
somewhat bewildered, like the boy.

Circumstances, however, soon brought me in contact with an uncle
of Emily Dickinson, a gentleman not now living: a prominent citizen
of Worcester, Massachusetts, a man of integrity and character, who
shared her abruptness and impulsiveness, but certainly not her poetic
temperament, from which he was indeed singularly remote. He could
tell but little of her, she being evidently an enigma to him, as to me. It
is hard to say what answer was made by me, under these circumstances, to this letter. It is probable that the adviser sought to gain time
a little and find out with what strange creature he was dealing. I remember to have ventured on some criticism which she afterwards
called "surgery," and on some questions, part of which she evaded, as
will be seen, with a naïve skill such as the most experienced and
worldly coquette might envy. Her second letter (received April 26,
1862) was as follows:—

MR. HIGGINSON,
—Your kindness claimed earlier gratitude, but I was ill, and write to-day
from my pillow.

Thank you for the surgery; it was not so painful as I supposed. I bring
you others, as you ask, though they might not differ. While my thought is
undressed, I can make the distinction; but when I put them in the gown,
they look alike and numb.

You asked how old I was? I made no verse, but one or two, until this
winter, sir.

I had a terror since September, I could tell to none; and so I sing, as the boy does of the burying ground, because I am afraid.

You inquire my books. For poets, I have Keats, and Mr. and Mrs. Browning. For prose, Mr. Ruskin, Sir Thomas Browne, and the Revelations. I went to school, but in your manner of the phrase had no education. When a little girl, I had a friend who taught me Immortality; but venturing too near, himself, he never returned. Soon after my tutor died, and for several years my lexicon was my only companion. Then I found one more, but he was not contented I be his scholar, so he left the land.

You ask of my companions. Hills, sir, and the sundown, and a dog large as myself, that my father bought me. They are better than beings because they know, but do not tell; and the noise in the pool at noon excels my piano.

I have a brother and sister; my mother does not care for thought, and father, too busy with his briefs to notice what we do. He buys me many books, but begs me not to read them, because he fears they joggle the mind. They are religious, except me, and address an eclipse, every morning, whom they call their "Father."

But I fear my story fatigues you. I would like to learn. Could you tell me how to grow, or is it unconveyed, like melody or witchcraft?

You speak of Mr. Whitman. I never read his book, but was told that it was disgraceful.

I read Miss Prescott's "Circumstance," but it followed me in the dark, so I avoided her.

Two editors of journals came to my father's house this winter, and asked me for my mind, and when I asked them "why" they said I was penurious, and they would use it for the world.

I could not weigh myself, myself. My size felt small to me. I read your chapters in the "Atlantic," and experienced honor for you. I was sure you would not reject a confiding question.

Is this, sir, what you asked me to tell you? Your friend,

E. DICKINSON.

It will be seen that she had now drawn a step nearer, signing her name, and as my "friend." It will also be noticed that I had sounded her about certain American authors, then much read; and that she knew how to put her own criticisms in a very trenchant way. With this letter came some more verses, still in the same birdlike script, as for instance the following:—

"Your riches taught me poverty,
Myself a millionaire

In little wealths, as girls could boast,
  Till, broad as Buenos Ayre,
You drifted your dominions
A different Peru,
And I esteemed all poverty
  For life's estate, with you.

"Of mines, I little know, myself,
  But just the names of gems,
The colors of the commonest,
  And scarce of diadems
So much that, did I meet the queen,
  Her glory I should know;
But this must be a different wealth,
  To miss it, beggars so.

"I'm sure 't is India, all day,
  To those who look on you
Without a stint, without a blame,
  Might I but be the Jew!
I'm sure it is Golconda
  Beyond my power to deem,
To have a smile for mine, each day,
  How better than a gem!

"At least, it solaces to know
  That there exists a gold
Although I prove it just in time
  Its distance to behold;
Its far, far treasure to surmise
  And estimate the pearl
That slipped my simple fingers through
  While just a girl at school!"

Here was already manifest that defiance of form, never through care-lessness, and never precisely from whim, which so marked her. The slightest change in the order of words—thus, "While yet at school, a girl"—would have given her a rhyme for this last line; but no; she was intent upon her thought, and it would not have satisfied her to make the change. The other poem further showed, what had already been visible, a rare and delicate sympathy with the life of nature:—

"A bird came down the walk;
He did not know I saw;
He bit an angle-worm in halves
And ate the fellow raw.

"And then he drank a dew
From a convenient grass,
And then hopped sidewise to a wall,
To let a beetle pass.

"He glanced with rapid eyes
That hurried all around;
They looked like frightened beads, I thought;
He stirred his velvet head

"Like one in danger, cautious.
I offered him a crumb,
And he unrolled his feathers
And rowed him softer home

"Than oars divide the ocean,
Too silver for a seam—
Or butterflies, off banks of noon,
Leap, plashless as they swim."

It is possible that in a second letter I gave more of distinct praise or encouragement, as her third is in a different mood. This was received June 8, 1862. There is something startling in its opening image; and in the yet stranger phrase that follows, where she apparently uses "mob" in the sense of chaos or bewilderment:

DEAR FRIEND,
—Your letter gave no drunkenness, because I tasted rum before.
Domingo comes but once; yet I have had few pleasures so deep as your opinion, and if I tried to thank you, my tears would block my tongue.
My dying tutor told me that he would like to live till I had been a poet, but Death was much of mob as I could master, then. And when, far afterward, a sudden light on orchards, or a new fashion in the wind troubled my attention, I felt a palsy, here, the verses just relieve.
Your second letter surprised me, and for a moment, swung. I had not supposed it. Your first gave no dishonor, because the true are not

ashamed. I thanked you for your justice, but could not drop the bells whose jingling cooled my tramp. Perhaps the balm seemed better, because you bled me first. I smile when you suggest that I delay "to publish," that being foreign to my thought as firmament to fin.

If fame belonged to me, I could not escape her; if she did not, the longest day would pass me on the chase, and the approbation of my dog would forsake me then. My barefoot rank is better.

You think my gait "spasmodic." I am in danger, sir. You think me "uncontrolled." I have no tribunal.

Would you have time to be the "friend" you should think I need? I have a little shape: it would not crowd your desk, nor make much racket as the mouse that dens your galleries.

If I might bring you what I do—not so frequent to trouble you—and ask you if I told it clear, 't would be control to me. The sailor cannot see the North, but knows the needle can. The "hand you stretch me in the dark" I put mine in, and turn away. I have no Saxon now:—

> As if I asked a common alms,
> And in my wandering hand
> A stranger pressed a kingdom,
> And I, bewildered, stand;
> As if I asked the Orient
> Had it for me a morn,
> And it should lift its purple dikes
> And shatter me with dawn!

But, will you be my preceptor, Mr. Higginson?

With this came the poem since published in one of her volumes and entitled "Renunciation"; and also that beginning "Of all the sounds dispatched abroad," thus fixing approximately the date of those two. I must soon have written to ask her for her picture, that I might form some impression of my enigmatical correspondent. To this came the following reply, in July, 1862:—

Could you believe me without? I had no portrait, now, but am small, like the wren; and my hair is bold like the chestnut bur; and my eyes, like the sherry in the glass, that the guest leaves. Would this do just as well?

It often alarms father. He says death might occur and he has moulds of all the rest, but has no mould of me; but I noticed the quick wore off those things, in a few days, and forestall the dishonor. You will think no caprice of me.

You said "Dark." I know the butterfly, and the lizard, and the orchis. Are not those *your* countrymen?

I am happy to be your scholar, and will deserve the kindness I cannot repay.

If you truly consent, I recite now. Will you tell me my fault, frankly as to yourself, for I had rather wince than die. Men do not call the surgeon to commend the bone, but to set it, sir, and fracture within is more critical. And for this, preceptor, I shall bring you obedience, the blossom from my garden, and every gratitude I know.

Perhaps you smile at me. I could not stop for that. My business is circumference. An ignorance, not of customs, but if caught with the dawn, or the sunset see me, myself the only kangaroo among the beauty, sir, if you please, it afflicts me, and I thought that instruction would take it away.

Because you have much business, beside the growth of me, you will appoint, yourself, how often I shall come, without your inconvenience.

And if at any time you regret you received me, or I prove a different fabric to that you supposed, you must banish me.

When I state myself, as the representative of the verse, it does not mean me, but a supposed person.

You are true about the "perfection." To-day makes Yesterday mean.

You spoke of "Pippa Passes." I never heard anybody speak of "Pippa Passes" before. You see my posture is benighted.

To thank you baffles me. Are you perfectly powerful? Had I a pleasure you had not, I could delight to bring it.

YOUR SCHOLAR.

This was accompanied by this strong poem, with its breathless conclusion. The title is of my own giving:—

The Saints' Rest

Of tribulation, these are they,
Denoted by the white;
The spangled gowns, a lesser rank
Of victors designate.

All these did conquer; but the ones
Who overcame most times,
Wear nothing commoner than snow,
No ornaments but palms.

"Surrender" is a sort unknown
  On this superior soil;
"Defeat" an outgrown anguish,
  Remembered as the mile

Our panting ancle barely passed
  When night devoured the road;
But we stood whispering in the house,
  And all we said, was "Saved!"

[Note by the writer of the verses.] I spelled ankle wrong.

It would seem that at first I tried a little—a very little—to lead her in the direction of rules and traditions; but I fear it was only perfunctory, and that she interested me more in her—so to speak—unregenerate condition. Still, she recognizes the endeavor. In this case, as will be seen, I called her attention to the fact that while she took pains to correct the spelling of a word, she was utterly careless of greater irregularities. It will be seen by her answer that with her usual naïve adroitness she turns my point:—

DEAR FRIEND,

—Are these more orderly? I thank you for the truth.

I had no monarch in my life, and cannot rule myself; and when I try to organize, my little force explodes and leaves me bare and charred.

I think you called me "wayward." Will you help me improve?

I suppose the pride that stops the breath, in the core of woods, is not of ourself.

You say I confess the little mistake, and omit the large. Because I can see orthography; but the ignorance out of sight is my preceptor's charge.

Of "shunning men and women," they talk of hallowed things, aloud, and embarrass my dog. He and I don't object to them, if they'll exist their side. I think Carlo would please you. He is dumb, and brave. I think you would like the chestnut tree I met in my walk. It hit my notice suddenly, and I thought the skies were in blossom.

Then there's a noiseless noise in the orchard that I let persons hear.

You told me in one letter you could not come to see me "now," and I made no answer; not because I had none, but did not think myself the price that you should come so far.

I do not ask so large a pleasure, lest you might deny me.

You say, "Beyond your knowledge." You would not jest with me, because I believe you; but, preceptor, you cannot mean it?

All men say "What" to me, but I thought it a fashion.

When much in the woods, as a little girl, I was told that the snake would bite me, that I might pick a poisonous flower, or goblins kidnap me; but I went along and met no one but angels, who were far shyer of me than I could be of them, so I have n't that confidence in fraud which many exercise.

I shall observe your precept, though I don't understand it, always.

I marked a line in one verse, because I met it after I made it, and never consciously touch a paint mixed by another person.

I do not let go it, because it is mine. Have you the portrait of Mrs. Browning?

Persons sent me three. If you had none, will you have mine?

YOUR SCHOLAR.

A month or two after this I entered the volunteer army of the Civil War, and must have written to her during the winter of 1862–63 from South Carolina or Florida, for the following reached me in camp:—

AMHERST.

DEAR FRIEND,

—I did not deem that planetary forces annulled, but suffered an exchange of territory, or world.

I should have liked to see you before you became improbable. War feels to me an oblique place. Should there be other summers, would you perhaps come?

I found you were gone, by accident, as I find systems are, or seasons of the year, and obtain no cause, but suppose it a treason of progress that dissolves as it goes. Carlo still remained, and I told him.

Best gains must have the losses' test,
To constitute them gains.

My shaggy ally assented.

Perhaps death gave me awe for friends, striking sharp and early, for I held them since in a brittle love, of more alarm than peace. I trust you may pass the limit of war; and though not reared to prayer, when service is had in church for our arms, I include yourself. . . . I was thinking to-day, as I noticed, that the "Supernatural" was only the Natural disclosed.

Not "Revelation" 't is that waits,
But our unfurnished eyes.

But I fear I detain you. Should you, before this reaches you, experience immortality, who will inform me of the exchange? Could you, with honor, avoid death, I entreat you, sir. It would bereave

YOUR GNOME.

I trust the "Procession of Flowers" was not a premonition.

I cannot explain this extraordinary signature, substituted for the now customary "Your Scholar," unless she imagined her friend to be in some incredible and remote condition, imparting its strangeness to her. Swedenborg somewhere has an image akin to her "oblique place," where he symbolizes evil as simply an oblique angle. With this letter came verses, most refreshing in that clime of jasmines and mockingbirds, on the familiar robin:—

The Robin
The robin is the one
That interrupts the morn
With hurried, few, express reports
When March is scarcely on.

The robin is the one
That overflows the noon
With her cherubic quantity,
An April but begun.

The robin is the one
That, speechless from her nest,
Submits that home and certainty
And sanctity are best.

In the summer of 1863 I was wounded, and in hospital for a time, during which came this letter in pencil, written from what was practically a hospital for her, though only for weak eyes:—

DEAR FRIEND,
—Are you in danger? I did not know that you were hurt. Will you tell me more? Mr. Hawthorne died.

I was ill since September, and since April in Boston for a physician's care. He does not let me go, yet I work in my prison, and make guests for myself.

Carlo did not come, because that he would die in jail; and the mountains I could not hold now, so I brought but the Gods.

I wish to see you more than before I failed. Will you tell me your health? I am surprised and anxious since receiving your note.

The only news I know
Is bulletins all day
From Immortality.

Can you render my pencil? The physician has taken away my pen. I inclose the address from a letter, lest my figures fail. Knowledge of your recovery would excel my own.

E. DICKINSON.

Later this arrived:—

DEAR FRIEND,

—I think of you so wholly that I cannot resist to write again, to ask if you are safe? Danger is not at first, for then we are unconscious, but in the after, slower days.

Do not try to be saved, but let redemption find you, as it certainly will. Love is its own rescue; for we, at our supremest, are but its trembling emblems.

YOUR SCHOLAR.

These were my earliest letters from Emily Dickinson, in their order. From this time and up to her death (May 15, 1886) we corresponded at varying intervals, she always persistently keeping up this attitude of "Scholar," and assuming on my part a preceptorship which it is almost needless to say did not exist. Always glad to hear her "recite," as she called it, I soon abandoned all attempt to guide in the slightest degree this extraordinary nature, and simply accepted her confidences, giving as much as I could of what might interest her in return.

Sometimes there would be a long pause, on my part, after which would come a plaintive letter, always terse, like this:—

"Did I displease you? But won't you tell me how?"

Or perhaps the announcement of some event, vast in her small sphere, as this:—

AMHERST.
Carlo died.
Would you instruct me now?

E. DICKINSON.

Or sometimes there would arrive an exquisite little detached strain, every word a picture, like this:—

The Humming-Bird
A route of evanescence
With a revolving wheel;
A resonance of emerald;
A rush of cochineal.
And every blossom on the bush
Adjusts its tumbled head;—
The mail from Tunis, probably,
An easy morning's ride.

Nothing in literature, I am sure, so condenses into a few words that gorgeous atom of life and fire of which she here attempts the description. It is, however, needless to conceal that many of her brilliant fragments were less satisfying. She almost always grasped whatever she sought, but with some fracture of grammar and dictionary on the way. Often, too, she was obscure, and sometimes inscrutable; and though obscurity is sometimes, in Coleridge's phrase, a compliment to the reader, yet it is never safe to press this compliment too hard.

Sometimes, on the other hand, her verses found too much favor for her comfort, and she was urged to publish. In such cases I was sometimes put forward as a defense; and the following letter was the fruit of some such occasion:

DEAR FRIEND,
—Thank you for the advice. I shall implicitly follow it.

The one who asked me for the lines I had never seen.

He spoke of "a charity." I refused, but did not inquire. He again earnestly urged, on the ground that in that way I might "aid unfortunate children." The name of "child" was a snare to me, and I hesitated, choosing my most rudimentary, and without criterion.

I inquired of you. You can scarcely estimate the opinion to one utterly guideless. Again thank you.

YOUR SCHOLAR.

Again came this, on a similar theme:—

DEAR FRIEND,

—Are you willing to tell me what is right? Mrs. Jackson, of Colorado ["H. H.," her early schoolmate], was with me a few moments this week, and wished me to write for this. [A circular of the "No Name Series" was inclosed.] I told her I was unwilling, and she asked me why? I said I was incapable, and she seemed not to believe me and asked me not to decide for a few days. Meantime, she would write me. She was so sweetly noble, I would regret to estrange her, and if you would be willing to give me a note saying you disapproved it, and thought me unfit, she would believe you. I am sorry to flee so often to my safest friend, but hope he permits me.

In all this time—nearly eight years—we had never met, but she had sent invitations like the following:—

AMHERST.
DEAR FRIEND,

—Whom my dog understood could not elude others.

I should be so glad to see you, but think it an apparitional pleasure, not to be fulfilled. I am uncertain of Boston.

I had promised to visit my physician for a few days in May, but father objects because he is in the habit of me.

Is it more far to Amherst?

You will find a minute host, but a spacious welcome. . . .

If I still entreat you to teach me, are you much displeased? I will be patient, constant, never reject your knife, and should my slowness goad you, you knew before myself that

Except the smaller size
No lives are round.
These hurry to a sphere
And show and end.
The larger slower grow
And later hang;
The summers of Hesperides
Are long.

Afterwards, came this:—

AMHERST.

DEAR FRIEND,

—A letter always feels to me like immortality because it is the mind alone without corporeal friend. Indebted in our talk to attitude and accent, there seems a spectral power in thought that walks alone. I would like to thank you for your great kindness, but never try to lift the words which I cannot hold.

Should you come to Amherst, I might then succeed, though gratitude is the timid wealth of those who have nothing. I am sure that you speak the truth, because the noble do, but your letters always surprise me.

My life has been too simple and stern to embarrass any. "Seen of Angels," scarcely my responsibility.

It is difficult not to be fictitious in so fair a place, but tests' severe repairs are permitted all.

When a little girl I remember hearing that remarkable passage and preferring the "Power," not knowing at the time that "Kingdom" and "Glory" were included.

You noticed my dwelling alone. To an emigrant, country is idle except it be his own. You speak kindly of seeing me; could it please your convenience to come so far as Amherst, I should be very glad, but I do not cross my father's ground to any house or town.

Of our greatest acts we are ignorant. You were not aware that you saved my life. To thank you in person has been since then one of my few requests. . . . You will excuse each that I say, because no one taught me.

At last, after many postponements, on August 16, 1870, I found myself face to face with my hitherto unseen correspondent. It was at her father's house, one of those large, square, brick mansions so familiar in our older New England towns, surrounded by trees and blossoming shrubs without, and within exquisitely neat, cool, spacious, and fragrant with flowers. After a little delay, I heard an extremely faint and pattering footstep like that of a child, in the hall, and in glided, almost noiselessly, a plain, shy little person, the face without a single good feature, but with eyes, as she herself said, "like the sherry the guest leaves in the glass," and with smooth bands of reddish chestnut hair. She had a quaint and nun-like look, as if she might be a German canoness of some religious order, whose prescribed garb was white piqué, with a blue net worsted shawl. She came toward me with two day-lilies, which she put in a childlike way into my hand, saying softly, under her breath, "These are my introduction," and adding, also under her breath, in childlike fashion, "Forgive me if I am frightened; I never see strangers, and hardly know what I say." But soon she began to talk, and thenceforward continued almost constantly; pausing sometimes to beg that I would talk instead, but readily recommencing when I evaded. There was not a trace of affectation in all this; she seemed to speak absolutely for her own relief, and wholly without watching its effect on her hearer. Led on by me, she told much about her early life, in which her father was always the chief figure,—evidently a man of the old type, *la vieille roche* of Puritanism,—a man who, as she said, read on Sunday "lonely and rigorous books"; and who had from childhood inspired her with such awe, that she never learned to tell time by the clock till she was fifteen, simply because he had tried to explain it to her when she was a little child, and she had been afraid to tell him that she did not understand, and also afraid to ask any one else lest he should hear of it. Yet she had never heard him speak a harsh word, and it needed only a glance at his photograph to see how truly the Puritan tradition was preserved in him. He did not wish his children, when little, to read anything but the Bible; and when, one day, her brother brought her home Longfellow's "Kavanagh," he put it secretly under the pianoforte cover, made signs to her, and they both afterwards read it. It may have been before this, however, that a student of her father's was amazed to find that she and her brother had never heard of Lydia Maria Child, then much read, and he brought "Letters from New York," and hid it in the great bush of old-fashioned tree-box beside the front door. After the first book, she thought in ecstasy, "This, then, is a book, and there are more of them." But she did not find so many as she expected, for she afterwards said to me, "When I lost the use of my eyes, it was a comfort to think that there were so few real books that I could easily find one to read me all of them." Afterwards, when she regained her eyes, she read Shakespeare, and thought to herself, "Why is any other book needed?"

She went on talking constantly and saying, in the midst of narrative, things quaint and aphoristic. "Is it oblivion or absorption when things pass from our minds?" "Truth is such a rare thing, it is delightful to tell it." "I find ecstasy in living; the mere sense of living is joy enough." When I asked her if she never felt any want of employment, not going off the grounds and rarely seeing a visitor, she answered, "I never thought of conceiving that I could ever have the slightest approach to such a want in all future time"; and then added, after a pause, "I feel that I have not expressed myself strongly enough," although it seemed to me that she had. She told me of her household occupations, that she made all their bread, because her father liked only hers; then saying shyly, "And people must have puddings," this very timidly and suggestively, as if they were meteors or comets. Interspersed with these confidences came phrases so emphasized as to seem the very wantonness of over-statement, as if she pleased herself with putting into words what the most extravagant might possibly think without saying, as thus: "How do most people live without any thoughts? There are many people in the world,—you must have noticed them in the street,—how do they live? How do they get strength to put on their clothes in the morning?" Or this crowning extravaganza: "If I read a book and it makes my whole body so cold no fire can ever warm me, I know that is poetry. If I feel physically as if the top of my head were taken off, I know that is poetry. These are the only ways I know it. Is there any other way?"

I have tried to describe her just as she was, with the aid of notes taken at the time; but this interview left our relation very much what it was before;—on my side an interest that was strong and even affectionate, but not based on any thorough comprehension; and on her side a hope, always rather baffled, that I should afford some aid in solving her abstruse problem of life.

The impression undoubtedly made on me was that of an excess of tension, and of something abnormal. Perhaps in time I could have got beyond that somewhat overstrained relation which not my will, but her needs, had forced upon us. Certainly I should have been most glad to bring it down to the level of simple truth and every-day comradeship; but it was not altogether easy. She was much too enigmatical a being for me to solve in an hour's interview, and an instinct told me that the slightest attempt at direct cross-examination would make her withdraw into her shell; I could only sit still and watch, as one does in the woods; I must name my bird without a gun, as recommended by Emerson.

After my visit came this letter:—

Enough is so vast a sweetness, I suppose it never occurs, only pathetic counterfeits.

Fabulous to me as the men of the Revelations who "shall not hunger any more." Even the possible has its insoluble particle.

After you went, I took "Macbeth" and turned to "Birnam Wood." Came twice "To Dunsinane." I thought and went about my work. . . .

The vein cannot thank the artery, but her solemn indebtedness to him, even the stolidest admit, and so of me who try, whose effort leaves no sound.

You ask great questions accidentally. To answer them would be events. I trust that you are safe.

I ask you to forgive me for all the ignorance I had. I find no nomination sweet as your low opinion.

Speak, if but to blame your obedient child.

You told me of Mrs. Lowell's poems. Would you tell me where I could find them, or are they not for sight? An article of yours, too, perhaps the only one you wrote that I never knew. It was about a "Latch." Are you willing to tell me? [Perhaps "A Sketch."]

If I ask too much, you could please refuse. Shortness to live has made me bold.

Abroad is close to-night and I have but to lift my hands to touch the "Heights of Abraham."

DICKINSON.

When I said, at parting, that I would come again some time, she replied, "Say, in a long time; that will be nearer. Some time is no time." We met only once again, and I have no express record of the visit. We corresponded for years, at long intervals, her side of the intercourse being, I fear, better sustained; and she sometimes wrote also to my wife, inclosing flowers or fragrant leaves with a verse or two. Once she sent her one of George Eliot's books, I think "Middlemarch," and wrote, "I am bringing you a little granite book for you to lean upon." At other times she would send single poems, such as these:—

The Blue Jay

No brigadier throughout the year
So civic as the jay.
A neighbor and a warrior too,
With shrill felicity
Pursuing winds that censure us
A February Day,
The brother of the universe
Was never blown away.
The snow and he are intimate;
I've often seen them play
When heaven looked upon us all
With such severity
I felt apology were due
To an insulted sky
Whose pompous frown was nutriment
To their temerity.

The pillow of this daring head
Is pungent evergreens;
His larder—terse and militant—
Unknown, refreshing things;
His character—a tonic;
His future—a dispute;
Unfair an immortality
That leaves this neighbor out.

The White Heat
Dare you see a soul at the white heat?
    Then crouch within the door;
Red is the fire's common tint,
    But when the vivid ore

Has sated flame's conditions,
    Its quivering substance plays
Without a color, but the light
    Of unanointed blaze.

Least village boasts its blacksmith,
    Whose anvil's even din
Stands symbol for the finer forge
    That soundless tugs within,

Refining these impatient ores
    With hammer and with blaze,
Until the designated light
    Repudiate the forge.

Then came the death of her father, that strong Puritan father who had communicated to her so much of the vigor of his own nature, and who bought her many books, but begged her not to read them. Mr. Edward Dickinson, after service in the national House of Representatives and other public positions, had become a member of the lower house of the Massachusetts legislature. The session was unusually prolonged, and he was making a speech upon some railway question at noon, one very hot day (July 16, 1874), when he became suddenly faint and sat down. The house adjourned, and a friend walked with him to his lodgings at the Tremont House, where he began to pack his bag for home, after sending for a physician, but died within three hours. Soon afterwards, I received the following letter:—

The last afternoon that my father lived, though with no premonition, I preferred to be with him, and invented an absence for mother, Vinnie [her sister] being asleep. He seemed peculiarly pleased, as I oftenest stayed with myself; and remarked, as the afternoon withdrew, he "would like it to not end."

His pleasure almost embarrassed me, and my brother coming, I suggested they walk. Next morning I woke him for the train, and saw him no more.

His heart was pure and terrible, and I think no other like it exists.

I am glad there is immortality, but would have tested it myself, before entrusting him. Mr. Bowles was with us. With that exception, I saw none. I have wished for you, since my father died, and had you an hour unengrossed, it would be almost priceless. Thank you for each kindness. . . .

Later she wrote:—

When I think of my father's lonely life and lonelier death, there is this redress—
Take all away;
The only thing worth larceny
Is left—the immortality.
My earliest friend wrote me the week before he died, "If I live, I will go to Amherst; if I die, I certainly will."
Is your house deeper off?

Your Scholar.

A year afterwards came this:—

Dear Friend,
—Mother was paralyzed Tuesday, a year from the evening father died. I thought perhaps you would care.

Your Scholar.

With this came the following verse, having a curious seventeenth-century flavor:—

"A death-blow is a life-blow to some,
Who, till they died, did not alive become;
Who, had they lived, had died, but when
They died, vitality begun."

And later came this kindred memorial of one of the oldest and most faithful friends of the family, Mr. Samuel Bowles, of the Springfield "Republican":—

DEAR FRIEND,
—I felt it shelter to speak to you.

My brother and sister are with Mr. Bowles, who is buried this afternoon.

The last song that I heard—that was, since the birds—was "He leadeth me, he leadeth me; yea, though I walk"—then the voices stooped, the arch was so low.

After this added bereavement the inward life of the diminished household became only more concentrated, and the world was held farther and farther away. Yet to this period belongs the following letter, written about 1880, which has more of what is commonly called the objective or external quality than any she ever wrote me; and shows how close might have been her observation and her sympathy, had her rare qualities taken a somewhat different channel:—

DEAR FRIEND,
—I was touchingly reminded of [a child who had died] this morning by an Indian woman with gay baskets and a dazzling baby, at the kitchen door. Her little boy "once died," she said, death to her dispelling him. I asked her what the baby liked, and she said "to step." The prairie before the door was gay with flowers of hay, and I led her in. She argued with the birds, she leaned on clover walls and they fell, and dropped her. With jargon sweeter than a bell, she grappled butter-cups, and they sank together, the buttercups the heaviest. What sweetest use of days! 'T was noting some such scene made Vaughan humbly say,—

"My days that are at best but dim and hoary."

I think it was Vaughan. . . .

And these few fragmentary memorials—closing, like every human biography, with funerals, yet with such as were to Emily Dickinson only the stately introduction to a higher life—may well end with her description of the death of the very summer she so loved.

"As imperceptibly as grief
The summer lapsed away,

Too imperceptible at last
To feel like perfidy.

"A quietness distilled,
As twilight long begun,
Or Nature spending with herself
Sequestered afternoon.

"The dusk drew earlier in,
The morning foreign shone,
A courteous yet harrowing grace
As guest that would be gone.

"And thus without a wing
Or service of a keel
Our summer made her light escape
Into the Beautiful."

7

The Sunny Side of the
Transcendental Period

I t happened to me once to be summoned on short notice to the house
of a most agreeable neighbor, then Dean of the Episcopal Theological
School at Cambridge, to assist in entertaining two English guests unexpectedly arrived. These guests were a husband and wife, both authors,
and visiting this country for the first time. They proved to belong to that
class of British travelers who, as the genial Longfellow used to say, come
hither, not so much to obtain information about America, as to communicate it. We were scarcely seated at table when the little lady—for
they were both very small in person—looked up at me confidingly and
said, "Don't you think it rather a pity that all the really interesting Americans seem to be dead?" It was difficult for a living man to maintain any
resistance against a conclusion so decisive, and all I remember is that our
talk became a series of obituaries. To those might now be added, were it
needful, similar memorials of my fair questioner, of her husband, and of
our gracious host himself, since these also have passed away. And why
should such remembrances be sad, one may well ask, if they are brought
together in a sunny spirit, and have for their motto, not the mournful-
ness of old-time epitaphs, but rather the fine outburst of Whitman's
brief song of parting, "Joy, Shipmate, Joy." Even the gloomy Carlyle had
to admit that "there is no life of a man faithfully recorded, but is a heroic
poem of its sort, rhymed or unrhymed."

Those who followed the chorus of affectionate praise which surrounded
the celebration of Emerson's hundredth birthday must have felt very
keenly its unlikeness to the ever renewing tumult of discussion around

the grave of Carlyle. The difference was in great measure the penalty of temperament, or in Emerson's case, its reward. No one recognized this more fully than Carlyle himself when he said sadly to me, "Ah! the dear Emerson! He thinks that everybody in the world is as good as himself;" just as he had said to Longfellow, years before, that Emerson's first visit to him was "like the visit of an angel." It is clear that the whole atmosphere of Emerson's memory breathes sunshine, but it gradually appears, in tracing it farther, that much of this traditional atmosphere extends—at least for those who lived through it and perhaps for their children also—over the whole intellectual period of which Emerson was the best representative. This period is now usually and doubtless vaguely known in America as the period of Transcendentalism. Unsatisfying as the word, when thus applied, must be, it may yet be employed for want of a better, without entering too profoundly into its source or its services. Originally a philosophic term, it can be used for the present to indicate a period.

The word "Transcendentalism" was apparently first employed by the leader among modern German philosophers, Immanuel Kant, to designate the intuitive method of reaching truth, as apart from the experimental or sensational method of Locke, which had held its own so stoutly. Kant died in 1804, but the word was handed on, so modified and, we might perhaps say, battered by later German thinkers, that it would now be useless to attempt to employ it further than as a landmark or guidepost, as it will be used here. If we wish to fix the birth-time of the American period bearing that name, we may place it somewhere near the publication of Emerson's "Nature" (1836), or the appearance of the first number of "The Dial" (July, 1840), or the formation of the "Brook Farm Institute," or "Community" as it was oftenest called, near Boston (1841). The special interest of this household for the world was not so much because it gave a new roof-tree for a little domestic experiment,—the Moravians and Shakers had long before done that,—but rather because it offered also an atmosphere of freedom.

It visibly relaxed restraint, suggested a substitute for the strict Puritan tradition, brought together the most open and hopeful minds of the community, sometimes uniting with them the fanatics, still oftener the do-nothings; giving conservatives and radicals alike something to talk about. Those whose names are now oftenest associated with the Brook Farm enterprise, as Emerson, Alcott, Margaret Fuller Ossoli, and William Henry Channing, never actually belonged to it; while its most noted members, as Hawthorne and George William Curtis, were there only during the first year. The only narrator who has written his personal remembrances of it was but a second-year member; and its more systematic historian, Mr. Lindsay Swift, says justly of it, "There was a distinct beginning, a fairly coherent progress, but a vague termination." He also touches the keynote of the whole history when he says in his preface, "It is more than fifty years since the last dweller in that pleasant domain turned his reluctant steps away from its noble illusions, and toward the stress of realities; but from no one of this gracious company has ever come the admission that Brook Farm was a failure." Surely this is much to say.

In going still farther back for the historic origins of American transcendentalism, we must recognize the earlier influence of Burns, Coleridge, and Wordsworth, as laying the foundations for all this new atmosphere of thought and living. This is a fact of much interest as compared with the first reception of all these poets in their own country. The "London Monthly Review"—the leading critical magazine in England before the "Edinburgh Review" appeared—pronounced Burns's first volume to be "disgusting," and "written in an unknown tongue," the editor adding his own partial version of "The Cotter's Saturday Night" translated into the English language! The same editor pronounced Coleridge's "Ancient Mariner" "the strangest story of a cock and bull that we ever saw on paper . . . a rhapsody of unintelligible wildness and incoherence, of which we do not perceive the drift," while "Christabel" was described by him as "rude, unfeatured stuff." Even of Wordsworth's "Tintern Abbey" the same critic complains that it is "tinctured with gloomy, narrow, and unsociable ideas of seclusion from the commerce of the world;" and yet on turning the pages of Dennie's "Portfolio" published in Philadelphia simultaneously with the English periodical just quoted (1786), we find these very poets and, indeed, these identical poems hailed as the opening of a new intellectual era. Such, indeed, it was, but an era heralded in America with an eagerness, cordiality, and, above all, a cheerfulness such as might well belong to a fresher and more youthful life.

Then followed Carlyle's great influence through his "Sartor Resartus," whose American editor, Charles Stearns Wheeler, I can well remember to have watched with timid reverence at the Boston Athenæum Library as he transcribed that exciting work from the pages of "Fraser's Magazine," for its first reprinting in book form. Still more must be recalled the influence of Kant and Fichte, Hegel and Schleiermacher, with the more transient eclectic philosophy of the Frenchmen Cousin and Jouffroy, whose books were translated from the French and used for a time as text-books in Harvard College and elsewhere, as early as 1839. The German poets also were just being translated, though of course in a fragmentary way, in America, especially Goethe, Schiller, and even Heine; and the poetic writings of Hoffmann, Novalis, Jean Paul Richter, and others lent their influence, first under the lead of Carlyle, and afterwards through direct American translators, the Rev. Charles T. Brooks and Mrs. Eliza Buckminster Lee. Many of these poetic translations appeared in "The Dial," and the prose versions in the series of volumes, fourteen in all, entitled "Specimens of Foreign Standard Literature," planned and edited by George Ripley. To him especial attention should be given, since if the sunny atmosphere of the period was personally incarnated in any one, it was undoubtedly in him.

George Ripley was the single consummate type, during that period, of that rarest of combinations, the natural scholar and the cheery good fellow. Evidence of the former quality might be found in the catalogue, had it only been preserved, of his library sold in aid of the organization of Brook Farm, and universally recognized as the best German library then to be found in America; while the clearest tribute to the other trait was the universal regret said to have been felt among his clerical brethren at the loss of the gayest companion and best story-teller in their ranks. He it was who, with Emerson, Hedge, and George Putnam, called together the first meeting of "what was named in derision the Transcendental Club," as Hedge writes; and he it was who resigned his clerical charge in 1840, with a view to applying to some form of action the newer and ampler views of life.

Even Dr. Channing, then the intellectual leader of Boston, had some conference with Ripley as to whether it would be possible to bring cultivated and thoughtful people together and make a society that deserved the name. Mr. Swift in his admirable book on "Brook Farm" reminds us that there was a consultation on this subject at the house of Dr. John C. Warren, then the leading physician of Boston, which ended "with an oyster supper, crowned by excellent wines." Undoubtedly, on that occasion, George Ripley told his best stories and laughed his heartiest laugh. But we may be sure that his jubilant cheeriness was no less when he turned his back on all this and left the flesh-pots of Egypt for a dinner of herbs at Brook Farm.

There is something very interesting and not wholly accidental in the way in which a German influence was thus early making itself felt in this country and contributing, as a matter of course, to its sunshine. This clearly came from a double influence, the appearance in America of a number of highly educated Germans, of whom Lieber, Follen, and Beck were types, who were driven from their country by political uproar about 1825; and, on the other hand, the return of a small number of highly educated Americans, at a period a little earlier, who had studied at the German universities. The most conspicuous among these men were Edward Everett, George Ticknor, George Bancroft, and Joseph Green Cogswell, the latter being the organizer of our first great American library, the Astor. Their experience and influence had a value quite inestimable, and the process of their training is shown unmistakably in a remarkable series of letters from them to my father, then steward of Harvard College, and in some respects their sponsor; letters published by myself in the "Harvard Graduates' Magazine" for September, 1897. In one of these letters, the cool and clear-headed Everett, going from the Continent to inspect the universities of Oxford and Cambridge, expressed the opinion that America had at that date (1819) "nothing to learn from England [in regard to university methods], but everything to learn from Germany," and I have been more than once assured by English scholars, on quoting to them the passage, that the remark was, at the period indicated, absolutely true. It is, however, also true that Mr. Everett himself practically recognized a subsequent change in conditions, when he sent his own son, forty years later, to an English and not to a German university.

It must not be supposed that the "Disciples of the Newness," as they liked to call themselves, were allowed to go on their way unchecked. Professor Bowen of Harvard, always pungent and often tart, followed them up vigorously in the "North American," as did Professor Felton more mildly. Yet there was always something behind the cloud, an influence which revived these victims like some cloud-concealed goddess in Homer; and however severe the attacks may have been, they were usually the fruit of narrowness, not of mere malice. They were rarely mixed with merely personal bitterness, as were the contests of the same period, under Poe's influence, among New York men of letters; nor were they so much entangled with money-quarrels as those, since money was a thing with which New England students had little to do. No one among them, however, fared so miserably, in financial negotiations, as did poor Cornelius Mathews in New York, who, after his "Big Abel and the Little Manhattan" had been announced as a forthcoming volume of a series, was offered by the repentant publishers $100 to allow them to withdraw the offer and leave the book unpublished, but who refused the request. The "North American Review"—then a Boston periodical—settled the case of this unfortunate author tersely by saying, "Mr. Mathews has shown a marvelous skill in failing, each failure being more complete than the last." Horace Greeley hit his merely political opponents as hard as this, but the New York "Tribune," under Margaret Fuller's influence, kept clear of bitter personalities in literature, something which she had not always quite done in "The Dial."

It must be remembered that the Transcendentalists never, in the early days, called themselves by that name. Their most ambitious title was, as has been said, that of Disciples of the Newness. It must also be remembered that this Newness itself was in some degree a reversion to the old, as in Margaret Fuller's case it came from a learned father who brought her up in direct inheritance of whatever was ancient. She was, by her own statement, early "placed in a garden with a great pile of books before her." She began to read Latin before she read English. The Greek and Roman deities were absolutely real to her, and she prayed, "O God, if thou art Jupiter;" or else to Bacchus for a bunch of grapes. When she was old enough to think about Christianity, she cried out for her dear old Greek and Roman gods. It was a long time, her friend Mrs. Dall tells us, "before she could see the deeper spirituality of the Christian tradition." Hence it is, perhaps, that we see rather less of sunshine in her than in the other Transcendentalists.

For the unbelieving world outside, it must be remembered, the Transcendental movement at least contributed some such sunshine through the very sarcasms it excited; as when Mrs. Russell, Father Taylor's brilliant daughter, did not flinch from defining the Transcendentalists as "a race who dove into the infinite, soared into the illimitable, and never paid cash;" or when Carlyle described Ripley, who had called on him in England, as "a Socinian minister, who had left the pulpit to reform the world by cultivating onions." Emerson compared Brook Farm to "a French Revolution in small," and a certain meeting of the Transcendental Club to "going to heaven in a swing." All the peculiarities of Brook Farm, we may be sure, were reported without diminution in the gossip of Boston society, even the jokes of the young people made upon themselves being taken seriously in the world outside; as when they asked at the dinner-table, "Is the butter within the sphere of your influence?" or proposed that a pie should be cut "from the centre to the periphery." There being more young men than young women, at first, an unusual share of household duties, moreover, fell upon the stronger sex. They helped in the laundry, brought water from the pump, prepared vegetables in the barn. The graceful George William Curtis trimmed lamps, and the manly and eminently practical Charles Dana organized a band of "griddle-cake servitors," composed of "four of the most elegant youths of the community."

There was also a Brook Farm legend that one of the younger members or pupils confessed his passion while helping his sweetheart to wash dishes; and Emerson is the authority for stating that as the men danced in the evening, clothespins sometimes dropped from their pockets. Hawthorne wrote to his sister, not without sarcasm, "The whole fraternity eat together, and such a delectable way of life has never been seen on earth since the days of the early Christians. We get up at half-past six, dine at half-past twelve, and go to bed at nine." An element of moral protest also entered into the actual work of the more serious members. Thus Mr. Ripley said to Theodore Parker of John Dwight, afterwards eminent as a musical critic, "There is your accomplished friend; he would hoe corn all Sunday if I would let him, but all Massachusetts could not make him do it on Monday." Rumor adds that Parker replied, "It is good to know that he wants to hoe corn any day in the week." The question is not how far these details were based on fact or were the fruit of fancy, but the immediate point is that they materially aided in keeping up the spirits of the unbelieving world outside.

It is possible that those seemingly vague and dreamy times might have communicated to those reared in them too passive and negative a character but for the perpetual tonic of the anti-slavery movement, which was constantly entangling itself with all merely socialistic discussion. At every crisis brought on by this last problem it turned out that mere moral purpose might impart to these pacific social reformers a placid courage which rose on occasion to daring. Thus it took years to appreciate the most typical of these men, Bronson Alcott. The quality that was at first rather exasperating in him became ultimately his greatest charm: the manner in which this idealist threw himself on the Universal Powers and left his life to be assigned by them. That life had seemed at first as helpless and unpromising as the attitude of the little Italian child who, having stopped at a certain door near Boston and received breakfast for sweet charity's sake, was found sitting placidly on the doorstep two hours later, and being asked why she had not gone away replied serenely, "What for go away? Plenty time go away!" The wide universe was to Alcott a similarly vast and tranquil scene. He had, as was said of his English friend Greaves, "a copious peacefulness." It was easy enough to see this in a humorous light, but when in later years, after those who had broken down the Boston Court House door for the rescue of Anthony Burns had been driven out, and the open doorway was left bare, it was Alcott who walked unarmed up the empty steps, calmly asking, "Why are we not within?" and on finding himself unsupported, turned back slowly, then walked placidly down again, he and his familiar cane, without visible disturbance of mind. It has lately come to light, since the publication of the memoirs of Daniel Ricketson, that Alcott afterwards offered to be one of a party for the rescue of Captain John Brown. It was still the same Alcott, only that he watched the slowly forming lines of his horoscope, and found them, in Emerson's phrase, "come full circle." In a similar way Thoreau, after all his seeming theories of self-absorption, ranged himself on the side of John Brown as placidly as if he were going for huckleberries.

Yet the effect of Transcendentalism on certain characters, a minority of its adherents, was seemingly disastrous; though the older we grow, the harder it is to be sure that we know all the keys to individual character. The freedom that belonged to the period, the sunny atmosphere of existence, doubtless made some men indolent, like children of the tropics. Some went abroad and lived in Europe, and were rarely heard from; others dwelt at home, and achieved nothing; while others, on the contrary, had the most laborious and exacting careers. Others led lives morally wasted, whether by the mere letting loose of a surge of passion ill restrained, or by that terrible impulse of curiosity which causes more than half the sins of each growing generation, and yet is so hard to distinguish from the heroic search after knowledge. I can think of men among those bred in that period, and seemingly under its full influence, who longed to know the worst of life and knew it, and paid dearly for their knowledge; and their kindred paid more dearly still. Others might be named who, without ever yielding, so far as I know or guess, to a single sensual or worldly sin, yet developed temperaments so absolutely wayward that it became necessary, in the judgment of all who knew the facts, for their wives and children to leave them and stay apart, so that these men died in old age without seeing the faces of their own grandchildren. Others vanished, and are to this day untraced; and yet all these were but a handful compared with that majority which remained true to early dreams, while the world called them erratic, and the church pronounced them unredeemed, or, in Shakespeare's phrase, "unhousel'd, disappointed, unaneled."

It must be remembered also that, in that period of general seething, all other reformatory movements alternated with efforts of the socialists and joined with them to keep up the spirits of the Community. The antislavery meetings, for instance, mingled sorrow with joy and sometimes even with levity. Nowhere in all the modern world could have been seen more strikingly grouped the various dramatis personæ of a great impending social change than on the platform of some large hall, filled with Abolitionists. There sat Garrison in the centre, his very attitude showing the serene immovableness of his mind, and around him usually two or three venerable Quaker Vice-Presidents, always speechless, while in themselves constituting an inexorable though unwearied audience. Grouped among them were "devout women, not a few," as the Scripture has it, and fiery orators brought together from different fields of action, where they had been alternately starved, frozen, or mobbed, according to the various methods adopted by unbelieving rural scoffers. Mingled with these were a few city delegates, the most high-bred men and women in appearance to be found in Boston, such as Wendell Phillips, Edmund Quincy, and Mrs. Chapman. Among these, strangest of all, were the living texts for all the impending eloquence of the platform: the fugitive slaves, black or mulatto or sometimes indistinguishably white, perhaps just landed from their concealment on Southern packet ships, or in covert corners of freight cars. There might be Henry Box Brown, so named from the box in which he had been nailed up and been borne, occasionally on his head, from slavery to freedom; or Harriet Tubman, who, after making her own escape from the land of slavery, had made eight or ten covert visits thither, each time bringing back by the underground railroad her little band of fugitives; or William and Ellen Craft, she going from city to city northward as a young Southern gentleman, wearing a tall hat and traveling-shawl after the manner of those days, and with spectacles to hide her still more, while her husband posed as her attendant slave. These, and such as these, passed across the stage in successive years. And no one who early saw Frederick Douglass just rescued from slavery could possibly have foreseen in him the princely and commanding aspect with which he was to tread in later years those same boards and prove himself, as the veteran reporter Yerrington used to say, one of the few speakers on the platform whose speeches needed absolutely no revision before printing.

These gave the tragic, the Shakespearean aspect of the anti-slavery movement, to be relieved by another side of the screen when Wendell Phillips and some other hero of the platform led beyond the door the shrieking Abby Folsom, with her unfailing cry, "It's the capitalists!" or Mellen was silenced by more subtle persuasions, and tempted away to continue his interminable harangue to some single auditor in the side scenes. Once take Garrison himself away from the convention, and no man better loved his placid joke. He could go to prison without flinching, but could not forego his pun, we may be sure, after he got there, and would no more have denied himself that innocent relaxation in jail than a typical French nobleman in Revolutionary days would have laid aside his snuff-box in the presence of the guillotine. A similar cheerful and unwavering tone pervaded those leaders generally, and I remember when Mrs. Chapman established the first outdoor anti-slavery festival, on the avowed ground that there was no reason why the children of this world should enjoy themselves better than the Children of Light.

It is needless to say that the tropical race in whose interest all this anti-slavery work was carried on took their share of levity, when opportunity came, the instances of habitual gloom being usually found, not among those who had escaped from slavery, but rather in those born free, bred at the North, having some worldly prosperity, and yet feeling that a modified subjugation still socially rested upon them. The inexhaustible sense of humor in Frederick Douglass, on the other hand, kept him clear of this, as was never better seen than on the once famous occasion when the notorious Isaiah Rynders of New York, at the head of a mob, interrupted an anti-slavery meeting, came on the platform, seated himself, and bade the meeting proceed. Douglass was speaking, and, nothing loath, made his speech only keener and keener for the interference, weaving around the intruder's head a wreath of delicate sarcasm which carried the audience with it, while the duller wits of the burly despot could hardly follow him. Knowing only, in a general way, that he was being dissected, Rynders at last exclaimed, "What you Abolitionists want to do is to cut all our throats!" "Oh, no!" replied Douglass in his most dulcet tones. "We would only cut your hair;" and bending over the shaggy and frowzy head of the Bowery tyrant, he gave a suggestive motion as of scissors to his thumb and forefinger, with a professional politeness that instantly brought down the house, friend and foe, while Rynders quitted the platform in wrath, and the meeting dissolved itself amid general laughter. It was a more cheerful conclusion, perhaps, than that stormier one—not unknown in reformatory conventions—with which Shakespeare so often ends his scenes: "Exeunt fighting."

One of the most curious circumstances connected with the whole Transcendental period, and one tending, whether in seriousness or through satire, to bring out its sunny side, was its connection with Horace Greeley. He himself was a strange mixture of the dreamy and the practical, and his very appearance and costume, his walk and conversation, combined these inconsistent attributes. The one great advertising medium possessed by the whole Brook Farm movement was the New York "Tribune," and it is a part of the quaintness of the whole affair that an enterprise which seemed physically so insignificant should have for its organ a journal then rapidly on its way to becoming the most widely circulated in the nation. Yet Greeley's own externals, when he first stood at the door at Brook Farm, might have suggested a visitor from any part of the land rather than New York city, and a delegate from any other sphere rather than that of metropolitan journalism. Miss Amelia Russell, a member of the Community, thus describes his appearance at first glance: "His hair was so light that it was almost white; he wore a white hat; his face was entirely colorless, even the eyes not adding much to save it from its ghostly hue. His coat was a very light drab, almost white, and his nether garments the same." No better samples could, perhaps, be given of the mirth-making aspects of that period than might be done by a series of extracts from Greeley's letters as published in the volume called "Passages from the Correspondence of Rufus W. Griswold," in which you find Greeley alternately moving heaven and earth to get for the then unknown Thoreau the publication of his maiden essay on Carlyle in "Graham's Magazine," and himself giving $75 to pay for it in advance; and about the same time writing to Griswold, "Gris, make up for me a brief collection of the best Epigrams in the Language—say three folio sheets of MSS.;" then cheerfully adding, "A page may be given to epitaphs, if you please, though I don't care!"

This suggests how much of the sunshine at that period came also to many from Thoreau himself, whose talk and letters, like his books, were full of delicate humor; and who gave to outdoor hours such an atmosphere of serene delight as made one feel that a wood thrush was always soliloquizing somewhere in the background. Walks with him were singularly unlike those taken with Alcott, for instance, who only strolled serenely to some hospitable fence at the entrance to some wood, and sat down there, oblivious whether frogs or wood thrushes filled the air, so long as they did not withdraw attention from his own discourses. As Alcott carried his indoor meditations out of doors, so Thoreau brought his outward observations indoors, and I remember well the delightful mornings when his favorite correspondent, Harry Blake, my neighbor in Worcester, Mass., used to send round to a few of us to come in and hear extracts from Thoreau's last letter at the breakfast-table; these extracts being the very materials that were afterwards to make up his choicest volume, "Walden;" letters which combined with breakfast and with sunrise to fill the day for us auditors with inexhaustible delight.

That period is long passed, and these few stray memories can at best give but a few glimpses of its sunnier side. The fact that it did pass and that it can never be reproduced is the very thing that makes its memories worth recalling. The great flood-tide of the civil war bore this all away, followed by the stupendous growth of a changed nation. Every age has its own point of interest; and the longest personal life, if lived wholesomely, can offer but a succession of these. But one question still remains, and will perhaps always remain, unanswered. Considering the part originally done by the English Lake Poets in bringing about this period of sunshine in America, why is it that the leaders of English literature on its native soil for the last half century have had a mournful and clouded tone? From Carlyle and Ruskin through Froude and Arnold to Meredith, Hardy, Stevenson, and Henley, all have had a prevailing air of sadness, and sometimes even of frightful gloom. Even Tennyson, during at least a portion of his reactionary later life, and Browning, toward the end of his, showed the same tendency. In America, on the other hand, during the same general period, the leading literary figures, with the solitary exception of Poe,—who was wont to be an exception to all rules,—were sunshiny and hopeful, not gloomy. This is certainly true of Emerson, Alcott, Thoreau, Longfellow, Lowell, Holmes, Whittier, Whitman. Even if Hawthorne may have seemed to the world an exception because of his reticence and sombre bearing, we must remember how he laid aside those traits within his own household. "Never was there such a playmate," said to me once his noble and stately daughter Una, describing her happy childhood. These and all the rest, save Poe, found joy, predominant joy, in life. Why this difference? It is not yet time, perhaps, to fathom the mystery and give a clear answer to the question.

8

The Literary Pendulum

After all," said the great advocate Rufus Choate, "a book is the only immortality." That was the lawyer's point of view; but the author knows that, even after the book is published, the immortality is often still to seek. In the depressed moods of the advocate or the statesman, he is apt to imagine himself as writing a book; and when this is done, it is easy enough to carry the imagination a step further and to make the work a magnificent success; just as, if you choose to fancy yourself a foreigner, it is as easy to be a duke as a tinker. But the professional author is more often like Christopher Sly, whose dukedom is in dreams; and he is fortunate if he does not say of his own career with Christopher: "A very excellent piece of work, good madam lady. Would 't were done!"

In our college days we are told that men change, while books remain unchanged. But in a very few years we find that the circle of books alters as swiftly and strangely as that of the men who write or the boys who read them. When the late Dr. Walter Channing, of Boston, was revisiting in old age his birthplace, Newport, R. I., he requested me to take him to the Redwood Library, of which he had been librarian some sixty years before. He presently asked the librarian, with an eagerness at first inexplicable, for a certain book, whose name I had never before heard. With some difficulty the custodian hunted it up, entombed beneath other dingy folios in a dusty cupboard. Nobody, he said, had ever before asked for it during his administration. "Strange!" said Dr. Channing, turning over the leaves. "This was in my time the show-book of the collection; people came here purposely to see it." He closed it with a sigh, and it was replaced in its crypt. Dr. Channing is dead, the librarian who unearthed the book is since dead, and I have forgotten its very title. In all coming time, probably, its repose will be as undisturbed as that of Hans Andersen's forgotten Christmas-tree in the garret. Did, then, the authorship of that book give to its author so very substantial a hold on immortality?

But there is in literary fame such a thing as recurrence—a swing of the pendulum which at first brings despair to the young author, yet yields him at last his only consolation. "L'éternité est une pendule," wrote Jacques Bridaine, that else forgotten Frenchman whose phrase gave Longfellow the hint of his "Old Clock on the Stairs." When our professors informed us that books were a permanent treasure, those of us who were studious at once pinched ourselves to buy books; but the authors for whom we made economies in our wardrobe are now as obsolete, very likely, as the garments that we exchanged for them. No undergraduate would now take off my hands at half price, probably, the sets of Landor's "Imaginary Conversations" and Coleridge's "Literary Remains," which it once seemed worth a month of threadbare elbows to possess. I lately called the attention of a professor of philology to a tolerably full set of Thomas Taylor's translations, and found that he had never heard of even the name of that servant of obscure learning. In college we studied Cousin and Jouffroy, and he who remembers the rise and fall of that ambitious school of French eclectics can hardly be sure of the permanence of Herbert Spencer, the first man since their day who has undertaken to explain the whole universe of being. How we used to read Hazlitt, whose very name is so forgotten that an accomplished author has lately duplicated the title of his most remarkable book, "Liber Amoris," without knowing that it had ever been used! What a charm Irving threw about the literary career of Roscoe; but who now recognizes his name? Ardent youths, eager to combine intellectual and worldly success, fed themselves in those days on "Pelham" and "Vivian Grey;" but these works are not now even included in "Courses of Reading"—that last infirmity of noble fames. One may look in vain through the vast mausoleum of Bartlett's "Dictionary of Quotations" for even that one maxim in respect to costume, which was "Pelham's" bid for immortality.

Literary fame is, then, by no means a fixed increment, but a series of vibrations of the pendulum. Happy is that author who comes to be benefited by an actual return of reputation—as athletes get beyond the period of breathlessness, and come to their "second wind." Yet this is constantly happening. Emerson, visiting Landor in 1847, wrote in his diary, "He pestered me with Southey—but who is Southey?" Now, Southey had tasted fame more promptly than his greater contemporaries, and liked the taste so well that he held his own poems far superior to those of Wordsworth, and wrote of them, "With Virgil, with Tasso, with Homer, there are fair grounds of comparison." Then followed a period during which the long shades of oblivion seemed to have closed over the author of "Madoc" and "Kehama." Behold! in 1886 the "Pall Mall Gazette," revising through "the best critics" Sir James Lubbock's "Hundred Best Books," dethrones Byron, Shelley, Coleridge, Lamb, and Landor; omits them all, and reinstates the forgotten Southey once more. Is this the final award of fate? No: it is simply the inevitable swing of the pendulum.

Southey, it would seem, is to have two innings; perhaps one day it will yet be Hayley's turn. "Would it please you very much," asks Warrington of Pendennis, "to have been the author of Hayley's verses?" Yet Hayley was, in his day, as Southey testifies, "by popular election the king of the English poets;" and he was held so important a personage, that he received, what probably no other author ever has won, a large income for the last twelve years of his life in return for the prospective copyright of his posthumous memoirs. Miss Anna Seward, writing in 1786, ranks him, with the equally forgotten Mason, as "the two foremost poets of the day;" she calls Hayley's poems "magnolias, roses, and amaranths," and pronounces his esteem a distinction greater than monarchs hold it in their power to bestow. But probably nine out of ten who shall read these lines will have to consult a biographical dictionary to find out who Hayley was; while his odd *protégé*, William Blake, whom the fine ladies of the day wondered at Hayley for patronizing, has since become a favorite in literature and art.

So strong has been the recent swing of the pendulum in favor of what is called realism in fiction, it is very possible that if Hawthorne's "Twice-told Tales" were to appear for the first time to-morrow they would attract no more attention than they did more than fifty years ago. Mr. Stockton has lately made a similar suggestion as to the stories of Edgar Poe. Perhaps this gives half a century as the approximate measure of the variations of fate—the periodicity of the pendulum. On the other hand, Jane Austen, who was for many years regarded by readers as an author suited to desolate islands or long and tedious illnesses, has now come to be the founder of a school; and must look down benignly from heaven to see the brightest minds assiduously at work upon that "little bit of ivory, two inches square" by which she symbolized her novels. Then comes in, as an alterative, the strong Russian tribe, claimed by realists as real, by idealists as ideal, and perhaps forcing the pendulum in a new direction. Nothing, surely, since Hawthorne's death, has given us so much of the distinctive flavor of his genius as Tourgueneff's extraordinary "Poems in Prose" in the admirable version of Mrs. T. S. Perry.

But the question, after all, recurs: Why should we thus be slaves of the pendulum? Why should we not look at these vast variations of taste more widely, and, as it were, astronomically, to borrow Thoreau's phrase? In the mind of a healthy child there is no incongruity between fairy tales and the Rollo Books; and he passes without disquiet from the fancied heart-break of a tin soldier to Jonas mending an old rat-trap in the barn. Perhaps, after all, the literary fluctuation occurs equally in this case and in ours, but under different conditions. It may be that, in the greater mobility of the child's nature, the pendulum can swing to and fro in half a second of time and without the consciousness of effort; while in the case of older readers, the same vibration takes half a century of time and the angry debate of a thousand journals.

9

HENRY JAMES, JR.

We are growing more cosmopolitan and varied, in these United States of America; and our authors are gaining much, if they are also losing a little, in respect to training. The early career of an American author used to be tolerably fixed and clear, if limited; a college education, a few months in Europe, a few years in some profession, and then an entrance into literature by some side-door. In later times, the printing-office has sometimes been substituted for the college, and has given a new phase of literary character distinct from the other, but not less valuable. Mr. Henry James, Jr., belongs to neither of the classes thus indicated: he may be said to have been trained in literature by literature itself, so early did he begin writing, and so incessantly has he written. We perhaps miss in his works something of the method which the narrower classical nurture was supposed to give; and we find few traces of that contact with the mass of mankind which comes through mere daily duty to the professional man, the business man, the journalist. Mr. James has kept a little too good company: we do not find in his books such refreshing types of hearty and robust manhood as Howells, with all his daintiness, finds it easy to depict in Colonel Ellison and the skipper of the Aroostook. Then Mr. James's life has been so far transatlantic, that one hardly knows whether he would wish to be accounted an American writer, after all; so that his education, his point of view, his methods, all unite to place him in a class by himself.

It is pleasant to see a man write, as he has always done, with abundant energy, and seemingly from the mere love of writing. Yet it is impossible to deny that he has suffered from this very profusion. Much of his early work seems a sort of self-training, gained at the expense of his readers; each sheet, each story, has been hurried into print before the ink was dry, in order to test it on the public,—a method singularly removed from the long and lonely maturing of Hawthorne. *"L'oisiveté est nécessaire aux esprits, aussi bien que le travail."* Even the later books of Mr. James, especially his travels and his essays, show something of this defect. What a quarry of admirable suggestions is, for instance, his essay on Balzac; but how prolix it is, what repetitions, what a want of condensation and method! The same is true, in a degree, of his papers on George Sand and Turgénieff, while other chapters in his "French Poets and Novelists" are scarcely more than sketches: the paper on the *Théâtre Français* hardly mentions Sarah Bernhardt; and, indeed, that on Turgénieff says nothing of his masterpiece, "Terres Vierges." Through all these essays he shows delicacy, epigram, quickness of touch, penetration; but he lacks symmetry of structure, and steadiness of hand.

We can trace in the same book, also, some of the author's limitations as an imaginative artist, since in criticising others a man shows what is wanting in himself. When he says, for instance, that a monarchical society is "more available for the novelist than any other," he shows that he does not quite appreciate the strong point of republicanism, in that it develops real individuality in proportion as it diminishes conventional distinctions. The truth is, that the modern novel has risen with the advance of democratic society, on the ruins of feudalism. Another defect is seen from time to time, when, in criticising some well-known book, he misses its special points of excellence. Take, for instance, his remarks on that masterly and repulsive novel, "Madame Bovary." To say of the author of that work that his "theory as a novelist, briefly expressed, is to begin at the outside,"[1] seems almost whimsically unjust. There is not a character in modern fiction developed more essentially from within than that of this heroine: all her sins and sorrows are virtually predicted in the early chapters; even Mr. James has to admit that it "could not have been otherwise"[2] with her, thereby taking back his own general assertion. Then he says "every thing in the book is ugly," whereas one of its salient points is the beauty of the natural descriptions in which its most painful incidents are framed. Finally,—and this is the most puzzling misconception of all,—Mr. James utterly fails to see the bearing of one of the pivotal points of the narrative, an unfortunate surgical operation performed by the heroine's husband, a country doctor: he calls it an "artistic bravado,"[3] and treats it as a mere episode of doubtful value,

---

[1] French Poets and Novelists, p. 256.
[2] Ibid., p. 261.
[3] Ibid., p. 265.

whereas it is absolutely essential to the working-out of the plot. The situation is this: Madame Bovary is being crushed to the earth by living in a social vacuum, with a stupid husband whom she despises, and has already deceived. She has just felt a twinge of remorse, after receiving an affectionate letter from her father; when suddenly this commonplace husband is presented to her eyes in a wholly new light,—that of an unappreciated man of genius, who has by a single act won a place among the great surgeons of his time. All that is left undepraved in her nature is touched and roused by this: she will do any thing, bear any thing, for such a husband. The illusion lasts but a few days, and is pitilessly torn away: the husband proves a mere vulgar, ignorant quack, even duller, emptier, more hopeless, than she had dreamed. The reaction takes her instantly downward, and with that impulse she sinks to rise no more. The author himself (Flaubert) takes the pains to warn us distinctly beforehand of the bearing of this incident;[4] but his precaution seems needless, the thing explains itself. It is one of the strongest and clearest passages in the whole tragedy, and it seems as if there must be some defect of artistic sensibility in any critic who misses his way here. Or else— which is more probable—it is another instance of that haste in literary workmanship which is one of Mr. James's besetting sins.

It may be one result of this extreme rapidity of production, that Mr. James uses certain catch-words so often as to furnish almost a shibboleth for his style; such words, for instance, as "brutal," "puerile," "immense." Another result is seen in his indifference to careful local coloring, especially where the scene is laid in the United States. When he draws Americans in Europe, he is at home; when he brings Europeans across the Atlantic, he never seems quite sure of his ground, except in Newport, which is in some respects the least American spot on this continent. He opens his "Europeans" by exhibiting horse-cars in the streets of Boston nearly ten years before their introduction, and his whole sketch of the Wentworth family gives a sense of vagueness. It is not difficult to catch a few unmistakable points, and portray a respectable elderly gentleman reading "The Daily Advertiser;" but all beyond this is indefinite, and, when otherwise, sometimes gives quite an incorrect impression of the place and period described. The family portrayed has access to "the best society in Boston;" yet the daughter, twenty-three years old, has "never seen an artist," though the picturesque figure of Allston had but lately disappeared from the streets, at the time mentioned, and

---

[4]"*Elle demeurait fort embarrassée dans sa velléité de sacrifice, quand l'apothécaire vint à propos lui fournir une occasion.*"—MADAME BOVARY, p. 210.

Cheney, Staigg, and Eastman Johnson might be seen there any day, with plenty of other artists less known. The household is perfectly amazed and overwhelmed at the sight of two foreigners, although there probably were more cultivated Europeans in Boston thirty years ago than now, having been drawn thither by the personal celebrity or popularity of Agassiz, Ticknor, Longfellow, Sumner, and Dr. Howe. The whole picture—though it is fair to remember that the author calls it a sketch only—seems more like a delineation of American society by Fortunio or Alexandre Dumas *fils*, than like a portraiture by one to the manor born. The truth is, that Mr. James's cosmopolitanism is, after all, limited: to be really cosmopolitan, a man must be at home even in his own country.

There are no short stories in our recent literature, I think, which are so good as Mr. James's best,—"Madame de Mauves," for instance, and "The Madonna of the Future." Even these sometimes lack condensation; but they have a thoroughly original grasp, and fine delineations of character. It is a great step downward from these to the somewhat vulgar horrors contained in "A Romance of Certain Old Clothes." The author sometimes puts on a cynicism which does not go very deep; and the young lovers of his earlier tales had a disagreeable habit of swearing at young ladies, and ordering them about. Yet he has kept himself very clear from the disagreeable qualities of the French fiction he loves. His books never actually leave a bad taste in one's mouth, as Charlotte Brontë said of French novels; and, indeed, no one has touched with more delicate precision the vexed question of morality in art. He finely calls the longing after a moral ideal "this southern slope of the mind,"[5] and says of the ethical element, "It is in reality simply a part of the richness of inspiration: it has nothing to do with the artistic process, and it has every thing to do with the artistic effect."[6] This is admirable; and it is a vindication of this attribute when we find that Mr. James's most successful social stories, "An International Episode," and "Daisy Miller," have been written with distinct purpose, and convey lessons. He has achieved no greater triumph than when, in this last-named book, he succeeds in holding our sympathy and even affection, after all, for the essential innocence and rectitude of the poor wayward girl whose follies he has so mercilessly portrayed.

It cannot be said that Mr. James has yet succeeded in producing a satisfactory novel: as a clever woman has said, he should employ some one else to write the last few pages. However strong the characterizations,

---

[5]French Poets and Novelists, p. 114.
[6]Ibid., p. 82.

however skilful the plot, the reader is left discontented. If in this respect, he seems behind Howells, it must be remembered that James habitually deals with profounder emotions, and is hence more liable to be over-mastered. Longfellow says to himself in his "Hyperion," "O thou poor authorling! Reach a little deeper into the human heart! Touch those strings, touch those deeper strings more boldly, or the notes shall die away like whispers, and no ear shall hear them save thine own." It is James rather than Howells who has heeded this counsel. The very disappointment which the world felt at the close of "The American" was in some sense a tribute to its power: the author had called up characters and situations which could not be cramped, at last, within the conventional limits of a stage-ending. As a piece of character-drawing, the final irresolution of the hero was simply perfect: it seemed one of the cases where a romancer conjures up persons who are actually alive, and who insist on working out a destiny of their own, irrespective of his wishes. To be thus conquered by one's own creation might seem one of those defeats that are greater than victories; yet it is the business of the novelist, after all, to keep his visionary people well in hand, and to contrive that they shall have their own way, and yet not spoil his climax. In life, as in "The American," the most complicated situations often settle themselves by events unseen, and the most promising tragedies are cheated of their crisis. But it is not enough that literary art should give a true transcript of nature; for the work must also comply with the laws of art, and must have a beginning, a middle, and an end. *"Un ouvrage d'art doit être un être, et non une chose arbitraire."*[7]

---

[7]Pensées de J. Joubert, p. 289.

BIBLIOGRAPHY

I. Works of Higginson Consulted or Used

Outdoor Papers Boston 1863
Army Life in a Black Regiment Boston 1869
   as reissued by Norton (paperback) Library New York 1984
Atlantic Essays Boston 1871
Oldport Days Boston 1873
Young Folks' History of United States Boston & New York 1875
Common Sense About Women Boston 1882
Hints on Writing and Speechmaking Boston 1887
Women and Men New York 1888
Travellers and Outlaws Boston 1892
The New World and the New Book Boston 1892
Concerning All of Us New York 1892
Margaret Fuller Ossoli, 6th edition Boston 1892 part of series American
   Men of Letters (sic)
Book and Heart New York 1894
Cheerful Yesterdays Boston & New York 1898
Contemporaries Boston 1899
Studies in History and Letters Boston & New York 1900
Women and the Alphabet Boston & New York 1900
John Greenleaf Whittier New York 1902
[Adult] History of the United States New York 1905
   update of first edition, *Larger History of the United States*, extending story to
   1905. Written with collaborator W. F. Channing.
Reader's History of American Literature (with Henry Boynton) Boston 1903
Part of a Man's Life Boston 1905
Carlyle's Laugh and Other Surprises Boston 1909

NOTE: Much of Higginson's own writing is autobiographical, particularly *Cheerful
Yesterdays* and *Contemporaries*.

II. Biographies and Dissertations

Biographies

Higginson, Mary Thacher, *Thomas Wentworth Higginson*   Boston   1914
Wells, Anna Mary, *Dear Preceptor*   Boston   1963
Meyer, Howard N., *Colonel of the Black Regiment*   New York   1967
Edelstein, Tilden G., *Strange Enthusiasm*   New Haven   1968
Tuttleton, James W., *Thomas Wentworth Higginson*   Boston   1978

Dissertations

Thomas Wentworth Higginson: Disciple of the Newness   Howard W. Hintz   NYU
   1939
Thomas Wentworth Higginson as a literary critic   Edgar L. McMormack   University
   of Michigan   1950
Thomas Wentworth Higginson: Reformer and Man of Letters   Sister T. C. Brennan
   University of Michigan   1958
Thomas Wentworth Higginson and the *Atlantic Monthly*   Leonard Brill   University of
   Minnesota   1968

III. Secondary Sources

Allen, Margaret A.   *The Achievement of Margaret Fuller*   University Park   1979
Bartlett, Irving   *Wendell Phillipps*   Boston   1961
Barzun, Jacques   *The Selected Writings of John Jay Chapman*   New York   1957 (biog-
   raphy of Garrison and essays on Emerson and others)
Bellamy, Edward   *Looking Backward: 2000–1887*   Boston   1887
Billington, R. A.   *The Journal of Charlotte Forten*   New York   1953
Bingham, Mary Todd   *Ancestors Brocades: The Literary Debut of Emily Dickinson*
   New York   1945
Blackwell, Alice S.   *Lucy Stone*   Boston   1930
Brooks, Van Wyck   *New England: Indian Summer*   New York   1940
_____   *The Flowering of New England*   New York   1955 (Everyman's
   Library Edition)
Commager, Henry S.   *The Era of Reform 1830–1860*   Princeton   1960
_____   *Theodore Parker: Yankee Crusader*   Boston   1962
Cornish, Dudley T.   *The Sable Arm*   New York   1956
Du Bois, W. E. B.   *Black Reconstruction*   New York   1935
_____   *John Brown*   Philadelphia   1909
Filler, Louis D.   *Abolition and Social Justice in the Era of Reform*   New York   1972
Flexner, Eleanor   *Century of Struggle*   New York   1972
Franklin, John Hope   *From Slavery to Freedom*   New York   1947
_____   *Reconstruction: After the Civil War*   Chicago   1961

Hirshon, Stanley P.   *Farewell to the Bloody Shirt*   Indiana   1962

Hixson, William A.   *Moorfield Storey*   New York   1972

Johnson, Thomas H., Ed.   *The Complete Poems of Emily Dickinson*   Boston   1960

Logan, Rayford W.   *The Negro in American Life and Thought: The Nadir 1877–1901*   New York   1954

McPherson, James   *The Negro's Civil War*   New York   1965

―――― *The Struggle for Equality*   Princeton   1964

Meyer, Howard N.   *Let Us Have Peace: The Life of Ulysses S. Grant*   New York 1966

Meyerson, Joel, Ed.   *The Transcendentalists*   New York   1984

Odell, Ruth   *Helen Hunt Jackson*   New York   1939

Rose, Willie Lee   *Rehearsal for Reconstruction*   Indianapolis   1964

Ruchames, Louis   *A John Brown Reader*   London & New York   1959

―――― *The Abolitionists*   New York   1963

Sargent, Mrs. John T.   *Sketches and Reminiscences of the Radical Club*   New York   1880

Stanton, Anthony Gage   *History of Woman Suffrage*   New York   1881–1922 (six volumes)

Stanton, Elizabeth Cady   *Eighty Years and More*   New York   1898

Stewart, James B.   *Wendall Phillips: Liberty's Hero*   Baton Rouge   1986

Tindall, George B.   *America: A Narrative History*   New York   1984

Tompkins, Beverly   *Anti-Imperialism in the United States*   Philadephia   1972

Tyler, Alice F.   *Freedom's Ferment*   New York   1944

Urbanski, Marie M. O.   *Margaret Fuller's Woman and the Nineteenth Century*   Westport & London   1980

Van Doren, Mark   *The Portable Emerson*   New York   1976

Walters, Ron G.   *American Reformers 1815–1860*   New York   1978

IV. Higginson in Print

In 1961 none of Higginson's works were in print, nor any biographies about him. As of 2000, the following books by Higginson are in print. The number next to a given title indicates the number of separate editions available of that particular work, by various publishers.

Army Life in a Black Regiment   4
Black Rebellion
Book and Heart
Carlyle's Laugh   2
Cheerful Yesterdays   3
Harvard Memorial Biographies
Henry Wadsworth Longfellow   2
John Greeleaf Whittier
Larger History of the United States
Letters and Journals (extracts)   3

Stephen Higginson
Francis Higginson
Malbone
Margaret Fuller Ossoli   4
Oldport Days
Reader's History of American Literature
Short Studies of American Authors
Women and the Alphabet
Young Folks' History of the United States
Definitive Edition (seven volumes)   2

The following books are also offered by a reprint service:

Army Life
Cheerful Yesterdays
Harvard Memorial Biography
Margaret Fuller Ossoli
Francis Higginson
John Greenleaf Whittier
Henry Wadsworth Longfellow
Stephen Higginson
Atlantic Essays
Carlyle's Laugh
Oldport Days
Young Folks' History of the United States
Larger History of the United States
Reader's History of American Literature
Letters and Journals
Malbone
Definitive Edition (seven volumes)

Publishing History

I. Abolitionist and Champion of Human Rights

1. Not by Bread Alone
   Newburyport Advertiser, January 2, 1848.
2. The School of Mobs
   John Greeleaf Whittier, Chapter V (New York: 1902).
3. Obeying the Higher Law: Attempts at Rescue
   Cheerful Yesterdays, Chapter V (Boston & New York: 1898).
4. A Ride Through Kansas
   Antislavery Tract #20, text originally published as "Letters from Worcester,"
   New York Tribune, 1856. On file Butler Library, Columbia University.
5. Assorted Lots of Young Negroes
   Mary T. Higginson, *Thomas Wentworth Higginson* (Boston: 1914).
6. The New Revolution: What Commitment Requires
   Pamphlet published Boston 1857. On file New York Public Library.
7. Why Back John Brown?
   Cheerful Yesterdays, Chapter VII (Boston & New York: 1898).
8. Miss Forten on the Southern Question
   Women's Journal, December 30, 1876.
9. Letter to the Editor
   New York Tribune, April 28, 1877.
10. The South Carolina Blacks
    Letter to the Editor, *The Nation*, April 30, 1874.
11. Letter to *The Nation:* "The Case of the Carpet-baggers"
    The Nation, March 2, 1899.
12. Southern Barbarity
    Boston Evening Transcript, March 10, 1899 (reported the meeting Higginson
    presided).

13. Lydia Maria Child
   Eminent Women of the Age (Hartford: 1869);
   Contemporaries (Boston & New York: 1899).
14. William Lloyd Garrison
   Atlantic Monthly, January 1886;
   Contemporaries (Boston: 1899).
15. Fourteen Years Later
   "Some War Scenes Revisited," *Atlantic Monthly*, July 1878;
   later as appendix to *Army Life in a Black Regiment*, 1900 edition.

II. Colonel of the First Black Regiment

1. The Black Troops: "Intensely Human"
   Atlantic Monthly, May 1904;
   Part of a Man's Life (Boston & New York: 1905).
2. Negro Spirituals
   Atlantic Monthly, June 1867;
   Army Life in a Black Regiment (Boston: 1870).
3. Camp Diary
   published as "Leaves from an Officer's Journal," *Atlantic Monthly*,
   November/December 1864 and January 1865;
   Army Life in a Black Regiment (Boston: 1870).
4. The Negro as Soldier
   Army Life in a Black Regiment (Boston: 1870).
5. Grant
   Atlantic Monthly, May & September, 1886;
   Contemporaries (Boston & New York: 1899).
6. Memo from *War of the Rebellion: Official Records of the Union and Confeder-
   ate Armies*
   United States Government records, 158-volume set, Series I, vol. XIV, 1885.

III Crusader for Women's Rights

1. Ought Women to Read the Alphabet?
   Atlantic Monthly, February 1859;
   reprinted many times in pamphlet form;
   Atlantic Essays (Boston: 1871);
   Woman and the Alphabet (Boston & New York: 1900)
2. Who Was Margaret Fuller?
   Eminent Women of the Age (Hartford: 1869).

3. The Shadow of the Harem

  Essay from *Harper's Bazar* (sic), collected in *Women and Men* (New York: 1888).

4. The Pleasing Art of Self-Extinction

  Essay from *Harper's Bazar*, collected in *Concerning All of Us* (New York: 1892).

5. Repression at Long Range

  Essay from *Harper's Bazar*, collected in *Concerning All of Us* (New York: 1892).

6. The Fact of Sex

  Essay from *Women's Journal*, collected in *Common Sense About Women* (Boston & New York: 1882);

  "*Women and the Alphabet*" (Boston & New York: 1900).

7. Womanhood and Motherhood

  Essay from *Woman's Journal*, collected in *Common Sense About Women* (Boston & New York: 1882);

  Women and the Alphabet (Boston & New York: 1900).

8. "Chances"

  Essay from *Harper's Bazar* collected in *Women and Men* (New York: 1888).

IV. ESSAYIST AS ACTIVIST

1. The Clergy and Reform

  Manuscript at Houghton Library, Harvard University, July 15, 1847.

2. A New Counterblast

  Atlantic Monthly, December 1861.

  Outdoor Papers (Boston: 1863).

3. Scripture Idolatry

  Lecture published with others in *The Secular Miscellany* (London: 1857).

4. The Sympathy of Religions

  The Radical, 1871;

  various pamphlets;

  World Parliament of Religions, Vol. I;

  Studies in History and Letters (Boston & New York: 1900).

5. Public and Private Virtues

  Editorial in *Women's Journal*, August 30, 1884.

6. "Tell the Truth"

  Editorial in *Women's Journal*, August 9, 1884.

7. More Mingled Races

  Book and Heart (New York: 1897);

8. Edward Bellamy's Nationalism
   Boston Sunday Evening Lectures (undated reprint).
9. The Complaint of the Poor
   Book and Heart (New York: 1897).
10. Where Liberty is *Not*, There is My Country
    Harper's Bazar, August 12, 1899;
    Broadside (flyer).
11. How Should a Colored Man Vote in 1900?
    Item in *Broadside* (flyer), originally printed in *Boston Herald*, October 11, 1900.
12. Higginson Answers Captain Mahan
    Report of public talk given February 15, 1900.

V. NATURALIST

1. Water Lilies
   Atlantic Monthly, September 1858;
   Outdoor Papers (Boston: 1863);
   Outdoor Studies (Boston & New York: 1900).
2. Snow
   Atlantic Monthly, September 1858;
   Outdoor Papers (Boston: 1863);
   Outdoor Studies (Boston & New York: 1900).
3. Oldport Wharves
   Atlantic Monthly, January 1868;
   Oldport Days (Boston: 1873);
   Studies in Romance (Boston & New York: 1900).
4. The Life of Birds
   Atlantic Monthly, September 1862;
   Outdoor Papers (Boston: 1863);
   Outdoor Studies (Boston & New York: 1900).
5. The Procession of the Flowers
   Atlantic Monthly, December 1862;
   Outdoor Papers (Boston: 1863);
   Outdoor Studies (Boston & New York: 1900).

VI. CRITIC AS ESSAYIST

1. Sappho
   Atlantic Monthly, July 1871;
   Studies in History and Letters (Boston & New York: 1900).

2. The Word Philanthropy
   Studies in History and Letters (Boston & New York: 1900).
3. Unconscious Successes
   Things Worth While (New York: 1908).
4. Longfellow as a Poet
   Henry Wadsworth Longfellow (Boston & New York: 1902).
5. A Letter to a Young Contributor
   Atlantic Monthly, April 1862;
   Atlantic Essays (Boston: 1871);
   Hints on Writing and Speechmaking (New York: 1887).
6. Emily Dickinson
   Atlantic Monthly, October 1891;
   Carlyle's Laugh (Boston & New York: 1904).
7. The Sunny Side of the Transcendental Period
   Atlantic Monthly, January 1904;
   Part of a Man's Life (Boston & New York: 1905).
8. The Literary Pendulum
   The New World and the New Book (Boston: 1892).
9. Henry James
   The Literary World, November 1879;
   Short Studies of American Authors (Boston: 1880);
   Dupee, F. W., ed. *The Question of Henry James* (New York: 1973).

About the Author

~~~~~~~~~~

Howard N. Meyer attended Columbia College and Law School, where he was editor of the *Law Review*. In his early public service, he worked for six years as Special Assistant to Attorneys General Francis Biddle and Tom Clark. Meyer then began a distinguished career as appellate and labor attorney, with further public service as a labor arbitrator with similar service in New York Civil Court.

Intrigued by a reference to Higginson's *Army Life in a Black Regiment* in Van Wyck Brooks's literary history, *New England: Indian Summer*, Meyer discovered that Higginson's book had been out of print for forty years and out of library circulation as well. Locating it after much searching in a New England used book shop, Meyer determined to seek the reissue of the book. He succeeded in doing so, adding his own introduction, which illuminated Higginson's power to prove the potential for human brotherhood. Meyer was especially moved by Higginson's deputy's farewell address to the ex-slave regiment, in which he pledged: "The nation guarantees to you full protection and justice." Despite the adoption of the Fourteenth Amendment, repeating that guarantee as the law of the land, the promise was broken. This was of importance as inspiration for Meyer's book *The Amendment That Refused to Die*, nominated at the request of one of the jurors for the Pulitzer Prize in 1974. A new, updated edition is in preparation.

Meyer has also written biographies of Higginson and of Ulysses S. Grant (*Let Us Have Peace*) and frequently contributes articles to national and international periodicals on civil rights and peace issues, particularly the neglected role of international law in peace studies and advocacy. On that theme, Meyer has a work-in-progress, tentatively titled *The Century of the World Court*.

INDEX